CW00542641

OXFORD
TWENTY-FIRST CENTURY
APPROACHES TO LITERATURE

OXFORD
TWENTY-FIRST CENTURY
APPROACHES TO LITERATURE

Middle English

Edited by

PAUL STROHM

OXFORD
UNIVERSITY PRESS

OXFORD
UNIVERSITY PRESS

Great Clarendon Street, Oxford OX2 6DP

Oxford University Press is a department of the University of Oxford.
It furthers the University's objective of excellence in research, scholarship,
and education by publishing worldwide in

Oxford New York

Auckland Cape Town Dar es Salaam Hong Kong Karachi
Kuala Lumpur Madrid Melbourne Mexico City Nairobi
New Delhi Shanghai Taipei Toronto

With offices in

Argentina Austria Brazil Chile Czech Republic France Greece
Guatemala Hungary Italy Japan Poland Portugal Singapore
South Korea Switzerland Thailand Turkey Ukraine Vietnam

Oxford is a registered trade mark of Oxford University Press
in the UK and in certain other countries

Published in the United States
by Oxford University Press Inc., New York

© Oxford University Press 2007

The moral rights of the authors have been asserted
Database right Oxford University Press (maker)

First published 2007

All rights reserved. No part of this publication may be reproduced,
stored in a retrieval system, or transmitted, in any form or by any means,
without the prior permission in writing of Oxford University Press,
or as expressly permitted by law, or under terms agreed with the appropriate
reprographics rights organization. Enquiries concerning reproduction
outside the scope of the above should be sent to the Rights Department,
Oxford University Press, at the address above

You must not circulate this book in any other binding or cover
and you must impose the same condition on any acquirer

British Library Cataloguing in Publication Data

Data available

Library of Congress Cataloging in Publication Data

Data available

Typeset by Laserwords Private Limited, Chennai, India
Printed in Great Britain
on acid-free paper byPrinted in Great Britain
on acid-free paper by
Biddles Ltd., King's Lynn, Norfolk

ISBN 978–0–19–928766–6

1 3 5 7 9 10 8 6 4 2

CONTENTS

LIST OF ILLUSTRATIONS

NOTES ON CONTRIBUTORS

Elizabeth Allen teaches in the English Department at the University of California, Irvine. Her book on *False Fables and Exemplary Truth in Later Middle English Literature* was recently published by Palgrave Macmillan. She is currently investigating narratives of sanctuary in late medieval England.   eallen@uci.edu

Christopher Baswell teaches medieval subjects at the University of California, Los Angeles. His interests include Arthurian literature, and is the author of *Virgil in Medieval England: Figuring the Aeneid from the Twelfth Century to Chaucer.*   baswell@humnet.ucla.edu

Jessica Brantley teaches Old and Middle English literature at Yale University. Her book on *Reading in the Wilderness: The Drama of Devotion in an Illustrated Carthusian Miscellany* is forthcoming with University of Chicago Press. She is currently engaged in a study of the iconography of Chaucer's 'Complaint of Mars'.   jessica.brantley@yale.edu

Diane Cady teaches English at Mills College. She has published essays on gender and money and on language and disease, and is completing a monograph on gender and medieval fears and fantasies about money.   dcady@mills.edu

Christopher Cannon is a member of the Faculty of English in the University of Cambridge. His most recent book is *The Grounds of English Literature*, published by Oxford University Press, and he is currently writing a cultural history of Middle English.   cdc1001@cam.ac.uk

Andrew Cole teaches in the Department of English at the University of Georgia. He is co-editor of the *Yearbook of Langland Studies* and his forthcoming book will concern England after heresy, 1382–1420.   awc@uga.edu

Lisa H. Cooper is a member of the Department of English at the University of Wisconsin-Madison. She has written on the grail legend and on Caxton's Dialogues, and is working on a book entitled *Crafting Narratives: Artisans, Authors, and the Literary Artifact in Late Medieval England.*   lhcooper@wisc.edu

Joyce Coleman is a member of the English Department at the University of Oklahoma. Recent articles have concerned Philippa of Lancaster, the frontispiece to a French City of God, and the prologue of Wynnere and Wastoure. Her next book will focus on book iconography in manuscript illumination.   joyce.coleman@ou.edu

Carolyn Dinshaw teaches in the Departments of English and of Social and Cultural Analysis at NYU. She is author of *Getting Medieval: Sexualities and Communities, Pre- and Post-Modern*, with Duke University Press. Her current project concerns medieval and post-medieval experiences of temporality.   carolyn.dinshaw@nyu.edu

Matthew Giancarlo teaches in the English Department at Yale University. Recent articles have appeared in *Representations* and *Studies in the Age of Chaucer*. His book *Parliament and Literature in Late Medieval England* is forthcoming from Cambridge University Press.   matthew.giancarlo@yale.edu

Alexandra Gillespie teaches in the English Department at the University of Toronto. Her most recent publication is *Print Culture and the Medieval Author: Chaucer, Lydgate, and Their Books, 1476–1557*, with Oxford University Press. She is currently co-editing a collection of essays on book production in England, 1350–1535.   alexandra.gillespie@utoronto.ca

Vincent Gillespie teaches English literature at the University of Oxford. A selection of his articles and papers will appear next year as *Looking in Holy Books*, to be published by the University of Wales Press. He is currently working on a study of fifteenth-century orthodox religious culture in England.   vincent.gillespie@ell.ox.ac.uk

Alfred Hiatt teaches Old and Middle English literature at the University of Leeds. He is author of *The Making of Medieval Forgeries: False Documents in Fifteenth-Century England*, published by the British Library, and is currently engaged in a study of terra incognita in the medieval and early modern geographical imagination.   a.hiatt@leeds.ac.uk

Bruce Holsinger teaches in the departments of English and Music at the University of Virginia. His most recent book is *The Premodern Condition: Medievalism and the Making of Theory*. His chapter in this volume is part of a longer-term project on liturgical culture and vernacular writing in England.   bh9n@virginia.edu

Sheila Lindenbaum is the editor of the forthcoming Westminster volume in the Records of English Drama series and the author of articles on medieval spectacle and dramatic entertainments. Formerly at Indiana University, she now lives in London, where she is completing a study of literate practice in late medieval London.   lindenb@indiana.edu

Sarah McNamer teaches in the Department of English at Georgetown University, where she specializes in medieval performance, meditative literature, and the history of devotion. She is writing a book on compassion.   mcnamer@georgetown.edu

Maura Nolan teaches English literature at the University of California, Berkeley. Cambridge University Press recently published her *John Lydgate and the Making of Public Culture*. She is currently finishing a book on Fortune as a literary idea, and plans to study the problem of the aesthetic in medieval literature.   mnolan@berkeley.edu

Susan Phillips teaches medieval and early modern literature and culture at Northwestern University. Her forthcoming book, with Penn State University Press, is *Transforming Talk: The Problem with Gossip in Late Medieval England*. She is currently studying premodern dictionaries, phrasebooks, and guides to conversation.   susie-phillips@northwestern.edu

Kellie Robertson directs Medieval and Renaissance Studies at the University of Pittsburgh. She is author of *The Laborer's Two Bodies: Labor and the "Work" of the Text in Medieval*

Britain, and co-editor of *The Middle Ages at Work*. She is currently writing a book entitled *Material Chaucer*.   krobert@pitt.edu

D. Vance Smith teaches medieval literature and continental philosophy at Princeton University, where he is director of the Program in Medieval Studies. His most recent book was *Arts of Possession*, and he is finishing a book called *Dying Medieval*. dvsmith@Princeton.EDU

Robert M. Stein teaches English and comparative literature at Purchase College and is also affiliated with the department of English and Comparative Literature at Columbia University. His most recent book is *Reality Fictions: Romance, History, and Governmental Authority 1025–1180*. He is currently studying crusade narratives.   rms9@columbia.edu

Emily Steiner teaches medieval literature in the department of English at the University of Pennsylvania. She is the author of *Documentary Culture and the Making of Middle English Literature*, published by Cambridge University Press, and is currently engaged in a book on the relationship between medieval political theory and vernacular poetics.
                                                    steinere@sas.upenn.edu

Paul Strohm teaches medieval literature and humanities at Columbia University. His most recent book is *Politique: Languages of Statecraft between Chaucer and Shakespeare*. He is currently thinking and writing about the vicissitudes of 'conscience', across the medieval-early modern divide.   ps2143@columbia.edu

Carol Symes teaches in the Department of History at the University of Illinois, Urbana-Champaign. Cornell University Press will publish her book *A Medieval Theatre: Plays and Public Life in Thirteenth-Century Arras*. She is currently studying the transmission of Greek tragedy and also the careers of professional entertainers in the pre-modern West.
                                                    symes@uiuc.edu

Stephanie Trigg teaches in the Department of English at the University of Mebourne. Her most recent book concerns *Medievalism and the Gothic in Australian Culture*, published by Brepols, and she is currently working on a cultural history of the Order of the Garter from 1346 to the present.   sitrigg@unimelb.edu.au

Marion Turner is a member of the English Department at King's College, London. Oxford University press is publishing her *Chaucerian Conflict: Languages of Antagonism in Late Fourteenth Century London*. Her current research is focused on Thomas Usk and London textual production.   marion.e.turner@kcl.ac.uk

Michelle R. Warren teaches in Comparative Literature at Dartmouth College. She is the author of *History on the Edge: Excalibur and the Borders of Britain*, published by University of Minnesota Press. Current projects include merchant translation in London and a colonial history of medieval French studies entitled *Creole Medievalism*.
                                                    michelle.r.warren@dartmouth.edu

Nancy Bradley Warren teaches English and religion at Florida State University. Her most recent book is *Women of God and Arms: Female Spirituality and Political Conflict, 1380–1600*, published by University of Pennsylvania Press. She is currently writing a book on female spiritualities, contested orthodoxies, and English religious cultures. nwarren@english.fsu.edu

Karen Winstead teaches in the Department of English at the Ohio State University. Her most recent book is *John Capgrave's Fifteenth Century*, and she is currently writing a book on late medieval and early modern English hagiography.   winstead.2@osu.edu

Nicolette Zeeman teaches at King's College, Cambridge. Her most recent publication is *Piers Plowman and the Medieval Discourse of Desire*. She is currently studying the impact of Latin literary theory on vernacular literature.   nz202@cam.ac.uk

CHAPTER 1

INTRODUCTION

PAUL STROHM

A publishing surge of the last twenty years has filled our shelves with 'companions', volumes designed to equip their readers with up-to-date and convenient surveys of the current state of knowledge about literary periods and major authors. Like many fellow teachers and researchers, I have previously ridden this wave. Here, now, is a volume that might *look* like one more 'companion' or its close kin. Its aspirations are, however, considerably—perhaps even completely—different. A companion or a handbook promises, at least by implication, to provide authoritative information, an accounting of what is 'known' and agreed upon by seasoned scholars in the field. By contrast, this volume seeks to enter the zone of the not-yet known, the less-than fully understood. Its contributors were asked to avoid settled consensus in favour of unresolved debate, to prefer the emergent, the unfinalized, the yet-to-be done.

Of course, contributors—especially the innovative and independent-minded ones sought out for this volume—make up their own minds about such things. As these essays have arrived in the mail, I have been constantly and delightedly surprised by the directions taken and the perspectives raised. My impression as editor is that this volume's aims have been realized, and in the best sort of way: along tangents I could never have predicted. One essay reads romances as scripts for the 'performance' of feelings, while another reads dramas not as performances at all but as instances of literate practice. An essay on the movement from script to print argues that the invention of 'the book' is what really matters, and that the emergence of the book spans and overshadows the apparent script–print divide. Another solicited on the subject of orality finds that medieval culture was less 'oral' than commonly supposed, but 'aural' through and though. Essays on translation and multilingualism agree that a single-language text can rest on a foundation of disguised multilingual presuppositions, even as another finds that many written texts are implicitly rooted in ways of seeing. Apparently theory-innocent vernacular texts are found by several writers to harbour refined ideas about beauty, aesthetics, and literary genre. 'Gossip' turns out to be less insurrectionary and more conservative than it ever seemed to be, and to have a good deal to do with narrative itself.

'Episodic' structure is seen not as happenstance but as design. The far-from-stable category of authorship is found lurking in the undiscovered space between manual and intellectual labour, as a by-product of other vocations, as an epiphenomenon of socio-political conflict. 'Literature' is discovered in camouflage, in apparently 'non-literary' surroundings, or as an incidental effect of writing practice, or dramatic convention, or even of manuscript arrangement or *mise-en-page*. Contrary to the dutifully learned lessons of a half-century, the 'I' of a text might end up having something autobiographical about it after all. And so on; readers will find these essays astir with new prospects and fresh research agendas.

My object in proposing topics was to avoid settled areas of discussion and 'bounded' subjects. Hence, this collection contains no 'major author' essays—even though citations and analyses of writings by Chaucer, Gower, Langland, and Lydgate constantly recur. It contains some 'genre' chapters, but wilfully new ones that violate customary categorizations: 'Vision, Image, Text' (embracing both secular visions and religious revelations) and 'Speculative Genealogies' (embracing romances, chronicles, and other narrative forms). Although its central subject is Middle English literary texts, it frequently sallies into Old and Early Modern English for its illustrative instances, and extra- or apparently 'non-literary' writings ('Learning to Live', 'The Poetics of Practicality') receive generous—even repeated—attention.

The last decade has been a period of restless exploration in Middle English studies. Several topics that would otherwise have ideally met this collection's criteria of innovativeness and wide-ranging enquiry have been extensively and expertly written about, already becoming subjects for collections and anthologies in their own right. Sexualities and queer theory, topics that would have been much at home here, have been splendidly covered in the writings of Carolyn Dinshaw,[1] and also in a stimulating collection edited by Glenn Burger and Steven F. Kruger.[2] Post-colonial writing has been comprehensively treated in a collection edited by Jeffrey Jerome Cohen,[3] and has received an even more recent and highly creative jolt in David Wallace's latest book.[4] James Simpson has opened new vistas on literary history with his take-no-prisoners assault on once-secure periodizations and generalizations.[5] Vernacularity has been treated by Jocelyn Wogan-Browne and her collaborators in a provocative collection—literally teeming with research ideas and agendas—that everywhere evinces a spirit to which the present volume aspires.[6] (If by mentioning these writings here I accomplish a sly and side-door augmentation of this volume's purposes, I can only say: ha! guilty as charged!) In

---

[1] *Chaucer's Sexual Poetics* (Madison: University of Wisconsin Press, 1989) and *Getting Medieval* (Durham, NC: Duke University Press, 1999).
[2] *Queering the Middle Ages* (Minneapolis: University of Minnesota Press, 2001).
[3] *The Postcolonial Middle Ages* (Basingstoke: Macmillan, 2000).
[4] *Premodern Places* (Oxford: Blackwell, 2004).
[5] *Reform and Cultural Revolution* (Oxford: Oxford University Press, 2002).
[6] *The Idea of the Vernacular* (State College: Pennsylvania State University Press, 1999).

the meantime, the swiftly moving assimilative energies of this field are displayed in the frequency with which all these topics, and their authors, are engaged in these pages. Those who employ the 'subject index' at the end of the volume will find each of these topics repeatedly addressed, not in theoretical isolation but concretely, in particular situations in which it rises to view.

In such aspects as its topical choices, its subject index, and its preference for future-oriented discussions of further reading over static bibliography, this volume elects an attitude. Rejecting premature or illusory closure and forgoing attempts to have the last word, it heads for the open ground of new speculation and continuing debate. The result is a collection equally suitable for new scholars just setting their own research agendas and for established practitioners ready to reconsider apparently 'settled' subjects.

PART I

CONDITIONS AND CONTEXTS

CHAPTER 2

MANUSCRIPT MATRIX, MODERN CANON

CAROL SYMES

The poem known to us as *Beowulf* is preserved in a single, early eleventh-century manuscript now housed in the British Library, which in the sixteenth century became part of a book bearing the designation Cotton Vitellius A.xv. This means that the volume in which the poem was rebound once occupied the fifteenth place on the first shelf of a bookcase topped by a bust of the Roman Emperor Vitellius in the famous library of Sir Robert Bruce Cotton (1571–1631). A precocious student of the antiquarian William Camden, Cotton had taken early advantage of the brisk trade in medieval books and documents that followed Henry VIII's dissolution of the monasteries (initiated 1536–7), and by the time of his death had amassed a collection to rival that of any European aristocrat, and more comprehensive than that contained in any official English archive. It included, among nearly one thousand handwritten artefacts, the Lindisfarne Gospels and two early redactions of Magna Carta. Although privately owned, the collection was generously opened to the use of contemporary scholars and literati during Cotton's lifetime, and was consulted by no less a person than King James I, to whom Sir Robert owed his knighthood: for already, in the eyes of his king and countrymen, this treasure-trove constituted the beginnings of a national library. Indeed, that is why it was confiscated by Charles I, restored to royal patronage after 1660, and eventually became one of the three foundational collections which formed the new British Museum chartered in 1753.[1]

Arguably, *Beowulf* owes its current celebrity to its manuscript's inclusion in this modern hoard of medieval memorabilia, now recognized as a repository of Britain's heritage. This is the first thing we should note about the strange

---

[1] Kevin Sharpe, *Sir Robert Cotton, 1586–1631: History and Politics in Early Modern England* (Oxford: Oxford University Press, 1979); C. J. Wright (ed.), *Sir Robert Cotton as Collector: Essays on the Early Stuart Courtier and his Legacy* (London: The British Library, 1997).

relationship, both symbiotic and dysfunctional, that has subsisted between medieval manuscripts and the modern canon: the post-medieval circumstances in which any medieval text is preserved will govern, to a large extent, its notoriety or obscurity. Packaging is key, and so is heightened visibility. If a text is decorative, large, distinctive, or bizarre, it will be remarked—so long as these qualities are obvious to the modern eye. But if, like most medieval texts, it is mutable, camouflaged, and chameleon-like, it may pass unnoticed beneath the gaze of bibliophiles. As a result, even the most thoroughly catalogued libraries of the world will continue, throughout the twenty-first century, to report spectacular 'finds' made by scholars leafing through manuscripts from which only a single, starring text has hitherto been extracted. Another thing to bear in mind is that the poem called *Beowulf* could just as easily have been consigned to oblivion by the same series of accidents that brought it to prominence, since Vitellius A.xv was one of many books severely damaged (many more were wholly destroyed) in a fire that broke out in a neighbouring house in Westminster on 23 October 1731, and which spread quickly through a room packed with parchment encased in dried leather and ancient wood. So slender is the thread which holds the sword of Damocles suspended over the fragile remnants of the medieval past, even—or especially—when they are gathered together for safekeeping.

Providentially, the half-scorched codex containing *Beowulf* made a narrow escape, probably through a window. But having survived the hazards of the English Reformation (Grendel) and evaded destruction by the elements (Grendel's dam) it found a dragon waiting, since the very attentions which the manuscript subsequently received have contributed disastrously to its present state of physical deterioration. For over a century after the Cottonian fire, the scorched leaves of Vitellius A.xv were worn away by the hands of philologists who sought access to its best-known text in ever-increasing numbers, Scandinavians and Germans vying with Englishmen to establish *Beowulf*'s pedigree as an early classic of their respective vernaculars. Hence, we owe our entire knowledge of the ephemeral words and phrases on the medieval pages' outer edges to modern transcriptions made by the Icelander Grimur Jonsson Thorkelin, who published the first edition of the poem in 1815, under the Latin title 'On the Deeds of the Danes in the Third and Fourth Centuries', with the artful subtitle 'A Danish Poem in the Anglo-Saxon Dialect'.[2] This neat appropriation—or repatriation, depending on one's perspective—quickly inspired a metrical translation into Danish by N. F. S. Grundtvig, who gave it a new name,

---

[2] Grimur Jonsson Thorkelin, *De Danorum rebus gestis secul. III & IV. Poema danicum dialecto anglo-saxonica. Ex bibliotheca Cottoniana Musaei britannici* (Copenhagen: T. E. Rangel, 1815). See Kevin Kiernan, 'The Conybeare–Madden Collation of Thorkelin's *Beowulf*', in Phillip Pulsiano and Elaine Treharne (eds.), *Anglo-Saxon Manuscripts and their Heritage* (Aldershot: Ashgate, 1997), 117–36. The dating and localization of the manuscript, not to mention the date and mode of *Beowulf*'s composition, are controversial: Kevin Kiernan, *Beowulf and the Beowulf Manuscript*, rev. edn. (Ann Arbor: University of Michigan Press, 1996), esp. pp. xv–xxviii, 120–2.

'Beowulf's Ballad' (*Bjowulfs Drape*), in 1820. Lest the Danes should have it all their own way, the first German verse translation, printed in Zurich in 1840, advertised the poem as 'the oldest hero-song of the German people', dating from the glorious epoch of Charles the Great.[3] Meanwhile, English patriots scrambled to regain lost ground, with John Josias Conybeare publishing a substantial extract and partial translation in his *Illustrations of Anglo-Saxon Poetry* (1826), where *Beowulf* was described 'as ranking among the most perfect specimens of the language and versification of our ancestors'.[4]

Here, then, is another irony: the threat of *Beowulf*'s material destruction at the hands of its latter-day evangelists was simultaneously countered by the constructions of their printed texts, whose purpose was to remove the poem as far as possible from the conditions of its circulation and transcription in manuscript. The modern editor's job—as conceived in the nineteenth century and as widely practised today—is to tame and regularize the barbarisms of medieval texts, rescuing them from the contaminating influence of their own scribes and teaching them to speak intelligibly for the first time. If the manuscript cataloguer is like Prospero, conjuring or drowning books at a whim, the editor plays Miranda to a series of unruly Calibans. At the same time, the newly schooled *Beowulf*, like many other medieval artefacts resurrected in the seventeenth and eighteenth centuries, became subject to another modern construct: the nation-state. All over Europe, claims to sovereignty were being staked in the medieval past, so that to colonize a text was to enter into a debate over identity and 'origins'. This process was at least as old as the new technology of printing. In 1476, the inaugural year of his press's operation in London, William Caxton (*c.*1422–1491) made a signal contribution to the modern canon of medieval literature when he published a first edition of Chaucer's *Canterbury Tales*; in 1485, acting out of overtly political motives, he released his own version of a long chivalric narrative by Sir Thomas Malory under the title *Le Morte Darthur*. In his preface, he explained that 'Many noble and dyuers gentylmen of thys royame of Englond' had been asking why he had not yet printed this 'noble hystorye', on the grounds that it was 'as wel of contemplacyon as of other hystoryal and wordly actes' and that the deeds of King Arthur 'ought moost to be remembred emonge vs englysshe men' and not consigned to Dutch, Italian, Spanish, Greek, and French audiences.[5] In the same combative spirit, a compendium of fabliaux published in Paris a decade before the French Revolution was selectively edited and translated into English in 1796—with the justification that these lively

---

[3] Ludwig Ettmüller, *Beowulf. Heldengedicht des achten Jahrhunderts* (Zurich: Meyer and Zeller, 1840), pp. [iii] and 1 ('dem ältesten Heldengedichte des deutschen Volkes').

[4] John Josias Conybeare, *Illustrations of Anglo-Saxon Poetry* (London: Harding and Lepard, 1826), 30.

[5] *Le Morte Darthur by Syr Thomas Malory: The Original Edition of William Caxton*, ed. H. Oskar Sommer (London: David Nutt, 1889), 1–2 (fos. 1^{r-v}); available online via the Corpus of Middle English Prose and Verse, **www.hti.umich.edu/c/cme/index.html**.

tales, 'written in a language which at that period was common to France and England, may be considered as equally connected with the literary history of both countries'. Their French editor, consequently, was accused of having been overly 'anxious to establish the pretensions of his countrymen to priority of romantick invention', as evinced by his 'violent invectives against the English nation'.[6] Tit for tat: when Paul Meyer published his inventory of French-language manuscripts in British libraries, an undertaking financed by the French government, the very title of his catalogue intimated that those texts were imprisoned in foreign lands: they were 'Manuscript Documents of the Ancient Literature of France Preserved in the Libraries of Great Britain'.[7] The struggle to secure *Beowulf*'s cultural capital is nothing compared to that over the *Chanson de Roland*, couched in the romance tongue of the Anglo-Norman empire of the Angerin Henry II, but claimed for France since 1835.[8]

So an obscure Anglo-Saxon epic was 'discovered', named, validated, edited, translated, glossed, and placed on the modern syllabus. The version of *Beowulf* with which we are familiar, in consequence, is less the product of two eleventh-century scribes than the composite production of the sixteenth to twentieth centuries, much less a version of the earlier entertainment(s) from which the manuscript's exemplar ultimately derived. For like most of the specimens that are now held up as 'works' of medieval 'literature', *Beowulf* began as a performance, not as a piece of writing; its gratuitous survival in this singular form therefore complicates the argument that it held a perennial place in the collective consciousness of pre- or post-Conquest England.[9] In fact, no independent witness to the story or its hero can be found prior to the poem's inclusion in Humphrey Wanley's survey of 'ancient literatures … extant in the libraries of England', published as a supplement to George Hickes's 'Grammatico-Critical and Archeological Thesaurus' in 1705. Here, for perhaps the first time since it had been copied, nearly seven centuries before, we find it described as an 'extremely noble treatise, written poetically' ('Tractatus nobiliissimus Poetice

---

[6] *Fabliaux or Tales, Abridged from French Manuscripts of the XII*[th] *and XIII*[th] *Centuries by M. Le Grand, Selected and Translated into English Verse* [by Gregory Lewis Way], with a preface and notes [by. G. Ellis] (London: W. Bulmer, 1796), pp. i and vi. Cf. Pierre Jean Baptiste Le Grand d'Aussy, *Fabliaux ou contes du XII*[e] *et du XIII*[e] *siècle, traduits ou extraits d'après divers manuscrits du tems* [sic]; *avec notes historiques et critiques, & les imitations qui ont été faites de ces contes depuis leur origine jusqu'à nos jours*, 4 vols. (Paris: E. Onfroy, 1779–81).

[7] Paul Meyer, *Documents manuscrits de l'ancienne littérature de la France conservés dans les bibliothèques de la Grande Bretagne. Rapports à M. le ministre de l'instruction publique*, Archives des Missions Scientifiques et Littéraires, 2nd ser. (Paris: H. Champion, 1871).

[8] Andrew Taylor, *Textual Situations: Three Medieval Manuscripts and their Readers* (Philadelphia: University of Pennsylvania Press, 2002), 26–70; and 'Was There a Song of Roland?', *Speculum*, 76 (2001), 28–65.

[9] Even if one accepts Kiernan's argument, that the eleventh-century manuscript 'preserves for us the artistic fusion of two originally distinct *Beowulf* narratives' (*Beowulf*, 249–78, at 271), neither those narratives nor their amalgamation were the product of a conscientiously *literary* poetics; see below.

scriptus')—a strange classification, indicating Wanley's discomfiture over the fact that the text, though metrical, was copied out like prose. (Inured to conventions of layout concretized by print, he and his contemporaries did not know that eleventh-century scribes did not waste valuable time and space delineating individual verses when they transcribed poetry.) Nor could Wanley attempt more than a cursory reading of the first and last pages of the poem he had 'found', since no scholar of his day had more than a rudimentary knowledge of Old English. 'In this book, which is an extraordinary example of Anglo-Saxon poetics, seem to be described the wars which Beowulf, a certain Dane, scion of a lineage from the kingdom of the Scyldings, fought against the chieftains of Sweden.'[10] Yet, wishing to be as thorough as possible in other respects, he concluded his analysis of the manuscript by noting that *Bewoulf* was followed by a 'Poetical Fragment, the History of Judith and Holofernes, written in Saxon after the Conquest', which had been published a few years earlier.[11]

How many students of English literature know that the sole text of *Beowulf* is juxtaposed with an Anglo-Saxon version of *Judith*, also in verse? How might our understanding of both poems be altered and informed if we entertain the notion that they occupied the same space, materially and perhaps conceptually, in the scriptorium where they were copied? In the seventeenth century, the contents of Vitellius A.xv consisted of two separate gatherings of Anglo-Saxon texts, which were themselves compilations put together at various times; for Cotton or his librarian, common dialect was their distinguishing characteristic. But the contents of the second miscellany, the 'Nowell Codex' which contains *Beowulf* and *Judith*, reveal earlier compilers' awareness of very different generic categories, since these two texts are combined with a prose life of St Christopher, an imaginative travelogue called 'The Wonders of the East', and a translation of Alexander the Great's letter to Aristotle, all copied by the same scribe who provided the first portion of *Beowulf*. How interesting to speculate on the tastes, the studies, the habits of thought exhibited by those responsible for these conjunctions! Still more fascinating is the connection suggested between *Beowulf* and *Judith*, the first of which was completed by the same scribe who copied the latter.[12] Although their eventual pairing may have

---

[10] George Hickes, *Linguarum vett. septentrionalium thesaurus grammatico-criticus et archaeologicus*, 2 vols. (Oxford: at the Sheldonian Theatre, 1705), ii: *Antiquae literaturae septenrionalis liber alter. Seu Humphredi Wanleii librorum vett. septentrionalium, qui in Angliae Bibliothecis extant, nec non multorum vett. Cod. Septentrionalium alibi extantium Catalogus Historico-Criticus*, 218ᵇ–219ᵃ ('In hoc libro, qui Poeseos Anglo-Saxonicæ egregium est exemplum, descripta videntur bella quæ Beowulfus quidam Danus, ex Regio Scyldingorum stirpe Ortus, gessit contra Sueciæ Regulos').

[11] Edward Thwaites, *Heptateuchus, liber Job, et Evangelium Nicodemi; Anglo-Saxonice. Historiae Judith fragmentum; Dano-Saxonice* (Oxford: at the Sheldonian Theatre, 1698). On the revival of Anglo-Saxon, see Timothy C. Graham and Andrew G. Watson, *The Recovery of the Past in Early Elizabethan England: Documents by John Bale and John Jocelyn from the Circle of Matthew Parker*, Cambridge Bibliographical Society 13 (Cambridge: Cambridge University Library, 1998).

[12] Kiernan, *Beowulf*, 140–58, 193–218 (the copying campaign), and 159–60 (the making of the Nowell Codex).

been dictated by practical considerations of a kind that frequently resulted in the making of strange bedfellows in the books of the Middle Ages—parchment quires of similar size were often bound together for that reason alone—this explanation does not adequately account for one copyist's singular investment in the two texts. Was there some perception of common themes, on his part or that of his supervisor? Both poems feature heroic cleansings of mead-halls and the successful slaughter of godless gluttons. Can Judith be understood as the female, Anglo-Saxon counterpart to the masculine foreigner, Beowulf? Both are superhuman, saintly, and sterile: Judith is a virgin, Beowulf dies childless. Was the effort of scriptural translation being compared to the expertise of those who recorded oral tradition? Both tasks called for ingenuity, and called forth new audiences.

These are mere conjectures, but they suggest some of the many questions still to be asked of even the most shop-worn medieval cultural commodities in the twenty-first century. Among the most immediate are: How have the heuristic methods, editorial practices, aesthetic judgements, and intellectual bigotry of many generations privileged some literary relics over others? Why, and with what justification, do we still adhere to these standards? And how have modern treatments of pre-modern manuscripts distorted or obscured the meanings their texts may have held for medieval readers or listeners? Composed under entirely different conditions, *Judith* and *Beowulf* may well have served similar purposes by the time they were recorded, and they were certainly relegated to obscurity at the same time, as the language in which they were couched gradually lost currency in England. But when they surface again, on desks in Cotton's library, their shared link with the religious community which had preserved them has long been severed, and their subsequent evaluation will be based on modern conceptions of what 'an extraordinary example of Anglo-Saxon poetics' *ought* to look like. *Beowulf*— manly, self-sufficient, bold, warlike, folksy, and complete—was a hero worth the having by any emerging nation-state defined by a Germanic language; *Judith*— feminine, derivative, duplicitous, elfin, Judaeo-Christian, and fragmentary—was a dangerous hybrid. Their total detachment from one another, and from their joint historical context, seemed necessary by the time *Beowulf* had found a place in the literary limelight: Conybeare separated the two in his 'Arranged Catalogue of All the Extant Relics of Anglo-Saxon Poetry', and *Judith*'s proximity to *Beowulf* goes unmentioned in the first textbook designed expressly for modern students of Anglo-Saxon. Until the middle of the twentieth century, as a result, *Beowulf* and *Judith* would be treated as entities bearing no conceivable relation to one another, and only in 1981 was the manuscript containing them both submitted to systematic analysis.[13] Still, one of them obviously holds a very ancillary place in the history of English literature.

---

[13] Conybeare, *Illustration*, pp. lxxvi–lxxviii; Edward Thorpe, *Analecta Anglo-Saxonica: A Selection, in Prose and Verse, from Anglo-Saxon Authors of Various Ages,* rev. edn. (London: John Smith, 1868),

The unequal treatment accorded to these two poems is paradigmatic of the issues that arise when any text formed in the medieval manuscript matrix is placed in the mouth of the modern canon.[14] When the influential critic Harold Bloom singles out certain 'authors' or 'writers' as 'canonical, that is authoritative in our culture', the very terms in which he articulates his project betray its inapplicability to the Middle Ages, since few of the medieval men and women whom we regard as producers of 'literature' thought of the creative act as being defined primarily by *writing*, or could oversee their work in such a way as to ensure its integrity or consistency, even if they did.[15] In reality, the four pre-modern 'authors' upon whom Bloom bestows the laurels of canonicity—Dante, Chaucer, Cervantes, and Shakespeare—all exhibit a marked self-consciousness when it comes to describing themselves as such, and only Cervantes can be said to have exploited the possibilities of mass publication on his own behalf with any degree of success. Shakespeare, in particular, appears to have invested minimal effort in the printing of his poetry and almost none in that of his plays, which were ephemeral by definition. That is why, in the prologue to *The Two Noble Kinsmen*, Shakespeare (or his associate, John Fletcher, or someone else) apologizes for having fashioned Chaucer's 'Knight's Tale' into a play and begs the audience to treat it kindly for the sake of a 'writer' 'of all admir'd', whose 'famed works' should not be demeaned by the 'light' touch appropriate to popular ballads and sketches. Of course, this view of Chaucer's poetics is almost as anachronistic as Bloom's: note how quickly modernizing forces have succeeded in occluding the aural and performative possibilities of *The Canterbury Tales*, perceived in Shakespeare's day (thanks to Caxton *et alia*) as a literary heirloom, 'constant to eternity'. By contrast, Shakespeare and Fletcher knew themselves to be play*wrights*, not play*writes*. They were craftsmen who sold dramatic materials to a company of actors in exchange for a fee, after which the performers were free to alter these materials at will. When Shakespeare does depict himself as a writer, as in the epilogue to *Henry V* ('Thus far, with rough and all unable pen, | Our bending author hath pursued the story'), there is a humble poignancy in that posture, since he knows that the page before him may well end up on the tiring

---

pp. iii–iv, x, and 141–52. See the bibliography of early editions, translations, and excerpts in Elliott van Kirk Dobbie (ed.), *Beowulf and Judith* (New York: Columbia University Press, 1953), pp. lxxv–c. On the history of the manuscript, its construction, and its present state of preservation, see Kiernan's *Beowulf*; on the importance of this study, see the foreword to the revised edition of 1996, by Katherine O'Brien O'Keeffe (pp. ix–xiii).

[14] I have borrowed the phrase 'manuscript matrix' from Stephen G. Nichols. See 'Philology in a Manuscript Culture', his introduction to a collection of essays on 'The New Philology' in *Speculum*, 65/1 (Jan. 1990), 1–10; 'Philology and its Discontents', in William D. Paden (ed.), *The Future of the Middle Ages: Medieval Literature in the 1990s* (Gainesville: University of Florida Press, 1994), 113–41; and Stephen G. Nicholas and Siegfried Wenzel (eds.), *The Whole Book: Cultural Perspectives on the Medieval Miscellany* (Ann Arbor: University of Michigan Press, 1996), 1–3.

[15] Harold Bloom, *The Western Canon: The Books and School of the Ages* (New York: Harcourt Brace and Company, 1994), 1.

room floor. And it probably did: the script of *Henry V* was halved from 3,400 to 1,700 lines before it received its original production at the Globe, and none of its Choruses may have made the cut. As Andrew Gurr remarks, 'Centuries of habituation to the written word have conditioned us to conceive as fixity what is really flux.'[16]

When Bloom marvels at Chaucer's 'power to represent his persons as to make them permanent', he is speaking metaphorically.[17] But how, in practice, can this permanence be assured in a world where texts are produced by human hands and as subject to whimsy and change as some of the stories told by Chaucer's pilgrims, which were already old when Boccaccio placed them in the mouths of his licentious Florentines? These pilgrims are the *tellers* of tales. Writing is merely the medium of the tales' transmission and, like any recording device, it is neither perfect nor permanent. Actually, the making of a medieval 'text' began long before a scribe put pen to parchment, and we can glimpse various approaches to the early stages of this process in another of Bloom's canonized confections, Dante's *Commedia*. Encountering the soul of his old friend Casella on the outskirts of Purgatory, Dante begs to hear one of his love songs, ' "If there is no new law that takes from you the memory or the skill" ' ('Se nova legge non ti toglie | memoria o uso'). Memory and skill alone are required for the making of music: songsters are not yet singer-songwriters, needing quills or parchment prompts. Casella sings. But we, the readers, are privy only to the song's intitulation, its first line; unlike Dante, we are not able to hear a performance so exquisite 'that the sweetness still sounds within me' ('che la dolcezza ancor dentro mi sona'). Dante himself withholds that pleasure, since he could easily have transcribed the lyrics. Yet he does not do so, fully aware that no talent of his could capture sound, forever lost. He gives us a little more satisfaction when he meets the Provençal poet Arnaut Daniel, approximating the effect of his voice by letting him speak in his native Occitan. Only on a more prosaic occasion, when Dante converses with the shades of the Lustful, does he present himself as a faithful clerk of anyone's testimony: ' "Tell me, so that I may take it down on parchment with my pen' " ('ditemi, ac ciò ch'ancor carte ne verghi'). Later, though, he will beg the reader's pardon for the limitations of his capacity 'to describe' ('A descriver'), to set down what he experiences in writing.[18]

These snatches of conversation, snatches of song, unheard of now and desiccated like the residue of ink left on a page, mimic the experience of the medieval reader who was all too aware that what he saw or heard was a pale shadow, or faint echo, of the lively happenings mediated by writing. The classicist Gregory Nagy, whose

---

[16] Andrew Gurr, *The Shakespeare Company, 1594–1642* (Cambridge: Cambridge University Press, 2004), pp. xiv, 14, 123; p. 120.

[17] Bloom, *The Western Canon*, 105.

[18] Dante Alighieri, *Commedia*, ed. Federico Sanguineti (Florence: Edizioni del Galluzzo, 2001), *Purgatorio*, II. 106–7 and 114; XXVI. 64; XXIX. 97–103.

work on the transmission of Homeric poetry has been informed by consideration of medieval composition and performance practices, helpfully distinguishes among three varieties of written artefact: the *transcript*, defined as 'a record of performance, even an aid for performance, but not the equivalent of performance', the *script*, 'a prerequisite for performance', and the *scripture*, the text that does not 'even presuppose performance'.[19] Most modern texts fall into the third category, but most ancient and medieval texts were of the first or second type, more often the first. As such, they often make anxious gestures toward their own textuality, or the oral traditions from which those texts derived. For the heroes of the *Chanson de Roland*—which began, as did *Beowulf* and the *Iliad*, as oral history—the worst fate imaginable is to become the object of sportive chatter (l. 1477) or the subject of mocking songs (l. 1517), while the best is to be the hero of just such a *chanson de geste* (l. 3181). However, because this poem (as we have it) is the product of a twelfth-century world in which the speech act was yielding some of its authority and potency to the written act, it also makes careful references to a charter inscribed at the cathedral of Laon (l. 2097) and to what 'is written in an ancient book of deeds' ('Il est escrit en l'anciene geste', l. 3742).[20]

The happenings preserved in medieval books, like the heroes of so many medieval romances, thus reveal different aspects of themselves through their encounters with unforeseen others, beginning with the process of their memorialization in written form. Thereafter, like Chaucer's pilgrims and their stories, they find themselves in mixed company. Medieval texts were not sold and circulated, as printed books and pamphlets were, in individualized formats: the vast majority of books were copied by or for people who had bespoken their contents, encasing favourite items between covers based on some similarity of theme, some convenient parity of size and shape, or some principle or preference not readily discernible to modern cataloguers. Consequently, most medieval books are miscellanies, and the texts in them are not always easily distinguishable from another, endowed with titles by their scribes, or provided with cleanly delineated incipits and explicits, beginnings and ends. Very often, these are added by later readers attempting to make sense of unfamiliar materials and unable to gauge 'in the telltale compression of the pages before them, that we are all hastening together to perfect felicity', as the narrator of Jane Austen's *Northanger Abbey* puts it. In some cases, we cannot even say by what names these texts were originally known. Whoever began to transcribe the poem we call *Beowulf*, for instance, either could not tell what it was called or assumed it to be so familiar that no title need be given. In other cases, 'literary' documents come to be entitled in the act of telling, by the

---

[19] Gregory Nagy, *Poetry as Performance: Homer and Beyond* (Cambridge: Cambridge University Press, 1996), 112.

[20] Gérard Moignet (ed.), *La Chanson de Roland: texte établi d'après le manuscrit d'Oxford* (Paris: Bibliothèque Bordas, 1969).

composer; or in the act of enjoyment, by readers and listeners; or in the act of publication, by a scribe; or in the act of editing, by the modern critic. In other words, the making of a medieval text is the result of an ongoing, multi-generational collaboration.

Who, then, among these many participants in the work of medieval literature, should be privileged to name an individual text and to designate its parameters? The author? But what if the author relinquishes these responsibilities by ascribing them to others, or has authority wrested from him by readers, copyists, continuers, and annotators? In the manuscript matrix, one cannot dictate the conditions of reception, any more than one can guarantee uniformity of format. Take, for example, the work of the first vernacular poet who tried to exercise the type of mastery which Bloom regards as essential to literary creation. Around the year 1180, Chrétien de Troyes (*fl.* 1160–83) was composing two Arthurian romances. According to the manuscripts in which these texts were later copied, he introduced one as being 'about the knight of the cart' ('del chevalier de la charrette', l. 24); the other he summarized, toward the end, as having been 'about the knight with the lion' ('del chevalier au lyon', l. 6804).[21] We call these heroes, and their stories, by the names Lancelot and Yvain; Chrétien's medieval audiences knew them by the salient features of the knights' adventures, by the former's shameful conveyance on a cart and the latter's heraldic association with the lion he had once carried on his shield. Moreover, these medieval listeners sometimes had to wait until a story's end before the title was pronounced, and routinely took in many verses of a romance before the identity of a protagonist was revealed, since a name could be a badge of honour and a potent chivalric weapon only to be deployed in special circumstances. (In *Milun*, a *lai* crafted by Chrétien's close contemporary Marie de France, the heroine falls in love with the eponymous hero on the strength of merely hearing him mentioned.) These elements of ambiguity and surprise are missing from our own reading experiences, since we have access to pre-packaged texts with obvious handles. There are certain things that we want to know up front, before we commit ourselves: What is it called? Who is it by? How long is it? For medieval readers, such questions were open-ended, and even the role of the author in answering them was equivocal. More often than not, the reader herself was enlisted in the acts of composition and interpretation.

The problem of authorial control does not end there. The first thing Chrétien tells us about the story of Lancelot (long before he tells us about Lancelot, or the cart) is that the ideas and impetus behind it come from someone else. That person—the real author?—is Marie of Champagne, daughter of England's Queen Eleanor of Aquitaine by her first husband, King Louis VII of France. 'Because my lady of Champagne | Wants a romance to entertain, | I will attempt it willingly,' he

---

[21] Chrétien de Troyes, *Le Chevalier de la Charrette*, ed. Charles Méla, and *Le Chevalier au Lion*, ed. David F. Hult, in *Romans* (Paris: Librairie Générale Française, 1994), 495–704 and 705–936.

begins ('Puis que ma dame de Champaigne | Vialt que romans a feire anpraigne | Je l'anprendrai molt volontiers', ll. 1–3). Really, he insists, he has no stake in the project at all.

> Mes tant dirai ge que mialz oevre
> Ses comandemanz en ceste oevre
> Que sans ne painne que g'i mete.
> Del chevalier de la charette
> Comance Crestiens son livre, 25
> Matiere et san li don et livre
> La contesse et il s'antremet
> De panser, que gueres n'i met
> Fors sa painne et s'antancion.

> For this I swear about this work:
> That her commands have done the work,
> Not any efforts on my part.
> About the knight upon the cart:
> Here Chrétien will begin his book,
> Matter and sense of which he took
> From the countess; he intercedes
> With thoughts, but he will not exceed
> Beyond his charge and its intent.

According to Chrétien, his role as the versifier of this tale constitutes a negligible aspect of the authorial project undertaken by Marie. Apparently, he was uncomfortable with the subject matter (adulterous love and courtly transgression): witness this strong disclaimer, and the fact that he never had the inclination to finish his task. Instead, the story was completed by one Godefroi de Lagny, who describes himself as a clerk who had received Chrétien's 'good accord' ('boen gré', l. 7106), so that 'no man should lay any blame' on him ('nus hom blasme ne l'an mete', l. 7104). Why? Was a stigma attached to unauthorized narrative interventions? Or is Godefroi hinting that such problematic tales are best left unfinished, at least on the page? They can certainly be completed in the fertile minds of the reader and her audience, who may take up the author's thread and unwind it as they please.

On the one hand, we catch Chrétien in the act of foisting the authorship of Lancelot's story onto others. On the other, surprisingly, we witness his audacious attempt to fix the contours of Yvain's tale by asserting his artistic authority.

> Del chevalier al lion fine:
> Crestiens son romant issi. 6805
> Onques plus dire n'en oï,
> Ne ja plus n'en orés conter
> Si on n'i velt mençonge ajoster.

> So ends the knight with the lion:
> Chrétien's own romance, it ends here.

> There is no more to say or hear,
> Nor will more e'er be told anon
> Unless some lies are added on.

But this unwonted display of hubris was too much for the scribe who produced the oldest surviving record of Yvain's exploits some decades later, in the second quarter of the thirteenth century.

> Explicit li chevaliers au lyon
> Cil qui l'escrit Guioz a non
> Devant nostre dame del val
> Est ses ostex tot a estal.[22]

> The knight with the lion here is closed.
> He who wrote it is called Guioz:
> In front of Notre-Dame-du-Val
> You'll always find his market-stall.

Using Chrétien's bravura finale as the hook on which to hang his own quatrain of self-advertisement, Guioz declares that the power of the professional writer trumps that of any professed author. Chrétien the poet had wanted to bring this tale to a point of closure for all time, to preclude the possibility of sequels, additional episodes, or variant readings; Guioz the scribe thumbs his nose at the author's attempt to dictate terms. In the manuscript matrix, he reminds us, no one ever has the last word.

Chrétien's conundrum would have resonated with Margery Kempe. In the preface to her book, a recent addition to the canon of Middle English, Margery chronicles the difficulties she encountered when attempting to record her spiritual adventures in writing, and reveals the extent to which authorship could be as much a collaborative effort in the early fifteenth century as it had been in the twelfth. She, too, seeks authorization for her endeavours with reference to someone else, the 'worshepful clerkys' who had bidden her 'wryten & makyn a booke of hyr felyngys & hir reuelacyons', although she also insists on retaining agency over her narrative. This was hard to do, because she was unable to 'to wrytyn hyr felyngys wyth her owen handys' and it took over twenty years to find a willing amanuensis. When she did, this man produced a script 'so euel wretyn' as to be illegible even to another man who was supposedly familiar with that writing. It took further prayer on Margery's part before a third man, the priest to whom she entrusted the task of transcription, was able to decipher it, and then his eyesight often failed. How strenuous, and tenuous, the operation that brought this book into being! And in the end, neither of these manuscripts, close enough to Margery to be termed autographs, has survived. We have her book because it was rewritten by a scribe

---

[22] Paris, Bibliothèque Nationale de France, fonds français 794, fos. 79ᵛ–105, at 105. See Keith Busby et al. (eds.), *The Manuscripts of Chétien de Troyes* (Amsterdam: Rodopi, 1993), i. 12–15 and ii. 28–33 and 389.

called Salthows sometime prior to 1450, commented upon by four different readers, and, after finding its way to the Carthusian monastery of Mount Grace in Yorkshire, became part of the library assembled by the ancestors of Colonel William Erdeswick Ignatius Butler-Bowdon, where it was identified by Hope Emily Allen in 1934.[23]

Not unlike *Beowulf*, *The Book of Margery Kempe* is the labour of many hands and the fruit of a long gestation in the manuscript matrix. It is also a testament to the power of individual and generational memory in the making of texts. Harold Bloom accordingly comes closer to a medieval idea of canonicity when he invokes pre-modern conceptions of the *ars memoriae*, the crafts of useful thought which were at once highly personal and necessary for public life, defining 'The Canon' (with a capital *C*) 'as the relation of an individual reader and writer to what has been preserved out of what has been written'.[24] In fact, though, the Greek word *kanón* means a rule, a support, the buttress of a shield; the imagery is protective and hints at frailty. Bloom's ideal, modern reader ranges obliviously through the shelves of some Elysian library unravaged by the failed transmission of oral traditions, the burning of books, the hard choices of copyists, the eccentricities of collectors. His confident judgements are predicated on the assumption that what has been lost is lost deservedly, and that what has lasted endures thanks to some inherent virtue. Obviously, this is not the case: *Beowulf* and *Judith* were 'preserved out of what has been written' by pure happenstance (and, for the record, do not figure in *The Western Canon*, which privileges the gods in Bloom's cult of genius); so was Margery's book. The mechanisms which assure the survival and promotion of some cultural artefacts and not others are complex, contingent, chancy, and chauvinistic. That is why *Beowulf* is on the syllabus and not *Judith*, why we have so much Homer and so little Sappho. If the Globe theatre had burned at night, and not in the middle of a performance, half of the known plays of Shakespeare, still in manuscript, would have been reduced to ash and Bloom's canon would carry a very different charge. In any case, his preferred reading list and that of the Elizabethans who frequented playhouses and printers' stalls are strikingly dissimilar. Shakespeare's contemporaries favoured *Mucedorus* over *Hamlet* by a ratio of 5 to 1, and *The Scornful Lady* was far more often seen than Bloom's beloved Falstaff.[25]

Whether or not a given text warrants inclusion in any canon, past or future, is beside the point. More important is the cultivation of an awareness that the very technologies which enable the wider circulation of some writings can be instrumental in eradicating others. Writing not only preserves and facilitates, it constrains and limits. Medieval performers were keenly aware of this. The

---

[23] London, British Library, Add. MS 61823. See *The Book of Margery Kempe: The Text from the Unique MS. Owned by Colonel W. Butler-Bowdon*, ed. Sanford Brown Meech and Hope Emily Allen (London: Oxford University Press, 1940; repr. 1961), pp. xxxii–xxxv and 1–6; *The Book of Margery Kempe*, ed. Lynn Staley (Kalamazoo: Western Michigan University, Medieval Institute Publications, 1996), 3–5. See below, Dinshaw, pp. 116–20.

[24] Bloom, *The Western Canon*, 17.   [25] Gurr, *The Shakespeare Company*, 88 and 126.

unscripted improvisations of the *commedia dell'arte* were a reaction against attempts at censorship, while most of the late medieval Corpus Christi pageants of England were transcribed in order to ensure that actors adhered to approved and orthodox scripts.[26] So, paradoxically, efforts to limit the power and purview of some entertainments have resulted in the making of the texts on which we rely for our study of the performances thus suppressed, while creating the conditions in which others could not survive. For example: when the Creed pageant performed annually at York was submitted to scrutiny in 1567, the Lord Mayor and his council took the precaution of asking an expert if it could be safely mounted under the new Protestant regime. Matthew Hutton, dean of York Minster, replied in the negative: 'For thoghe it was plausible XL yeares agoe, & wold now also of the ignorant sort be well liked; yet now in this happie time of the Gospell, I knowe the learned will mislike it: and how the State will beare with it, I knowe not.' The fact that the script of this pageant is missing from the official register is not coincidental; its disappearance signals that untold numbers of texts met with similar fates within a generation or two of that 'happy time'.[27] Not a decade later, the laws governing the official registry of playscripts in London made the licensing of certain entertainments profitable to an increasingly authoritarian state. At the same time, entrepreneurs' desire to circumscribe other acting companies' access to their approved playbooks meant that some plays would not be published so long as they remained in a repertory, in order to maintain a semblance of copyright. Hence, Andrew Gurr estimates that over half of the plays produced by Shakespeare's company during the productive years of 1594–1600 have 'been lost without a trace'.[28] These measures could not stop rival troupes from performing pirated versions of protected plays, nor did they prevent the theatres' clowns from speaking more than was set down for them, as Hamlet was to complain. But they do mean that we have far fewer scripts than there were plays.

The bottom line? Medieval processes of textual transmission have exercised less effect on the reception and interpretation of medieval 'literature' than modern trends in preservation, proscription, and 'recognition', or modern habits of collection, categorization, and use. Postmodern revisionism has done little to alter this pattern, since successive schools of literary criticism have largely focused on re-editing and reinterpreting the texts already deemed canonical; they have scarcely begun to transgress the boundaries of that canon, to ask when and how they were set,

---

[26] Domenico Pietropaolo, 'Improvisation in the Arts', in Timothy J. McGee (ed.), *Improvisation in the Arts of the Middle Ages and Renaissance* (Kalamazoo, Mich.: Medieval Institute Publications, 2003), 1–28, at 22–3.

[27] 'Matthew Hutton's Letter to the Mayor and Council of York (1567)', in Greg Walker (ed.), *Medieval Drama: An Anthology* (Oxford: Blackwell, 2000), 206. For a facsimile edition of the register, kept up to date until 1583, see Richard Beadle and Peter Meredith (eds.) *The York Play* (Leeds: University of Leeds School of English, 1983).

[28] Gurr, *The Shakespeare Company*, 126.

or to become inquisitive about the texts that have been excluded. Nearly everything that we take for granted about the identification, classification, and evaluation of texts must therefore be subjected to rigorous scrutiny in the twenty-first century, so that we gain a new appreciation of the very different conditions in which *all* medieval writings came into being, while acknowledging that many of the texts that make up the medieval segment of the modern canon were elevated to that status based on a variety of criteria which does not account for the aesthetic, cultural, or social values of medieval people, nor the media through which these values were conveyed. This alienating process, already discernible in the early decades of print, was exacerbated by the mass migration and redistribution of medieval books during the Reformation and the Counter-Reformation, the French Revolution, and a series of other crises; in their aftermaths, many manuscripts wandered abroad for the first time, encountering readers unfamiliar with the traditions in which they had been manufactured and read. Their eventual concentration in Europe's nascent national libraries then led to more or less systematic efforts to create a series of generic categories into which their now confusing contents could be apportioned. Forces as powerful as nationalism and imperialism played a role, as we have noted. So did the embryonic techniques of ethnography, anthropology, and evolutionary biology. *The Origin of Species by Means of Natural Selection, or, The Preservation of Favoured Races in the Struggle for Life*, published by Charles Darwin in 1859, galvanized philologists and literary critics who were at once fascinated, repelled, and puzzled by some of the medieval texts on which modernity was shedding its harsh light. The eminent Shakespearian E. K. Chambers accordingly drew strong parallels between the rites of 'primitive' peoples and the drama of the Middle Ages, in order to argue that the advancement of civilization would make both obsolete. (All hail the 'favoured races' of the Renaissance, brandishing their translations of Aristotle's *Poetics*.) Corroborating this account, Karl Young redated and reorganized the fossils of medieval plays in order to demonstrate that they had evolved from simple to complex forms, applying critical techniques developed in direct response to Darwin.[29] The damage has been lasting. Not until the latter part of the twentieth century did scholars begin to discern that medieval conventions did not die a 'natural' death with the 'evolutionary progress' of humanism.[30] Even now, the prejudices underlying such theories die hard.

---

[29] Ernest Kerchever Chambers, *The Mediaeval Stage*, 2 vols. (Oxford: Oxford University Press, 1903); Karl Young, *The Drama of the Medieval Church*, 2 vols. (New Haven: Yale University Press); John Matthew Manly, 'Literary Forms and the New Theory of the Origin of Species', *Modern Philology*, 4 (1906–7), 577–95.

[30] Harold C. Gardiner, *Mysteries' End: An Investigation of the Last Days of the Medieval Religious Stage* (New Haven: Yale University Press, 1946); O. B. Hardison, *Christian Rite and Christian Drama in the Middle Ages: Essays in the Origin and Early History of Modern Drama* (Baltimore: Johns Hopkins University Press, 1965). See Carol Symes, 'The Appearance of Early Vernacular Plays: Forms, Functions, and the Future of Medieval Theatre', *Speculum*, 77 (2002), 778–831; 'The Performance and Preservation of Medieval Latin Comedy', *European Medieval Drama*, 7 (2003), 29–50.

FURTHER READING

On pre-modern poetics and techniques of composition: Sylvia Huot, *From Song to Book: The Poetics of Writing in Old French Lyric and Lyrical Narrative Poetry* (Ithaca, NY: Cornell University Press, 1987); Joaquín Martínez Pizarro, *A Rhetoric of the Scene: Dramatic Narrative in the Early Middle Ages* (Toronto: University of Toronto Press, 1989); Paul Zumthor, *Toward a Medieval Poetics,* trans. Philip Bennett (Minneapolis: University of Minnesota Press, 1992). On the working methods of medieval scribes as, or in relation to, authors: Michael T. Clanchy, *From Memory to Written Record: England 1066–1307,* 2nd edn. (Oxford: Basil Blackwell, 1993); Armando Petrucci, *Writers and Readers in Medieval Italy: Studies in the History of Written Culture,* ed. and trans. Charles M. Radding (New Haven: Yale University Press, 1995); Jeff Rider, *God's Scribe: The Historiographical Art of Galbert of Bruges* (Washington: The Catholic University of America Press, 2001). On the treatment of medieval texts by modern editors, and the effects of modern editions on scholarship and interpretation: Bernard Cerquiglini, *In Praise of the Variant: A Critical History of Philology,* trans. Betsy Wing (Baltimore: Johns Hopkins University Press, 1999); John Dagenais, *The Ethics of Reading in a Manuscript Culture: Glossing the* Libro de buen amor (Princeton: Princeton University Press, 1994); John Haines, *Eight Centuries of Troubadours and Trouvères: The Changing Identity of Medieval Music* (Cambridge: Cambridge University Press, 2004); Siân Echard and Stephen B. Partridge (eds.), *The Book Unbound: New Directions in Editing and Reading Medieval Books and Texts* (Toronto: University of Toronto Press, 2004). On the history of the Middle English canon and other vernacular literatures: Lee Patterson, *Negotiating the Past: The Historical Understanding of Medieval Literature* (Madison: University of Wisconsin Press, 1987; Seth Lerer, *Chaucer and his Readers: Imagining the Author in Late-Medieval England* (Princeton: Princeton University Press, 1993); Michèle Goyens and Werner Verbeke (eds.), *The Dawn of the Written Vernacular in Western Europe* (Louvain: Leuven University Press, 2003). On the uses of the medieval past in forging modern ideologies: Patrick J. Geary, *The Myth of Nations: The Medieval Origins of Europe* (Princeton: Princeton University Press, 2002); John M. Ganim, *Medievalism and Orientalism: Three Essays on Literature, Architecture, and Cultural Identity* (New York: Palgrave Macmillan, 2005).

CHAPTER 3

MULTILINGUALISM

ROBERT M. STEIN

Homo erat eloquens, Gallice et Latine, magis rationi dicendorum quam ornatui uerborum innitens. Scripturam Anglice scriptam legere nouit elegantissime, et Anglice sermocinare solebat populo, set secundum linguam Norfolchie, ubi natus et nutritus erat.

(Jocelyn of Brakelond).[1]

[He was eloquent in both French and Latin, striving for clarity rather than verbal ornament. He could read English letters elegantly, and he used to give sermons in English to the people, but in the speech of Norfolk, where he was born and raised.]

And Frenssh she spak ful faire and fetisly [elegantly]
After the scole of Stratford atte Bowe,
For Frenssh of Parys was to hire unknowe. (I. 124–6)

Even before the Norman Conquest introduced a significantly large population of French speakers to the Island of Britain, England was polyglot. Not only did various dialects of Old English coexist along with the progressively standardized literary language of the West Saxons and the learned Latin of the liturgy and monastery, but North Germanic and Celtic speakers formed significant portions of the settled population of the island. The marriage of King Æthelred to Emma of Normandy and her subsequent remarriage to King Cnut is a typical example of what Robert Bartlett has called the Aristocratic Diaspora[2]: strategic intermarriage among the European nobility and territorial conquest and colonization served to create a pan-European international culture that crossed political boundaries and resulted in continuous linguistic interchange. Such movements on the part of international elites could also result in shifts in the social meaning of indigenous languages or other local vernaculars that resulted from prior conquest. In the case of early Britain, for example, the Celtic languages became progressively marginalized by the

---

[1] *The Chronicle of Jocelyn of Brakelond,* ed. and trans. H. E. Butler (Oxford: Oxford University Press, 1949), 40.

[2] Robert Bartlett, *The Making of Europe: Conquest, Colonization, and Cultural Change, 950–1350* (Princeton: Princeton University Press, 1993), 24–59.

waves of settlement and ultimate conquest by Germanic speakers, just as the Slavic languages in the eastern Empire were supplanted by German. England after 1066, with its two vernaculars and a third learned language in active and multiform use, is less an anomaly than a particularly striking example of the generally polyglot reality of much of medieval life.

Trilingual England after the Conquest

The sociolinguistic situation of England between 1066 and the end of the thirteenth century has been much studied;[3] the literary consequences of this situation have just begun to be thought about in productive ways. I want to discuss some of the reasons for the neglect in a moment, but first let me broadly outline the linguistic facts on the ground after the Conquest. Celtic speakers were a twice-conquered minority. Danish was still in circulation in the north and east. The great mass of the population was English speaking and probably never learned more than the most rudimentary French. The royal court was francophone. A thin, but very significant, portion of the upper echelons of the aristocracy was similarly francophone. This group, in proximity to royal power and needing to interact in many spheres with the English-speaking population, developed as a truly bilingual elite. This group was fluid and changed over time; many of its members arrived from the Continent in various waves of immigration, especially after the marriage of Henry II to Eleanor of Aquitaine further unified the Angevin and English elites; many of its members were born in England to descendants of conquerors who had settled, intermarried with native elites, and—although still French speaking—had developed a sense of themselves as English. Although English law differentiates between 'Angli' and 'Franci' throughout this period, various contemporary witnesses point out the difficulty of keeping the two groups separate from each other.[4] Language choice

---

[3] See the suggestions for further reading for a list of studies on which this section is based.

[4] Richard Fitzneale's often-quoted remark in the *Dialogus de Scaccario*, written during the reign of Henry II, that the English and Normans had so mingled by his time that it was impossible to distinguish them is the classic witness. See Richard Fitzneale, *Dialogus de Scaccario*, ed. Charles Johnson, F. E. L. Carter, and Diana E. Greenway, Oxford Medieval Texts (Oxford: Clarendon Press, 1983). At the same time, twelfth-century writers often characterize ideas, opinions, and points of view as typically English or typically French. For example, in the *Historia pontificum* William of Malmesbury reports a variety of opinions regarding the integrity of Earl Waltheof of Northumbria, characterizing some of them as the opinions of the French and others as English; see William of Malmesbury, *De gestis pontificum Anglorum*, ed. N. E. S. A. Hamilton, Rolls Series 52 (London: Longman, 1870; repr. Wiesbaden: Kraus, 1964), book 4, section 182. For ethnic identity as legal categories see George Garnett, 'Franci et Angli: The Legal Distinction between Peoples after the Conquest', *Anglo-Norman Studies*, 8 (1986); Ian Short, 'Tam Angli quam Franci: Self-Definition in Anglo-Norman England', *Anglo-Norman Studies*, 18 (1996).

is throughout the period determined more by the relation of language to power than by any other reason including ancestry or a strong sense of ethnic or national identity.

Contemporary sources present William's conquest of England in such a way as to disavow the fact of conquest as such. This contradiction–in which a conquest, that is to say a violent transfer of regimes, is not represented as a conquest but rather as a routine event in the regular affairs of royal succession–is at the heart of William's own ideological programme, and is an important determinant of the linguistic relations among Latin, French, and English during this period. William claimed the English throne first of all by descent, then by election, and finally by feudal right.[5] The conquest is taken to be both the recovery of what was rightfully already William's own while also being a continual manifestation of the justice of that recovery, a judgement of God in a large-scale aristocratic trial by combat over the rights of land tenure. In the period after 1066 the legitimization achieved by casting the conquest as a recovery develops into a strong coherently contradictory assertion that the Normans were already English even before they arrived on the island. In historical and hagiographical texts, Norman rulers find English ancestors for themselves, and otherwise present themselves as natives rather than settlers in new territory. The violence of the civil war after the death of Henry I and the particular ideological investments of Henry II's claim to the throne raise the stakes of the English identity of the francophone elite with the paradoxical effect of greatly enhancing the prestige of the French language at exactly the moment when it was becoming less and less a native vernacular in England.

A curious scene in Wace's *Roman de Rou*, written for Henry II, makes plain how Norman history is made English in this fashion.[6] William asks his feudal council composed of both Normans and English to choose what laws they would live under and thus to choose their ethnic identity. English and French together choose to live

---

[5] For a good summary of the grounds on which William rested his claim to the English throne, Guillaume de Poitiers, *Histoire de Guillaume le Conquérant*, ed. Raymonde Foreville (Paris: Societe d'Édition 'Les Belles Lettres', 1952), p. xvi.

[6] The process by which the Norman rulers of England found English ancestors for themselves and otherwise asserted the legitimacy of their being in England began to attract scholarly attention in the 1980s. More recently scholars have begun to examine the converse possibility, the self-identification of prosperous Englishmen with Norman elites. See S. J. Ridyard, 'Condigna veneratio: Post-Conquest Attitudes to the Saints of the Anglo-Saxons', in R. Allen Brown (ed.), *Anglo-Norman Studies IX: Proceedings of the Battle Conference 1986* (Woodbridge: Boydell Press, 1987). David Townsend, 'Anglo-Latin Hagiography and the Norman Transition', *Exemplaria*, 3 (1991). Frank Barlow, 'The Effects of the Norman Conquest', in *The Norman Conquest: Its Setting and Impact. A Book Commemorating the Ninth Centenary of the Battle of Hastings* (London: Eyre & Spottiswoode, 1966), Ralph V. Turner, 'Changing Perceptions of the New Administrative Class in Anglo-Norman and Angevin England: The Curiales and their Conservative Critics', *Journal of British Studies*, 29 (1990), 28–65. Ralph V. Turner, *Men Raised from the Dust : Administrative Service and Upward Mobility in Angevin England* (Philadelphia: University of Pennsylvania Press, 1988).

under the customs and laws that they all declare to have been their own laws from the time of the Anglo-Saxon King Edward:[7]

> Poist fist toz les barons mander
> e toz les Engleis assembler
> a chois les mist quels leis tendreient
> e quels costumes li voldreient
> ou des Normans ou des Engleis.   (ll. 8997–9001)
>
> [Then he had all the barons sent for
> and all the English assemble
> and had them choose what laws they would hold
> and what customs they wanted
> whether Norman or English.]

They choose the laws and customs of King Edward, a choice that William confirms:

> E cil distrent del rei Ewart
> les soes leis lor tienge e gart
> les costumes qu'il conoisseient
> qu'al tens Ewart tenir soleient
> celes voldrent, celes requistrent,
> celes lor plorent, celes pristrent.
> Issi lor fu a volenté
> e li reis lor a graanté.   (ll. 9003–10)[8]
>
> [And they said of King Edward
> they would hold and preserve his laws
> the customs that they knew
> and that they were accustomed to hold from the time of Edward
> Those they wanted, those they requested
> those pleased them, those they prized
> Those were what they desired
> And the King granted these to them.]

This is the ideological context in which French begins to take on some of the official and literate functions that since the Conquest had been the preserve of Latin—it becomes a language of record, of instruction, and a status marker demonstrating one's proximity to royal governance. As such, having a certain degree of proficiency in spoken and written French becomes a matter of practical urgency during the course of the thirteenth century.[9]

---

[7] Several codifications of law, all purporting to be of venerable date, are composed during the reign of Henry II. One of the most important of these texts is titled *Leges Edwardi Confessoris*. See Felix Liebermann, *Die Gesetze der Angelsachsen* (Halle: Max Niemeyer, 1903–11).

[8] Wace, *Le Roman de Rou*, ed. A. J. Holden, Société des Anciens Textes Français (Paris: Picard, 1970).

[9] Especially given the long passage of time, one cannot be certain about degrees of influence back onto French by the social usages of early English, but it is perhaps no accident that before the Conquest a standardized English had been similarly used as a language of record and instruction alongside Latin in both lay and clerical circles.

At this time books of instruction emerge, advertising themselves as necessary for the mastery of French. Some of these books of instruction are written in Latin and modelled directly on the modes of instruction for practical Latin literacy in public affairs, the *ars dictaminis*. They clearly are meant to help those who need to write letters, contracts, or other documents that might have public or legal ramifications. Other books of instruction are in the vernacular. None of them is addressed to raw beginners, and all presuppose that their users will have already attained a certain degree of literacy. Walter de Bibbesworth's *Tretiz* provides a good example of the trilingual relations of the early thirteenth century.[10] Addressed to a noblewoman as an aid in teaching her son French, the book is primarily a French vocabulary list in rhymed octosyllabic couplets with English glosses. It emphasizes terms necessary for estate management and the running of a great house. After beginning with a quick tour through the vocabulary necessary for naming the parts of the body and items of clothing, most of the text is devoted to the outdoors, and it frequently takes the form of a walk around the estate. 'Ore aloms as prés e as champs | Pour enformer vos enfaunz' (ll. 326–7) is a typical transition. The layout of the book (in which French terms—with much attention to homonyms and near homonyms—are explained by English glosses[11]) demonstrates Bibbesworth's assumption that his audience was familiar with French, even as English was still the vernacular spoken most comfortably. Other indications of familiarity with French are his choice of octosyllabic rhymed lines, as well as several places of direct address where he assumes that his addressee knows some French—for example,

> Mes n'ad mester ke vous dioms
> De tute manere de blé les nouns,
> De segle, orge ne forment,
> Ke commune sunt a tote gent.   (ll. 334–7)
>
> [But there is no need to tell you
> The names of all sorts of grain
> or of rye, barley, or wheat
> For these are commonly known by everyone.]

---

[10] Walter de Bibbesworth and William Rothwell, *Le Tretiz* (London: Anglo-Norman Text Society, 1990). I cite by line number parenthetically in the text.

[11] Typical is the following run of lines:

Vous avez la levere e le levere,	lippe hare
la livere e le livre	the pount bock
la levere, c'est ke enclost les dens	
le levere ki boys se tent dedeins	
la livere sert de marchandie,	
le livere nous aprent aprent clergie	(ll. 61–7)

The passage as a whole may be translated as 'You have the lip and the hare | The pound and the book | The lip, that's what encloses the teeth | The hare, who hides in the woods | The pound is used in the market | The book teaches us Latin learning.'

His observation that one learns one's Latin from a book ('le livere nous aprent clergie', l. 66) attests as well to the spread of a certain degree of pragmatic Latin literacy among the laity. And his comparison of his own instructional text to the kind of book from which one learns Latin shows that French, although a spoken language for his addressee (and the sixteen extant manuscripts of *Le Tretiz* demonstrate that his particular addressee is but one of many actual readers), needs the aid of more formal instruction for perfection.

Literary relations

The polyglot reality of medieval life, while often acknowledged, has barely received its due as a literary phenomenon. The reasons for this neglect are manifold, complex, and trickily entangled with the historical development of literary studies during the nineteenth and twentieth centuries and with the ghosts of earlier moments in their history that still haunt current academic configurations. Although medievalists study a period prior to the state, they do this, if they are literary scholars, as part of the historical study of national literatures. The departmental structures of our universities, as well as the 'specialization category codes' of our professional associations and granting institutions, are organized directly by the idea of national languages, national literatures, and national history.

This disciplinary organization still rests directly on the fundamental, even if now highly contested, assumption of philology; namely that the essential ethnic characteristics of a nation are embodied most profoundly in the deepest characteristics of its language. In these linguistic characteristics the truth of the nation progressively realizes itself and becomes most profoundly manifest in its literature and in its law. In this manifestation, we can call philology the sister discipline of the kind of philosophical history that since the time of the early German Romantic writers and especially since Hegel sees the formation of the secular state as the highest achievement of human culture.[12] The philological study of literary works and legal texts thus intends to bring the truth of the nation to critical self-consciousness just as Romantic philosophy of history sees this same truth embodied in the state. Philology so construed requires the identification of the state with the nation, an

---

[12] Erich Auerbach was extremely aware of the debt of his own work to Hegel and German Romanticism as well as to Vico. In the 'Epilegomena to Mimesis', in *Mimesis* (Princeton: Princeton University Press, 2003), he writes that *Mimesis* would be 'conceivable in no other tradition than in that of German romanticism and Hegel. It would never have been written without the influences that I experienced in my youth in Germany' (p. 571). See also the brilliant analysis of the work of Auerbach and its reception in America in Paul Bové, *Intellectuals in Power: A Genealogy of Critical Humanism* (New York: Columbia University Press, 1986). For the importance of Vico see Erich Auerbach, 'Giovambattista Vico e l'idea della filologia', *Convivium*, 4 (1956); Edward W. Said, *Beginnings: Intention and Method* (New York: Columbia University Press, 1985).

imaginary structure that maps political sovereignty onto territories presumed to be ethnically and linguistically homogeneous. We have not yet escaped the fact that the study of national literatures emerged during the period of high imperialism. During this period the linguistic and ethnic purity of the European national state was taken to be the sign of both its rationality and its modernity, and it granted Europe its 'mission civilisatrice' and authorized its right to rule. Hence, for medieval literary studies, the great privilege granted to writing in the European vernaculars: they were presumed to contain the national soul in its most direct manifestation. Indeed, in the birth of national literary studies, the medieval vernaculars occupied the same intellectual slot as Greek and Latin had done in the pan-European humanist curriculum. And hence, too, the emphatic assertion—despite all evidence to the contrary—that the European vernaculars were themselves linguistically homogeneous entities. For creoles and pidgins, it long went without saying, belonged to the polyglot, lawless, disorderly world of the darker races, the races 'without history' who needed to be ruled and directed along the path to the modern world.[13]

The orderliness that once was asserted to be the universal sign of culture itself was also manifest in the orderliness of the map: the grand historical narrative maintains that the division of the world into ethnically and linguistically bordered national states began in Europe when the 'not yet modern' medieval associations coalesced into the early modern state, and thence spread by the 'modernizing' and 'civilizing' imperial project to the rest of the world.[14] The great early twentieth-century reference collections such as the eleventh edition of the *Encyclopaedia Brittanica* or *Shepherd's Historical Atlas*[15] present the nationalist historiographical narrative and its colonialist correlatives with particular clarity. Paging through *Shepherd's*, one sees visually laid out the 'progress' of European state sovereignty. The European nation-states are there, even if only spectrally, from the beginning of recorded history. Thus, map 29 'The Growth of Roman Power in Italy to 218 B.C.' shows Rome progressively occupying the territorial outlines of the modern unified Italian state as if the state were already in place. England, France, and 'Central Europe' are presented map after map in their progressive development to modernity. We follow France, for example, from 1035 (map 61) to 1154–84 (69), 1328 (76), 1453 (81), 1455–94 (84), and finally 1789 (101). Only with map 104 does Asia enter the

---

[13] The process is by no means over. The Medieval Academy of America Annual Meeting, Spring 2000, Austin, Tex., devoted a session to examining whether Middle English is a creole. The answer was a definite no—in fact, the answer was a no in thunder—and emotions ran very much higher than one would ever expect to find in response to a panel presentation attempting to use quite precise criteria and quantitative historical linguistic methodology.

[14] Edward W. Said, *Culture and Imperialism* (New York: Vintage Books, 1994) for the way that late nineteenth- and early twentieth-century documents of culture speak empire. For medievalism and its imperial entanglements, Jeffrey Jerome Cohen, *The Postcolonial Middle Ages* (New York: St Martin's Press, 2000); Allen J. Frantzen, *Desire for Origins: New Language, Old English, and Teaching the Tradition* (New Brunswick, NJ: Rutgers University Press, 1990).

[15] William R. Shepherd, *Shepherd's Historical Atlas*, 9th edn. (New York: Barnes & Noble, 1973).

story, and it enters in a map entitled 'Medieval European Commerce (Asia)'. The New World comes into existence in 1492 (105), of course, followed immediately by a large double foldout tracing the European voyages of discovery and entitled 'The Expansion of Europe'. Africa makes its first appearance only in map 174, entitled 'The Partition of Africa', which shows the pre- and post-First World War colonial divisions of the continent. This map is followed directly by the only linguistic map in the volume. It is a world map titled 'Distribution of the European Languages', dividing the world into the seven languages of English, French, German, Spanish, Dutch, Portuguese, and Russian. The legend reads: 'In the colonial dominions of the European powers in Asia and Africa, the coloring shows the language of the dominant nation' (176). Lest my reader find this all an old story and too often told, I note that the copy I consulted advertised how very up-to-date it had become: it was 'revised and updated' to 1973 and ends with map 226 'Europe in 1973'. This colonialist historiography is not only a product of popular culture or outdated reference volumes. Even modern, historically self-conscious, scholarly discussions of medieval Northumbria, for example, treat it as already part of England long before English monarchs were able to assert any kind of hegemony in the territory, describing, for example, the struggle against William I as a 'rebellion', as if medieval England were already in existence and always in the process of achieving its current borders.[16] The historical paradigm that has determined the institutional structure of medieval studies rests today, still, on this nineteenth-century teleology: all history is nothing but the history of modernity; the rest of the world possesses a history only insofar as it is a prelude to modernity, as the not-yet modern, and medieval studies witnesses modernity at its origin.

In the case of England this imperial historiography was doubled by a local search for the origins and persistence of English enlightened institutions. This search necessarily identified English writing with writing in the English language. The metaphor of the Norman yoke, for example, combines this desire for origins with the whiggish sense of history as progressive so that an English nation and English state turn out to be both the precursor and the preordained outcome of post-Conquest history. The essentializingly nationalist rhetoric of R. W. Chambers's famous introduction to the EETS edition of Harpsfield's *Life of More*, 'On the continuity of English prose from Alfred to More'[17] might now seem easily dismissible, as does the nationalist, ideological programme of Gaston Paris and Francisque Michel[18] as they combed through English libraries seeking to 'repatriate' the cultural patrimony of France—to restore the *Chanson de Roland, La Vie de Saint Alexis, Tristan,* the writing

---

[16] For further discussion of this matter, see Robert M. Stein, *Reality Fictions: Romance, History, and Governmental Authority 1066–1180* (Notre Dame, IN: University of Notre Dame Press, 2006), 87–103.

[17] Nicholas Harpsfield et al., *The Life and Death of Sr Thomas Moore, Knight, Sometymes Lord High Chancellor of England,* EETS, os 186 (London: Oxford University Press, 1932).

[18] Andrew Taylor, 'Was There a Song of Roland?' *Speculum,* 76 (2001), 28–65.

of Wace, Benoît de Saint Maure and all the *romans d'antiquité* to their 'native' soil. (For without these texts, all written under Anglo-Norman or Angevin auspices and many written entirely in England for English audiences and reflecting English experience, early medieval French literature is virtually non-existent.) However transparently visible the nationalism that underlies these scholarly efforts might be, it is far more difficult to imagine the revisionary extent—both theoretically and practically considered—of reading the literature of England not only within an international context, as Elizabeth Salter began to show us before her untimely death,[19] but also as a fluid entity within an internally fissured, polyglot field.

How then to begin? Deeply entrenched theoretical presuppositions must be called into question. Huge practical difficulties immediately arise. Training in multilingual and multinational medieval studies necessarily takes place in what is now a departmental dispersal, departments in which medieval studies have themselves become marginal to the departmental mainstream. Yet the future of medieval studies, and perhaps the future of literary studies, lies precisely at this theoretical and practical juncture.

Learning from the manuscripts

Perhaps the easiest point of theoretical and practical entry to the multilingual reality of medieval literary relations is provided by the manuscript evidence. A very large number of twelfth- and thirteenth-century manuscripts produced in England cross linguistic boundaries in their contents while also crossing boundaries separating literary from non-literary, sacred from secular, serious from comic, popular from learned—to name only a few categories that seem inescapably necessary in organizing our habitual understanding of literature and culture. These categories are frequently and often puzzlingly transgressed by medieval habits of compilation. The Oxford manuscript of the *Chanson de Roland* (Digby 23), for example, binds the poem together with Chalcidius' translation and commentary on Plato's *Timaeus*. Reading the *Lais* of Marie de France in a modern edition or finding 'Sumer is icumen in' in an anthology of Middle English lyrics are entirely different experiences from finding them together in Harley 978. Let me spend a moment describing this fascinating manuscript. First of all, Harley 978 was owned and may well have been produced at Reading Abbey, a Benedictine foundation.[20] The manuscript begins

---

[19] Elizabeth Salter, Derek Albert Pearsall, and Nicolette Zeeman, *English and International: Studies in the Literature, Art, and Patronage of Medieval England* (Cambridge: Cambridge University Press, 1988).

[20] With regard to Marie's *Lais* in this manuscript, John Frankis remarks with characteristic understatement, 'It is striking to find such courtly secular poetry, with traces of moral ambiguity and of paganism, preserved in a Benedictine abbey.' John Frankis, 'The Social Context of Vernacular Writing in Thirteenth Century England: The Evidence of the Manuscripts', *Thirteenth Century England*, 1 (1986), 177.

with a collection of Latin antiphons, many with musical notation. Included among the antiphons is the text of 'Sumer is icumen in' accompanied by an alternative set of words in Latin, 'Perspice Christicola', to be sung to the same tune, and Latin instructions for singing it polyphonically. The Latin poems are followed immediately by a liturgical calendar and a series of prose essays, some in Latin and some in French, giving practical medical advice on such matters as preparing oil for the elimination of headlice (fo. 33), how to tell whether a wounded man is alive or dead (fo. 30), or what to do in case of snakebite (fo. 32), and also discussing such things as the distance from the earth to the moon, to the sun, and to the throne of God (fo. 35). These useful essays are followed by an important collection of Latin satires and goliardic verse, Marie's *Fables*, Latin material from the cult of Thomas Becket, a French praise of Simon de Montfort's victory at the battle of Lewes, Marie's *Lais*, and a concluding set of Latin motets. The quality of much of this material—and its interest for us—is striking; the range of this trilingual compilation is quite characteristic for the period.

A manuscript like Harley 978 not only provides information about the trilingual reading habits of its compiler and of its audience, but also provides a material context for questions about our own construction of the field that we call medieval English literature. What are the exclusions, identifications, filiations, and generic associations that create the intellectual and institutional context within which a medieval text becomes an object of study for us? What might it mean, to stay with this manuscript for another moment, that the only 'complete' French text of Marie's *Lais* is to be found in this company? And what does it further mean, that the only other 'complete' medieval text of the *Lais* is an Old Norse translation,[21] especially in the light of Marie's own continual meditation on translation, cultural friction, and multilingualism throughout all her work?

Multilingual relations within manuscripts open very wide theoretical perspectives. Multilingual relations between related manuscripts similarly raise complex theoretical questions. The St Albans Psalter, for example, made for Christina of Markyate, is intimately related to her Latin *vita*, written as part of a campaign to have her canonized as a saint. The *vita* carefully registers the tensions between the prosperous English families of Huntingdonshire, including Christina's own, and the French ecclesiastical and secular officials with whom they were entangled in all aspects of public and private life.[22] Indeed the English language makes a stunning appearance in the *vita*, when the hermit Roger affectionately calls her 'myn sunendaege [Sunday] dohter'. The St Albans Psalter, while having been made

---

[21] See Robert Cook and Mattias Tveitane (eds.), *Strengleikar: An Old Norse Translation of Twenty-One Old French Lais* (Oslo: Norsk Historisk Kjeldeskrift-institutt, 1979).

[22] As C. H. Talbot, the *vita*'s modern editor, notes, 'The people with whom Christina was intimately connected-seem to have belonged exclusively to the Anglo-Saxon element of the community.' See C. H. Talbot, *The Life of Christina of Markyate: A Twelfth Century Recluse* (Oxford: Clarendon Press, 1987), 12.

for the obviously anglophone Christina, contains no English. It weds the Latin texts of the Psalms to the French *Chanson de Saint Alexis* and to an elaborate picture cycle accompanied by Gregory's famous letter justifying images as the Bible of the illiterate. This letter is followed in the text by a French translation. The circulation of languages within this textual community corroborates our general sociolinguistic account of the period, and the stakes in the dominant linguistic choices seem clear enough. A Latin *vita* is an inextricable part of the ecclesiastical process of canonization that the text wishes to perform; French seems by the early twelfth century to be the ordinary language of instruction in the monastic milieu. Yet these texts in their relations also can provide an entry point to the largest questions of cultural translation in a polyglot milieu. These dominant choices are destabilized not only by the presence of English—even if an absent presence—but even more radically by the social tensions the languages themselves continuously record.

Even shifting between dominant linguistic possibilities is never a straightforward matter and can indeed have large-scale effects. Consider, for a moment, a small example from the diglossic milieu of the Continent. An anonymous French translator, possibly writing as late as the fifteenth century, translates Galbert of Bruges's characterization of Count Charles, 'fortissimus vir', as 'un prince bon e vaillant'.[23] Galbert's Latin assimilates Charles to Republican Roman canons of virtue; the translator places him directly into the chivalric world, an aristocratic scale of values that in many ways Galbert's text otherwise calls quite seriously into question. More seismic effects occur as Geoffrey of Monmouth's vastly influential *Historia regum Brittaniae* crosses into Wace's French octosyllabics, and in the process becomes both a *roman d'antiquité* and a song of Norman victory, and then into Layamon's archaic alliterative English where the English conquest of the Britons cannot help but recall the subsequent conquest of the English themselves by the Normans. Where Wace's French text is a victor's song of victory, Layamon's English speaks victory always as abjection. In the new language the text not only is transformed in itself and in its genre but enters into networks of intertextual affiliation that create very different meanings out of even its smallest elements. What I want to emphasize here, though, is not the special effect of translation on a single text. I am rather using the example of translation to say that any choice to speak is simultaneously a choice not to speak otherwise. This is true even within a single language: Layamon's Old English-looking verse appears in the same manuscript as the elegantly 'modern' English of the *Owl and the Nightingale*, written in octosyllabics and laid out in an unmistakably French *mise-en-page*; at about the same time, someone at the Cistercian nunnery at Wintney copied an Old English translation of Benedict's Rule, 'in a form of language that may well

---

[23] Galbert de Bruges, *De multro, traditione, et occisione gloriosi Karoli comitis Flandiarum*, ed. Jeff Rider, Corpus Christianorum Continuatio Mediaevalis 131 (Turnholt: Brepols, 1994).

have posed some problems of comprehension to the nuns who were to use it'.[24] In the polyglot world, literary language is fissured not only internally by words not spoken but also continuously by always gesturing to the language of the other that inescapably inhabits one's own. Perhaps the francophone Galbert while writing 'fortissimus vir' was himself thinking 'prince bon e vaillant' even as he resisted the pull of its meanings.

No points of stability can be found within the fluid and shifting multilingual field. Neither English nor Latin nor French can be definitively attached either to a place of production or to a specific use during this period. The law of genre, as Derrida remarked, or rather the law of the law of genre, is contamination;[25] so too, I follow his spirit to add, the law of the law of literary production is constant dissemination. Among the writings of the Cistercian monk Ailred of Rievaulx are found the *Institutione inclusarum*, written in the learned Latin of philosophical meditation as a manual of private devotion for his sister, and the *Vita Edwardi regis*, a piece of distinctly Angevin propaganda written for Henry II on the occasion of the translation of Edward the Confessor to Westminster, a grand state occasion. Soon after, the *Vita Edwardi* appears again twice, now in French, once written by a nun of Barking Abbey, where it now seems to provide a hagiographical starting point for private meditation within a devotional community, and again elaborately remade by Matthew Paris in St Albans with beautiful and copious illustrations, to be read as national and spiritual history alongside his chronicles. The *Institutione inclusarum* is later translated into English, where it joins the *Ancrene Wisse*; this latter text is also continuously remade in various English, French, and Latin versions, addressed now to a small group of recluses, now to much larger communities, sometimes to women, sometimes to men, and in the fourteenth century it becomes part of the library of Lollard writings.[26]

The three languages circulate among court, monastery, cathedral, and baronial hall; history, hagiography, romance, and books of private devotion similarly circulate—Jordan Fantosme's history, written in French, using the verse structures of epic, and having manifest baronial interests, is bound together in several manuscripts with Gaimar's *Estoire des Engleis*, written in the octosyllabics of French romance, and Wace's *Roman de Brut*, the one with provincial, the other with royal, interests. Read together, they form a continuous history; more interestingly, this is

---

[24] Frankis, 'The Social Context of Vernacular Writing', 178.

[25] 'Avant d'en venir à l'epreuve d'un certain exemple, je tenterai de formuler, de manière aussi elliptique, économique et formelle que possible, ce que j'appellerai la loi de la loi du genre. C'est précisément un principe de contamination, une loi d'impureté, une économie du parasite.' Jacques Derrida, 'La Loi du genre', *Glyph*, 7 (1980), 179. My debt to the life's work of Jacques Derrida throughout the whole of this essay is beyond citation.

[26] For further bibliography see Bella Millett, George Jack, and Yoko Wada, *Ancrene Wisse, the Katherine Group, and the Wooing Group*, Annotated Bibliographies of Old and Middle English Literature V. 2 (Rochester, NY: D. S. Brewer, 1996).

a continuous history told from conflicting perspectives. In the fluid, multilingual social space no single text ever stays comfortably in its generic place or maintains a fixed political alignment.

Polygot literature: literature without nations

No name exists for the kind of literary studies we do, nor for its aims. Without the authorization provided by the grand historical narrative of modernity and without the assurance that both works of art and their analysis are, at their best, 'doctrinal for a nation', we carry on a critical practice filled with uncertainties of all kinds yet rich in implication. We make do with the term literary criticism, while recognizing that we are no longer quite in the business of separating the artistically compelling wheat from the historical chaff. Techniques of close and extremely attentive reading that historically were elaborated to come to grips with the complex, evocative, and highly self-conscious linguistic procedures of the great artistic works of high culture have, since the linguistic turn throughout the human sciences, been brought to bear with extremely fruitful results—inside and more often outside departments of literature—on linguistic and symbolic material of all sorts, and with a manifold of scholarly aims. Medieval literary studies began in a philology tied to a certain national self-consciousness and to national interests. It claimed the great privilege of witnessing the beginning of a preordained development—the triumph of modernity, enlightenment, and civil society incarnate in the emergence of the secular state. Our literary criticism now takes place in the context of a crisis of the secular state, if not of its outright failure, and at a moment of a striking desecularization of both political discourse and civil society.[27] This critical practice is rather thoroughly decoupled from the philological presuppositions and historical aims that both authorized it and endowed it with a promise of positive knowledge for its end. It is necessarily theoretically self-reflexive, interminably calling into question the enabling suppositions of its own critical operations, and yet it is inescapably historically conscious. International and multilingual, it finds its most pregnant textual examples rather in border territories and areas of shifting sovereignties than in hegemonic centres, yet it shares neither the presuppositions nor disciplinary aims of comparative literature as conventionally understood. For comparative literature, too, bears the burden of the nationalist ghost bequeathed it by philology, and it preserves national boundaries in the act of comparison even as it would transgress them in theory. That the unquestioned confidence in the truth of

---

[27] In this context of failure and of rapid desecularization the secular state is still in no hurry to wither away or otherwise disappear. See for some important recent discussion Anne-Marie Slaughter, *A New World Order* (Princeton: Princeton University Press, 2004) and Gauri Viswanathan, *Outside the Fold: Conversion, Modernity, and Belief* (Princeton: Princeton University Press, 1998).

philology has vanished utterly is a pregnant moment in the history of globalization. At an earlier moment in that history, one dreamed optimistically of a *Welt-literatur*, a huge library of ethnic and national diversities conversing together polyphonically in a multitude of languages that demonstrated the richness of human experience and the vast range of human possibility. Revisionary multilingual medieval literary studies stand at a place where their version of the past can no longer imply a preordained future. Yet, perhaps the beginnings of their awareness of the multiple perspectives opened by the continuous, fluid, polyglot circulation of expression and representation in the past might allow them to hear a new and as yet unheard whisper from the world to come, to begin to create a knowledge new enough that one does not know before it has arrived what it might be or where it might lead.

FURTHER READING

The foundational work for the modern study of multilingual literacy in post-Conquest England is M. T. Clanchy, *From Memory to Written Record: England, 1066–1307* (Cambridge, MA: Harvard University Press, 1979). R. M. Wilson's magisterial 'English and French in England 1100–1300', *History*, NS 28 (1943), 37–60 is still the best starting point for exploring the relations between English and French during this period. The monograph by Douglas A. Kibbee, *For to Speke Frenche Trewely: The French Language in England, 1000–1600: Its Status, Description, and Instruction* (Philadelphia: J. Benjamins, 1991) provides an excellent overview of the field. Much of the best work on English multilingualism has been done by major scholars of Anglo-Norman. William Rothwell for example has devoted many articles to determining the precise relations between English and French. Among them one should definitely consult 'Aspects of Lexical and Morphosyntactical Mixing in the Languages of Medieval England', in D. A. Trotter (ed.), *Multilingualism in Later Medieval Britain* (Woodbridge: D. S. Brewer, 2000); 'À quelle époque a-t-on cessé de parler français en Angleterre?', in *Mélanges de philologie romane offerts à Charles Camproux* (Montpellier: CEO, 1978); 'The Role of French in Thirteenth Century England', *Bulletin of the John Rylands Library*, 58 (1976), 445–66; 'The Teaching of French in Medieval England', *Modern Language Review*, 63 (1968), 37–46. Ian Short and Susan Crane have made major contributions to our understanding of the implications of English multilingualism. See Short's 'On Bilingualism in Anglo-Norman England', *Romance Philology*, 33 (1979–80), 467–79 and Susan Crane's 'Social Aspects of Bilingualism in the Thirteenth Century', *Thirteenth Century England*, 6 (1997), 103–16, 473–86.

Some very interesting work has recently begun to be done on the persistence of Old English into the post-Conquest period. Notable is the anthology edited by Mary Swan and Elaine M. Treharne, *Rewriting Old English in the Twelfth Century* (Cambridge: Cambridge University Press, 2000).

Literary critical work from a multilingual perspective is still in its early stages. Notable exceptions are Elizabeth Salter's posthumously published *English and International: Studies in the Literature, Art, and Patronage of Medieval England*, ed. Derek Albert Pearsall, and Nicolette Zeeman (Cambridge: Cambridge University Press, 1988) and the extraordinary book by Susan Crane, *Insular Romance: Politics, Faith, and Culture in Anglo-Norman and Middle English Literature* (Berkeley and Los Angeles: University of California Press, 1986). As is the case among the more purely linguistic studies, Anglo-Norman scholars are leading the way in the literary field. Outstanding is the series of studies on francophone women's writing and women's textual communities by Jocelyn Wogan-Browne. Two of her articles in particular stand out: '"Clerc u lai, muïne u dame": Women and Anglo-Norman Hagiography in the Twelfth and Thirteenth Centuries', in Carol Meale (ed.), *Women and Literature in Britain, 1150–1500* (Cambridge: Cambridge University Press, 1993); 'Queens, Virgins, and Mothers: Hagiographic Representations of the Abbess and her Powers in Twelfth- and Thirteenth-Century Britain', in Louise O. Fradenburg (ed.), *Women and Sovereignty* (Edinburgh: Edinburgh University Press, 1992). Wogan-Browne's book *Saints' Lives and Women's Literary Culture c.1150–1300: Virginity and its Authorizations* (Oxford: Oxford University Press, 2001) is an especially good indication of the riches that lie buried in this field. The multiple relations between the vernaculars of England and Latin are especially noticeable in hagiography and historiography. Three articles among recent studies that have approached these fields from the perspective of multilingualism are theoretically rich and especially thought-provoking for literary studies in general: Robert Bartlett, 'The Hagiography of Angevin England', *Thirteenth Century England*, 5 (1995), 37–52; Annie Samson, 'The South English Legendary: Constructing a Context', *Thirteenth Century England*, 1 (1986), 185–95. David Trotter, 'Oceano Vox: You Never Know Where a Ship Comes From: On Multilingualism and Language-Mixing in Medieval Britain', in Kurt Braunmüller and Gisella Ferraresi (eds.), *Aspects of Multilingualism in European Language History* (Amsterdam: Benjamins, 2003). Of particular theoretical interest for multilingual studies is a recent article on continental material, Sara S. Poor, 'Mechthild von Magdeburg, Gender, and the "Unlearned Tongue"', *Journal of Medieval and Early Modern Studies*, 31 (2001), 213–50.

CHAPTER 4

MULTILINGUALISM ON THE PAGE

CHRISTOPHER BASWELL

England in the fourteenth and fifteenth centuries inherited the very complex and shifting linguistic situation that Robert Stein has outlined for the twelfth and thirteenth, in both social use and literary settings. While English continued its slow and uneven ascent to political and literary prominence across the fourteenth and earlier fifteenth centuries, French remained an important presence, and in places a dominant one. The appearance of treatises on French usage and writing as early as the middle of the thirteenth century, however, suggests that even by that point some French speakers felt the need for technical help. Walter de Bibbesworth's probably mid-thirteenth-century *Tretiz de langage* (also called *Femina*), mentioned by Stein, was used by its powerful patron Dionysia de Munchesni to teach her sons and daughters correct French, including the vocabulary of estate management, law, and trade, not just courtly exchange. An early fifteenth-century language text derived from the *Tretiz* was called *Femina nova*, most likely in recognition of the users who taught from it. Manuscripts of the *Tretiz*, as of related works, multiply across the fourteenth century (nine surviving copies) and the fifteenth (five copies). Twenty copies of guides to French letter-writing, or collections of sample letters, survive from the same centuries.[1] The focus of such works suggests the continuing practical uses of Anglo-French in the later Middle Ages in England. Many mercantile and civic records, too, where we might expect an early use of English, continued to be kept in French.[2]

I am indebted to Jocelyn Wogan-Browne for help with this chapter.

[1] For the most recent discussion of the *Tretiz*, see Renate Haas, '*Femina*: Female Roots of "Foreign" Language Teaching and the Rise of Mother-Tongue Ideologies', in Lynn Arner (guest ed.), *Exemplaria: In Honor of Sheila Delany*, currently available online at **www.english.ufl.edu/exemplaria/SD/**. For manuscript survival of this and related teaching texts, Andres Kristol, 'L'Enseignement du français en Angleterre (XIIIe–XVe siècles): les sources manuscrites', *Romania*, 111 (1990), 289–330.

[2] W. Rothwell, 'English and French in England after 1362', *English Studies*, 82 (2001), 548.

The young Chaucer would have known and used the self-consciously provincial French of 'Stratford atte Bowe' that he later mocks in his Prioress; he would have learned the French of Paris as well, though, by means of books like those mentioned above, or through court contact and diplomatic work. As a servant of Prince Lionel he would have carried diplomatic documents, carefully written in continental French, back to London from the negotiations of the Treaty of Brétigny.[3] As an adult working in a number of administrative posts, too, he would have needed many of the skills in account-keeping and letter-writing purveyed by the French treatises. And he often depends on French versions for access to Latin (and perhaps Italian) texts that were apparently a greater challenge to him. Throughout the *Canterbury Tales*, Chaucer moves with brilliant ease among the diction worlds of his upbringing, from the Man of Law's portrait, which draws heavily on technical law French, to Chauntecleer's condescending courtly French and passable Latin, to the quite learned citation of Statius that Chaucer (or his Knight) seems to have placed at the head of the 'Knight's Tale'.

Despite the rise of urbane literary English around the court of Richard II, in which we take so much interest, practical French remained widespread in later medieval England—notwithstanding John Trevisa's often quoted assertion that by 1385 Latin education took place in English: 'in all the gramer scoles of Englonde children leveth Frensh and construith and lerneth in English.'[4] Specialized official versions of French were important in records such as the Rolls of Parliament and court documents across the fourteenth and fifteenth centuries, at least until the 1430s in the Rolls, and much longer in law reports. There, French finally became 'an arcane trade jargon, albeit a socially elevated one', even as oral pleading was increasingly conducted in a syntactically English language still dependent on the French vocabulary of law.[5] Edward III's Statute of Pleading of 1362, often seen as a watershed in the rise of official English, did call for pleading in 'la lange anglaise', but it made no parallel demand about record-keeping, and of course it was issued in Anglo-French.[6] In the face of rising competition from French in the public sphere across the thirteenth century and after, Latin too retained its multiple roles, albeit increasingly specialized and divided, in public documents, the Church and devotional books (such as psalters and the enormously popular Books of Hours), university discourse, and in diplomacy. At the turn of the fourteenth century, wrangling with the Scots about his claims to be their overlord,

---

[3] Ibid. 550.

[4] *Polychronicon Ranulphi Higden*, ed. C. Babington and J. R. Lumby (London: Rolls Series, 1865–86), ii. 161.

[5] Rothwell, 'English and French', 557.

[6] For a nuanced discussion of the multiple contexts of the statute—national political negotiations, legal practices, and diplomacy with France—see W. M. Ormrod, 'The Use of English: Language, Law, and Political Culture in Fourteenth-Century England', *Speculum*, 78 (2003), 750–87.

Edward I writes to the Pope in Latin, but receives word of the Scots' reply at the curia through a French report. His son Edward II takes his coronation oath in French.[7]

In what follows, rather than tracking further these complex, large-scale social moves and convergences among the dominant languages of Britain, I want to pay attention to multilingualism on the page itself—occasions and usually specific written spaces where contextually unexpected languages make sudden, even dramatic appearances. These occasions display a sometimes explosive emergence of what I will hesitantly call languages of authenticity. The languages themselves shift widely in varied settings from the twelfth to the fifteenth century, although I will concentrate on what appears to be a broad move from authenticating French in the emergent period of Middle English earlier in the fourteenth century, to authenticating Latin in the later fourteenth and fifteenth centuries. I hope that my discussion will distinguish these occasions of authenticating language from the broader notion of prestige language in multilingual settings, as well as from occasions of multilingualism and code-switching as discussed by sociolinguists.[8]

Although my focus here is on the later English Middle Ages, I want to note briefly some exemplary moments when such 'authenticating language' appears in earlier centuries. Robert Stein anticipates me with a key instance, the brief English phrase in the Latin record of the life of Christina of Markyate, whom her spiritual mentor calls 'myn sunendaege dohter'.[9] A more poignant, equally constrained glimpse of homely English occurs not long after, in Walter Daniel's highly rhetorical life of Ailred of Rievaulx. On his deathbed, the old man seems to see angels, and urges them, in English, to hurry—'Festinate, for crist luue'—perhaps because that language is, Walter notes, 'in some ways sweeter to hear'.[10] Yet at this liminal moment, when a dying holy man witnesses agents of divinity, the brief appearance of English also has an authenticating force absent from most of Walter's Latin.

Such use of authenticating language need not be intimate in the manner of these two instances. William the Conqueror exploited the—to him—probably little comprehensible language of his conquered subjects to similar effect, issuing a number of early charters in Old English as well as Latin, exploiting thereby the alternative antiquity and legal prestige of his Anglo-Saxon royal forebears. His

---

[7] Christopher Baswell, 'Latinitas', in David Wallace (ed.), *The Cambridge History of Medieval English Literature* (Cambridge: Cambridge University Press, 1999), 146; for increased mixing of French (and some English) with the dominant learned Latin of the thirteenth and fourteenth centuries, pp. 145–8.

[8] These categories are usefully deployed in relation to the French-language teaching texts such as the *Tretiz*, in Kathleen Kennedy, 'Changes in Society and Language Acquisition: The French Language in England 1215–1480', *English Language Notes*, 35 (1998), 1–15.

[9] Stein, 'Multilingualism', p. 32.

[10] Maurice Powicke (ed. and trans.), *The Life of Ailred of Rievaulx* (Oxford: Clarendon, 1978), 59–60.

grandson Henry I did the same in 1123; and Henry II did so yet again in 1155, virtually quoting the charter of 1123, now in a language perhaps rich with archaic associations but in an alphabet so foreign to his scribe that Henry I's 'thurh [through] godes gefu' gets written for Henry II as 'kurh'.[11] A similarly evocative but confused gesture appears in the roughly contemporary Eadwine Psalter (from Christ Church Canterbury), with ill-chosen and awkwardly copied Old English interlinear glosses parallel to a correct, quite lively set in Anglo-French. Even if almost functionless, though, Old English here makes a powerful gesture toward the monastery's prestigious antiquity and institutional continuity.[12]

A more self-consciously elaborated, even playful, deployment of language is regularly encountered in yet another roughly contemporary text, the *Roman d'Eneas*, almost certainly produced in connection with the Angevin court. That text's gestures toward its own origin in Latin manuscripts and the schoolroom are nowhere denser than in the passage where a love-lorn Lavine thinks of herself as being put to school by Love, and urges him to turn the unhappy page she has been reading. She then decides to write Eneas a letter, explicitly said to be *en latins*, thus exercising a skill few young Angevin women were likely to possess (though some did), and implying the insertion of a Latin-language letter in the Old French text. Lavine's choice pulls Latin out of chronology, and into a timeless emblem of her learning and wisdom, perhaps too her brief power as the unmarried heiress to Latium, before marriage pulls her into the task of royal succession.[13]

As noted in the instances of late Old English, these occasions of fairly restricted but intensified authenticity need not occur in languages of broad (or even any) direct access. The original users of the *Ancrene Wisse* may have had only the most mediated acquaintance with Hebrew, yet some key definitions of the recluse's identity and acts in that text occur through citation and glossing of Hebrew names: 'hire leor lufsum to ure lauerdes ehnen. For swa muchel seith þis word. Davith. On ebreische ledene' (her face is lovely to our Lord's eyes. For the name 'David' means this in the Hebrew language); 'For iudith on ebreisch; is schrift on englisch' (for Judith in Hebrew is 'confession' in English).[14] The appropriation of such Hebrew etymologies draws these female recluses—patrons of yet another language still

[11] London, BL, Harley Charters 111, B.49. Reproduced in Wolfgang Keller, *Angelsächsische Palaeographie*, ii (Berlin: Mayer & Müller, 1906), pl. XIII.

[12] Margaret Gibson, T. A. Heslop, and Richard W. Pfaff (eds.), *The Eadwine Psalter: Text, Image, and Monastic Culture in Twelfth-Century Canterbury* (London: MHRA and Pennsylvania State University Press, 1992), 132–7, 142–56.

[13] For text and further discussion, see Christopher Baswell, *Virgil in Medieval England: Figuring the Aeneid from the Twelfth Century to Chaucer* (Cambridge: Cambridge University Press, 1995), 168–73.

[14] J. R. R. Tolkien (ed.), *The English Text of the Ancrene Riwle*, EETS, OS 249 (London: Oxford University Press, 1962), 69, 72; translation *Anchoritic Spirituality: Ancrene Wisse and Associated Works*, trans. Anne Savage and Nicholas Watson (New York: Paulist Press, 1991), 97, 99. I am grateful to my student Dorothy Kim for bringing these instances to my attention.

unusual in extended religious prose, Middle English—into analogy with heroic Old Testament figures, both male and female.

More political uses of contextually unexpected language occur when a language group briefly gains the attention of, or even threatens, powerful agents of a dominant language practice. We see this in the circulation of French copies of Magna Carta and a related royal writ, as well as the Latin copies in which they were mostly recorded; this is a unique instance of vernacular being used in such an official setting as early as 1215. Such a language gesture certainly had practical ends, to make certain that noble listeners across England would understand the freedoms guaranteed in the document. But it also publicly recorded, and thereby authenticated, the influence of a new cohort of language users, barons with good Anglo-French but presumably limited Latin. By 1258, in a culture by now adapted to French in royal records, copies of the Provisions of Oxford circulate in English, again placing in the record a new vernacular identity group and a new medium of verbal power.[15]

In what is surely a more self-conscious gesture, English suddenly erupts from the mouth of a man verging on royalty in the Rolls of Parliament for 1399, when Henry Bolingbroke rises to claim the throne left empty by Richard II's deposition. Even the frequently used Anglo-French vernacular (perhaps too associable with the Francophile Richard himself) is evacuated from this lengthy narrative, delivered wholly in anxiously official Latin, until Henry stands up:

> prefatus Henricus dux Lancastrie de loco suo surgens, et stans adeo erectus quod satis intueri posset a populo, … dictum regnum Anglie … vendicavit in lingua materna, sub hac forma verborum:

> [Henry duke of Lancaster, rising from his place, and standing upright so that he could be seen sufficiently by the people, … claimed the realm of England … in his mother tongue, in this form of words:]

> 'In the name of Fadir, Sone, and Holy Gost, I, Henry of Lancastr' chalenge this rewme of Yngland, and the corone with alle the membres and the appurtenances, als I th(a)t am disendit be right lyne of the blode comyng fro the gude lorde Kyng Henry therde, and thorghe that ryght that God of his grace hathe sent me, with helpe of my kyn and of my frendes to recover it; the whiche rewme was in poynt to be undone for defaut of governance and undoyng of the gode lawes.'[16]

Henry's claim gains at least part of its authenticity, I would claim, from his speech being delivered in a language recent and still rare in the Rolls of Parliament, used here for the very first time by a claimant to the throne.

English has at once a surprising and authenticating force, then, in the immediate Latinate and francophone context of the Rolls of Parliament for 1399; boyish,

---

[15] Michael Clanchy, *From Memory to Written Record: England 1066–1307* (Oxford: Blackwell, 1993), 219–20; J. C. Holt, *Magna Carta* (Cambridge: Cambridge University Press, 1992), 474–7.

[16] I quote from the recent CD-ROM edition and translation, *The Parliament Rolls of Medieval England*, ed. Chris Given-Wilson (Leicester: Scholarly Digital Editions, 2005). For further discussion of the episode, see Ormrod, 'The Use of English', 784–5.

French-loving Richard makes way for the manly and English-speaking Henry, king by acclamation of all the estates once he delivers his speech. But the two vernaculars had been in subtle apposition in literary contexts since early in the century. Literary Anglo-French suffers an apparent eclipse in the famous Auchinleck manuscript (National Library of Scotland, Advocates' MS 19.2.1), copied in London between 1330 and 1340.[17] In fact, the one French text in the manuscript is decidedly un-literary: the Battle Abbey Roll, which lists over five hundred names of Norman knights said to have fought at the Battle of Hastings. Otherwise, this is famously the first ambitious literary (and devotional) anthology wholly in English. It represents a sea-change in patronage as well: a manuscript produced probably for a well-off mercantile (hence urban) buyer, rather than the provincial gentry who seem to have sponsored the earlier multilingual anthologies like Oxford, Digby 86 or Jesus College 29. Highly consistent in language choice, the Auchinleck manuscript is famously varied in content, ranging from saints' lives and devotional treatises to a metrical chronicle, popular romances, the Breton lay *Sir Orfeo*, and heroic verse such as *Kyng Alisaunder*.

The last of these, now only fragmentary in the manuscript due to lost leaves, interests me here. Largely a narrative based on the later twelfth-century Anglo-French *Roman de toute chevalerie*, *Kyng Alisaunder* uses (unsurprisingly) a richly French-derived diction. At a few points of high narrative drama, moreover, leading characters—and only leading characters—break directly into French. One instance occurs when Alisaunder calls his troops out of ambush and into battle:

> Alisaunder made a cry hardy:
> 'Ore tost, a ly! A ly!' (ll. 3814–15)[18]

Soon after, a knight sneaks up and tries to spear Alisaunder from behind. Alisaunder notices though, and turns on his assailant: ' "Fitz a puteyne!" he seide, "lecchoure!" ' (l. 3912). At such moments in *Kyng Alisaunder*, the brief emergence of French creates an effect something like pentimento in paintings, with key leaders speaking in the recognizably authentic voice of the antique aristocrat. Similar effects occur in the whole 'Kyng Alisaunder' group, probably by one author, which includes *Richard Coer de Lyon* and *Arthur and Merlin*, both of which also appear in Auchinleck. Alisaunder's French ejaculations assert his status as a militant aristocrat and empire builder who, at moments of defining drama, operates in a language by now verging toward the antique (although still widely used) and perhaps still associated with the greatest of England's more recent conquerors, William, duke of Normandy. Given these brief but intense emergences of the Anglo-French language of aristocratic authenticity, is the reader invited to experience these poems primarily as English,

[17] Available on line at **www.nls.uk/auchinleck/**. For a print facsimile, Derek Pearsall and I. C. Cunningham (introd.), *The Auchinleck Manuscript: National Library of Scotland Advocates' MS 19.2.1* (London: Scolar Press with National Library of Scotland, 1977); date and audience, pp. vii–viii.

[18] Ed. G. V. Smithers, vol. i: Text (London: EETS, 1952).

or rather as fundamentally French but largely coded in a more accessible tongue that is nonetheless easily penetrated, at intense moments, by its genuine voice? Is the narrative universe of this Middle English poem still, in fact, French?

The Holkham Bible Picture Book (London, BL, Add. MS 47682), from *c.* 1325–30 and hence roughly contemporary with the Auchinleck manuscript, offers at one point an even more complex interplay of languages on the page, with two languages of authenticity at work simultaneously, one might say in a certain competition. Made for a Dominican patron, to instruct an explicitly wealthy audience ('mustré serra a riche gent'), the book does much of its narrating through a series of vigorous and detailed illustrations, but it also tells its biblical and apocryphal stories by means of an Anglo-Norman text above, below, and sometimes within the images.[19] On fo. 13[r], the rhymed text and images narrate the Annunciation to the shepherds (in the upper scene) and their visit to the Holy Family (in the lower scene).

The upper scene and its text record an episode of multilingual blockage, attempted revelation but actual incomprehension between shepherds who speak Anglo-French and an angel who only sings, and does that only in Latin:

> Coment un ange aparuth
> A pastureus ou ioye muth,
> 'Gloria in excelsis' venyst chantant
> E dyst: 'Alez loer li tut puysant,
> Veez la signe de grant poer,
> Alez tot, ne fetes targer.'
> Li un et li autre grant poer mettoyt
> Por dire le chant qe le angel chantoyt.
> Li un dist 'Glum glo, ceo ne est rien.
> Allums la, nous la saverums been.'

[How an angel appeared to the shepherds with great joy; he came singing 'Gloria in excelsis', and said, 'Go and praise the all-powerful, see the sign of great power; go quickly, make no delay.' Each of them tried very hard to speak the song that the angel sang. One said 'Glum glo—that's nonsense. Let us go there, there we'll understand well.']

The only mutually acknowledged sign in the upper scene is visual: the 'signe de grant poer', a star to which both the angel and one of the shepherds point, and toward which the other two shepherds direct their gaze. All they can conclude is that by following the star they may understand better: 'Allums la, nous la saverums been.'

In the lower scene of the same page, though, a far more complex, and suddenly unimpeded linguistic exchange occurs. The shepherds have arrived at the manger

---

[19] F. P. Pickering (ed.), *The Anglo-Norman Text of the Holkham Bible Picture Book* (Oxford: A-NTS, 1971), 3. Pickering's edition is rather interventionist; I quote his text verbatim, since his emendations nowhere affect my argument here. The manuscript is described in Lucy Freeman Sandler, *Gothic Manuscripts: 1285–1385* (London: Harvey Miller, 1986), no. 97. A facsimile was edited by W. O. Hassall, *The Holkham Bible Picture Book* (London: Dropmore, 1954).

where the Holy Family is sheltering, and where the same 'signe de grant poer' now hovers, above the roof and directly over the infant Christ.

> Coment les pastureus de leur cheverie
> Feseyent ioye a la Vyrge Marie.
> E le chant que le angel out chaunté
> En le honour de la nativité
> Songen alle wid one steuene
> Also the angel song that cam fro heuene:
> 'Te deum et Gloria.'
> La contenance veyez cha.[20]

[How the shepherds with their bagpipes rejoiced before the Virgin Mary. And the song that the angel had sung in honour of the nativity they all sang with one voice, just as the angel sang who came from heaven: 'Te deum et Gloria.' You see the picture here.]

One shepherd plays the bagpipes, as indicated in the text. In scrolls from the mouths of the other two come the Latin hymns also named in the narrative:

> Gloria in excelsis deo et in terra …
> Te deum laudamus …

The shepherds now seem to understand not just the angel's message, but also his Latin hymns. One aspect of this scene, then, returns the book's audience to a traditional, even predictable, transcendent and unifying Latin, almost magically available to all when the shepherds, Holy Family, and 'signe de grant poer' are present together at the manger.

This musical, angelic Latin might well be the language of revelation expected by the wealthy audience viewing the book under the direction of a friar. Just as important, though, is the presence and position on the page of the Middle English couplet, the unique and explosive appearance of that language in the Holkham Bible Picture Book: 'Songen alle wid one stevene | Also the angel Song that cam fro hevene.' If not necessarily a language of transcendence here, Middle English is certainly a language of union ('alle wid one stevene'). Middle English provides the authenticating narrative of the shepherds' miraculous song, and records their ability to penetrate the barrier between their Anglo-French and the angel's Latin. Further, by happy accident, and possibly more than an accident, 'alle' is actually divided into its component syllables—'al—le'—on each side of the 'signe de grant poer', the star that in the upper scene had been the only sign that had indeed communicated to all.[21]

---

[20] Pickering (ed.), *The Anglo-Norman Text*, 22. The verse lines are written continuously in the manuscript. I alter Pickering's punctuation in the second passage. The translation is mine; I am grateful for the assistance of Jocelyn Wogan-Browne.

[21] Ian Short mentions an analogously miraculous access to Anglo-French for monoglot English speakers, 'Tam Angli quam Franci: Self-Definition in Anglo-Norman England', *Anglo-Norman Studies*, 18 (1996, for 1995), 159.

These two contemporary instances, *Kyng Alisaunder* and the Holkham Bible Picture Book, occupy two distinguishable but reciprocal positions in the shifting negotiations of Latin, French, and English during the first half of the fourteenth century. Both reflect an interweaving of the two vernaculars as Middle English was beginning to emerge as a central literary medium, and as ideas of Englishness were being explored under a variety of pressures. But where *Kyng Alisaunder*, I think, holds onto Anglo-French as the palimpsest language that authenticates heroic antiquity and aristocratic hierarchy, the Holkham Bible Picture Book might be claimed to offer English as a language of secular union and of linguistic authentication rising from below, through the language and song of shepherds. If angelic, biblical Latin remains the actual medium of revelation, the earthly transmission of revelation is emphatically narrated in English.

Manuscripts of the emergent Middle English literary canon, produced just before 1400 and roughly a quarter-century after, offer another, much broader arena for the interplay of dominant and authenticating languages in later medieval England. I will focus on perhaps the most famous of them all, the 'Ellesmere Chaucer' (San Marino, Huntington Library, MS EL 26 C 9), and a small group of vernacular manuscripts related to it by scribal links, or by similar ambitions toward codicological prestige. In each, the use of Latin in the *mise-en-page* represents a form of authenticating language that lays implicit claims for the prestige and canonicity of the English text it accompanies.[22]

The 'Hengwrt manuscript' (Aberystwyth, National Library of Wales, Peniarth 392) is generally thought to be our earliest surviving copy of the *Canterbury Tales*.[23] Both it and the Ellesmere manuscript were copied by the same scribe, recently identified by Linne Mooney as Adam Pinkhurst.[24] The Hengwrt manuscript is carefully produced, but in size (292 × 210 mm), layout, and decoration it is more modest than the slightly later Ellesmere copy. Ellesmere and Hengwrt share their use of English for running titles and rubrics at beginnings and ends of tales. Its size (394 × 284 mm), excellent parchment, and elaborate decoration help Ellesmere lay larger claims for the *Tales* as a canonical text, the object of careful editing and costly production. Equally, however, an elaborate system of carefully planned and mostly Latin marginalia also serves implicitly to locate the *Canterbury Tales* in the context of ancient Latin learning, and more specifically that crucial site of canonicity, the schoolroom. The Latin marginalia in Ellesmere are

---

[22]   A persistent contemporary encounter of Latin and English, of a rather different kind, is explored by Tim William Machan, 'Language Contact in *Piers Plowman*', *Speculum*, 69 (1994), 359–85.

[23]   Geoffrey Chaucer, *The Canterbury Tales: A Facsimile and Transcription of the Hengwrt Manuscript, with Variants from the Ellesmere Manuscript*, ed. Paul G. Ruggiers, introd. Donald C. Baker and A. I. Doyle and M. B. Parkes (Norman: University of Oklahoma, 1979).

[24]   'Chaucer's Scribe', *Speculum*, 81 (2006), 97–138. Mooney generously acknowledges the series of articles by Malcolm Parkes and A. I. Doyle on which her new research depends; for citations see esp. p. 97 nn. 1 and 2.

sporadic but numerous, most dense around those tales that explicitly summon up Latin books (for instance the 'Merchant's Tale', 'Franklin's Tale', and 'Melibee') or—more intriguingly—challenge the authority of Latin books and the men who control them (the 'Wife of Bath's Prologue and Tale').[25] Hengwrt too has Latin marginalia, though far fewer; what distinguishes the ambitions of Ellesmere is the care with which this authenticating Latin element has been planned in the book's layout and ruling. Hengwrt's Latin marginalia are cramped into often narrow margins without special ruling. By contrast, the denser Latin marginalia in Ellesmere often occupy their own ruled column in the manner of annotated schoolbooks, accommodated by putting the Middle English text column slightly off centre.

Latin as used in Hengwrt and Ellesmere is a far distance from the highly mediated Hebrew etymologies in *Ancrene Wisse* mentioned above; and such Latin presence in high-end vernacular manuscripts does not create the element of surprise I suggest the verbatim French does in the Auchinleck manuscript, or English in the Holkham Bible Picture Book. Nonetheless, Latin would be a less accessible language for most (though by no means all) of the early users of Hengwrt and Ellesmere, especially if we credit recent suggestions that many of them were of the urban mercantile classes. And the position of most Latin in these manuscripts, in the margin, gives it a paradoxical authenticating cachet, associating the manuscripts with the activities and prestige of learned Latin texts and ambitious university manuscripts.

Other Middle English manuscripts that Mooney associates with Adam Pinkhurst make comparable use of authenticating Latin in their *mises-en-page*. The Hatfield House fragment of *Troilus and Criseyde* uses 'liber' in its running titles. Trinity College Cambridge R.3.2 (Gower, *Confessio Amantis*) of necessity has some Latin in its text, but also Latin marginalia, though its format does not allow even as much space as in the Hengwrt manuscript.[26] Pinkhurst worked on the Trinity College Gower in collaboration with the Gower specialist 'Scribe D', whose manuscripts have been studied by Malcolm Parkes and A. I. Doyle.[27] Scribe D too uses Latin in his *mise-en-page* in the Trinity College Gower, as well as in other manuscripts such as Oxford, Corpus Christi College 198 (*Canterbury Tales*). In New York, Columbia University, MS Plimpton 265, another copy of the *Confessio Amantis*,

---

[25] For further discussion and references, Christopher Baswell, 'Talking Back to the Text: Marginal Voices in Medieval Secular Literature', in Charlotte Morse, Penelope Reed Doob, and Marjorie C. Woods (eds.), *The Uses of Manuscripts in Literary Studies: Essays in Memory of Judson Boyce Allen* (Kalamazoo, MI: Medieval Institute, 1992), 121–60, esp. 141–7.

[26] For a current list of manuscripts that Mooney associates with Adam Pinkhurst, see www.medievalscribes.com/scribes.html. For Latin in the two manuscripts mentioned here, see 'Chaucer's Scribe', figs. 2a,2b, and 3.

[27] 'The Production of Copies of the *Canterbury Tales* and the *Confessio Amantis* in the Early Fifteenth Century', reprinted in M. B. Parkes, *Scribes, Scripts, and Readers* (London: Hambledon, 1991), 201–48. Pinkhurst is Parkes and Doyle's 'Scribe B'.

Scribe D makes the Latin in both his main text and margins particularly prominent by writing all of it in red.[28]

A similar, perhaps more purposeful deployment of authenticating Latin in the context of Middle English is to be found in John Trevisa's translation of Ranulph Higden's *Polychronicon*, produced under the patronage of Sir Thomas Berkeley. Trevisa prefaces his translation with a dialogue between a 'dominus' and 'clericus' in which the claims and merits of Latin and English are debated. Intriguingly, sophisticated Latin is an attribute of the less aristocratic clerk, while the lord claims a modest command of Latin yet prefers English for its accessibility to 'mo men'. The actual presence of Latin within the translation and the *mise-en-page* of its manuscripts, though, is so dense (as I have claimed elsewhere) as to restrain access to the English book for those who do not have the kind of bilingual resources of the dialogue's 'dominus', who is clearly to be associated with Berkeley himself. Indeed, most of the manuscripts of Trevisa's *Polychronicon* are large, quite grand affairs that give considerable prominence to their marginal Latin apparatus, sometimes by rubrication. One such manuscript with rubricated Latin (London, BL, Add. 24194) is written by a scribe Parkes and Doyle name the 'Delta scribe' because of the great similarities between his hand and that of the Gower specialist Scribe D; they propose some kind of close contact between the two. The Delta scribe is responsible for at least one, and probably two, other similarly grand manuscripts of Trevisa's *Polychronicon*.[29]

Scribes unconnected with this circle were also using Latin as one part of the many codicological gestures by which they claimed prestige, even canonical status, for the texts they copied. It would be worthwhile, however, to explore systematically the place of authenticating Latin in manuscripts produced by Pinkhurst, Scribe D, and the cluster of other scribes with whom they have been associated, producing Middle English manuscripts in the very late fourteenth and first half of the fifteenth centuries.

What these sometimes disparate instances of authenticating language have in common is some degree of the virtual. The language of authenticity is most emphatically present because of its unexpectedness and, often, its varying degrees of inaccessibility. W. M. Ormrod has remarked of royal government in the later thirteenth and earlier fourteenth centuries that 'the employment of French as a

---

[28]   For Oxford, CCC 198, see Parkes and Doyle, 'Production', fig. 43. For a number of images of Plimpton 265, see http://dpg.lib.berkeley.edu/webdb/scriptorium/ds_search?&MsID=1001084&Ms-PtID=1001113&EDocID=1001265. Thomas Dankastre, the scribe of Langland's *Piers Plowman* in San Marino, Huntington Library, MS HM 137, similarly writes all of Langland's Latin in red, in a textura script that contrasts with the slightly more informal Anglicana formata of the English parts of the text. See http://sunsite.berkeley.edu/scriptorium/hehweb/HM137.html.

[29]   For full references and further discussion, see Christopher Baswell, 'Troy, Arthur, and the Languages of "Brutis Albyoun"', in Robert Stein and Sandra Pierson Prior (eds.), *Reading Medieval Culture: Essays in Honor of Robert W. Hanning* (Notre Dame, IN: University of Notre Dame Press, 2005), 178–80, 185–6. In n. 71 of that essay, I mistakenly collapse scribes D and Delta into one, and take this opportunity to correct my error.

formal and authoritative language of process actually increased in inverse proportion to its use as a language of generalized social exchange'.[30] I claim that a related phenomenon—of slightly disorienting surprise associated with obscurity—gives these language gestures their impact on the page. The wealthy audience of the Holkham Bible Picture Book would understand perfectly well the Middle English into which the text so briefly breaks, literally as the Incarnation is displayed to the shepherds. Yet in a manuscript of such costly execution, which otherwise privileges only Latin in addition to its dominant Anglo-French, English might have an impact at once intense and somewhat alienating. Suddenly it is the shepherds—common men whose labouring status is carefully depicted—who have special access to the divine, and who shift from incomprehension of angelic Latin to univocal performance ('wid one stevene' (with one voice)) of the angel's own song. The Hebrew etymologies that help create anchorite identity in *Ancrene Wisse* are far more mediated, almost certainly unknowable in any direct sense to their users, yet that inaccessibility also functions to draw attention to the mystery and power of the Hebrew names, their capacity to authenticate identities still under textual construction. What is surprising or unknowable—moments, we might say, of linguistic aporia—is also what makes language work, in these instances, with a force that can, in its extreme cases, border on the uncanny.

FURTHER READING

The classic study of language and demographics after the Conquest, especially individuals' command of two or three of the primary languages, is Rolf Berndt, 'The Linguistic Situation in England from the Norman Conquest to the Loss of Normandy (1066–1204)', in Roger Lass (ed.), *Approaches to English Historical Linguistics: An Anthology* (New York: Holt, Rinehart and Winston, 1969), 369–91. W. Rothwell offers an accessible survey in 'The Trilingual England of Geoffrey Chaucer', *Studies in the Age of Chaucer*, 16 (1994), 45–67. Largely linguistic in focus but very useful is D. A. Trotter (ed.), *Multilingualism in Later Medieval Britain* (Cambridge: D. S. Brewer, 2000). Several essays there investigate questions of code-switching and language use.

In addition to these and references in the footnotes above, a number of studies also address issues of multilingualism while focusing on other topics. Malcolm B. Parkes, 'The Literacy of the Laity', in *Scribes, Scripts and Readers* (London: Hambledon, 1991), 275–97. Douglas A. Kibbee, *For to Speke Frenche Trewely: The French Language in England, 1000–1600: Its Status, Description, and Instruction* (Amsterdam: J. Benjamins, 1991). Full of useful material, but note the cautions expressed by W. Rothwell at several points in 'English and French in England after 1362' (n. 2 above). John H. Fisher, *The Emergence of Standard English* (Lexington: University Press of Kentucky, 1996). Christopher Cannon, *The Making of Chaucer's English: A Study of Words* (Cambridge: Cambridge University Press, 1998). Tim William Machan, *English in the Middle Ages* (Oxford: Oxford University Press, 2003).

[30] 'The Use of English', 755.

Multilingualism has a role in several essays in David Wallace (ed.), *The Cambridge History of Medieval English Literature* (Cambridge: Cambridge University Press, 1999) especially: Lesley Johnson and Jocelyn Wogan-Browne, 'National, World, and Women's History: Writers and Readers in Post-Conquest England', 92–121; Christopher Baswell, 'Latinitas', 122–51; Andrew Galloway, 'Writing History in England', 255–83; Sheila Lindenbaum, 'London Texts and Literate Practice', 284–309.

CHAPTER 5

TRANSLATION

MICHELLE R. WARREN

The translated text has long occupied a relatively low status within academic culture, due to its seemingly derivative and secondary nature. Lacking the 'originality' still valued by many teachers and students of literature, translations generally only gain firm purchase in literary history when they somehow manage to surpass their source and to function as 'autonomous' expressions. And yet translation is ubiquitous in medieval writing practices, literary and non-literary alike. It underwrote not only cultural and ideological transfers from distant times and places, but also the practical transaction of daily life in much of the so-called Middle English period. Given these tensions between the mundane and the aesthetic, the desirable and the dismissed, I would like to consider here what 'Middle English literature' might look like if we adopt new approaches to and definitions of translation. Indeed, what might happen to the literary tradition if translated texts constituted an aesthetic grouping independent from authorial and generic categories? And if this grouping were granted the same critical value as the most prestigious authors and genres? Perhaps more importantly, how might our understanding of seemingly monolingual compositions change if we locate them in a cultural environment saturated with translating activities?

Translation theory, cultural studies, analyses of *translatio studii et imperii*, and source studies all contribute necessary and vital elements to the repositioning of translated literature that I would like to explore. Nevertheless, in keeping with the spirit of this volume, my purpose here is neither to survey this body of work nor to transcend it. Rather, I would like to propose a decentred aesthetic order, one that would set aside the very notion that 'originals' are worth more their translations, 'originality' more than repetition, 'uniqueness' more than similarity. This involves placing texts in relation to each other via strategic alliances that depend less on genre and language than on culture. It also means adopting the 'cultural turn' taken by translation studies in the 1990s, and treating translations less as linguistic events and more as manifestations of culture. In this perspective, relations between sources and translations become more flexible and varied (not limited to hierarchies of relative value, aesthetic or otherwise). At the same time, translations themselves invite investigations into their relations to texts that are not, in fact, their sources (and written in any language).

From this cultural perspective, translated texts represent the monolingual product of specifically multilingual alliances. These relations emerge from various occasions and motivations, including class-consciousness, political persuasion, theological dispute, cultural rivalry, and personal admiration. In each case, translation offers an opportunity to redefine audiences, social relations, historical inheritance, and ethnic identities. Finding value in the translated text does not therefore mean liberating it from its sources, but making their relations as concrete and complex as possible. This critical endeavour necessarily involves a broad range of issues, each potentially implicated in an even broader range of theoretical questions: domination and resistance, geographical and regional sites, ethnic and national identity, class and intercultural relations, gender and status constructions, linguistic and aesthetic values. Translation can become, then, one of the most theoretically rich topics of research, taking us far beyond the traditional notions 'accuracy' and 'slavishness'.

While the translated text can be seen as the monolingual product of a multilingual process, the untranslated text also operates in a multilingual environment. In other words, 'Middle English' functions as a language in contact, a language best understood as a 'translated' expression and whose literature does not make full sense unless studied within the dynamics that generally pertain to translated texts. Translation and (apparent) monolingualism meet most dramatically in the modern pedagogy of Middle English in English-language classrooms. This is, in fact, an encounter fraught with unspoken translations. I would like to suggest, ultimately, that the silent presence of pedagogical translation demands attention as a research problem of equal importance to more properly 'medieval' topics.

Translation and the amateur

The professionalization of writing via chancery and clerkship has been an important part of defining the content and value of the canon of Middle English literature. As a result, criticism has tended to treat translation as a primarily a professional activity, the purview of individuals highly trained in the forms and structures of (Latin) language. The epitome of the professionalization process is of course Chaucer, the textbook case of an 'author-translator' whose status as an 'author' seems to overcome the aesthetic pitfalls generally attributed to translation. The relative autonomy of Chaucer's translations offers a lesson for approaching figures who have do not have the same iconic status in the Middle English tradition. First, translation is not, by definition, a secondary form of writing. Further, the value accorded to a translated text does not depend, by definition, on its relations with sources. Finally, implicit theories about translation (derived from analyses of technique, etc.) can be as richly 'theoretical' as explicit theorization. Chaucer, for example, not only talks about translation but practises it in such a way that *translatio* turns rhetorically into a new kind of *auctoritas*.[1]

Paradoxically, vernacular *auctoritas* can diminish the primacy of professional training in the definition of literary value: the vernacular itself gradually becomes a self-sufficient authority. Professional translation thus leads us toward amateurs, especially when we also approach translation as a cultural phenomenon. Cultural translation studies bring critical attention to incidental fragments of daily life, idiosyncratic personal commentary, and 'derivative' or stylistically unremarkable literary texts. Their status as 'mere translations' has perhaps discouraged investigation into their cultural significance. What Middle English texts might become newly compelling for scholars and students when approached with felicitous combinations of basic textual histories and open-minded theoretical and/or cultural questions?

As a case in point, consider Henry Lovelich, one of the least-loved writers of Middle English literature—the polar opposite, if you will, of all that Chaucer represents as an author-translator. Lovelich, a skinner of London, translated the *History of the Grail* and *Merlin* from thirteenth-century French prose into English verse in the 1420s.[2] Because of his amateur relation to literature, Lovelich's project challenges some generally held assumptions about linguistic competence and the social roles of books in fifteenth-century London. Dismissal of Lovelich's poems has typically rested on identifying him as a 'hack translator'.[3] Yet, critics have taxed Lovelich with incompetence without actually knowing what he was translating. The French prose sources exist in a number of different versions and, unless one knows Lovelich's exact sources, one does not in fact know what he translated, how he translated, and what he 'created'. With a direct source, we can evince implicit theories of translation, even in the absence of an overt articulation of translation methods. Moreover, if we pose cultural as well as linguistic questions, these theories have broad implications that do not depend on professional training in rhetoric and poetics. In Lovelich's case, comparative textual analysis reveals linguistic transfer as a profoundly social act.

As autonomous artefacts, the French and English texts already embed implicit translation theories within their general theories of narrative. Narrative itself in the French *Grail* and *Merlin* is conceived of as a process of translation. Every narrator

---

[1] Cf. Rita Copeland, *Rhetoric, Hermeneutics, and Translation in the Middle Ages: Academic Traditions and Vernacular Texts* (Cambridge: Cambridge University Press, 1991), 193–202.

[2] *History of the Holy Grail*, ed. Frederick Furnivall (London: Early English Text Society, 1874–1905); *Merlin*, ed. Ernst Kock (London: Early English Text Society, 1904–32).

[3] Roger Dalrymple surveys salient deprecations in 'Evele knowen ɜe Merlyne, jn certeyn': Henry Lovelich's *Merlin*', in Judith Weiss, Jennifer Fellows, and Morgan Dickson (eds.), *Medieval Insular Romance: Translation and Innovation* (Cambridge: D. S. Brewer, 2000), 155–67.

acts a kind of translator, even as the romances thematize rewriting and translation in an infinite regression of ever-receding sources. One figure, however, counteracts this narrative tendency—Merlin's personal scribe, Blaise. He displays the same desire for true knowledge that Lovelich will adopt as his defining mode: Blaise remarks, as he transcribes Merlin's stories, that he did so 'car aussi avoie ge grant desirrier de savoir en la verité' (because I had a great desire to know the truth about them).[4] Lovelich will take this spirit further by revising the French romances' circular structure of translation (where the source can never be found in the endless chain of narrative substitutions) into a linear model that recognizes no source other than the narrator.

In this newly linear narrative, Lovelich uses a variety of terms for textual creation, which collectively reveal a sustained social theory. Most concretely, Lovelich refers to his work as a 'book' that has been made (*Grail*, XXXIII. 542); he later prays that it comes to a good end (*Grail*, LVI. 537). A great deal could be said about the idea of the book in the late Middle Ages; suffice it here to recall some of its social attributes: books organize knowledge, preserve it in memory, and negotiate exchange-values (monetary and symbolic).[5] Lovelich emphasizes especially the 'making of memory' (*Grail*, XXVII. 478–9), purveying a spirit of conservation in which readers acquire social status by possessing historical knowledge. The historical implication is made explicit when Lovelich uses the word 'cronycle' (*Merlin*, l. 23433). All of these terms point to the text as an embodied object that travels through time, 'translating' the past for the present. This metaphorical translation implies an active communication beyond the object, and inserts the book into a social environment.

A second set of narrative terms articulates the text's engagement with the immediate environment, the community of the city of London. Lovelich periodically characterizes the narrative as a 'schewing' (e.g *Merlin*, l. 1831), aligning it with the various processions that wended their way through the London streets throughout the year. Public 'schewing' is designed to present truth, to display the real (be it religious, political, etc.) for the benefit of the social community.[6] Processions often included particular props or dramatic scenes, called 'pageants'—yet another of Lovelich's preferred terms for narrative scenes.[7] In these references, the narrative itself becomes a landscape of social transactions. Lovelich inherits a spatial notion of narrative from the French romances, which frequently mark transitions with the

---

[4] Marc-René Jung, *La Légende de Troie en France au moyen âge* (Tübingen: Francke, 1996), 504; see also my *History on the Edge: Excalibur and the Borders of Britain* (Minneapolis: University of Minnesota Press, 2000), 204.

[5] e.g. Jesse Gellrich, *Discourse and Dominion in the Fourteenth Century* (Princeton: Princeton University Press, 1995); Lesley Lawton, 'The Illustration of Late Medieval Secular Texts, with Special Reference to Lydgate's *Troy Book*', in Derek Pearsall (ed.), *Manuscripts and Readers in Fifteenth-Century England* (Woodbridge: Boydell and Brewer, 1983), 41–69.

[6] Mary-Rose Mclaren, *The London Chronicles of the Fifteenth Century: A Revolution in English Writing* (Woodbridge: D. S. Brewer, 2002), 61.

[7] Dalrymple, 'Evele Knowen', 158.

phrase 'ci endroit le conte dit ... ' (here in this place the story says ...). The French 'ci' focuses perspective inward, on the story itself. Lovelich, however, translates the French formula in a wide variety of ways, all of which turn the perspective outward to the audience, with frequent direct address that casts the audience as physical participants in narrative: 'Now forth this Storye gynneth to procede, | and to Othere Materis it wyle vs lede' (*Grail*, LIII. 1–2); 'But let vs now resten here a whyle' (*Merlin*, l. 17261). In these and many other ways, Lovelich maps the narrative onto a civic landscape, where one moves from place to place, 'pageant to pageant', in a 'processe' towards true understanding. Indeed, 'processe' is perhaps the most used term. This is a linear, visual term linked both to procession and procedure in general.[8] Lovelich thereby implies that by following the necessary steps one can arrive at a true narrative and a coherent social community.

Lovelich's English terminology for textual creation says a great deal about his ideas of translation. We can learn even more through a detailed comparison with an appropriate source, for in this particular case the drama of translation unfolds largely on the micro-linguistic level. In the precise definition of translation techniques (abridgement, amplification, adaptation, etc.), the amateur emerges as author. For reasons that I will develop elsewhere, I have identified Lovelich's source as a book of the same content and form as Bodleian, Douce MS 178. In this context, Lovelich's techniques for rendering French recognize clearly the urban social space: his text is socially inclusive where the French is hierarchical ('menus peuples' becomes 'every manne'), urban where the French is rural ('la terre la commencent a degaster & a essillier' (fo. 235) becomes 'and maden there mochel destruction both of city, borough, and town' (*Merlin*, ll. 17318–26)). These are just a few examples among many. They reveal a sustained effort to bend the aristocratic source to the civic milieu. If translation often involves a tension between the creation of access and the achievement of status, Lovelich's translation engages both sides: he provides access to elite, historical culture for his fellow guildsmen while simultaneously documenting that they have collectively acquired enough status to borrow from the aristocracy.

Lovelich's nuanced perception of urban politics and social status inspires his striking representation of the process by which Arthur takes the throne in *Merlin*. This more extended passage highlights the social theory that shapes both translation and narration in Lovelich's poems. Just after the discovery of the sword in the stone, Lovelich portrays a two-tiered social order according to which the 'more and lasse' enter the church (l. 7042) and the Archbishop cautions no one to envy God's choice, 'whethir to pore or to riche it happe, trewlye, | that non man ayens this elexioun ne be' (ll. 7054–5). Lovelich here defines social difference in terms of quantity (associated with mercantile values) not quality (associated with aristocratic values). When disagreement breaks out over who should have the right

---

[8] Ibid.

to try removing the sword, Lovelich offers a somewhat different portrayal of social categories: 'thanne began there ful gret discord | betwixen comunes, gentyles, and lord' (ll. 7071–2). While 'lord' seems clearly to refer to an aristocracy, 'gentyles' might refer to merchants as well as to noblemen. 'Comunes' also might include merchants, as well as poorer citizens and labourers. These overlapping distinctions represent the complex social and political life of fifteenth-century London, where wealth often meant more than status, but even the commons could successfully petition the king. Later in *Merlin*, for example, Lovelich refers to the 'riche men' (l. 7504) when he clearly means to designate the barons. This conflation of nobles and merchants (those who have 'more') brings together two groups who otherwise remain separated by qualitative social differences. The conflation does not so much imply social mobility as the contingency of social categories and allegiances.

As the Archbishop seeks to calm the boisterous crowd around the sword, he reminds everyone that no one is so worthy as to know God's will, and 'neither gentility or riches' (l. 7084) will determine the outcome. Describing the great responsibility of justice to be assumed with the sword, he enjoins the 'hygh, prowd, other Riche' to be humble and the 'pore men' to be patient:

> For vnknoweng hit is to yow alle
> yit on whom the lot schal falle,
> whethir on Lord, knyht, or sqwyer,
> On powr, comown, other on bacheler ...   (*Merlin*, ll. 7125–38)

While allowing the radical possibility of a king from any sector of society, the Archbishop affirms clear social differentiation. In the interest of law and order, he argues for the acceptance of election in general, whatever one's personal feelings or social status relative to the elected. This kind of 'law and order' conservatism aligns him with merchant values: responsible for peace in the city as a condition of their freedom to govern, city leaders supported social stratification. The specific social actors identified by the Archbishop reflect the multifarious forces at work in civic politics. Lord, knight, and squire all pertain to the nobility, although not strictly; poor, common, and bachelor refer to those without landed status. Common, however, could include the wealthy 'gentle' who is not noble, while bachelor might refer to a poor young noble. The list may be arbitrary or partial, but it aims to designate comprehensively all those concerned with the election. In contrast to the earlier economic division of the public into 'rich and poor', this list of six categories suggests the profound difficulty of defining clear social boundaries in the urban community.

According to the Archbishop's plan, 250 of the 'worthyest' lords try the sword first (l. 7144), but all fail; then the 'comunes' and 'powre men' have their turn (l. 7150). Lovelich returns to three groups here, distinguishing commons and poor from lords. But that the common and poor try at all is a remarkable innovation from the French romance. Of course, just as in the French romance, the barons subsequently resist and finally revolt, complaining that they should not be ruled by a knave of low birth. Lovelich's narrative thus ultimately supports a conservative aristocratic ordering, but with a definite and powerful place for all citizens. In fact, during the barons' rebellion that follows Arthur's election, Lovelich privileges the role of the citizens: 'and the Barowns the contrarye helden anon | ayens Arthewr and the comunes echon'. (ll. 7427–8). Highlighting the loyalty of London citizens, Lovelich makes them the main supporters of legitimate royal succession. Indeed, the guard of the sword while the barons delay their acceptance is specifically divided among five clerks and five 'lower men of good lyve' (l. 7530). Throughout the ensuing battles, the citizens of London act as Arthur's most loyal and effective supporters.

Lovelich's emphasis on London citizenry derives in part from his use of the word 'Logres' to designate both London and the realm as a whole. This doubling also occurs in the French romance, but, when transferred to London English, the effect differs dramatically. Standing for both city and country, 'Logres' contains a specifically urbanized nationalism. To explain this name, Lovelich turns to the island's etymological history. The island was once called 'Bretaigne Londe' after Brutus and its capital 'New Troy'. 'Long aftyr' an ambitious king named 'Logrius' renewed the city and renamed it 'Logres' after himself: this king 'Logrius' is a conflation of Lud and Brutus' son Locrinus (traditionally, the eponymous ruler of one section of the island, not the city or the whole realm). So, each time Lovelich speaks of the 'rewm of logres' (e.g. *Merlin*, l. 17922), London accedes implicitly to dominion of the whole island. 'Logres' urbanizes the romance landscape, turning royal Arthurian history into a civic chronicle. Lovelich thus infuses the narrative with an urban ethos as he merchandizes the French romance, bending it to the urban social order as he draws it into English. Social and linguistic theory together determine the results of this translation process.

These results, however, are not only linguistic (the English language poem) but also visual and physical—the manuscript pages on which the poem survives. In fact, the book of Lovelich's poems, Cambridge, Corpus Christi, MS 80, is designed for illustrations that were never completed. The spaces for images, the chapter initials, and the double-column layout mirror exactly the structure of Bodleian, Douce MS 178, suggesting that Lovelich was involved in a project whose aspirations were far more than textual. Here, translation involves a physical transfer irrespective of the languages involved. Lovelich's project, in other words, performs multiple kinds of *translatio*—and the multiple dimensions of the poems' signification depend on both the language and form of the source. These processes reveal an intensely transformative dialogue between an inherited vision of noble chivalry and an emerging concept of urban citizenship, a concept documented both linguistically and materially on an illustrated paper manuscript designed for craftsmen.

Translation and the monolingual text

Medievalists know well that *translatio* is a multivalent concept meaning 'translation' *and* a number of other things (transfer, travel, etc.). Yet the latter should probably take precedence over the former more often: *translatio* per se does not require interlingual translation. Indeed, in a certain vein it excludes translation. In the logic of *translatio studii*, the transfer of learning from Greece to Rome involved both a geographical movement and a linguistic translation. Yet the transfer from Rome to northern Europe was essentially monolingual: Latin learning moved geographically, but remained expressed in Latin. Monolingualism, as Rita Copeland has shown, was, in fact, central to the medieval ideology of continuity with ancient authorities. Only belatedly did multilingualism become part of the enterprise and interlingual linguistic translation a relatively common dimension of knowledge transfer.[9]

Taking a cue from the idea of monolingual *translatio*, I would like to look at the potential role of translation in analysing monolingual Middle English texts—that is, texts conceived and written originally in English, whose significance depends at least partly on their relationship to translation. This approach combines the multilingualism of late medieval *translatio* with the monolingual undercurrent that continued to shape historical perceptions. In the context of Middle English, monolingual *translatio* involves at least two broad areas, the one philological and the other theoretical. Philologically, the inherent multilingualism of seemingly monolingual situations suggests research opportunities in linguistic, rhetorical, and literary histories. Theoretically, connections between Middle English and actual other languages may not even be necessary for a form of translation to have occurred.

In relation to the history of language, Middle English could be fruitfully approached as a translated and actively translating language. This concerns not only the obvious multilingual history of the language (Germanic and Romance, along with regional variations of both), or etymology, but something like the socio-historical linguistics proposed recently by Tim Machan, which addresses phenomena such as language in contact, bilingual speakers, language and conquest, code-switching, and self-translation.[10] Traces of multilingual histories at the lexical level unsettle the cultural homogeneity of the language: how many translations are needed to render sense to a word like 'sentence', which is formally identical to French 'sentence' and a translation of Latin 'sententia'? This and other English words modelled on Latin forms alter the hermeneutic significance of the mono-lingual text by creating multiple layers of linguistic and cultural signification.[11] In these ways, 'monolingual' texts become networks of multilingual transactions.

[9]   e.g. Copeland, *Rhetoric*, 97–107, 127–50.
[10]   Tim William Machan, *English in the Middle Ages* (Oxford: Oxford University Press, 2003).
[11]   e.g. Andrew Cole, 'Chaucer's English Lesson', *Speculum*, 77 (2002), 1128–67, at 1157–8.

The diversity of 'Middle English' itself makes even monolingual communication a translation process. Transfers between dialects and social registers invite translation into the heart of monolingual culture.[12] The oft-cited lines from the conclusion of Chaucer's *Troilus and Criseyde* articulate just one explicit example of the potential challenge of monolingual translation:

> And for ther is so gret diversite
> In Englissh and in writing of oure tonge,
> So prey I God that non miswrite the,
> Ne the mysmetre for defaute of tonge;
> And red wherso thow be, or elles songe,
> That thow be understonde, God I beseche!   (ll. 1793–8)

The technicalities of dialect, sociolinguistic register, and regional pronunciation (to name just a few of the linguistic variables) impinge directly on literary expression and reception (medieval and modern). Whether viewed diachronically or synchronically, the cultural dimension of multilingual English opens a number of new paths for investigations of Middle English texts.

Translation also enters monolingual English whenever texts, translated or not, rhetorically assert their linguistic identity as 'English'. By drawing attention to the language of expression as English, these kinds of assertions subtly remind us that a different choice could have been made—that translation in one form or another could be taking place. Monolingual identity, in other words, depends deeply on the option to translate. Here, I am thinking of exclamations such as Chaucer's in the Prologue to the *Legend of Good Women*, 'Allas, that I ne had Englyssh, ryme or prose, | Suffisant this flour to preyse aryght!' (F, ll. 66–7). As Copeland has pointed out, the passage references Chaucer's relation to French Marguerite poetry (*Rhetoric*, 191). This relation, however, is not one of literal translation; instead, Chaucer proclaims the theoretical difficulty of translation, or even of adequate monolingual creation.[13] In this sense, the difficulty of translation corresponds precisely to the difficulty of expression per se (a leitmotif of this and other Chaucerian works). The thematization of monolingual creation as a translation problem contributes directly to the conflation of source and target, of monolingualism and multilingualism, of literal and metaphorical translation. For the *Legend of Good Women* includes both literal linguistic translation and 'original' poetry—along with a fairly sufficient praise of the flower in question.

Finally, monolingual texts that engage translations intertextually thematize the cultural significance of translation itself. These engagements, of course, may not always be immediately apparent. By simply adopting the habit of wondering about

---

[12] e.g. Christopher Baswell, 'Troy, Arthur, and the Languages of "Brutis Albyoun"', in Robert Stein and Sandra Pierson Prior (eds.), *Reading Medieval Culture: Essays in Honor of Robert W. Hanning* (Notre Dame, IN: University of Notre Dame Press, 2005), 170–97.

[13] Cole discusses other Chaucerian examples in a similar vein ('Chaucer's English Lesson', 1148).

translation and linguistic identity as often as possible, whenever words or books arise as narrative objects, we may further enrich the significance of well-known texts and render those less well known newly compelling. My first example, appropriately enough, comes not from a Middle English text but from Geoffrey of Monmouth's Latin *Historia regum Britanniae*. In the conclusion, as Geoffrey considers the etymology of the Welsh, *Guallenses*, he proffers the possibility that it might derive from *barbarie*. In Latin, the connection is obscure, but in English it makes perfect sense: as T. D. Crawford demonstrated, the translation of 'barbarian' as 'Welsh' depends on the silent mediation of English translation, from *wylisc* meaning 'foreign'.[14] The shadow presence of translation here renders sense into Latin etymology, and affords an example of latent translation, of the presence of English even where it is not immediately visible. This example also shows that research in Middle English cannot be confined to English-language texts. Any number of texts written in contact with English could turn out to engage in multilingual conversation.

English-language texts themselves, even when not translated, often encode references to translations and non-English texts. These references imply a reader-translator, whose informed apprehension of the English text includes previous or concurrent experiences of textual translation. Seemingly English-only expressions, in other words, may be anything but. Returning again to the authorial translator, Chaucer, we find in the 'Nun's Priest's Tale', for example, a story partly translated from one or more French fables. The tale includes, further, a wide array of references to non-English books—from the biblical to the classical to the medieval, primarily in Latin and French.[15] These allusions set the context for the tale's direct naming of the 'book of Launcelot' at the end of Chauntecleer's joyful speech to Pertelote:

> But sodeynly hym fil a sorweful cas,
> For evere the latter ende of joye is wo.
> God woot that wordly joye is soone ago;
> And if a rethor [rhetorician] koude faire endite,
> He in a cronycle saufly might it write
> As for a sovereyn notabilitee.
> Now every wys man, lat him herkne me;
> This storie is also trewe, I undertake,
> As is the book of Launcelot de Lake,
> That women holde in ful greet reverence.
> Now wol I torne again to my sentence.   (ll. 3205–14)

The book of Lancelot is of course a French book, reputedly held in great esteem by women (the book itself or else its hero, or both). The passage thematizes

---

[14] Geoffrey *Historia*, l. 303; T. D. Crawford, 'On the Linguistic Competence of Geoffrey of Monmouth', *Medium Aevum*, 51 (1982), 152–62. In Warren, *History on the Edge*, 50.

[15] e.g. Macrobius, Cicero, Dares Phyrgius, *Chanson de Roland*, *Aeneid* (or *Eneas*), Geoffrey of Vinsauf, Cato, Augustine, Boethius (ll. 2940, 3122–56, 3227, 3241–2, 3347, 3357–9).

truth—how it can be translated into chronicle by a 'rethor', into a tale such as 'this storie', or into a historic book such as Lancelot's. Of course, the passage also implies the utter absence of truth—in a chronicle of joy, an animal fable, and a romance of a famously adulterous lover. The only 'truth' of the book of Lancelot is its prose form. The women readers, moreover, are readers of French, and therefore potential translators (literal and metaphorical) who are enmeshed in 'double dealing'. At the end of the passage, the narrator disavows these dubious complexities with a return to the 'sentence'—a return to the story that signals a return to 'meaning'. But this claim provides no hermeneutic certainty since it follows closely upon a mistranslated 'sentence' of Latin, quoted a few lines earlier as part of Chauntecleer's meditation on joy:

> 'Now let us speke of myrthe, and stynte al this.
> Madame Pertelote, so have I blis,
> Of o thing God hath sent me large grace;
> For whan I se the beautee of youre face,
> Ye been so scarlet reed aboute youre yen,
> It maketh al my drede for to dyen;
> For al so siker as *In principio*,
> *Mulier est hominis confusio*—
> Madame, the sentence of this Latyn is,
> 'Womman is mannes joye and al his blis.'   (ll. 3157–66)

This performance of mistranslation suggests the extent to which the tale is largely about translation, a process shown here to engage a number of other issues central to the tale—from gender relations to classical authority to persuasive speech.

A more direct appeal to the reader-translator can be drawn from Hoccleve's address to Oldcastle, where latent translation operates on several different levels at once. Here, in the aftermath of the failed uprising of 1414, Hoccleve admonishes Oldcastle to reform his heterodox ways. Among his recommendations he includes a reading list, a list whose surface impression of monolingualism disintegrates almost immediately upon closer investigation:

> Bewar Oldcastel & for Crystes sake
> Clymbe no more in holy writ so hie [high]!
> Rede the storie of Lancelot de lake,
> Or Vegece the aart of Chivalrie
> The seege of Troie or Thebes. thee applie
> To ething that to thordre of knight longe
> To thy correccioun now haaste and hie,
> For thow haast been out of ioynt al to longe.
> If thee list thing rede of auctoritee,
> To thise stories sit it thee [it is fitting for you] to goon:
> To Iudicum Regum, and Iosue,
> To Iudith & to Paralipomenon,
> And Machabe & as siker as stoon [as sure as stone],

> If that thee list in hem bayte [feast] thyn ye,
> More autentike thing shalt thow fynde noon,
> Ne more pertinent to Chiualrie.   (ll. 193–208)

This list of readings seems quite disparate, if one thinks of the texts themselves as genres, but finds its unity in the knightly reader seeking models of knighthood.[16] From this perspective, Hoccleve offers a fairly straightforward catalogue of righteous chivalry: if heterodox religion has made Oldcastle a bad knight, attention to proper knightly conduct can make him a proper Christian once again. The content of these books, however, suggests something more complicated. Indeed, for all of Hoccleve's apparent faith in the reformative power of reading, one wonders if he could have read these books very deeply. Lancelot, for example, pales sinfully in comparison to his pure son Galahad in the very first pages of the romance that bears his name. And his story is more commonly associated with 'women's reading', not the manly conduct of battle (as Chaucer's allusion suggests). Thebes and Troy fare no better upon any close scrutiny: they are filled with valorous, flawed knights who fail all reasonable tests of 'correction' other than strong battlefield performance. Vegetius might seem a safer source, but successful reading of this practical guide to war would seem only to aid Oldcastle further in evading the champions of orthodoxy. The biblical books offer clearer models of proper and improper conduct, although their status as 'holy writ' suggests a latent danger, for they are found in association with the biblical readings that led Oldcastle astray in the first place.

But what if Hoccleve means to recommend a particular *form* of reading, rather than just a particular content? While embracing the powerful effects of books (a view of reading that made people fear Lollardy), Hoccleve subtly turns the question away from reading per se to the issue of choosing one's books wisely. And the choice here may be for particular translations—specifically, translations into French. For while some of the sources suggested were available in English in 1414–15, *all* of them were available in French. The opening reference to Lancelot orients us immediately toward French, the extensive thirteenth-century prose romance cycle that did not reach English until the later fifteenth century with Malory's translations. *Lancelot*, then, invites us to think next of a French *Art de chevalerie* translated from Vegetius' Latin treatise. These translations, including one by Jean de Meun, were numerous in the thirteenth and fourteenth centuries. By contrast, a single English translation had been made in 1408 for Thomas of Berkeley.[17] In this line of thought, the 'seege of Troie' evokes the twelfth-century verse *Roman de Troie* or even a French prose version of the kind that Lydgate would later use for his own English

---

[16] Ruth Nisse, ' "Oure Fadres Olde and Modres": Gender, Heresy, and Hoccleve's Literary Politics', *Studies in the Age of Chaucer*, 21 (1999), 275–99, at 294–8; John M. Bowers, 'Thomas Hoccleve and the Politics of Tradition', *Chaucer Review*, 36 (2002), 352–69, at 354–5.

[17] Geoffrey Lester, *The Earliest English Translation of Vegetius'* De re militari (Heidelberg: Carl Winter, 1988).

translation. Of course, two English versions already existed in 1414-15, along with Chaucer's *Troilus* (not primarily a 'seege' story) and the Latin account by Guido delle Colonne.[18] A French *Troie* leads most directly to a French *Thèbes*, in either verse (twelfth century) or prose (thirteenth century). Despite Chaucer's various references, Thebes did not come fully into English until Lydgate's translation from French prose completed in 1422; the Latin account by Statius would of course also have been available.[19]

In the context of heretical 'correccioun', English is certainly not the first option that comes to mind for reading the Bible, even if Hoccleve emphasizes that the goal is to apprehend historical chivalry, not to contemplate theological subtleties or spiritual truths.[20] And while Latin, as in several of the other references, could also be an option, the Old French Bible may be the most appropriate form for orthodox biblical reading by a knight. The Old French Bible (*c*.1260), also used as a basis for the *Bible historiale* (*c*.1300), would be an especially appropriate source: widely available by Hoccleve's time, the Old French Bible offers a quite orthodox rendering of the Latin Vulgate, including glosses that focus on literal interpretations for a lay audience.[21] So, when Hoccleve opens the reading list passage with the exhortation 'Clymbe no more in holy writ so hie' (l. 194), he does not in fact enjoin Oldcastle against biblical reading per se but rather against a certain kind of reading—an overly interpretative reading that seeks 'higher' meanings, spiritual interpretations that should be left to experts. Instead, Oldcastle should mine the Old Testament for literal, historical examples of noble service and chivalric feats of arms. Hoccleve may even be suggesting that certain translations serve this purpose better than others: in French, biblical chivalry looks all the more like that depicted in French historical romances like *Troie, Thebes,* and *Lancelot*. Or, as Ruth Nisse has put it, 'In [Hoccleve's] knightly idea of translation, so different from the Lollards', the military virtues of *Maccabees* lend biblical "auctoritee" to those in *Lancelot* and other works of chivalry' ('"Oure Fadres Olde and Modres"', 296). The common authority that links these sources of disparate tone, genre, and period is ultimately French prose translation. Prose, associated with truth-telling, resists in its very form the dangers of interpretation (poetic or spiritual) that Hoccleve has identified as the source of Oldcastle's heterodoxy.

In all events, none of the stories Hoccleve mentions was originally written in English, and so, if he envisioned English as a language for Oldcastle's reading,

---

[18] David C. Benson, *The History of Troy in Middle English Literature: Guido delle Colonne's Historia destructionis Troiae in Medieval England* (Woodbridge: D. S. Brewer, 1980), esp. 156–8.

[19] Dominique Battles, *The Medieval Tradition of Thebes: History and Narrative in the OF Roman de Thèbes, Boccaccio, Chaucer, and Lydgate* (New York: Routledge, 2004).

[20] Nisse, '"Oure Fadres Olde and Modres"', 297–8.

[21] Clive R. Sneddon, 'On the Creation of the *Old French Bible*', *Nottingham Medieval Studies*, 46 (2002), 25–44. On the specifics of technique in the Old French Bible, Sneddon, 'Translation Technique and the *Old French Bible*', *Forum for Modern Language Studies*, 35 (1999), 339–49.

he also envisioned translations. If Hoccleve thus uses French chivalry to oppose Lollards and to redefine English literature as an antidote to heresy,[22] that literature is in fact only rarely expressed in the English language, and then only in recent translation. Whether the reading list was intended or received as multilingual (French, English, and/or Latin) or monolingual (French), the necessary absence of English is a matter of theological import in the context of arguments against heresy. The heresy that Hoccleve enjoins Oldcastle to abandon is of course strongly associated with unauthorized English translation of sacred texts. Linguistic transfers underwrote knowledge transfers that disrupted established institutional and social hierarchies. In this context, the necessary presence of translation in Hoccleve's reading list problematizes the very idea of 'right' reading that he proposes.

Nor can Hoccleve's poem itself be apprehended without translation. The autograph manuscript, Huntington MS 111, opens and closes each work with French tags; in the Oldcastle poem, side notes reference Latin sources for several key points. There are seven of these notes, of varying lengths, in the first half of the poem; there are no notes in the second half, which begins with the narrator's direct address to the heretics who have induced Oldcastle's fall. This is in fact the only densely commented section of the entire manuscript (a handful of notes appear later, in Latin and French (fos. 25^v, 26^r, 28^r, 41^r)). The marginal notes to the Oldcastle poem actually reveal the accompanying English passages to be translations.[23] In the poem's larger poetic design, the aesthetic value of these passages equals that of the 'original' poetry, for no formal or semantic differences distinguish the two Englishes. This seamlessness destabilizes a supposed hierarchy of original creation over translations. At the same time, the presence of the 'original' Latin sources enhances the value of the translated passages, demonstrating visually and linguistically that English operates as a functional equivalent to Latin. The passage outlining Oldcastle's reading list comes between the last two Latin notes. At this point, readers of this manuscript have learned to see the poem itself as a partial translation—but also to engage sources directly. The reading list, in other words, now looks certain to include both translations and 'originals', perhaps without significant distinction.

These several brief examples suggest some of the pressures that translation exerts on seemingly monolingual expressions. In each case, other languages intervene unexpectedly to broaden the linguistic and cultural references of texts that appear committed to narrower terms of signification. At this point, it seems that monolingualism does not exist, for even monolingual texts engage multilingual histories. Conversely, translation operates even in the absence of multiple languages. For any text, even one that is not, philologically speaking, a translation, implies antecedents and precedents. This approach reverses the traditional relation between source text

---

[22] Nisse, '"Oure Fadres Olde and Modres"', 278–80; Bowers, 'Thomas Hoccleve', 354–5.
[23] Fos. 1^v (ll. 33–44), 2^r (ll. 51–6), 2^v (ll. 81–8, 89–96), 8^v (ll. 139–44), 9^v (ll. 185–92), 10^v (ll. 217–32).

and target, suggesting that every text creates its own original. The translated text, in other words, is as much an original as the source.[24] Ultimately, to say that every text is an original, or that every text is a translation, amounts to the same thing. As such, all kinds of methods adapted from translation studies proper may be pertinent to Middle English and offer prospects for new approaches to well-travelled ground.

Translation and (our) teaching

A theoretically engaged approach to monolingual translation poses some fresh research questions for the pedagogy of Middle English. Courses in Middle English literature include both medieval texts that derive from other medieval (or earlier) texts and medieval texts that have been themselves translated into modern languages. If we accept the former as critically compelling, why not the latter? How can we then legitimize both moments of translation as locations for analytic research? What kinds of questions can they support, such that students work on genuine literary and cultural problems even if they do not read 'original' texts? What distinguishes a reading of Chaucer in Modern English from one in Turkish or Korean?

Beginning again with philological issues, direct comparative study of translations provides an obvious starting point for querying the diversity of 'English'. Indeed, Peter Beidler proposed some time ago that medievalists (especially Chaucerians) try to 'teach the problem' rather than ignoring modern versions of medieval texts.[25] Invigorated by the theoretical resources of translation studies, this diachronic approach to the literary 'variant' legitimizes each version as an authentic source of literary analysis, while provoking critics (students and professionals) to define clearly and carefully the historical and cultural locations of their conclusions. Classroom translations thus become yet one more location for studying the long history of reception and rewriting that characters medieval literature itself. Sustained, theorized approaches to modern versions bring into the open the silent, hidden translations (literal and metaphorical) already taking place both in and outside of the classroom.

A pedagogy of translation also focuses attention on the role of mediation in the reading experience. In translation theory, mediation pertains to the collection of processes, centred on the figure of the translator, that together enable some level of communication between source culture or language, and 'target' culture or language. In a simple version, mediation theory makes of the teacher a translator—a provider of equivalences (literal translation) and explanatory context (metaphorical

---

[24] Edwin Gentzler, *Contemporary Translation Theories* (London: Routledge, 1993), 149–53 (on poststructural translation theory).
[25] Peter Beidler, 'Chaucer and the Trots: What to Do about Those Modern English Translations', *Chaucer Review*, 19 (1985), 290–301.

translation). In a more theoretically complex way, mediation involves interpretation of historical and contemporary contexts; it touches both the teacher and the material text itself as a site of and product of multiple translating operations. Ultimately, essay-writing students also take on the identity of mediators in their translations of the past. By marking, and then theorizing, these various modes of mediation, a pedagogy of translation can transform theory into analytic critical practice and ultimately produce new forms of criticism (amateur and professional).

Finally, in broader theoretical terms, I would like to delegitimize the very idea of the 'untranslated' text. No one of the twenty-first century has a 'native' knowledge of any medieval language, and so even the 'original' text is apprehended through various literal and metaphoric translations (cultural, editorial, linguistic, etc.). Our status as migrant readers in the field of the past conditions everything we think, write, and teach about literature. The encounter with the medieval text is a multilingual encounter, even when one appears to be reading 'English' texts in 'English' in an 'English' classroom. In other words, one of the primary conditions of reading Middle English is translating it (linguistically, culturally, historically, etc.). In a very real sense, the way we translate the past (for students, for ourselves) creates knowledge of the past. As such, it may be one of the most powerful and least examined procedures of Middle English pedagogy—and by extension, of Middle English research.

A pedagogy of translation, then, would dismantle the putative monolingualism of English literature. The effects of this procedure represent much more than a 'mere' teaching issue or question of pedagogical strategy. In a very real sense, they represent a research opportunity for the twenty-first century. What methods and theories of translation are at work in the English classroom? How do these shape the kinds of interpretations considered convincing, or even considered possible? What would it mean to consider the reader a multilingual subject? If talking about Middle English literature is always a form of talking about translation, then how can we bring the dynamics of translation theory and practice to bear upon the task of vivifying Middle English literature for new generations of students and future scholars? These generations might be native speakers of one of the Englishes wrought by anglophone globalization. Or they might come to English as non-native speakers. Perhaps, on the multilingual side of globalization, they will have more than one 'native' language. Whatever the case may be, the place of translation in modern daily life, in academic life, and in the historic life of Middle English writers can all provide fruitful points of comparison.

FURTHER READING

Research on translation coming out of medieval studies offers opportunities to broaden dialogues across language areas and regions. Some particularly inspiring recent works include: Christopher Cannon, *The Making of Chaucer's English: A Study of Words* (Cambridge: Cambridge University Press, 1998); Maria Tymoczko, *Translation in a Postcolonial Context: Early Irish Literature in English Translation* (Manchester: St Jerome Publishing, 1999); Anne Appel, 'Extremes of "Remembering:" Translation as "Figura"', *Forum Italicum*, 36 (2002), 447–56; Claude Buridant, 'La "Traduction intralinguale" en moyen français', *Moyen Français*, 51–3 (2002–3), 113–57; Fiona Somerset and Nicholas Watson (eds.), *The Vulgar Tongue: Medieval and Postmedieval Vernacularity* (University Park: Pennsylvania State University Press, 2003); Anne E. B Coldiron, *Canon, Period, and the Poetry of Charles of Orleans* (Ann Arbor: University of Michigan Press, 2000). Coldiron also shows some of the possibilities for redefining literary corpora through translation in 'Translations Challenge to Critical Categories: Verses from French in the Early English Renaissance', *Yale Journal of Criticism*, 16 (2003), 315–44 (this issue contains a number of other thought-provoking essays).

One of the greatest opportunities for new insights comes from the exploration of translation through theories and methods that appear to have little to do with the medieval context. This kind of 'achronic' (not to say anachronistic) thinking might propel research in unexpected directions. Some recent publications that have attracted my attention include: Sherry Simon, *Changing the Terms: Translating in the Postcolonial Era* (Ottawa: University of Ottawa Press, 2000); Antonio Sousa Ribeiro, 'Translation as a Metaphor for our Times: Postcolonialism, Borders and Identities', *Portuguese Studies*, 20 (2004), 186–94; Sergio Waisman, *Borges and Translation: The Irreverence of the Periphery* (Lewisburg, PA: Bucknell University Press, 2005); *India's Shakespeare: Translation, Interpretation, and Performance* (Newark: University of Delaware Press, 2005); Susan Bassnett, 'Translating Terror', *Third World Quarterly*, 26 (2005), 393–403; Emily Apter, *The Translation Zone: A New Comparative Literature* (Princeton: Princeton University Press, 2006) (and everything else published in the *Translation/Transnation* series Apter edits at Princeton University Press).

Further thought and research attention could certainly be given to pedagogical translation, perhaps drawing on some of the following: Mary Ramsey (ed.), *Beowulf in our Time: Teaching Beowulf in Translation* (Kalamazoo: Medieval Institute, Western Michigan University, 2002); Tereas Bargetto-Andrés, 'Teaching Medieval Translation Culture of Fifteenth-Century Spain', *Studies in Medieval and Renaissance Teaching*, 8 (2000), 5–20; William D. Paden, 'Why Translate?', *TENSO* 15 (2000), 85–96; Lene Petersen, 'Literary Translations between Philology and Aesthetics', in Hans Hansen (ed.), *Changing Philologies: Contributions to the Redefinition of Foreign Language Studies in the Age of Globalisation*, (Copenhagen: Museum Tusculanum Press, 2002), 137–40; Carol Maier, 'Gender, Pedagogy, and Literary Translation', in Brian Baer and Geoffrey Koby (eds.), *Rethinking Translation Pedagogy* (Amsterdam: Benjamins, 2003), 157–72; Kristen Prevallet, 'Risking It: Scandals, Teaching, Translation', *Journal of Scholarly Publishing*, 25 (2004), 148–58.

CHAPTER 6

AURALITY

JOYCE COLEMAN

One evening in 1437, James I of Scotland and his lords passed the time 'att the playing of the chesse, att the tables [backgammon], yn redying of Romans, yn syngyng and pypyng, in harpyng, and in other honest solaces of grete pleasance and disport'.[1] A few hours later, one of the lords came back to murder James—which is why we know about the earlier part of that day. Nobody would have bothered to record the evening's romance-reading otherwise; it was too ordinary.

James I was literate, of course; he was the author of a book himself, *The Kingis Quair*. And as a king, he probably had a decent library. If he'd wanted to sit down and read a romance as we would read one today, alone in a chair, he could have. So why didn't he? Obviously, he would have had less fun. The object of the evening was to socialize; all the other activities were communal, and if the king went off by himself to read, that would have ended it for everyone. Plus, off alone in his room or corner, the king would not have been reinforcing his primus-inter-pares status by visibly presiding over the action.

The shape of that evening in 1437 was not determined by its being in Scotland. Rusticity was not an issue, that is: James had spent his youth at the English court (after they captured him at the age of 10). In any case, ample evidence exists for similar evenings in London too, and generally throughout England. And the date, long after the death of Chaucer, is equally unremarkable. Up to his death in 1491, William Caxton, England's first printer, was sending his books out with prologues explaining how good they were to read or hear.

The practice has come to be called 'aurality'. 'Aurality' is different from 'orality' (though the two words are difficult to distinguish in speech). 'Orality', like 'literacy', means a lot of things, depending on the individual, the discipline, and the context. For the purposes of discussing medieval European literary reception, I've defined 'orality' as 'the shared hearing of texts' and 'literacy' as 'the private reading of

---

[1] John Shirley (trans.), *The Dethe of the Kynge of Scotis*, in Joseph Stevenson (ed.), *The Life and Death of King James the First of Scotland* (Edinburgh: Maitland Club no. 42, 1837), 47–67, at 54.

written texts'. 'Aurality', 'the shared hearing of written texts', combines aspects of both.[2]

To date, aurality has remained a little-understood, rarely acknowledged, and—I would argue—historically crucial arena of medieval literary experience. For reasons to be suggested below, most scholars steer around it. The only critics to have explored it in any detail are D. H. Green, writing on earlier medieval German literature, and myself, concentrating on later medieval English, French, and Burgundian literature and illumination. This essay will trace some of the issues involved, explicate the practice of aurality, and indicate some of the many potential directions for future research. I will attempt to stay within reports of British reading, though I will occasionally dip into the more abundant evidence about French and Burgundian reading. I will also confine myself mostly to recreational literature—material read for entertainment and relaxation—but with some reference to other contexts of reading.

The theory of aurality

A long-standing and still, often, current assumption is that orality (understood in such contexts as 'the oral delivery of texts') gave way to literacy (here, 'the private reading of texts') over the course of the Middle Ages. Defined in this way, the two entities are mutually exclusive, which allows them to be placed in a relationship of evolution: orality giving way to literacy as dinosaurs gave way to mammals. Tracing this evolution has been an exciting scholarly occupation, especially when the scholar has followed Walter Ong in equating 'literacy' with critical thinking, individuality, and a variety of other desirable traits.[3] For scholars of Middle English literature, such evolutionary dazzle has attached particularly to Geoffrey Chaucer, whose injunction (to those unlikely to enjoy the 'Miller's Tale') to '[t]urne over the leef and chese another tale'[4] has been hailed repeatedly as evidence that he embraced the ethos of privately and critically read literature.

So where does that leave James I? Not to mention Chaucer himself? Although Chaucer depicts his persona reading in a number of his texts, he consistently addresses a listening audience throughout his works, using phrases such as 'as ye shall hear' and 'as ye have heard'. A historiated initial in a copy of the *Canterbury Tales* (see Fig. 1) shows Chaucer holding the book open before himself, perhaps as though ready to read it aloud to the viewer. His writings, moreover, include

[2] For a fuller discussion of this terminology, see Joyce Coleman, *Public Reading and the Reading Public in Late Medieval England and France* (Cambridge: Cambridge University Press, 1996). Unless otherwise referenced, further details on the aural texts cited in this article can be found in this book.
[3] Walter S. Ong, *Orality and Literacy: The Technologizing of the Word* (London: Methuen, 1982), 36–57.
[4] Geoffrey Chaucer, *The Riverside Chaucer*, ed. Larry D. Benson, 3rd edn. (Oxford: Oxford University Press, 1987); *Canterbury Tales*, I. 3177. All citations of Chaucer's works are to this edition.

Figure 1
Chaucer prelects from the opening W
of 'Whan that aprill ... ' (London, BL
Lansdowne 851, fo. 2; by permission
of the British Library)

detailed accounts of two aural readings at different ends of the social scale: the literate noblewoman Criseyde and her ladies listening to a maiden read *The Siege of Thebes* (*Troilus and Criseyde*, II. 81–4); and the probably illiterate weaver Alisoun of Bath listening to her husband read his 'book of wikked wives' (*CT* III. 669–793). Even the celebrated injunction to 'turne over the leef' is addressed to 'whoso list it [the 'Miller's Tale'] nat yheere' (*CT* I. 3176–7)—to whoever doesn't want to *hear* it. A hearer turning a page? This is not a self-cancelling paradox: if you don't want to hear the tale, you're to ask the person reading the *Canterbury Tales* aloud to look for some other, less offensive story.

The problem with the Great Divide model of orality and literacy—the model that sees them as polar opposites—is that it generates such apparent paradoxes as this.[5] In this model, orality and literacy can coexist only in the period during which literacy is replacing orality. Points at which literacy and orality clearly seem to coexist—such as Criseyde's group-reading, for example—are perceived as transitional, and therefore fugitive, and therefore unimportant. To do otherwise depletes the dazzle attached to the claim that Chaucer—or whatever other figure or period one is writing about—marks the emergence of a new, more sophisticated and ambitious understanding of literature and self, etc.

---

[5] The term 'Great Divide' is widely used now to designate the theories of orality propagated by Walter Ong, *Orality and Literacy*; Eric Havelock, *Preface to Plato* (Cambridge, Mass.: Harvard University Press, 1963); and Jack Goody and Ian Watt, 'The Consequences of Literacy' (1963), repr. in Goody (ed.), *Literacy in Traditional Societies* (Cambridge: Cambridge University Press, 1968), 27–68. The term was introduced by Ruth Finnegan in her 1973 article 'Literacy Versus Non-Literacy: The Significance of "Literature" in Non-Literate Cultures', reprinted in Finnegan's *Literacy and Orality* (Oxford: Blackwell, 1988).

But aurality was not transitional. The ancient Greeks and Romans read their books in aural groups, the early medievals did, the late medievals did, and the Renaissance did. People kept reading books aloud to each other until they got radios, at which point they began listening to programmes such as the English 'A Book at Bedtime'. And I can't explain my research to someone I meet at a party without being told how much they love listening to audio-books. What *did* phase out in the late Middle Ages, relatively, was the minstrel performance of texts: recitation from memory of material learned either by hearing or reading (or both). This is sometimes called 'memoriality'. If 'orality' is defined as 'the hearing of texts', then both memoriality and aurality are subsets of orality, and it is easy to equate the disappearance of minstrel performance with the disappearance of aural reading.

Easy, but not accurate. Not only did aurality not disappear, it was, in fact, the predominant means of experiencing written texts throughout the Middle Ages, both in Latin and in the vernaculars. University education consisted of listening to the lecturer read the set text aloud, sometimes with explications. (This was called *praelectio*—'reading before', in the sense of 'before a group of auditors'. The English form *prelection*—along with *prelect* and *prelector*—appears in the *Oxford English Dictionary*, with citations from 1586 to 1907. I have revived the terms to give us a means of distinguishing reading aloud from private reading.) Oxford collegians relaxed by prelecting 'poems, chronicles of kings, and wonders of this world' ('poemata, regnorum chronicas, et mundi hujus mirabilia') in the evening,[6] as did law students, as did kings like James I, as did courtiers such as the esquires described in a household book of Edward IV (see below), as did nobles like Criseyde, as did gentry such as Sir John Berkeley (whose hospitality included damsels ready to 'rede him oright romance'),[7] as did lower middle-class people like Alisoun of Bath, if they had someone literate to read to them. Depending on the audience and the text, the prelected material was in Latin, French, or English (or Cornish, Welsh, or Gaelic). Much of Christian devotion centred on aural reading: not just the biblical passages read in church, but Scripture and patristic writings prelected in monastic refectories, devotional manuals prelected in lay households, and saints' lives prelected probably everywhere.

This is not to say, of course, that no one read books privately. Anyone who was literate could and probably did. A social map of medieval reading would show a variety of oralities, auralities, and literacies in operation, adapted to different individuals, genres, and situations. Criseyde, for example, liked to hear history read aloud with her companions (*The Siege of Thebes*) but went into a private room to read her letter from Troilus. This makes sense: the history-reading was intended to entertain a whole group, whereas most people would choose to keep their love letters secret. The university students who heard books read aloud in lectures and

---

[6] *Statutes of the Colleges of Oxford*, i (Oxford: Royal Commission, 1853), New College, 40–2.
[7] Thorlac Turville-Petre (ed.), 'The Lament for Sir John Berkeley', *Speculum*, 57 (1983), 332–9; l. 44.

in the college hall no doubt also studied them in private (if they had or could obtain copies). Literate individuals moved back and forth between kinds of reading, depending on circumstances. Most recreational literature seems to have been read publicly, but nothing stopped a literate individual from picking up the book and reading it alone. Dennis Green has labelled such reading 'the intermediate mode of reception ... in which a work was composed with an eye to public recital from a written text, but also for the occasional private reader'.[8] To avoid the evolutionary implications of 'intermediate', I've called this kind of reading 'bimodal', meaning it mixes modalities, or ways of receiving texts. One night, you might hear a portion of the book read aloud; the next afternoon, you might pick it up again to read the same or a different passage to yourself, or to look at the pictures. That night, you might hear the prelector read the next instalment.

Outweighing Chaucer's references to and depictions of aural reception, for some scholars, is the author's own frequently described and depicted habit of private reading. The Chaucerian persona, so fond of reading Ovid in bed (*Book of the Duchess*, ll. 44–51) or of spending his evenings 'sitting at another book' (*House of Fame*, l. 657), is hailed as the forerunner of the new era of literacy. But authors—and Chaucer's persona, unassuming as he is, is always an author—were special cases. They had to go off by themselves to read a lot of books so that they could write their own books, which came out of those other books. Thus, the dreamer in *The Book of the Duchess* no sooner closes his *Metamorphoses* then he has turned the Ceyx and Alcyone story into English verse. Once the new text is produced, out of extensive private reading, it is handed over to its patron and audience, who, usually, would read it aloud together. References in many medieval texts describe or imply such a cycle of production and reception.

The practice of aurality

The core of what made aurality unique—not a fugitive hybrid of orality and literacy but an independent, important (and long-term) literary phenomenon—is the social presence it gave texts. That is why I define aurality as 'the shared hearing of written texts', with 'orality' as 'the shared hearing of texts' and 'literacy' as 'the private reading of written texts'. Whether private readers vocalized as they read—i.e., read the text aloud to themselves—or read it silently, they still read it alone. Their experience of the text was not influenced by a performer or by the reactions of fellow listeners. By contrast, when someone participated in an aural reading, either as prelector or listener, many new factors entered into the experience and understanding of the text.

---

[8] See D. H. Green, 'Orality and Reading', *Speculum*, 6s (1990), 277; see also Green, *Medieval Listening and Reading* (Cambridge: Cambridge University Press, 1994), esp. chs. 7–8.

What were these new factors, and how did they influence the text? Starting with the reading event, I will move on to consider how the dynamics of aurality arguably affected medieval literature, and why it matters. Finally, I will review work that has been done, and suggest areas as yet unexplored.

To return to James I on that night in 1437; at some point the king and his lords had had enough of chess, harping, and so on, and decided to listen to a romance. Modern discussions of medieval aural readings often assume that they disenfranchised the audience—another way in which such readings allegedly hindered the exercise of critical intelligence. But medieval audiences did not sit in submissive silence, at the mercy of a powerful reader who determined the text and controlled the event. Rather, the prelector was usually a person of equal or lower status to the audience, whose members were quite comfortable about determining the direction of any given reading event. When a clear social superior was present, as in James's court or among Criseyde's ladies, that person may have chosen the text to be prelected. Or the prelector may have consulted the group. Criseyde tells Pandarus that '[t]his romaunce is of Thebes that *we* rede' (*T&C* II. 100; emphasis added), though she was not the prelector. British prelection (unlike French and Burgundian) tended to downplay issues of status, emphasizing instead the mutual enjoyment and bonding the reading would produce.

Equally, the group or its leader would have chosen a certain portion of the text to read that particular evening, since clearly they could not get through a whole romance in one session. They might have been progressing through a given text in regular instalments—the famous example of this is a French one, Jean Froissart taking ten weeks to read his *Méliador* to the count of Foix and his court.[9] Or the group might have called for a favourite episode from an already-familiar text. Even a king's household would have had a limited number of recreational works available, and over time most of the court would have become familiar with their contents. This enabled them, as Andrew Taylor has described, to read in excerpts, or fragments, with their memories filling in the context.[10]

The prelector might have been one of their own group—perhaps a younger man, with better eyesight—or might have been one of James's household clerks. The audience would seat themselves in a casual group facing the reader, perhaps discussing the text they were going to hear. Medieval illuminations that depict reading aloud (which is what most medieval pictures of reading depict) usually show the audience in a tight cluster—even when there is enough room for them to spread around. An example shows Guillaume de Machaut, a French poet who greatly influenced Chaucer, reading from a master's chair to six people who sit

[9] Jean Froissart, *Œuvres: poesies*, ii: *Le Dit du florin*, ed. Auguste Scheler (Brussels: Devaux, 1871), ll. 282–314, 340–87; Froissart, *Œuvres: Chroniques*, xi: *1383–1386*, ed. Kervyn de Lettenhove (Brussels: Devaux, 1870), 85.

[10] Andrew Taylor, 'Fragmentation, Corruption, and Minstrel Narration: The Question of the Middle English Romances', *Yearbook of English Studies*, 22 (1992), 38–62.

Figure 2 The audience that listens together sits together. (Paris, BnF fr 22545, fo. 75ᵛ; by permission of the Bibliothèque Nationale de France)

piled together on a little clump of ground (see Fig. 2). I know of no English pictures that present this iconography, but the famous *Troilus and Criseyde* frontispiece (Cambridge, Corpus Christi, MS 66, fo. 1; see Fig. 3), which shows Chaucer apparently reciting (not prelecting) the text to a courtly group, similarly crowds its audience in front of the speaker. The arrangement is emphasized by its contrast with the scene in the background, where people are spread out over the available space. The implication is that the shared experience bonds the audience into a group.

The situation may not resemble how we read books today, but it might remind us of how we'd view a DVD of a favourite movie with family or friends—mutually choosing which film to watch, preparing drinks and food, settling in and chatting as the DVD is loaded up. The DVD, however, would not give us a different performance of the movie every time we watched it—whereas different prelectors, or the same prelector on different occasions, would present the same text in different ways. There would be the simple issue of competence: how well the prelector could decipher the script and read the words clearly and accurately. Then there's skill: how well the prelector could convey the action and organization of a text. And then there's talent: how well the prelector could bring the story to life, creating drama and fleshing out characters as a good actor would—as a good audio-book reader does today.

Figure 3 Chaucer's audience clusters around him. (Cambridge, Corpus Christi College 61, fo. 1ᵛ, by permission of the Master and Fellows of Corpus Christi College, Cambridge)

All of this considers the prelector/performer alone. But the prelector was not, of course, reading into a vacuum. As many of us do today watching a movie in company—even, notoriously, in theatres—the audience had a tendency to comment and critique during the course of a reading. Froissart reports proudly that the count of Foix wouldn't let anyone interrupt him as he read[11]—which implies that such interruption was usual. Medieval preachers frequently mentioned the enthusiastic reaction of those who listened to tales of King Arthur or Robin Hood or Guy of Warwick (in order to compare it disparagingly with the tepid response the same auditors give to the story of Christ's passion). If members of an aural audience disliked a given reading (outside of church), they might very well terminate it—as we would eject the DVD, and as the Canterbury pilgrims terminated the Squire's, the Monk's, and Chaucer's tales, while the Wife of Bath went so far as to tear three pages out of her husband's book and knock him into the fire. But an audience's running commentary could just be part of their mutual enjoyment—since the whole point of an aural reading is that it is shared, it is intended as a social occasion. A household book of Edward IV describes his esquires spending their downtime in lords' chambers 'talkyng of cronycles of kinges and of other polycyez, or in pypyng, or harpyng, synging, other actez marciablez, to help ocupy the court and acompany straungers' (note the resemblance to James I's last evening).[12] The phrase 'talkyng of cronycles' seems to equate the prelection of a text with discussion of its content. Aural audiences probably commented as readings progressed on the action, the battles, the heroes and villains. Equally, depending on the audience and the text, they might have commented on the author's skill, might have recognized sources and evaluated the new interpretation, might have reflected (as glossators liked to) on citations from Latin authorities.

Such reactions would have shaped the prelection in various ways. The prelectors might have stopped periodically, as some point was debated among the group, perhaps contributing their own opinion. Prelectors might have adapted their reading to some consistent preference or dislike expressed by the group. They could emphasize the dastardliness of a character who was proving unpopular, for example; they might even have interpolated further comments, plot-points, or analyses out of their memory of other texts. To this extent an aural reading recalls the sort of extempore adaptation of texts documented by Milman Parry and Albert Lord in their famous research on oral-formulaic performance.[13]

But aural reading differs crucially from extemporaneous composition because of the clear presence of the book. When a given day's prelection was done, the text did not vanish, but remained, reverting back to its 'ur' form as a Shakespeare play does

---

[11] Froissart, *Chroniques*, xi. 85.

[12] A. R. Myers (ed.), *The Household of Edward IV: The Black Book and the Ordinance of 1478* (Manchester: Manchester University Press, 1959), 129.

[13] See Albert Lord, *The Singer of Tales* (Cambridge, MA: Harvard University Press, 1960).

no matter how avant-garde the latest production. Even in the Scottish case—the prelection of a romance by an unspecified, perhaps anonymous author—the book was the third player in the communication loop of aural reading. Its very presence, and its function as source of the text being shared, communicated authority, and when the author was well known, perhaps carried a sense of venerability. Both Chaucer and Gower talk of how 'these olde wyse'[14]—a phrase that seems to cover both books and their authors—remain for us in the books they wrote. The prelectors of such prestigious material must have picked up some aura of the *auctor* they were voicing—especially when, like Chaucer, that *auctor* wrote in the first person. Medieval illuminators were not simply inspired by naive anachronism to dress Cicero, for example, in the robes of a 'modern' university master (see Fig. 4). Rather, they were responsive to the almost mystical sense that the book effaced time, that the manuscript brought Cicero into our world, gave him voice through the voice of the prelector, and drew the entire reading group into communion with a transhistorical and highly valued cultural heritage.

James I's evening of mixed entertainments among an all-male group follows a pattern evidenced by a number of other historical and literary texts from Britain (we have already seen this with Edward IV's esquires). This was the best-attested pattern—probably because male experience is the best attested generally—but it was not the only pattern. Criseyde and her ladies listening to the *Siege of Thebes* is another one. Pandarus' entry with his intimations of a love affair in the offing retrospectively emphasizes the security and chastity of that all-female reading group. Nonetheless, the 'historical' nature of the women's chosen text arguably reflects an attempt to understand their position as residents of another besieged city, Troy. Jankyn's reading to his wife depicts a less affluent, more intimate form of prelection. Sometimes aural reading served as a means of seduction or was exploited as an excuse for staring at a beautiful young woman. An anonymous poet reports visiting Ribblesdale, for example, to consort with 'wilde wymmen'; he praises his chosen one for having 'a mury mouht to mele, | with lefly rede lippes lele, | romaunz forte rede' (a merry mouth to speak with, | with lovely loyal red lips, | romance for to read).[15]

Prelections of devotional material in lay households tended to mimic religious settings. Duchess Cecily Nevill had a priest read to her and her household at dinner, and herself recapitulated the reading—apparently from memory—at supper.[16] A spiritual director instructed a middle-class man to have his family members take

---

[14] Chaucer, *Legend of Good Women*, F. Prol. 19; John Gower, *Complete Works*, ii–iii: *Confessio Amantis*, ed. G. C. Macaulay (Oxford: Clarendon Press, 1901), Prol. 7.

[15] 'The Fair Maid of Ribblesdale', in *The Harley Lyrics*, 2nd edn., ed. G. L. Brook (Manchester: University of Manchester Press, 1956), ll. 2, 37–9.

[16] 'Orders and Rules of the House of the Princess Cecill, Mother of King Edward IV', in *A Collection of Ordinances and Regulations for the Government of the Royal Household* (London: Society of Antiquaries, 1790) *35–*39 (*37).

Figure 4 Cicero lecturing at the Sorbonne. (Ghent, Univ. Bibl. 10, fo. 37ᵛ; by permission of the Universiteitsbibliotheek Gent)

turns prelecting religious texts at meals, which he would then explain to them.[17] One reason for the practice was to control the babble that a family meal might otherwise involve. Margery Kempe, famously, had her priest take her through an aural course on theology—congratulating herself on how useful the sessions were for the prelector, since it caused 'hym to lokyn meche good scriptur & many a good doctowr whech he wolde not a lokyd at that tyme had sche [Kempe] ne be'.[18]

Why aurality matters

So say medieval English reading was bimodal—with a bias towards the aural. So what? We have relatively little evidence about how such readings worked, and no detailed descriptions. No field videos or medieval equivalents survive documenting a series of Chaucer readings, for example, in any given household or across different households. All we have are the texts, and we might as well get on with reading them.

References to aural readings, in early eras of scholarship as now, may acknowledge that such things existed but rarely remember that fact once analysis of the text commences. The issue is evidently considered peripheral—an aspect of book history, or of sociology, not really relevant to literary interpretation itself. This recalls the classic tension between study of Shakespeare's plays as literature and as performance—only in this case, without institutional compensation, no Drama Department ready to champion the aural issues sidelined in the English Departments.

Obviously, I think aurality matters. In the first place, aurality is a fact, multiply attested. So when we talk about how a medieval reader would have read some text or other, we should factor in that that reader would as likely as not have been hearing the text, not reading it privately. An example involves John Gower's *Confessio Amantis*.[19] This English-language compendium of mostly Ovidian love exempla is heavily glossed with prose Latin moralizations and ornamented by complex Latin verses. The fact that the moralizations often don't seem to match the tales has produced a good deal of scholarly commentary, crediting Gower with various deconstructive intentions. Almost invariably, these discussions assume, without exploration, a private, Latinate reader assiduously engaged in cross-indexing the text's multiple registers. But not only does Gower explicitly invoke aurality as

[17] 'Instructions for a Devout and Literate Layman', ed. William Abel Pantin, in J. J. G. Alexander and M. T. Gibson (eds.), *Medieval Learning and Literature: Essays Presented to Richard William Hunt* (Oxford: Clarendon Press, 1976), 398–400 (English) and 420–2 (Latin).

[18] Margery Kempe, *The Book of Margery Kempe*, i, ed. Sanford Brown Meech, EETS, os 212 (London: Milford, 1940), 143.

[19] See Joyce Coleman, 'Lay Readers and Hard Latin', *Studies in the Age of Chaucer*, 24 (2002), 209–35.

the reception format of his and other such works—he speaks of written works remaining 'to the worldes eere' (*CA* Prol. 10)—but he tells us in the book's Prologue that he wrote it at the request of Richard II. While the love stories would no doubt have delighted Richard, the young king would have been highly unlikely to possess the Latinity or the interest to pore over Gower's disjunctive glosses and tricky Latin verses. The only solution that scholars have offered for this paradox, if they acknowledge it, is that Gower made up the story about writing the book for Richard, and that he really wrote it for scholarly friends. Anyone who was erudite enough to decipher Gower's Latin verses, however, could have read Ovid for himself. Why, then, have an Englished Ovid at all—why, indeed, would the typically very serious Gower have turned, in old age, to love stories, and why would he have made up the story about Richard's commission?

The solution might be that Gower put these disparate texts together in the expectation that Richard would have one of his household clerks read the book to him and his court. This clerk would prepare the reading in advance, taking time to master the different texts and their interrelationships. Gower presumably hoped that the prelector would pause over each entertaining love story to expound the moralization that went with it, engaging the king (whom Gower was eager to instruct) in discussion of its lessons—maybe even of its contradictions. The prelector could also read, translate, and explicate the Latin verses. In the event, if such readings ever took place, the Latin may or may not have received the attention Gower craved for it. Richard would have been unlikely to take as much interest as in the story, or to be an appreciative audience for highly rhetorical Latin verses with no courtly content. Other audiences may have been more amenable, though the manuscript tradition shows a continuous struggle to accommodate the Latin elements, and a tendency in some cases to curtail or omit them altogether. In this example, then, aurality matters. At least scholars should distinguish between what Gower may have intended in creating the complex bilingual *Confessio* and what readers would actually have made of it.

Aurality can matter, too, when we try to understand the language of medieval texts. Scholars in recent times have become much more tolerant of repetitive language in memorial genres such as the popular romance. Clearly, redundancy helps an oral performer remember and/or improvise, as it helps the audience follow. Further, repetition can have a esthetic effect, each reiteration or variation of a word, phrase, or theme adding layers of meaning to the text. When done poorly, repetition is hackwork; when done well, it can be art. Hardly anyone, however, has taken that insight into texts that circulated in writing—that is, to aural or bimodal texts. Once the minstrel is out of the picture, such recursive language has seemed to lose its rationale. Yet if the prelectors had simply to read what was before them, they still played to a listening audience whose comprehension would be facilitated by familiar phrasing. And the play of meaning made possible by this oral/aural esthetic would apply as well.

Sir Thomas Malory's *Le Morte Darthur*, for example, is renowned for its 'hackneyed' phraseology—all knights are noble, all ladies are fair, and so on. Mark Twain had great fun with it in his *Connecticut Yankee in King Arthur's Court*, presenting direct quotes from Malory as amateur sports reporting on tournaments. Yet Malory is also credited with a style that 'will bear comparison with the greatest and most distinctive styles in English prose'.[20] Another paradox! By now I almost think that paradox is a symptom of unattended-to aurality. A few years ago I was involved in a project to record a reading of Malory in late fifteenth-century English.[21] Individually and collectively, as the group practised, we kept swooning over the sheer beauty of Malory's language. Yet what we were reading was all noble knights and fair ladies. What we realized, though, as we practised excerpts from different sections, was that Malory achieves quite extraordinary and complex effects with variations and reiterations of his stock diction. The phrase 'destroyer of good knights', for example, is applied originally to sorceresses and outlaws. Lancelot, ambushed by four witchy women, exclaims: 'sore am I of thes quenys crauftis aferde, for they have destroyed many a good knyght'.[22] Many pages later, as the adultery of Lancelot and Guenevere begins to overshadow Camelot, Guenevere herself is denounced as 'a destroyer of good knyghtes' (p. 617). Finally, as Arthur and Gawain are besieging Lancelot in his French castle (while Mordred is starting his rebellion back home), Gawain tells Lancelot that he has 'many longe dayes overlad me and us all, and destroyed many of oure good knyghtes' (p. 689). The whole decline and fall of Arthur's kingdom is implied in the trajectory of this one phrase.

One more example. Early in the *Morte*, the brothers Balin and Balan end up killing each other in battle, not having recognized each other until too late. The whole episode is characterized by the phrase, 'Alas, that was great pity', culminating in Arthur's exclamation, upon hearing of the brothers' death: 'Alas! ... thys ys the grettist pité that ever I herde telle off of two knyghtes, for in thys worlde I knewe never such two knyghtes' (p. 59). Five hundred pages further on into the *Morte Darthur*, when Lionel deliberately attempts to kill his brother Bors, he swears: 'Thou shalt have death, for hit were pite ye leved any lenger' (p. 573). The echo is chilling, tragic accidental death contrasted with premeditated fratricide—but nothing on the surface of the narrative alerts us to the contrast. Malory does not editorialize; he lets the echo speak for itself—if we can catch it. By seemingly reducing information through redundancy on the verbal level, Malory has increased the semantic power of context, opening up many artistic possibilities for a (literally) soundless underlining of changes in character or situation. This is an aural esthetic, and though it works

[20] P. J. C. Field, *Romance and Chronicle: A Study of Malory's Prose Style* (London: Barrie & Jenkins, 1971), 102.

[21] *Malory Aloud: A Dramatic Reading of Excerpts from 'Le Morte Darthur'*, The Chaucer Studio, 2003.

[22] Sir Thomas Malory, *Works*, 2nd edn., ed. Eugène Vinaver (Oxford: Oxford University Press, 1971), 152.

on us (over some 700 pages of text, even modern readers have time to internalize the system), we lack the vocabulary and the simple awareness to understand what is affecting us so much.

Finally, a clue that aurality matters may be a persistent scholarly trend to act as if it didn't—didn't matter, or simply didn't exist. As I noted above, a critical discussion may begin with a nod to aurality, giving a pro-forma citation or two, but will often proceed as if there were no such thing. Instead, the scholar will retell the satisfying, value-adding tale of the triumph of literacy over orality in the late Middle Ages, celebrating the many intellectual and literary achievements that came with it. I do not necessarily dispute that any such changes occurred; I just dispute that they were inconsistent with aurality, or, of course, that aurality can be subsumed into and thus eliminated with 'orality'. The other scholarly strategy, when confronting a text that invokes a hearing audience, is to dismiss the reference as a fictionalization of orality, as a transitional (and therefore unimportant) phenomenon, or as a meaningless convention.

This point can be illustrated from the case of *Wynnere and Wastoure*.[23] In the prologue to this alliterative dream-vision, the author aligns himself with an older 'maker of myrthes' who is offended by the popularity of beardless boys who 'jangle als a jaye and japes telle'.[24] The first editor of this poem, Sir Israel Gollancz, was so convinced that the contrast recorded the displacement of orality by literacy that he moved lines around and changed words to 'clarify' the relationship. In particular, 'Wyse wordes withinn that wroghte were neuer' (l. 22) became 'Wyse wordes with-inn, that wr[iten] were neuer' (Gollancz's brackets).[25] Even with Gollancz's help, the maker of mirths and the jangling boy both seem to be delivering texts orally. Nonetheless, the scholarly consensus developed that the maker was an oral poet being displaced by a boy who was reciting someone else's written work. The restoration of the manuscript readings by later editors didn't destroy that argument, but added another, designed to ease any misgivings: the maker's complaints were all 'conventional', which meant that they meant nothing.

In fact, the situation described in *Wynnere and Wastoure* echoes comments by clerical authors and later literary authors. Ongoing through the period, and through most periods, was a competition between more 'worthwhile' sorts of texts and performances and more scurrilous ones. It wouldn't be hard to find examples in many cultures today. The maker of mirths used to produce wise words for his appreciative patron; whether he wrote and then prelected them, recited

---

[23] See Joyce Coleman, 'The Complaint of the Makers', in Evelyn Birge Vitz, Nancy Freeman Regalado, and Marilyn Lawrence (eds.), *Performing Medieval Narrative* (Cambridge: Boydell & Brewer, 2005), 27–39.

[24] *Wynnere and Wastoure*, ed. Stephanie Trigg, EETS 297 (Oxford: Oxford University Press, 1990), ll. 19, 26.

[25] Sir Israel Gollancz (ed.), *A Good Short Debate between Winner and Waster* (London: Oxford University Press, 1920).

them from memory, or improvised them is not specified. Now, he fumes, the fashion is for young men to entertain with lighter fare—presumably, jokes, songs, patter, probably performed from memory or improvised. This 'jangling' is explicitly differentiated from 'making', that is, from true and useful textualizing. The contrast is between the moral value of the performances and texts involved, not between orality and literacy.

Aurality must matter—otherwise, why have such strategies evolved to pretend that it does not? What is at stake, I think, is a favourite scholarly creation myth, the saga of literacy's triumph over orality. In the *Wynnere and Wastoure* case, the stakes are clear if we look at the estimated date of the poem's composition: *c*.1352. That is some twelve years after Chaucer was born, just five years before he entered the court of Elizabeth of Ulster, and who knows how many—but not too many—years before he began composing those '[d]itees and ... songes glade' (*CA* VIII: *2945) that his friend Gower cites at the close of the *Confessio Amantis*. We want to think of Chaucer as the privately reading, intellectually subtle 'first finder' of English whose work bespeaks a sophistication possible only within a literate, privately reading environment. We do not like to think of him as a jangling child reciting frivolous poetry before a countess, or even an earl or a king.[26] And if he is uncomfortably close in time and genre to that beardless boy, we would like to transform that figure somehow into an avatar of literacy, however disruptive that may be to the text that presents him.

Potential areas for research

For all the various reasons explored here, aurality is a pretty open field for future research. My own work has concentrated on late medieval recreational literature; upcoming projects focus on Malory's diction and on 'book iconography', the illustration of reading and writing in medieval manuscripts. Aurality played into the creation and reception of religiously oriented literature as well as into the social and political penumbra of literature. How did the peasants who embraced the figure of Piers Plowman actually read the book itself, for example?[27] Even if some of them were literate, who among them could have understood the Latin sprinkled throughout, especially as the reader is often expected to know the rest of a partial quote and its context? Were clerical prelectors available to read the book and explicate it, in a low-end version of Richard II's readings of the *Confessio*

---

[26] Over his youth, Chaucer moved from the household of Elizabeth, countess of Ulster, to that of her husband, Lionel of Antwerp, to that of Lionel's father, Edward III (Derek Pearsall, *The Life of Geoffrey Chaucer: A Critical Biography* (Oxford: Blackwell, 1992), 306–8).

[27] For the peasant audience of *Piers Plowman*, see Stephen Justice, *Writing and Rebellion: England in 1381* (Berkeley and Los Angeles: University of California Press, 1994).

Amantis? What about other politically sensitive material, from royal propaganda to dissident poetry, that was posted on doors and walls, or circulated in small quires, the medieval equivalent of pamphlets? Were these read aloud and discussed in the streets? This leads to the issue of public sphere: from pamphlets to *specula principis*, aurality was a means of promoting public discussion and opinion formation in a way that private reading could not achieve.

Gender is implicated as well. Margery Kempe's dependence on a prelector and scribe has distressed some scholars, who resent or resist the implication that she was illiterate. Not enough research has been done on women and aurality, nor on the implications of the fact that for medieval readers, status was invested in the audience, not in the prelector. Another rich area as yet unexplored is the erotic potential of aural reading, reflected in the 'wild woman' of Ribblesdale—presumably a prostitute—whose lips and teeth displayed so attractively as she prelected a romance.[28]

Manuscripts themselves possibly bespeak aurality, through many features of *ordinatio* and script: indexing, glossing, punctuation, the bracketing of rhymes, and so on. The medieval preference for short tales, exempla, *de casibus* stories, etc. may reflect aurality, as they chop texts up into the length of a reading session or two.

FURTHER READING

Early work on orality in Middle English was done by Ruth Crosby, in two still-cited articles: 'Oral Delivery in the Middle Ages', *Speculum*, 11 (1936), 88–110; and 'Chaucer and the Custom of Oral Delivery', *Speculum*, 13 (1938), 413–32. Like many earlier (and later) scholars, Crosby doesn't clearly distinguish between aurality (reading aloud) and memoriality (performance from memory, by minstrels or reciters).

Counter-arguments to the Great Divide view of orality have been mounted most effectively by anthropologists alarmed at its ethnocentricity; see Ruth Finnegan, *Oral Poetry: Its Nature, Significance and Social Context* (Cambridge: Cambridge University Press, 1977); Brian V. Street, *Literacy in Theory and Practice* (Cambridge: Cambridge University Press, 1984); and Finnegan, *Literacy and Orality: Studies in the Technology of Communication* (Oxford: Blackwell, 1988).

D. H. Green was the first scholar to consider public reading as a significant phenomenon for medieval European (especially German) literature; see his 'On the Primary Reception of Narrative Literature in Medieval Germany', *Forum for Modern Language Studies*, 20 (1984), 289–308; 'Orality and Reading: The State of Research in Medieval Studies', *Speculum*, 65 (1990), 267–80; and *Medieval Listening and Reading: The Primary Reception of German Literature 800–1300* (Cambridge: Cambridge University Press, 1994).

---

[28] For an exploration of erotic aurality and the French romance, see Evelyn Birge Vitz's 'Erotic Reading in the Middle Ages: Performance and Re-performance of Romance', in Vitz et al. (eds.), *Performing Medieval Narrative*.

For a discussion of theories of orality, aurality, and literacy with special application to English, Scottish, and Franco-Burgundian material, see Joyce Coleman, *Public Reading and the Reading Public in Late Medieval England and France* (Cambridge: Cambridge University Press, 1996). Other Coleman articles exploring issues related to medieval English aurality include 'Lay Readers and Hard Latin: How Gower May Have Intended the *Confessio Amantis* to Be Read', *Studies in the Age of Chaucer*, 24 (2002), 209–35; and 'The Complaint of the Makers: *Wynnere and Wastoure* and the "Misperformance Topos" in Medieval England', in Evelyn Birge Vitz, Nancy Freeman Regalado, and Marilyn Lawrence (eds.), *Performing Medieval Narrative* (Cambridge: Boydell & Brewer, 2005), 27–39. A recent issue of *Arthuriana* (13/4, winter 2003) was devoted to the implications of aurality for medieval and modern readings of Malory's *Morte Darthur*; see especially the articles by Rosamund Allen and Michael Twomey. The issue includes a CD of the group Malory reading mentioned above.

Evelyn Birge Vitz has written extensively on the memorial and aural performance of medieval French romance; see her *Orality and Performance in Early French Romance* (Cambridge: Brewer, 1999). Sioned Davies has explored Welsh aurality in 'Written Text as Performance: The Implications for Middle Welsh Prose Narratives', in Huw Pryce (ed.), *Literacy in Medieval Celtic Societies* (Cambridge: Cambridge University Press, 1998), 133–48.

Articles exploring orality, literacy, and (sometimes) aurality are collected in a recent anthology edited by Mark Chinca and Christopher Young, called *Orality and Literacy in the Middle Ages: Essays on a Conjunction and its Consequences in Honour of D. H. Green* (Turnhout: Brepols, 2005). See Chinca and Young's introduction for a short, readable overview of the development of the field. A similar mix of articles, emphasizing performance, can be found in Evelyn Birge Vitz, Nancy Freeman Regalado, and Marilyn Lawrence (eds.), *Performing Medieval Narrative* (Cambridge: Boydell & Brewer, 2005).

CHAPTER 7

BOOKS

ALEXANDRA GILLESPIE

In Chaucer's words

Adam scriveyn, if ever it thee bifalle
Boece or Troylus for to wryten newe,
Under thy long lokkes thou most have the scalle [scabrous skin],
But after my makyng thow wryte more trewe;
So ofte adaye I mot thy werk renewe,
It to correcte and eke to rubbe and scrape,
And al is thorugh thy negligence and rape [haste].[1]

'Chaucers Wordes unto Adam, His Owne Scriveyn' is a slight and yet appealing poem: our routine, readerly desire to *know* is concentrated by the constraints of poetic form, by the narrowness of the fissure through which we, like John with his eye to the hole in the door to Nicholas's chamber in the 'Miller's Tale', glimpse just what we always wanted to see—something of the maker himself. Chaucer the man is in there, writing to his own scribe about the scribal form of his 'owne' words. His words are most ironic, most 'Chaucerian', if they are hastily copied out by that scribe, who only notices his own name, 'Adam', as he starts to write from a draft that the author has slipped into a pile of papers or scratched onto a wax tablet. These are intimate textual moments, which, to layer irony on irony, we share in because it so 'bifell'. Someone did copy these 'Wordes'—perhaps Adam, certainly the Exchequer scribe, household retainer, and Londoner John Shirley (copyist of the only fifteenth-century manuscript of this poem) and after him the London merchant tailor, editor, and antiquary John Stow (who first had the poem printed in 1559).[2] In doing so they provided a basis for further copies, including the one printed here.

---

[1] References to Chaucer's texts are from *Riverside Chaucer*, ed. Larry D. Benson, 3rd edn. (Boston: Houghton Mifflin, 1987).
[2] Shirley's version is Trinity College, Cambridge, MS R. 3. 20 and Stow's is in *Workes of Geffray Chaucer* (London, 1561), STC 5075, sig. 3R3ᵛ. See Seth Lerer, *Chaucer and his Readers* (Princeton: Princeton University Press, 1993), 117–46.

But readerly intimacy always comes at a cost. In Adam's, Shirley's, Stow's, and then our own books, the connection with Chaucer is imaginary. Thus, while the joke in this poem is on Adam, who must share his namesake's burden and remake his author's 'making' in some imperfect form, the joke is also on us. As past becomes present, just when we see Chaucer the maker, he loses his capacity to be meaningful in his 'owne' terms. Like Adam Scriveyn's 'Boece or Troilus', his text is 'renewed', but by some copyist, and then by a reader, not by him. What we want as we peer through the small opening offered by 'Chaucers Wordes', like gullible John, is 'a secret origin—so secret and so fundamental that it can never be quite grasped in itself'.[3] What we get is not authority, but the unruly bodies and corrupting fictions that exist in its absence. Through Nicholas's door in the 'Miller's Tale', John sees a clerk's disingenuous divination of 'Goddes pryvetee' (l. 3454). When John fails to resist temptation and believes what he sees, the ineluctable logic of the fabliau into which he has fallen undoes all of his looking. 'Goddes pryvetee' is just the ready way to Alisoun's 'pryvetee', and the 'hole' (l. 3442) in Nicholas's door, promising so much, reveals about as much as the hole that we see next: the crack through which we get a view, 'pryvely', of Nicholas's 'ers' (l. 3802).

The imagery of 'Chaucers Wordes' is less exuberant than that of the 'Miller's Tale', but it is similarly visceral. Adam's body is unregulated: it is decaying and scabrous. And because the scribe's 'scalle' is formally (figuratively, phonetically, and as a word copied onto a page, literally) connected to what Chaucer must 'scrape', Adam's body is akin to the book itself. Both suffer from the damage done by time, from imperfect existence in the world—from 'negligence and rape'. Carolyn Dinshaw has argued that 'rape' in 'Chaucers Wordes' means more than 'haste' (the usual gloss for the word; a meaning drawn from *raptus*, a carrying off by force). It is a gendered and sexualized metaphor by which Chaucer imagines himself and his 'makyng' violated by 'the pen of the scribe'.[4] I would press this observation further: 'rape' is literally as well as metaphorically bodily in 'Chaucers Wordes'. It is Chaucer's *book*—his textual corpus—that is borne off in haste, opened, fingered, and defiled, because it is the book that stands in the place of the author (or his scribe), that represents what happens to human 'makyng' and so what happens to all of the things that we want to know.

The point I wish to make here is a general one about books. Books provide us with our knowledge of the past, but because they are the material result of inevitably imperfect human labour, and because they are further disordered by time, they are unstable witnesses to that past. My general concern is framed by a more specific interest. In this discussion I will use the word 'books' to refer to a

---

[3] Michel Foucault, *The Archaeology of Knowledge*, trans. A. M. Sheridan Smith (London: Tavistock, 1972), 25.

[4] Carolyn Dinshaw, *Chaucer's Sexual Poetics* (Madison: University of Wisconsin Press, 1989), 10.

wide range of legible surfaces for texts, from scraps of parchment to substantial codices. This is how the word was used in the Middle Ages, and my particular interest is medieval 'books'.[5] I am interested in them *because* their forms and their meaning—the very words associated with them—are fluid and changing. I am also interested in them because we have a new occasion to think about them and Chaucer's 'Wordes' about them in particular: Linne R. Mooney's remarkable discovery of the identity of the copyist of the Hengwrt and Ellesmere manuscripts of the *Canterbury Tales* as a London Scrivener called Adam Pinkhurst—and therefore, perhaps, the 'Adam' whom Chaucer calls his 'scriveyn'.[6] Mooney's discovery is important to the study of medieval literary culture, but it is also important to the broader, burgeoning field of book history. In what follows, I propose that texts such as 'Chaucers Wordes' and the fluid forms and meanings of medieval manuscripts offer specific answers to this field's central, often-repeated question: 'What is the history of books?'[7]

In the dust of books

When Anthony Grafton writes that 'book history exploded into print' in recent decades he inadvertently conflates two accurate observations about the field.[8] First, it is of growing significance to the study of culture and literature, and second, most of its best-known practitioners focus their energy upon 'print'. The importance of the press and the nature of the 'print culture' associated with it—which, in the field's rather reductive terms, is 'the nature of the book' itself—is a matter of some contention. On one side of the debate about print culture are scholars, most famously Elizabeth Eisenstein, who maintain that the press was 'an agent of change'. The invention of movable type allowed for the mass production of fixed, standardized texts. Mass production also allowed for a large-scale, speculative, and more profitable book trade which in turn enabled the wide dissemination of knowledge in fixed forms. The counter-argument to these claims emerges most recognizably in Adrian Johns's study *The Nature of the Book*. Johns and others argue that 'fixity', a proliferation of titles, capitalist investment in book production, possessive authorship, and the invention of copyright were effects of the advent of print, but they were not its inevitable result. These were uses that a culture found

---

[5] For definitions of Middle English words in this discussion, I use the *Middle English Dictionary* (henceforth *MED*) from *The Middle English Compendium*, University of Michigan, 2006 (**http://ets.umdl.umich.edu.myaccess.library.utoronto.ca/m/mec/**).

[6] Linne R. Mooney, 'Chaucer's Scribe', *Speculum*, 81 (2006), 97–138. In what follows I will use the name 'Adam' if I am discussing an imaginative depiction of a fourteenth-century 'Scriveyn' or scribe, and Pinkhurst when referring to Adam Pinkhurst's particular history.

[7] This is the title of Robert Darnton's influential essay 'What is the History of Books?', in Kenneth E. Carpenter (ed.), *Books and Society in History* (New York: R. R. Bowker Company, 1983), 3–26.

[8] Grafton, 'Introduction', *American Historical Review*, 107/1 (2002), 85.

for a new technology and the authority that was ascribed to that technology. They were and still are ways of *thinking* about books.[9]

If the study of 'print culture' is not the study of technologically determined change, but study of various ways that people think about books, the question 'what is the history of books' can be rephrased—how have books been imagined and then used over time? With this newly framed question in mind, the field of book history can be broadened, its usual limits opened up to work by medieval codicologists that is usually overlooked in a field so preoccupied with the work of the press. 'Chaucers Wordes' is a useful place to begin this process, in part because as the poem describes a medieval context for book production, it suggests what Johns suggests—that the press was not the necessary condition for the development of the cultural habits that we associate with printing.

Consider that Chaucer describes Adam as a 'Scriveyn'. In Chaucer's London, scriveners were either members of the Scriveners' Company—makers of legal documents such as indentures, deeds, wills, and petitions in cursive hands—or just scribes who were referred to as scriveners (the term was used loosely). I will return to these matters below, and here simply note that work of Chaucer's 'scriveyn' is, like the work of a printer, something to speculate about: 'if ever it thee bifalle | ... for to wryten newe'. This is not to suggest that the medieval manuscript is described as a product made speculatively (as most printed books were), but rather to suggest that the labour of bespoke book production can here be anticipated, and that a text can therefore be imagined as a book written not for an author or even a patron, but for an as-yet unidentified customer. This 'newe' work imagined for a 'scriveyn' (as well as the more familiar concern about scribal error) seems to frame Chaucer's anxiety about his texts. He claims the texts as his own, 'my makyng', the author's possession, and then claims that, as the author, he retains the power to fix them and make them 'more trewe'. In 'Chaucers Wordes', possessive authorship and textual fixity, key features of both Eisenstein's and Johns's conception of print culture, are thus imagined as conditions of a specific, late medieval manuscript culture. The poem makes the medieval book a way for us to think about the new technology of print, which was accommodated by pre-existing, even familiar, ways of using and describing 'newe' books.

Chaucer's poem, however, has more to offer the field of book history than precedents for ideas about printing. As he describes some of the ways in which we invent a stable, authoritative 'nature' for books, as he makes them 'my making', he also lets them go; he reminds us that an imaginary order for things is one vulnerable to error and susceptible to 'rape'. The ideas we come up with as we think

---

[9] Eisenstein and Johns summarize their debate, and the contributions of other scholars to it, in *American Historical Review*, 107/1 (2002), 87–128. Their studies are, respectively, *The Printing Press as an Agent of Change: Communications and Cultural Transformations in Early Modern Europe*, 2 vols. (Cambridge: Cambridge University Press, 1979) and *The Nature of the Book: Print and Knowledge in the Making* (Chicago: University of Chicago Press, 1998).

about books are not, that is, inevitable or natural, but various, often contested, and slipping from every individual grasp. So much is evident from books themselves: not many of those who made or read medieval manuscripts, for instance, saw the need to imagine or describe authors. Most Chaucer manuscripts are anonymous. Likewise, not all of those who used the printing press were interested in the fixity of texts. In the early modern period, and still today, books are sometimes printed in haste, without much concern for textual fidelity.

If my first point is that there are lots of different ways of thinking about books, my second is that no one way of thinking about a book is secure in itself. A book is something that must be worked on and made sense of. It is discursively formed—and discursive formations, the forms of human knowledge, are partial and unstable. I would go further: instability is especially apparent in books, because books promise stability and then fail to deliver it. Books are here, in the present, as if their past is available to us, but they are also old and a bit ragged. They have carried knowledge away from the imaginary, authoritative conditions of their own 'makyng'; they contain tangible evidence of our failure to hold fast to our ways of describing the world.

This is the sense in which one of bibliography's most important theorists, D. F. McKenzie, argues, in *Bibliography and the Sociology of Texts*, that the history of the book has 'a massive authority' to recover 'the human presence in any recorded text'. McKenzie's point is not that, when our other critical and historical endeavours fail, we can open an old book and find what we wanted there. His point is that there is something material, some 'form' of the text, at the heart of every imperfect encounter we have with its author—or even its printer or scribe.[10] To make new meaning from texts we must therefore do what Chaucer is doing in his 'Wordes'. We must rub and scrape at old books, dig out forms and ideas, imaginatively recreate some authoritative meaning—something beyond our physical reach—from whatever imperfect material object is within our grasp.

The 'nature of the book', I am arguing, is shifting and unstable. Books are made, and made meaningful, by a variety of localized and specific attitudes and practices and—rather like Adam's festering body—they are subject to further disordering. Our ideas about the world (including our ideas about books themselves) are contingent. In books, those ideas remain open to change. The book's instability gives it a special capacity to describe the past. In *The Archaeology of Knowledge*, Michel Foucault argues, likewise, that our powerful desire for a fixed origin for what we know, and the naive teleological histories that result from this desire, bind us to conventional ways of thinking. We can usefully undo what we think we know if we instead,

> receive every moment of discourse in its sudden irruption; in that punctuality in which it appears, and in that temporal dispersion that enables it to be repeated, known,

---

[10] 'The Book as an Expressive Form' in *Bibliography and the Sociology of Texts* (Cambridge: Cambridge University Press, 1999), 19.

forgotten, transformed, utterly erased, and hidden, far from all view, in the dust of books.[11]

To know the world in less conventional ways, Foucault suggests, we need to read books—to read their very 'dust'. 'The dust of books' is an evocative description of their history. It suggests their most minutely meaningful physical forms: the fibres of a linen-based stock of paper; the strings with which quires were bound; the nails hammered into leather and bevelled boards. A sense of 'human presence' and also pastness attends dusty, scholarly work on such *minutiae*. But dust is also what rises up when you dislodge an old book from its place on an orderly shelf. It is the evidence of physical wastage—motes of paper and vellum that time has scraped from the page. Dust reminds us that a book was made and exists in the world, imperfectly. This observation can be broadened, until the idea of 'dust' includes not only the materials from which books were made, but all our ideas about books. At the moment of its production, the book was 'caught up in a system of references to other books, other texts, other sentences' in the dust-like swirl of its possible meanings (Foucault, *The Archaeology of Knowledge*, 23). It has since gathered dust. It has been caught up by (or lost to) new systems of reference; it has been 'forgotten' at times, and at other times 'transformed'. The books that Chaucer describes as having issued from Adam's hands are 'dusty' because, as they bear texts to us, they dislodge any naive trust we have in texts'—or books'—original, ideal, inviolable form.

In a mixed bag of medieval books

The history of medieval manuscript production is a history of diffuse and dispersed activity. Medieval English books were not made, as is sometimes supposed, in monastic scriptoria. Nor does any evidence support the idea of 'commercial' scriptoria in England. Medieval books were instead made by a range of people in localized conditions. Monks did copy texts (probably at desks in the cloister or in their own cells). So did other regular clergy and clerics attached to cathedrals, parish churches, and large households. Books facilitated the secular clergy's own pastoral and catechistic work and priests probably copied material at the request of devout members of the laity. Educated lay people made their own books. Surviving books from the households of merchants and the lower gentry contain business accounts, poems, recipes—whatever seemed worth writing down at the time. In English royal and noble households—and more broadly around 'courts', including judicial courts—an increasing number of scribes were employed to meet the needs of a growing bureaucracy in England. Clerks copied letters, bills, receipts, writs,

---

[11] Foucault, *The Archaeology of Knowledge*, 25.

proclamations, and other official documents, and were presumably available for bookwork of other kinds. Ready-made books were also sold directly. The books carted to fairs or sold in urban shops were probably second hand for the most part, but liturgical and school texts, for which there was steady demand and continental supply, may also have been sold new. Some of those involved in selling books were likely also to have been involved in local, bespoke production of manuscripts: in late medieval England, writing, decorating, and binding books were skills for hire.[12]

Those who were paid to make or supply books concern me most in this discussion. By the end of the Middle Ages, such artisans and merchants were increasing in number, but their activities, or at least ways of thinking about those activities, were rather fluid. The history of the word 'stationer' usefully illustrates this point. 'Stationer' is a term sometimes applied by book historians to the men who sold medieval books and employed scribes to do bespoke work on manuscripts. In medieval records, the word's meaning and the processes it describes are more slippery. In the thirteenth century, academic booksellers in Oxford and Cambridge came to be known as 'stationers', which was the fashionable, Parisian word for university booksellers. In fourteenth-century London, the same word was applied to men who are elsewhere recorded as text-writers, limners, scriveners, and bookbinders. Thus, a 'stationer' might *be* a limner, bookbinder, or some other book artisan, and he might also receive a commission—for a 'Boece or Troilus' perhaps—and subcontract the labour *to* a binder, limner, text-writer, or scrivener who lived nearby (though commissions were probably regularly executed abroad, as well). A 'scrivener' who was also a 'Scrivener' (my capital here signals membership of the fourteenth-century London Scriveners' Company) might be busy working on regular commissions for legal documents, and unable to take on much extra work. Text-Writers (who were often called 'scriveners', who wrote in more formal hands than Scriveners, and who had their own fourteenth-century London Company) probably handled most demand for non-legal texts. But they too might have been busy with direct orders. So a 'stationer' might assemble an ad hoc team to fulfil a contract. To do so, he might turn to other scribes available in his locale: chaplains in large households, functionaries in royal offices, literates at the Inns of Court. In the Trinity College, Cambridge copy of Gower's *Confessio Amantis* (MS R. 3. 2) and in the Hengwrt *Canterbury Tales* we find the hand of Thomas Hoccleve, Clerk of the Privy Seal and poet, alongside that of Adam Pinkhurst, Scrivener, and also scrivener (a vernacular poem is not, strictly, the work of a legal 'Scriveyn').[13] There

---

[12] For London courtly and other medieval English documentary culture, see M. T. Clanchy, *From Memory to Written Record: England 1066–1307*, 2nd edn. (Oxford: Blackwell, 1993); for other kinds of book production, see Jeremy Griffiths and Derek Pearsall (eds.), *Book Production and Publishing in Britain 1375–1475* (Cambridge: Cambridge University Press, 1989).

[13] M. B. Parkes and A. I. Doyle, 'The Production of Copies of the *Canterbury Tales* and the *Confessio Amantis* in the Early Fifteenth Century', in M. B. Parkes and Andrew G. Watson (eds.), *Medieval Scribes, Manuscripts and Libraries: Essays Presented to N. R. Ker* (London: Scolar Press, 1978), 163–210.

was never a single way of making a medieval manuscript, nor a singular way of thinking about how a manuscript was made. The story about medieval stationers, for instance, goes on. By 1450, a new guild—founded in 1403 by booksellers and the previously distinct companies of the Limners and Text-Writers—was routinely described as the Stationers' Company. From about that time, the meaning of the word 'Stationer' was more restricted, but never static: in the sixteenth century, the Incorporation of the London Stationers established a monopoly over the trade in printed books, and the word 'Stationer' came to describe a print-publisher. Every answer to the question 'what is the history of medieval books?' must accommodate this sort of uncertainty, this evidence of flux and change.

The instability that characterizes medieval book production, I contend, is the very heart of what Emily Steiner has usefully described as late medieval 'documentary poetics'.[14] In Chaucer's texts, or in a poem like the 1409 *Mum and the Sothsegger*—to whose account of manuscript production I now turn—books made in the contexts I have just described are imagined as sites for disruption and disorder; imagined again, more hopefully, as a place where authority can be renewed; and finally imagined as they *are*—objects that unravel the meaning that has been rather awkwardly assigned to them.

The alliterative poem *Mum and the Sothsegger* is situated in the context of a review of the officers of a king—presumably, given that its date is about 1409, Henry IV. A narrator leaves the court and wanders England in search of a 'Sothsegger' (or some news of him). He sees his quarry in a shop, but the truth-teller is badly wounded. The narrator then falls asleep. He dreams of an idyllic and orderly garden and a beekeeper, who directs him to make his own books, in his heart. The narrator wakes to find a bag of books in his hands, and in this bag he renews his search for texts 'forto conseille the king' (l. 1343).[15] In the fragmentary surviving manuscript, the text of *Mum* breaks off before the narrator can get to the bottom of the bag, which seems appropriate; we know from other texts in the *Piers Plowman* tradition, to which *Mum* belongs, that there can be no worldly end to our search for truth.

The absence of truth is, instead, a precondition for the narrative of *Mum and the Sothsegger*. There is no truth in late medieval England because the world is in the hands of 'Mum'. Mum is not silence (as his name might imply); when he appears and speaks, he is a loquacious and effective rhetorician, whose truths sometimes please the narrator. Mum is instead someone who 'knittith a knotte' in utterances (l. 693). In *Mum*, the word 'knit' describes an end to debate (as it does when Chaucer's Parson uses it). However, it also retains its earlier, material sense—to tie loose things together. This material world—a world of bodies and

---

[14] Emily Steiner, *Documentary Culture and the Making of Medieval English Literature* (Cambridge: Cambridge University Press, 2003).

[15] All citations from *Mum and the Sothsegger* are from Helen Barr's superb edition, *The Piers Plowman Tradition* (London: Everyman, 1993).

books—constrains utterance in *Mum and the Sothsegger*. Truth is suppressed by threat of external sanction: 'yf a burne bolde hym to bable the sothe | ... | He may lose his life and laugh here no more' (ll. 165–7). Liars and flatterers are rewarded materially. Coins are printed into the flesh of each corrupt 'palme' (l. 61). Finally, truth is undermined by the exigencies of its material existence: it is uttered by men whose bodily needs and frailties betray them, or copied into quires of paper and vellum that are then, as the poet tells us, 'knitted'—stitched together and sewn onto binding bands. In such tangible, material forms, truth is not truth any more. It is worldly, and so subject to Mum. Mum's mastery, in this poem, is therefore not only of speaking, but also of the making and the makers of English books.

As he makes his way through the allegorical landscape of the poem, the narrator therefore finds Mum among all kinds of medieval book producers. Mum has mastered the notaries, lawyers, sergeants, 'scribes and clercz that to the court longen' (l. 15): the London-based, bureaucratic functionaries amongst whom I numbered Hoccleve, above, and in whose company we also find Chaucer, Gower, and perhaps the *Mum*-poet himself. The words, including the poems, written by these clerks endure—manuscripts of texts made or copied by members of this clerkly class survive in unprecedented numbers[16]—but Mum ensures that these words are bound by political and pecuniary self-interest. 'Writing' and 'waxe eke' will merely earn a courtier his advancement and a lawyer or clerk his 'fee' (l. 25).

The narrator finds men of letters elsewhere: at the university and in 'priories and personages many | ... abbeys of Augustyn and many hooly places'. But religious foundations, like the sites of England's increasingly centralized government, are 'parfitely y-closed' (ll. 536–8). Mum has made sure that England's clerics make their books in 'doutz' (l. 360) and for innumerable corrupt ends. So the narrator wanders on to town. There he catches sight of the Sothsegger:

> And as I lokid the loigges along by the streetz,
> I sawe a sothe-sigger, in sothe as me thought,
> Sitte in a shoppe and salwyn [salve] his woundes.   (ll. 845–7)

The use of the word 'shoppe' here is suggestive. It was a relatively new addition to the English poetic lexicon in 1409 and it refers specifically to the space in which urban merchants and artisans produced, distributed, or retailed wares.[17] The shop is the next logical stop for the narrator: having visited courts, offices, churches, and schools where books are made, he arrives at the lodging place of artisans and

---

[16] A. S. G. Edwards and Derek Pearsall, 'The Manuscripts of the Major English Poetic Texts', in *Book Production and Publishing in Britain, 1375–1475*, 257, describe an almost tenfold increase in the survival rate for vernacular literary manuscripts from this period.

[17] The first use of the word 'shop' in English is Robert of Gloucester, *c.* 1300; all other uses before that in *Mum* listed in *MED* are Chaucer's. See Derek Keene, 'Shops and Shopping in Medieval London', in L. M. Grant (ed.), *Medieval Art, Architecture and Archaeology in London* (London: British Archaeological Association, 1990), 29–40.

merchants, whose numbers included, at this time, stationers, scriveners, binders, and limners. It seems that truth might lodge within such a community—except that the world has done its worst. An alderman explains to the narrator that '[s]ith Mvm and the mayer were made suche frendes', the truth-sayer has drunk deep of the 'dum-seede' (ll. 839–40). He is silent. Like Adam Scriveyn, he bears the bodily 'woundes' of corruption. He has been harmed, and he has lost the salve for his ills, because 'Mum and his ferys | ... bar a-weye the bagges and many a boxe eeke' (l. 1342). Truth has proven subject to depredation and to 'rape', and the last dwelling place for the Sothsegger in *Mum* has been emptied of all utterance.

Immediately after his visit to the shop, the narrator in *Mum* falls into the reverie of dream-vision. There, he finds bookish solutions for the world's seemingly insolvable problems. The beekeeper whom the narrator meets in the garden explains that the only secure 'hovsing' for truth is 'man-is herte' (l. 1224) and that the heart is a place for books. There they can and should be made 'complete to clapsyng'; 'lete no feynt herte', says the beekeeper, '[a]bate thy blessid bisynes of thy boke-making' (ll. 1280–2). When he awakes, the narrator is meant to find the end of his wandering is in his grasp, but what he actually finds is something close to, but not quite, this perfect ending. He finds one of the missing 'bagges' from the Sothsegger's shop:

> Now forto conseille the king vnknytte I a bagge
> Where many a pryue poyse [secret verse] is preyntid withynne
> Yn bokes vnbredid [unbound] in balade-wise made.[18]

The bag of books in *Mum and the Sothsegger* is brimful. It contains a 'quayer' (l. 1348); 'penyworth of papir' (l. 1350); 'a volume ... of viftene leves' (l. 1353); more than one 'rolle' (ll. 1364, 1565); 'a paire of pamphilettz' (l. 1370); a 'copie' (l. 1388); a 'scrowe' (scroll) (l. 1489); a 'writte' (l. 1498); something in frayed 'forelle' (a limp vellum cover) (l. 1586); a schedule with 'tuly [red] silke intachid right atte rolle-is ende' (l. 1735). The poem provides us with a richly knowing account of what it was like to make a book in the Middle Ages. Here is the earliest use of the word 'forrel' to refer to a cheap, limp binding; reference to 'paper', still a relatively new material for the production of written records in 1409 in England; description of the process ('intachen' or 'attachen') by which one appended strings to an official rolled document; and the earliest use of the English verb 'print' to refer specifically to marks 'yn bokes'.[19]

---

[18] Barr glosses 'vnbredid' as unopened, which is a possible reading (for meaning here is 'pryue') but it is also problematic, in that the books in the bag *are* open to the narrator. The word may be un-braided, and refer to the ties which were sometimes used in place of clasps to keep medieval books closed. Cf. 'The Ragman's Roll', in T. Wright (ed.), *Anecdota literaria* (London: J. R. Smith, 1846), where the strings attached to each misogynist verse in imitation of an charter are described as sewn 'in brede' (l. 5).

[19] See *MED*: the word 'forrel' originally meant a sheath or box; it became a way to describe cheap vellum binding in the sixteenth century (see Nicholas Pickwoad, 'Onward and Downward:

The word 'print' should be a cue here, reminding us that the meaning of books is not simply technologically determined, but discursively shaped and subject to change. A manuscript can be described as 'preyntid' if that is a useful way to think about its forms. The same word, 'print', will later be appropriated to describe the impressions left on a page by metal type. The problem with the world, in *Mum and the Sothsegger*, is that this process—the process by which books are described, authorized, and so made useful—is routinely corrupt. The 'quayer', for example, is 'of quitances [receipts] of quethyn [bequeathed] goodes, | That bisshoppz han begged to binde al newe' (ll. 1348–9). Greedy bishops catalogue their receipt of the goods of the dead, and then spend their beggarly riches on new book bindings for their catalogues. All the books in the bag are made for a specific and usually a corrupt purpose: the 'volume' is of a 'visitacion' (l. 1353), but it erases evidence of priestly licentiousness; the scroll is 'for squyers' (l. 1489) who walk the other way when confronted by the wicked practices of the nobility; the 'writte' (l. 1498) is for rich men who accuse each another of crimes as they jostle for social status.

Meaning, in the bag of books, is thus localized and contested. But my argument in this essay is further that, even as each book is appropriated, even when it serves a bishop or a lord directly (or is sent back to a grouchy author, his penknife in hand), its meanings remain fractured and unstable. The forms of books, however authorized, are always waiting to be 'vnbredid'. The books in the bag in *Mum and the Sothsegger* are designed, for the most part, to maintain the power and self-interest of those who possess them. But, discharged from the bag, books speak volumes *about* power and self-interest. The bishops' 'quayer' teaches the narrator a lesson in anticlericalism and the 'copie of couertise' (1683) may be the means by which a greedy man seizes riches (l. 1686), but the ambiguous wording suggests that it is also a text *about* corrupt practices. Consider, moreover, the other 'copie' described in *Mum and the Sothsegger*. It contains 'culmes [columns of text] for comunes' against the spread of seditious rumours (l. 1388).[20] The poet remarks that rumours 'been so trouble' (l. 1392) and in her edition of the text, Helen Barr notes that in 1405 English sheriffs issued a royal proclamation against rumour-mongering. Perhaps the 'culmes' is a copy of the proclamation, and perhaps the poet approves of this. Perhaps it is a copy of the petition, that Barr describes, presented by the prince

---

How Binders Coped with the Printing Press before 1800', in Robin Myers and Michael Harris (eds.), *A Millenium of the Book: Production, Design and Illustration in Manuscript and Print, 900–1900* (Winchester: St Paul's Bibiliographies, 1994), 61–106. Mum's 'forell' is 'frayed' (l. 1486) which suggests it is limp and cloth-like. On paper, see R. Lyall, 'Materials: The Paper Revolution', in *Book Production and Publishing in England*, 11–29. On rolls and their seals and strings, see Clanchy, *Memory to Written Record*, 310–13, plates I–VII. 'Printed' is also used to describe words written in books in *The York Plays* and (more obliquely) in the *c*. 1400 *Gest Hystoriale of the Destruction of Troy*.

[20] 'Culmes' is unique to *Mum*: *MED* tentatively derives its meaning from Latin *culmus* (which it defines as 'stipulation'; in every medieval and classical use I can trace it means 'straw', 'dust', 'ridge', or 'culmination of authority'). I think the directly related *columen* or column (the medieval Anglo-Latin word *column/a* was used to describe pages in books) provides the more likely etymology here.

of Wales to parliament in 1406 against the seditious rumours of the religious. Or perhaps the copy is simply a list of dangerous ideas—the sort of document that might be posted, like a bill, on a column, to stir up political dissent.[21] The meaning of the 'culmes' (both the word and the material object described) is open, and will remain so as long as these 'culmes' subsists.

The narrator of *Mum and the Sothsegger* still dreams of ways to recover stable meaning from books and words. He opens the bag 'forto conseille the king'. He means to impose an order on knowledge that centres on a stable relationship between true saying and monarchical authority. But his reasoning comes full circle—from faith in books, which is something encouraged by the beekeeper, who describes the natural law by which kings turn utterance into common profit, back to the books themselves, which might counsel this king, but which are readily 'vnbredid' to new purposes. The stable meaning of the book in our own hands, *Mum and the Sothsegger*, falters at this point. There is only one king in the *Mum*-poet's incomplete narrative: 'Changwys' (l. 1414). The name is the poet's for Ghengis Khan (from the French of *Mandeville's Travels, Changuys Can*). Ghengis is a king who legislates for the execution of the elder sons of the nobility after he takes the throne. He is praised for his strong rule, but he also casts a shadow on the poem, which may be that of the belligerent usurper Henry IV. Even a sack of royal counsel may be what the narrator calls 'cunseille of Changwys' (l. 1486). It may—like the poem itself—teeter on the brink of changefulness and radicalism, and unsettle all the stability that it purports to sustain.

In Adam's shop

The argument I am making about books in *Mum and the Sothsegger* and about books in general has two parts. We need ideas about them to authorize their existence and make use of their forms—ideas about authors, about the pragmatic uses of record, or about the counsel of kings, for instance, but because books are the result of human labour, because they are constrained by worldly concerns, and because they are material, slowly turning to dust, they are always unfixed. They unravel the already contested authority that has been assigned to them. The two parts of this argument have never been separable—but I now want to propose a slightly different link between them. The openness of books—whether manuscript or print—is what necessitates the attempt to limit their meaning, define their value, 'renewe' their authority, to close down bookshops and carry off all the stock.

I make this connection in order to return to an evocative image—the image of the empty shop and the wounded Sothsegger—and to a residual question. Of all the

---

[21] See Wendy Scase, '"Strange and Wonderful Bills": Bill Casting and Political Discourse in Late Medieval England', *New Medieval Literatures*, 2 (1998), 225–47.

estates, merchants seem to fare the best in *Mum and the Sothsegger*. The narrator only comes across one 'shoppe' and it is not a site for corruption, but somewhere close to the narrator's own 'herte', somewhere that might accommodate a Sothsegger and, perhaps, 'blissid bisynes of ... boke-making'. The question that follows is: if shopkeepers, and specifically the keepers of bookshops, are not themselves corrupt, what then has silenced the Sothsegger and borne away the bags and boxes?

The poem's final answer, I have argued, is the world itself, where things are too transitory for truth to settle. But the contingency of truth—and the mutable forms of books—only create a problem if we want meaning to be absolute and unchanging. 'We' may be happy with all of the dust stirred up by books. The *Mum*-poet is probably not: he harbours conventional hopes of heavenly security. However, those with whom the narrator of the poem dwells have more immediate concerns. In *Mum and the Sothsegger*, the disorderly work of the bookshop threatens established arrangements of power. This includes, I would suggest, the arrangements made by members of the merchant classes. Lesser merchants and artisans are not directly described as corrupt in *Mum*, but those who structure and control mercantile business are. The poem states explicitly that Mum keeps company with the 'mayer' (l. 840) and we may infer that he is still keeping this sort of company when he and his 'ferys' come to the Sothsegger's shop (l. 1341). Mum's 'ferys' are not merely henchmen, though the word's sense of 'soldiers' is one of its meanings here. They are also 'ferys' in the sense of fellows or equals: the 'frendes' (l. 840) Mum finds in a late medieval English town—a powerful urban, oligarchical elite.

To conclude my discussion of medieval books, then, I turn back further—to 'Chaucers Wordes' and 'Adam Scriveyn'. Adam Pinkhurst must have kept shop. Whatever space a Scrivener occupied was, after 1373, formally designated in this way by the Scriveners' Company. His shop was subject to guild authority, and that authority was enforced by the London mayor and his aldermen. Pinkhurst's work on legal documents, petitions, and accounts was not, therefore, 'blissid' or idealized 'boke-making', but an activity bound by the particular concerns of his milieu. But, while the 'werk' done by Scriveners like Pinkhurst was newly and narrowly defined in the late fourteenth century, book-making was not entirely bound by civic regulation. If we peer further into the gloom of the seemingly empty shop inhabited by 'Adam', it is messier than it first appeared. The petitions he copies create disorder as well as order in the world, and he is at work, quite unexpectedly, on poems. We see him, that is, making books, whose meanings are never absolute or immutable.

In 1385, Adam Pinkhurst was involved in a transaction over a tenement adjoining the Hospital of St Thomas of Acon. St Thomas of Acon was a meeting place for the Mercers' Guild, for whom Pinkhurst appears to have compiled accounts in the 1380s. Professor Mooney speculates that he may have had 'a foothold at the hospital as well and conducted his scribal work out of it' ('Chaucer's Scribe', 111). Pinkhurst must have worked somewhere, and whatever 'foothold' he found is described in

more certain terms by the petition of the Scriveners' Company of 1373, addressed
to the men with whom we last saw Mum, 'the honourable lords, the Mayor and
Aldermen'. The ordinances proposed by the petition and approved in 1373 state
that '[n]o one may be suffered to keep shop [*tenir shope*] of the said craft in the
said City … if he is not free of the City and also made free of the craft by men of
it'.[22] The authority of the Scriveners' Company was already established by 1373
(the Company first appears in London records, named along with the guilds of
Text-Writers, Limners, and Barbers, in 1357), but the 1373 petition asks permission
to extend that authority by several ordinances,

> for want of good rule, many mischiefs and defaults are, and have often been, committed
> in the said craft by those who resort to the said City from divers countries, as well
> chaplains and others, who have no knowledge of the customs, franchises and usages
> of the said City, and who call themselves scriveners [*escryveyns*].

The 1373 ordinances were not enough: men from 'divers countries' (not free of city
or craft) continued to set up shops and bring the trade into disrepute, or so the
Scriveners argued in 1392, when, seeking to impose better order on the business of
book-making, they required all members to compose and swear a Company oath,
and to copy the oath in their own hand into a Common Paper. Adam Pinkhurst,
who had probably been a member of the Company for a while, took his oath at
about this time,

> for the total avoidance and also removal (as far as possible) of disinheritances par-
> ticularly and all other scandals, deceptions, disgraces and falsehoods of all kinds
> [*exheredationibus praecipue quibuscumque scandalisque deceptionibus oprobriis et falsi-
> tatibus universis pro posse totaliter evitandis pariter et deponendis*], and as much for the
> increase of honour and the good and praiseworthy reputation of the said craft as for
> preserving the status of the whole nation.

The historical contexts for all this rule-making and oath-swearing have often
been described. Growth in and competition for London trade and craft business
prompted the formation and consolidation of increasingly specialized guilds and
strengthened the authority of the London mayoralty and aldermanic elite. Londoners of all sorts were regularly caught up by civic and courtly factional wrangling,
violence, and 'disgraces'. And a new legal culture, more dependent on written
record, was sometimes used for 'deceptions' (often respecting forged deeds and
'disinheritances'). Centralization of the English legal system produced work for
Scriveners, but it also produced what Richard Firth Green has described as 'a

---

[22] The translation of the ordinances and the oaths of Pinkhurst and Grantham that follow is adapted
from Francis W. Steer (ed.), *The Scriveners' Common Paper 1357–1628* (London: London Record
Company, 1968), pp. xx, xxi, 2; I provide the Latin and French from London, Guildhall Library, MS
5370 (pp. 2, 56 and 59), where I deem this useful. As I have not been able to consult the manuscript
myself, I do not provide a full transcription.

crisis of truth'.[23] In such fraught conditions for textual activity, Mum is best kept close at hand. That is what the Scriveners intend to do. There will be no unknitting of 'scandals ... and falsehoods'. Anything transgressive, anything disorderly, will be subject to 'removal' and oaths and ordinances will restrict the use of the term 'scrivener' and tidy up the work of book production.

The scant records we have from the Scriveners' Company indicate that the new rules for book-making were enforced and those who breached ordinances punished by fines, disenfranchisement, and imprisonment. In 1395/6, for instance, five Scriveners were charged with rebellion and expelled from the Company on the authority of the mayor and aldermen; another was imprisoned.[24] The loosely cooperative arrangements by which books were made in late medieval towns—made 'complete to the clasping', or, as Pinkhurst puts it, 'for the status of the whole nation'—were slowly reshaped by guild concerns. A Scrivener was not someone in the business of 'clasping'; he was, or was *meant* to be, in the business of legal document production and other reputable work 'of the said craft'. The 'bagges and boxes' of those who did not conform to new trade custom were, in this sense, carried off by Mum and his 'ferys'.

I do not, however, mean to suggest that, prior to the consolidation and specialization of the London book crafts (when scriveners could be binders, when mayors and aldermen had no say over book business), book production was some idealized, community-minded affair. Book-making always was (and still is) a matter of competing and localized concern. Earlier cultures are not simpler than later ones; they just establish their 'customs', 'usages', and authority in different ways. Nor do I mean to imply that a few newly formed London guilds had comprehensive control of medieval English book production—or even their localized corner of it. On the contrary, books continued to be made, and to be made meaningful, in disorderly ways. Adam swears he will keep his oath 'as far as possible'. He will work in the sort of unstable world where it was customary to ignore or resist or just fail to live up to fixed expectations. If Professor Mooney is right in identifying him as copyist of the 1387/8 Mercers' Petition to the King's Council, then Pinkhurst, as Marion Turner argues elsewhere in this volume, was embroiled in 'scandal'. He produced an accessible, vernacular petition that accused the former London mayor, Nicholas Brembre, of tyrannous conduct, in the midst of a factional fracas that cost another London scrivener, Thomas Usk, his life.[25]

---

[23] See Sylvia L. Thrupp, *The Merchant Class of Medieval London* (Ann Arbor: University of Michigan Press, 1948); Sheila Lindenbaum, 'London Texts and Literate Practice', in D. Wallace (ed.), *Cambridge History of Middle English Literature* (Cambridge: Cambridge University Press, 1999), 284–309; and Green's *Crisis of Truth: Law and Literature in Ricardian England* (Philadelphia: University of Pennsylvania Press, 2002).

[24] For a succinct account of the enforcement of Company rules, see Francis W. Steer, *A History of the Worshipful Company of Scriveners of London*, vol. i (London: Phillimore, 1973), 1–6.

[25] See Marion Turner's discussion of 'Conflict' in this volume.

Much English book production, moreover, remained loose and ad hoc. Scriveners were not restricted to work on official documents (recall Hoccleve and Pinkhurst's collaborative work on the Trinity Gower and Hengwrt manuscripts) and some 'chaplains' presumably continued to 'call themselves scriveners'. Certainly, all manner of 'other' men continued to copy all manner of books. The sites for English medieval book production remained multiple and shifting: Chaucer's desk; the household of the earl of Warwick (where the scribe John Shirley sometimes worked); Hoccleve's Office of the Privy Seal; the cells of monks like John Lydgate at the monastery at Bury St Edmunds; the room of William Abell, fifteenth-century London Limner (and so, by 1450, 'Stationer'); and eventually the print shop kept by Caxton in Westminster from 1476.[26] Book-making was never the idealized arrangement imagined by the beekeeper, nor the perfectly customary one protected by the Scriveners' ordinances. Books were made, as Chaucer suggests Adam's books are made, in an imperfect and fallen world, by hasty arrangement, according to a guild's custom one moment, and using some newfangled technology the next.

In conclusion

The making and meaning of books is authorized in a variety of ways. We say that a book is 'counseille', the oeuvre of an author, the 'werk' of a 'Scriveyn', or the product of a printing press. Under whatever term it is authorized, the book remains an imperfect thing. In his *c.*1392 Common Paper oath to the Company, one of Adam Pinkhurst's fellow Scriveners, Nicholas Grantham, makes this observation very plainly. We are human not divine, he writes; we cannot know 'every single thing by heart; the idea is absurd [*omnia et singular cordetenus quod absurdum*]' (an error worthy of gullible John in the 'Miller's Tale', perhaps). Grantham goes further. The book itself, he says—'to write [*scribere*]'—is evidence of our imperfection. A book calls to mind worldly things that 'sink and stagger through the instability of human ingenuity [*per ingenii labilitate … subsidiunt et vacillant*]'. A book is not evidence of singularity or total recall; it is always a mark of multiplicity and loss.

Remarkable as it is, Professor Mooney's identification of Adam Pinkhurst has not, therefore, given us the window on the Middle Ages that we might want—a clear view of the author. 'Adam scriveyn' is probably Pinkhurst, but the relationship between poet and scribe is only imagined in Chaucer's poem—and thus uncertain. The poem's title in the *Riverside Chaucer*, 'Chaucers Wordes unto Adam, His Owne Scriveyn', is probably not Chaucer's (the author is not inclined to name himself so plainly), but a characteristically gossipy addition by its first copyist, Shirley (whose

---

[26] See Linne R. Mooney, 'John Shirley's Heirs', *Yearbook of English Studies*, 33 (2003), 182–98 for the most recent work on Shirley; C. Paul Christianson, *A Directory of London Stationers and Book Artisans 1300–1500*, (New York: Bibliographical Society of America, 1990), lists Abell.

title in R. 3. 20, 'Chaucers Wordes a Geffrey vnto Adame his owen scryveyne', is the *Riverside* editors' source). Chaucer may never call Adam his 'owne'. Not only were fixed arrangements unlikely in the book trade at this time, but Chaucer takes trouble to distance his 'making' from Adam's. Adam's copying of 'Boece and Troylus' is a matter, I argue above, of *speculation*—of futurity, conditionality, and happenstance ('if ever it thee bifalle'). *Boece* and *Troilus* are probably named in the poem *not* because Pinkhurst was employed in the 1380s to copy them, as has been suggested, but because their titles scan perfectly; they are themselves perfectly complete; their completeness is an ideal counterpoint to Adam's imperfect work. Who knows, then, when Chaucer wrote this poem, or which of Adam's texts, poetic or otherwise, he expected to correct? We do know that Pinkhurst copied multiple Chaucerian texts—but we cannot, in consequence, look at Hengwrt and see right through its erasures to Chaucer, rubbing and scraping at the page. Hengwrt is still a disordered and incomplete witness to Chaucer's *Tales*: both it and Ellesmere have the same complicated status they ever had.[27] What Mooney's discovery shows us is what I have argued throughout: the books on which medieval scribes laboured are not neutral objects by which someone bagged up a text and moved it along. They are a record of 'human presence', and, like all written documents, like all worldly things, they 'sink and stagger', presenting us not with inviolable meaning, but dust: dispersed and thickly layered ways of thinking about the past.

A history of 'the dust of books' is the sort of book history that interests me. It recognizes that books are things about which people have ideas. It argues that these ideas are not determined by the technologies invented for book production—by the ways of making manuscript, print, or for that matter electronic records—but by all the localized, multiple, and sometimes irreconcilable concerns of a particular culture at a given time. It looks past conventional periodic and disciplinary boundaries, and accepts that the objects of its enquiry are not singular or fixed. Such a history might usefully begin, as it has here, with the bag of books in *Mum and the Sothsegger* or with 'Chaucers Wordes'—because both texts remind us that it is the nature of the book, in manuscript or print, to mean, and move, and change. For all the cost to Chaucer's authority in saying it, medieval books are still *here*, still waiting to be written new.

---

[27] Phyllis Portnoy, 'The Best-Text/Best-Book of Canterbury: The Dialogic of the Fragments', *Florilegium*, 13 (1994), 161–72 is a helpful introduction to the debate generated by the inconsistencies between Ellesmere and Hengwrt; these have not been solved but rather further complicated by the discovery of the scribe's identity.

FURTHER READING

This essay arises out of my graduate work on printed editions of Chaucer and Lydgate's work, recently published as *Print Culture and the Medieval Author: Chaucer, Lydgate, and their Books, 1473–1557* (Oxford: Oxford University Press, 2006). It is meant to elaborate upon matters I touch on in that study—the differences between, and sameness of, the two bibliographical cultures on which I work—manuscript and print; and my sense of what a book *is*, and why it is important.

Joseph A. Dane's work on 'print culture', especially in *The Myth of Print Culture: Essays on Evidence, Textuality and Bibliographical Method* (Toronto: University of Toronto Press, 2003) has influenced me in both respects. Alexandra Halasz's *The Marketplace of Print: Pamphlets and the Public Sphere in Early Modern England* (Cambridge: Cambridge University Press, 1997); Roger Chartier's *The Order of Books*, trans. Lydia G. Cochrane (Cambridge: Polity Press, 1994); and David McKitterick's *Print, Manuscript and the Search for Order, 1450–1830* (Cambridge: Cambridge University Press, 2003) have been important as I have revisited the transition from manuscript to print; my views are closest to McKitterick's as the way I think about 'order'. I find the order of manuscript books to be different in some detailed respects from the order imposed upon printed books—but also rather similar, because I presume that any 'order' is discursive and so unstable, something for negotiation and something liable to change. I regret not having the space, here, to contend with Joseph Loewenstein's persuasive arguments about the relationship between printing, speculation, and possessive authorship in *The Author's Due: Printing and the Prehistory of Copyright* (Chicago: University of Chicago Press, 2002) and *Ben Jonson and Possessive Authorship* (Cambridge: Cambridge University Press, 2002). I acknowledge Foucault's *Archaeology of Knowledge* as an influence on my thinking in this regard; another unspoken influence is Jacques Derrida: see 'Plato's Pharmacy', in *Dissemination*, trans. Barbara Johnson (Chicago: University of Chicago Press, 1981), 63–171 in particular. I was alert to the possibilities of Foucault's description of the 'dust of books' after reading Carolyn Steedman's *Dust: The Archive and Cultural History* (New Brunswick, NJ: Rutgers University Press, 2002).

The best practical guide to medieval book production is Christopher de Hamel, *Scribes and Illuminators* (London: British Library and University of Toronto Press, 1992). I recommend Ralph Hanna III's *London Literature 1300–1380* (Cambridge: Cambridge University Press, 2005), and Andrew Taylor's *Textual Situations: Three Medieval Manuscripts and their Readers* (Philadelphia: University of Pennsylvania Press, 2002) as books that suggest that study of late medieval English culture would be enriched by more detailed and integrated codicological research.

PART II

VANTAGE POINTS

CHAPTER 8

TEMPORALITIES

CAROLYN DINSHAW

What does it feel like to be an anachronism? In an episode of her *Book* that has fascinated me since I first read it, fifteenth-century English mystic Margery Kempe visits the grave of her loyal supporter and sometime confessor, Richard Caister of Norwich. She makes such a ruckus in the churchyard and then in front of the high altar—weeping, screaming, throwing herself to the ground, and writhing in the extreme devotional practice that is her trademark—that people around her are completely annoyed. Suspecting her of 'sum fleschly er erdly [earthly] affeccyon', these onlookers snarl, 'What eylith the [you] woman? Why faryst thus wyth thi-self? We knew hym as wel as thu.'[1] Among the backbiters Margery finds a sympathetic local woman and proceeds with her to her church. There Margery gets into yet another face-off with a believer less zealous than she: Margery sees an image of the blessed Virgin Mary holding the dead Christ—a *pietà*—and is absolutely overcome by this sight:

> And thorw [through] the beholdyng of that pete [*pietà*] hir mende was al holy ocupyed in the Passyon of owr Lord Ihesu Crist & in the compassyon of owr Lady, Seynt Mary, be [by] whech sche was compellyd to cryyn ful lowde [loud] & wepyn [weep] ful sor, as thei [though] sche xulde a [would have] deyd. (p. 148)

The good lady's priest holds a more distanced perspective, however: 'Damsel', he says to the convulsed Margery, 'Ihesu is ded long sithyn [Jesus is long since dead]'

I thank the many colleagues who have heard or read this material in various stages and made suggestions, comments, and queries; the imprints of these many contributions are clear and deep. Limitations of space prevent me from acknowledging each one, but I must mention particular debts to Kathleen Davis and to Heather Love for crucial references, formulations, and insights in the early stages of writing, and to John Hirsh for his invaluable work on Hope Emily Allen and his collegial generosity. Thanks to Wilber Allen for permission to quote from Hope Allen's papers. I gratefully acknowledge permission to draw on my essay 'Margery Kempe' in Carolyn Dinshaw and David Wallace (eds.), *The Cambridge Companion to Medieval Women's Writing* (Cambridge: Cambridge University Press, 2003), 222–39.

[1] *The Book of Margery Kempe*, ed. Sanford B. Meech and Hope Emily Allen, EETS 212 (Oxford: Oxford University Press, 1940), 147. My glosses throughout are informed by the modern English translation by B. A. Windeatt, *The Book of Margery Kempe* (Harmondsworth: Penguin, 1985).

(p. 148). Provoked by this dismissal, Margery responds to his cool detachment with a scorching rebuke:

> Sir, hys deth is as fresch to me as [as if] he had deyd this same day, & so me thynkyth it awt [ought] to be to yow & to alle Cristen pepil. We awt euyr [ever] to han mende of hys kendnes [kindness] & euyr thynkyn of the dolful deth that he deyd for vs. (p. 148)

In this striking confrontation, we hear a clash of temperaments, of estates, of spiritual commitments: the moist, restless, righteously angry laywoman versus the dry, satisfied, and complacent clergyman. This contrast is structured by Margery's point of view, of course, which produces the narration of this episode: it is all part of what has been called her 'active propaganda', her angling for sainthood via her *Book*.[2] But can a priest really have said that—'Lady, Jesus died a long time ago'? How can Margery have even imagined such a confrontation?

Radically different experiences of time divide Margery from this cleric and inform the narrative construction of this episode. His words sound secular, almost incredibly so, but they are not necessarily as disenchanted as they might at first seem. Perhaps he is making the implicitly reassuring point, in the face of Margery's grief, that the Church (and he himself as the embodiment of that Church) has been able to conserve access to the body of Christ over the centuries. In the priest's world, time passes but the Church reclaims it; his words separate the past from the present and brandish it in an affirmation of institutional power. Margery, in his view, is a pathetic anachronism—a creature stuck in the past and not availing herself of the comforts that the Church can provide in a present defined by time's inexorable loss.

For Margery, however, the point is immediate access to Christ *now*. The conflict with the priest in front of the *pietà* goes to her core and tests the immediate reality of her being. Her response is ethical and moral, focused in the now and distanced neither by institutional structures nor by the chronological time they seek to control. Her time, her present, her now, is defined by its being invaded or infused by the other: the *pietà* out there becomes the pity in her. That's what it feels like to be an anachronism; she is a creature in another time altogether—with another time *in* her, as it were. We can read this episode as a historical allegory of theological conflict, or place it in a historical narrative about the institution of Catholicism and the challenge of emergent Protestantism. But still, there's something about Margery that will not be assimilated into these historical paradigms; there's something out of joint. Even a historical narrative that links her with holy women of the European continent such as Catherine of Siena marks Margery as living in the wrong country and a generation late.[3]

---

[2] Hope Emily Allen, in the Hope Emily Allen Papers, Special Collections Department, Bryn Mawr College Library; quoted by Marea Mitchell, ' "The Ever-Growing Army of Serious Girl Students": The Legacy of Hope Emily Allen', *Medieval Feminist Forum*, 31 (spring 2001), 17–29, at 20. Mitchell's superb work with the minimally processed Bryn Mawr papers supplements my own here.

[3] See David Wallace, 'Mystics and Followers in Siena and East Anglia: A Study in Taxonomy, Class and Cultural Mediation', in. Marion Glasscoe (ed.), *The Medieval Mystical Tradition in England*,

This clash of temporalities—the priest's pragmatic observation of a progressive everyday chronology, Margery's absorption in the everlasting *now* of the mystic—is what piques my interest here. The serial chronology of this chapter is in fact more disrupted than I have yet mentioned. By the end of the scene the prophecy that prompted Margery's visit to Norwich in the first place proves on her return home to Lynn to be true. That is, Margery has foreseen her current priest's recovery and goes to the grave of Richard Caister, her (past) priest confessor, in a gesture of thanks to God for that (future) recovery. In Margery's narrative world, past-present-future times are collapsed into a very capacious now. And she seems in this very episode to inhabit a different time zone, a more extensive now, from the other people whom she encounters in Norwich. Roaring and weeping when that priest approaches her, she does not stop her conniption just because of his remark that may well be an attempt at consolation. She *takes her time*, as it were: and 'Whan hir crying was cesyd [ceased]', when she stops crying, when the pressure of Christ's presence subsides, then she rebukes the priest for his apparent indifference. It is as if she is in another temporal dimension even from the people who take her under their wings; others insist that Margery eat, others speak for her (the good lady 'was hir auoket [advocate] and answeryd for hir', as if Margery is elsewhere), others take her as an 'exampyl' (p. 148). They put her into, or connect her to, the stream of mundane, everyday life, out of which she has precipitated.

These complex temporal reckonings, and especially an expanded understanding of contemporaneity, the now, begin my rumination here on history and time, past and present. Such thinking leads me to a concept of queer history, for in my view a history that reckons in the most expansive way possible with how people exist in time, with what it feels like to be a body in time, or in multiple times, or out of time, is a *queer* history—whatever else it might be. Historicism is queer when it grasps that temporality itself raises the question of embodiment and subjectivity. Michel de Certeau has written in *The Mystic Fable* that 'time is ... the question of the subject seized by his or her other, in a present that is the ongoing surprise of a birth and a death'.[4] In its emphasis on the endlessness of the present, oriented around the Incarnation and Crucifixion, this definition of time perfectly describes Margery's experience before the *pietà*.

It is not just a coincidence that Margery Kempe would lead me to queer history, Margery, who, whatever else she was, was a mystic.[5] For all their differences, including profound disagreement on the status of truth and the relationship of

(Cambridge: D. S. Brewer, 1984), 169–91; cf. Susan Dickman, 'Margery Kempe and the Continental Tradition of the Pious Woman', in Glasscoe, (ed.), *Medieval Mystical Tradition*, 150–68.

[4] Michel de Certeau, *The Mystic Fable*, i: *The Sixteenth and Seventeenth Centuries*, trans. Michael B. Smith (Chicago: University of Chicago Press, 1992), 11.

[5] Here I differ from John C. Hirsh in *Revelations of Margery Kempe: Paramystical Practices in Late Medieval England* (Leiden: Brill, 1989), who develops a concept of the 'paramystical' to explain Margery's experiences. As I suggest below, I want to extend the category of the mystical itself to make

subjectivity to it, both mysticism and queer historicism intensely problematize the body in time and reject the protocols of any historicism grounded in coherent temporal progress. Mysticism and queer historicism thus bear a similarity to one another (at least with regard to corporeality) that might help us expand each concept. Understanding mysticism helps us open up the potentials of multiple temporalities of queerness. Such problematizations may allow us to broaden the category of mysticism, in turn, as we tune in to the multiplicities and irrationalities of bodily life in the present. The expansion of the realm of queer history is my specific goal in this essay, and to that end, I find it specifically useful to see a mystic like Margery Kempe as a subject of queer history. As it is useful to see Margery's first modern editor, Hope Emily Allen, as such a subject—Hope Allen, who mused, 'I seem to have always a craving to touch the great human mystery of Time.'[6] There is something corporeal—queer—about an extended now, a shared contemporaneity, as Margery feels the body of Christ now, as Hope Allen tries to touch time itself.

I will return to Hope Emily Allen shortly, but I want to stay for the moment with the very fact of multiple temporalities operating in the same moment—the priest's, for example, and Margery's, working simultaneously. I am not uncovering anything new, I'll be the first to admit, when I talk about multiple temporalities, and neither are the post-colonial historians whose work on non-Western, non-Enlightenment historiography has inspired my thinking here.[7] Moreover, for all the uniqueness of the *Book of Margery Kempe*, its multiple temporalities are not unusual in its medieval context. In fact, as Dipesh Chakrabarty has seen, medievalists can usefully guide queers and other historians in search of ways of talking about expanded temporalities. Aron Gurevich, the Russian medievalist, has remarked that all medieval people in fact felt themselves 'on two temporal planes at once: on the plane of local transient life, and on the plane of those universal-historical events which are of decisive importance for the destinies of the world—the Creation, the birth and the Passion of Christ'.[8] Thus, as do her neighbours and fellow community members, Margery participates in pilgrimages, retracing the steps of Christ and his family and disciples in the Holy Land, and in Easter pageants, bringing biblical time into the present. Indeed, her imaginative participation in Christ's life derives from the tradition of that immensely popular treatise on affective devotion, *Meditations on the Life of Christ*. Gurevich analyses the different and sometimes

it more inclusive and thus to expand our sensitivity to the heterogeneity of times in what we know as the present.

    [6] Hope Emily Allen, 'Relics', in John C. Hirsh, 'Past and Present in Hope Emily Allen's Essay "Relics"', *Syracuse University Library Associates Courier*, 24 (1989), 49–61, at 54.

    [7] Primary among these is Dipesh Chakrabarty, *Provincializing Europe: Postcolonial Thought and Historical Difference* (Princeton: Princeton University Press, 2000), esp. 'Minority Histories and Subaltern Pasts', 97–113.

    [8] A. J. Gurevich, 'What is Time?', in *Categories of Medieval Culture*, trans. G. L. Campbell (London: Routledge and Kegan Paul, 1985), 93–151, at 139.

contradictory kinds of time perception operating at once in the Middle Ages: agrarian, genealogical, cyclical, sacral/biblical, and historical. These are all other 'attitudes to time' than what Gurevich identifies as modern 'awareness of its swift and irreversible onward flow and ... the identification of only one present' (p. 102).

When I read, then, in Gurevich that among the ancestors of the medieval world model, 'time was not so much apprehended as experienced' (p. 102), I am moved to explore experiences of time falling outside the apprehension of time that constitutes modern historical consciousness. Thus my emphasis on experiencing temporal heterogeneities in my opening question: 'What does it *feel like* to be an anachronism?' To begin to answer, we must disobey Fredric Jameson's famous imperative, 'Always historicize!'—not only because of the importance of causal sequences in the Marxism that informs his historicizing, as Christopher Lane has argued, but also because we understand that the 'always' in that command, as Chakrabarty puts it, presumes 'a continuous, homogeneous, infinitely stretched out time' that is belied by such plural temporalities as we find in Margery's *Book*.[9] What are other ways of experiencing time besides objectifying it, segmenting and claiming it, deploying it in an exercise of power or defence of some institution? If this is what the priest in Margery's *Book* does, as he would control time past and access to it, what else is there?

Foucault helps us pose the question, though his answer to it, while provocative, is quite indirect. Nietzschean genealogy should be a help, for it is anti-foundational and anti-institutional, emphasizing the fragmentary and contingent: genealogy theoretically accounts for the heterogeneities of times. Foucault declares it, in fact, to be the 'transformation of history into a totally different form of time'.[10] The genealogical project is an 'ontology of the present', which is what Foucault calls the enquiry into the ' "now" in which all of us find ourselves'.[11] Such a formulation clearly expands the conventional modern historical consciousness of fleeting time and a singular, ever-vanishing present. But in practice, as various critiques have suggested, Foucault's commitment to periodization in *The History of Sexuality*, volume i, the introduction to what he had planned as his largest genealogical project, tends to cut off the past from the present, and selectivity of his sources isolates temporalities.[12] Nevertheless, Foucault conveys something of

[9] Christopher Lane, 'The Poverty of Context: Historicism and Nonmimetic Fiction', *PMLA* 118 (2003), 450–69; Chakrabarty, *Provincializing Europe*, 111. Jameson's admonition opens his preface to *The Political Unconscious: Narrative as a Socially Symbolic Act* (Ithaca, NY: Cornell University Press, 1981), 9.

[10] Michel Foucault, 'Nietzsche, Genealogy, History', in *Language, Counter-Memory, Practice: Selected Essays and Interviews*, ed. Donald F. Bouchard, trans. Donald F. Bouchard and Sherry Simon (Ithaca, NY: Cornell University Press, 1977), 139–64, at 160.

[11] Quoted by Wendy Brown, *Politics out of History* (Princeton: Princeton University Press, 2001), 106.

[12] See, for example, Kathleen Biddick, 'The Cut of Genealogy: Pedagogy in the Blood', in John Dagenais and Margaret Greer (eds.), *Decolonizing the Middle Ages*, spec. issue, *Journal of Medieval and*

the feeling of an expanded present, a temporally multiple now, in his remarkable 1977 essay 'The Life of Infamous Men'.[13] In this introduction to an anthology that never actually appeared in the form in which he projected it, Foucault recalls his physical reaction to stories found years earlier while researching *Madness and Civilization*. He experienced the terrifying, austere, lyrical beauty of *lettres de cachet* and other documents consigning atheistic monks, obscure usurers, and other wretches to confinement: this is the 'intensity' (p. 77), he says in this essay, that motivated his analysis in *Madness and Civilization* but that his discourse in that book was 'incapable' of bearing. He wants now, he writes, to present an anthology of documents that provoked that feeling, that 'vibration' (p. 77), that sensory experience of being-made-an-outsider which these unfortunate men lived.

Such a moment in the archive introduces temporal multiplicity, an expanded now in which past touches present, making a 'physical' impression (p. 77). In a genealogical framework that seeks to overcome the denial of the body in traditional historicism, we could attempt an analysis of the experience of such times. But Foucault acknowledges that 'the primary intensities which had motivated me ... might not pass into the order of reasons'. In insisting on the importance of these feelings occurring outside rational analysis, Foucault thus opens up other kinds of questions for us to ponder, questions that are queerly historical: What are these feelings, when a past rises up in the present? What does it feel like to experience 'a totally different form of time'? To live asynchronously? To be out of time? And what will allow us to analyse these feelings, these experiences?

The following remarks don't provide an exhaustive answer to such questions, I hasten to note before my claims get ahead of me. Or maybe that's exactly what I should be promoting, claims that race out ahead, arguments that disrespect the temporal and causal demands of conventional historicism or even of some versions of genealogy. I don't intend to do a full reading of the *Book of Margery Kempe* in these few pages. I offer, rather, a description of temporal experiences of being out of joint, using the examples of Margery Kempe, and her first editor, Hope Emily Allen, and, finally, me. My meditation here is prompted by the juxtaposition of three temporally unruly phenomena: first, Margery's expansive now, her own resistance to institutional, church time as recorded in the temporal jumble that is her *Book,* juxtaposed with, second, an exploration of the struggles of Hope Allen trying to manage an ever-expanding history of Margery, juxtaposed with, third, my research into Hope Allen's archive which is also, you could say, my own.

Early Modern Studies, 30 (2000), and Didier Eribon, 'Michel Foucault's Histories of Sexuality', trans. Michael Lucey, *GLQ: A Journal of Lesbian and Gay Studies*, 7 (2001), 31–86, esp. 52–3.

[13] Michel Foucault, 'The Life of Infamous Men', trans. Paul Foss and Meaghan Morris, in *Michel Foucault: Power, Truth, Strategy*, ed. Meaghan Morris and Paul Patton (Sydney: Feral Publications, 1979), 76–91.

For I read Allen's papers on the Bryn Mawr College campus where both she and I were undergraduates, both of us earnest students in the process of becoming medievalists. We were both touching a past that would become for each of us—as the past was for Margery—part of an absorbing now.

How Soon Is Now?

'[T]he mystic is seized by time as by that which erupts and transforms', writes de Certeau of the mystic's temporality. Few people give a better account of this physical experience than Margery Kempe. Time erupts in Margery's body, and the ensuing temporal struggle turns her, in the memorable phrasing of her *Book*, 'blue as lead'. Used at least three times in the *Book*, this phrase describes Margery's livid, mottled skin, her blotchy, pent-up complexion as she weeps, sobs, and screams. 'Sche with the crying wrestyd [wrested] hir body turnyng fro the o [one] syde in-to the other & wex [turned] al blew & al blo as it had ben colowr of leed' (p. 105). 'Blue as lead' is a common simile in Middle English, indeed a cliché, as you can sense from the syntax of this line: 'turned blue ... blue as lead'. Because of the rhyme word 'dead', which appears in numerous other works alongside this simile, and because of lead's associations with heaviness as well as its pale, ashen, bruised colour—'my heart is heavy as lead', as one medieval romance character moans (in *Sir Amadace*, c.1475)—the image carries a feeling of sadness, desperation; being weighed down, as the *Middle English Dictionary* puts it, by sin, by grief; even a feeling of death.

In her desperate agonies of devotion, it seems that Margery will indeed die. Her extraordinary bouts of crying originated at the scene of Christ's death, on Calvary, while she made her pilgrimage to Jerusalem: the actual place triggers her bodily act of compassion, her suffering together with Christ. Chapter 28 tells us that she locates that place in her soul—it becomes 'the cite [city] of hir sowle' (p. 68), where she sees 'freschly' how the Lord was crucified. Her body is thus transfixed by the time and the place—in fact it becomes the space, physical image of the time—of Christ's death. Christ's death should always be fresh to us, she admonished the priest in the passage with which I began; that event in Norwich occurred chronologically later than this trip to Jerusalem, but no matter: Margery is in the everlasting now of the fresh prince of heaven.

Margery tries to resist these intense eruptions of crying, chapter 28 tells us, because she knows that they irritate people.

> As [A] sone as sche parceyvyd that sche xulde [would] crye, sche wolde kepyn it in as mech as sche myth [might] that the pepyl xulde not an [should not have] herd it for noyng [annoying] of hem. For summe seyd it was a wikkyd spiryt vexid hir; sum seyd it was a sekenes [sickness]; sum seyd sche had dronkyn to mech [too much] wyn ... And therfor, whan sche knew that sche xulde cryen, sche kept it in as long as sche myght & dede al that sche cowde to withstond it er ellys [else] to put it a-wey til

> sche wex as blo as any leed, & euyr it xuld labowryn in hir mende mor and mor in-to
> the tyme that it broke owte.   (p. 69)

'It' boils in Margery's 'mende'—her mind, her memory, where images are stored, where past, present, and future interact—while Margery's body, stuck in history's chronological time, pushes back. I am fascinated by this use of 'it' for her emotion, her compassion, but 'it' is not a thing, despite the apparent reification. 'It' will not be withstood or 'put away'; to do so would turn 'it' into an object or event in chronological time, something that can be made part of the past or deferred into the future. 'It' is *now*. The seething, leaden body, overwhelmed, blue, yields to the now that is so powerful that 'it' bursts forth, overtaking any other temporality or causality. This is what it feels like to experience a totally different form of time: Margery is overtaken by an eternal now. Her crying becomes a performative with no separable content, the meaning in the movement, enacted in an all-inclusive present. Such weeping is not subject to historical comparisons: even the Blessed Virgin didn't cry this much, her companions observe wryly, but that matters not. Rather, her crying absorbs the historical past, present, and future into a panoramic now where all God's creatures can, and should, live.

Margery's wearing of white clothes, her other very controversial bodily practice that is marked by colour, may in fact be performing a similar temporal disjunction from people around her. I have written previously that her clothes—which cause her such trouble that in Leicester she is put under house arrest virtually for wearing them—mark her sexual queerness; they are the colour worn by virgins, and as such they mark the impossible virginity of the mother of fourteen children.[14] But now I add that they also mark her temporal singularity, which is a major aspect of Margery's queer life. Margery may in fact claim by wearing her white garb on earth that she is in heaven already. How arrogant, think her companions, or at the very least, how annoying: 'Why speke ye so of the myrth that is in Heuyn' (p. 11), they snap at her. 'ye know it not & ye haue not be ther no mor than we.' But aren't they in some fundamental way wrong? Margery's narrative, of course, intimates that they are. Perhaps she *has* been to heaven, the *Book* suggests; perhaps she is there now. As the late twelfth or early thirteenth-century prose treatise on virginity *Hali Meiðhad* repeatedly asserts, virginity on earth in itself foreshadows the angelic life in heaven: it *is itself* an angelic and heavenly life.[15] Julian of Norwich, whose spiritual authorization Margery solicits, further explains in her own *Showings*: 'we be more verely in hevyn than in erth.' That is, when our lives are fulfilling their mystical promise, we *are* in heaven.[16]

---

[14] *Getting Medieval: Sexualities and Communities, Pre-and Postmodern* (Durham, NC: Duke University Press, 1999), 143–65.

[15] Bella Millett and Jocelyn Wogan-Browne (eds.), *Hali Meiðhad, Medieval English Prose for Women* (Oxford: Clarendon, 1990), esp. 4, 10.

[16] *Showings*, ch. 55, revelation 14, in E. Colledge and J. Walsh (eds.) (Toronto: Pontifical Institute, 1978), 566, cited in Evelyn Underhill, *Mysticism* (1930; New York: Doubleday, 1990), 68.

When we experience the *Book of Margery Kempe* by engaging the heterogeneity of its temporal modalities, we not only begin to appreciate the immensely productive instability of the world of the *Book*, but also allow the *Book* to reveal the heterogeneity of our times. Margery's is not the only world in which various disparate chronologies operate: the medieval inheres in our modernity (that is, our postmodernity), as many people have observed. And further, Margery's times can touch ours as well. An experience of contemporaneity, Chakrabarty argues, in fact makes historical understanding possible: if we did not already in some sense connect with Margery, we could not even begin to understand or historicize her. Some connection must exist (at the least, in the very fact of a mutually intelligible language, which links past and present, creates a simultaneity) before any connection can be made (information shared, understanding reached). This hermeneutic circle is inevitable: in all acts of interpretation, as James Simpson has demonstrated for the medieval context, some such crossing the gap between beings is a necessary condition of intelligibility.[17] Hermeneutics, then, is the beginning of one answer to the question I posed earlier about what might allow us to analyse the experience of 'noncontemporaneous contemporaneity'.[18] Jan Davidse tries to explain this hermeneutic condition by suggesting that our 'understanding' or hermeneutic connection with the past *includes*—in fact is based on—distance: the fact that we attribute meaning to something in the past already links it to us in the present and 'turns the people inhabiting the past into contemporaries on the basis of the awareness that this is something that is really past and will stay past'. I cannot claim to understand this formulation completely, but I recognize in it a valiant attempt (in the context of scholarship on medieval historiography) to insist on contemporaneity *and* difference, to analyse a complex sense of simultaneously belonging to one's own time as well as to other times, and to reckon with ambivalence in our experience of time and history, including the past's own intransigence.[19]

What we do with such knowledge of these unavoidably complex hermeneutic conditions, what we do with the awareness of our expanded and heterogeneous present, riven with the time of the other, punctuated with the drastically unfamiliar, and edged by the unknown, is what I care about here. The *Book of Margery Kempe*, with its various temporalities, allows us to see that modern historical consciousness—with its singular timelines—is, as Chakrabarty puts it, but a 'limited good'.[20] This is knowledge that Hope Emily Allen had, and it attended an ambivalent experience indeed: while it was a source for her, I will argue, of considerable joy, it may as well underlie conditions that eventually prevented her great work from appearing.

[17] James Simpson, 'Faith and Hermeneutics: Pragmatism versus Pragmatism', *Journal of Medieval and Early Modern Studies*, 33/2 (2003), 227 ff.

[18] The phrase is from Jan Davidse, 'The Sense of History in the Works of the Venerable Bede', *Studi Medievali*, ser. 3, 23/2 (1982), 647–95, at 657.

[19] Ibid. 657, 666, *et passim*.   [20] Chakrabarty, *Provincializing Europe*, 112.

The Time of Hope

The story of editing the *Book of Margery Kempe* is the stuff of legend, at least for medievalists. Scholarship on the English Middle Ages is deeply indebted to Hope Emily Allen, whose well-regarded work on early English spirituality—as well as familial ties and a bit of good luck—situated her in just the place to get the call about the manuscript of the *Book of Margery Kempe*. In the summer of 1934, as John Hirsh notes, when others had left London on holiday, this American medievalist was in the city and able to make what would be one of the biggest medieval literary identifications of the century.[21] The famous English scholar of mysticism Evelyn Underhill had been contacted by the Victoria and Albert Museum, and sensing she was out of her depth, she recommended her distant American relation. Hope Allen's career from this point onward changed utterly: an independent scholar, she was invited to produce the scholarly edition of the *Book* for the Early English Text Society (EETS), and 'an element of haste' entered her research life which had earlier been temporally unfettered.[22] 'It is so exciting it needs speed', she wrote to her chosen collaborator, Sanford Brown Meech, shortly after the identification.[23]

Allen became so 'immersed' in Margery's *Book* that her other researches virtually ceased.[24] In compiling the volume, she struggled with Meech over the scope of their individual responsibilities, particularly what should be covered in her introduction and notes. After tense exchanges and much anxiety, a compromise was found: the edition was completed and published in 1940, with signed notes, a brief prefatory note, and two appendices by Allen, but Allen would be allowed to issue a second volume (entirely her own) for what she really wanted to produce, a general introduction synthesizing the mystical elements with social history. For the 1940 edition she worked on her notes until the very last minute before publication, extending the present moment until she could no longer, until her temporality had to give way to the press's and the present had at last to be declared finished, closed, past. Peppered throughout the 1940 edition, though, are promises of the large work to come: already, in the 1940 addenda section, the past was proliferating: 'My research on these topics became too complicated to be summarized now', she wrote, in her characteristically harried style. But the time of the second volume never came.

---

[21] John C. Hirsh, *Hope Emily Allen: Medieval Scholarship and Feminism* (Norman, OK: Pilgrim Books, 1988), and *passion*, has substantially informed my work on Allen here.

[22] Hope Emily Allen Papers, Special Collections Department, Bryn Mawr College Library, letter to Revd Paul Grosjean, SJ, 4 Apr. 1938.

[23] Oxford, Bodleian Library, MS Eng. Letters c. 212, fo. 2, letter to Sanford Brown Meech, 22 Oct. 1934.

[24] Hope Emily Allen Papers, Special Collections Department, Bryn Mawr College Library, letter to Revd Paul Grosjean, SJ, 30 Mar. 1938.

BMK II, as she referred to it in her voluminous correspondence, was to be a 'synthesis of Margery, the mystic and the woman' (*BMK*, p. lvii). Her approach to Margery was multiple, engaging both the time of the mystic and the temporalities of everyday life. Allen always, to echo Jameson, historicized—in fact, one of her sharpest scholarly debates about Margery was with a theologian who, she thought, misunderstood her position towards Margery because of his ahistorical disciplinary disposition. But her work on Margery drew on her literary as well as her scholarly impulses, as she reflected in a letter; Allen, I want to show you, felt a lively contemporaneity with Margery.[25] Such a contemporaneity does not just create a counter to that rigorous chronological historicizing, but provides its lifeblood, makes it possible in the first place.

Thus we hear the affectionate familiarity with which Allen and her scholarly correspondents refer to their subjects of research: theirs is the intimacy born of 'living with' their authors (as Roland Barthes would say). 'Dear Miss Allen', wrote Mabel Day, retired secretary of the EETS, 'Here is St. Elizabeth, with many thanks for the parcel, which is most delicious. I like her very much indeed, and I like the way the B. V. M. talks to her.'[26] A correspondent at Ohio State wrote a few years earlier about the *vita* of a German saint: 'Dear Hope, Many thanks for Dorothea—I bound her and sent her back to you (registered) on Friday.'[27] A professor wrote from Mount Holyoke College: 'Elizabeth of Schönau has come to life again: I am just sending back my revised article … '[28] In a long letter replying to a graduate student, Allen writes, 'I have such an even personal interest in Margery Kempe that I was very pleased to have your kind words about her.' The student had written not about Margery, per se, but about the *Book of Margery Kempe*.[29] Yet the distinction is too fine; Allen in fact (and not insignificantly) often conflated reference to the manuscript with reference to the woman. Moreover, she expressed a sense of being almost corporeally coextensive with Margery: in her projected 'magnum opus', BMK II, she wrote, 'all the absorptions of my various incarnations coalesce'.[30] Tracing a curious time-knot (a term Chakrabarty uses), Allen wrote in another letter, 'I hope Margery comes to her own in our life-time.'[31] And in a resonant

---

[25] Oxford, Bodleian Library, MS Eng. Misc. c. 484, fo. 151, letter to Donald Goodchild, 20 Dec. 1935.

[26] Hope Emily Allen Papers, Special Collections Department, Bryn Mawr College Library, letter from Mabel Day, 11 July 1952.

[27] Hope Emily Allen Papers, Special Collections Department, Bryn Mawr College Library, letter from 'Bud' (H. N. Milnes) at Ohio State, 20 Jan. 1948.

[28] Hope Emily Allen Papers, Special Collections Department, Bryn Mawr College Library, letter from Ruth J. Dean, 23 July 1939.

[29] Hope Emily Allen Papers, Special Collections Department, Bryn Mawr College Library, letter to Hester R. Gehring, 19 Apr. 1947.

[30] Oxford, Bodleian Library, MS Eng. Letters c. 212, fo. 125, letter to Mabel Day, 17 Mar. 1949.

[31] Hope Emily Allen Papers, Special Collections Department, Bryn Mawr College Library, note (perhaps to E. I. Watkins?), n.d. 'Time-knot' is from Ranajit Guha, via Chakrabarty, *Provincializing Europe*, 111–13.

phrase, alluding to the horrors of the Second World War but with an intersubjective twist: 'Margery gives me hope.'[32] (I am tempted to capitalize that last word.)

Such may be the common passion of many a historian, this feeling of familiarity, inspiration, even identification with one's subject. When another correspondent of Allen's refers to a friend of his, asserting, 'She knows Margery Kempe,' we feel that more than textual comprehension is at stake for her, too.[33] But the pull of the past was at once thrilling, complicated, and problematic for Allen, as witnessed in much of her writing over the years, literary and scholarly.[34] In an early essay, 'Relics', whose publication Allen (finally unsuccessfully) pursued for over a decade, she wrote that she experienced the past every day in 'relics', the word she used for material things 'surcharged with the personalities of the past' (p. 58). An 'antiquary bred in the bone' (p. 54), as she described herself, Allen felt connectedness through such 'antiquities developed in indigenous America' (p. 53) in her upstate New York home. She wished to communicate with others beyond her own mortal being, wanting 'to transcend the narrow limitations of the individual' by connecting with the past—even while acknowledging the 'vital impulse of life' to be 'placed in the real immediate present' (pp. 55, 58). But she felt that this approach to antiquities and the past isolated her from her fellow citizens. 'My inclination for "relics" is something inscrutable and inevitable in my composition,' Allen wrote. '[T]his is a civilization that makes no provision for my own type . . . . I said to [a woman in a nearby hill village], "I am very fond of all old things", and she replied in a puzzled way, "How very queer that is!"' (pp. 54–6). At the very end of this essay, Allen finds, after all, in this village woman's attitude a shared interest in continuities with the past, stressing not the dead but the living. But this resolution in the article comes quickly, too quickly; I have a feeling that Allen's sense of her own singularity, her queerness, her bodily absorption in the past, may indeed have persisted beyond that perfunctory essayistic ending.

Allen concedes in 'Relics' that 'life in an environment solidly filled in with memorials from the past might in certain moods and circumstances, be a torment haunted by incessant ghosts' (p. 58). Was Margery Kempe one such ghost? Perhaps; Allen writes—in the informal context of a letter to another medievalist—of being 'buried alive' by the Book of Margery Kempe, 'almost, as it were'.[35] BMK II finally overwhelmed her, though she remained hopeful throughout the experience: an old

[32] Oxford, Bodleian Library, MS Eng. Letters d. 217, fo. 113ᵛ, letter to Dorothy Ellis, 18 Apr. 1941.
[33] Hope Emily Allen Papers, Special Collections Department, Bryn Mawr College Library, letter from R. Gordon Wasson, n.d.
[34] Hope Allen was born, raised, lived, and died in the Oneida community, about whose controversial past she expressed a careful ambivalence, simultaneously celebrating the community's controversial history and distancing herself from it. See especially Oxford, Bodleian Library, MS Eng. Misc. c. 484, fos. 97b–q. For further literary reflections on relations to the past, see also 'A Glut of Fruit', Atlantic Monthly, 131 (Sept. 1923), 343–52, and 'Ancient Grief', Atlantic Monthly, 131 (Feb. 1923), 177–87.
[35] Hope Emily Allen Papers, Special Collections Department, Bryn Mawr College Library, letter (to Kenneth Sisam?), n.d.

Figure 5
Wooden statue of St Bridget at Vadstena. (Hope Allen's papers, Oxford, Bodleian Library MS. ENG. MISC c. 484, fo. 222.) On reverse Allen noted that the expression, 'not quite ecstasy', is 'MK's "laughing countenance"'.

friend had 'sent word that she expected me somehow to "ooze through" what I set out to do and I am optimist enough to agree with her', she wrote, late in the 1950s.[36] Those researches on the past kept proliferating in the present; even Allen's own scholarly past—her earlier unpublished work on recluses and on the *Ancrene Riwle*, set aside because of the 'advent of MK'—became engulfed in the vast BMK II now.[37] If this fact of the expansive now was not the failure, but rather the very condition, as Chakrabarty would say, of Allen's historicizing work on Margery Kempe, nonetheless the form of the book could not accommodate it. As we have seen, in trying to understand a sense of simultaneous belonging to one's own time as well as to other times, the balance between contemporaneity and difference, connection and distance, is a very delicate one. 'I am sorry not to be self-controlled in libraries', she confesses—Harvard's library in particular 'sends me into spasms of excited research'—and that physical reaction might signal a deeper psychic refusal to draw boundaries, set limits, exercise final interpretative power over the material.[38] If, as de Certeau suggests, history (Chakrabarty would say disciplinary history, Enlightenment history) requires a lost object, a death that it then is said mystically to 'resuscitate', the endlessness of Allen's book project, never finally killing Margery off by sending her to press, may in fact be the necessary condition for Allen to inhabit multiple temporalities.[39]

Allen's felt experience of temporality was in great part fatigue: her past work on the *Book of Margery Kempe* and earlier projects had fundamentally worn her out. 'Over-stimulation', as she put it, left her drained and exhausted as she worked on

[36] Oxford, Bodleian Library, MS Eng. Misc. c. 484, fo. 116, letter to P. M. Kean, 30 Apr. 1956.

[37] 'Advent of MK': Oxford, Bodleian Library, MS Eng. Letters c. 212, fo. 80, letter to Mabel Day, 28 Apr. 1946.

[38] Oxford, Bodleian Library, MS Eng. Letters c. 212, fo. 128ᵛ, letter to Mabel Day, 27 July 1949; Hope Emily Allen Collection, Special Collections, Bryn Mawr College Library, letter to [J. S.?] Purvis, 17 Feb. 1945.

[39] See Michel de Certeau, *The Writing of History*, trans. Tom Conley (New York: Columbia University Press, 1988), esp. 46–7.

BMK II; that had always, in fact, been both the condition of and the impediment to her working, and it may indeed both re-enact and result from Margery's own *modus operandi*.[40] From her letters—with their rushes of words at all angles on every inch of the page and their excited admixtures of scholarly business with domestic news—one gets the feeling of her entire awareness of the past and all its particularities rising up at once in the present. There was pleasure in this, alongside guilt and bewilderment: unpublished work burdened and embarrassed her, and she rued her lack of 'self-control', but listen to the nervously gleeful figures of speech she used to describe her non-progress and non-method—language that Marea Mitchell notes in making the same point: in a letter to Mabel Day, who was helping her try to finish, Allen declared: 'I sent you yesterday a fearful budget—to demonstrate my difficulties in composition thro my mind sprouting like a potato brot [*sic*] from the cellar, when anything comes up that interests me.'[41] Another letter to Mabel Day: 'I realize that if I were dealing with money instead of research, I would be a defaulter who didn't balance my books, I am so much behind.' Moreover, shame-facedly but cheerfully: 'I am as irresponsible as a child at times in giving way to enthusiasms which only time will dispel.'[42] In fact, that forward-moving aspect of time, time as discipline, is what—with Margery, that other woman queerly connected to a past that is all—Hope was pleased finally to refuse. She gratefully quoted an old friend's adage: 'Forecast is as good as work.'[43]

Time Is on my Side

Nothing could have fitted me out better to do research on the *Book of Margery Kempe* than the *Book* itself. Its robust depiction of 'asynchronous temporalities' (the term is Ernst Bloch's) has demonstrated to me vividly—helped me feel—the reality of multiple temporalities operant and lived in the world every moment.[44] The research took me to Bryn Mawr College, where Hope Allen was an undergraduate, Class of 1905, and in whose library's 'feminist collection', as she put it, she wanted

---

[40] Bodleian Library, MS Eng. Letters c. 212, fo. 127, letter to Mabel Day, 3 May 1949; fos. 119–23, letter to Mabel Day, 16 Mar. 1949; Cf. Hope Emily Allen Collection, Special Collections, Bryn Mawr College Library, letter to Col. William Butler-Bowdon, 26 Mar. 1936: 'When I spoke of Margery's "killing" her son, I meant by overstimulating and over-tiring him, by talking (and perhaps writing) about her revelations.'

[41] Oxford, Bodleian Library, MS Eng. Letters c. 212, fo. 125, letter to Mabel Day, 17 Mar. 1949.

[42] All three passages quoted by Mitchell, ' "The Ever-Growing Army" ', 21; the latter two (including the letter to Mabel Day, 12 Apr. [no year]) are in the Hope Emily Allen Papers, Special Collections Department, Bryn Mawr College Library.

[43] Hope Emily Allen Papers, Special Collections Department, Bryn Mawr College Library, letter to Helen [Cam?], 21 Aug. 1956.

[44] Bloch quoted by Paul Strohm, *Theory and the Premodern Text* (Minneapolis: University of Minnesota Press, 2000), 82.

at least some of her papers deposited.[45] I was an undergraduate at Bryn Mawr, too, Class of 1978, and going back there, I found, was inevitably as much about my own past as it was about Allen's. The journey to Bryn Mawr from New York City, my current, hectic home, felt like a journey back in time: the serenity of the campus, in relation to the intense post-9/11 world of New York, seemed to be itself part of another chronology. But the hush I perceived at Bryn Mawr was the sound of my *own* timeline, as I stepped back into the formative locus of my young adulthood, rather than anything anyone else was hearing there now. Time present and time past collapsed as I made my way to the archive.

And time future: for when I sat in the archive (in Canaday Library, a modern building on that Collegiate Gothic campus), doing the work of a professional medievalist, I was sitting in the very building where I had started training a quarter-century ago to become a literary historian and critic. And I was sitting on the grounds where Hope Allen, her papers now archived there, had herself received her training as a medievalist. Our pasts touched in my reading her pages, an experience of bodily absorption into a moment in which time seemed indeed to stop its forward motion. Allen's papers were even more 'non-organised' than her notes in her edition, full of fits and starts, beginnings and dead ends, wormholes of optimism in the face of a task threatening to bury her.[46] The multiplicity of times in the archive that day was composed of temporalities that went back to Margery through Hope Allen and up to me (both in my 1970s incarnation and my early twenty-first-century one), meeting in my now that if not divine, as was Margery's, nonetheless shared with Margery's and Hope Allen's a refusal of the evanescence of chronological time in favour of an expanded present. The intricacy of this experience is matched, in my mind, by its queer intimacy.

Foucault wondered if his infamous men should not after all have been left alone in 'the darkness of night', the obscurity in which they lived, away from the glare of power—not only seventeenth- and eighteenth-century monarchical power, but also his own twentieth-century discursive power. He imagined that these wretches might get their revenge in the mere chance that would allow them once again (in his planned volume) to 'manifest their rage, their affliction, or their invincible obstinacy of divagation' (p. 81). What of any obstinacy of Margery or Hope Allen, their rage against institutional or discursive power? My experience in the archive was certainly structured by ambivalence, not only an ambivalence between hermeneutic connectedness and historical distance, such as I've been

---

[45] Hope Emily Allen Papers, Special Collections Department, Bryn Mawr College Library, note, n.d., n.p.

[46] 'Non-organised' notes: letter to [J. S.?] Purvis, 17 Feb. 1945, Hope Emily Allen Papers. The disorganization of her papers is in part an artefact of the minimally unprocessed state of the Bryn Mawr collection, but see Allen's letter to W. A. Pantin, 22 May 1956: 'When my brother died, nearly two years ago, the mere state of confused papers in my own rooms was terrific.' Hope Emily Allen Papers, Special Collections Department, Bryn Mawr College Library.

describing, but also the ambivalence generated by the different temperaments of the historical subjects themselves. On the one hand, there was the desiring call of the medieval figure—Margery, who was evidently eager for a cult to follow her death and proceed with her canonization—and, on the other, there was the unknowability of a person as nervous, prickly, and radically centripetal as Hope Allen apparently was. Not to mention, moreover, the disoriented and scared undergraduate that I was in the 1970s. My experience of shared contemporaneity on that day in the archive—its queer intimacy—necessarily included the ambivalences, awkwardnesses, abrasions that accrued to those bodies so temporally out of joint in the world: as the now invades Margery, there is the resistance of her own body, 'blue', as well as the constant irritation of onlookers; as the *Book of Margery Kempe* buries Hope Allen, there is her own outrage at her co-editor for the 1940 edition as well as the frustration of her colleagues about BMK II; as I opened boxes in the archive, there was all of that plus my own guarded defensiveness as a displaced kid from San Jose at Bryn Mawr College, frustrating the touch of my friends then, and perhaps even my own touch now.

What does it feel like to be an anachronism? It can have its downside: Margery Kempe, pierced by an eternal now, remained an outsider, albeit an outsider with social usefulness[47] and a righteous sense of salvation. Hope Emily Allen never finished her work, absorbed as she was in an uncontrolled, if not uncontrollable, past. Michel Foucault never produced that book of *The Life of Infamous Men* in which his feelings would form a principle of selection and would be subject to critical scrutiny. So there is nothing intrinsically positive about the experience, or indeed the condition, of multiple temporalities—which condition, I would argue, defines life on this earth. Nonetheless, the recognition of multiplicity and the break with discipline are themselves exhilarating. At the least, we can use a queer historical awareness of multiplicity to expand our apprehension and experience of bodies in time—their pleasures, their agonies, their limits, their potentials—to contest and enlarge singular narratives of development; and to begin to imagine collective possibilities for a post-disenchanted—that is to say, queer—future.

FURTHER READING

For explorations of non-synchronous temporality from varying disciplinary perspectives, see Johannes Fabian, *Time and the Other: How Anthropology Makes its Object*, new edn. (New York: Columbia University Press, 2002); Ernst Bloch, *Heritage of our Times*, trans.

---

[47] Richard Kieckhefer, *Unquiet Souls: Fourteenth-Century Saints and their Religious Milieu* (Chicago: University of Chicago Press, 1984), 190.

N. and S. Plaice (Oxford: Polity Press, 1991); Jacques Derrida, *Specters of Marx: The State of the Debt, the Work of Mourning, and the New International*, trans. P. Kamuf (New York: Routledge, 1994). For thinking about multiple temporalities in the context of medieval literature, see Paul Strohm, *Theory and the Premodern Text* (Minneapolis: University of Minnesota Press, 2000). Queer studies has taken a temporal turn: for projects that resonate with mine, see Christopher Nealon, *Foundlings: Lesbian and Gay Historical Emotion before Stonewall* (Durham, NC: Duke University Press, 2001); Elizabeth Freeman, 'Time Binds, or, Erotohistoriography', *Social Text*, 23/3–4 (2005), 57–68, and 'Packing History, Count(er)ing Generations', *New Literary History*, 31 (2000), 727–44; Heather Love, *Feeling Backward: Loss and the Politics of Queer History* (Harvard University Press, forthcoming); Judith Halberstam, *In a Queer Time and Place* (New York: NYU Press, 2005); and Carla Freccero, *Queer/Early/Modern* (Durham, NC: Duke University Press, 2005). For exploration of scholarly study of mysticism as itself a mystical exercise, see Jeffrey J. Kripal, *Roads of Excess, Palaces of Wisdom: Eroticism and Reflexivity in the Study of Mysticism* (Chicago: University of Chicago Press, 2001).

There are many answers to my question about the felt experience of asynchrony: I haven't even touched on sexualization and racialization here. Elsewhere I have written that I experience my own queerness as an anachronism, complexly related to my father's dark foreignness, his Indianness, his 'backwardness'. For sexuality, after all, is chronic—as are, moreover, race and ethnicity. See my 'Pale Faces: Race, Religion, and Affect in Chaucer's Texts and their Readers', The 2000 Biennial Chaucer Lecture, *Studies in the Age of Chaucer*, 23 (2001), 19–41. For analysis of race and temporality see José Esteban Muñoz, 'Cruising the Toilet: LeRoi Jones/Amiri Baraka, Radical Black Traditions and Queer Futurity', *QLQ* (forthcoming).

For institutional and social contexts of Hope Allen's work, see Jane Chance (ed.), *Women Medievalists and the Academy* (Madison: University of Wisconsin Press, 2005). For social contexts and a different emphasis on Allen's psychic identification with Margery Kempe, see Deanne Williams, 'Hope Emily Allen Speaks with the Dead', *Leeds Studies in English*, 35 (2004), 137–60.

CHAPTER 9

SYMBOLIC ECONOMIES

DIANE CADY

Money haunts discussions of language. Writers and thinkers as varied as Chaucer and Nietzsche, Boethius and Saussure, Langland and Derrida mine the language of money to talk about linguistic practice. On virtually a daily basis, money smuggles itself into our discussions of the use and abuse of language. We 'coin' a term, 'counterfeit' another's literary style or vision, 'clip' or 'debase' the language, and give 'credit' or are 'indebted' to others for our ideas. The pervasiveness with which money and language intersect suggests a relationship that is more than metaphorical. In *The Economics of the Imagination*, Kurt Heinzelman observes that all metaphor might be considered economic since the very idea of transfer or exchange is rooted in its etymology. Marc Shell makes a similar argument, noting that money serves as an 'internal participant' in the organization of language.[1] Nor is the relationship between money and language unilateral. Despite the objectivist claims of neoclassical economists, their discipline is also a language, one comprised of metaphors, foundational myths, and fictional underpinnings. Money and language reside in one another not because they are like each other, but because they are philosophically and structurally alike.

Jean-Joseph Goux probes these philosophical and structural links in *Symbolic Economies*.[2] *Symbolic Economies* is best understood as a project of intellectual history and political intervention. Goux wants to identify and deconstruct what he sees as a pervasive 'style of thought' that traverses seemingly distinct social domains: economics, linguistics and psychoanalysis. He argues that only a fourfold challenge to patricentrism, phallocentrism, logocentrism, and monetarocentrism will provide an exit from metaphysics—if such an exit is even possible.[3] Goux describes money, language, and psychoanalysis as symbolic economies because they share a similar

---

[1] Kurt Heinzelman, *The Economics of the Imagination* (Amherst: University of Massachusetts Press, 1980). Marc Shell, *The Economy of Literature* (Baltimore: Johns Hopkins University Press, 1978).

[2] Jean-Joseph Goux, *Symbolic Economies: After Marx and Freud*, trans. Jennifer Curtiss Gage (Ithaca, NY: Cornell University Press, 1990).

[3] Ibid. 2–5.

investment in exchange and value, an investment that is gendered. For Goux, Marx's genesis of money serves not just as a roadmap for tracing gold's rise from one among several products to the general equivalent of all commodities, but as a larger model for how privileged signifiers are selected in other domains—that is, how the phallus becomes the general equivalent of objects, the Father the general equivalent of subjects, and the spoken word the general equivalent of communication. Intrinsic to the selection of a general equivalent in any field is its idealization and its designation apart from other signs. Such a process establishes a hierarchy of values in which the majority of signs are subordinated to the authority of a few. The items that the general equivalent measures may change, but the general equivalent itself remains inviolate. While the general equivalent is marked by stability, the commodities, objects, subjects, actions, and gestures measured by their various general equivalents are marked by mobility and instability: they can be changed and exchanged and the differences among them are absorbed by the power of the general equivalent.

Goux identifies in this process a conceptual inheritance of Aristotelian ideas of gender difference, although how this is so is less transparent in terms of money and language than it is in terms of the phallus or the Father. In texts like *Physics* and *On the Generation of Animals*, Aristotle locates gender difference in the differing roles that men and women play in procreation. According to Aristotle, the father plays an active role, providing the foetus with form. The mother, on the other hand, plays a passive role, providing the chaotic matter that is shaped by the imprint of the father. Aristotle imagines women as unstable because of their association with this chaotic, unformed matter, whereas the father's association with form marks him as stable. Goux sees in the gendered division of reproductive labour a conceptual framework for the division between various general equivalents and the signs they measure. Like the father, the general equivalent is assigned an active role and serves as the creator of value. Like the mother, most signs lack value until they have been 'imprinted', in the sense of measured, by the general equivalent. These signs are in the passive and secondary position, whereas general equivalents play an active and primary role. In short, general equivalents are masculine, whereas signs measured by them are feminine. In a large part, the general equivalent is idealized and its privileged position secured because the history by which it has been selected has been erased. The gendered aspects of that process are part of that concealed history. But in Lévi-Strauss's claim that women and words are both items of exchange, or in Baudrillard's observation that all objects for sale are feminine, we might detect a trace of that history.[4]

Symbolic Economies identifies a prominent mode of symbolization in Western culture. However, at times an absence of historical contextualizing gives Goux's

---

[4] Claude Lévi-Strauss, *Elementary Structures of Kinship*, trans. James Harle Bell et al., ed. Rodney Needman, rev. edn. (Boston: Beacon, 1969), 496. Jean Baudrillard, *Le Système des objets* (Paris: Gallimard, 1968), 98.

theories a universalizing and structuralist bent. Goux has also been criticized for insisting that the relationship among money, language, and psychoanalysis is homologous rather than isomorphic. If registers are homologous they share an anthropogenic root and a hierarchy among them is lacking. Therefore, Goux frequently insists that money, language, and psychoanalysis should be understood as systems that are equally entangled, and that no one register holds a position of privilege over the others. However, it is difficult to discuss the relationship among systems without slipping into the language of hierarchy. Thus, while Goux insists that the domains he describes are homologous, he privileges the economic register by turning to it as a model for understanding the linguistic and psychoanalytic fields. Perhaps a more useful way of thinking about the relationship among these registers is that it is isomorphic. That is, that they are not identical but, as Howard Horwitz suggests, 'have related morphologies and arise out of kindred networks'.[5]

Nor do Goux's theories translate seamlessly into the Middle Ages. For example, while today money might be seen as something masculine because of its status as the general equivalent of commodities, in the Middle Ages money is more frequently associated with women. Money and women are imagined to have the same *character*: both are supposedly passive yet potentially powerful; both are unstable and do not hold their 'imprint' (whether that imprint is from the royal mint or from a husband); both endanger homosocial bonds; and both are seen as items of exchange. We might understand this difference as a product of money's differing status in the Middle Ages. Money does not serve as the general equivalent of commodities until fairly late in the Middle Ages. During the Carolingian period, for example, soldiers paid by the government in currency were hard pressed to find vendors who would accept their currency. Laws had to be passed threatening fines and even flogging if sellers refused to take currency as payment. These laws were amended and expanded over a seventy-year period, suggesting a stubborn resistance to the adoption of currency.[6]

Nonetheless, Goux's theories make important contributions to our understanding of exchange and value in the linguistic, monetary, and psychoanalytic fields. Perhaps most important among them is his exposure of the role that gender ideology plays in the construction of those values. This idea points us in new directions in our examination of money and language in the Middle Ages. The last twenty years have produced exciting work on the relationship between money and language, from R. A. Shoaf's exploration of the metaphoric links between money

---

[5] For a useful discussion of the differences between homologies and isomophisms, see Martha Woodmansee and Mark Osteen's introduction in *The New Economic Criticism: Studies at the Intersection of Literature and Economics* (New York: Routledge, 1999), 18–19. Howard Horwitz is quoted on p. 19.

[6] Alexander Murray, *Reason and Society in the Middle Ages* (Oxford: Oxford University Press, 1978), 31–7.

and language in *Chaucer, Dante and the Currency of the Word* to D. Vance Smith's stunning examination of the household imaginary in *Arts of Possession*.[7] While studies of the relationship between money and language in the Middle Ages have sometimes touched upon gender it has tended to be an ancillary concern. Yet the role that gender plays in the construction of value, and the anxieties, transformations, and trends these studies trace, may have as much to tell us about gender and sexuality as they do about money and language. To take one brief example, why does the troubadour Guillaume IX of Aquitaine imagine the profit economy as a vagina that increases with use? How are we meant to read such an image? Is it, as William Burgwinkle suggests, 'a challenge to traditional, uni-directional economic thinking', rather than a crude comment on women's sexual appetites?[8] Or, is the image intended to elicit horror and fear in the audience—perhaps a simultaneous horror about the monstrous appetites of the profit economy and women's bodies? What does the introduction of a woman's body in the middle of a discussion of economics tell us about the metaphorical 'equivalency' of money and women and about their fungibility as signs in medieval discourse?

Examining the gendering of monetary and linguistic discussions not only enriches our understanding of these domains in the Middle Ages, but as medievalists we are poised to make unique contributions to the history of the general equivalent and its gender ideology. The burgeoning field of new economic criticism explores both the isomorphic links between money and language, as well as the effects of political economy on particular writers and on the production, circulation, and transmission of writing during particular historical moments. New economic critics tend to focus their attention on eighteenth- and nineteenth-century literature—the time when economics and the humanities split into separate fields and the gap between aesthetic and economic value widened. In both cases, these events were gendered. In the eighteenth century, political economy emerged as a public and masculine discourse at the same time that the novel fashioned femininity and domesticity. Likewise, the separation between commercial and aesthetic value developed at precisely the moment when women began to write with some commercial success. Little surprise, then, that in the first quarter of the eighteenth century the term 'hack' becomes synonymous with both 'drudge' and 'prostitute' (*OED*, def. 4 and 4b). The Middle Ages occupy the time before the split and therefore offer fresh perspectives on the relationship between money and language, which, although gendered, is gendered in different ways. These differences also provide an important opportunity to call into question the hegemony of the general equivalent by recovering part of the obscured early history of its genesis.

[7] R. A. Shoaf, *Dante, Chaucer and the Currency of the Word: Money, Images, and Reference in Late Medieval Poetry* (Norman, OK: Pilgrim Books, 1983); D. Vance Smith, *Arts of Possession: The Middle English Household Imaginary* (Minneapolis: University of Minnesota Press, 2003).

[8] William Burgwinkle, 'For Love or Money: Uc de Saint Circ and the Rhetoric of Exchange', *Romanic Review*, 84/4 (1993), 347–78.

As a way to begin mapping some of that history, I turn my attention in the remainder of this essay to an anxiety shared by medieval discussions of money and language. Although medieval writers often recognize that language and money are socially constructed, they still cling to the idea that they are based on nature. This tendency towards the natural protects a vulnerable conceptual framework around gender, money, and language. All three domains are central to medieval society, organizing daily life and underwriting institutional hierarchies in the Middle Ages, just as they do our own. Without recourse to the natural, these concepts appear arbitrary and malleable—a potentially frightening situation for those who might wish to retain the status quo. Indeed, discussions of proper language, proper sexuality, proper gender roles, and proper money often drift into more general discussions about the need to maintain proper social order. In addition, contradictions inherent in theories about language and money are projected onto women and feminized men as a way to maintain naturalistic fantasies about these systems—bad practitioners, and not the systems themselves, are assigned responsibility for their gaps and disruptions. Finally, analogical logic is summoned in support of naturalistic claims. Writers turn to conventions about one of these registers in order to 'prove' their claims about another. Such explorations demonstrate gender's role in the formation of medieval theories about language, money, and value, my disclosing gender's function as a malleable intellectual category that organizes not only knowledge about the body, but also knowledge about other social systems.

Nature, convention, and the anxieties of the sign

Like their classical predecessors, medieval grammarians debated whether language was a socially constructed system or one based on nature. Most medieval theorists rejected the more rigid, naturalistic position asserted by the Stoics, who traced the roots of language back to the human body itself. Yet few advocates of the conventional position went as far as Saussure to argue for the arbitrariness of signs. Although one might assume the two positions would be diametrically opposed, grammarians often argued for both the conventionality and the naturalness of language in the same treatise—and sometimes in the same sentence. In John of Salisbury's *Metalogicon*, for example, one finds the coexistence of such seemingly contradictory positions:

> Since grammar is arbitrary and subject to man's discretion, it is evidently not a handiwork of nature. Although natural things are everywhere the same, grammar varies from people to people. However, we have already seen that nature is the mother of the arts. While grammar has developed to some extent, and indeed mainly, as an invention of man, still it imitates nature, from which it partly derives its origin. Furthermore, it tends, as far as possible, to conform to nature

in all respects ... The very application of names, and the use of various expressions, although such depends on the will of man, is in a way subject to nature, which it probably imitates (at least) to some modest extent. In accordance with the divine plan, and in order to provide verbal intercourse in human society, man first of all named those things which lay before him, formed and fashioned by nature's hand.[9]

In the beginning of this passage, John of Salisbury admits that language is a social construct. Verbal signs are not natural, but arbitrary, something created by consensus ('ad placitum sit'). Yet almost immediately he dilutes this statement by reminding the reader that nature is the mother of all arts; therefore, she gives birth to language as well. The vacillations present in these first three lines continue in the rest of the passage. Language is a human invention, dependent upon the will of man ('ab hominum institutione processerit; etsi arbitrio humano processerit'), and it is through this invention that man can conduct a literal commerce of words ('verbi commercium'). As John Alford notes, this passage is replete with qualifiers.[10] Language has developed to some extent and indeed mainly as a human invention ('aliquatenus, immo ex maxima parte'); it tends, as far as possible, to conform to nature, from which it springs ('naturam tamen imitatur, et pro parte ab ipsa originem ducit, eique in omnibus, quantum potest, studet esse conformis'); it depends on the will of man and yet is subject to nature, which it imitates to some modest extent ('nature quodammodo obnoxia est, quam pro modulo suo probabiliter imitatu'); and it is, despite its human origins, in accordance with a divine plan ('divine dispensationi'). John of Salisbury's qualifying words and phrases reveal the tensions endemic to medieval language theory. On the one hand, grammarians are well aware of the Aristotelian precept, transmitted through Boethius, that words are sounds that have meaning due to convention alone. On the other, they exhibit nostalgia for a language (usually associated with the time before the Fall) when words supposedly derived 'naturally' from the objects that they signified and the meanings of words remained fixed. Thus, an awareness that language is not natural coexists with a desire for it to be so. Howard Bloch calls this the 'anguished ambiguity' of medieval linguistics.[11]

One way that medieval grammarians manage this 'anguished ambiguity' is by trying to contain the instability of language through rules. For example, in his *Etymologies*, Isidore of Seville identifies straightness as grammar's main

[9] John of Salisbury, *Metalogicon*, ed. J. B. Hall (Turnhoult: Brepols, 1991) 1. 14. *The* Metalogicon *of John of Salisbury: A Twelfth-Century Defense of the Verbal and Logical Arts of the Trivium*, trans. Daniel D. McGarry (Berkeley and Los Angeles: University of California Press, 1962), 1. 14. 38–9. All quotations and translations are from this text and will be cited parenthetically.

[10] John Alford, 'The Grammatical Metaphor: A Survey of its Use in the Middle Ages', *Speculum*, 57 (1982), 728–60, at 736.

[11] For discussions of medieval linguistic theory and its anxieties, see R. Howard Bloch, *Etymologies and Genealogies: A Literary Anthropology of the French Middle Ages* (Chicago: University of Chicago Press, 1983), 30–63 and Alford, 'The Grammatical Metaphor'.

attribute: 'Grammatica est scientia straighte loquendi.' Drawing on the etymology of 'gramma', John of Salisbury makes a similar argument: ' "Gramma" means a letter or line, and as a result grammar is "literal", in that it teaches letters, namely both the symbols which stand for simple sounds and the elementary sounds represented by the symbols. It is also [in a way] linear' (1. 13. 32, 37–8).

One of the most extensive and well-known discussions of 'straight' writing is found in Alain de Lille's *Complaint of Nature*. In Alain's text, Nature complains that some men have abandoned 'straight' writing ('orthography') in favour of 'falsigraphia', writing riddled with solecisms that occurs when the laws of grammar are extended too far by 'barbarians'. Alain's text reflects a similar kind of nostalgia for a time when things were natural—before man had, as Nature puts it, 'denatured the nature of natural things' ('nature naturalia denaturare pertemptans').[12] It is not clear precisely what Nature means by this phrase. Alain's text is generally read as an indictment of sodomitic pleasure, an indictment that uses the trope of bad grammar and figurative language to make its point. However, given the pervasiveness of sexual tropes in medieval discussions of language, it can just as easily be read as an indictment of the pleasure inherent in bad grammar and figurative language which works through the trope of sodomy.[13]

The links between sexuality and language in Alain's text imply a larger method of symbolization in the Middle Ages, one that relies on the hegemonic logic of analogy. In order to buttress arguments about the nature of one domain (whether linguistic, sexual, or monetary) medieval writers often draw upon discussions of the nature of another. Thus, Alain may be using improper sexuality as a way to 'prove' his argument that certain linguistic practices are improper or using improper linguistic practices as a way to 'prove' that certain sexual practices are improper. Either way, Alain's text reveals why such shoring up is necessary. The 'natural' distinctions that Alain's text sets up between proper sexuality and linguistic practice are continually undercut.[14] Nature wants to insist that rigid rules govern speech and sexuality, only to demonstrate, time and time again, that these rules are constantly breaking down,

---

[12] Alan of Lille, *De planctu Naturae*, ed. Nicholas Häring, *Studi Medievali*, ser. 3, 19/2 (1978), 797–879. Translations are from *The Plaint of Nature*, trans. James J. Sheridan (Toronto: Pontifical Institute of Medieval Studies, 1980), 833. 8. 201. Subsequent citations are made parenthetically.

[13] Alain never uses the word 'sodomia' in *De planctu*. Throughout the text, the vice or vices under attack are left unnamed and rendered unspeakable; they are called 'monstra nefanda' (808. 1. 52) and the reader is told that they should be covered with euphonious speech (839. 8. 194–5). Yet as Larry Scanlon notes, the term 'nefandum' has been associated with sodomitic desire since late antiquity and at least one medieval reader viewed Alain's text as a condemnation of sodomy. On the one hand, the unspeakability of sodomy illustrates the horror with which Christian theology viewed this crime. Yet on the other, the refusal to name sodomy gives tacit permission for its existence. See Larry Scanlon, 'Unspeakable Pleasures: Alain de Lille, Sexual Regulation and the Priesthood of Genius', *Romanic Review*, 86 (1995), 213–42. On the unspeakability of sodomy, see also Jonathan Goldberg, *Reclaiming Sodom* (London: Routledge, 1994), 5.

[14] For a discussion of this aspect of Alain's text, see Mark Jordan's 'Alain of Lille: Natural Artifices', in *The Invention of Sodomy in Christian Theology* (Chicago: University of Chicago Press, 1997), 67–91.

thus belying their supposedly natural origins. The inconsistencies and instabilities in theories about language and sexuality reflect a larger cultural anxiety about the instability of society itself and explain the attraction of the theory of natural origins, which attempts, much like the laws of grammar, to 'fix' social institutions and cultural practice.

This cultural anxiety and the symptomatic desire to 'fix' social practice also may account for the frequency with which discussions of money, language, and sexuality drift into broader discussions of the need to preserve social order. In *The Complaint of Nature*, for example, Nature criticizes the 'barbarians of grammar' for deviating from her modulated tones and running in a frenzy to the sound of Orpheus' lyre: 'Man alone turns with scorn from the modulated strains of [Nature's] cithara and runs deranged to the notes of mad Orpheus' lyre' (834. 8. 54–9; 133). Turning away from 'nature' translates into turning away from God and from his laws, which he 'regulated by agreement from law and order; He imposed laws on them; He bound them by sanctions' (840. 8. 208–10; 145). Beyond a desire for a straight language or straight sexuality, Nature desires a straight society, one in which people stay in their place, rather than running in a frenzy, turning away from law and order.[15]

Turning to money, we find the discussion again framed by naturalistic and conventional theories. Central to medieval understandings of money was Aristotle's exploration of the nature of currency in the *Politics*. He asks, does money, like any other commodity, have its own inherent value? (The metallist theory of money.) Or is money worthless except as a means of measuring the value of other commodities? (The sign theory of money.) Although seemingly inconsistent, Aristotle finds validity in both positions. On the one hand, money is not simply an abstraction. Money has physical properties: it is fashioned from gold, silver, or other precious metals and its value can fluctuate. On the other, money's status among commodities is unique. According to Aristotle, most commodities have both a proper and improper (or primary and secondary) use—what Marx will call 'use-value' and 'exchange-value'. For example, if a person wears a pair of shoes, she is employing their proper and primary use. But if she exchanges those shoes for another commodity, the shoes become a kind of currency, a secondary use. Unlike shoes, money only has a secondary use: its function is to measure the value of all other commodities. In addition, while gold and silver exist in nature, money does not. Money has no intrinsic value because, if another commodity served as the means of measuring value, money would become worthless. In addition, even though money may in some cases purchase the necessities of life (food, shelter, and clothing) it is not itself a necessity and therefore not a form of real wealth. Aristotle

---

[15] In referencing 'straight' sexuality, I do not mean to invoke here heterosexuality per se, which is as much a product of nineteenth-century medical and legal discourse as is homosexuality. However, Alain's text does clearly link heteronormativity with 'straight' sexuality.

gives the example of Midas, who had all the gold he could possibly wish for and yet was unable to eat. If money could not supply Midas with the most basic of needs, Aristotle asks, how can it be deemed intrinsically valuable? For this reason, Aristotle calls money 'nonsense'.[16]

Aristotle makes such an effective case for the two positions that scholars have seen him as an advocate for both the metallist and sign theories of money. Sign theory, however, becomes more influential in the Middle Ages, especially among the scholastics. Thomas Aquinas, for example, identifies two sources of value in his *Summa theologica*: use-value and labour. Commodities that fulfil basic human needs (food, shelter, and clothing) have use-value and are a form of 'natural' wealth. Labour (the sowing of seeds, the breeding of animals, etc.) is the only way that value can be added naturally to wealth. Like Aristotle, Aquinas sees money as a secondary sign, a means of indicating use-value and thus a form of 'artificial' wealth. Albert the Great, also pointing to the artificiality of money, calls it madness.[17]

Despite the prominence of the conventional theory of money, we find the same tensions, contradictions, and anxieties present in discussions of money that we find in discussions of language. This is perhaps best illustrated by Nicholas Oresme's *De moneta*, one of the most extensive treatments of money matters written in the Middle Ages. Oresme's treatise is a critique of the French crown's practice of debasement. When a currency is debased, its metal content is decreased, either by reducing the fineness of the metal from which coin is made, or by reducing the coin's weight, or both. As a result, more coins can be made from a given mark or pound of precious metal. The opposite of debasement, 'strong' money, returns the currency to its weight and fineness prior to debasement. Both abrupt debasements and returns to 'strong' money had dramatic social consequences. Debasement harmed most those who lived on fixed incomes, such as landowners, whose main income came from money rents. The poor, on the other hand, generally benefited from a debasement of the currency because it usually was followed by a decrease in prices and an increase in the amount of coinage in circulation. Landowners benefited when the currency was made strong, whereas the poor generally suffered. Price- and wage-fixing and new taxes often followed a return to strong money and people were compensated less for the old coins they brought in for minting.[18]

Debasement was not a new practice in the fourteenth century. Throughout the twelfth and thirteenth centuries minor adjustments were made to the currency as

---

[16] *Politics*, 1. 3. 10–17, ed. H. Rackman (Cambridge, MA: Harvard University Press, 1977), 39–45.

[17] *Summa theologica*, Ia, 2ae, quaestio 2, ad primum. Following Aristotle, Aquinas viewed usury as an unnatural way to make money because it did not involve labour. See Odd Langholm, *Economics in the Medieval Schools* (Leiden: Brill, 1992), 221–39. For a wider discussion of the Church's prohibition on usury, see Jacques LeGoff, *Your Money or your Life* (New York: Zone Books, 1988). On Aristotle's influence on scholastic theories about money, see Odd Langholm, *Price and Value in the Aristotelian Tradition* (New York: Columbia University Press, 1979).

[18] For a useful discussion of debasement and its social impact see Peter Spufford, *Money and its Use in Medieval Europe* (Cambridge: Cambridge University Press, 1988), 289–318.

coins in circulation wore thin. However, in the fourteenth century, kings actively sought to debase the currency in order to raise revenues. In France the need for money was particularly acute at the beginning of the Hundred Years War. The war was a high-priced venture, not only because of the more mundane expenses associated with battle (including the payment of soldiers, supplies, etc.) but also because of the need to secure allies through financial compensation. These costs increased significantly when the war lasted longer than either side envisioned. France did not have a direct system of taxation, so, unlike his English counterpart, Philip VI could not extract money from his people. Instead, Philip had to rely heavily on debasement for raising revenues. Within a space of five and a half years, Philip had decreased the weight and fineness of the coinage by one-half.[19]

In the first chapter of *De moneta*, Nicholas Oresme, like Aquinas and Albert the Great, acknowledges that money is an instrument, governed by convention: 'For money does not directly relieve the necessities of life, but it is an instrument artificially invented for the easier exchange of natural riches.'[20] Yet almost immediately, Oresme reveals his naturalistic tendencies. He points out that the material used to coin money must be sufficiently available, but it cannot be too abundant or else the money will have no value. Given these conditions, gold and silver make excellent choices:

> that may be the reason why Providence has ordained that man should not easily obtain gold and silver, the most suitable metals, in quantity, and that they cannot well be made by alchemy, as some try to do; being, if I may say so, justly prevented by nature, whose works they vainly try to outdo.   (p. 6)

Like the qualifiers in the passage from John of Salisbury discussed above, Oresme's 'if I may say so' ('ut ita dicam') may signal an ambivalence. Oresme, too, understands that money is artificial, but he still wants to permit the possibility of its naturalness by having Providence ordain and nature dictate the amount of precious metals available on earth. Oresme's dream of a fixed currency, one in which money would remain stable and unadulterated, is not dissimilar to the desire for a 'straight' language, in which words do not wander from their fixed meaning.

Early on in his treatise, Oresme, like Alain de Lille, reveals that his concern extends beyond a desire to see a return to 'strong' money:

[19] Ibid. 305: While in England debasement never reached the levels found on the Continent, it was, nevertheless, an issue of concern. Although Edward III had recourse to direct taxation, Parliament often resisted his repeated requests for money to fund the war with France. As a consquence, Edward began a series of debasements in 1344. By 1351, he had debased the currency three times within seven years. While the reduction in the value of the coinage was insignificant in comparison to France (it amounted to a reduction in value of only 6%) the rapidity with which it happened, as well as the series of debasements occurring simultaneously in France and Spain, contributed to anxieties about the instability of the coinage in England as well. On this point, see 318.

[20] Nicholas Oresme, *De moneta*, ed. and trans. Charles Johnson (London: Thomas Nelson and Sons Spufford, Ltd., 1956), 4–5. All citations and translation are from this edition and will be cited parenthetically.

First of all we must know that the existing laws, statutes, customs and ordinances affecting the community, of whatever kind, must never be altered without evident necessity. Indeed, as Aristotle says in the second book of the *Politics*, an ancient positive law is not to be abrogated in favor of a better new law, unless there is a notable difference in their excellence, because changes of this kind lessen the authority of the laws and the respect paid them and all the more if they are frequent. For hence arise scandal and murmuring among the people and the risk of disobedience. Now it is the case, that the course and value of money in the realm should be, as it were, a law and a fixed ordinance.   (pp. 12–13)

In this passage Oresme is not only advocating 'strong' money—a currency that does not change—but also a strong society, where institutions and customs remain fixed. Alterations of any kind, he argues, only lead to scandal and disobedience.

Although neither Alain nor Oresme explains why institutions and customs should remain fixed, I would suggest that changes in systems that comprise the infrastructure of society—whether economic, linguistic, or sexual—call attention to their conventionality and trouble the naturalistic fantasies that exist in all three registers in the Middle Ages. If actions highlight the arbitrariness of a convention, the danger is that people might begin to question other social conventions and seek to change them. This larger concern about social order explains why the instability of money and language produces anxiety for some writers and why these discussions often drift into larger discussions about the need to maintain social order and the status quo. The instability of money—and its ability to destabilize social relations—needs to be managed by rules and arguments based on nature just as language does.

The anguished ambiguity associated with language and money is associated with women as well. As medieval misogynistic discourse reiterates, *ad nauseam*, women are defective men: incomplete, chaotic, and changeable. In part this view of women has to do with the Middle Ages' inheritance of ancient Greek notions of the world and gender difference, which Goux argues also inform value and exchange. Medieval theories about reproduction draw on the ancient Greek belief that the world is comprised of two elements, 'form' and 'matter'. In reproduction women provide the 'matter', the shapeless, raw material from which life is moulded, and men provide the 'form', the active agent that shapes this raw material. In *De generatione animalium*, Aristotle claims that the different roles performed by the sexes during reproduction are at the heart of gender difference: 'The female always provides the material, the male provides that which fashions the material into shape; this, in our view, is the specific characteristic of each of the sexes: that is what it means to be male or female.'[21] This difference is, in turn, used by misogynistic discourse as a way to explain why women are 'naturally' more inconstant than men.

---

[21] Aristotle, *De generatione animalium*, 5 (729a).

Yet medieval discussions of gender contain the same tensions between naturalistic and conventional theories that we have seen in discussions of money and language. Although Aristotelian theories about gender would naturalize the difference between men and women, medieval theories about the body seem to contradict this argument. If, as Thomas Laqueur argues, medieval science understood women to simply be men turned inside out,[22] then Aristotelian theories about a 'natural' difference between the sexes could more accurately be said to be conventional theories masquerading as 'natural'. Indeed, Alain's Nature makes this point herself when she describes the 'barbarians of grammar' as unmanning themselves. Like language and money, gender is 'nothing natural'—an 'ars humana'. Yet, as with language and money, gender is a construct that is essential to the infrastructure of medieval society. Therefore, there is a similar investment in both manufacturing seemingly 'natural' origins for gender difference and attempting to stabilize the slipperiness of gender through rigid notions of masculinity and femininity. We find once again a larger concern about social order and a phobic distaste for blurry boundaries.

As I noted earlier, the cross-pollination among money, language, and gender serves as a way to shore up claims regarding natural order. Perhaps because medieval views of gender difference were so well entrenched (even though clearly they are not as stable as some medieval writers and thinkers would have liked to have believed) gender becomes a particularly important tool for differentiating propriety and impropriety in the linguistic and monetary spheres. If we recall Goux's observations, the general equivalent is ascribed a masculine status, whereas the unstable quantity or quantities are ascribed a feminine status. Just as the establishment of the general equivalent requires idealization, so, too, does the construction of theories of natural origins. Such a mandate necessitates projecting somewhere else the instabilities endemic to language and money, and in these discussions, women—or femininity more generally—serve as that screen.

Femininity and signification

William Langland's *Piers Plowman* provides a particularly sustained example of both the instantiations among money, language, and gender and the projection of social instability onto women. Throughout the poem, one finds discussions of money, sex, and language sliding into one another. For example, in Passus I, Holy Church begins by citing Lot's incestuous coupling with his daughters as an example of the kind of vice caused by excessive drink.[23] The narrator praises

[22] Thomas Laqueur, *Making Sex: Body and Gender from the Greeks to Freud* (Cambridge, MA: Harvard University Press, 1990), 4.

[23] All quotations are from Derek Pearsall's edition of the C-text (Exeter: University of Exeter Press, 1994) (I. 24–39) and will be referenced parenthetically within the text.

Holy Church's wisdom, saying 'A madame, mercy, me lyketh wel youre wordes' (I. 41), but his next question is not about illicit sexuality or drunkenness, as one might expect from the conversation that just took place, but about money: 'Ac the moneye of this molde, that men so faste kepen, | Telleth me to wham that tresour bylongeth' (I. 42–3). One might dismiss this sudden change of subject as characteristic of Langland's free-flowing, sermon-like style, characterized by an associative movement from topic to topic. However, the same kind of slippage occurs in Passus II, this time beginning with a discussion of false language. As Holy Church explains to the narrator, Fauel is associated with 'fals speche', and provokes people 'To bacbite and to boste and bere fals witnesse, | To skorne and to skolde and sklaundre to make, | Unbuxum and bold to breke the ten hestes' (II. 85–7). Immediately after these lines, she describes Fauel's relationship to false monetary practices and lechery:

> The counte of coueytise he consenteth to hem bothe,
> With vsurye and auaryce and other fals sleythus [tricks]
> In bargaynes and brocages [brokered deals] with the borw [pledge] of thefte,
> With al the lordschip of leccherye in lenghe and in brede,
> As in werkes and in wordes and in waytynges of yes [oogling looks],
> In woldes and in weschynges and with ydel thouhtes
> There that wille wolde and werkmanschip faileth.   (II. 90–6)

The movement from sex to money, as in the first example, or from language to money to sex in the second, suggests the isomorphic relationship among these three systems. These sins go hand in hand because they are understood in basically the same way—as kinds of excess that cause individuals to stray from the 'straight' path, thereby producing chaos in society.

In the grammatical metaphor in the C-text of *Piers Plowman*, Langland uses the images of straight and wandering language to distinguish 'mede' and 'mercede':

> Thus is mede [reward] and mercede [due reward] as two maner relacions,
> Rect and indirect, reninde [running] bothe
> On a sad and a siker [certain] semblable to hemsuluen,
> As adiectif and sustantif vnite asken
> And acordaunce in kynde, in case and in nombre,
> And ayther is otheres helpe—of hem cometh retribucoun,
> And that the gyft that god gyueth to alle lele lyuynge,
> Grace of good ende and gret ioye aftur.   (III. 332–9)

As readers of *Piers Plowman* and *Piers Plowman* criticism know, the difference between 'mede' and 'mercede' is not always clear in the poem.[24] Part of this

---

[24] For a good summary of the different interpretations of mede and mercede, see Robert Adams, 'Mede and Mercede: The Evolution of the Economics of Grace in the *Piers Plowman* B and C Versions', in Edward Donald Kennedy, Ronald Waldron, and Joseph S. Wittig (eds.), *Medieval English Studies Presented to George Kane* (Suffolk: D. S. Brewer, 1988), 217–32. Many of the questions surrounding

confusion, I would suggest, is because Mede represents more than just monetary excess. She is first introduced in the poem at the behest of the narrator, who asks Holy Church for 'sum craft to knowe the false' (II. 4). She tells him to ' "Loke vppon thy left half and loo where he standeth. | Fals and Fauel and fikel-tonge Lyare | And mony mo of here maners of men and of wymmen" ' (II. 5–7). But instead of seeing a multitude, as Holy Church's description might lead one to expect, the narrator sees only one lone woman, 'wonderly yclothed' (II. 9). Mede becomes the representative of 'the false' in all its forms. That 'the false' encompasses illicit sexuality and the improper use of language is revealed in Conscience's pithy description of Mede: 'she is tikel of here tayl, talewys [gossipy] of tonge, | As comyn as the cartway to knaues and to alle, | To monekes, to alle men, ye, musels in hegge [lepers in hedges]; | Lyggeth by here when hem lust lered and lewed' (III. 166–9). Mede is a gossip and a storyteller—clearly her speech is off the 'straight' path advocated by Isidore of Seville and John of Salisbury. And her body follows suit. Her body does not stay on the path, but rather it *is* the path that others wander onto. She is sexually available to all who can pay the price—whether they are knaues, monks, or lepers. As Holy Church complains, she is as 'pryve' as herself in the Pope's palace—a word that suggests not only her privileged access to the Church through simony and bribery, but also her lasciviousness. Understanding Mede's larger function as the emblem of a more general excess in the poem helps to explain certain aspects of her behaviour, such as her request that a confessor be lenient towards those who commit fornication—instead of those who use money improperly—as one might expect if she was simply the representative of the profit economy (III. 556–8).

Mede's gender in particular plays a pivotal role in conveying the connection between improper speech and sexuality. As John Alford points out, medieval grammarians used the literal meanings of terms like 'casus' and 'declinatio'—both of which signify 'fall'—as an opportunity to draw comparisons between grammar and the story of Adam and Eve: 'original sin is referred to as "the first declension," and Adam and Eve are "oblique" nouns that fell away or "declined" from God'.[25] But, as is well known, the blame for this 'declension' falls largely on Eve's head. Some theologians and philosophers see the creation of woman herself as the moment when language's literalness is lost—when it becomes metaphoric.[26] That this linguistic fall is sexual in nature is suggested by the word 'impropria', which is a word for metaphor as well as sexual impropriety. Unlike the parts in a grammatically correct

the terms stem from Langland's own handling of them. For example, St Lawrence is said to have 'Lokede vp to oure lord and alowed sayde | "God of thy grace heuene gates opene | For y, man, of thy mercy mede haue diserued" ' (II. 131–4). The use of 'mede' here—by no less authoritative a figure than Theology—points to the ambiguous nature of the terms.

[25] Alford, 'The Grammatical Metaphor', 728.

[26] R. Howard Bloch, *Medieval Misogyny and the Invention of Western Romantic Love* (Chicago: University of Chicago Press, 1991), 37–8.

sentence, where 'ayther is the otherer helpe' (l. 337), Eve turns away from her duties as a helpmate and leads Adam to sin. The punishment for this transgression, and the way to prevent its repetition, is to put her under the control of patriarchal institutions, just as language and money are put under the control of systems that keep them on the 'straight' path.

One sees just such a reaction to Mede's transgression. For example, when the dream-narrator first encounters her, he is instantaneously 'ravished' by her rich array, and immediately asks Holy Church 'Whos wyf a were and what was here name' (II. 17). This is a question he does not ask of Holy Church, nor does he request even her name until she has spoken for some sixty lines: 'Thenne hadde y wonder in my wit what woman she were | That suche wyse wordes of holy writ shewede, | And y halsede here on the hey name or she thennes wente | What she were wytterly that wissede me so and taughte' (I. 68–71). His question is motivated by the wisdom of her speech, not the beauty of her body. She is a lovely lady of 'lere'—perhaps of face, but also of teaching. In contrast, Lady Mede's prodigious sexuality produces a kind of disempowering desire in the dream-narrator. He is 'ravished'—a reaction that he seeks to control by trying to incorporate her into some form of socially sanctioned sexuality, such as marriage. The king responds in a similar fashion. He suggests she marry Conscience, but if she refuses, promises to enclose her as a religious recluse where she will serve as an example, so 'That alle wantowen women shal be war be the one | And bitterliche banne the and alle that bereth thy name (III. 142–3). Mede serves not only as a warning to other wanton women of what will be in store for them if they go outside the bounds of sanctioned activity, but also a symbol of wantonness—in the sense of wandering off the 'straight' path in general. Enclosure within the bounds of a socially sanctioned system becomes the way of dealing with those who wander off the 'straight' path.

If following Mede leads to deviation from the 'straight' path, how does one stay on it? On one level, Langland's advice seems strikingly similar to that of Oresme and Alain—obey God and king. In Passus I, Holy Church explains to the narrator how that archetype of 'wantoness', Satan, ended up in hell: 'He was an archangel of heuene, on of goddes knyghtes; | He and other with hym helden nat with treuthe, | Lepen out in lothly forme for his fals wille | That hadde lust to be lyke his lord that was almyghty. | "Ponam pedem meum in aquilone, et similus ero altissimo"' (I. 107–11). As Derek Pearsall points out, Langland makes a curious change here to Isaiah 13: 13–14, for which there is no textual precedent—he alters 'sedem' to 'pedem'. He suggests that Langland might have in mind Augustine's notion of 'the foot of pride', or perhaps simply wants to emphasize the idea of movement (n. 110a). This latter possibility is further supported by Langland's choice of verbs, which convey a sense of action, such as 'lepen out' (l. 109) and 'lupen' (l. 112). They not only indicate physical movement, but also a psychological and spiritual movement away from God and authority ('To break out in an illegal or disorderly way' (OED, II, def. 1b, 1591)). The connection between physical movement and apostasy is made even clearer a few lines later, when Holy Church describes what happens when Satan places his foot in the north: 'For theder as the fende fly his fote for to sette, | Ther he faylede and ful and his felawes alle' (I. 118–19). Like 'lepen out' and 'lupen', 'faylede' is a double entendre, meaning both to misstep and to miss the mark, in the sense of being at fault or going astray (*OED*, 11, def. 11a and 11b). Satan's fall happens just as he is placing his foot where it does not belong—in the north and away from God, who is himself the 'straight' path. As Langland notes later, God is the 'ground of al' (III. 353)—perhaps a reference to Psalm 26: 12, 'My foot stands on level ground.' Satan falls because he steps away from God and off the stable ground of obedience and onto the shaky ground of apostasy.

Langland continues to play with this pun throughout Passus I. For example, in l. 182 he notes that 'fayth withouten the feet is feeblore than nautht'. 'Feet' can mean 'deed' and, as Pearsall observes, Langland is probably referring to James 2: 26: 'Faith without works is dead' (n. 184a, 52). But it is also a playful reference back to Satan's misstep. Charity is essential for heavenly reward, but so is obedience. Without feet that walk the 'straight' path, we are, in this afterlife, 'ded as dore-nayl' (III. 183). This is a point that Holy Church makes in discussing Satan's fall. He may have seemed free, leaping and cavorting where he willed, in both the physical and spiritual sense, but now 'helle is ther he is, and he there *ybounde* [my emphasis]' (I. 120). Rather than freedom, a wandering foot leads to everlasting bondage.

Langland seems to suggest that God's authority—and the obedience that it demands—is also transferred onto the king. The commune has the right to demand certain things of him, such as 'lawe, loue and lewete' (III. 378), but in the end his rule is absolute. He is the 'lord antecedent' (III. 378), just as God himself is 'a gracious antecedent' (III. 353). He is also the establisher of boundaries—boundaries that are meant to contain the behaviour of people and keep them on the 'straight' path. He is like a 'stake that stikede in a mere | Bytwene two lordes for a trewe marke' (ll. 380–1). The king's role as boundary-maker is doubly emphasized in these lines. He is the 'true marke'—the boundary that stands in the 'mere' (the marsh). But the word 'mere' itself can also mean boundary (*OED*, def. 1). Like God, who is the 'ground of al', the king and the limits he sets on people's actions are the stuff on which a stable society sits.

Immediately after discussing the duties and functions of the king, Langland turns to what he suggests is the current problem with society today:

> Ac the moste partie of peple now puyr indirect semeth,
> For they wilnen and wolden as beste were for hemsulue
> Thow the kyng and the comune al the coest hadde.
> Such inparfit peple repreueth alle resoun
> And halt hem vnstedefast for hem lakketh case.
> As relacoynes induréct reccheth thei neuere
> Of the cours of case so thei cache suluer.   (III. 382–8)

Like Mede (III. 333), people are now 'indirect' and 'imparfit' (III. 385), wandering off the 'straight' path, which Langland describes as 'rhytful custume' (III. 373)—an idea that is similar to Oresme's belief that long-standing customs, laws, and ordinances should remain fixed, except in the case of 'evident necessity'. Instead of staying within the boundaries marked by God and king, people do as they wish—like Satan with his 'fals wille'. Their indulgence in individual desires not only puts them in jeopardy because they stray off the beaten path (they are 'vnstedefast'), but it also damages society as a whole. The king and the commune pay the 'coest' for their wilful choices. This is a theme to which Langland returns again and again. In the Prologue he notes that now that charity has become a 'chapman', 'Mony ferlyes han falle in a fewe yeres, | And but holi chirche and charite choppe adoun such shryuars [confessers] | The moste meschief on molde mounteth vp faste' (Prol. 63–5). In Passus III, the narrator notes that 'many sondry sorwes in citees falleth ofte', such as fires, flood, fever, and plague (III. 90–7). People damaged by the greed and wickedness of others ask God for retribution. He responds, but his punishment falls on the heads of the innocent as well as the wicked: 'And thenne falleth ther fuyr on fals men houses | And goode mennes for here gultes gloweth on fuyr aftur' (III. 102–3). Sinners may burn in hell in the next life, but innocent victims 'gloweth on fuyr' in this life for the crimes of others. Those who follow their own desires and behave 'indirectly', rather than conforming to the laws established by God and king, pattern themselves after Eve and Mede, who cause damage to their fellow man instead of being 'ayther otheres helpe' (III. 337a).

Further directions: misogyny and money

I have sought in this essay to be investigative rather than prescriptive—to sketch with broad strokes some of the links among money, gender, and language in the realm of value and its accompanying anxieties. I want to close by briefly mentioning other possible avenues of exploration that are opened by thinking about the links among money, language, and gender. We might enrich our discussions of the relationship between money and language by exploring the role that gender ideology plays in its construction. For example, well-entrenched stereotypes about women provide detractors of the profit economy with a ready vocabulary for demonizing money and articulating anxieties about the cultural and social transformations that some writers fear it will produce. In turn, economic and monetary metaphors provide misogynistic discourse with a new way of imaging women's supposedly debased natures.

We might also supplement the excellent recent work on the gendering of medieval rhetoric and poetry by examining how poetics intersect with value and the marketplace. Medieval rhetorical texts often use the language of the marketplace to describe rhetoric's potent effects. Medieval rhetoricians like Geoffrey of Vinsauf and Alberic of Montecassino imagine figurative language as a form of advertising and urge their readers to use metaphor and other rhetorical techniques as a way to display and sell their poetic wares. In his *Flores rhetorici*, Alberic claims that figurative language has an additional advantage. It is a way to take a text that is well-known to readers (and therefore less valuable) and make it seem unfamiliar, thus converting it into a costly commodity. In Alberic we see how economic and gendered images converge: he not only describes a well-known text as a used and thus less valuable commodity, but also as a sexually 'used' woman—as damaged goods. Vestiges of these ideas still linger, albeit in subtle ways, in more modern discussions of what makes a text valuable, in both the economic and aesthetic sense.

FURTHER READING

For a discussion of the tropic exchange between money and language, see Kurt Heinzelman's *The Economics of the Imagination* (n. 1 above) as well as the work of Marc Shell, especially *The Economy of Literature* (n. 1) and *Money, Language and Thought: Literary and Philosophical Economics from the Medieval to the Modern Era* (Berkeley and Los Angeles: University of California Press, 1982). The English translation of Jean-Joseph Goux's *Symbolic Economies: After Marx and Freud* (n. 2), provides a useful introductory essay by Goux, which outlines his theory of symbolic economies (see pp. 1–8). Martha Woodmansee and Mark Osteen's introduction in *The New Economic Criticism: Studies at the Intersection of Literature and Economics* (n. 5) provides useful background on the history of new economics and recent directions, as well as an excellent collection of essays written by both economists and literary theorists working in this field. On the subject of money and gender, also see Diane Cady, 'The Gender of Money,' *Genders* 44 (2006). http://genders.org/g44/g44_cady.html.

CHAPTER 10

AUTHORITY

EMILY STEINER

Authority is something that one is always in relation to, that one is never absolutely identical to, and that one can only provisionally be said to possess. This is true not simply because authority can be acquired or lost. The very fact that authority sometimes refers to persons (I am an authority), sometimes to a quality that people possess (I have the authority to enforce something), sometimes to a governing institution (I work for the local authority), sometimes to a text containing crucial information or founding principles (the Ten Commandments), and sometimes to an exemplary event (a miracle, a usurpation), suggests that authority is never properly one thing. Authority sometimes works instrumentally: like force, it is used to obtain an end, and, like force, it serves as an aspect of power. Authority sometimes works through substitution: it serves in place of something or someone else, or it expresses the substitutive relation between two things ('vested in me'). Authority sometimes works as a precedent, serving as an exemplar, standard, or guide.

Recognition is an integral part of authority, insofar as the signs of power or status are encoded or displayed (a heraldic device, for example, or a banner signifying speech, or a monumental script). Recognizing authority entails thinking about how it is embodied in persons or conveyed through signs. Texts register the cultural symbols of authority, and, in doing so, allow readers to ascribe authority to texts. Genres are characterized by conventions, which, in turn, make tradition; and they refer, if indirectly, to a hierarchy of institutions or classes. Yet if the work of literature, of all writing and art, is to aid the recognition of authority, it is also to depict those abstract principles that lie behind manifestations of authority, principles that may be intuited but are rarely represented in practice.

Medievalists have always attended to questions of authority, in part because medieval writers are themselves devoted to the subject. Legislators and reformers

I thank Barbara Fuchs, Ann Matter, Sarah McNamer, Kevin Platt, and Maurice Samuels for their insightful comments on earlier drafts.

constructed models of social hierarchy, which, if increasingly untenable in the fourteenth century, nonetheless illustrated 'the sheer pleasure in working out the details of relative status';[1] canonists explored the intricacies of jurisdiction; and political philosophers participated in centuries-long debates about papal and imperial sovereignty. All medieval writers, whether hagiographers or legal theorists, tend to valorize tradition, appealing to custom and origin and privileging the past over the present. Medieval theories of authorship, found largely in academic glosses on canonical works, consistently identify authorship with authority, situating both in established traditions, with ultimate reference, at least in the case of biblical texts, to the supreme author, God. A medieval *auctor*, such as Augustine or Virgil, possesses *auctoritas*, but not simply because he has put his own text in the 'principal place' (following St Bonaventure's classic definition of the *auctor*, which he ranks above the commentator, compiler, and scribe).[2] A person composes a text and that person (or text) becomes authoritative only if what he brings into being becomes an exemplar, fashioning rules for language, form, or belief, or offering expertise, which medieval writers generally tried to incorporate rather than surpass. As Rita Copeland has shown, however, incorporation or reiteration often involved elements of competition or even displacement.[3] For example, medieval academic commentaries, which often included defences of both the credentials of the *auctor* and the intentions of the commentator or compiler, were translated along with texts, creating opportunities for literary innovation, as well as topoi with which vernacular poets such as Geoffrey Chaucer or Robert Henryson might claim authority for themselves. Principles of compilation and translation also helped found other kinds of literatures, such as biblical redactions, legendaries, and universal histories. Many of these, in turn, provide new insights into the complex relationship between Latin and vernacular authorship, transactions between university, pulpit, and court, and the work of genre in the later Middle Ages.

For modern critics of medieval literature, authority is perhaps the most persuasive link between art and context. Because medieval English writers were not especially invested in the 'literary' as a category, the idea of textual authority helps scholars adapt modern conceptions of literature to the peculiar conditions of medieval textual production: a taste for didactic literature; a high regard for translations and commentaries; small communities of literates, which were rapidly expanding the meaning of 'clergie' (learnedness); manuscript culture; various modes of

---

[1] Rosemary Horrox, 'Servitude', in Horrox (ed.), *Fifteenth-Century Attitudes: Perceptions of Society in Late Medieval England* (Cambridge: Cambridge University Press, 1994), 61.

[2] Alistair Minnis, *The Medieval Theory of Authorship: Scholastic Literary Attitudes in the Later Middle Ages* (London: Scolar Press, 1984 repr. Philadelphia: University of Pennsylvania Press, 1988), 94–103. According to Minnis, this hierarchy of written authority can be found in the *accessus* before Bonaventure.

[3] Rita Copland, *Rhetoric, Hermeneutics, and Translation in the Middle Ages* (Cambridge: Cambridge University Press, 1991).

performance (oral/aural/written); and the presence of at least three languages of letters (Latin, French/Anglo-Norman, English). By 'textual authority' we mean the credibility of a given text—the status of its claims or its plausibility as a textual form—or its capacity to serve as a model. Following this definition, textual authority extends the purview of medievalist literary criticism by historicizing textual production and by offering new perspectives on how status is assigned and traditions made, that is, how texts command readerships and generate interpretation.

Textual authority also helps us see how literary authority is constituted by the relation of a given text not only to established literary traditions but also to discourses that modern readers usually classify as non-literary, such as penitential manuals, parliamentary records, and medical treatises. Relatedly, it helps make connections between authorship and institutions of 'practical' or 'extra-literary' authority, such as patronage, prohibition, or rule. In this way, the idea of textual authority effectively blurs distinctions between what is 'internal' and what is 'external' to a text: the authority that a text claims for itself or for its author is always determined by the conditions—material, formal, ideological—that help to produce it. To cite a much-discussed example, the Prologue to Chaucer's *Legend of Good Women* (*c*.1386) has become the ideal text for talking about vernacular authority, and all the more so because it raises questions about translation that precede English debates about Bible translation (which dealt more explicitly and contentiously with the problems of shifting authority from one language or estate to another). In the Prologue, the poet-narrator, a social marginal gleaning in the fields of courtly love, finds himself in trouble with his patron-sovereign, the God of Love, for translating into English classic 'antifeminist' texts, such as *Troilus and Criseyde* and the *Roman de la Rose*. These translations, apparently rendered without explanatory gloss, mark the narrator as either an apostate (he has committed 'heresy' against God's law) or a drone, both of which have serious implications for a royal servant and subject.[4]

Naturally, the way that an *auctor* makes tradition differs from the way that practical authority functions. For example, an *auctor* might lend sanction but cannot actively regulate or prescribe, as much as medieval writers fantasized about the relation between writerly *auctoritas* and political authority. In the *Canterbury Tales*, for instance, Chaucer's English Clerk fears the posthumous correction of the Italian laureate poet Francis Petrarch, whose reputation as a great Latinist was enhanced by the control that he exerted over his readership during his lifetime.[5] Yet, as this last example suggests, an *auctor* and an authority both express the relationship between tradition and legitimization, that is, how official sanction informs historical

---

[4] For other examples, see John Trevisa's *Dialogue between a Lord and a Clerk* (*c*.1387), and Christine de Pisan's *Letter from Othea to Hector* (*c*.1400).

[5] David Wallace, *Chaucerian Polity: Absolutist Lineages and Associational Forms in England and Italy* (Stanford, CA: Stanford University Press, 1997), 261–98.

acts of writing. Indeed, as we saw with the example from the *Legend of Good Women*, any discussion of authorship, medieval or modern, implicitly refers to an analogy between authorship and authority. That analogy may highlight differences between the two, but it also suggests that the process by which status is translated into power or influence always depends on the means with which such a process may be conceived. Authority, like authorship, is a *theoretical proposition* as well as a lived experience. Both an *auctor* and an authority, for example, assume the existence of a person, whether an actual person who wields official power or is subject to the demands of others; or a figure of speech, a personified agent, such as the Crown or Bible; or a text that serves in place of an authorial person (Peter Lombard, the Master, the *Sentences*). Like an *auctor*, too, an authority depends on the fiction that the authority precedes the act of writing. For modern critics, authority often works like a legal precedent: insofar as the act of composing, or copying, or illustrating a text always 'comes after' the moment at which an authority is constituted, the text is always determined in some way by the authority in question, even if it also helps to produce that authority as an authority. This 'time' of authority is a back-formation, sometimes even a myth, but it has a critical effect on the way that we classify traditions and texts, as when we speak of Boethian or Ricardian literature.

As this brief summary suggests, both medievals and medievalists use textual authority to understand literary innovation, which, at least for modern critics, always seems to involve a tension between the act of writing and an authority that belongs to its past, as well as between persons, texts, and institutions. This approach can yield valuable insights into the relationship between literature and other discourses such as penitence or law, while showing how literature serves as a political or social force in its own right. However, several problems with this approach may also open up new lines of enquiry. One problem has to do with the way that we tend to link tradition with authority and innovation with dissent. What becomes artistically interesting in this view are the moments at which authority is appropriated or contested. Texts that challenge neither traditional hierarchies nor traditional assignations of power tend to be regarded by modern critics as both ideologically and formally conventional. To be sure, later medieval England, with its concerns about the English language, its peasant revolts and royal depositions, and its identification of Lollardy as a punishable heresy, offers attractive connections between risk, innovation, and tradition. I am proposing that, if textual authority helps extend our object of study, it sometimes imposes unnecessary constraints on the way that we understand both 'authority' and 'innovation'.

The idea of authority may, however, be used to recover the inventiveness of medieval literature, while still preserving a relationship between innovation and politics. Most importantly, we should be asking how medieval texts go about theorizing authority rather than simply responding to it. In fact, I would argue, where medieval texts are most formally inventive they also are best equipped to isolate the principles that inform different kinds of authority. How, we might ask, do medieval literary texts conceive of authority as an artefact, something that inheres in and directs social life, but, when represented, is necessarily re-formed? And if we accept that authority is not something coherent or uniform, an entity or quality that may be transferred in the same form from an author to a text, or from an institution to a person, or from a language to a genre, we might ask how textual forms of authority are constructed with respect to other forms, while still maintaining the structural differences between them. From this perspective, we might think about medieval representations of or encounters with authority not merely as sites of appropriation or legitimization but as *acts of imagination*. These imaginative acts may reveal something new about the politics of form.

A reconsideration of medieval authority in these ways might reveal new alternatives to author or author-centred criticism. As mentioned above, 'authority' always refers to the existence of a person, and critical investments in risk, in sanction or censure, continually return us to the question of authorial intention, either the political intentions of the text's author or the intent behind expressions of official power. A related way of using authority to shift focus from the author, while at the same time rethinking the relationship between innovation and politics, might be to examine the relationship that texts construct between authority and its reception. Here I refer not to history of textual reception, which, in the last two decades has become an enormously rich area of medieval studies, addressing questions such as, what becomes of a text despite or because of the constraints of manuscript production, the politics of reading, or the gender of ownership. Rather, I refer to the way that authority, and specifically lordship, was imagined to achieve its effects: how it was exercised, and what it was thought to require in terms of recognition or response.

Medieval political and juristic commentary, while devoted to questions about counsel, representation, and dominion, lacked a coherent discourse about lordly authority. Certainly, the practical operations of lordly authority can be traced in legal handbooks, such as *The Customary Laws of the Region of Beauvais* (*c.*1290), compiled by Philippe de Beaumanoir, or Henri de Bracton's *On the Laws and Customs of England* (*c.*1260); treatises on estates management, such as those of Walter of Henley (*c.*1275) and Elizabeth de Burgh (*c.*1330s); allegorical visions, such as the *Parlement of the Three Ages* and *Wynnere and Wastoure* (*c.*1350–70); fifteenth-century courtesy books, such as Caxton's *Boke of Curtasye* (1478?) and Wynkyn de Worde's *Boke of Noblesse* (1498?); and correspondences, such as the Paston letters (1422–1529). Only occasionally does practical lordship tackle more abstract concepts. So for example, in the *Seneschaucy*, Walter of Henley observes that a servant's accountability is tied to the kind of access he has to his lord: to the lord's commandments, to his physical presence, and to his 'advantages', i.e., his ability to confer favour and profit.[6] Yet observations such as these are rare and are

---

[6] Dorotha Oschinsky, *Walter of Henley and Other Treatises on Estates Management and Accounting* (Oxford: Clarendon Press, 1971), ch. 11, c. 73.

usually lodged between explanations of the merits of swan flesh, and why not to pet a dog during dinner.

Literary examinations of lordship fill a gap in medieval political philosophy by directing sustained attention to the *nature* of lordship, asking questions such as, is lordship inherently plural or singular, and, if the former, to what extent does it rely on written instruments, impersonation, or mediation? In what sense do the operations of authority assume the existence of an audience? In the interest of space I shall examine just two sets of texts that offer complex investigations into the nature of lordship: the fifteenth-century biblical cycle plays and the great fourteenth-century alliterative poem *Piers Plowman*.

Theorising authority in the cycle plays

The medieval English theatre is well known for its powerful representations of authority. The biblical cycle plays, for example, depict salvation history as a series of divine judgements, provoked by humanity's failure to recognize divine authority. Many of the pageants, moreover, use transgressions against God as an occasion to critique contemporary abuses of official power, to negotiate between competing civic authorities, or to valorize new symbols or customs. As many scholars have noted, moreover, the dramatic authority to challenge existing beliefs or practices is predicated on a real or imagined audience. What has received less attention is the way that the cycles go about theorizing authority in the process of creating dramatic conventions. In addition to its performance of authority, for example, in imitation of liturgical and legal rituals or as a vehicle for civic institutions, or in perpetuation of dramatic traditions, theatre also concerns ideas about authority that emerge in the ongoing construction of audience. As we shall see, many of these ideas are introduced elsewhere and earlier, namely in *Piers Plowman*, but they are insistently rehearsed in the cycles as the conditions of dramatic production.

The pageants compiled in the Towneley manuscript (*c*.1480), and especially those attributed to the Wakefield Master, are particularly interested in the nature of lordship. An obvious example is the 'Creation' play. All four major cycles begin with Deus, who describes what he has accomplished in the six days of creation. The 'Creation' plays, in short, propose to dramatize the original event of linguistic performance, an event in which the authority of the Word is synonymous with divine sovereignty. In Genesis, an omniscient narrator reports past events ('And God said, "Be light made." And light was made'), thus serving as a context or witness to divine performance ('and it was done'). In the plays, Deus is solely responsible for telling and enacting the events of creation:

> All maner thyng is in my thoght,
> Withoutten me ther may be noght,
> For all is in my sight.

> Hit shall be done after my will:
> That I haue thoght I shall fulfill
> And manteyn with my might.
> (Towneley 'Creation', p. 3, ll. 13–18)[7]

Deus's speech is supposed to explain total presence: what God wills, he speaks, and what he says, he does in the course of his speech, accompanied, presumably, by dramatic spectacle. In doing so, however, the speech highlights the necessity of both description and context, the visible manifestation of creation. God speaks and creates effects, but those effects are judged, not by the original events, but by the medieval dramatic audience. In this way, theatrical representation invests divine sovereignty with a reflexive quality: both God and the audience must see the effects in order for them to be said to have taken place. This attention to the visible manifestation of creation is most fully dramatized in the Chester 'Adam and Eve' play, in which Deus faithfully recounts the whole of Genesis 1.[8] In Chester, Deus witnesses his creation not simply by judging it but also by acknowledging that its effects are 'expresse'—plain and open, created in the presence of others: 'At My byddynge made be light. | Light is good, I see in sight ... This morne and evene, the first day | is made full and *expresse* ... Now Heaven and Earth is made *expresse*, | Make wee man to our likeness' (Chester, 'Adam', p. 14, ll. 9–10, 15–16, 81–2; my emphasis).[9]

The question at stake is how the dramatic commitment to a first-person account of Creation generates new questions about the nature of supreme authority.[10] First-person narration acknowledges that a context always exists within which the exercise of authority can be recognized, even or precisely at the moments at which authority is declared to be sovereign. In the case of Deus' speech, it also suggests that authority is intrinsically plural: in the cycle plays, the biblical narrator is replaced, not only by God himself, but also *and therefore* by a description of the means through which God creates, the multiple instruments of supreme authority.

> Darknes we call the nyght
> And lith also the bright;
> It shall be as I say.

---

[7] Martin Stevens and A. C. Cawley (eds.), *The Towneley Plays*, EETS, SS 13–14 (Oxford: Oxford University Press, 1994). All subsequent citations are to this edition.

[8] See Meg Twycross, 'The Theatricality of Medieval English Plays', in *The Cambridge Companion to Medieval English Drama* (Cambridge: Cambridge University Press, 1994), 37–84.

[9] R. M. Lumiansky and David Mills (eds.), *The Chester Mystery Cycle*, EETS, SS 3 (Oxford: Oxford University Press, 1974), 14–16.

[10] Every 'Creation' play opens with a first-person speech by Deus, the first line of which is drawn from Revelation 1: 8/22: 13 ('I am alpha and omega, the first and last, beginning and end'), given either in Latin, English, or both, and in different scripts. One issue, then, which I can't address here, is the relative status of languages and their capacity to represent divine presence. See Janette Dillon's response to Martin Stevens and Peter Meredith in *Language and Stage in Medieval and Renaissance England* (Cambridge: Cambridge University Press, 1998), 35–8.

After my will this is furth broght: ...
In medys the water, *bi oure assent,*
Be now maide the firmament ...

(Towneley, 'Creation', p. 4, ll. 25–8, 31–2; my emphasis)

Starres also *through Myne entente*
I will make one the firmamente, ...
all make I *with a thoughte*—
bestes, fowles, fruit, stone, and tree—
These workes are good, well I see.
Therfore to blesse all well liketh me,
This worke that I have wrought. ...
This morne and evon *through my might*
of the fiveth day and the night
Is made and ended well aright,
all *at my owne will.*

(Chester, 'Adam and Eve', pp. 15–16, ll. 49–50, 60–4, 69–72; my emphasis)

In these passages, it falls to Deus to elaborate the relationship between speaking and effects: what does it mean to say, 'God said', and what does it mean to say, 'it was done'? What God accomplishes according to his 'will' or 'entente' or 'assent' he makes 'with a thought' or 'through his might'. Scholastic theologians succeeded in proving divine sovereignty in the act of creation: nothing compels God to create, and he creates *ex nihilo*, entirely through his own (will) power, motivated purely by his own goodness. According to this reasoning, Deus' elaboration of the means of creation need not compromise divine unity or autonomy. Further, as Thomas Aquinas explains, we tend to reduce particular effects to particular attributes—e.g., 'God creates through his power'; along similar lines, although in God attributes such as will and thought are essentially the same, each of these faculties still has to proceed in a certain order ('through My might', 'at My owne will'). By having Deus describe his own process, however, the plays call attention to the multiple means through which God creates, thus reading theology back into the biblical narrative, and, in doing so, reflecting upon the operations of authority more generally.

The nature of authority, illustrated by Deus' first-person account of creation, implicates the audience at the same time that it underlines the plurality of the creative process. The playwrights seem to have had difficulty conceiving divine sovereignty, or indeed, any authority, as a singly constituted entity: the plurality of authority seems to have been fundamental to its expression, and plurality seems to have been inseparable from both instrumentality (how God makes things happen) and reception (the contexts within which authority is seen and received). Yet the different ways in which authority might be imagined as multiple or plural are hardly commensurate. For example, in the 'Creation' plays, Deus' account of creation is preceded by a credic assertion of divine sovereignty, which is explicitly located in

God's plural nature(s): God is the first and last, beginning and end, and he is three Persons in one God.

> Ego sum alpha et o [omega],
> I am the first, the last also,
> Oone god in magesté;
> Meruelus, of myght most,
> Fader, and son, and holy goost,
> On God in Trinyté.
>
> I am without begynnyng,
> My Godhede hath none endyng,
> I am god in tron [throne],
> Oone God in persons thre
> Which may neuer twynnyd [divided] be,
> For I am God alone.   (Towneley, 'Creation', p. 3, ll. 1–12)

If first-person narration is supposed to be the ultimate dramatization of sovereign presence, it is also an invitation to consider the troublesome first-person plural: 'Et ait faciamus hominem ad imaginem et similitudinem nostram' (And God said, 'Let us create man after our own image and likeness') (Genesis 1: 26). That Trinitarianism is invoked at the beginning of a play about creation is not surprising. The plural subject of 'faciamus' was usually glossed as the Trinity and served as an occasion for catechistic instruction, as it does here. Moreover, the self-generation of the Trinity within the Godhead was crucial to medieval proofs of divine unity with respect to creation: because the three Persons are of one essence, they all help to create.[11] What is surprising is the way medieval writers apply the various pluralities of divine sovereignty (persons, means, attributes) to theorizations of human lordship. Specifically, the comparison between divine and human lordship allowed them to posit a relationship between the multiple instruments of lordly authority and its reception, a relationship that, in the cycle plays, becomes a function of the dramatic audience.

Piers Plowman and the Nature of Sovereignty

In *De Trinitate*, Augustine discusses the generative relations that bind the Trinity but refuses to go so far as to create an analogy between the Trinity and the first family.[12] In *Piers Plowman*, however, Langland directly compares the Trinity to Adam, Eve, and their progeny, and to the forces of production, desire, and loss that characterize human procreation.[13] Just before he launches into the family analogy,

---

[11] Thomas Aquinas, *Summa theologica*, I. 45. 6 (following Dionysius, *Divine Names*, II).

[12] See Augustine, *Confessions*, Book 13, ch. 11, v. 12.

[13] See Andrew Galloway, 'Intellectual Pregnancy, Metaphysical Femininity, and the Social Doctrine of the Trinity in *Piers Plowman*', *Yearbook of Langland Studies*, 12 (1998), 117–52; M. Teresa Tavormina, *Kindly Similitude: Marriage and Family in 'Piers Plowman'* (Cambridge: D. S. Brewer, 1995), 140–50; and Lawrence Clopper, *'Songes of Rechelesnesse': Langland and the Franciscans* (Ann Arbor: University of Michigan Press, 1997), 115–23.

Langland with equal daring compares the persons of the Trinity to another form of social experience, the execution of lordly authority:

So thre bilongeth for [pertains to] a lord that lordshipe cleymeth:
Might, and a mene (his owene myghte to knowe),
Of hymself and of his servaunt, and what suffreth hem bothe. [endure, experience]
So God, that gynnyng hadde nevere, but tho hym good thoughte [seemed good to him],
Sente forth his sone as for servaunt that tyme,
To ocupien hym here til issue were spronge—
That is, children of charite ...   (B. XVI. 191–7)[14]

In this passage, true lordship is tripartite: it involves (1) might; and (2*a*) an intermediary ('mene'), through which a lord comes to know both his own might and that of his servant; or (2*b*) a 'meinie': servants, members of the household, those in relation of dependence to the lord (both readings mutually supported by l. 195); and (3) what both of them, the lord and his servant, experience ('suffreth') as a result. By analogy, God the Father sent forth his servant, Christ, until he had achieved results (the children of charity, i.e. the 'fruits' of the Holy Spirit).[15]

Langland's analogy was probably modelled on chapter 7 of Augustine's *De Trinitate*, which argues that the Son is said to be the servant of the Father, not because he is less in nature, but rather because he is less in fashion: God takes on different forms of the same nature in order to accomplish different objectives with respect to human salvation. The plurality of divine persons, designated in Genesis by 'faciamus', proves that God doesn't change his nature, even though he works through three Persons.[16] By invoking the very analogy that Augustine tried to explain away, Langland wants to show, as he does elsewhere in the poem, God's commitment to experiencing creatureliness through Christ ('what suffreth hem both'). But surely the plurality of authority that pertains to human lordship is qualitatively different from that which pertains to divine sovereignty! Lordship doesn't exclude the possibility of sovereignty, but the comparison between divine sovereignty and lordly authority involves a concession to the kind of analogy that only human lordship realizes literally. A servant is an instrument of lordly authority precisely because he doesn't possess the same authority as the lord. He makes lordly authority manifest, both to the lord and to others, by extending the lord's command: he neither emanates from the lord nor does he partake of the lord's nature.

To be sure, a servant may function as a legal expression of the will of the lord, insofar as he helps to execute it. According to Beaumanoir, for example, if

---

[14] All citations of *Piers Plowman* are to *The Vision of Piers Plowman*, ed. A. V. C. Schmidt (London: J. M. Dent, 1995).

[15] For a very different reading, see Clopper, '*Songes of Rechelesnesse*', 121–4.

[16] Augustine, *De Trinitate*, 1. 7. 14.

a lord invests his employee with the power to administer justice, and while doing so the employee does something wrong, the lord may not disavow the action of his employee.[17] Similarly, according to Bracton, a procurator may represent his absent lord in certain transactions provided that he has letters from the lord conveying the lord's will.[18] In this way, the servant could be said to have a symbolic relationship to the lord but not an essential one. The lord and servant might uphold each other's interests, but service nevertheless implies fundamental inequality.[19] By 'servant', Langland surely doesn't mean a menial labourer. He was probably thinking about gentle servants, household officers or administrators, men who were asked to act as the lord's executors, deputies, and ambassadors. These were the men who reflected and extended the lord's authority because they wore his livery and represented, his interests through his direct command. It is certainly possible that Langland's contemporary, the great translator John Trevisa, understood his own service to his patron, the Lord Thomas Berkeley, in precisely these ways, and Langland, despite his sometimes marginal authorial persona, may have served in a similar capacity. *Piers Plowman* returns continually and knowledgeably to topics of gentle service, such as aristocratic prerogative, the nature of dominion, alienation of property, and courtly manners, including modes of address and proper hall conversation.

This idea of service would explain Langland's peculiar emphasis on the reflexive quality of lordly authority: 'and a mene (his owene myghte to knowe), | Of hymself and of his servaunt, and what suffreth hem both.' Reflexivity, in this case, is bound up in relations of service and dependence, rather than essential sameness and equality. Moreover, in Langland's analogy, lordly authority, insofar as it is reflexive—relying, therefore, on instruments or persons external and, in this case, inferior to the lord—must inherently be demonstrated through something and to someone other than the lord himself. (Most C-text manuscripts underline the reflexivity of lordly authority by giving l. 192 as 'Mighte, and a mene [his owene myghte to shewe]'.) However much the Incarnation—Christ's human agency—serves the divine plan for human salvation, God's visible manifestation is not strictly necessary to the operations of divine sovereignty.

By comparing the creative work of the Trinity to the operations of lordly authority, Langland means to emphasize the similarities rather than the differences between the two. But in doing so, he proffers some challenging questions about lordship: to what extent must lordly authority be demonstrated in order to be

---

[17] Phillipe de Beaumanoir, *Coutumes de Beauvaisis*, trans. F. R. P. Akehurst (Philadelphia: University of Pennsylvania Press, 1992), 291.

[18] Henri de Bracton, *De legibus et consuetudinibus Angliae/On the Laws and Customs of England*, trans. and rev. Samuel Thorne (Cambridge, MA: Published in association with the Selden Society [by] the Belknap Press of Harvard University Press, 1968–), 124.

[19] Horrox, 'Servitude', 77.

effective, and further, must authority be reflexive—that is, manifest to the lord himself—in order to be recognized by others? To what extent does authority rely on human agents, on relations of dependence, and could it be said to be, in that sense, an ethical practice or labour? Do the mediatory aspects of authority compromise or affirm it?

Langland's investigation into the nature of authority can be traced back to an earlier passage in the poem, in which Wit explains the nature of the Creator (Kynde). Wit avers that the nature of the Creator can be discovered through a reading of Genesis 1 ('faciamus'). Peculiarly, however, he omits all discussion of Trinitarianism, reading the first-person plural as a treatise on human lordship:

> Dixit et facta sunt.
> And made man [moost lik] to hymself one
> And Eve of his ryb bon withouten any mene.
> For he was synguler hymself seide *Faciamus*—
> As who seith, 'Moore moot [is required] herto than my word oone:
> My myght moot helpe now with my speche.'
> Right as a lord sholde make lettres, and hym (ne) lakked parchemyn,
> Though he koude write never so wel, if he [wel]de no penne,
> The lettre, for al the lordshipe, I leve [believe] were never ymaked!
> And so it semeth by him, as the Bible telleth, there he seide—
> (Dixit, 'Faciamus')—
> He moste werche with his word and his wit shewe. ...
> And that he wroghte with werk and with word bothe:
> Thorgh myght of the mageste man was ymaked.   (B. IX. 32a–43, 51–2)

Once again, what does it mean that God spoke certain things and they were done ('dixit et facta sunt')? On the one hand, the Latin line attests to the performativity of the divine Word, or the unity of a God who creates woman from man 'withouten any mene'. On the other hand, the first-person plural ('faciamus') suggests that lordship without intermediary is inconceivable: plurality suggests the existence of intermediaries, human agents or written instruments. It likewise suggests, at least in this passage, that authority is a *labour* of lordship. A lord doesn't simply speak and his expressed will produces results. A lord requires might, and he requires the tools—here pen and parchment—the materials with which to make his will known and to translate intention into action.[20] In this passage, Langland is positing an analogy between divine authority and human lordship (although he doesn't mention the Trinity explicitly, the parchment surely invokes the incarnate Word). Yet, as in the passage from B. XVI, the contrast between divine authority and human lordship opens up a discussion with profound implications for human lordship.

---

[20] According to Bracton, the lord, when present at a transaction, need only declare his intention; only the absence of the lord necessitates the mediatory work of writing. See E. Steiner, *Documentary Culture and the Making of Medieval English Literature* (Cambridge: Cambridge University Press, 2003), 21–8.

Lordship involves instruments distinct from the lord's person, which extend and implement the lord's authority. Unlike servants, documents are not persons but they do impersonate the lord's will and render it material, thus constituting his work. This, says Langland, is what God meant when he said 'faciamus': he was referring to lordly labour ('werche with his word', 'wroghte with werk and with word bothe'), that is, to the way that authority is constituted by the means through which it achieves effects. According to this analogy, moreover, sovereign labour is something that must be made visible, not just through creation itself (the effect), but also through the instruments of command. God's authority is effective because he works 'with his word and his wit shewe': the parchment and pen matter, not simply because they transform legal will into legal instrument but also because they make it, in the words of Chester, 'expresse'.[21]

Deus' speech dramatizes some basic principles about the nature of sovereignty, specifically, that it is plural, reflexive, and manifest; his speech also offers new forms through which those principles may be expressed. In this sense, *Piers Plowman*, by pursuing analogies between divine and human authority, formulates some of the principles (re)presented by the drama. In both cases, divine sovereignty offers a way of thinking through what is necessary to the operations of supreme (human) authority. But what, then, is the relationship between *Piers Plowman* and the drama? Are both innovative in the same way? Does *Piers* posit theories about the operations of lordship that only theatre can fully develop, insofar as theatre performs the performance of authority by addressing a real audience?

The lordship analogies in *Piers Plowman* are characteristic of a poet who specializes in unlikely comparisons that always exceed the terms with which they begin. These moments in the poem are ostentatiously beautiful, theoretically bold, and formally complex. The plays, by contrast, do not call attention to literary experiment per se, but they do reiterate certain choices, often exceeding the conventional perimeters they set for themselves. In that sense, both texts showcase formal innovation as a way of articulating fundamental principles about the nature of authority. Specifically, in the cycle plays, audience address is key to the way that lordly authority is imagined to operate. Indeed, it is the Wakefield Master's relentless, sometimes perverse attention to audience address that gives special force to the dramatic theorization of sovereignty: what is the relationship between audience recognition and the construction of sovereignty, and, critically, what are

---

[21] In William Thorpe's *Testimony*, Archbishop Thomas Arundel examines Thorpe on the question of image-worship, arguing that the cross is Christ's insignia, attesting to his authority, to which is owed worship. In this way, argues Arundel, might we not compare Christ's cross to the letters that earthly lords send out, sealed with personal devices ('armes') or privy seals? After all, when men receive these letters 'in which thei seen and knowen her willis and the heestis of her lordis, in worship of her lordis thei don of her cappis or her hoodis to her lettris' (Anne Hudson (ed.) *Two Wycliffite Texts*, EETS, OS 301 (Oxford: Oxford University Press, 1993), ll. 1086–91) Thorpe answers simply that temporal lordship can't be compared to divine sovereignty.

the limits to that relationship? How is supreme authority extended or reflected through intermediaries, and what do mediating persons or instruments have to do with the way that authority is imagined to be received?

Authority and audience

Medieval literary texts are notoriously exhortative, alternately reassuring and reproving an audience imagined to be sceptical or disruptive. The narrator who exhorts the audience tries to establish the credentials of the narrative, its truth claims or entertainment value, or to explain the events to come. The unruly audience takes on a new incarnation in late medieval drama, in which the characters themselves are responsible for securing the audience's attention, as well as establishing claims to absolute authority, to power or truth. The Croxton 'Play of the Sacrament' (after 1461), for example, opens with elaborate 'heroic' boasts by the merchants Jonathas and Aristorius, who brag, not about martial or amorous conquest, but about the influence over others their wealth has bought them. Dramatic addresses such as these, not unlike God's creation speech, direct the boast to the imagined real audience, an audience supposed to be awed by the claims of the speaker, whose character the audience also helps to create.

Of course not all bids to supreme authority have equal weight. Lucifer's classic mistake is confusing mastery ('maistré') with sovereignty: as he declares to the audience and angels, 'For I am lord of blis, | Ouer all this warld, iwis, | My myrth is most of all; | The[r]for my will is this: | Master y[e] [s]hall me call' (Towneley, 'Creation', p. 6, ll. 94–8). God's authority, of course, is derived not from displays of mastery but rather from the infinite gap between creator and created. In the Towneley manuscript, however, exhortations to the audience tend to situate all claims to authority, and not just the claims of villains, in the context of audience recognition. In the 'Prophets' play, for example, Moses demands that the audience recognize the signs of authority embodied in the procession of prophets to follow: those who believe the prophets will be saved and those who doubt will be outlawed:

> When his tyme begynnys to day [approaches],
> I rede no man fro hym draw,
> In way ne stand on strut [offer resistance];
> For he that will not here his sagh [what he has to say],
> He be shewed as an outlagh,
> And from his folkys be putt [taken]. ('Play of the Prophets', pp. 63–4, ll. 13–18)

Moses is speaking from the long view of salvation history: the medieval Christian audience (the Church) stands in for the 'folk of Israel' who, if they believed the prophets, would later be saved with them. His address secures the attention of the viewers, and persuades them to suspend disbelief, both in the theatrical representation and in the content of the prophecies.[22] Yet, even though Moses is talking about salvation, the threat of outlawry recalls the rants of *potentates*, such as Pharaoh, Herod, and Caesar Augustus, for whom the presence of the audience is indispensable to the construction of authority, with dire consequences for those who fail to acknowledge it. These characters suffer from an overdeveloped sense of audience: to silence the audience is to dominate it.

Pharaoh, for example, identifies audience attention with submission to the will of a legitimate authority—to pay attention to the play is 'take tente to' the 'soferand syre' and obey his will.

> And of youre wordys look that ye seasse;
> Take tent to me, youre soferand [sovereign] syre,
> That may youre comfort most increasse,
> And to my lyst [pleasure] bowe lyfe and lyre [flesh and blood].
>
> ('Pharoah', p. 72, ll. 21–4)

In the cases of meglomaniacs such as Herod and Caesar Augustus, the declaration of supreme authority entails violent punishments for uncooperative members of the audience:

> Be styll, beshers [sirs], I commawnd yow,
> That no man speke a word here now
> Bot I myself alon;
> And if ye do, I make avow
> Thys brand abowte youre nekys shall bow;
> Forthy be styll as ston.   ('Caesar Augustus', p. 84, ll. 1–6)

In the Wakefield 'Killing of Abel' play, Cain takes pains to resemble these other bullies, yet his confrontation with the audience launches a complicated investigation into the nature of sovereignty and its relation to audience. Throughout the 'Killing of Abel', Cain assumes not only that supreme authority, human or divine, requires an audience to be realized, but also that authority operates entirely with an audience in mind. The play supplies a motive for Abel's murder by portraying Cain as a deeply angry person, whose character is initially formed by Cain's complaint to God at Genesis 4: 14, 'every one therefore that findeth me, shall kill me.' Well before God accuses him of homicide, Cain presumes that the audience will judge him, and tries to intimidate them accordingly ('And if any of you think I did amis, | I shal it amend wars than it is, | That all men may it se', ll. 331–3). And from the very beginning of the play, Cain is already the hounded outcast that he becomes after Abel's death. The problem with Cain, we discover, is that he has pathologically subjected himself to the recognition of others, through which he attempts to demonstrate supreme authority.

---

[22] On audience address in the cycle plays, see Hans-Jürgen Diller, *The Middle English Mystery Play: A Study in Dramatic Speech and Form*, trans. Frances Wessels (Cambridge: Cambridge University Press, 1992), 122–44.

The 'Killing of Abel' begins with Cain's warm-up man, his sassy farmhand, who, claiming to represent the will of his master, threatens the audience with curses should anyone dare to speak: 'Be peasse youre dyn, my master bad, | Or els the dwill you spede. | Wote ye not I com before? | Bot who that ianglis any more, | He must blaw my blak hoill bore ... ' (Quiet your noise, orders my master | or may the devil cause you to prosper. | Don't you know who's before you? | He who continues to chatter | Must blow my black hole) (p. 12, ll. 3–7). If Cain's servant exists to point up the difference between master–servant and God–Man relations, he also shows how authority operates through the intermediary effects—persons or instruments—that are the province of theatre. Indeed, Cain goes on to dismiss divine authority, not precisely because he holds God to be categorically irrelevant,[23] but rather because he insists upon substituting for divine authority those manifestations of human lordship that require recognition. It is telling that it is a peculiar feature of the play that God never gives Cain the protective mark. He merely assures Cain that no one will hurt him, but Cain discounts this assurance, prompting his servant to proclaim a fictive royal pardon. A comic interlude ensues in which Cain cues the lines and his servant spoofs them.

> Caym: The kyng wrytys you vntill,
> Garcio: Yit ete I neuer half my fill.
> Caym: The kyng will that thay be safe.
> Garcio: Yey, a draght of drynke fayne wolde I hayfe   (ll. 429–32)

In this way, the pardon functions as a reprise of the servant's opening address: in Cain's view, there is little distinction between blasphemous rant and official address: both reduce authority to its intermediary instruments and commit it into the hands of an audience.[24] Cain's proclamation is supposed to be the expression of the will of the sovereign, extended through the written document, as well as through the lord's servant who proclaims it. In the 'Killing of Abel', the proclamation is disconnected from any authorizing body; in presenting it, moreover, the servant executes the will neither of his master nor of the absent king.

This scene is comic because it shows Cain's ineffectual appropriation of supreme authority based on a misreading of all authority, whether human or divine. At the same time, it uses dramatic conventions to lay bare the structures with which authority works. As this essay shows, medieval writers, poets and playwrights, invented theories about lordly authority, not by exposing contradictions or urging

---

[23] V. A. Kolve, *A Play Called Corpus Christi* (Stanford, CA: Stanford University Press, 1966), 217.

[24] The pardon itself is a strange cross between a royal protection, requesting that the bearers be given safe conduct, and a royal pardon, releasing Cain and his servant from blame. Technically royal pardons for homicide pardoned the offence and not the guilt of the crime, either because the motive for the act was excusable, as in the case of self-defence, or because someone of high rank had supplicated the king on behalf of the accused. See Naomi D. Hunard, *The King's Pardon for Homicide before A.D. 1307* (Oxford: Clarendon Press, 1969), and numerous examples of these pardons in the *Calendar of the Patent Rolls Preserved in the Public Record Office, 1383–84* (London: HM Stationery Office, 1891–).

reform, but by expressing ideas and principles that had not yet emerged in other discourses, discourses in which those ideas and principles would seem more likely to appear. These writers seem to have recognized an intrinsic link between the articulation of fundamental principles and the 'produced effects' of literary texts, as if the capacity to innovate formally were related to the capacity to create new categories of thought. Further exploration of the link between formal experiment and social and political theory promises to open up new ways of thinking about medieval authority.

FURTHER READING

On authority and political symbolism, see Susan Crane, *The Performance of Self: Ritual, Clothing and Identity in the Hundred Years War* (Philadelphia: University of Pennsylvania Press, 2002); Helen Barr, *Socioliterary Practice in Late Medieval England* (Oxford: Oxford University Press, 2001); Paul Strohm, *England's Empty Throne: Usurpation and the Language of Legitimation, 1399–1422* (New Haven: Yale University Press, 1998). For examples of studies of the relationship between hierarchy and discourse, see Emily Steiner and Candace Barrington (eds.), *The Letter of the Law: Legal Practice and Literary Production in Medieval England* (Ithaca, NY: Cornell University Press, 2002); David Wallace, *Chaucerian Polity* (n. 5 above); Steven Justice and Kathryn Kerby-Fulton (eds.), *Written Work: Langland, Labor, Authorship* (Philadelphia: University of Pennsylvania Press, 1997); Rita Copeland (ed.), *Criticism and Dissent in the Middle Ages* (Cambridge: Cambridge University Press, 1996); Lawrence Scanlon, *Narrative, Authority, and Power: The Medieval Exemplum and the Chaucerian Tradition* (Cambridge: Cambridge University Press, 1994); and David Aers, *Community, Gender and Individual Identity in English Writing: 1360–1430* (London: Routledge, 1988).

On medieval theories of authorship, see Alistair Minnis and Ian Johnson (eds.), *The Cambridge History of Literary Criticism*, ii: *The Middle Ages* (Cambridge: Cambridge University Press, 2005); Rita Copeland, *Rhetoric, Hermeneutics and Translation* (n. 3); and Alistair Minnis, *The Medieval Theory of Authorship* (n. 2). On Chaucer, the Chaucerians, and authorship, see Seth Lerer, *Chaucer and his Readers: Imagining the Author in Late Medieval England* (Princeton: Princeton University Press, 1993); Ethan Knapp, *The Bureaucratic Muse: Thomas Hoccleve and the Literature of Late Medieval England* (University Park: Pennsylvania State University Press, 2001); Andrew Galloway, 'Authority', in Peter Brown (ed.), *Blackwell Companion to Chaucer* (Oxford: Blackwell, 2000), 23–39; and Maura Nolan, *John Lydgate and the Making of Public Culture* (Cambridge: Cambridge University Press, 2005).

On biblical translation and Latinity, see Kantik Ghosh, *The Wycliffite Heresy: Authority and the Interpretation of Texts* (Cambridge: Cambridge University Press, 2002); Fiona Somerset, *Clerical Discourse and Lay Audience in Late Medieval England* (Cambridge: Cambridge University Press, 1998); and Nicholas Watson, 'Censorship and Cultural Change in Late-Medieval England: Vernacular Theology, the Oxford Translation Debate, and Arundel's Constitutions of 1409', *Speculum: A Journal of Medieval Studies*, 70/4 (1995), 822–64.

For the practical operations of lordship, see D. Vance Smith, *Arts of Possession: The Medieval Household Imaginary* (Minneapolis: University of Minnesota Press, 2003), ch. 4; Ffiona Swabey, *Medieval Gentlewoman: Life in a Gentry Household in the Later Middle Ages* (New York: Routledge, 1999); C. M. Woolgar, *The Great Household in Late Medieval England* (New Haven: Yale University Press, 1999); Christopher Dyer, *Standards of Living in the Later Middle Ages* (Cambridge: Cambridge University Press, 1989), chs. 2–4; and Chris Given-Wilson, *English Nobility in the Later Middle Ages* (London: Routledge, 1987).

On authority in medieval English theatre, see Ruth Nisse, *Defining Acts: Drama and the Politics of Interpretation in Late Medieval England* (Notre Dame, IN: Notre Dame University Press, 2005); Lynn Forest-Hill, *Transgressive Language in Medieval English Drama* (London: Ashgate, 2000); Lawrence M. Clopper, 'English Drama: From Ungodly *Ludi* to Sacred Play', in David Wallace (ed.), *The Cambridge History of Medieval English Literature* (Cambridge: Cambridge University Press, 1999), 739–66; Claire Sponsler, *Drama and Resistance: Bodies, Goods, and Theatricality in Late Medieval England* (Minneapolis: University of Minnesota Press, 1997); Sarah Beckwith, *Christ's Body: Identity, Culture, and Society in Late Medieval Writings* (London: Routledge, 1993); and Lauren Lepow, *Enacting the Sacrament: Counter-Lollardy in the Towneley Cycle* (Teaneck, NJ: Fairleigh Dickinson University Press, 1991).

CHAPTER 11

INSTITUTIONS

D. VANCE SMITH

Literature is that ensemble of objects and rules, techniques and works, whose function in the general economy of our society is precisely to institutionalize subjectivity.

(Roland Barthes, 'History or Literature')

Dying before writing: institutional histories of institutions

The hall of Fame in Chaucer's *The House of Fame* may be as close as the Middle Ages comes, outside the monastery, to what Erving Goffman called in his famous study of asylums a 'total institution'.[1] In Fame's hall, the afterlives of works and their writers are subjected to her arbitrary but supreme judgement, and she consigns them justly or unjustly to oblivion or renown. Even speech acts, 'tydynges', lose their identity, becoming 'fals and soth compouned' (l. 2108) because of their sheer profusion.[2] Tellingly, the narrator observes that there are more of these 'tydynges' than all the people who have died (l. 2040). This sort of institution demands a compliance from its members so extreme and depersonalizing that Goffman described the process of joining as one of 'mortification'.[3] In obvious and brutal ways, but also in insidious slights and insults, a total institution leaves no room for idiosyncrasy and little for personal identity.

The monastery, of course, differs from modern institutions in both the willingness of its inmates to belong to it and the metaphysical and religious ideas that are its justification and purpose. Mortification, in that context, is the deeply fulfilling exercise of becoming dead to the world in order to live more fully. The third

---

[1] Erving Goffman, *Asylums: Essays on the Social Situation of Mental Patients and Other Inmates* (New York: Anchor, 1961), 4.

[2] *The Riverside Chaucer*, ed. Larry Benson (Boston: Houghton Mifflin, 1987).

[3] An indication of the extent of mortification is given by Goffman's synonyms for it: 'disidentification' (*Asylums*, 23), 'contaminative exposure' (p. 25), 'disfigurement' (p. 35), 'defilement' (p. 35), and 'loss of self-determination' (p. 44).

degree of humility in the Benedictine Rule is 'that for the love of God a man subject himself to a Superior in all obedience, imitating the Lord, of whom the Apostle saith: "He became obedient unto death" (Phil 2: 8)'.[4] As readers of *The Canterbury Tales* will remember, however, monasteries in practice, and even in imagination, were seldom totalizing in Goffman's sense of the word. Chaucer's Monk deviates so far and so flagrantly from the austere precepts of the Benedictine Rule that his portrait has become a condensation of various relaxations of monastic discipline, whether real or imagined. It embodies this relaxation, of course, in the form of the Monk's outrageous sophistry, but also in the form of affiliation with other institutions, such as the free-floating but ubiquitous institution of aristocratic hunting.

The reforms of the Benedictine order, and particular, local reassertions of its precepts, were not undertaken because the application of the Rule had become too strict and depersonalizing—as the Monk says, 'somdeel streit'—but because the institutional identity of monasteries had become contaminated by the practices of other institutions. They had begun, in some ways, to become other institutions than the places of mortification imagined in the Rule. Abbots certainly attempted to realign their institutions with their primitive principles, both by creating new ordinals and prohibiting, as Abbot de le Mare of St Albans did, monks from keeping dogs, bows, and knives.[5] But other changes occurred precisely because other institutions inevitably contaminated the original sixth-century vision of the cenobitic life. The success of the mendicant orders in England encouraged fourteenth-century Benedictine houses to increase the resources and duration of novitiate education, even to the extent of setting up separate *studia* at places like St Albans and larger ones at Oxford.[6]

One lesson of the Monk's portrait is the limits of what I would call the institutional history of institutions, reliance on the documents and archives that institutions themselves generate in order to come to terms with the means by which they established their identities and practices. At some level, we can become members of, if not collaborators in the creation of, total institutions that obliviate our own initiative, our own ability to see how institutions operated in more complex, that is to say, in less perfect, ways. This is a problem we as literary historians need to confront even when we think about the context of a work: we obviously need to understand how the various social institutions within which a work was written shape it, and how it stands—to the degree that any work of literature is exceptional—outside the institution. But we cannot forget to ask how the concept

[4] *The Rule of St. Benedict*, ed. Timothy Fry (Collegeville, MN: Liturgical Press, 1981).
[5] James G. Clark, *A Monastic Renaissance at St. Albans: Thomas Walsingham and his Circle, 1350–1444* (Oxford: Oxford University Press, 2004), 23–4. For fuller discussions of the relaxations and reassertions of monastic rule in the fourteenth century, see Barbara Harvey, *Living and Dying in England, 1100–1540: The Monastic Experience* (Oxford: Clarendon Press, 1993), 77–81.
[6] Clark, *A Monastic Renaissance*, 45–72.

of a work emerges in the first place. In other words, we need also to ask ourselves whether we can, in any way, stand outside of *our institution of the literary*.[7]

In a formal sense, this problem is true of any writing: as long as we believe it to possess powers of continuity and expression that no individual can have, we invest it with a sacrality—some people call it formalism—that keeps us incomplete, profane, and, in the root sense of the word, idiotic. I think most of the power of that unforgettable passage from Hoccleve's *Regement of Princes* comes from his extraordinary awareness of how the quotidian, institutional work of writing for the Office of the Privy Seal keeps him outside of himself:

> ...we labour in trauaillous stilnesse;
> We stowpe and stare vp-on the shepes skyn,
> And keepe muste our song and wordes in.[8]

Like Hoccleve, we imagine the institution within the horizon of the written, as the enduring legacy of the contingent choices and whims of human individuals. Institutions come about because we need to believe that an agency beyond us can collate and keep our desires, moments, words, in a form that will outlast each of those evanescent instants. But more importantly institutions are necessary because they keep from us the very act of willfulness that initiates them, the imposition—the institution—of the individual will on social flux. In a sense, they inaugurate death, because they extend the duration of desire and will beyond the span of an individual life, and their very being commemorates the incapacity of a human to act in that stead.

In a more sinister fashion, as Hoccleve realized, institutions create, especially for the people who labour in them, that peculiar state of disaffection, that is, an alienation from our own affections, that Durkheim, in *The Division of Labor in Society*, first described as anomie. In a fascinating extension of this logic, Lukács, in his early and eloquent work *The Theory of the Novel*, recognized that not only do institutions figuratively and literally deaden experience, the initiatives we take through our senses, but they themselves are the archive of our senses: 'the nature of man-made structures ... is a complex of senses which has become rigid and strange, and which no longer awakens interiority; it is a charnel-house of long dead interiorities.'[9] Institutions embody and reify dead labour time, the living death of the worker. But sometimes we want them to do that, not just to take us from ourselves but also to record our presence and to plead on our behalf.

---

[7] Important works in this question include John Guillory, *Cultural Capital: The Problem of Literary Canon Formation* (Chicago: University of Chicago Press, 1993); Susan R. Horton, 'The Institution of Literature and the Cultural Community', in Joseph Natoli (ed.), *Literary Theory's Future(s)* (Urbana: University of Illinois Press, 1989), 270.

[8] Thomas Hoccleve, *The Regement of Princes*, ed. F. J. Furnivall, EETS, ES 72 (London, 1897; repr. New York: Krauss, 1988), ll. 1009–29.

[9] Georg Lukács, *Theory of the Novel: A Historico-Philosophical Essay on the Forms of Great Epic Literature*, trans. Anna Bostock (Cambridge, MA: MIT Press, 1971), 64.

The accumulated death of those not yet dead gives mortuary guilds their institutional effectiveness. By paying into a guild and commemorating the deaths of former members, one could, in effect, institutionalize one's own death. In order to save your life, you had to turn it into a communal property. It becomes a no-longer-individual form of being, a category not of being, but of registration, subject to the capacity of the guild to record and enact your commitment to death.[10] On the face of it, this submission to an institution is, in terms of economic anthropology, not much different from what is wrested from us, anyway, by the institutions of capital. This account of the necessity of dying communally in order to die fully, too, might be precisely the inauthentic kind of death that Heidegger argued depends upon the institution of representation, that is, the insistence of what 'they' tell me my own death means, my own willingness to be caught in and by representation. But Heidegger's refusal of representation and sociality in his adequation (a word I use advisedly, given his profound knowledge of medieval Parisian logic) of authenticity and the 'ownmost' makes institutionality an aspect of the *Gesell* of which he was so suspicious. His student Hannah Arendt was suspicious, too, of the force of 'normalization that takes us away from ourselves', yet her critique of Heidegger suggests how we might begin to think of mortuary institutions in complexly productive ways. As Julia Kristeva's eloquent framing of Arendt's critique of Heidegger puts it, 'the gravity of being-for-death [in Heidegger is] transformed by Arendt into a succession, less desolate than shining, of *ephemeral strangers* who disappear only when dislodged by the surprising birth of newcomers'.[11] The mortuary guild as an initiative—indeed, the institution as an initiative—would then encompass, if not anticipate, wait eagerly for, the newcomer, whose presence is crucial and necessary precisely because it is expected but not understood by 'those who are already there', as Arendt puts it, 'and are going to leave in a short while'.[12]

A fuller account of the institutional work of mortuary guilds and chantry chapels, in other words, need not rest on our institutionalized inheritance of notions of authenticity, individuality, and a hermeneutics of suspicion. Coming to terms with the instituting work of medieval institutions, that is, requires us at the very least to allow the representations by which they institute themselves to continue to do their work. Perhaps because institutions become successful by appearing to do something that can be done in no other way, or even by appearing to be rooted in nature or necessity, the means by which they reproduce their authority seems to be a mere epiphenomenon of the continuity that they guarantee. Mary Douglas's critique of

---

[10] On mortuary guilds, see Caroline M. Barron, 'The London Middle English Guild Certificates of 1388–9. I: Historical Introduction', *Nottingham Mediaeval Studies*, 39 (1995), 108–18; for chantry chapels see K. L. Wood-Legh's classic *Perpetual Chantries in Britain* (Cambridge: Cambridge University Press, 1965).

[11] Julia Kristeva, *Hannah Arendt: Life is a Narrative* (Toronto: University of Toronto Press, 2001), 25.

[12] Hannah Arendt, 'The Concept of History', in *Between Past and Future* (Harmondsworth: Penguin, 1993), 61.

Durkheim reminds us of how institutions, at least in Durkheim's understanding of them, encourage us to forget just this structural dependence upon individual initiative. Where Durkheim thought of institutions as macrocosmic minds that think for each of us, Douglas argues that the relation is just the other way around: a mind is a microcosmic institution.[13] More recently, Samuel Weber and other theorists of social formation have been more insistent about the insidious effects, including on the institution of sociology itself, of this forgetting of initiative in institutions.

As others have done, Weber locates two opposing impulses in institutions. The first, which Douglas described as the naturalizing tendency of institutions, Weber describes as 'the instituted [*l'institue*], the established order, the already existing norms'. This aspect of institutions tends to become stronger over time, and stronger, as Weber argues, in theory as well, so that it eventually comes to be confused with the state of law itself. Institutions strengthen their authority in this way because their second impulse tends to be forgotten. Their

> instituting aspect [*l'instituant*] ... has been increasingly obscured. The political impli-
> cation of the sociological theories appears clearly here. By emptying the concept of
> institution of one of its primordial components (that of instituting, in the sense of
> founding, creating, breaking with an old order and creating a new one), sociology has
> finally come to identify the institution with the status quo.[14]

Yet sociological theory has tended to efface this distinction also by emphasizing its radically subjective alternative, in the form of rational choice theory, which suggests that institutions are formed out of a continuous voluntary relinquishment of self-determination in order to preserve self-autonomy.[15] And even influential theorists of the relation between the constitution of subjectivity and institutions, such influential thinkers as Max Weber, Foucault, and Cornelius Castoriadis, have tended to analyse the 'instituting' as a function of the institution's reproduction. Apart from Arendt, few theorists of the institution have pursued Heidegger's argument that this instituting function represents both the potentiality of a radical break with the institution and its potential for originality. As it happens, Heidegger works this out most clearly in a reflection on poetry: 'Poetry is a founding [*Stiftung*, instituting] by the word and in the word ... Poetry is the founding [*Stiftung*] of being in the world.'[16] Lurking behind this assertion, however, is his equation of poetry with Romantic original genius, an equation that is not entirely accurate for

---

[13] See *How Institutions Think* (Syracuse, NY: Syracuse University Press, 1986).

[14] Samuel Weber, *Institution and Interpretation* (Palo Alto, CA: Stanford University Press, 2001), p. xv.

[15] For an attempt to recuperate this aspect of rational choice theory, see Meir Dan-Cohen, 'Conceptions of Choice and Conceptions of Autonomy', in *Harmful Thoughts: Essays on Law, Self, and Morality* (Princeton: Princeton University Press, 2002), 125–49.

[16] 'Holderlin and the Essence of Poetry', in *Elucidations of Hölderlin's Poetry*, trans. Keith Hoeller (Amherst, NY: Humanity Books, 2000), 58–9.

thinking about medieval writing. Poetry (*Dichtung*) opens up a 'truth that … is never to be proven by or derived from what came before it … Instituting is an excess.'[17] How, then, can we understand the relationship between the institution and writing in a period before writing is itself an institution?

From writing to institution

We can begin by thinking of writing as the act of *instituting*, breaking not from an institution of writing—that is, literature—but from institutions of being, in which being is contained, represented, held, for the sake of individuals. That is, we can begin by thinking of writing as a *break* with the homologies between institutional forms of inscription and tropes, or between the causes of literature and the pressures of an institution. Much recent work on late medieval devotion has done that well, but always leaves us with the questions of what is left behind, what order of experience and sensation might be encrypted by the relation of writing to institution, what complex of senses remains unawakened in it. Why write instead of pray? Why turn to rhymed stanzas instead of to the already mysterious and complex words of the daily offices? Why turn to poetry, if poetry is really ethics, which is really philosophy? We discover a different relation between the work of literature and the work of human institutions when we think of the institutions that need to be produced within the written, institutions which are the product of imagination and of a struggle for identity. I want to think about institutions that need to be invented—invented as things already existing, waiting to be found beyond the horizon of the writing that produces them—rather than merely the formal institutions of government, Church, and sociality. In order to achieve this vantagepoint, we must accept that the form of a work—something about its *literary* quality—allows us to discover its own institution.

I do not mean that institutional documents cannot amount to a kind of poetry—a possibility Paul Strohm demonstrated in several chapters of *Hochon's Arrow* and that Lisa Cooper weighs elsewhere in this collection—and that they cannot embody a kind of initiative. I do want to argue that once we read them in this way, we have ceased to read them for their institutional importance and have begun to read them for their deviant sensibility. This sensibility enables them to accomplish a work that we do not quite recognize but with which we find ourselves sympathizing. Every registration in an archive of an injunction, an obligation, a debt, is also a wish that it were otherwise, a wish that such a registration were not necessary, that one did not have to come before the institution in the first place. To identify with the movement of the institution is to identify with what undoes us, to efface something

---

[17] 'The Origin of the Work of Art', in *Poetry, Language, Thought*, trans. Albert Hofstadter (New York: Harper and Row, 1971), 61.

of the particularity of the act of inscription if not the act of literature in an age before its institution.

This argument might seem to imply little more than a crude formalism, an insistence that we understand the literary on its own terms. To insist that we do is also to resist the work of specifically literary institutions, the encouragement to think that what we read can never really change things, can never really alter the constitution of the world, of the institutions in which we, now, are caught. We need to keep in mind the active work that institutions do to propagate themselves, to define themselves, and to draw on the resources of narrative form in order to do so. T. F. Tout's extraordinary, vast history of the development of just two departments of the government in the years after the Norman Conquest in his *Chapters in Mediaeval Administrative History*, for example, shows how dynamic and contingent institutions are, even when at any given point they define themselves as unchanging and permanent. Diachronic institutional studies like Tout's remind us that institutions also carry with them their inbuilt critique, the exceptions to the permanence of their registrations that are, in the end, the exceptions on which they are founded: the flux of social change and individual initiative that makes institutions 'law positive' rather than natural law.

The question of how we get from writing to institutions is especially complex for the Middle Ages, because there were no institutions of writing, in the sense that we know them, yet, no sociological category for the possibility of non-instrumental writing. The question is how to think of the relation between writing and institutions before, for example, the Academie Française, the introduction of literature as a formal academic study in the university, the appearance of technologies that made it possible for literature to be appear as more—or less—than an expensive, hieratic, and fetishized object.

There were certainly institutions that produced writing, and for which writing was often a central, even constitutive, activity. But for these institutions writing was always a mere trace of more important activity, for which it served as the formal registration of decisions made and disputes settled off the page. No prisoner was ever set free, no fortune restored, no life saved or lost *solely* because of the act of writing. That may never have come about, although such narratives as Kafka's *The Penal Colony*, in which death is administered by a writing machine, make literal and immediate a vaguer, and more abstract, sense in which writing is a metonym of the array of extra-subjective technologies of order, containment, and repression that come into being—or are at least intensified—in the current situation.

The Middle Ages has its own fantasies about the institutional force, the energy of imposition, that writing represents. We live, after all, in a world that is a book written by the hand of God. But a book is not the same thing as an institution, especially before the advent of the repeatable—that is, the printed—book. Indeed the book often implies a deeply anti-humanist position, the impossibility of the individual initiative, at the very least, and, at the very worst, the impossibility of human initiative in general. In Bernardus Silvestris's wonderful 1147 poem *Cosmographia* Physis writes a book that records the ceaseless movement of the cosmos in the form of a register of being:

> Here was shown the coming-to-be of all that generation draws forth to substance and the passing away from substance of those things whom corruption destroys. In such a great multitude of natures Physis discovered only with great labor the shadowy [form] of man, faint at the very end of the final page.[18]

The metabolism, the change and exchange of the cosmos, is not what resists resolution here, but the location of the human, the one creature, or so say Aristotle and Nietzsche, subjected to the burden of recollection, the compulsion to preserve, to fix things, above all themselves and their experiences, outside of change—that is, to engage in the activity of institution. Within the initiative of human memory, driven by the impulse to preserve, we discover that we have actually undone the lucid form of our incessant contingency. That is, if we could actually see what we bequeath to the cosmos, as in the kind of thing we might write, we would find that we have only succeeded in dwindling to the shadowy form of a general thing.

We might expect this kind of anti-humanist scepticism in an idealizing Neoplatonist work of the twelfth century, but we find the same result in writers celebrated for their deep humanism. In Geoffrey Chaucer, for example, whose *Canterbury Tales* Dryden famously celebrated as 'God's plenty', we often glimpse deep and disquieting encounters with the disjunction between the principles institutions embody and the practices they not only tolerate but seem to generate. It is not surprising beginning students often mistake the General Prologue's critique of deviations from institutional obligation for a critique of the institutions themselves. But this may not be an altogether naive reading, especially when it comes to institutions that are being deliberately and systematically rearranged, reoriented, and rethought in the fourteenth century—above all chivalry, whose internal contradictions Chaucer charts more astutely than any other writer does in the Middle Ages. But a large part of the attraction, the sheer enjoyment, of his engagement with chivalry, is the overwhelming sense that it is a proxy for the impossibility of writing that way, of writing as a cosmological exercise, or at the very least as an institution among other institutions. In *The House of Fame* Chaucer's dreamer discovers that the institution of literature is completely unmoored from human initiative, that it has absolutely nothing to do with judgement or value. At the end of the poem the dreamer finds himself in a vast house of twigs, whirling around as fast as the speed of thought, hearing everything that has been uttered before in the world. As anyone who has read the poem knows, it breaks off just at the point where we are about to meet a 'man of gret auctoritee', and we never find out, in effect, how order can be imposed

---

[18] *The Cosmographia of Bernardus Silvestris*, trans. Winthrop Wetherbee (New York: Columbia University Press, 1973), 2. 11.

on the cacophony of the poet's sensorium, how to extricate a practice out of the institution of writing as Chaucer imagines it at that point, a scene that is less an institution than what Jean-Luc Marion has called a saturated phenomenon.[19]

Of course, because the wicker house includes all the sounds there are, the question here might be 'the institution, as opposed to what?' We hear nothing, literally, that is not part of the institution that lies at the end of the dream. It is both the genesis and the limit of aurality, which is shaped and determined by what must be contained in the house, or by the way in which sound must be contained there. Anyone who had studied elementary grammar in the Middle Ages, as Chaucer surely had, could not forget that words are a special case of sound. They are the product of human intelligence and, furthermore, mean anything at all because of what humans have arbitrarily agreed that they mean, by what various writers called convention, habit, or imposition. We can also call speech an institution.

The logic of institutions

Yet, again and again both Chaucer and the garrulous eagle demonstrate that the only principles that shape the institution of speech are physical (the 'breaking' of air, the melting of writing), and that it, too, is putatively subject to the sorting institutions of nature. Everything returns eventually to its limit, its starting and ending point, by what the eagle describes, in his beautiful borrowing of Boethius, as 'kindly enclyning'. That is, the disorder—really the complete anarchy—found in both the temple and the house is the result, the *production* (the leading forth) of principles of absolute regularity and determinacy. If a shadow did not keep the sun's heat from melting some of the names inscribed on ice, if some of the sounds uttered did not happen to return all the way to their origin, then the institution of fame would really be as arbitrary as we are supposed to think that it is. This is another way of discovering that the *House of Fame*'s real trick is to convince us of the necessity of institutions, especially when we can see that their work, in effect, deranges what we know to be the order of things. The principles of taste or judgement we use to demonstrate, in a dialectical sense, that one author is better than another do not matter, precisely because those principles are not institutionalized. That is, they are not part of the institution of fame (as Chaucer imagines it), not enough to save or recuperate a writer with the logic of institution. The point in the poem is not to know what that logic is, just to demonstrate that there is one, and that it supersedes any human initiative, no matter how capaciously, humanely, or beautifully imagined it is.

---

[19] See Jean-Luc Marion, *In Excess: Studies of Saturated Phenomena*, trans. Robyn Horner and Vincent Berraud (New York: Fordham University Press, 2002).

The way in which institutional logic trumps human initiative and covers over the law of *kynde* with its inscrutable set of impulses and commands, the way we are fascinated and horrified by Fame's unthinking enthusiasms and hatreds, suggests that one of the poem's topics is the inquietude of human agency. Fame's institution is both deeply human—the desire and capacity for narrative, for something that extends beyond the moment—and exclusive of the human. We want to be more than ourselves, but to want that requires us to give up our own will, to subordinate it to the demands of something that is not quite human—for then we would just be wanting to be someone else, which is not what writing is about. Or perhaps we can just think of *The House of Fame* as the institution of, to paraphrase Ethan Knapp, the bureaucratic imaginary.[20]

The House of Fame's temple and house are uncannily like the central offices of English government, to which all discord and dissatisfaction ultimately returned in one form or another. Whether in the form of an unpleasant, unexpected tax that someone did not want to pay to the Exchequer, an inquiry over that refusal, an order to pay the resultant fine, hearings over the ensuing violence, what the central departments of the royal household collected was sowed in arbitrariness—the king's will, or the will of the barons or nobles who prevailed on him—and yielded dissatisfaction and discord. The extent to which the records of the poll taxes of 1379–81 and of the inquisitions that followed the Rising of 1381 have in recent years been treated as traces either of broader social strategies of resistance or of the failures of institutions partially misses the point, which is that these records demonstrate the perfection of the institution. I do not mean the obvious point that these records all emanate from institutions that opposed the Rising. I mean that all institutions fail in just this way, although not often as visibly. They are all founded on a logic that purports to be utterly internally consistent—that is what makes them institutions, what gives and continues an institution's singularity. But something about that logic must be inscrutable, or an institution would be identical to a self. We would always know how others will act, or know that we can merely think their actions into being (violence is, after all, just the first institution). What must remain inscrutable are the means by which institutions persuade us that they are acting on our initiative (the crude version is George Bush's declaration that the 'American people' want security, or something else) when in principle they act despite our will. I am not trying to make the merely deconstructive claim that institutions are impossible, but to argue that it is the very capacity of institutions to act that must, necessarily, deprive us of our own capacity to act, and yet to believe—and to truly believe—that they embody the human capacity for initiative.

Allowing institutions and their representations to continue to work may involve, in fact, an assumption that at first seems to be another version of the hermeneutics

---

[20] Ethan Knapp, *The Bureaucratic Muse: Thomas Hoccleve and the Literature of Late Medieval England* (University Park: Pennsylvania State University Press, 2001).

of suspicion. There is often more that lurks behind transactions and records than we may at first suspect, and *that* 'more' is sometimes precisely what we would like to know more about. Yet that is often just what medieval institutions do not record because it is so much a part of the ground people walked on that they would not necessarily think to explain it. Nowhere in the copious records of the four major *Curia militaris* trials in the fourteenth century over the right to bear a particular coat of arms is there an explanation of why that right mattered so much that fortunes were spent in prosecuting or defending these rights.[21] We might be able to glimpse the importance the fourteenth century attached to heraldry in imaginative literature, which unravels part of the complex tangle of ideas that the institution of heraldry gathered together. But such accounts are adjacent, at best, to the real practice of institutions, and, at worst, vestigial. How do we explain the great reluctance to join the institution of knighthood in the fourteenth century on the part of men who not only could become knights but were legally required to? Nothing in *Curia militaris* records, Exchequer records (from where so-called writs of distraint were issued), or, at least directly, in imaginative literature explains this. But, as I argue in my *Arts of Possession*, we can begin to understand what happens when we read the documents generated by these different institutions in conjunction with each other.

Institutions sometimes tell us more than we ought to know. We can misread the stories institutions tell about themselves as accounts of their practices, rather than as the stories they tell to legitimize themselves. An institution will always confirm accounts of its own genesis and function, since part of its job is to produce forms of sameness and identity among both its subjects and its representations. Compare Chaucer's description of the institution of heraldry in *The House of Fame*, which is subjected to the same kinds of defamiliarization and objectification that other institutions in the poem are. One group of people, which at first seems to be a crowd of kings, turns out to be simply a throng of heralds in their tabards and crowns of office. Instead of describing them as registrars of bloodlines, signs, and historical prerogative, Chaucer simply describes them as a group who 'crien riche folks laudes'. That may be what they did, but no account of heraldry internal to the institution describes its work in anything like those terms.

In two completely different discursive registers, the institutional story of heraldry seems to follow the same plot: it concerns a group of men identified by blood and the quality of being 'armigerous'. In the case of witnesses called before the *Curia militaris*, that double designation obviously worked practically. Using a formula established at the beginning of each trial, each witness testified that he was of 'gentil

---

[21] See G. D. Squibb, *The High Court of Chivalry: A Study in the Civil Law in England* (Oxford: Oxford University Press, 1959), 1–28. Transcripts of two hearings have been published in scarce editions: Harris Nicolas, *The Scrope and Grosvenor Controversy*, 2 vols. (London, 1832); C. G. Young, *An Account of the Controversy between Reginald Lord Grey of Ruthyn and Sir Edward Hastings* (London, 1841).

sanc' *and* stated the number of years that he had borne arms, either in the form of weapons or an escutcheon. The conflation of the two kinds of arms betrays a kind of confusion in the institutional history of heraldry itself, a confusion that reappears insistently despite the deliberate effort of heraldic writers to rationalize it. A large number of English treatises on heraldry from the first two decades of the fifteenth century begin with an account of how heraldry was instituted during the Trojan War, but their explanation of the term 'arms' is etymological rather than etiological. The term for a coat of arms arose simply because it records some previous, even ancestral, act of prowess: it was 'getten with strengith of mennis armis'. This account's contingency and indebtedness to locality and language is only revealed more clearly by other attempts in the early fifteenth century to legitimize the authority of the institution of heraldry in England. The Latinity of some treatises on heraldry mimics the scholarly, even institutional, authority with which the first treatise arrived in England with Queen Anne, written by the great jurist Bartolo di Sasseferrato. Yet they are obviously translated from those English treatises: the term 'armas', they say, comes from the 'strenuitas brachiorum', an explanation that only makes sense in English. But only in English does the confusion between the metonymic and symbolic functions of heraldry persist that widely and that long, and precisely because of the heraldic institution's effort to maintain the integrity of its own genesis, its own institutionalizing moment.

Even within its own history, however, institutional heraldry must include a revision of its genesis in order to protect its signifying prerogatives. It does so, at least in England, by inventing a moment of institution, at Troy, the birthplace of so many English institutions, including the governance of London itself. The descendants of the Trojans instituted heraldry a second time later in its history, however, because they 'had grete dispirite that the merchauntes shulde call theys merkes as they dide there [and] | they concentyd that they shulde no lenger be called markes but the merchants shulde calle them merkes And these men of worship that cam from Troye there merkes shulde be turnid and callyd armes in tokenyng that they were gotten with strengthe of men is armes.'[22] The very term 'arms' is a deliberate trope, at least for the institutional history of heraldry, that reminds its members that it has the power to nominate, delegitimize, or institute new conventions in order to preserve, paradoxically, its guarantee of natural legitimacy.

The institutional logic of logic

This is part of what we mean when we talk about the logic of an institution, its ability to shape what one can, and even wants to do, within its confines, to think

[22] British Library, Harley MS 992, fo. 14ʳ.

for us rather than *of* us. But in the most literal way logic is the act of thinking, and its discipline not only delimits but can open up the scope of thought. The institutional logic of logic in the late Middle Ages did differ between universities, and we can see a relation between it and the kinds of thinking that occurred in them. I want to examine the writing on logic that comes out of a very particular institution—Oxford in the thirteenth and fourteenth centuries. Logic would seem to be the very expression of institutional and impersonal knowledge, the trace of a *ratio* that has succeeded in winning the great battle with the passions, that might have had piss poured on its head but calmly continues to ask questions, as Socrates himself did. And indeed its own stated goals are to express nothing less than the truth, to extricate the mind from its own contingent, prejudiced, and arbitrary impulses.

A logic is the modus of an institution, but is it recognizable as such because of its institutional identity, its mere vicariousness, or because a logic produces the institution of which it is the expression? To answer this, I would like to consider the differences between the institutional logics of Oxford and Paris in the fourteenth century. In one sense, logic at Paris was the legacy of an abstract and enduring debt to institutionality. Its field of enquiry was the way in which the terms of language related to the structure of reality, and it assumed generally that the modes of signifying, understanding, and being are equivalent or isomorphic—in their language, adequate. What made this possible, though, was the assumption that language is artificially instituted, the result of acts of *impositio* that artificially and conventionally established a link between a term and a real object or event. It is, in short, a logic that assumes that language is an institution, and an institution that preserves its original act of institution, the *impositio* that enables the adequation of those three essential modes.[23]

This Parisian logic can be seen as the formal equivalent of the university's own institutional history and practice, which combined, in the fourteenth century, an unparalleled cosmopolitanism—drawing students from further afield than any other European university—a porous pedagogical system, in which students could move between masters easily, and a political structure made up of smaller micro-institutions that had their own historical and administrative independence. Paris logic, predicated on a series of ontological, epistemological, and representative isomorphs, was isomorphic with the institution itself. But the difference between Oxford and Parisian logic can also be attributed to the effect of each institution on the development of logic. Modistic grammar turned out to be, as Parisian masters were beginning to realize by the mid-fourteenth century, something of a dead

---

[23] For general discussion of *impositio* and its centrality to modistic or speculative grammar, see Jan Pinborg, 'Speculative Grammar', 254–69; Christian Knudsen, 'Intentions and Impositions', 479–95, both in Norman Kretzmann et al. (eds.), *The Cambridge History of Later Medieval Philosophy* (Cambridge: Cambridge University Press, 1982).

end, but because it was the dominant analytic mode and because a large, complex institution like Paris had a certain intellectual inertia, its logic continued largely unchanged until the third quarter of the fourteenth century. It changed under the increasing influence of Oxford logic, in fact, a discipline that was rooted in what was thought in Paris earlier in the century to be an old-fashioned terminist logic. Yet it was a logic that allowed Oxford to develop a highly supple, subtle, and powerful analytic logic known as supposition theory.

The conditions that allowed this to happen had a great deal to do with Oxford's pedagogical conservatism, which was due to its situation, at least in the late thirteenth century when modistic grammar was being developed at Paris, out of the academic mainstream, and its smaller size. The work of the members of a single college, Merton, is famous because of its extraordinary innovation, in both quantity and quality, but Merton stands for a larger school of Oxford thinking. Oxford logicians responded to the work of their colleagues in a variety of ways, and the textbooks themselves tended to change rapidly—unlike Paris, where the same texts remained important through the same period. And supposition theory itself, loosely speaking, allows us to think in more accommodating, discriminating ways about the condition of things, rather than continually requiring us to acknowledge an original institutional moment that we are powerless to change. Oxford masters, indeed, defended their right to debate *probabiles opiniones*, arguments capable of being proved regardless of their canonical or doctrinal status, in 1411 when Archbishop Arundel visited Oxford to excise the influence of Wyclif.[24] What has not been recognized before is the degree to which the dominance of supposition theory at Oxford determined specific modes of reading that almost certainly found their way into the writing of vernacular literature in England, and indeed may be related to the vernacularization of the Bible in the fourteenth century.

Against the logic of institution

Supposition theory is, in some ways, a remarkably anti-institutional mode of reading. It is not bound by the linkage of sign and object as in modistic grammar, and focuses on the particular quality of a proposition—its constituent elements and their interaction. It is a kind of suspension of belief in ontological fundamentals that we now would call the phenomenological reduction, and pursues a kind of reading that in literature departments has for a long time been known as formalism or close reading. Supposition theory concentrates on the givenness of a proposition, not on its context, its origin, or its instrumentality. It describes how a proposition works by analysing how its terms are modified, restricted, or expanded in a given

---

[24] See J. M. Fletcher, 'Developments in the Faculty of Arts', in *A History of the University of Oxford* (Oxford: Oxford University Press, 1992), 316–17.

sentence. In its simplest form, it recognized that in particular sentences the word 'homo', 'man', for example, could refer to itself as a term in a sentence (as it does here), it could refer to the universal concept 'man', it could refer to a particular man, it could refer to *this* man, it could refer to *every* particular man.

By analogy—what Oxford logicians would call 'improper supposition'—we can see how the work of Wyclif might emerge out of this rigorous formalism, how the work of that man opens up the work of logic to every man. Most important, his work opens up the Bible and its logic to a wider audience than just Mertonians and Oxford terminists. He opens it to those who read only the vernacular, and to those who have no training in the rigours of supposition theory. What Wyclif urges instead is a logic that emerges out of the reading of the Bible: 'the logic of scripture inheres in the form of the words and the mode of speaking.'[25] More explicitly than anywhere else in Oxford logical writing, that is, Wyclif urges a mode of close reading in which the very principles of reading are discovered by that process, an *immanente Deutung*. But it is also a kind of work that emerges out of (originating in, and moving beyond) the institution of logic at Oxford. Wyclif's career at Oxford is usually imagined as a fairly conventional, orthodox, although brilliant, one. His logic (in a massive two-part work), for example, has recently been described by Kantik Ghosh in his extraordinary book on Wyclif as 'uncontentious' because of its incorporation into unexceptionable collections of schools texts.[26] So it is, to the extent that Wyclif is representative of a logic that analyses propositions rather than primarily things, as at Paris. Yet his logical work at Oxford already intimates that he is moving out of the institution.

In his work on *insolubilia*, Wyclif moves beyond the contradictions and impasses that they pose not by refining the means by which they could be resolved, which was the traditional approach, nor by showing how an *insolubilium* referred back to a fundamental problem in the syllogism, but by denying that they have a particular power of self-referentiality.[27] In other words, he denies that they might be linguistic institutions, unassailable in any terms other than their own or any procedures that they did not themselves initiate. Clearly, Wyclif is already working to undo or move beyond what we would now call the linguistic turn in Oxford logic of the fourteenth century. His insistence that logic should literally move beyond its narrow linguistic institution at Oxford informs much of the logical work in his massive *Summa de ente*. In the section on universals (the question of whether, say, humanity is the aggregate of all humans, or a general and abstract concept)

---

[25] Kantik Ghosh, *The Wycliffite Heresy: Authority and the Interpretation of Texts* (Cambridge: Cambridge University Press, 2002), 48, citing *De veritate Sacrae Scripturae* 1. 51/26–52/10.

[26] Ghosh, *Wycliffite Heresy*, 49. See also J. A. Robson, *Wyclif and the Oxford Schools* (Cambridge: Cambridge University Press, 1961). For him, Wyclif's metaphysics represent the work of a 'cautious and conservative Oxford don' (p. 218).

[27] See Wyclif, *Summa insolubilium*, ed. Paul Vincent Spade and Gordon Anthony Wilson (Binghamton, NY: MRTS, 1986).

Wyclif criticizes the *doctores signorum*, obviously the Oxford-influenced theorists of supposition, for their 'lengthy and tangled heaps of words to expound everything as being principally about signs'.[28] What is remarkable is that Wyclif attempts, in his logical work, to move toward a philosophical realism, the implication of language in the real world, within the orbit of supposition theory. Even more remarkable is his insistence not only that language has something to do with the real world, but that a realist theory of predication makes certain ethical and political demands. Because universals are real, what we must love in another human is 'in natura communi', not any of his or her properties as a particular individual, and certainly not, using a word that became very politically loaded after the 1370s, by virtue of 'affinitatis'.[29] We have an obligation to the universal, not to the particular, not to the individuating conditions that are precisely what we tend to favour: familial bonds, political allegiances, geographical accident.[30] Not much later, the history of possible institutions would change radically with his departure from Oxford and the burgeoning of individuals, groups, communities that would oppose, openly and privately when they had to, the 'secta signorum', the institution of a Church from which they differed, individually, in ways we are only beginning to understand within our own institutions.

FURTHER READING

For the ways in which chivalry is constituted and represented, see L. O. Aranye Fradenburg, *City, Marriage, Tournament: Arts of Rule in Late Medieval Scotland* (Madison: University of Wisconsin Press, 1991). On the institutional history of feudalism, see Susan Reynolds, *Fiefs and Vassals: The Medieval Evidence Reinterpreted* (Oxford: Oxford University Press, 1994); Joseph Strayer, 'Feudal Institutions', in Marshall Clagett (ed.), *Twelfth-Century Europe and the Foundations of Modern Society* (Madison: University of Wisconsin Press, 1961); and especially Kathleen Davis, 'Sovereign Subjects, Feudal Law, and the Writing of History', *Journal of Medieval and Early Modern Studies*, 36(2006), 223–61. Susan Crane's 'The Writing Lesson of 1381' is a useful account of the relation between writing and institution in the Rising: in Barbara Hanawalt (ed.), *Chaucer's England: Literature in Historical Context* (Minneapolis: University of Minnesota press, 1992), 201–22. On the medieval university see Gordon Leff, *Paris and Oxford Universities in the Thirteenth and Fourteenth Centuries: An Institutional and Intellectual History* (New York: Wiley, 1968); J. M. M. H. Thijssen, *Censure and Heresy at the University of Paris 1200–1400* (Philadelphia: University of Pennsylvania

---

[28] 'diffusas et imbrigabiles rangas verborum exponere totum principaliter de signis' (2. 40, p. 53).
[29] 3. 125; p. 76. On the politics of affinity in the 1388 Cambridge parliament, see Paul Strohm, *Hochon's Arrow: The Social Imagination of Fourteenth-Century Texts* (Princeton: Princeton University Press, 1992). On the institution of affinity, see Simon Walker, *The Lancastrian Affinity, 1361–1399* (Oxford: Oxford University Press, 1990).
[30] On this last point, Wyclif actually refers to the preference of place (3. 125).

Press, 1998). Many chapters in volume ii of J. I. Catto and R. Evans (eds.), *The History of the University of Oxford* (Oxford: Oxford University Press, 1992), are helpful. A good introduction to the differences between Parisian and Oxford logic can be found in many chapters of Norman Kretzman (ed.), *The Cambridge History of Later Medieval Philosophy* (Cambridge: Cambridge University Press, 1982). On Wyclif, Lollardy, and institutionality, see Anne Hudson's foundational *The Premature Reformation: Wycliffite Texts and Lollard History* (Oxford: Oxford University Press, 1988); Fiona Somerset, *Clerical Discourse and Lay Audience in Late Medieval England* (Cambridge: Cambridge University Press, 1998); Wolfgang Hübener, 'Wyclifs Kritik an den Doctores signorum', in W. Vossenkuhl and R. Schönberger (eds.), *Die Gegenwart Ockhams* (Weinheim: VCH, 1990), 128–46. On Wyclif and the afterlife of persecution, see Paul Strohm, *England's Empty Throne: Usurpation and the Language of Legitimation, 1399–1422* (New Haven: Yale University Press, 1998), 36–40.

The indispensable sociology of institutions remains Pierre Bourdieu's, especially in *Homo academicus*, trans. Peter Collier (Cambridge: Polity Press, 1998); *The Logic of Practice*, trans. Richard Nice (Palo Alto, CA: Stanford University Press, 1990). Cornelius Castoriadis's *The Imaginary Institution of Society*, trans. Kathleen Blamey (Cambridge: Polity Press, 1987) is more philosophically interesting. More positivist is Edward Shils's *The Constitution of Society* (Chicago: University of Chicago Press, 1982). In classical sociological theory, indispensable works are *Georg Simmel on Individuality and Social Forms*, ed. Donald N. Levine (Chicago: University of Chicago Press, 1971); Émile Durkheim, *On the Division of Labor in Society* (New York: Free Press, 1964); Max Weber's monumental *Economy and Society*, 2 vols., ed. Guenther Roth and Claus Wittich (New York: Bedminster Press, 1968); Robert K. Merton, *Social Theory and Social Structure* (New York: Free Press, 1968).

CHAPTER 12

FORM

CHRISTOPHER CANNON

'Form' is a slippery concept and this has long been true. As Plato had it, a 'form' was external to the material world, a notion or idea or 'thought, which cannot properly exist anywhere but in a mind'.[1] As Aristotle critiqued and revised this view, 'form' was always a part of some material thing ('in everything which comes to be matter is present, and one part of the thing is matter, and the other form').[2] In both of these broad formulations 'form' referred as fully to natural objects (a tree, a person, the sea) as it did to made things (a house, a vase, a statue). But, at the border between the view that form is the idea that precedes the thing and the view that form is the attribute that gives things their distinctive being is a way of conceiving of the process of creation or making as a movement from one of these states to the other, as the *in*forming of raw materials according to the script of some idea, as the *forming* of an object guided by some thought:

> For everi wight that hath an hous to founde [build]
> Ne renneth naught [does not rush] the werk for to bygynne
> With rakel [hasty] hond, but he wol bide a stounde [while],
> And sende his hertes line out fro withinne
> Aldirfirst [first of all] his purpos for to wynne.[3]

This description comes from Chaucer's *Troilus and Criseyde*; it does not use the word 'form', and yet it describes a process that could be summarized with the word 'formation'. Plato and Aristotle and their respective followers might argue about what, in this description, is properly called 'form', but it is the very range of possible meanings here that makes the concept so very useful. The slipperiness

---

[1] Plato, *Parmenides*, 920–56 in *The Collected Dialogues*, ed. Edith Hamilton and Huntington Cairns, Bollingen Series 71 (Princeton: Princeton University Press, 1961), 132b (p. 926).

[2] Aristotle, 'Metaphysics', 1552–728 in *The Complete Works of Aristotle*, ed. Jonathan Barnes, 2 vols., rev. edn. (Princeton: Princeton University Press, 1984), book 7, 1033b (p. 1632).

[3] *Troilus and Criseyde*, I. 1065–9 in *The Riverside Chaucer*, ed. Larry D. Benson, 3rd edn. (Boston: Houghton Mifflin, 1987). Hereafter, all quotations from Chaucer will be taken from this edition and cited in the text.

that causes the controversy ensures that 'form' (as both concept and term) always allows analysis to build a bridge between the immaterial and the material: 'form' is necessarily the 'werk' seen in terms of the 'thoughte' behind it, the brute physicality of some thing as it is rooted in the realm of ideas conceived in some mind.

In this essay I shall try to show the advantages of a literary analysis that embraces such a broad definition of form, particularly in the sphere of Middle English writing. I shall argue that such a method is, above all, uniquely *comprehensive*, for it amounts to the insistence that the form of a text not only consists of all the structural levels we traditionally anatomize when we refer to 'literary form' (as we look, almost always by turns, at its metre, rhyme scheme, or style; at its metaphors or patterns of imagery; at its generic affiliations or plot), but of the integration of all those levels, along with any other aspect of a particular text which may be seen to structure it. In assuming that every attribute of text is either the elaboration or entailment of some originating 'thought', this method necessarily recruits a very great part of that structure to any account of a text's meaning.

While English literature in all periods might benefit from such careful attention to form, this method is also uniquely valuable for the understanding of Middle English because of three distinctive qualities of the writing of that period, each one enchained with the other. First, since Middle English writers often had few (or no) vernacular models to rely upon, their productions are often *formally unique*, and a great deal of the distinctive meanings of Middle English texts must be wrested from the unusual and unpredictable figures they cut upon the page. As a result of this uniqueness, these texts, second, tend to *resist interpretation*, and what is both passionate and unusual in their shape often tends to appear as tediousness (when referred to our reading experience) or ineptitude (where referred to an author's activities). Both of these attributes of Middle English form are shaped by the third: a general *absence of explanatory context*, as the passage of time has ensured that framing documentation and the key cultural knowledge that would place or explain the extravagance of a given form has been lost. A mode of analysis that can move from a given structure alone back to an initiating thought (or thoughts) is itself a valuable resource for generating contexts from texts—a way of excavating lost cultural facts and a wide range of historical determinants from nothing but the surviving, solitary work.

It is not surprising that a writer as curious about form as Chaucer—and as inventive in this particular area—should be the one Middle English writer to lay his finger so squarely on the crucial elements of the concept of form that I wish to trace, nor that the passage in question should count as his one and only direct borrowing from a medieval handbook on literary technique.[4] The influence of this

---

[4] Robert Payne cites the passage I have quoted from *Troilus* as 'the only serious statement of general aesthetic principle that Chaucer takes directly from the theorists', *The Key of Remembrance: A Study of Chaucer's Poetics* (New Haven: Yale University Press, 1963), 16.

borrowing would itself have been great simply because the handbook in question
was Geoffrey of Vinsauf's popular *Poetria nova* (*c*.1210):

> Si quis habet fundare domum, non currit ad actum
> Impetuosa manus: intrinseca linea cordis
> Praemetitur opus, seriemque sub ordine certo
> Interior praescribit homo, totamque figurat
> Ante manus cordis quam corporis; et status eius
> Est prius archetypus quam sensilis.

[If a man has a house to build, his impetuous hand does not rush into action. The
measuring line of his mind first lays out the work, and he mentally outlines the
successive steps in a definite order. The mind's hand shapes the entire house before
the body's hand builds it. Its mode of being is archetypal before it is actual.][5]

Chaucer uses this elaborate image of formation in *Troilus* to refer to nothing more
momentous than the beginnings of Pandarus' plot to snare Criseyde for Troilus ('Al
this Pandare in his herte thoughte, | And caste his werk ful wisely or he wroughte',
I. 1070–1). Such misdirection is typical of Chaucer (who tends to mock or deflate
the poetic principles on which he most relies), but it is also typical of discussions of
form in the Middle Ages (if not in all periods), where governing theories are more
usually *embedded* than stated. The absence of the term *forma* in the creation of
this image in the *Poetria nova* is the originating subtlety, a symptom of the degree
to which ideas of 'form' can enable thought about creation or making almost in
inverse proportion to their explicitness. But, for the same reason, each element of
a comprehensive theory of literary form is spread wide in thinking and writing in
the Middle Ages (with the crucial exception of the passages I have just quoted).
Because such a theory is, necessarily, more steadily present in poetic *activity*—in
the making of texts and the texts themselves—the clearest account of its elements
and advantages will therefore come from the description of the formal properties
of particular works. I shall therefore conclude this essay by detailing crucial aspects
of the form of two representative Middle English texts, *Handlyng Synne* and *Pearl*.

Medieval theories of form

The most explicit attention given to the concept of form in the late medieval centuries
occurred in Latin commentaries on Scripture and the classics. This discussion
habitually focused on a distinction between the *forma tractandi*, or 'the form of
treatment' in a particular work, and the *forma tractatus*, or the 'form of the treatise'.

---

[5] Geoffrey of Vinsauf, *Poetria nova*, 194–262 in *Les Arts poétiques du XIIe et du XIIe siècle*, ed.
Edmond Faral (Paris: Champion, 1958), ll. 43–8 and *Poetria nova*, trans. Margaret F. Nims (Toronto:
University of Toronto Press, 1967), 16–17. Subsequent quotations from this text will come from this
edition and this translation, cited by line and page number in the text.

The first of these is the most elusive, but it is, loosely speaking, the devices a given writing uses to make its point or to produce a certain emotional effect (or both). In his commentary on Ovid's *Metamorphoses* (1322–3), Giovanni del Virgilio defines the *forma tractandi* as a 'mode of proceeding' and, by way of explanation, he suggests that in the case of the *Metamorphoses* this must refer, at a general level, to 'the quality of the style and the genre of the poem' and, more specifically, to the 'discursive or inferential ... definitions' it offers.[6] This is vague, to be sure, but this particular *forma* seems to have been typically general in conception, and even when Dante actually lists the particular modes he employs in the *Divine Comedy*, the specifications are no more precise ('the form or manner of treatment is poetic, fictive, descriptive, digressive, and figurative; and further, it is definitive, analytical, probative, refutative, and exemplificative' (Minnis et al. (eds.), *Medieval Literary Theory*, 460)).

If the *forma tractandi* is too broad, however, the *forma tractatus* is a category so fine that it is often impossible to relate its elements to any of a text's larger meanings. For Giovanni del Virgilio the *forma tractatus* of the *Metamorphoses* consists of no more than the broadest divisions and subdivisions of its books and chapters ('the putting together and arrangement [*ordinatio*] of the fifteen books in this volume, and of the chapters into the aforesaid books, and of the parts within the chapters' (ibid. 364)). Although the *forma tractatus* of the *Divine Comedy* may be unique in its terms and parts (for Dante it consists of a 'first division ... whereby the whole work is divided into three *cantiche*; the second, whereby each *cantica* is divided into cantos; and the third, whereby each canto is divided into rhymed lines' (ibid. 460)), Dante's anatomy might also be said to state the obvious.

If pressed, medieval writers would probably have professed deep faith in a continuity between the *forma tractandi* and the *forma tractatus* because, as Erwin Panofsky has shown, the most striking and majestic human creations in the Middle Ages were born out of a faith in 'the unity of truth', in the general ambition that man-made things—particularly great works of art or learning—should be governed by such unity at every formal level as well as in the relationship between each of their hierarchized parts.[7] Panofsky's key example is the medieval cathedral and the 'progressive divisibility' governing the whole of its architecture: such buildings were not only systematically and visibly subdivided into three main parts (nave, transept, and chevet), but these subdivisions were further and further divided (by aisles and chapels, then by supports, ribs, and arches, and then by window tracery and mouldings) with each successive part connected to all the others by the continuous process of subdivision (Panofsky, *Gothic Architecture*, 47–8). That this was a 'mental habit' of the period, as Panofsky also termed it (21), means that progressive divisibility was

---

[6] A. J. Minnis and A. B. Scott, with David Wallace (eds.), *Medieval Literary Theory and Criticism, c.1100–c.1375: The Commentary Tradition* (Oxford: Clarendon Press, 1988), 364. Hereafter, quotations taken from this reader will be cited in the text.

[7] Erwin Panofsky, *Gothic Architecture and Scholasticism* (London: Thames and Hudson, 1957), 28.

also the defining feature of the sort of text called the *summa* in which the 'customary apparatus of parts, distinctions, questions and articles' produced similarly continuous relations between hierarchized parts (ibid. 58–9). Such a strong commitment to comprehensive order rarely led to any explicit connection of *forma tractatus* to *forma tractandi*, but a revealing and frequently cited passage in a commentary on the Song of Songs by Giles of Rome (1243/7–1316) shows exactly how these two modes of analysis might be explicitly connected.[8] Giles begins by acknowledging that 'it has been usual to distinguish two kinds of form', but he concludes with the claim that the *forma tractatus* 'can be ascertained' *from* the *forma tractandi* (or 'mode of procedure' as he also glosses this term) because the *forma tractatus* 'must be such as is required by the mode of proceeding' (Minnis et al. (eds.), *Medieval Literary Theory*, 246).

Although the more specific analysis of written forms tended to elide this key connection, a more comprehensive attitude toward form was available in the Middle Ages. It occurs in discussions that would simply never stoop to describing a text because they were concerned with the divinely made shapes of the natural world. This rich tradition conceived of form as an originating idea—the thought that shaped created things—but it understood that idea to have originated in the mind of God. A key text here is the *Summa theologica* of Thomas Aquinas, and it takes this relationship to be fundamental: 'When matter [*materia*] receives form [*forma*] the result is something with a definite and specific nature, like air or fire.'[9] In such a view, Aquinas—like many who think about form in the Middle Ages—is a firm Aristotelian, for he understands form as an attribute of material objects ('form limits matter', Ia. 7. 1 (ii. 96–7)); but he is also a Platonist to the extent that he grants form the possibility of floating free of matter in the realm of thought ('the intellective soul is a form just so and absolutely, and not something composed of matter and form', Ia. 85. 5 (xii. 76–9)). The result is a constant tension in the concept of form, but a tension that allows it to name the relations, movements, and moments where the material and the immaterial meet. This defining blending of the Aristotelian and Platonic makes form, here, and in many later formulations, that which thought has in common with things:

> Now there is both a sense in which matter is limited by form, and a sense in which form is limited by matter. Form limits matter because before assuming form matter is potential of many forms, but afterwards is determined by the one assumed. Matter limits form because a form as such may be shared by many things, but when acquired by matter becomes determinately the form of this thing. (Ia. 7. 1 (ii. 96–7))

---

[8] The passage is carefully marked out by Judson Boyce Allen as one of the few in which 'the normal medieval doubleness of form is collapsed into unity', *The Ethical Poetic of the Later Middle Ages* (Toronto: University of Toronto Press, 1982), 91–2.

[9] St Thomas Aquinas, *Summa theologiae*, 60 vols., gen. ed. Thomas Gilby (London: Eyre & Spottiswoode, 1964), Ia. 50. 2 (ix. 12–13). Subsequent references to Aquinas's *Summa* will be taken from the facing-page translation in this edition, cited in the text (with volume and page number given parenthetically).

Aquinas is still thinking of forms such as 'air' or 'fire' in this passage, but this understanding of divine creation can be adapted very easily to a view of human making. To substitute the mind of the architect or the writer for the mind of God in such a view is to make form the immateriality that 'determines' the form of the cathedral or treatise or poem; it is the idea that, by informing a given raw material, gives the object its particular (and defining) shape.

Geoffrey of Vinsauf and then Chaucer absorb this general idea of form to their understanding of the forms of a plot (as in the case of Pandarus) or a poem. This understanding is also further expanded in the *Poetria nova* not long after the passage that Chaucer borrows for *Troilus*, where it is even more clearly a way of moving a theory of natural forms into the arena of writing. In this case, the poem begins as formless matter that is shaped by the mind that guides the hand, which in turn 'moulds' or shapes matter into the solidity of a given text:

> Formula materiae, quasi quaedam formula cerae
> Primitus est tactus duri: si sedula cura
> Igniat ingenium, subito mollescit ad ignem
> Ingenii sequiturque manum quocumque vocarit,
> Ductilis ad quicquid. Hominis manus interioris
> Ducit ut amplificet vel curtet.   (ll. 213–18)

[The material to be moulded, like the moulding of wax, is at first hard to the touch. If intense concentration enkindle native ability, the material is soon made pliant by the mind's fire, and submits to the hand in whatever way it requires, malleable to any form. The hand of the mind controls it, either to amplify or curtail.   (pp. 23–4)]

The 'matter' in question is not, of course, what Aquinas posits when he imagines 'air' or 'fire' before they take on their particular nature—it is, in fact, closer to what is sometimes called a text's 'contents'—and, again, Geoffrey's Latin does not use the word *forma* (but its close synonym, *formula*). What this rich and elegant description specifies, however, is all that unites the immaterial realm of thought (here figured as the 'mind's fire' ('ignis ingenii')) and the solidity of the finished poem (here, never quite named, but imagined as a thing as solid as 'wax' ('cera')). Geoffrey captures this connection in the beautiful image—itself neatly immaterial and material—of 'the hand of the mind' ('hominis manus interioris'), but my point here is that the term that most generally captures the powerful and salient relations is 'form' (or *forma*). In fact, such an equation of thought and thing, when applied rigorously to a textual form, necessarily defines every contour that might be discerned in a text, not just as a clue to an originating thought (or set of them), but as a version of it. This is an understanding of form that, while simultaneously a theory of literary making (a set of views about how thoughts become things), allows criticism to move from the most trivial of details to the most complex of ideas. It is a theory, then, with the unusual status of a rigorous and practical interpretative *tool*.

A theory in practice

The notion of form I have just outlined frequently reappears in Western under-standings of the relationship between the immaterial and material because its roots run so deep in our philosophical traditions.[10] These traditions are not always easily visible, however, and in late medieval England the kind of clear statements we find in Geoffrey of Vinsauf are highly unusual. In fact, in Middle English the word *forme* was only common in the general, Aristotelian sense of the physical shape of an object (Chaucer used it in this sense in the *Boece* to refer to 'the forme of the body ... withowte', 4. pr. 3. 90–2). It was very occasionally used to describe an immaterial idea or archetype in the Platonic sense ('thilke same symple forme of man that is perdurably in the devyne thought', *Boece* 5. pr. 4. 165–6). Where the Middle English word *forme* was applied to writing, it was always with a sense so general as to make it a synonym for writing as such (so, for Chaucer, the whole of *Troilus and Criseyde* was 'the forme of olde clerkis speche | In poetrie', V. 1854–5).[11]

Aspects of the form of Middle English texts were discussed, even in the absence of this word, but—as in the analysis that passed under the rubric of the *forma tractatus*—such discussion tended to focus on the obvious, usually characterizing a text's diction or versification: the 'lel letteres loken' ('locked together letters') or alliterative metre of *Sir Gawain and the Green Knight* (*c*.1380), for example, or the 'ryme couwee' (tail-rhyme stanzas), 'enterlace' (entwined or alternating rhyme), or 'baston' (stanzaic verse) listed as a set of alternatives for Middle English poetry in Robert Mannyng's *Chronicle* (1338).[12] On the very rare occasion that the whole of a text was described in Middle English, such minute particulars were equated with the whole of a form:

> And, for rude wordes and boystous [rough] percen the herte of the herer to the inrest [inmost] poynte, and planten there the sentence [meaning] of thynges, so that with lytel helpe it is able to spring: this boke, that nothyng hath of the greet floode of wit ne of semelych colours [rhetorical ornament], is dolven [dug] with rude wordes and

---

[10] For a more comprehensive version of the theory of form I advance here see the 'Introduction' (esp. pp. 1–10) to my book on early Middle English, *The Grounds of English Literature* (Oxford: Oxford University Press, 2004).

[11] For these meanings and citations see Hans Kurath et al. (eds.), *The Middle English Dictionary* (Ann Arbor: University of Michigan Press, 1954–2001), s.v. 'forme n.', 1a a ('the physical shape of something'), 6a ('style of writing'), 14a a ('the Platonic idea').

[12] See *Sir Gawain and the Green Knight*, l. 35 in A. C. Cawley and J. J. Anderson (eds.), *Pearl, Cleanness, Patience, Sir Gawain and the Green Knight* (London: J. M. Dent, 1976). Robert Mannyng of Brunne, *The Chronicle*, ed. Idelle Sullens, Medieval & Renaissance Texts & Studies (Binghamton, NY: Binghamton University Press, 1996), ll. 85–9.

boystous, and so drawen togyder, to maken the catchers thereof the more redy to hent [comprehend] sentence.[13]

In this description of his own *Testament of Love* (*c.*1385) it is as if Thomas Usk has expanded the *forma tractatus* so as to take in the whole of the *forma tractandi*: as a result, the text's 'rude wordes and boystous' have become equivalent to the whole of the *Testament*'s meaning, these details of language somehow *are* the 'sentence' of a whole 'boke'.

The form of a Middle English text could be described as lying somewhere between what might be said about it and what it actually was. This is, however, exactly the converse of what has often been said about created forms in this period: Panofsky has suggested, for example, that the progressive divisibility of the cathedral or *summa* was part of a more general principle of *manifestatio* or 'transparency' in made forms of the period (*Gothic Architecture*, 43), a kind of 'self-analysis and self-explication' whereby individual objects were not only governed by a certain formal logic, but that logic was pressed upon any observer by means of the careful and precise articulation of each and every formal level (ibid. 59). The forms of Middle English writings were almost never progressive in this careful way, and, even though they were equally rich, they tended toward the opposite of such transparency, usually employing governing logics so unusual that they have remained virtually invisible to critical analysis, often appearing to such analysis in the guise of their opposite, as the very absence of structure. The result is a collection of texts that have seemed almost uniquely resistant to formalism of any sort, despite the complex formal richness that is the very cause of that resistance. In all these ways, Middle English is a body of writing that has long required comprehensive formal analysis—but to precisely the extent that it has not seemed to allow it. For this reason, although the theory of form I have just described is necessarily applicable to texts in all languages and all periods, Middle English texts are more likely than most to appear to *have* a form only in situations where we are willing to employ this theory: where we are willing to insist that every aspect of every 'line' *must* relate to every other such aspect, and that, whatever the obfuscating complexities, all such details can be brought together as the parts of a shape that discloses an originating, if complex, thought.

Since the task of such description is inherently difficult, but never more so than in the Middle English case, formalism in this sphere must be, in every case, active, flexible, and resourceful; it must be everywhere happy to experiment with the elements that constitute a text's form, and particularly willing to look at any apparent oddity and credit its importance in a larger meaning and structure. For this same reason, such a formalism can only really be described in the specific and accretive analysis of a large number of Middle English texts. Within the necessarily

---

[13] Thomas Usk, 'Prologue' to *The Testament of Love*, 28–34 in Jocelyn Wogan-Browne, Nicholas Watson, Andrew Taylor, and Ruth Evans (eds.), *The Idea of the Vernacular: An Anthology of Middle English Literary Theory, 1280–1520* (Exeter: University of Exeter Press, 1999), 29–30.

limited scope of this essay, however, something of the nature of what is usually entailed can be shown by way of two texts that represent different extremes of the common recalcitrance.

The first of these texts, Robert Mannyng's *Handlyng Synne* (c.1303) possesses the kind of form that resists analysis because its shape seems so simple and obvious: 'like other penitential handbooks of the thirteenth and fourteenth centuries ... [it is] highly schematic in layout, divided into sections, on the Ten Commandments [ll. 147–2988], the seven deadly sins [ll. 2989–8582], sacrilege [ll. 8583–9492], the seven sacraments [ll. 9493–11302], and confession [ll. 11303–12630] ... [and it] proceeds by alternating between exemplary narratives and a combination of commentary, ethical and religious instruction, and a general description of the topic or topics at hand.'[14] Its versification is simple and unvaried (four-stress couplets throughout), and the majority of its instructions and examples are taken directly from Mannyng's source, the Anglo-Norman *Manuel des pechiez* (c.1270).[15] The most substantial additions Mannyng makes to the givens of the *Manuel* are roughly seven predominantly new narratives sprinkled widely throughout the text's 12,638 lines.[16] These narratives are also interesting because they are so difficult to relate to the principles they are meant to illustrate, so often do they seem to cut directly across the particular doctrine they are meant to help teach, but such stories actually function as nodal points in *Handlyng Synne*'s form precisely in the awkwardness with which they fulfil their pedagogical role: they are, in fact, disproportionately important moments in which the governing logic of a whole form only appears to fail because of a boldness that allows that logic to appear—in those moments—as if in isolation.

The most revealing of these nodal points—and one that may stand here for all—is the narrative to which F. J. Furnivall gave the appropriately sensational title 'The Witch and her Cow-Sucking Bag' (ll. 501–61). The narrative occurs in the section of the poem devoted to the First Commandment ('Thou shalt have no god but one', l. 148), and it describes a witch who possesses a magical bag of leather which she uses to steal milk from all the cows in a town. She is summoned before the Bishop, but, rather than condemn her, the Bishop asks to be taught how to use this bag, which he fails to make work, because, although he repeats the spell that the Witch has taught him, he does not share the Witch's faith in its power (as the Witch puts the point, 'Ye beleve nought as y do', l. 544). The story certainly

---

[14]   Mark Miller, 'Displaced Souls, Idle Talk, Spectacular Scenes: *Handlyng Synne* and the Perspective of Agency', *Speculum*, 71 (1996), 606–32 at 608–9.

[15]   For the relationship between the two texts see the old but still-invaluable parallel text *Robert of Brunne's* Handlyng Synne *and its French Original*, ed. Frederick J. Furnivall, EETS, os 119, 123 (London: Oxford University Press, 1901, 1903).

[16]   These added narratives—as well as all the other narratives Mannyng tells—are carefully anatomized in appendix II (pp. 381–7) of Robert Mannyng of Brunne, *Handlyng Synne*, ed. Idelle Sullens (Binghamton, NY: Medieval and Renaissance Texts and Studies, 1983). Hereafter lines of *Handlyng Synne* will be cited in this edition by line number, in the text.

makes the wrong doctrinal point: rather than condemn those who disobey the
First Commandment—or those who subscribe to a 'fals thyng' (l. 497), such as
witchcraft—a bishop is shown to fail because he lacks 'fals beleve' (l. 496). Yet, at
the join between this story and subsequent discussion of true and false belief, the
ability to share others' beliefs turns out to be as important as doctrinaire allegiance:

> Heyr mow we wete [perceive], beleve wyle make
> There the wrde [word] no myght may take.
> The bysshop seyd the wrdys echoun,
> But, beleve ther yn hadde he noun.
> No more shal hyt avayle the
> That belevyst not there [where] beleve shulde be.   (ll. 557–62)

As the story is rounded off by this injunction, it is fitted into a complicated
shape that gives false belief a clear and useful relationship to doctrine: rather than
encouraging simple and rectilinear adherence to a principle (a belief that simply
is truth), *Handlyng Synne* here roots belief in a multiculturalism generous enough
to pass through other understandings; it therefore holds, subtly but forcefully, that
only a belief supple enough to encounter and understand its antithesis will finally
come to rest where it 'shulde be'.

Once detected and accepted in this extreme form, the shape of this nodal point
is not only characteristic of the use of narrative in *Handlyng Synne* as a whole
(most of its narratives are misaligned in equally surprising ways), but basic to the
larger lesson this poem wishes to teach.[17] The most global statement of that lesson
occurs in relation to the work's explanation of its title and the surprisingly literal
translation that Mannyng gives for the Anglo-Norman 'manual' (from Latin *manus*,
'hand'), the word 'handling'. Part of the force of this translation is to insist on the
tangibility of sin ('we handel synne every day; In worde and dede, als we may'), but
Mannyng also insists upon another, more obscure, meaning of 'handling', 'dealing
with something', or 'acting upon something', a meaning he also represents as key
to his text's programme of instruction: [18]

> Handlyng yn speche ys as weyl [the same as]
> As handlyng yn dede everydeyl [in every way]
> On thys manere handyl thy dedys
> And lestene and lerne whan any hem redys [speaks of them].   (ll. 115–18)

The sinner must 'handle' his belief by moving it through the various ways and
circumstances that life throws at him, in much the same way that the Bishop's belief

---

[17]   Miller offers a very detailed analysis of the problems of 'exemplarity' in relation to another of
the narratives Mannyng adds to his source, 'The Dancers of Colbek' ('Displaced Souls', 610–28). This
narrative can be found at ll. 9011–237 of *Handlyng Synne*.

[18]   See *MED*, s.v. 'hondlen v.', 1a ('to touch with the hands') and 3c ('to deal with (sth.), have to
do with, consider, act upon'). The lines I quote from *Handlyng Synne* are cited in the last of these
subsections.

is moved through successive degrees in the story of the 'Witch and her Cow-Sucking Bag' and the reader's attention is moved through a complicated theory of belief as he or she reads that story.[19] Such a merging of narrative procedure and pedagogy ensures that the misfit of Mannyng's stories to Christian doctrine provides its own solution. Their very awkwardness is a method for arming the potential sinner with a set of narrative experiences that will not only teach him the content of wrong belief, but will help him to resist it. Mannyng's more lurid stories are commonly said to have 'attracted his audience', as if their acts of exemplification were a way of sweetening the bitter pill of doctrine.[20] But a more comprehensive account of the text's form suggests that the bold and extraordinary achievement of these narratives is to unfold doctrine in ways so difficult and complex—requiring such efforts on the reader's part—that their very apprehension makes them a part of lived experience. Such a comprehensive treatment is therefore also coextensive with the comprehensiveness of a form, a deeply subtle but complex integration of a variety of formal levels into a larger meaning in which the ostensible problems of any particular story are a manifestation, not of a formal failure but of a general richness.

With *Pearl*, my second example, we can begin with such richness, since, on its face, and from almost any angle of approach, this poem not only parades its form's extravagance, but the intricacy of that design is itself a way that the poem clearly announces a commitment to the integration of formal levels, to a comprehensive order in which every contour has a meaningful part to play. Thus, *Pearl* is carefully arranged not only at the level of many of its words (which are drawn together by alliteration), but at the level of each line (as it is woven into a twelve-line stanza in the rhyme scheme *abababababcbc*), every stanza (as it is grouped into units of five—or, in one significant case, six—by a shared word in the first line and a common last line), and every one of these stanza units (each of which is linked to the previous unit by the repetition of some word or phrase central to that unit's repeated last line). The repetition of the poem's last line as its first draws all such progressive and extensive linking into a kind of circle (the poem ends where it begins), with the consequence that the organization of its words presents itself as the shape those words often name and generally describe: the pearl. *Pearl* generally relates the events of a dream in which a female figure—who is at once 'a perle' and the embodiment of the spiritual perfection the pearl generally represents in this poem—reveals the spiritual beauty of the afterlife for good Christians.[21] The poem's elaborate structure is therefore a correlative for the ornament that

[19] Miller also discusses the importance of the 'handleability of sin' for Mannyng, though he places less emphasis on the kinds of power this notion gives to stories, and more on the complexity it necessarily gives to the idea of 'sin' itself ('Displaced Souls', 612–14).

[20] D. W. Robertson, 'The Cultural Tradition of *Handlyng Synne*', *Speculum*, 22 (1947), 162–85, at 162.

[21] For the maiden as a 'perle' see esp. *Pearl*, ll. 241–52 in Cawley and Anderson (eds.), *Pearl, Patience, Cleanness* and *Sir Gawain and the Green Knight*.

characterizes the dreamscape, which is itself a correlative for the perfection of every aspect of the 'pearl' ('the consequence … is an art which … produce[s] a verbal effect as bejewelled as the other world').[22] And yet, all such layered order and ornament also, everywhere, deny the poem's main subjects: an overwhelming loss (the dreamer is mourning the death of someone deeply beloved), a consequent and irremediable anguish (as the dreamer puts it, 'And ever me longed ay more and more', l. 144), and an irreducible confusion about how Christian grace can be understood in the face of such sorrow—how, in particular, an infinite mercy can be accepted by a mind equipped to do nothing but measure a loss ('For the grace of God is gret inoghe', l. 612). Where the progressive, self-explicating, omnipresent order of the poem's form constantly emphasizes circularity, in other words, the dreamer is desperate for progressive and linear movement toward some relief for his overwhelming confusion, or some comfort for his unbearable grief. And yet this sought-after movement is precisely what the poem's form thwarts.[23]

The disjunction has attracted some attention, and Spearing has written in detail about a 'constant dialectic' between 'pattern and resistance to pattern' throughout the poem (*Readings*, 208). What a comprehensive theory of form must add however—a theory which insists, right across such difficulties, that there is *still* a necessary and constant relationship between a poem's originating thought and the shapes in which it unfolded—is that such a misfit is, therefore, the poem's point (the flaw in the pearl that actually constitutes its larger and more complex symbolic function). The nodal point here is *Pearl*'s penultimate stanza which (by virtue of the poem's circularity) also functions as its prologue:

> To that Prynces paye [will] hade [if I had] I ay bente [submitted],
> And yerned [yearned for] no more then was me gyven,
> And halden me [restrained myself] ther in trwe entent,
> As the perle me prayed that was so thryven [fair],
> As helde [very likely], drawen to Goddes present,
> To mo of his mysterys I hade [would have] ben dryven,
> Bot ay wolde man of happe [good fortune] more hente [seize]
> Then moghte by ryght upon hem clyven [belong to them].
> Therefore my joye was sone toriven [destroyed],
> And I kaste of kythes [places] that lastes aye,
> Lorde, mad hit arn [they are] that agayn the stryven,
> Othere proferen [propose] the oght agayn thy paye. (ll. 1189–201)

[22] A. C. Spearing, *The Gawain-Poet: A Critical Study* (Cambridge: Cambridge University Press, 1970), 98.

[23] Spearing suggests that the 'form of the line' is an important 'symbolic opposite' for the circle in *Pearl*, but he sees its force as 'dissolved … in the heavenly world'. See A. C. Spearing, *Readings in Medieval Poetry* (Cambridge: Cambridge University Press, 1987), 209–10. The importance of the line as a figure in *Pearl* was first pointed out, as Spearing notes, by Marie Boroff ('*Pearl*'s "Maynful Mone": Crux, Simile, and Structure', in Mary J. Carruthers and Elizabeth D. Kirk (eds.), *Acts of Interpretation* (Norman, OK: Pilgrim Books, 1982), 159–72, at 163–4).

The dreamer's sense that he would have fared better had he not 'yearned' for more than he was 'given' is undercut, first, by the claim that a man will 'always' yearn in this way, and, second, by the connection made between such striving ('therefore') and blighted hope (a 'joy' that is, by this model, *inevitably* 'destroyed'). That the dreamer should pause long enough in his strivings to reflect upon them is something new at this point in the poem, and one might emphasize, as Spearing does, the extent to which the dreamer has progressed through his self-reflection and 'we have been shown a new way of looking at things' (*Readings*, 215). But I also think that the assertion that such a conclusion is in any way 'consoling' (as Spearing does (ibid. 213)) is contrary to the movement of the poem, and to the dreamer's emphatic sense that he has hit a brick wall ('Lorde, mad hit arn that agayn the stryven'). The dreamer may now recognize that his strivings are as 'mad' as the *Pearl*-maiden first found them to be (as she puts it, very early on in their conversation, 'So madde ye be!', l. 290), but his confusions and sadness not only persist in this stanza, they have been very much deepened by another realization: that these thoughts and feelings can *never* be ameliorated.

Once accepted as part of the poem's meaning, however, the circularity of the dreamer's attempts to cope acquires obvious and determinate meanings all its own. At the level of affect, such circularity is a method for emphasizing the unremitting pain of grief and for measuring a believer's necessary frustration in the face of a divinity who is defined by his capacity to exceed human understanding. The poem's attempts at consolation and explanation become less significant for their failure or inconclusiveness, and more meaningful as an insistent movement toward the closing of a loop (as every link of word, line, stanza, and unit is there in order to turn every thought of the poem back to its beginning at the poem's close). Although the poem presents itself as the most passionate of searches for a resolving comfort or knowledge, viewed in this comprehensive way, it clearly proffers the much more difficult observation that consolation and understanding are processes without destination. Part and parcel of the attempt at progressive movement that defines such emotional need is the larger fact that, in so many ways, human grief *is* permanent and a human mind never *can* comprehend the ways of divinity.

This description of the form of *Pearl*, like my description of the form of *Handlyng Synne*, is only slightly different from accounts of these poems that one may find elsewhere, although the emphasis I have laid on the co-extension of meaning and form serves to absorb certain neglected elements of these texts to the general account. This is, as I see it, the principal strength of the theory of form I have been describing—and the grounds on which I would particularly advocate its use in the study of Middle English. The defining analytic question of such a theory is probably the following: how can *this* fit into the whole (where 'this' may be not only what criticism has neglected or found confusing, but some aspect of the text which has made the whole of it seem confused or self-contradictory). In my experience, such a question is often the Archimedean lever which, by shifting the most recalcitrant aspects of a form from the periphery of our attention to the centre of our analysis, also tends to crack open those parts of a textual surface that had, heretofore, seemed impenetrable. Since so much of this literature has successfully resisted not only our careful reading, but our critical interest, an abundance of Middle English writing still awaits such shifting and opening.

FURTHER READING

Because it considers forms more material than those of literary texts, art history often provides the most eye-opening accounts of form. I have relied particularly on Panofsky's seminal *Gothic Architecture and Scholasticism* (n. 7) in the discussion above, but, in the larger study of form from which my account is derived, I have found particularly useful Michael Baxandall, *Patterns of Intention: On the Historical Explanation of Pictures* (New Haven: Yale University Press, 1985), especially chapter 1, and W. J. T. Mitchell, *Iconology: Image, Text, Ideology* (Chicago: University of Chicago Press, 1986). My larger study, *The Grounds of English Literature* (n. 10), may also be understood as a set of practical illustrations of such a theory in relation to a number of early Middle English texts (though the book also makes a progressive argument about the peculiar conditions of literature in this period). Ernst Robert Curtius offers a foundational discussion of the *forma tractandi* and *forma tractatus* in *European Literature and the Latin Middle Ages*, trans. Willard R. Trask (Princeton: Princeton University Press, 1948), 221–5. The seminal text on this matter is A. J. Minnis, *Medieval Theory of Authorship: Scholastic Literary Attitudes in the Later Middle Ages*, 2nd edn. (London: Scolar Press, 1988), especially the chapter on 'Literary Forms' (pp. 118–59). Equally valuable is the reader of primary texts assembled to accompany Minnis's study, *Medieval Literary Theory and Criticism*, ed. Minnis and Scott, with Wallace (n. 6), from which I have drawn much of the contemporaneous discussion of form quoted above. Some of the discussions of literary form that occurred in Middle English are collected in the section of *The Idea of the Vernacular* (ed. Jocelyn Wogan-Browne, et al.; n. 13) on 'authorizing text and writer' (pp. 1–105). There is a dearth of criticism on Mannyng's *Handlyng Synne*, but the best account of the text that I know is Miller's ('Displaced Souls'; n. 14). The literature on *Pearl* and the *Pearl*-poet is, on the other hand, vast, but Spearing's writings (also cited above, nn. 22–3) are among the most congenial to the theory of form I have advanced here. Spearing has also written searchingly about 'the detailed analysis of literary texture' in Middle English works (and the problems attendant upon such a critical programme) in chapter 1 of *Criticism and Medieval Poetry*, 2nd edn. (London: Edward Arnold, 1972), an approach he calls 'practical criticism' or 'close reading'. The second of these terms is not itself a bad description of the mode of analysis I have here advocated, though I tend to think of my method as a more fully theorized—and, in its insistence that texts are, above all, determinate shapes, a more materialist—version of the traditional practice.

CHAPTER 13

EPISODES

ELIZABETH ALLEN

Medieval narratives, like those of any other period, create order based on causal sequences in time: one thing happened, which caused the next, and so on. But even the most cursory survey of prominent medieval narratives suggests that the ordering power of narrative causality can be offset by cyclical and episodic structures, formal fragmentation, incompletion, and the existence of multiple versions. Although some may think of twentieth-century modernism as 'the great epoch of experiment', later Middle English narratives conduct deliberate as well as accidental challenges to the expectation of coherence.[1] My aim is neither to praise a late medieval experimental aesthetic, nor to condemn narrative incoherence as an aesthetic liability; I ask instead how narrative discontinuity reveals social concerns, and how, as a result, episodic form functions as a method for anticipating and shaping audience response. With respect to the inevitable alliance of form with content, I want to examine anew the link between narrative incoherence and dynastic discontinuity.

Generational coherence relies on successive iterations of family identity—father, son, grandson—whose juxtaposition can signal continuity or its absence, even as one generation, ideally, produces the next, or fails to do so. Although episodic narratives resist coherent moral or social injunction on such matters, they raise the question of social continuity because they typically expose the artifices necessary to the creation of both narrative and social order. On display in these narratives is the often-temporary nature of both narrative coherence and generational continuity. Social anxiety supplies not only the thematic material but the structural basis of

---

[1] The quotation is from Frank Kermode, *The Sense of an Ending* (Oxford: Oxford University Press, 2000), 127. Experimentation with narrative incoherence can also be taken as a postmodern phenomenon, which in turn has influenced medieval studies. There has been significant attention to the ways in which manuscript vicissitudes create such challenges to the coherence of texts, from the work of Paul Zumthor on *mouvance* in *Toward a Medieval Poetic*, trans. Philip Bennett (Minneapolis: University of Minnesota Press, 1992) to Ralph Hanna's studies of 'scribal poetics' in *Pursuing History: Middle English Manuscripts and their Texts* (Stanford, CA: Stanford University Press, 1996).

narrative; in turn, narratives serve to reveal the fundamental instability of familial structures, to reconceptualize inheritance claims, and to expose the provisional nature of dynasties.

Episodic structure, as Auerbach long ago pointed out, strings *aventures* together in paratactic relationships; rather than relying on formal density, romances in particular unfold events in series.[2] Like their earlier French cousins, later Middle English romances avoid clear causation and even subordination, relying on readers to connect one scene to another. Episodic juxtaposition of this kind challenges readers to assess the sort of truth an individual episode conveys, often based on events in previous episodes, which imply retrospective explanations for undermotivated events.[3] Tag-lines, apostrophe, narrative endorsements ('That trytour has no pere!'), inconsistencies in name or social status, noticeable reiterations, ill-fitting juxtapositions—all such formal disruptions call readers' attention to repetition and renewal, the structural building-blocks of episodic romance. According to Peter Brooks, repetition is a 'major operative principle' of plot; it shapes what he calls the 'energy' of a story, 'giving it perceptible form, form that the text and the reader can work with in the construction of thematic wholes and narrative orders'. Through repetition, narratives master otherwise formless or boundless human needs and desires.[4] Episodes, elements which etymologically 'go on the road beside' one another, rely strongly on reiterated symbols and language, precisely because they eschew causality.

Yet repetitions loosen as well as bind; repeated names, motifs, or events look back to an origin but at the same time work toward an unknown future. 'Factual' disagreement between episodes, awkward interdependence between one event and the next, and incomplete closure can fragment narrative structures, producing irreconcilable strands of meaning. Paradoxically, even as they detach or disorient readers, such ruptures also encourage symbolic or associative connection. The conceptual challenge of episodic structure, then, lies in recognizing the ways in which ruptures both violate coherence and make sense.[5] The communicative function of episodic narrative lies not so much in the formation of order based on

---

[2] 'The Knight Sets Forth', in *Mimesis: The Representation of Reality in Western Literature*, trans. Willard R. Trask (Princeton: Princeton University Press, 1953), 123–42.

[3] On 'backwards' motivation see Morton W. Bloomfield, 'Episodic Motivation and Marvels in Epic and Romance', in *Essays and Explorations: Studies in Ideas, Language, and Literature* (Cambridge, MA: Harvard University Press, 1970), 97–128, at 108–10.

[4] Peter Brooks, *Reading for the Plot: Design and Intention in Narrative* (Cambridge, MA: Harvard University Press, 1984), 123.

[5] Bakhtin writes that 'adventure-time … emerges only at points of rupture (when some hiatus opens up) in normal, real-life, "law-abiding" temporal sequences', and that such ruptures become normalized or 'generally applicable' in chivalric romances, so that 'the unexpected, is what is expected'. Jumping off from Bakhtin, I find that later Middle English romances demand serial adjustment to such ruptures. See *The Dialogic Imagination*, ed. and trans. Caryl Emerson and Michael Holquist (Austin: University of Texas Press, 1981), 152.

coherence and closure as in this tactical breaking or fraying of narrative strands, which in turn reveals the making of meaning itself as partial and temporary.

Irresolution in *Athelston*

Repetition, the 'core of fictionality', maintains links between episodes but, at the same time, opens gaps between them.[6] In *Athelston*, one of the most compact of Middle English romances, repetition calls into question the finality of closure itself, despite the just rewards of the innocent and the just punishment of the guilty. King Athelston is the cousin, not son, of a king. His anxiety of inheritance shows when he immediately believes his friend Wymound's false accusation against his friend Egelond; it culminates when, because his wife defends Egelond, he kicks her angrily in the pregnant stomach, killing his only heir.[7] In response to Athelston's injustice, the Bishop institutes trials by fire. Each trial is announced with virtually the same six lines, including the tag-line 'in romaunce as we read' (ll. 567–72, 777–82), asserting the orderliness and symmetry of the trials but also marking their extravagance—twice, the fire is nine furlongs long. Repetition also encourages us to register narrative progress through changes in detail: where Egelond's trial is hedged about with explanations and amplified by the testing of his wife and children, Wymound's trial concludes quickly when he endures only two plough-lengths of fire.[8] Repetition calls attention to Wymound's heirlessness in contrast to Egelond's productivity: out of his wife's trial, Egelond's third son St Edmund is born. Thematically, Wymound's heirlessness emerges as the 'backward motivation', the cause of his original treason. And the birth of Egelond's son resolves the dynastic problem of King Athelston himself: Edmund is named heir to Athelston's kingdom (ll. 657–62). In many ways, the narrative coheres around this essentially fractured dynasty.

Despite the narrative's apparent structural coherence, the theme leaks into the structure, creating narrative impropriety at the end. Although the pairing of trial-by-fire episodes clearly emphasizes the Bishop's sanctified power over the King's injustice, it also raises, without answering, profound questions about the political costs of oblique inheritance. Repetition and juxtaposition undo the tale's effort to imbue a fractured dynasty with sanctity because, despite the dichotomy between innocent child-saint and guilty traitor, the tale stresses the resemblance between

[6] Matilda Tomaryn Bruckner, *Shaping Romance: Interpretation, Truth, and Closure in Twelfth-Century French Fictions* (Philadelphia: University of Pennsylvania Press, 1993), 107, 91.

[7] Elizabeth Ashman Rowe, 'The Female Body Politic and the Miscarriage of Justice in *Athelston*', *Studies in the Age of Chaucer*, 17 (1995), 79–98.

[8] I quote from *Athelston*, in Ronald B. Herzman, Graham Drake, and Eve Salisbury (eds.), *Four Romances of England*, TEAMS Middle English Texts Series (Kalamazoo, MI: Medieval Institute Publications, 1999), 341–84.

Athelston's violent justice and the Bishop's punishment of Wymound.[9] The king, now called 'goode king Athelston' (l. 774), retains a violent control expressed in the tale's concluding image: the body of Wymound 'left dangling by decree' (*Four Romances*, 343). In narrative terms, Edmund's miraculous body born in fire gives way to the burned, drawn, and hanged symbol of the divided realm; the episodic juxtaposition of birth and death binds them inextricably, exposing the high costs of social order and rendering the child's body a proleptic dynastic fantasy, inadequate to end the tale's brutality. Wymound's body bespeaks Athelston's rule by fear, for the populace is afraid to take down the remains. To varying degrees, any narrative exposes the limited authority, the benightedness, of its own efforts at coherence (Brooks, *Reading for the plot*, 113–42). But these disturbances in the conclusion of *Sir Athelston* suggest a potentially endless spiral of oblique inheritances, violent judgements and dismembered bodies, and ever-contested iterations of power. Later Middle English narrative is characterized by just such a tendency to link dynastic ruptures to narrative inconclusiveness—indeed, to theorize social problems as problems of narrative form.

Extravagance in *Sir Degaré*

The urge to subsume narrative discontinuity within unified conceptual wholes—for Auerbach, the 'chivalric ideal' ('The Knight Sets Forth', 139); for Bloomfield, the 'divine erupting into the world' ('Episodic Motivation', 122)—can obscure the ways in which narrative rupture can expose profound cultural anxieties. One of the most provocative recent expressions of the urge to coherence is James Simpson's incisive essay on *Sir Degaré*, Malory's 'Sir Gareth', and the *Folie Tristan d'Oxford*. Simpson demonstrates one way in which romances theorize social problems as matters of form: each of his texts, he argues, seeks to restore social propriety by reintegrating the hero with his proper name. In these romances, narrative movement unfolds as a result of a mismatch or 'extravagance' in the thematic relationship between name and social place.[10] 'Significant violence' (p. 127) produces narrative movement toward stasis and reintegration. Simpson's view of romance narrative as the drive through disintegration toward oneness elucidates an essential insight of romance scholars and narrative theorists alike.[11] His essay demonstrates that the

---

[9] Some have argued that the poem is anti-monarchical; see A. Inskip Dickerson, 'The Subplot of the Messenger in *Athelston*', *Papers on Language and Literature*, 12 (1976), 115–24.

[10] 'Violence, Narrative and Proper Name: *Sir Degaré*, "The Tale of Sir Gareth of Orkney," and the *Folie Tristan d'Oxford*', in Ad Putter and Jane Gilbert (eds.), *The Spirit of English Popular Romance* (London: Pearson Education Ltd., 2000), 122–41, at 123.

[11] Simpson's theory of romance as expending the 'semantic force' of a name (pp. 130–1) strongly resembles Peter Brooks's psychoanalytic theory, in *Reading for the Plot*, that all narratives discharge or spend desire.

genre is constituted by the 'wandering' of words—that romances are in this sense 'about' themselves—and that such wandering is ultimately contained within fairly restricted ideological parameters. In the case of *Sir Degaré*, the hero's adventures and the rediscovery of his nobility confirm the 'wholeness of the kinship group' (ibid. 130) and indeed, the 'genetically pre-given order of things' (p. 131).

However persuasive this line of argument, episodic structures cannot finally be reduced to a drive toward order. Even relatively brief lays like *Sir Degaré* give rise to vital interruptions that heighten the narrative's ideological complexity, exposing generational continuity as effortful, costly, precarious, and accidental, rather than 'pre-given'. Degaré's reunification of his own family begins when, having unhorsed his grandfather, he marries his mother; in the nick of time, he reveals his identity by producing gloves that fit only his mother's hands, creating familial continuity and avoiding incest. Yet the scene of their union is shot through with ambivalence. Repetition pauses the narrative, emphasizing the daughter's reluctance: she is 'sori' (l. 585) that she has to marry a man she has never seen, sorry he is unknown and foreign.[12] Narrative dilation here calls attention to a social fact embedded in dynastic structure: exogamy requires that women marry unknown men.

The daughter's sorrow also connects to an earlier episode, the scene in which she encountered the unknown fairy knight who would be Degaré's father. In the earlier scene, she wanders away from her father's party, a separation associated with sadness even before the fairy knight appears and rapes her. Afterward, as her pregnancy progresses, she laments that men will think her father begot the child (ll. 168–9). The daughter's repeated sorrow reveals a constitutive ambiguity: whether the daughter's rape symbolizes the exogamous knight's transgression against the family's integrity, or whether, instead, the rape stands in for the father's incest with his daughter. This equivocation oddly attenuates the 'significant violence' of the rape itself: the daughter might be resisting her father's excessive dynastic conservatism or its opposite, exogamy. Rather than render incest simply transgressive or 'extravagant', the daughter's response to her rape, pregnancy, and, later, marriage registers a profound ambivalence about the symbolic replacement of the father necessary to dynastic continuation. Her sorrow in the marriage scene, then, points toward a fantasized alternative: if the father could live forever and never be unhorsed, incest would, in fact, be the ideal means of achieving coherence between generations.

This fantasy comes to the fore when, during the marriage feast, the narrator remarks the amazing coincidence of strangers who turn out to be kin: 'Lo, what aventoure fil hem thar!' (l. 626). The metatextual 'Lo!' suggests that the happenstance of discovering one's unknown kin is less a 'pre-given' providential event than a narrative artifice barely achieved. Here too, Degaré suddenly recalls

---

[12] For *Sir Degaré*, see Anne Laskaya and Eve Salisbury (eds.), *The Middle English Breton Lays*, TEAMS Middle English Texts Series (Kalamazoo, MI: Medieval Institute Publications, 1995), 101–44.

the heretofore neglected gloves. Narratologically, though, it is too late: even as the incest is quickly averted, the audience has been made uncomfortably aware of the hero's distraction from his search for identity, and, more important, of the uncanny desirability—indeed, the generational coherence—of marrying one's own kin. Moreover, the gloves themselves carry another equivocation, because although they look like a symbol that should identify the proper wife (Degaré should not love any woman *unless* the gloves fit, ll. 215–16), actually they signal the improper wife (he should *not* marry the woman they fit). The gloves, like the tale itself, point to discordant meanings. These meanings do not produce layered complexity so much as oscillation, or a kind of serial shifting of gears; they are not a tension resolved in the story's drive toward stasis and reintegration, so much as a set of potentialities that remain engaged even once Degaré's family relationships resolve into exogamous marriages. The narrative could—and indeed *did*—get rewritten in terms that enhance its fragmentation, for example, by downplaying Degaré's progressive development of chivalric skill.[13]

In *Sir Degaré*, rape substitutes for incest, and eventually marriage replaces rape. The sheer incommensurability of these substitutions leaves the initial equivocation between incest and exogamy both unresolved and visible. The episodic structure of *Sir Degaré* opens time and space for such discord. Episodes mark undermotivated events, unreconciled details, and awkward transitions; even in the relatively coherent and closed *Sir Degaré*, ruptures in narrative continuity defer or thwart unified meanings, reveal alternative stories, and make extraneous connections. A narratorial 'Lo!' when Degaré happens to meet his father in battle reminds us again of the artifices involved in linking father to son, and hence, for a brief moment, suggests a kind of ghostly Oedipal remainder wherein the son might overthrow the father (ll. 1028–31). Narrative, so often understood as the creation of order, cannot simply keep the inexplicable and extravagant under containment. *Aventure* occurs in narrative *as* uncanny experience—wandering away from the familiar—neither wholly 'providential' nor wholly accidental, but pointing to the ways in which accidents form the basis of any human aspiration toward meaning, even the 'natural' continuation of a family line, and even the attribution of its meaning to the mysterious intentionality of God.

Inconsistency in *Beves of Hampton*

More fully and loosely than *Athelston* or *Degaré*, *Beves of Hampton* plays with the ways in which episodic structure undermines the basic teleology of reclaiming lands, depicting instead a potentially infinite series of random and fragmented

---

[13] W. C. Stokoe Jr., 'The Double Problem of *Sir Degaré*', *PMLA* 70 (1955), 518–34.

peregrinations.[14] The sheer diversity and frank inconsistency of *Beves*'s adventures raises with particular force the question of audience response. For any romance, dynasty offers the fantasy of stability across generations, guaranteed by land tenure. By the time romances are circulating in later Middle English, property becomes a manifestation of abstract ideas of stability, defined both in literature and in lived history by combinations of wealth, status, profession, and familial continuity. Within the narrative of *Beves of Hampton*, the world of aristocratic luxury and beauty is attenuated by roughshod journeying; the narrative's pace and content anticipate a 'bourgeois-gentry' audience rather than providing 'a *mise en abyme* of contemporary feudal society' (Bruckner, *Shaping Romance*, 6–7).[15] Although the correspondence between fiction and 'reality' is never exact, the distance between them widens in the case of later Middle English romance, and the English embrace of disjunctive episodic forms rather than the elaborate interlace of the French cycles reflects this situation. As Felicity Riddy points out, direct links between the content of a narrative and the values of either author or audience are difficult to confirm; modern viewers watch westerns, for instance, without having any necessary tie to either the west or the frontier heroism that they depict (238). Precisely because chivalric truth is figured as an ideal operative in Beves's invisible past, his more visible present appears aimless, fragmented, even empty.[16] While the perpetuation of inheritance provides a socially rooted structure of comprehension, episodic structure disjoins both text and audience from the actual economic basis of property's function.

Yet, as Corinne Saunders astutely points out, *Beves* is 'dominated by the idea of "right"'.[17] The hero operates on the assumption that he has a right or just entitlement to his father's lands, a situation in which his identity corresponds to his property claim. Gradually, Beves finds that his own right to property is not natural, but a social artifice created by human organization and affirmed through martial and marital enterprises. In a strand of the plot particularly indicative of the social register of episodic narrative, Beves moves from frank, even vehement identification with his lands to a series of disguises and tricks that allow him finally to reclaim (and then forgo) his property. We might say that the irregular progress

---

[14] In this sense, the events in *Beves* resemble the chronotope of Greek romance as described by Bakhtin: between the beginning and the end adventures 'are strung together in an extratemporal and in effect infinite series' (*Dialogic Imagination*, 94). Yet their arrangement suggests certain strands of narrative progress, giving a characteristically medieval sense of 'playing around with time' and deliberately distorting space (p. 155).

[15] The analysis of romance's audience and relationship to 'history' are indebted to Felicity Riddy, 'Middle English Romance: Family, Marriage, Intimacy', in Roberta L. Krueger (ed.), *The Cambridge Companion to Medieval Romance* (Cambridge: Cambridge University Press, 2000), 235–52, at 238.

[16] For the empty present, see Bakhtin, *Dialogic Imagination*, 147. His analysis of nostalgia in the folklore chronotope gets at an aspect of late chivalric romances which readers have often seen as 'debased' (Bloomfield, 'Episodic Motivation') or otherwise emptied of richness.

[17] 'Desire, Will and Intention in *Sir Beves of Hamtoun*', in Phillipa Hardman (ed.), *The Matter of Identity in Medieval Romance* (Cambridge: D. S. Brewer, 2002), 29–42.

of *Beves of Hampton*—its years-long digressions, its geographical mobility—enacts temporally and spatially Beves's constitutive loss of the lands after which he is named.[18]

But the tale theorizes the problem of 'right' as an episodic problem—an ever-returning need for inheritance narratives. Despite the coherence of this general theme, *Beves*'s structure remains fragmented. The inconsistencies that break its continuity demand from an audience either passive assent to any and all narrative activity or continual querying of social values. For example, the hero's lord and protector King Ermin suddenly turns against him when enemy knights accuse Beves of sleeping with Ermin's daughter Josiane. The King has earlier offered Beves his daughter's hand in marriage (ll. 559–60); but he now sends his protégé into enemy hands with a sealed letter, which Beves promises to bear 'treuliche and wel' (l. 1246) even as he 'bereth with him is owene deth' (l. 1261).[19] The irony surrounding Beves's role as the loyal messenger calls attention to questions of narrative causality: why does Ermin, for whom Beves has fought against the enemy knights, suddenly believe those enemies? Why does the King suddenly seek to prevent his daughter's marriage? Why, in fact, does he never accuse Beves directly but instead take advantage of Beves's frank investment in 'truth' in order to make him a bearer of untruth? Seeking answers to these questions involves acknowledging the disjunctive nature of Ermin's 'protection' in the first place. Beves landed in Armenia after his mother helped a foreign king usurp his father's lands, initiating Beves's need to test himself in exile until he can return to reclaim Hampton. We can confer various causes upon the narrative: Ermin's betrayal ends Beves's subordination entirely, so he never has another lord; or, kissing Josiane makes the Christian Beves from Hampton a threat to the dynastic integrity of the heathen kingdom.[20] Ermin is, however, emphatically *not* Beves's kin, or even his 'true' lord, but a substitute lord in an adopted (heathen) realm. Any presumed continuity between early events at Hampton and later events in Armenia is here exposed as a product of temporary acts of substitution.

Even the vocabulary of substitution proves inadequate to explaining Ermin's betrayal. This is signalled when the narrative itself pauses to issue a truth-claim before Ermin's decision to trick Beves: 'He dede nothing, boute ones hire kiste,

---

[18] *Beves of Hampton* has topical links to Southampton's lords of Arundel; see M. Dominica Legge, *Anglo-Norman Literature and its Background* (Oxford: Clarendon Press, 1963), 159–60. Judith Weiss argues persuasively that the romance was written in two chunks, in honour of the second and then the third earl of Arundel. See 'The Date of the Anglo-Norman *Boeue de Haumtone*', *Medium Aevum*, 55 (1986), 237–41.

[19] All quotations from *Beves of Hampton* are from the edition in Herzman et al. (eds.), *Four Romances*.

[20] Bloomfield writes, 'In the eyes of God, in another dimension, all these episodes are no doubt explicable … The center of the story is not within the tale but beyond it' ('Episodic Motivation', 106–7). For him, the 'irrational' motivation of romance opens toward 'another realm of meaning beyond human ken' (p. 111), even the 'numinous' (p. 112).

[Beves had done nothing but kiss Josiane once] | Nought elles bi hem men ne wiste. | Tharfore hit is soth isaide | And in me rime right wel ilaide' (ll. 1213–16). Here, defensive narrative commentary points out a gap in causal progress that suggests just how easily the story might have gone another way, if only 'men … wiste' something more. Beves's betrayal does not arise necessarily from the previous series of episodes; Ermin's haste and violence are undermotivated, and the very structure of the narrative appears contingent upon his unheralded weakness or corruptibility. Rather than portray romance events as given, mysterious, magical, and predestined, this moment invites readers to regard narrative developments as provisional, and to view bonds of lordship as artificial and impermanent.

The narrative's frequent transitions emphasize this impermanence as well, relying on sudden transitional language rather than unified, self-enclosed structures. Immediately following Ermin's betrayal of Beves, a shift in time and place apparently signals a wholly new episode: 'Terne we aghen, thar we wer er, | And speke we of is em Saber!' (ll. 1263–4). The narrative returns to Hampton, where Beves's loyal master Saber suddenly sends his own son, Terri, to seek the lost hero. But Terri's story returns again to Beves's, in a scene of non-recognition between them. Non-recognition, of course, is structurally meaningless unless it recalls a past or anticipates a future recognition, so the episode depends thematically upon other events. Throughout the romance, events continually reach toward other episodes in ways that foil their own internal coherence, raising questions about geographical, temporal, and causal 'progress'. Terri has not appeared in the narrative before now; Saber has suddenly become Beves's uncle or 'em' rather than simply his father's loyal knight; later in the narrative, Saber's wife crops up as interpreter of prophetic dreams. This shifting family constellation has many potential causes, all of them provisional and functional, not fully coherent at the level of content. Most noticeably, having lost a substitute father, Ermin, Beves apparently gains an uncle. The meeting with Terri also provides the opportunity for Beves's first lie: he says Beves of Hampton has been hanged by Saracens, suggesting symbolic loss of his own initially frank character. But the 'counterfactual' possibility of reunification with uncle and cousin does not simply demonstrate Beves's developmental stage; the invitation to go home calls attention to the tenuousness of Beves's connection to his lands, the inconsistency of his relationship to Saber and his family origins, and the penitential brutality of his exile. Although on the one hand Beves must continue on his way in order to deliver his message 'treuliche and wel', his fantasy of his own destruction suggests the degree to which he already knows he 'bereth with him is owene deth'. Again, causal links can be made here. We might say that Beves embraces his status as exile precisely in order to direct his plot himself, entering into a world of trickery by playing his own trick on Terri. We might, alternatively, argue that his penitential acceptance of subordination causes his rebirth, later, when he emerges weak and vulnerable from seven years' imprisonment and makes his way to Jerusalem. But these (rather contradictory) readings are inadequate to the emotional pain registered by Terri and Saber, who weep sorely at their loss; inadequate to their shifting roles as vassals and as kin; inadequate even to the possibility of reunification their sudden presence seems to hold out; and formally, inadequate to explain their presence in this episode at all. Why should Beves not simply land in prison, avoiding such radically inconsistent elements of plot?

When interrupted causality performs improprieties, the plot appears, as it were, under construction. If the misrecognition episode raises the possibility of a new family unit as 'answer' to narrative disjunctions, it still fails to 'fit' structurally. When Beves finally escapes prison and makes his way to Jerusalem, his visit to the Patriarch for confession arguably turns him from escapee to returning hero and sacralizes his 'treuthe' (l. 1966) in a conversion or rebirth. Yet the entire sojourn in Jerusalem comprises only eleven lines, an abbreviation strangely inadequate to such seemingly pivotal content. Such disjunctions between content and form foil efforts to view episodes as a series of discrete steps in a synthetic process.

Yet ruptures in causality do not undo meaning; instead they encourage various and plural meanings, indeed a multiplicity of meanings, and require continual readerly readjustment. The tactical incoherence of episodic narrative invites readers to seek out connections that prove partial and temporary—as if we too are involved in the tricks and fiction-making of Ermin and Beves—and that, in turn, reveal lineage itself as a consequence of fiction-making. In the radically inconsistent depiction of Saber, family constellation becomes an instrument of plot, rather than a given social structure. The landed wealth that produces dynastic continuity emerges as itself fundamentally episodic: far from a stable sequence of events from land tenure to marriage to dynastic perpetuation, romances thematize the gaps between family members, especially between successive generations, that make it continually necessary to reimagine family inheritance. If Saber's family is constituted by the needs of Beves's plot, then so too Beves's own family—his age-enfeebled father, his treasonous mother, his opportunistic stepfather—can be understood as the narrative emanations of dynastic anxiety. Self-referential transitions, narrative inconsistencies, blurry lines between episodes, and 'counterfactual' plots depict as temporary almost any imaginative solution to such problems. Dynastic interruption itself, then, is more than thematic: episodic ruptures express the culture's most profound social anxiety.

The Seven Sages of Rome, 'Sothe Sawe', and the next generation

The social significance of narrative incoherence may be especially salient in romance, but it characterizes many later Middle English narratives that appear both structurally and ideologically far more coherent and closed. English romances share the techniques of disjunction with compiled works like sermon collections and conduct books. Of course, many other kinds of medieval narrative texts are essentially collections of episodes, from Chaucer's *Canterbury Tales* and Gower's *Confessio Amantis* to preaching manuals; from dream-visions to penitential manuals; from the *Legenda aurea* to the *Miroir des bonnes femmes* to its offspring, the *Book of the Knight of the Tower*, and from the Auchinleck manuscript to miscellanies and commonplace books. Whatever the differences between long, unframed, episodic romance narratives and self-contained episodes within a frame narrative, both forms lie along a continuum, and both use disjunctive form to manifest social content. A representative case is *The Seven Sages of Rome*, which originated in India and reached Europe via Arabic and exists in eight fourteenth- and fifteenth-century English manuscripts translated from the French.[21] The narrative contains fifteen tales within a larger dynastic conflict. Each episode is a distinct story, whose teller explicitly applies it to a framing situation.[22]

The framing narrative relates a Phaedra-Potiphar's wife plot in which the Emperor Diocletian remarries, and his wife accuses his son Florentine of trying to rape her. Following prophetic advice, Florentine remains mute while his seven teachers engage in a storytelling competition with the Empress. Each night, she tells a tale that convinces Diocletian to execute Florentine; each day, a sage convinces him not to. Strikingly, the Emperor subordinates the enactment of justice to his own enjoyment of narrative: each sage agrees to tell a tale only if the Emperor agrees *first* to issue a reprieve, to which the eager Emperor repeatedly agrees. Despite Diocletian's distraction and indecision, the audience is aware that the Empress propositioned Florentine rather than vice versa. The delay before Florentine's self-defence arguably gives the Emperor time and opportunity to mitigate his fury, listen to counsel, and ready himself for his son's claim; thus a set of stories that could be an endless courtly debate instead drives toward closure and condemnation of the Empress. On the eighth day, when Florentine finally tells a fable and then reveals the truth about his encounter with the Empress, Diocletian condemns his wife and burns her at the stake.

The structure of the *Seven Sages* appears relatively closed, and the content is conclusively antifeminist. The text ends in version E with Florentine's foundation of an abbey in honour of his father, and in version B with the 'good endyng' (l. 3820) of Florentine's successful reign after his father's death. These conclusions clarify what the frame narrative has been doing all along: seeking to close the gap

---

[21] On the complexities of the English manuscript tradition, see Killis Campbell, 'A Study of the Romance of the Seven Sages with Special Reference to the Middle English Versions', *PMLA* 14 (1899), 1–107.

[22] On the various versions of the English *Seven Sages* see Karl Brunner (ed.), *The Seven Sages of Rome*, EETS, os 191 (London: Oxford University Press, 1933). I quote from Brunner's edition of the version from the Auchinleck manuscript (A), substituting variants where necessary from MSS Egerton 1995 (E), Balliol College, Oxford 354 (B), and Cambridge, Ff II, 38 (F), which he prints in parallel columns. For analysis of the structure of the French text, see Mary B. Speer, 'Recycling the *Seven Sages of Rome*', *Zeitschrift für romanische Philologie*, 99 (1983), 288–303.

opened between father and son. In essence, the Empress manifests Diocletian's own resistance to the passing of the throne to his son: he is old, and has sent his son away and married a new wife, who herself wants power. Instead of an old man desperately clinging to his throne, Diocletian becomes a susceptible and wayward, but finally truthful, judge.

The principal formal expression of the Emperor's effort to create affective familial connection is application of individual tales: every 'moral of the story' seeks to create continuity between tale and frame. With each application, the Emperor is newly convinced not only of the truth and attractiveness of the story's message, but also of his intimacy with the teller, based on his acceptance of the story's argument in favour of one or the other judgement. Because of the Emperor's serial susceptibility to plot, each closure also appears utterly temporary, contingent upon his momentary absorption in the story—dependent, that is, upon his odd refusal to assert his own story, to *be* Emperor. If the Empress aspires to stay on the throne at any cost, the Emperor veers toward the opposite, a kind of anticipatory abdication. He views stories as emanating from the needs of their tellers, putting him entirely at their mercy. This coercive view of narrative allows Florentine to assert his dynastic claim, even as it risks making Florentine's 'victory' appear just as temporary as any other convincing story. Still, Florentine's tale finally forces his father to cede to the dynastic, rather than erotic, organization of justice—an organization in which the son will ultimately displace his father entirely. The *Seven Sages* thus employs episodic structure as a way of theorizing dynasty.

Florentine's fable—which both narrates and performs an inheritance claim— plainly asserts a son's right to inheritance, even in a foreign land, divorced from the envious parent. The story tells how a powerful man and his son, while sailing one day, hear two crows who predict the son's social ascent above his father's degree. The son translates the birds' speech to his uncomprehending father:

> 'I shalle so ryche a man be,
> That with youre yeen [eyes] ye shall se,
> The whylys my hondys waschyn bene,
> Ye shalle be fayne to holde the bason,
> And my modyr, withowtyn fayle,
> Shalle serue me of the towele.'   (E. 3302–7)

In wrath at this prophecy of parents serving the child, the father casts his son into the sea; but the child is saved by a fisherman and raised by a constable. Later, the King of the realm is plagued by three ravens, and offers his daughter and half his land to the man who can stop their racket. The son once again offers a translation: two male ravens fighting over a female are seeking the King's judgement about who should have her as a mate. The King issues a judgement in favour of the younger raven; the older raven shrieks with grief and flies off. The outcast son now receives daughter, lands, and eventually title as king. Meanwhile, his now-impoverished parents appear in his own kingdom; he visits them incognito, but when offered a basin and a towel he will not accept their service. Instead he announces his identity and forgives the father's wrong.

This tale, designed to reassure Florentine's father of his forgiveness, nonetheless encodes the costs of inheritance to the older generation. In a classically Oedipal structure, the father tries to stave off his replacement by the son, and is later replaced by the King who grants the son a new dynasty. The father's return nearly realizes the original threat that the son's prosperity will constitute usurpation. Oedipal doom is averted because of the son's interpretative and rhetorical skill. Even before the conclusion, the son 'rewrites' his initial act of translation: his second act of translation is instrumental, not prophetic. Still, the love triangle echoes the earlier raven-speech in suggestive ways. The famine that has separated the elder male from the female echoes the poverty of his father, and the elder male's shrieking flight into exile suggests a darker mirror of the father's fate.

This displacement of father–son conflict onto erotic conflict underlies the structure of the *Seven Sages* as a whole. Both raven episodes tell stories of the demise of impoverished older males and the achievement of younger generations. Despite the son's refusal to lord it over his father as he had feared, then, the tale—and the *Seven Sages* as a whole—everywhere drives toward displacement of fathers by gifted and prosperous sons. The son's secret knowledge of bird language, like Florentine's mute knowledge of the Empress's transgression, makes his generational usurpation at once a disavowal of aggression and a privilege of youth. The story mystifies his competitive urge, displacing it onto ravens, who fly away. Florentine's story and his subsequent exposure of the Empress's transgression can then express the 'real' son's loyalty to his father. His fable makes every effort to show that the son does not have to destroy the father; the family line can continue seamlessly and project a fantasy of stable and timeless bonds sustained by loyalty and truth between the generations. But the mystification only partly covers over the reality of death and replacement that motivates the larger narrative. After Diocletian has proven himself a willing servant to every narrative, this story demands the Emperor's ultimate acceptance of more than counsel: he must accept Florentine's authority, both as teller of a 'sothe sawe' and as his heir—that is, like the son in the story, his replacement.

The effect here resembles that of episodic romance. In *Athelston, Sir Degaré, Beves of Hampton,* and so many other English romances, the son has no father, or the father dies leaving behind a steward or a false uncle; the task is to retrieve the father, or the father's lands, but rarely to overcome him directly. A notable exception is Malory's Mordred, whose direct generational violence transgresses Arthurian codes. The fundamental structure of replacement lies at the heart of even the most apparently clear situation of inheritance, that which excludes the mother entirely because she is a 'vile houre' or a wicked stepmother. The evil uncle or the aggressive queen is overthrown in order to mystify the violent destruction of one generation by the next. Yet the replacement of fathers, in turn, destabilizes identity and inheritance, repeatedly depicting an imaginative system that emphasizes the contingency of property rights, prosperity, and family name, revealing the episodic character of dynasty itself. The ruptures between episodes are not only analogous to disjunctions between generations, but formally enact the most profound anxieties about the possibility of establishing and perpetuating lineage. Episodic narratives, finally, make audiences aware of the artifices necessary to create inheritance. Diocletian finally acts within a structure of 'justice, the fundamental basis on which human society can function as a stable entity'—but it is a precarious justice indeed, because it is dependent upon so susceptible a reader.[23]

Episodic isolation

In a climate of exemplification, the 'wandering' will of the Emperor suggests a profoundly unstable situation, in which an audience's every effort to create a bulwark against death through procreation must be constructed anew. Episodic structures communicate with an audience by demanding continual adjustments to uneven or ruptured development. Indeed, the lack of formal coherence critics often note in medieval narrative can be understood as a constitutive call for audience response, the basis for audience participation and contribution to meaning. The tactical incoherence I have described invites audiences to make conceptual 'sense', however temporary, in order to partake in narratives of social continuity. Rupture and inconsistency puts pressure upon readers to imagine, and continually reimagine, the terms of their communities. This continual effort lies at the heart of conduct books, sermon collections, and penitential manuals as well—books whose unified moral truths are almost always exceeded, and troubled, by narrative.

Indeed, dynastic anxiety lurks within even radically non-dynastic texts like the vernacular penitential manual *Jacob's Well*. As an exemplum of wrath, the *Well*-author tells the tale of a gambler who curses, despite his friend's warnings, until God strikes him dead with a thunderbolt. Next, as an exemplum of patience, comes the story of St Theodora, who is falsely accused of adultery and suffers beatings from her husband. To save herself, she dresses in her husband's clothes and joins a monastery. Accused of adultery again and exiled from the monastery, she lives at the abbey gates—alone and in public—and raises her accuser's child until, when she dies, the abbot discovers she is a woman. The connective tissue between these two tales, of the gambler and the saint, urges alignment between anger and punishment, patience and reward. An angry man, says the author, should be shunned like a raving dog: of course sin isolates the sinner, taking him far from God.

---

[23] Peter Haidu, 'The Episode as Semiotic Module in Twelfth-Century Romance', *Poetics Today*, 4 (1983), 655–81, at 678.

Yet Theodora, despite her evenness of temper, is also shunned, apparently because of her beauty (both of her accusers are people she resists sexually). Her reward lies as much in her 'procreative' success as in heavenly reward, for the fostered child will eventually become the new abbot of the monastery. Like Edmund born out of fire, this child holds a promise for the future that creates a dynastic fantasy through sacred miracle. Still, because Theodora raises someone else's child, and because she dies, she renders the family as discontinuous and happenstance as anything we have seen in romance. Of course, hagiography can veer close to romance, so perhaps this is no surprise. But the thematics of this story unfold within a larger structure: when devotional handbooks combine moral purposes and relatively closed, disconnected narratives, they isolate episodes from one another, creating discontinuities that often rob their exempla of even the barest contextualization. Such formal disjointedness highlights the social disjunction we have seen elsewhere in the interstices between episodes. The paratactic structure of any manual renders exempla provisional and incomplete: they demonstrate one sin in a world of endlessly subdivided sins, give rise to excoriations, produce further tales, demand application. Episodic narrative, even in *Jacob's Well*, does not finally create pearl-like wholeness and self-enclosure, but evokes deliberation on the difficult question of how morals can become conceptually and socially coherent, even across ruptures in time and space. Thematically, in the chapter on anger in *Jacob's Well*, radical social isolation connects the penitent Theodora to the ever-impenitent gambler—and finally, the spectre of isolation urges audiences toward the socially binding act of application.

Romances, conduct books, even a text like *Cleanness*, the most episodic work in the *Pearl* manuscript—all seem to call upon the imaginative energy of an audience to achieve not only formal but social continuity. Later Middle English narrative is particularly obsessed with its capacity to mediate between an imagined world and an actual society—to make vernacular storytelling morally applicable—rather than crystallize the world into formal conclusions. Adventure in romance normalizes narrative rupture, using what is unexpected, unfinished, extravagant, and inconsistent to activate audiences. But many other sorts of episodic narrative also register the constant and arduous aspiration toward social coherence through formal structures. Behind Diocletian's dynastic unease—and indeed behind the dynastic anxieties portrayed in *Athelston*, the resistance to exogamy in *Degaré*, and the homeless wandering in *Beves*— lurks the ultimate rupture, solitude. Dynasties represent a bulwark against the loss of property, social place, and connection to the things of this world; they imagine that inheritance overcomes solitude and death; they narrate social life after death.[24] Yet because dynasty is episodic, and because episodic structures trouble narrative continuity by assembling many events

---

[24] For a different reading of romance that foregrounds the ways in which wealth becomes bound up with death, see D. Vance Smith, *Arts of Possession: The Medieval English Household Imaginary* (Minneapolis: University of Minnesota Press, 2003).

paratactically, the fantasy of dynastic wholeness also raises the spectre of social isolation and failure of causality. What Riddy calls 'the catastrophe of sonlessness' in romance expresses that lived disaster wherein the episodes of a family's life fail to cohere. In asking audiences to register formal disjunction, episodic narratives ask them both to acknowledge and to resist, provisionally and continually, social separation and catastrophe.

FURTHER READING

My understanding of the dynastic struggles registered in medieval narrative is shaped by Felicity Riddy's brief but incisive 'Middle English Romance: Family, Marriage, Intimacy' (n. 15 above). Other recent work on Middle English romance stresses its engagement with economic issues; see especially D. Vance Smith, *Arts of Possession* (n. 24) and Christopher Cannon's chapter 'The Spirit of Romance', in *The Grounds of English Literature* (Oxford: Oxford University Press, 2004). A particularly haunting historical record indicates the connection between dynasty and death that underlies my analysis of episodic structure: Reynold Peckham, a bachelor, provides for the engraving of his tombstone with a picture of a wife and children. His will is cited in F. R. H. Du Boulay, *An Age of Ambition: English Society in the Late Middle Ages* (New York: Viking Press, 1970), 90–1.

I find the most convincing general account of romance in Northrop Frye, *The Secular Scripture: A Study of the Structure of Romance* (Cambridge, MA: Harvard University Press, 1976). For several scholars, romance provides a generic basis for analysing the temporary coherences of any episodic structure, though less in relation to exemplary narrative than in relation to epic, as in Morton W. Bloomfield, 'Episodic Motivation and Marvels in Epic and Romance' (n. 3). But see also Matilda Tomaryn Bruckner, *Shaping Romance* (n. 6), and Peter Haidu, 'The Episode as Semiotic Module in Twelfth-Century Romance' (n. 23). In the vast body of writings on narratology, I have found most useful for medieval texts Peter Brooks, *Reading for the Plot: Design and Intention in Narrative* (n. 4) and M. M. Bakhtin, *The Dialogic Imagination* (n. 5). With respect to exempla, I have found particularly cogent the analysis in Claire M. Waters, *Angels and Earthly Creatures: Preaching, Performance, Gender in the Later Middle Ages* (Philadelphia: University of Pennsylvania Press, 2004). My understanding of exemplary discourse as fundamentally episodic and discontinuous differs from other accounts of such texts, including that of Larry D. Scanlon in *Narrative, Authority, and Power: The Medieval Exemplum and the Chaucerian Tradition* (Cambridge: Cambridge University Press, 1994).

On the ways in which narratives call up audiences, I am generally indebted to the work of Paul Strohm; in particular, *Social Chaucer* (Cambridge, MA: Harvard University Press, 1989) and 'Chaucer's Audience(s): Fictional, Implied, Actual', *Chaucer Review*, 18 (1983), 137–45. I also have in mind Wolfgang Iser, *The Act of Reading: A Theory of Aesthetic Response* (Baltimore: Johns Hopkins University Press, 1974), which stresses the gaps and blanks that audiences are asked to fill in during the process of reading.

CHAPTER 14

BEAUTY

MAURA NOLAN

The experience of 'being in error' so inevitably accompanies the perception of beauty that it begins to seem one of its abiding structural features.

(Elaine Scarry, *On Beauty and Being Just*)[1]

The association between beauty and error that Elaine Scarry articulates, in which error is part and parcel of the human understanding of beauty, is a particularly appropriate beginning for an essay on beauty and late medieval poetry. Not only was beauty regarded with some suspicion by medieval writers, for whom it tended to mean feminine beauty and thus to imply sexual desire, but it has also fallen dramatically out of fashion in the modern era, in which it is usually understood to mean 'taste' and to imply judgement—just the kinds of categories that literary critics eschew in favour of more objective standards (like history) or more abstract thinking (as in philosophy). Even though both 'objectivity' and 'generalization' have themselves been thoroughly critiqued, they remain available as standards by which to impeach other modes of apprehending the literary text. At the same time, beauty remains a working, and workable, concept largely in the introductory classroom; one begins by teaching about beauty, and progresses to teaching about history or theory. It is all the more pressing, then, to wonder about beauty and what its hold over readers and writers *really* is; to wonder, in an old-fashioned way, what medieval poets thought about beauty and if those thoughts had discernible effects on what and how they wrote. If they did, then we must ask ourselves why we routinely exclude beauty from our considerations of medieval writing, and what it would mean to add to our critical repertoire a working notion of the beautiful.

Many thanks to Andrew Cole, Anne Middleton, Geoffrey O'Brien, and Paul Strohm for advice and commentary, and to Dan Blanton and Jill Mann for straight talk about metre.

[1] Elaine Scarry, *On Beauty and Being Just* (Princeton: Princeton University Press, 1999), 28.

I have chosen a text to focus on that is familiar to all medievalists, Chaucer's 'Miller's Tale', and within it, his description of Alisoun, the lively main actor in the plot. Even within that passage I have narrowed my focus, in large part, to eleven lines:

> She was ful moore blisful on to see
> Than is the newe pere-jonette tree,
> And softer than the wolle is of a wether.
> And by hir girdel heeng a purs of lether,
> Tasseled with silk and perled with latoun.
> In al this world, to seken up and doun,
> Ther nis no man so wys that koude thenche
> So gay a popelote or swich a wenche.
> Ful brighter was the shynyng of hir hewe
> Than in the Tour the noble yforged newe.
> But of hir song, it was as loude and yerne
> As any swalwe sittynge on a berne.[2]

This portrait is traditionally seen in one of two ways, either as a brilliant synthesis of the poetic and the natural, with Alisoun representing the essence of the harmonious natural world evoked by the Miller's sense of poetic justice, or as a subtly but profoundly lascivious leer at Alisoun's body, particularly her midsection, or 'queinte'. In what follows, I will suggest that though both of these readings are possible, they are deeply limited because they fail to read the text closely enough. Subjecting the portrait to severe scrutiny yields not only new insight, but also an appreciation for the degree to which it produces and then sustains an aesthetic tension between the natural and the artificial as a way of preserving its own vision of the beautiful. I have chosen the eleven lines above because they contain the exact midpoint of the thirty-eight-line-long passage, which is structured around the image at its centre: Alisoun's purse, 'Tasseled with silk and perled with latoun' (l. 3251). Chaucer has taken this purse from the *Romance of the Rose*, where it appears in the Old Woman's discourse on love as a crucial element of a young woman's seductive costume: the maiden wishes 'particularly to show off her purse, which should be right out for everyone to see' ('Et l'aumoniere toute voie, | Que bien est drois que l'en la voie').[3] In the *Romance of the Rose*, of course, the purse is a sexual metaphor pure and simple. But as I will show, Alisoun's purse is in fact quite real, with very specific design features and a very different set of referents from that

---

[2] *The Riverside Chaucer*, ed. Larry Benson (Cambridge, MA: Houghton Mifflin, 1987), ll. 3247–58. All subsequent references to Chaucer will be in the text by title and line number.

[3] See Guillaume de Lorris and Jean de Meun, *Le Roman de la Rose*, ed. Daniel Poiron (Paris: Garnier-Flammarion, 1974), ll. 13563–4, and *The Romance of the Rose*, trans. Charles Dahlberg (Princeton: Princeton University Press, 1971), 233. For a discussion, with illustrations, of *aumonières* and their sexual implications in medieval texts, see Michael Camille, *The Medieval Art of Love: Objects and Subjects of Desire* (New York: Harry N. Abrams, 1998), 63–5.

of Jean de Meun. In Chaucer's rendering, the purse is further framed by a series of comparative similes, the only ones in the passage to assert Alisoun's superiority to the world that she inhabits; she is 'moore blisful', 'softer', and 'brighter' than the pere-jonette tree, than wool, than a gold coin. These comparatives are themselves formally set off from the remainder of the passage with the repetition of the word 'newe'; both pere-jonette tree and 'noble' are described as 'newe', creating a ring in which the purse is nestled, drawing our attention away from the closing couplet of the passage—'For any lord to leggen in his bedde, | Or yet for any good yeman to wedde' (ll. 3269–70)—which usually serves as the rubric for interpreting its function within the tale as a whole.[4]

Like Alisoun's clothes, her purse is highly decorated and elaborately made, with silk 'tassels' (which can mean either gatherings of fringe or a kind of fastening) and little beads of 'latoun' embedded in the leather.[5] Everything about the purse is artificial, from the worked leather, to the tassels, to the 'perles' made of 'latoun'; it is not even a *useful* thing, as we hear nothing about its contents or even if it can be opened, given the ambiguity of 'tassel'. Indeed, both 'perling' and 'latoun' are the end results of processes highly alienated from the natural world. To 'perle' is to craft little pearl-like studs of metal and embed them in leather or cloth, thus making ersatz versions of a natural object; 'latoun' or 'latten' is an alloy of copper, tin, and various metals that is then polished to shine like gold.[6] It, too, is a *made* object, something constructed by human beings and used here for decoration, for the creation of an object with no discernible purpose in either the text or Alisoun's life. In some senses, it represents the high point of one distinct element of the description, its anti-naturalistic aspect, in which the seeming naturalism of Alisoun's portrait is undermined by the highly artificial and decorated quality of her appearance and her body.

How are we to judge this artifice? A modern understanding of beauty—by which I mean, very loosely, post-Kantian beauty—favours the natural, the unadorned, the pure contingency of beauty, a quality given sparingly to some persons and landscapes and not at all to others. From paintings to advertisements we see this understanding of beauty at work in our own culture, deeply embedded in modern consciousnesses; for a medieval version, we have only to look as far as Criseyde and her joined but *unplucked* brows. Chaucer's aristocratic heroine has a flaw in

---

[4] For example, Kevin Kiernan has argued that the entire description is characterized by the Miller's leering optics. See 'The Art of the Descending Catalogue, and a Fresh Look at Alisoun', *Chaucer Review*, 10 (1975), 1–16, 14, 15. E. T. Donaldson more subtly suggests that Chaucer makes conventional romance heroines into the 'targets of a lewd whistle'. See *Speaking of Chaucer* (London: Athlone Press, 1970), 25. An exception to this tendency can be found in Jill Mann's 'Speaking Images in Chaucer's "Miller's Tale"', in *Speaking Images: Essays in Honor of V. A. Kolve* (Asheville, NC: Pegasus Press, 2001), 237–56, in which she suggests that the sheer excessiveness of the details in the portrait suggest a kind of sexual excess coming from *Alisoun* herself, an 'overspilling energy' that asks 'to be realised in narrative action' (p. 241).

[5] See *MED*, s.v. 'tassel' and 'tasselen'.   [6] See *MED*, s.v. 'perled', a, and 'latoun', a.

her beauty but does not rectify it; plucking appears to be associated firmly with the loveliness of 'wenches' rather than the 'deignous' attractiveness of a Criseyde or Emelye, as Alisoun's eyebrows are 'ful smale ypulled' (l. 3245).[7] Think, too, of the antifeminist discourse that inveighs against women's use of artificial beauty enhancements, in such texts as the *Romance of the Rose*.[8] Alisoun's purse links her to a world in which artifice supersedes nature and enhances what the contingencies of natural reproduction have wrought. Indeed, all of her actions are apparently for pleasure, an excessive and expressive aesthetic of artifice for its own sake. Here she distinctly differs from that other Alisoun, the Wife of Bath, whose artifice—both sartorial and rhetorical—is all designed for a *purpose*, gaining 'maistrye', a new suitor, clerkly approbation.

What of nature can be salvaged from this vision of beauty? Or perhaps not nature at all, but beauty itself requires salvage. After all, it would be entirely Chaucerian to expose underneath the seeming loveliness of a 'wenche' her artificiality and thus undermine her claim to beauty. That would perhaps be the Ovidian reading of the passage, one in which the secrets of femininity are revealed in order to expose its fundamental ugliness, the 'thyng al rough and long yherd' (l. 3738) Artificial Alisoun is *soft*, 'softer than the wolle is of a wether' | (l. 3249); Alisoun stripped of her artifice is rough and frightening, repulsive, distasteful. Is beauty then only a surface designed to conceal and seduce, form overlaying horrible content? While this may be Absolon's conclusion, his is not the only perspective in the tale, nor is it at all privileged. Chaucer clearly performs this reading precisely in order to reject it. It is the clerical reading *par excellence*, the vision of beauty as seduction and concealment that figures like Jerome (and indeed Jankyn) persistently promote. Over and against this dark vision of beauty Chaucer constructs an aesthetic in which both nature and artifice have roles to play.

When Chaucer's Miller interrupts the progression of tales from Knight to Monk, a new aesthetic enters the poem and with it an attempt to redefine both poetry and beauty. Even the simple gesture of cataloguing a wench rather than a lady, and doing so in affirmative and not parodic terms (we see an example of the latter in the 'Reeve's Tale' and its description of poor Malin), represents an attempt to recalibrate the reader's aesthetic sensibility and to introduce new terms of judgement and evaluation.[9] Chaucer asks us to look anew (at a wench),

---

[7] Though, we should recall, Emelye is plucking flowers to make a garland for her head when first seen by Palamon ('Knight's Tale', l. 1053), a scene that Mark Miller has recently analysed in relation to questions of agency, self-fashioning, and freedom; see *Philosophical Chaucer: Love, Sex and Agency in the Canterbury Tales* (Cambridge: Cambridge University Press, 2004), 84–91, esp. 86; for Miller's reading of the 'Miller's Tale', see pp. 36–81.

[8] For the Old Woman's discussion of feminine artifice, see Guillaume de Lorris and Jean de Meun, *Le Roman de la Rose*, ll. 13265–600, and *The Romance of the Rose*, trans. Charles Dahlberg, 229–34.

[9] The 'Weddyng of Sir Gawain and Dame Ragnell', as Kevin Kiernan has noted, is a good example of the 'inverted' blazon, with each characteristic of the beautiful lady parodied and turned upside down. Alisoun's description is strikingly different. See 'Art of the Descending Catalogue', 12.

to touch, listen, taste, and smell again (at, to, and of nature), and finally to think hard about the relationships among standards of beauty, class-based discourse, and vernacular poetry. The formal structures at work in the poem thus bear a strong resemblance to Alisoun's ornamented vision of beauty, in which she decks herself out in elaborate garments from head to toe, each of which is embroidered, beaded, gored, laced, barred and girdled on every available surface ('bifore … bihynde … aboute … withinne … withoute' (ll. 3238–40)).[10] Emelye's simple garlands look dignified and austere by contrast. Chaucer articulates multiple aesthetics in his portrait of Alisoun, linked to rank, gender, and poetic stature, and these aesthetics mingle in such a way that traditional understandings of 'medieval beauty' are rewritten and radically reshaped.

First, Alisoun herself must be credited with a notion of beauty, expressed through her clothing and her alterations to her body. Chaucer conceals this aspect of the portrait by consistently using the passive voice in his descriptions of her dress and face ('broyden', 'ypulled', and so on). But who else would have chosen her clothing or plucked her brows? Alisoun has presented herself for viewing, and clearly has a very particular notion of beauty, one in which artifice and decoration play central roles. Beauty is here gendered feminine and is modified by the word 'wenche' ('swiche a wenche' (l. 3254)), which tells us both her sex and her place in the social order. Perhaps today it might be described as 'busy' or 'ornamental' and, then as now, it is linked to her non-aristocratic status; Alisoun has imitated great ladies, but has done so with an excess and verve that lead to her wearing a brooch 'as brood … as a bokeler' (l. 3266) A second aesthetic at work defines beauty as pleasure for the senses, a kind of Epicureanism of the feminine, in which every human sensory capacity is sated with delightful sensations: she can be seen (she shines), she can be touched (she is softer than ram's wool), tasted (sweet as bragot or meath), smelled (sweet as apples), and heard (lively as a swallow). In this vision, which is surely masculine (as the final lines of the passage suggest), Alisoun is an object for use *and* delight, a kind of sensorium of pleasures. We see a distinction between estates; lords simply enjoy her while yeomen wed her, and, presumably, beget children with her. Beauty, in this vision, is a means to a sexual end for both men and women; Alisoun's ornamentation becomes *her* means of achieving a goal it is assumed that both men and women desire, sexual intercourse and marriage.

We find ourselves in a world of art 'for profit or delight' (to use the Horatian formulation beloved of medieval poets), in which uses and endings supersede pure beauty, natural or artificial, and replace the pleasure of the moment ('solaas') with the goal-directed drive of 'sentence'—in this case, marriage.[11] Or so things stand

---

[10] See Mann, 'Speaking Images', 241.

[11] Horace, *Satires, Epistles and Ars Poetica*, trans. H. Rushton Fairclough (Cambridge, MA: Harvard University Press, 1936), 478–9, l. 333, 'aut prodesse volunt aut delectare poetae' (Poets aim either to benefit or to amuse).

for yeomen. Lords, in contrast, are allowed to enjoy the pleasures of beauty with none of the pains of labour or the 'wo in mariage' that the lower orders must endure. That is why, for a noble, a 'wenche' like Alisoun represents an aesthetic of useless pleasure, far more so than an Emelye, for whom deeds must be done and enterprises undertaken. Even knowing, however, that lords and yeomen, ladies and wenches have different standards of beauty and different responses to beautiful objects, cannot blind readers to the universalizing drive of the portrait, to the ways in which it solicits consensus by embedding the artificial in the natural. This claim rests on the assertion that 'the natural' represents some kind of universal human experience, some notion of shared sensory perception such that apples always taste and smell sweet, skipping calves are always appealing and joyous, 'softness' is always delightful, and so on. One might not like Alisoun's dress sense, finding it too gaudy or too revealing (that 'lowe coler' (l. 3265)), but the portrait seems to assume that when she is compared to, or supersedes, nature, all readers will agree that she must be, in fact, beautiful.

I have been describing the mixture of aesthetic perspectives that Chaucer establishes throughout his portrait of Alisoun, and suggesting that in each of them we find a different emphasis on the natural and the artificial, with some particularly interested in artifice and others captured by the pleasing images from nature embedded in the text. By 'artifice' I mean those elements in the description that derive from the hand of a human being, which betray their human origin in one way or another—from a 'barred ceynt' (l. 3235) to a 'brood brooch' (l. 3265–6) to 'bragot' or 'meeth' (l. 3261) 'Nature' becomes, by process of elimination, everything else. Or so it would seem. Where do Alisoun's eyebrows fit into this model? Or indeed, the 'wolle of a wether', which can be in its natural state, on the sheep, or sheared and processed by human beings? The apples Chaucer mentions have been harvested; even the swallow sits on a 'berne', symbol of cultivation and agriculture—the human control over the natural environment. The more closely we examine the natural imagery in the passage, the more artificial it seems to become, the more we realize that human hands have left their imprints upon almost every element of the natural world, every seemingly untouched and innocent created thing. But in general the effect of Chaucer's description is to blur the distinction between nature and artifice with which I began, to break down the seeming opposition between natural beauty and women's artifice, and to call into question thereby the value judgements associated with the two poles of the binary.

To address such questions, we have to move backward to two moments of oddity in the description itself, one that is formally privileged (that ubiquitous purse) and one that is strikingly out of step with the vision of nature and sensation that I have been articulating above (Alisoun's 'loud' voice). These odd moments are linked, I will argue, by their connection to poetry itself, by the way in which they bring together the artifice of Alisoun's dress with the art of 'making', linking the human tendency to shape and reshape the natural (shearing sheep or brewing bragot) with Chaucer's vision of what poetry fundamentally *does* and whence it ultimately derives. To begin with the purse:

> And softer than the wolle is of a wether;
> And by hir girdel heeng a purs of lether
> Tasseled with silk and perled with latoun.
> In al this world, to seken up and doun.

What, we might usefully ask at this juncture, is Chaucer making, or what has been made? It could be a woman, or a purse, or a purse as a metaphor for a 'queinte' which is a synecdoche of a woman, or 'woman-ness'. Certainly this purse could be said to be 'queinte' in the neutral sense of the term, meaning only 'ingeniously made, skilfully wrought; elaborate, intricate'.[12] But a close analysis of the purse yields two crucial observations: first, Chaucer describes it in such a way as to emphasize its ersatz quality, the sense in which it has been decorated ('perled') *as if* with gems, and *as if* in gold. No real pearls are in sight, and 'latoun' is merely an alloy, a made substance, something that *represents* the real thing (gold) but is not itself that thing. Second, the thing itself, the purse, is not the only the leather object fastened with a tassel and decorated with latoun that Chaucer would have known. The other such object would be a book. Medieval books were bound with leather-covered boards, which were often decorated with metal—gold, silver, brass—and they sometimes featured clasps with tassels.[13] In an entry in Edward IV's Wardrobe accounts, we see a suggestive payment 'to Alice Claver for the makyng of xvj laces and xvj tasshels for the garnysshing of divers of the Kinges bookes, ij s. viij d'.[14] Though this entry is dated almost a century after Chaucer composed the 'Miller's Tale', other evidence confirms that fasteners and clasps were often decorated with tassels, and that book covers were adorned with metalwork from a very early date.[15] They thus functioned as tangible symbols of their

---

[12] *MED*, s.v. 'queinte', 2c.

[13] For a history of early bookbinding, from the Nag Hammadi codices to the end of the Middle Ages, see J. A. Szirmai, *The Archaeology of Medieval Book Binding* (Brookfield, VT: Ashgate Press, 1999).

[14] Nicholas Harris Nicolas (ed.), *Privy Purse Expenses of Elizabeth of York: Wardrobe Accounts of Edward IV* (London: William Pickering, 1830), 125 (for 1480). For a much later (1572), but still interesting, image of a bound Spanish charter with gold tooling, and silk ties and a tassel, see fig. 65 in P. J. M. Marks, *The British Library Guide to Bookbinding: History and Techniques* (Toronto: University of Toronto Press, 1998), 74. In the Beinecke Library there is also a manuscript with tassels; see Marston MS 268, a twelfth-century French manuscript that has 'two strap-and-pin fastenings, the pins on the lower board and the kermes pink, tawed skin strap ending in a catch with a twisted, tawed skin cord and tassel attached, later additions [?]'. In Barbara Shailor, *Catalogue of Medieval and Renaissance Manuscripts in the Beinecke Rare Book and Manuscript Library, Yale University*, 4 vol. (Binghamton, NY: Medieval and Renaissance Texts and Studies, 1984–2000), iii. 528. It is also possible that manuscripts had bookmarkers with tassels; Graham Pollard describes the tabs on the upper spines of some books, sometimes with holes in the centre stitched round with coloured silk, to which bookmarkers were tied with knots; see his 'Describing Medieval Bookbindings', in *Medieval Learning and Literature: Essays Presented to Richard William Hunt* (Oxford: Clarendon Press, 1976), 50–65, at 62.

[15] For discussions of metal decorations and furnishings on Gothic manuscripts, including illustrations of metal stamping and punching, see Szirmai, *Archaeology*, 263–71. For illustrations of fasteners

owners' wealth and prestige, communicating visually a message that the text inside the covers could not be relied on to produce, depending on its purpose and frame. Like 'perling' and 'latoun', books are not things-in-themselves so much as they are representations of things—and people, places, actions, objects, events. They are, as Francesca famously reminds us, go-betweens, and sexualized go-betweens at that.

It is precisely this connection that Chaucer exploits and indeed, reaches beyond in the next few lines, when he compares Alisoun's 'hewe' to a coin:

> Ful brighter was the shynyng of hir hewe
> Than in the Tour the noble yforged newe.   (ll. 3255–6)

These lines set in place an unsettling link between the image of the purse-as-book—which encourages a kind of metapoetic, self-referential reading—and the image of a gold coin, an object that combines image and text, abstraction and particularity, in a succinct and disturbing way. A coin is a mimetic object. It is a thing that functions in the abstract. It links the 'real' world of Alisoun's costume, in which she *wears* a purse, to the 'poetic' world of comparison, in which she is *like* a coin: the purse becomes metaphorical, and the coin becomes 'real', as something that might be inserted in the 'real' purse. This coin has a specific identity and a specific point of origin: it is a 'noble yforged newe' in the 'Tour', the London Mint. Historically, the noble bore the image of the king, and was an unusual and very popular English coin; first struck in 1344, on the back it depicted Edward III sitting in a ship, with a large sword and shield, and probably commemorated the battle of Sluys in 1340. As Donald Baker showed long ago, the ship itself was unusually realistic, and represented a one-masted, square-rigged cog; the coin also bore a legend from the Gospel of Luke, 4: 30, 'Ihc avtem transiens per medivm illorvm ibat' ('But Jesus Christ, passing through the midst of them, went his way').[16] Like a book, or the image of the king on a coin, Alisoun's description is a substitute for Alisoun, and along the way, a substitute for a good many other ideas—like nature and beauty—as well. The comparison of Alisoun to a coin helps to make sense of the motivation at work behind the description itself, for when we examine the particularity of the coin, its *specificity*, we find not only the king, but also images that Chaucer picks up again further on. Alisoun is 'Long as a mast and upright as a bolt. | A brooch she bar upon hir lowe coler, | As brood as is the boos of a bokeler' (ll. 3264–6). These martial images fit oddly with the natural world

---

with tassels, see the discussions of Late Coptic and Byzantine bindings on 42–3 (fig. 3.10) and 81–2 (fig. 6.15). For a description of 'treasure bindings', with metal and jewels, see p. 81. Evidence for the fastening and furnishing of decorated English manuscripts before 1450 is very thin, as is evidence for fourteenth- and fifteenth-century 'treasure bindings', because the majority were destroyed during the Reformation or have suffered the 'ravages of time and moths'; see Mirjam Foot, 'English Decorated Bookbindings', in Jeremy Griffiths and Derek Pearsall (eds.), *Book Production and Publishing in Britain, 1375–1475* (Cambridge: Cambridge University Press, 1989), 65–86, at 65.

[16]   Donald Baker, 'Gold Coins in Mediaeval English Literature', *Speculum*, 36 (1961), 282–7, at 285. For an illustration of a noble, front and back, see plate I, number 3.

evoked by most of the similes that sit between the image of the coin and that of the 'brood brooch'. But in the context of the noble, they become clearer; Edward III sits beside a mast, carrying a large shield and sword. By rendering Alisoun in terms of the noble, Chaucer enables us to see her as parallel to, and literally made of, imagery from a facsimile—a near-sacred facsimile, but a form of imitation or mediation nonetheless. She commemorates a commemoration, and it thus lends to her some of its own qualities of stability and thingness. Coins, that is, are forms of representation that both imitate an absent thing or event or person, and have a particular identity and value of their own. At the same time, they are concrete forms of abstraction, things that act like ideas. Alisoun's description acts as a memorial to a person. It acts as a concrete textual object that stands in for an idea—about 'wenches', about nature, about beauty. Inserting an Alisoun made up of the elements of a 'noble' allows us to see the text itself, the thirty-eight lines, as a thing, an artistic object in its own right.

At this point we must heed the words on the coin. They are drawn from Luke 4, which recounts Jesus' temptation in the desert and his preaching in Galilee, where he so offended the Galileans that they cast him out of the city, intending to hurl him down the hill upon which it sat; instead, 'Ihc avtem transiens per medivm illorvm ibat' ('But Jesus Christ, passing through the midst of them, went his way'). Baker suggests that the quotation functions as a kind of amulet against coin-clipping, and indeed, the link that it establishes between Christ and the king does sacralize the coin, making clipping equivalent to an attack on the body of the king; as we know from the Statute of Treasons, enacted only eight years after the coin was first struck, this equivalence was not only noted but actively promoted by both king and parliament.[17] The statute asserted that both counterfeiting and coin-clipping constituted treason, just as did attacks on the king's body and those of his immediate family; as Hoccleve would insist sixty years later, physical damage to a coin was equivalent to damage to the body of the king, and deserved the same punishment.[18] When Alisoun is compared to a noble, then, she is being linked very appropriately to an object designed for circulation and use, but not for damage or penetration; as critics have often remarked, even though she is sexually handled by three men over the course of the story (two willing, one unwitting), she is not punished at tale's end, nor does her honour or reputation seem to suffer the same drastic consequences as those Virginius fears for Virginia, or Lucrece experiences so painfully in the Legend of Good Women. Neither she nor her 'purse' is ever described as less than intact or as injured in any way; her beauty remains fresh and shining throughout time and despite use. Here we see, perhaps, the optimism of the description and the fear that lurks beneath it.

[17] Ibid. 285; see also John Evans, 'The First English Gold Coins', Numismatic Chronicle, 3rd ser. 20 (1900), 27–31. For the Statute of Treasons, see J. G. Bellamy, The Law of Treason in England in the Later Middle Ages (Cambridge: Cambridge University Press, 1970), 85–6.

[18] See Hoccleve's 'Dialogue', ll. 99–196, in 'My Compleinte' and Other Poems, ed. Roger Ellis (Exeter: University of Exeter Press, 2001), 134–6.

To return once more to the problem of nature and artifice, it is the ephemerality of the natural that lends to the passage its emotional force, its capacity to engage the reader in more than a sexual way by arousing his anxiety about the passage of time and the inevitable decay of beauty. The provisional solution that Chaucer proffers is itself time honoured, but no less effective or meaningful for that: the *representation* of an object or a person can outlast its beauty, capturing it both through the meaning of the words on the page ('Alisoun is beautiful') and with their very form (the poetry itself is beautiful). Reading the passage becomes itself an experience of, an engagement with, the beautiful. This process appears in miniature in the section of the passage framed by the repetition of 'newe', which begins with the 'pere-jonette tree' and ends with a coin, the noble. The tree, as Langland knew, was an emblem of ephemerality; in a passage added to the C-text of *Piers Plowman*, Rechelesnesse tells 'lordes … and ladyes': 'Hit lasteth nat longe that is lycour-swete, | As pesecoddes, pere ionettes, plommes and cheries; | That lihtlich launseth vp litel while dureth, | And that rathest rypeth rotieth most sonnest' (C. XII. 220–3).[19] Alisoun's ripe young beauty, which evokes proleptic sorrow for its loss in the image of the pere-jonette, is transformed over the course of eight lines into the shining light of a new coin. The natural becomes artificial; the organic thing becomes an inorganic image, the tree is transformed into a text. What was once ephemeral has been reified and thus commodified; a 'wenche' transformed into a 'wenche', a maid into a prostitute. That this is not merely a cynically described instance of the pere-jonette's quick decay is indicated by the specificity with which the coin is identified: it is not any gold coin, but a *noble*, made in a particular mint, with a particular inscription—and as I have shown, lest we fail to get the point, Alisoun is reinscribed as the image on the coin a few lines later.

The specificity of the noble is significant, because it allows us to begin to see what might be the broader implications of Chaucer's lavish description of Alisoun, his clear investment in the portrait and its complexity, his refusal to reduce her to raw sexuality or to deny that she is sexual. Despite many attempts to link Chaucer to one or another medieval scholasticism—to nominalism, or Aristotelianism, or Neoplatonism—such readings have never fully captured the literary critical imagination in the way that (for example) Charles Muscatine's exposition of Chaucer's debt to the French tradition continues to do.[20] This failure has nothing to do with the skill of the critic, or the objective relevance of the research; after all, it would be hard to say in the present day that various

[19] William Langland, *Piers Plowman: The C Version*, ed. George Russell and George Kane (London: Athlone Press, 1997), 449.

[20] Charles Muscatine, *Chaucer and the French Tradition: A Study in Style and Meaning* (Berkeley and Los Angeles: University of California Press, 1957). Muscatine's reading of Alisoun's portrait focuses on the relationship of convention to naturalism, suggesting that 'the literary effect is as if to present Alisoun as the one precious illusion in the poem' but that, at the same time, 'the animalism and the ideality must be intertwined' (pp. 229–30).

poststructuralist theoretical models were irrelevant to the work of contemporary poets. But Chaucer so resolutely vernacularizes everything he touches—including even Boethius, the one philosopher he translates and quotes in depth—that such turns to philosophy never quite explain the motivation, function, or effect of his poetry on readers. It is as if ideas about philosophy were floating in the House of Rumor and occasionally made their way into his work, becoming transformed in the process from abstractions into concrete particulars, into characters, events, plots, ecphrases, images, and the like. These particulars, taken together, come closest to constituting what we might call an 'aesthetic' in Chaucer's poetry, something for which neither history (as in the 'contexts' of historicism') nor philosophy (whether Ockham, Aquinas, or Derrida) can account in any specific way. Chaucerian verse demands close reading; close reading disrupts abstraction. In the case of Alisoun's description, what we find when we look closely at a noble is the same structuring tension with which I began this consideration of beauty, that between the abstract and particular, and it is a tension that *must be sustained* in order for Alisoun's beauty to become meaningful. Sustained, that is, in order that Alisoun does not become an idealization (like Emelye) or an assemblage of particular body parts (her 'queinte'). Only if she is both of these and neither of these at once can beauty be said to be authentically present.

Beauty, for Chaucer, must be considered an entity whose essential characteristic is its tendency to mediate, to stitch together part and whole. Without falling into the well-worn trap of considering Chaucer to be a singularly modern figure, or singularly innovative, we may nevertheless note that he seems strongly conscious, in his description of Alisoun, that he is doing something new. To take some pages from Umberto Eco's lucid exposition of beauty in the Middle Ages, he is combining notions of beauty available to him 'in the air' and vernacularizing them in such a way that he forges a text both particularized in its beauty, and paradigmatic in its definitions of the beautiful and of art. We see in Alisoun's 'shining hewe', for example, what Eco describes as the central value in medieval aesthetics, crossing boundary after boundary between schools of thought and philosophies of beauty: *claritas*, or light.[21] That it is instantly reified as a gold coin—instantly particularized—brings us immediately to the 'haeccitas' of Duns Scotus, the nominalism of Ockham, to the 'universe of particulars' in which 'beauty had to be sought in that uniqueness of the image which is generated by felicity or genius'.[22] In other words, Chaucer enacts what Eco sees as the fundamental transformation at work in medieval aesthetics, in which 'beauty changed from being a property of the ideal order to being a property of concrete particulars'.[23]

---

[21] Umberto Eco, *Art and Beauty in the Middle Ages*, trans. Hugh Bredin (New Haven: Yale University Press, 1986), 43–51; see also his discussion of Aquinas and the 'expressive capacity of organisms', pp. 74–83.
[22] Ibid. 86, 89.   [23] Ibid. 116.

Lest this seem like mere rewriting of the oldest Chaucerian story in the book—the story of how Chaucer conquered the Middle Ages and induced the Renaissance—let us remember how thickly he renders the tension between idealization and particularity, and in what register. For Chaucer to ask us to see a 'wenche' as an illustration of 'beauty' is an act that turns the Emelyes and Criseydes of the world on their well-coiffed heads. But of course, *only* a wench could be flexible enough to cross the boundary between the ideal and the real, the light and the shining coin. Nor should nature be forgotten here. The pere-jonette tree becomes both more and less than a figure for decay over the course of the passage; less, because it is particularized in Alisoun and stripped of its moralizing character, and more, because it becomes beautiful in itself, as a metaphor. This final move allows us to see Chaucer's motivation at work. What he loses in the move from abstract idealism to particularized description is authority, the capacity to moralize and to instruct. What he gains is a form of cultural capital, in that the verses suddenly acquire a market value, a beauty that lends them a market share. Nobles are not the only objects upon which the beautiful can be etched and engraved; we have Alisoun's purse, a closed book waiting to be opened—perhaps waiting for a coin before disgorging its secrets.

This thought—that perhaps art, in the form of the beautiful book or the beautiful description, itself participates in the commodity logic that Chaucer has elucidated in relation to Alisoun—directs us to the biggest point of ambiguity in the passage, her 'loude and yerne' song, or voice. In turning to this point, I will be broadening my scope a bit to suggest some ways in which the poetic conception of beauty might be brought into play in medieval literary criticism, in part by simply acknowledging that the category had meaning for Chaucer and for other late medieval poets as a contested and strained concept that nevertheless offered a way to achieve a certain freedom from didacticism and exemplarity. Immediately after comparing Alisoun to a 'noble', Chaucer deploys one of his famous adversative conjunctions, telling us, 'But of hir song, it was as loude and yerne | As any swalwe sittynge on a berne' (ll. 3257–8).[24] Almost everything in the description, up until this point, has been unabashedly positive, a celebration of Alisoun's highly individualized beauty and her skill at manipulating and enhancing it. The passage builds to a climax (the 'noble yforged newe' (l. 3256)) and we find ourselves stopped short by a 'But' and a seemingly negative comparison between Alisoun and a loudly twittering swallow—a bird traditionally associated with lust.[25] That world of sensuality I

---

[24] For Chaucer's adversative conjunctions, see E. Talbot Donaldson, 'Adventures with the Adversative Conjunction in the General Prologue to the *Canterbury Tales*; or, What's Before the But?', in Michael Benskin and M. L. Samuels (eds.), *So meny people longages and tonges: Philological Essays in Scots and Mediaeval English presented to Angus McIntosh*(Edinburgh: M. Benskin and M. L. Samuels, 1981), 355–66.

[25] For this association, see Beryl Rowland, *Blind Beasts: Chaucer's Animal World* (Kent, OH: Kent State University Press, 1971), 24; her reading focuses on the sexuality of the portrait, as revealed in

described earlier, the natural world filled with universally appealing delights, comes suddenly to an end. 'But' introduces a new series of similes focused on Alisoun as an *active* figure, who 'skippes', who 'wynses' and 'makes game', perhaps with the idea that this frenetic activity compensates for the loudness of her voice and emphasizes the sheer sexual energy of her being; as Chaucer says, '*Thereto* she koude skippe and make game' (l. 3259), with 'thereto' implying a structure of purposiveness.[26] But looking closely at the image of the bird, we find that the easy association between the swallow and lust is undone by Chaucer's own use of the image in *Troilus and Criseyde*, where he associates it with the sorrowful 'Proigne', who 'cheter[s] … How Tereus gan for hire suster take' so loudly that Pandarus is awakened 'with the noyse of hire (II. 68–70).[27] By embedding this association with Philomela—both in his own poetry and in Ovid's *Metamorphoses*—within the description of Alisoun, Chaucer creates a simile of tremendous complexity, in which the horrifying story of a woman whose silencing produces art, the woven image of her own rape and mutilation, flickers at odd intervals through the consciousness of the reader, never explicitly declaring itself but never quite absent, either. Alisoun's 'song' functions as an embedded figure for poetry itself, and for the uneasy relationships encoded in the passage among beauty, sexual desire, and the making of art.

I have argued throughout this essay that Chaucer uses his description of Alisoun to stage an investigation or exploration of the relationship of beauty to individual perspectives (dictated by such categories as rank and gender), and the idea of a universal aesthetic based on nature. He further, and obsessively, returns to the problem of use and uselessness; what seems like the mere crudeness of a crude man, the Miller, is in fact a fairly roundabout way of addressing the usefulness of beauty in a world of sexuality and commercial exchange. Alisoun is the proximate cause of such meditation, but Chaucer is not really interested in Alisoun per se. He is interested in what happens to poetry—to making—once it has been written. Does it circulate like a coin? Does it 'cheter'? Does it delight, and, if so, is it consumed for pleasure or reproduction? He chooses Alisoun (and her purse, and her 'song') as his figure because, like him, she lives in a world where others make the rules and create the endings—where lords bed and yeomen wed the objects of their desire. Only if some vision of beauty can be constructed that embraces the tension between

---

the simile of the weasel and in the Miller's focus on Alisoun's clothing and her 'likerous ye' (see pp. 24–30).

[26] See *MED*, s.v. 'thereto', 8c, 'with ref. to a desired end or event, goal, etc …. (d) with verbs expressing notions of making, devising, designating, etc.: for that purpose, for that, to that end, to realize that plan'. One example given is from Chaucer's 'Knight's Tale', 'For every wight that lovede chivalrye … Hath preyed that he myghte been of that game; | And wel was hym that therto chosen was' (ll. 2106, 2108–9).

[27] Some manuscripts record 'chitering' instead of 'sittynge' in the description of the swallow in the 'Miller's Tale', thus strengthening the association between these passages. See J. M. Manly and E. Rickert, *The Text of the Canterbury Tales* (Chicago: University of Chicago Press, 1940), iii., 135, notes to l. 3258.

the particularity of human making and using (artifice and construction), and the universality of pleasure and pain in the natural world will art have done its job. That is the task Chaucer sets himself, and it is a task left largely unfinished, a Pandora's box that has yet to be closed.

Poets like the *Gawain*-poet, Langland, and Lydgate all understood beauty in similarly troubled terms, though not always with Chaucer's clarity. The ecphrasis of the alliterative tradition is one link we might establish between Chaucer's attempt to rethink the beautiful and other Middle English texts and traditions. It is clear that the *Gawain*-poet similarly engaged with the relationship between the natural and the artificial, between the created and the made, in such passages as the dissection of the deer, where the full impact of alliterative ornamentation and artifice is put to use in the service of unmaking a created thing and making it into something that serves human needs, i.e. meat. In the same way, Langland constructs a vision of nature and the beauty of nature in Passus XI (B-text), only to severely reprove both Will and (by implication) readers for being attracted to it in the very next passus. In this case, the emblematic figure is the peacock, 'merveilled' at by Will in Kynde's vision, and 'unmade' by Ymaginatif shortly afterward: 'For pursue a pecok or a pehen to cacche, | They may noght flee fer ne ful heighe neither; | For the trailynge of his tail ouertaken is he soone. | And his flessh is foul flessh and his feet bothe, | And vnlouelich of ledene and looth for to here.'[28] For Langland, the natural world must be read properly, that is, with human reason, before it can be safely engaged; its beauty is the index of its dangerousness for human beings, who are seduced by it because they lack the proper aesthetic. It is the humble lark, with her 'louelich ledene' (XII. 264), that Will must *learn* to embrace, rather than the showy peacock, or indeed, the ravishing Mede and Fortune, both women extravagantly and artificially decorated. As in *Sir Gawain and the Green Knight*, some form of readerly 'unmaking' must take place before the hero or the reader can safely encounter the beautiful. This distinction between genuine and false beauty is one that Chaucer considers, but rejects; like Langland's bird, his 'peacock' Alisoun has an 'unlovelich' voice, a 'song ... loude and yerne'. But while Langland imagines the humble voice of the lark as the appropriate voice for both poetry and nature, Chaucer wants to embrace the loudness of the vernacular, its aggressivity, as part of an aesthetic mode with which he is experimenting and in which he is thoroughly invested. That loudness resonates with the flashy alliteration of the *Gawain*-poet, and later, with the extravagant aureation of Lydgate and his followers, for whom excessiveness in poetry—sweetness, shininess, and the like—becomes an end in itself. In all of these cases, the fault lines I have articulated here between human making and divine creation, particularity and abstraction, troubled the poets and remain to trouble us. Beauty became for them one locus of

---

[28] William Langland, *Piers Plowman: The B-Version*, ed. George Kane and E. Talbot Donaldson (London: Athlone Press, 1988), XII. 242-6. Subsequent references will be in the text by passus and line number.

tectonic stress, one hotspot in which these varied pressures came together in contra-dictory fashion, with Kynde's vision of love competing with Ymaginatif's exposure of the peacock's dirty tail, with Alisoun's soft and shiny self crying out like a lustful sparrow, or the doe leaping in the air and falling to the ground as mumbles and guts.

In all of these examples—and more could be given, including the frightening cyborg that is Hector in Lydgate's *Troy Book*—we see that dialectic between natural and artificial that so deeply structures Alisoun's description. The term that stitches them together, and that marks their distinctive character as literary works in a thriving and self-aware tradition, is beauty. I don't mean beauty as a Kantian universal, or as a Platonic form, but beauty as a medieval category that allowed poets to explore critical aspects of their own practice and its meaning in a broader frame. As readers of medieval poetry, we could perhaps do no better than to think through and with the idea of beauty as a way of grasping what is at stake in the literary tradition itself and its relation to those histories and philosophies that would seem to reject beauty in favour of either specificity or generality. Like light—the preferred medieval metaphor for beauty—the beautiful is both wave and particle, both abstract and particular, and cannot be grasped as one or the other. That is what Chaucer knew, and that is why Alisoun, purse and all, will always mean more than she seems to mean: she too, with her embellished purse and her plucked brows, insists on the beautiful as a category worth thinking about.

FURTHER READING

The place to start is Umberto Eco's *Art and Beauty in the Middle Ages* (n. 21 above); the interested reader can follow any one of many different paths leading through the labyrinth of medieval philosophical texts that engaged with aesthetics and the beautiful, including St Thomas Aquinas, Robert Grosseteste, William of Auvergne, Roger Bacon, William of Conches, Thierry of Chartres, Bernard of Tours, Alain de Lille, Duns Scotus, William Ockham, and many others. For a deeper examination of Aquinas, see Eco's *The Aesthetics of Thomas Aquinas*, trans. Hugh Bredin (Cambridge, MA.: Harvard University Press, 1988). Immanuel Kant's *Critique of the Power of Judgment*, trans. Eric Matthews (Cambridge: Cambridge University Press, 2001) includes his paradigmatic consideration of the aesthetic and of the place of beauty in it. Two works that have influenced my thinking are Theodor Adorno's *Aesthetic Theory*, trans. Robert Hullot-Kentor (Minneapolis: University of Minnesota Press, 1998), which explores the question of beauty in chapters on 'natural beauty' and 'art beauty', and Elaine Scarry's *On Beauty and Being Just (n. 1 above)*. The latter is a lyrical exploration of the parameters of beauty as a concept, as well as an argument for reintroducing beauty as a category for analysis and consideration in the study of art.

CHAPTER 15

IMAGINATIVE THEORY

NICOLETTE ZEEMAN

Schools theory and the figurative text

The ground-breaking volume *The Idea of the Vernacular* has put pre-modern English 'literary theory' firmly on the intellectual map.[1] However, the full extent of literary self-theorization—whether Latin or vernacular—only becomes apparent when we recognize that much of it is expressed in figured and even metaphorical form. Scholarship in Middle English literature should pay more attention to 'imaginative' articulations of literary theory. In this essay, I shall look at one particular literary-theoretical figure, the *chanson d'aventure* ('the song of adventure'). Both a genre of lyric in its own right, but also in due course a narrative unit inserted into longer narratives, the *chanson d'aventure* can perform a diverse range of literary self-commentaries.

In contrast to such figurative, 'literary' expressions of literary theory, the literary theory of the medieval schools tends to be articulated in a language that is analytical and explicit. Indeed, in Middle English studies the dominance of research into schools literary theory may explain scholars' relative lack of interest in figuratively expressed literary theory. And yet schools literary theory, despite its own analytical and explicit forms of articulation, also valorizes the use of radically figurative and imaginative language in literature as a way of describing textual issues. Even when an imaginative literary-theoretical figure such as the *chanson d'aventure* derives from a vernacular tradition, pre-modern awareness of its potential *as literary theory* is, I propose, underpinned by the literary theory of the schools.

Medieval school views of 'poetic' figuration are helpfully encapsulated in Lactantius' words, cited across the Middle Ages by Isidore of Seville, Rhabanus Maurus, Vincent of Beauvais, and Pierre Bersuire: 'it is the business of the poet elegantly and

---

[1] Jocelyn Wogan-Browne, Nicholas Watson, Andrew Taylor, and Ruth Evans (eds.), *The Idea of the Vernacular: An Anthology of Middle English Literary Theory 1280–1520* (Exeter: University of Exeter Press, 1999).

with oblique figures to turn and transfer things that have really occurred into other representations'; in the work of the poet 'something is carried over and obscured by the indirections of tropology'. This notion of classical poetry as a form of figurative 'other speaking' is fundamental to medieval grammatical teaching—and glossatory practice: language is equivocal and opaque—and provides a constant opportunity for verbal 'rewriting'. What Lactantius and the fourth-century *Aeneid* commentator Servius call poetic 'licence' ranges from local refiguration to the cultivation of various narrative conceits and to fiction itself; to use any of these modes is to write 'in the poetic manner'.[2] To describe the figured text as 'imaginative' also portrays it as appealing to the partly rational, image-combining, and hypothetical 'imaginative' power of the mind.[3] As described in Hermannus Alemannus' translation of Averroes' commentary on Aristotle's *Poetics*, figured poetry offers an imagistic *assimilatio* ('likening') that ranges from apparently 'convincing' narrative, described as if it were 'before our eyes', to highly troped and 'transferred, extraneous, altered and enigmatic' types of representation.[4] All these ideas about textuality are reflected in later medieval theories of the various biblical modes, which bring new formal awareness to long-standing practices of biblical exegesis as well as to the rhetoricized, affective, and inspirational languages of pastoral care and devotion.[5] Even later scholastic interest in the 'literal sense' of Scripture and 'exemplary' modes of writing, moreover, involves the recognition that they are still part of a wide spectrum of imaginative *assimilatio*.[6] Although they need not be, both 'poetical' and biblical writing can be figured, exemplary, particular, multiple, enigmatic, 'difficult', and inexplicit.

The full implications of these theories, and the glossatory practices that lie behind them, have only been partially recognized. Of course at one level theories about the figured and imaginative text serve as cues for various forms of grammatical, ethical, or other 'glossatory' recuperation, that is, for the production of more

---

[2] See Nicolette Zeeman, 'The Schools Give a License to Poets', in Rita Copeland (ed.), *Criticism and Dissent in the Middle Ages* (Cambridge: Cambridge University Press, 1996), esp. 156–7, 163, 171; also A. J. Minnis and A. B. Scott with the assistance of David Wallace (eds.), *Medieval Literary Theory and Criticism c.1100–c.1375. The Commentary Tradition* (Oxford: Clarendon Press, 1988), chs. 1, 4, 8, 9 (esp. pp. 428–32); Vincent Gillespie, 'The Study of Classical Authors: From the Twelfth Century to c. 1450', in Alastair Minnis and Ian Johnson (eds.), *The Cambridge History of Literary Criticism*, ii: *The Middle Ages* (Cambridge: Cambridge University Press, 2005), ch. 6.

[3] See Alastair J. Minnis, 'Langland's Ymaginatyf' and Late-Medieval Theories of Imagination', *Comparative Criticism: A Yearbook*, 3 (1981), 71–103.

[4] Minnis and Scott (eds.), *Medieval Literary Theory*, 305; Nicolette Zeeman, 'Alterations of Language', *Paragraph*, 13 (1990), 217–28, at 224–6; also Minnis, 'Langland's Ymaginatyf '; 'Medieval Imagination and Memory' in Minnis and Johnson (eds.), *Literary Criticism*, ii, ch. 7; Judson Boyce Allen, *The Ethical Poetic of the Later Middle Ages: A Decorum of Convenient Distinction* (Toronto: University of Toronto Press, 1982), esp. ch. 4.

[5] See Minnis and Scott (eds.), *Medieval Literary Theory*, chs. 4, 5, and 6.

[6] See ibid., ch. 6; Rita Copeland, *Pedagogy, Intellectuals, and Dissent in the Later Middle Ages: Lollardy and Ideas of Learning* (Cambridge: Cambridge University Press, 2001), chs. 1 and 2; identifying this with *assimilatio*, see Allen, *Ethical Poetic*, 95.

explicit readings in the form of 'literally', preceptively, or logically expressed interpretations that accord with the various pedagogies of Church and academia. Pre-modern alertness to the multivalency of language cannot, however, always be disciplinarily circumscribed and reincorporated in this way. On the contrary, extracted from the intellectual and ethical framework in which they were developed, schools theories about the figuratively and imaginative text—and the practices that accompany them—may become something more than mechanisms for conceptual control.[7]

These theories may, for instance, point to a rather different view of the figurative and imaginative text. While they clearly attribute a very real place to the figurative or imaginative text within the disciplines of grammar, rhetoric, ethics, or biblical studies, they also point to its discursive 'otherness'. In fact, precisely because schools 'science' and pedagogy attribute a certain primacy to analytical and explicit language, these theories raise the possibility that the figuratively and tropologically oriented text has the potential to speak from a different place altogether, *from outside the disciplines of the schools*. The distinction between explicit and implicit, literal and figural (however tenuous), may not only be internal to the various school disciplines, but also a means of defining their boundaries. Acknowledgement that the figural and imaginative text is formally 'other' grants it the capacity to stand apart from the institutions of clerical knowledge and power. Although this observation may not sound surprising to readers of pre-modern literature (Latin or vernacular), it must in the Middle Ages have acquired substantial authorization from having been articulated from within the schools. Ironically, then, the schools may themselves have encouraged forms of textuality that had the potential to query the schools' own intellectual and ethical project.

Nevertheless, historians of the literary theory of the schools remain reluctant to acknowledge this possibility, stressing instead the place of schools theories about figurative and imaginative textuality within an overarching academic and ecclesiastical hermeneutic. Writing on 'imaginative art', Alastair Minnis concludes that it 'is allowed considerable purchase within its own sphere of operation (personal ethical behaviour), but within the grand scheme of things that sphere occupies a lowly position'. Even Vincent Gillespie's capacious and subtle chapter on later medieval grammar and the study of the poets concludes that the 'perceived ethical indirectness [of the Classics] ... argued for a war[y] exegetical approach', putting 'commentators on their guard for the slipperiness of poetic meaning'. Similarly, the editors of *The Idea of the Vernacular* claim that emphasizing the literary theory of the schools leads to seeing only 'a theoretical field rooted in academic origins and spheres of influence'.[8]

---

[7] See Zeeman, 'The Schools Give a License', 156, 171–4.
[8] Minnis, 'Medieval Imagination and Memory', 255; Gillespie, 'The Study of Classical Authors', 161, 164, 192; Wogan-Browne (ed.), *The Idea of the Vernacular*, 314, 316.

Nevertheless, the schools' valorization of discourses that are *by definition* 'latent' must authorize the development of figured and imaginative literary writing in the vernacular: writers of literary texts must have assumed figuration to be a fundamental tool of their trade. Indeed, such formal recognition may also have facilitated a sense that the literary text—especially in the vernacular—was in a disciplinary sense 'different', a site from which to enter into dialogue with, or even counter, the teachings of the schools. Pre-modern vernacular literature is, after all, full of literary 'arts of love' and parodic 'science's, secular remakings of Boethius and medieval 'philosophy'. Later fourteenth-century English writers such as Chaucer and Langland signal in a variety of ways their distance and disengagement from the traditional intellectual formulations and teaching methods endorsed by the schools: ethics, philosophy, and spiritual teaching look very different in the new forms of vernacular literature. When 'Langland' is challenged about the ethical value of his poetic undertaking, for instance, it transpires that his 'work' is militantly premised on the view that traditional ethical teaching is no longer adequate: 'if ther were any wight that wolde me telle | What were dowel and dobet and dobest at the laste, | Wolde I nevere do werk ... '[9]

Imaginative literary theory

And what about the expression of literary theory in vernacular literature? Pre-modern literature contains a number of elaborate allegories of literary composition, such as Machaut's 'Prologue'.[10] In this essay, however, I want to point in the direction of more widespread, recognizable figures that need less overt explication, such as the dream, the mirror, the reading of a book, or the conversation overheard. Some of these more widespread figures first appear in Occitan and Old French songs, where 'metaphors describing the art of composition are common': even in these songs, the lover who 'must' sing, the spring setting, and the *chanson d'aventure* function as literary 'signposts'.[11] Once such figures are elaborated and appended to longer texts, they

---

[9] *Piers Plowman: The B Version. Will's Visions of Piers Plowman, Do-well, Do-better and Do-best*, ed. George Kane and E. Talbot Donaldson, rev. edn. (London: Athlone Press, 1988), B. XII. 25–7.

[10] Guillaume de Machaut, *Œuvres*, ed. Ernest Hoepffner, 3 vols. (Paris: SATF, 1908–21), i. 1–12.

[11] See Simon Gaunt and John Marshall, 'Occitan Grammars and the Art of Troubadour Poetry', in Minnis and Johnson (eds.), *Literary Criticism*, ii, ch.16, at 476. On the lover, see Simon Gaunt and Sarah Kay (eds.), *The Troubadours: An Introduction* (Cambridge: Cambridge University Press, 1999), 33, 43. On the spring setting in Latin, Occitan, and Old French, see Ernst Robert Curtius, *European Literature and the Latin Middle Ages*, trans. Willard R. Trask (New York: Routledge and Kegan Paul, 1953), 183–202; Gaunt and Kay (eds.), *The Troubadours*, 33, 168–9; David F. Hult, *Self-Fulfilling Prophecies. Readership and Authority in the First* Roman de la Rose (Cambridge: Cambridge University Press, 1986), 208–13, 266–8. On the *chanson d'aventure*, see the formalist analysis of M. Zink, *La*

take on developed literary-theoretical connotations, becoming part of what modern readers have identified as the literary 'prologue'.[12] In the theoretically self-conscious later Middle Ages, writers would have regarded such passages as forms of literary theory, marked by their particular hospitality to the medieval sense of the multiple forms in which language can signify and, more important, comment on itself.

Modern scholars, especially those working in the ambit of schools literary theory, have remained reluctant to acknowledge the possibility of literary theory expressed in 'literary' form. This reluctance may stem partly from the refusal to consider how schools theory might be re-expressed or even mutated outside the overarching hermeneutic of the schools; and partly from a related tendency to recognize as literary theory only propositions expressed in an analytical, preceptive, and explicit language. So, in *The Cambridge History of Literary Criticism, ii*, the chapter on vernacular literary theory explains: 'we shall synthesise the explicit comments about literature to be found often, though not exclusively, in prologues.' Another chapter notes the lack of explicitly articulated vernacular literary theory, and when it does find some, this turns out to conform closely to the disciplinary teachings of the schools; when the poetry of Dante acquires an overtly ethical and theological agenda, the authors comment regretfully, 'there was a price to pay: love had to recede before wisdom'.[13] Such critical prioritization of the explicit often leads to a very delimited notion of vernacular literary theory, one that is often largely made up of pastoral and scholastic commonplace. The editors of *The Idea of the Vernacular* also prioritize explicit articulation, though they do argue for the importance of what they call 'situatedness'—the 'pressing awareness' of a 'complex cultural context' in vernacular textual theory. Later on, too, they note the function of the vernacular 'prologue' as a praxis, ritual, or 'work', and, within this frame, they acknowledge its formal variety, its inclusion of 'narratives, lyrics, letters, exhortations and prayers'.[14] Nevertheless, the selections from this volume confirm that its editors espouse an essentially explicit and analytically expressed version of vernacular literary theory. Whereas, in fact, Middle English literary texts often allude to textual matters—even to the grammatical and rhetorical theories of the schools—in figured modes.

Pastourelle (Paris: Bordas, 1972), 77–80; and Anne Middleton, 'The Audience and Public of *Piers Plowman*', in David Lawton (ed.), *Middle English Alliterative Poetry and its Literary Background: Seven Essays* (Cambridge: D. S. Brewer, 1982), 101–23, at 114–20.

[12] Middleton, 'Audience', 114; on the vernacular prologue see Ruth Evans in Wogan-Browne (ed.), *The Idea of the Vernacular*, 371–8.

[13] Kevin Brownlee et al., 'Vernacular Literary Consciousness c.1100–c.1500: French, German and English Evidence', 423; Ralph Hanna et al., 'Latin Commentary Tradition and Vernacular Literature', 420.

[14] pp. 316, 374–8, 372; compare Walter Haug, *Vernacular Literary Theory in the Middle Ages: The German Tradition, 800–1300, in its European Context*, trans. Joanna M. Catling (Cambridge: Cambridge University Press, 1997), who both foregrounds the explicit (pp. 58, 93) and attributes a role to figuratively expressed theory (pp. 160–72).

Chanson d'aventure

The *chanson d'aventure* is one of many medieval figures—whether construed as textual units or genres—that signify by allusion to a tradition of similar usages, bringing with them a distinct set of textual connections and conceptual implications. Specification often comes either through particularization within the paradigm, or through combining several different tropes or narrative elements. In this respect the high degree of formal awareness to be found in vernacular literature (according to Zumthor, the result of vernacular literary *mouvance*[15]) is of special relevance: at all levels of composition, ranging from the verse line to a whole piece of narrative, juxtaposed forms often dialogue and comment upon each other, both across texts and within them. In such cases, the interplay of forms itself serves to specify meaning.

The *chanson d'aventure* appears in many Old French trouvère songs, dialogues, or *pastourelles*, most of which are amorous or erotic; it also occurs in Middle English lyrics, but many more of these are religious. What does it mean in these original contexts?

> Nou sprinkes the sprai;
> Al for love icche [I] am so seek [sick]
>   That slepen I ne mai.
>
> Als I me rod [rode] this endre [recent] dai
>   O mi playinge,
> Seih [saw] I hwar a litel mai [maid]
>   Bigan to singge:
>   'The clot him clingge!
> Wai es him [Woe is the one who] i lovve-longinge
>   Sal libben ai [shall ever live].'
>
> Son [as soon as] icche herde that mirie note,
>   Thider I drogh [went];
> I fonde hire in an herber [arbour] swot
>   Under a bogh
>   With joie inogh.
> Son I asked, 'Thou mirie mai,
>   Hwi sinkes tou ai [do you sing all the time]?'
>
> Than answerde that maiden swote [sweet]
>   Midde wordes fewe:
> 'Mi lemman me haues bihot [promised]
>   Of louue trewe.

[15] On *mouvance*, see Paul Zumthor, *Toward a Medieval Poetics*, trans. Philip Bennett (Minneapolis: University of Minnesota Press, 1992), 41–67.

He chaunges anewe;
Yiif I mai, it shal him rewe
Bi this dai.'[16]

In the *chanson d'aventure* the singer goes out into a rural landscape, where he has an encounter that, whatever else it involves, takes the form of a dialogue; sometimes he is riding, reinforcing a second level of allusion to the *aventure* of chivalric romance. Readers tend to agree that the *chanson d'aventure* signals the song, the figured and literary text. This fourteenth-century lyric also exemplifies the formal interplay of this genre, as its narrative of *aventure* interfaces with song in its various manifestations, that is, with the 'whole' song, but also with its inset songs—both the songs in the narrative and the song's inner refrains. Not only does the lyric's dialogue involve both words and song, but the formal attributes of song—its assumed delights and 'playfulness'—are paralleled in the singing and 'playinge' of the narrator and the 'litel mai' who sings 'With joie inogh'.

The narrator is also characteristically 'errant', that is, without an explicit intent or object of desire. Middleton notes that 'chanson d'aventure' is similarly contingent and 'eccentric': 'every encounter offers itself as a deflection of an intentional act, which turns aside the speaker's attention to a new centre'—'a decentred and decentring experience' ('Audience', 114–16). Nevertheless, 'intent', feeling, and desire are at stake. Even if the singer is not initially able to articulate his desire, he usually finds it in the landscape—sometimes his own desire, and sometimes that of another person. The two protagonists are not always in accord and many songs and *pastourelles* exploit the uncertain engagement of their protagonists' intentions or affective states. In 'Nou sprinkes the sprai' different readings result from attributing the refrain about being sick for love to the narrator or the 'litel mai', both at the beginning and then again at the end; 'he' seems to take pleasure in her, but she seems to be lamenting the loss of someone else. Yet, in the last lines of the lyric, her threat to her former lover may also in fact be an oblique offer to the narrator. Here and elsewhere, the *chanson d'aventure* is centrally about the partialities of the two protagonists and the possibility of some kind of felt engagement between them, and it usually involves a dialogue in words or song.

The same formal self-consciousness and an interaction involving song can be found in the following lyric (from MS Harley 1317, *c.*1500). Here too the *aventure* seems both random and intense; although this time without apparent mutual attraction, but still with empathy, recognition, and even a sense of possible likeness:

---

[16] RichardsKalamazoo Leighton Greene (ed.), *The Early English Carols*, 2nd edn. (Oxford: Clarendon Press, 1977), no. 450; see Helen Estabrook Sandison, *The 'Chanson d'aventure' in Middle English*, Bryn Mawr College Monographs 12 (Philadelphia: Bryn Mawr College, 1913); for a French analogue to this lyric, pp. 47–8; also William D. Paden (ed. and trans.), *The Medieval Pastourelle*, 2 vols. (New York: Garland, 1987); Susanna Greer Fein (ed.), *Moral Love Songs and Laments* (Kalamazoo, MI: Medieval Institute Publications, 1998), 165–7, 176, 262–3, 266.

Wep [weep] no more for me, swet hart,
  Wepe no more for me;
As scharpe as a dart hathe perysht [?been destroyed? pierced] My
    hart
  That you shod [should] morne for me.

Apon a mornyng of May,
In the mornyng grey,
  I walkyd plesantly
To a garden gren,
So freshe besen,
  That joy hyt was to se.

Ther walkyd I
Al soburly,
  Musyng myselffe alon,
Tyll sodeynly
I blenkyd myn y
  Wher I spyyd won [one].

Whych in gret payn,
Me thowt sarteyn,
  Hyt semed that he was;
Hys gown al blake
Apon hys bake,
  Lyke lede [lead] hys colore was.[17]

In this encounter, the man in black seems to be oblivious of the narrator; but
hearing and seeing him transforms the narrator from one who walks 'plesantly',
though 'Al soburly', to one seemingly transfixed. The apparent lack of a predatory
sexual agenda here brings out the potentially reflexive dimension of the *chanson
d'aventure*, the possibility that its narrative reflects some aspect of the narrator. In
this respect it echoes the way that chivalric *aventure* is, as Jill Mann has put it, both
active and in some central way passive, a submission to what events have to show
and tell.[18] Like the literary-theoretical dream prologue, the *chanson d'aventure*
offers the possibility that the landscape and what the narrator finds in it are a
manifestation of something in him.

These points are all illustrated in my third song, a fifteenth-century instance of
the many Middle English religious 'chansons d'aventures'. Here the *aventure* is in
'mynd', overtly metaphorical or spiritual:

In the vaile of restles mynd
  I sowght in mownteyn and in mede,
  Trustyng a treulofe [true love] for to fynd.

[17] Greene (ed.), *Early English Carols*, no. 462.
[18] Jill Mann, ' "Taking the Adventure": Malory and the *Suite du Merlin*', in Toshiyuki Takamiya
and Derek Brewer (eds.), *Aspects of Malory* (Cambridge: D. S. Brewer, 1981), 71–91.

Upon an hyll than toke I hede,
   A voise I herd (and nere I yede)
In gret dolour complaynyng tho,
   'See, dere soule, my sydes blede,
Quia amore langueo [Because I languish with love].'

Upon thys mownt I fand a tree,
   Undir thys tree a man sittyng;
From hede to fote wowndyd was he,
   Hys hert blode I saw bledyng,
   A semely man to be a kyng,
A graciose face to loke unto.
   I askyd hym how he had paynyng.
He said, '*Quia amore langueo.*'

'I am treulove, that fals was never.
   My sister, mannys soule, I loved hyr thus ... [19]

Again we observe the combination of narrative errancy and desire. The narrator meanders through the landscape, notices a voice, and draws near to an emotive figure, who is himself a feeling and desirous subject—'In gret dolour', '*Quia amore langueo*', 'I am treulove.' The underlying implication is that this narrative may reveal some hitherto-unexpressed desire in the narrator, who seeks with 'restles mynd ... Trustyng a treulofe for to fynd'. Again we see the formal self-consciousness of the *chanson d'aventure* as the narrator's *aventure* leads to an encounter with words and a song, this time a line from the Song of Songs: '*Quia amore langueo.*' In fact, such encounters with song, words, or text are a special feature of many English religious and moral *chansons d'aventure*: in one, the narrator finds 'a lettre of love ... That was wyrtyn on a wall', in another he sees 'a Clerk a book forth bringe', and in many more he hears someone speak words that then become the refrain of the song.[20] This pervasive orientation towards the sung, spoken or written word can only reinforce the literary-theoretical potential of the *chanson d'aventure*.

In fact, these *chanson d'aventure* openings even articulate aspects of the literary theory of the schools, describing very incisively the rhetoricians' notion of *inventio* ('finding'/'composition'), a combination of textual 'discovery' and 'invention' (in the modern sense). This rhetorical reworking assumes that composition is an erratic but sense-making encounter with 'found' texts or *materia*, whether textual or otherwise.[21] This school notion of rhetorical 'finding' is of course written into the

---

[19] Douglas Gray (ed.), *A Selection of Religious Lyrics* (Oxford: Clarendon Press, 1975), no. 43; also Fein (ed.), *Moral Love Songs*, 57–86.

[20] Carleton Brown (ed.), *Religious Lyrics of the XIVth Century* (Oxford: Clarendon Press, 1924), no. 105 (ll. 5–6); no. 96 (l. 5); also nos. 107, 119, 121 (also Fein (ed.), *Moral Love Songs*, 255–88); and Sandison, 'Chanson d'aventure', 110–26; Gray (ed.), *Religious Lyrics*, no. 80.

[21] See Rita Copeland, *Rhetoric, Hermeneutics and Translation in the Middle Ages. Academic Traditions and Vernacular Texts* (Cambridge: Cambridge University Press, 1991), 27–9, 35–6, and ch. 6; for *inventio* as 'finding', 151; on *materia*, 72–9, 108–9, 166–8.

names of the earliest practitioners both of documented vernacular song and of the *chanson d'aventure* opening, the troubadours and trouvères ('finders', 'inventors', 'composers').[22] In this way, the iconography of *chanson d'aventure* intersects with other explicitly articulated literary-theoretical descriptions of composition. Its mysterious or marvellous 'findings' recall 'difficult' rhetorical tropes such as 'ornatus gravis' or *enigma*, or the romance *merveille*. Just as 'discovery' assumes that composition involves something 'new', so rhetoricians discuss composition with *materia* that is 'new', while vernacular writers describe composition as a 'renewing' and their songs as 'new'. Even the 'finding' of song in the landscape reflects the fact that by the thirteenth century song could itself be an 'authority'.[23]

The *chanson d'aventure* is also a way of alluding figuratively to writerly subjectivity. As an expression of personal investedness and partiality, the pursuit of *aventure* reflects the role of desire in the literary text and the way that the text inevitably reflects the concerns of its writer. This is one area where vernacular literature is from an early period very self-conscious, with its writerly self-representations within the text—see above, for instance, the troubadours' and trouvères' claim, 'love makes me sing'. By the thirteenth century, however, rhetorical theory and the grammatical *accessus* have also led to more sophisticated notions about authorial *intentio* in the mechanics of textual composition, as well as the author's capacity to choose textual strategies and forms of expression.[24] As the *chanson d'aventure* comes to be used more widely, it offers a means of signalling not just the subjectivity of the lover or knight, but literary subjectivity and reflexivity per se.

The *chanson d'aventure* also locates the text socially, pointing (as does so much vernacular literature) to issues of class and gender. In its secular manifestations, it is a tale about the discovery/pursuit of affect, eroticism, or entertainment; it imagines itself shaped by youth, seasonal renewal, and 'the natural'. However, these imaginings mask its (aristocratic or clerkly) masculinist, homosocial, and predatory agenda. The religious *chanson d'aventure* is, by contrast, much less clearly marked in terms of class or gender, and is more open in its audience appeal (even the predatory

[22] Gaunt and Kay (eds.), *The Troubadours*, 294; my thanks here to Bill Burgwinkle.

[23] For 'difficult' figures of diction that '[depart] from the ordinary meaning of the words', see *[Cicero] ad C. Herennium (Rhetorica ad Herennium)*, trans. Harry Caplan, Loeb Classical Library (London: Heinemann, 1954), 4. 31. 42–34. 46 (citation 4. 31. 42); Geoffrey of Vinsauf, in Ernest Gallo, *The 'Poetria nova' and its Sources in Early Rhetorical Doctrine* (The Hague: Mouton, 1971), ll. 770–98; also pp. 197–207; for these and for *enigma* in Hermannus Alemannus' Latin translation of Averroes' commentary on Aristotle's *Poetics*, see Zeeman, 'Alterations of Language', 223–6; for *merveille*, see Douglas Kelly, *Medieval Imagination: Rhetoric and the Poetry of Courtly Love* (Madison: University of Wisconsin Press, 1978), 33, 49, 165. On 'new matter' in rhetorical theory, see Copeland, *Rhetoric, Hermeneutics*, 170–2; on vernacular composition as 'renewing', see Brownlee et al., 'Vernacular Literary Consciousness', 429–30. On song as textual 'authority', Ardis Butterfield, *Poetry and Music in Medieval France from Jean Renart to Guillaume de Machaut* (Cambridge: Cambridge University Press, 2002), chs. 13–15.

[24] Copeland, *Rhetoric, Hermeneutics*; Minnis and Scott (eds.), *Medieval Literary Theory*, chs. 1, 3, and 4.

dynamic of secular *chanson d'aventure* is reversed by the didactic and emotionally demanding spiritual figures found in the landscapes of these religious songs). In fact, these religious *chansons d'aventure* echo the revelatory or inspirational 'encounters' by which in the later Middle Ages 'unauthorized' or female devotees often valorize their religious compositions and thinking.

The *chanson d'aventure* also situates the text conceptually and textually. With its 'experiential', exemplary, and embodied narratives, it reveals proleptically the 'experiential', exemplary, and embodied forms of the text that is to follow. A writer can also nuance ecphrasis or description within the *chanson d'aventure* (treating it, for instance, as emotive, visionary, or 'realistic') to indicate the nature of the text to come. Here again, the *chanson d'aventure* is a means of pointing to categories of textuality and textually simulated 'experience' that are extensively theorized in the schools.[25] Finally, the *chanson d'aventure* also says something about vernacularity. It does this not just because it is written in the vernacular, but by virtue of its clear allusion to specific genres of writing—songs, *pastourelles*, and chivalric romances—that evolved only in the vernacular. What is more, various kinds of 'realistic' specifications can point this allusion to the vernacular by presenting it as a language grounded in personal, temporal, and geographical experience. Poets refer to the passing of time or the seasons, and to locations, such as a wood, a church, under a tree, in a garden, or even a specific place—Arthur's Dale or Rybbesdale. Poems begin 'By one foreste as I cone, ryde', 'In Bowdoun on blak monunday', 'In somer bi-fore the asceniun', or 'Upon the Midsummer ewin, the mirriest of nichtis'; and,

> Nou skrynketh [withers] rose and lylie flour
> That whilen [once] ber that suete sauour
> In somer that suete tyde …
> From petres-bourh in o morewenyng,
> As y me wende o my pleyghyng … [26]

Such passages provide exemplary, figured instances of the vernacular 'situatedness' that Wogan-Browne and others have found theorized more explicitly elsewhere.[27]

Even in the simplest of forms, then, the *chanson d'aventure* prologue or frame carries *in potentia* a substantial burden of figuratively expressed literary-theoretical implications. At the most fundamental level, it describes composition both as process and as discovery; a form of 'unconcealing', it is as much a 'finding' as it is a 'making' of text. And, from the *Roman de la Rose* onwards, the *chanson d'aventure*

---

[25] On 'experience' see Nicolette Zeeman, *'Piers Plowman' and the Medieval Discourse of Desire* (Cambridge: Cambridge University Press, 2006), 167–74.

[26] Brown (ed.), *Religious Lyrics*, no. 10 (1–3, 11–12); for the previous references, Sandison, 'Chanson d'aventure', 'Alphabetical Register of Middle English Chansons d'aventure' (pp. 130–47): Amorous, nos. 20, 30, 8, 45; Religious, 15, 21.

[27] According to Wogan-Browne, Watson, Taylor, and Evans, the English vernacular is attributed with 'idiom', 'situatedness', 'familiarity', 'immediacy', 'accessibility', 'emotional directness', even 'orality' (*The Idea of the Vernacular*, 324–30).

appears in many longer narrative and debate poems: here its literary-theoretical potential becomes fully manifest.

Chanson d'aventure as literary-theoretical prologue

Chaucer's *Book of the Duchess* has multiple 'literary prologues'—the sleepless night, the reading of a book, the tale of Seys and Alcyone, the dream, the building whose windows are glazed with the tale of Troy. Amongst these is an elaborate hunting *chanson d'aventure*. As he sets out on this *aventure* of courtly *inventio*, the narrator, like that of the *Roman de la Rose*, is simultaneously aimless and desirous, eager to wander and yet also lured on by delightful features in the landscape; amongst these is a little hound:

> I wolde have kaught hyt, and anoon
> Hyt fledde, and was fro me goon;
> And I hym folwed, and hyt forth wente
> Doun by a floury grene wente
> Ful thikke of gras, ful softe and swete.[28]

It should be no surprise when, amongst the animals wandering in the wood, the narrator comes across a man:

> so at the laste
> I was war of a man in blak,
> That sat and had yturned his bak
> To an ook, an huge tree.
> 'Lord,' thoght I, 'who may that be?
> What ayleth hym to sitten her?'   (ll. 444–9)

Even less surprisingly, the grieving man in black is also a singer.

> For-why he heng hys hed adoun,
> And with a dedly sorwful soun
> He made of rym ten vers or twelve
> Of a compleynte to hymselve—
> The moste pitee, the moste rowthe,
> That ever I herde; for, by my trowthe,
> Hit was gret wonder that Nature
> Myght suffre any creature
> To have such sorwe, and be not ded.   (ll. 461–9)

The narrator quotes the 'lay, a maner song', voiced by the man in black; this is a song about the death of his lady, which the narrator inexplicably seems not

---

[28] *The Riverside Chaucer*, gen. ed. Larry D. Benson, 3rd edn. (Oxford: Clarendon Press, 1987), 329–46 (ll. 395–9).

to hear, and about which he spends the rest of the poem quizzing the man in black. At the very end of the poem the man tells the narrator—this time not in song—that the lady is dead. Chaucer's poem conforms to the *chanson d'aventure* model remarkably closely, in that it involves an intensely emotional encounter in a landscape with a person who sings a song; this song becomes in a very real sense the 'text' of the poem, to which it repeatedly returns. Spearing has argued that in this poem Chaucer is meditating on the difficulty of hearing the hyperbolic genre of song properly: 'death' can be heard only as a courtly-poetic metaphor until it is explicated in prosaic conversation.[29] Whether or not this is the case, in this poem *chanson d'aventure* figures *inventio* on the sad *materia* encapsulated in the text of a song.

Chanson d'aventure here also points to a courtly and clerical version of the predicament of the writer, simultaneously acknowledging his desire to initiate a text and figuring this desire as subject to his social milieu—in particular, the desires of the patron, John of Gaunt. Chaucer uses the ambiguous way that *chanson d'aventure* situates desire to portray himself in the classic courtly role of clerical amanuensis to the desire of the lord. This desire, expressed in song, is the poem's text, on which the poet must perform his imaginative work. Rhetorically speaking, the dominant trope of the text is the *chanson d'aventure* trope of *enigma* or *merveille*—a trope that Chaucer will maintain throughout until finally he replaces it with ones of *exclamatio* and *brevitas*:

> 'She is ded!' 'Nay!' 'Yis, be my trouthe!'
> 'Is that youre los? Be God, hyt ys routhe!'   (ll. 1309–10)

Chaucer also seems to exploit the *chanson d'aventure* in another somewhat surprising way in his depiction of a suffering man by a tree. Despite the striking likenesses between the *Book of the Duchess* and the song of the man in black found in the later MS Harley 1317, direct influence cannot be presumed. Both poems can, however, be located within the rich Middle English tradition of religious *chanson d'aventure*, in which the figure in the landscape is a moral or biblical 'sufferer'.[30] I am not suggesting that Chaucer imagines John of Gaunt as Christ. Nevertheless, the peculiar intensity of Chaucer's suffering man found in a courtly landscape surely owes much to the devotional *chanson d'aventure*, with its images of Christ and its affective language of religious pathos (a language that the later Chaucer was happy to exploit in secular as well as religious tales):

> Hys sorwful hert gan faste faynte,
> And his spirites wexen dede;

---

[29] A. C. Spearing, 'Literal and Figurative in *The Book of the Duchess*', *Studies in the Age of Chaucer, Proceedings*, 1 (1984), 165–71 (Spearing's description of medieval poetry tallies closely with the one proposed here).
[30] See Greene (ed.), *Early English Carols*, 497.

> The blood was fled for pure drede
> Doun to hys herte ...   (ll. 488–91)

Just as the *Book of the Duchess* is an audacious appropriation of the courtly *dit amoureux* for a new and serious purpose, so Chaucer invokes the religious connotations of the *chanson d'aventure* to prefigure the seriousness of his poetic enterprise.

In my second example, the opening frame of *Piers Plowman* (B- and C-texts), *chanson d'aventure* brings a very different set of connotations:

> In a somer seson, whan softe was the sonne
> I shoop [dressed] me into a shroud as I a sheep weere;
> In habite as an heremite unholy of werkes,
> Wente wide in this world wondres to here.
> Ac on a May morwenynge on Malverne Hilles,
> Me bifel a ferly [wonder], of Fairye me thoghte.
> I was wery forwandred [exhausted with wandering] and wente me to reste
> Under a brood bank by a bourne [stream] syde,
> And as I lay and lenede and loked on the watres,
> I slombred into a slepyng, it sweyed [flowed] so murye.   (B. Prol. 1–10)

This B-text opening not only echoes the broad genre of the *chanson d'aventure*, but also the elaborate, detail-laden nature descriptions of other Middle English alliterative *chansons d'aventure* such as *Wynnere and Wastoure*. B-text Langland claims a place in a self-consciously vernacular tradition of subjective and imaginative verse *inventio*, one that also has specifically English (even West Midlands), alliterative, and even oral connotations.[31] The *materia* that Langland's narrator 'finds' in the landscape is again simultaneously random and sought, subjective and objective; voiced by a series of visionary speakers and verbalized texts, it will again be formulated as poetic *enigma* and 'marvel'.

In the C-text, however, Langland revises this prologue. After replicating the first four lines of the B-text, he picks up as follows:

> ... wondres to here
> And say many selles [strange things] and selkouthe [wondrous] thyngus.
> Ac on a May mornyng on malverne hulles
> Me biful for to slepe, for werynesse ofwalked,
> And in a launde as y lay lened y and slepte
> And merueylousliche me mette [dreamed], as y may yow telle.
> Al þe welthe of the world and the wo bothe,

---

[31] Ralph Hanna, 'Alliterative Poetry', in David Wallace (ed.), *The Cambridge History of Medieval English Literature* (Cambridge: Cambridge University Press, 1999), ch. 18; this poetry is 'not simply marked, but over-marked, as vernacular. Alliteration and alliterative diction ... self-consciously mark the poetry off as English'; 'alliterative poets over-emphasise their vernacularity through flaunting their own (thoroughly fictive) orality—and its social implications' (501–2; on Langland, 498–9).

> Wynkyng as hit were, witterliche [truly] y sigh hit:
> Of treuthe and tricherye, tresoun and gyle
> Al y say slepynge as y shal yow telle.[32]

The fact that this passage retains the rhetoric of *wondres* and the *merueylous*, and replaces the 'ferly, of Fairye me thoghte' with what appears to have been an earlier variant, 'selles and selkouthe thyngus', affirms Langland's commitment to visionary enigma. However, as readers have noted, the passage also omits much distinctively pastoral detail. The C-poet loosens the 'pastoral-alliterative-poetic' affiliations of the B-prologue in favour of a briefer and possibly more 'directly' referential *chanson d'aventure*. Developments of the frame over the rest of the B- and C-texts reveal that the general tendency is to show the waking narrator in plainer and sometimes harsher landscapes, though their continued correspondence with his angst-ridden state indicates that they are as much a sign of poetic subjectivity as of any increasing 'realism'.[33] But the C-text also adds new lines—'Al the welthe of the world and the wo bothe ... | Of treuthe and tricherye, tresoun and gyle'—lines that refer the reader to ethical and satirical concerns. Even this language, however, is drawn from the nexus of romance, and especially alliterative romance, recalling lines such as these from *Wynnere and Wastoure*:

> Sythen that Bretayne was bigged [built] and Bruyttus it aughte [possessed it]
> Thurgh the takynge of Troye with tresone withinn,
> There hathe selcouthes [wonders] bene sene in seere [many] kynges tymes,
> Bot never so many as nowe by the nynedele [ninefold].[34]

Langland's changed C-prologue may be not a repudiation of alliterative *chanson d'aventure* but a reworking to foreground its ambivalent romance *wondres*, its characteristic *aventure*.

Langland's imitators seem to have picked up on the incipient 'realism' of his pared down but visionary *chanson d'aventure*—though they do not lose sight of poetic subjectivity either. The Lollard or dissidently religious *Pierce the Ploughman's Crede* takes Langland's brevity for granted: 'Thanne wende y to wyten [learn] and with a whight [man] y mette, | A Menoure [Franciscan friar] in a morwe-tide and to this man I saide ... '[35] However, later in the poem, with his narrator already in a

---

[32] *Piers Plowman: The C Version. Will's Visions of Piers Plowman, Do-well, Do-better and Do-best*, ed. George Russell and George Kane (London: Athlone Press, 1997), C. Prol. 4–13.

[33] See B. XVIII. 1–4; B. XX. 1–5; the C versions tend to be briefer: B. XV. 1–11 is not in C-text; compare B. XVI. 167–71 with C. XVIII. 179–80; however, the idyllic pastoral scenario of B. VIII. 63–9 is retained in C. X. 61–7.

[34] Thorlac Turville-Petre (ed.), *Alliterative Poetry of the Later Middle Ages: An Anthology* (Washington: Catholic University of America Press, 1989), 38–66 (ll. 1–4); also *Sir Gawain and the Green Knight*, in Malcolm Andrew and Ronald Waldron (eds.), *The Poems of the Pearl Manuscript*, rev. edn. (Exeter: University of Exeter, 1987), 207–300 (ll. 1–29).

[35] Helen Barr (ed.), *The Piers Plowman Tradition: A Critical Edition of 'Pierce the Ploughman's Crede,' 'Richard the Redeless,' 'Mum and the Sothsegger' and 'The Crowned King'* (London: Dent, 1993), 61–97 (ll. 32–3).

state of heightened distress, this poet also develops a graphically naturalistic version of *chanson d'aventure*:

> Thanne turned y me forthe and talked to my-selve
> Of the falshede of this folk—whou faithles they weren.
> And as y wente be the waie wepynge for sorowe,
> I seie a sely [poor] man (...) upon the plow hongen.
> His cote was of a cloute that cary [coarse cloth] was y-called,
> His hod was full of holes and his heer oute ...
> His ton toteden [peeped] out as he the londe treddede ...   (ll. 418–23, 425)

This reworking of the devotional *chanson d'aventure* (many Lollard texts after all use the language of affective piety) introduces a harsh rural scene containing the figures of the good ploughman and his family: his wife is 'wrapped in a wynwe [winding] schete to weren hire fro weders' and their baby lies on 'a litell crom-bolle [scrap bowl] ... lapped in cloutes' (ll. 435, 437–8). The family even sing a 'song', though this is a 'song' of dearth:

> And alle they songen o songe that sorwe was to heren,
> They crieden alle o cry a careful note.
> The sely man sighede sore, and seide 'Children, beth stille!'[36]

This harsh *chanson d'aventure* landscape may reflect the poet's grim state of mind, but it is also an unidealized winter landscape, into which the poet can really 'walk out'. It signposts the imaginative tradition from which the poem speaks and points in a specific and English-vernacularized way to its political concerns. Unlike *Piers Plowman*, however, this poem does not present its speakers or visionary content as enigmatic or 'difficult'. On the contrary, in line with the Lollard project of religious and social reform, Pierce is utterly and vernacularly accessible—' "Dere brother," quath Peres ... ' Of corrupt clerics he says: 'Thei schulden delven and diggen and dongen the erthe, | And mean-mong [ordinary] corn bred to her mete fongen [take] ...' (ll. 785–6). Pierce speaks his *crede* from within a landscape refigured in exaggeratedly naturalist terms to reflect on the social and theological purposes of the poem.

My last two *chansons d'aventure* are even more formally self-conscious. Henryson's *Fables* pivot on three central tales, each containing a *chanson d'aventure*. Numbers 7 and 8, 'The Lion and the Mouse' and 'The Preaching of the Swallow', form a contrasting diptych. The first of these has a special prologue, set in a hot June and a blossomy, bird-filled landscape:

> In ane morning betuix mid day and nicht
> I rais and put all sleuth and sleip asyde,
> And to ane wod I went allone but [without] gyde.[37]

---

[36] ll. 440–2; see Langland's 'songs' ('*dieu save dame Emme*' and the tradesmen's cries) at C. Prol. 229–34.

[37] Robert Henryson, *Fables*, in *The Poems*, ed. Denton Fox (Oxford: Clarendon Press, 1981), 3–110 (ll. 1325–7).

Out in the wood, the narrator sleeps and dreams that he meets Aesop, 'the fairest man that ever befoir I saw' (l. 1348), who in due course tells the tale. Before he begins, however, Aesop expresses despair about human beings' reluctance to acquire moral teaching, 'That now my taillis may lytill succour [benefit] mak' (l. 1397). This idyllic and pastoral literary prologue, with its dream and noble old *auctor*, then, stands in some contrast to Aesop's expressed pessimism about the didactic potential of the fable.

'The Preaching of the Swallow' is set up quite differently. It begins with a description and expansive survey of the exemplary world through which 'we may haif knawlegeing | Off God almychtie be his creatouris' (ll. 1650–1). This time, however, the fable is not framed with a prologue, dream, or *auctor*, and the narrator *walks out* directly into a 'realistically' described, seasonably variable, and agricultural world. This is the planting season, and he hopes 'Off lauboraris to se the besines':

> That samin seasoun, in to ane soft morning,
> Rycht blyth that bitter blastis wer ago,
> Unto the wod ...
> I passit furth, syne lukit to and fro,
> To se the soill, that wes richt sessonabill,
> Sappie [moist], and to resave all seidis [seeds] abill.
>
> (ll. 1721, 1713–15, 1717–19)

Contrasting sharply with the preceding prologue, this naturalistic, unframed *chanson d'aventure* allows Henryson to signal not only 'realism' of content, but also something textual: the literary form of the 'exemplary', a literalistic mode that simulates unmediated encounter with the world.

Once out in this agricultural *chanson d'aventure*, the narrator comes across the inevitable birds, but along with them, the labouring farmer, planting seed to grow hemp and make bird nets. A swallow 'preaches' to the birds on how to thwart the fowler, but they are defiantly indifferent. The year progresses, and again the narrator sets out into the naturalistic, exemplary landscape:

> I movit furth betuix midday and morne
> Unto the hedge under the hawthorne grene,
> Quhair I befoir the said birdis had sene,
> And as I stude, be aventure and case [chance],
> The samin birdis ...
> Thay lychtit [alighted] doun ...   (ll. 1780–4, 1787)

Again the swallow preaches and again they ignore him. Winter comes, vividly described, and the fowler catches the birds. Once more, Henryson imagines himself seeing the events happen before him, 'Allace, it wes grit hart sair [sorrow] for to se | That bludie bowcheour [bloody butcher] beit thay birdis doun.'[38] This, then,

---

[38] ll. 1874–5. Compare *Fable* 6: 'Bot of this scheip and of his cairfull cry | I sall reheirs, for as I passit by | Quhair that he lay, on cais I lukit doun, | And hard him mak sair lamentatioun ... ' (ll. 1282–5).

is a fable *about* the fact that birds/people cannot learn moral teaching; whereas a similar pessimism was expressed verbally by Aesop in the prologue of *Fable 7*, in the exemplary narrative of *Fable 8* it is 'seen'. This formal move to exemplary 'seeing' in the world is precisely what is anticipated in Henryson's realistic and unframed version of the *chanson d'aventure* prologue.

My last *chanson d'aventure*, Chaucer's prologue to the *Legend of Good Women*, seems to be an ironic literary theory reference. Although time does not permit a detailed exploration of the differences between the two 'drafts' of this prologue, their existence indicates that even here the nuancing of the *chanson d'aventure* is important to Chaucer. The Prologue indubitably refers to the courtly literature of love. As in the *Book of the Duchess*, the narrator is figured as the masculine courtly amanuensis of love, subservient to the aristocratic patron of the poem's metaphorical 'court' and able to speak to him only in the evasive and inexplicit terms of courtly literature. The landscape is full of song. Here birds sing 'layes of love', songs to St Valentyn, and, as in Henryson, their defiance of the bird-catcher ('This was here song, "The foulere we defye, | And al his craft" '[39]); in G a lark announces the God of Love accompanied by Alceste, and a troop of ladies sing the *ballade* 'Hyd, Absalon'. The person the narrator meets, the God of Love, also turns out to have a very particular textual preoccupation, in this case with Chaucer's own writings, in particular *Troilus and Criseyde*, which he denounces for not conforming to a traditional notion of love literature as praise of love and ladies.

> Thow mayst it nat denye ...
> Thow hast translated the Romauns of the Rose,
> That is an heresye ageyns my lawe ...
> Hast thow nat mad in Englysh ek the bok
> How that Crisseyde Troylus forsook,
> In shewynge how that wemen han don mis?   (G, ll. 253, 255–6, 264–6)

As readers have noted, this is a piece of *coterie* literary theory. The joke is on the God of Love and all who subscribe to his programmatic notion of love literature, those who cannot see the innovations of *Troilus*. Chaucer invites the reader to supply the 'defence' that 'Chaucer' and Alceste (in the courtly manner) can only make by insinuation. Although Chaucer's last exquisite *chanson d'aventure* initially seems to be traditional, then, it is in fact the ironic staging of a literary tradition with which Chaucer no longer fully identifies.[40]

The pre-modern *chanson d'aventure* is a precise and supple vehicle for imaginative articulations of literary theory. Although the medieval schools may have articulated their literary theory in analytical and explicit terms, other philosophers have in fact

---

[39] *Riverside Chaucer*, 587–630 (G. 126–7).

[40] Indeed, one small index of the innovations of *Troilus and Criseyde* might be the inversions of gender and psychology that occur in its inset *chanson d'aventure*, when it is a woman, Criseyde, who goes out into a garden to hear a song (ibid. 471–585; II. 811–910).

shared with medieval literary writers the sense that theory can be expressed in figural terms. At the risk of distorting just one of them, we might say that the pre-modern 'chanson d'aventure' describes the coming into being ... of the literary text both as a 'work' and as a 'happening,' an opening of 'paths' in the midst of concealment, a woodland 'clearing'—a process of discovery in an imaginary landscape.[41]

FURTHER READING

Essential compendia and bibliographies on the literary theory of the schools are to be found in: A. J. Minnis and A. B. Scott with the assistance of David Wallace (eds.), *Medieval Literary Theory and Criticism c.1100–c.1375: The Commentary Tradition* (n. 2 above); Rita Copeland, *Rhetoric, Hermeneutics and Translation in the Middle Ages; Academic Traditions and Vernacular Texts* (n. 21); Alastair Minnis and Ian Johnson (eds.), *The Cambridge History of Literary Criticism*, ii: *The Middle Ages* (n. 2), esp. chs. 6 and 7; see also Nicolette Zeeman, 'The Schools give a License to Poets', in Rita Copeland (ed.), *Criticism and Dissent in the Middle Ages* (n. 2), 151–80. For vernacular literary theory, see Douglas Kelly, *Medieval French Romance* (New York: Twayne, 1993); Jocelyn Wogan-Browne, Nicholas Watson, Andrew Taylor, and Ruth Evans (eds.), *The Idea of the Vernacular. An Anthology of Middle English Literary Theory 1280–1520* (n. 1); Minnis and Johnson (eds.), *The Cambridge History of Literary Criticism*, ii: *The Middle Ages*, chs. 15 and 16. Studies of 'figured' vernacular literary theory include: Anne Middleton, 'The Audience and Public of *Piers Plowman*' in David Lawton (ed.), *Middle English Alliterative Poetry and its Literary Background. Seven Essays* (n. 11), 101–23, at 114–20; Nicolette Zeeman, 'The Verse of Courtly Love in the Framing Narrative of the *Confessio Amantis*', *Medium Aevum*, 60 (1991), 222–40; Steven F. Kruger, *Dreaming in the Middle Ages* (Cambridge: Cambridge University Press, 1992), ch. 6. For innovative recent readings inspired by theories of gender and sexuality: Sylvia Huot, 'Seduction and Sublimation: Christine de Pizan, Jean de Meun and Dante', *Romance Notes*, 25 (1984–5), 361–73; Rita Copeland, 'The Pardoner's Body and the Disciplining of Rhetoric', in Sarah Kay and Miri Rubin (eds.), *Framing Medieval Bodies* (Manchester: Manchester University Press, 1994), 138–59; Susan Schibanoff, 'Sodomy's Mark: Alan of Lille, Jean de Meun and the Medieval Theory of Authorship', in Glen Burger and Steven F. Kruger (eds.), *Queering the Middle Ages* (Minneapolis: University of Minnesota Press, 2001), 28–56.

---

[41] Martin Heidegger, 'The Origin of the Work of Art', in *Poetry, Language, Thought*, trans. Albert Hofstadter (New York: Harper and Row, 1971), 15–87, at 54–6.

CHAPTER 16

FEELING

SARAH MCNAMER

It's a good time to think about feeling. The past few decades have witnessed a surge of interest in affective states and processes: in neurology, philosophy, psychology, anthropology—wherever one turns, as a recent *Chronicle of Higher Education* article observes, emotions have become 'all the rage'.[1] No one has yet proclaimed an 'emotional turn' in academia, and perhaps rightly so: this interest across the disciplines may prove to be mere fashion, or a contingent symptom of millennial hopes or fears that will dissipate as we find our bearings in a post-millennial world. But I expect that emotions are here to stay. Why? Not only because they are so fundamental to human experience, but because their exclusion from so many branches of academic study has been predicated on prejudices that we now recognize as such—chiefly the reason/emotion dichotomy itself, with the privileging of the former reinforced by its associations with 'the masculine'. In fact, given the historical designation of emotion as 'feminine', what we are witnessing, in the emergence of emotion out from under, may well be one among the many lasting consequences of the feminist movement, structurally akin to the entry of women into academia and the intellectual impact of feminism: there is no going back. Whatever the case, the serious study of emotion is not only shifting the focus of attention within the disciplines, but generating important interdisciplinary conversations—conversations that are, in turn, opening up new methodologies and new fields.

Of these, the field with the clearest relevance to medievalists is the 'history of emotion'.[2] My thoughts in this essay will revolve around how scholars of Middle English literature might participate more fully in this discipline-in-the-making, not only by absorbing more fully its concerns as they have been articulated so

---

[1] Scott McLemee, 'Getting Emotional', *Chronicle of Higher Education*, 49/24 (21 Feb. 2003), A14.

[2] Another obvious area for investigation is that of psychoanalytic criticism and its application to Middle English texts. I am not treating this here because it is not my field of expertise, but I suggest staying tuned to the work of Aranye (Louise O.) Fradenburg, Peter Travis, and Elizabeth Scala, among others. Cultural studies offers another richly productive framework for considering emotion; see Further Reading.

far by historians, but by enlarging the aims, scope, and methods of the field itself. At present, we are facing a moment of real opportunity, one that can be recognized only by first registering a fundamental problem: oddly enough, given all the interdisciplinary buzz, historians and literary scholars interested in getting emotional have yet to seriously conspire on how to do so.[3]

In the first half of this essay I will look at some of the disciplinary assumptions and practices that currently limit, even as they enable, work in the history of emotion, and will advocate performance and performativity as concepts that can move us to a new level in thinking about emotion historically via literary texts. I will then bring this down to a more concrete level by giving brief readings of two Middle English texts, *The Wooing of Our Lord* and *Sir Gawain and the Green Knight*, as scripts for the performance of historically specific emotion.

Literature and the history of emotion

Historians devised the term 'the history of emotion' twenty years ago, in part as a means of isolating more specifically the affective dimension of *mentalités* as conceived by the *Annales* school, but only in the past decade or so has what began as an enterprise of a few pioneers come into its own.[4] That the field is still under construction is clear: witness the publication of William Reddy's attempt to articulate a comprehensive 'framework for the history of emotion' as recently as 2001, and the ongoing efforts of Barbara Rosenwein to chart a course for medieval historians in particular.[5] Much methodological borrowing has gone on in this process, chiefly from the fields of anthropology (where the deep cultural construction of emotion was first posited), cognitive science (which has demonstrated how deeply cognition and feeling are intertwined), and linguistics (with its close attention to affective discourse and the issue of translation). Much ingenuity has also gone into thinking about what kinds of sources to use, and how. It is therefore quite striking that literature and the methods of literary analysis have been so little valued as the history of emotion works toward defining itself as a discipline.[6] Literature, after all, is the chief archive of the emotions, isn't it?

---

[3] Fredric L. Cheyette and Howell Chickering, however, have recently offered a compelling example of how collaborative work might proceed; see their 'Love, Anger, and Peace: Social Practice and Poetic Play in the Ending of *Yvain*', *Speculum*, 80 (2005), 75–117.

[4] Peter N. Stearns has been the most energetic leader in this field; see his books and others in the 'History of Emotion' series he founded with New York University Press.

[5] William Reddy, *The Navigation of Feeling: A Framework for the History of Emotions* (Cambridge: Cambridge University Press, 2001); Barbara Rosenwein, 'Worrying about Emotions in History', *American Historical Review*, June 2002 (**www.historycooperative.org/journals/ahr/107.3/ah030 2000821.html**, 28 Apr. 2006).

[6] Rosenwein, for instance, refers to literary scholarship in a single footnote in the essay cited above; see 'Worrying', n. 47. Even the collaborative essay by Cheyette and Chickering (see n. 3, above)

Yes, many historians seem to acknowledge; but it is unfortunately of limited use. Why? Precisely because it is 'literary'—for the literary is, by its very nature, thought to be untrustworthy: disorienting in its instability, disarming in its beauty, never meaning what it says—in short, a tease. If the goal is to discover the historical truth through the veils of compromised sources, the less opaque those veils, the better. In practice, then, when historians of emotion have sought evidence from literature, they have gravitated towards what appear to be its least dishonest forms—letters, chronicles, conduct books—genres, in other words, with a minimum of what Jakobson defined as the 'poetic function', in which 'a word is perceived as a word and not merely a proxy for the denoted object or an outburst of emotion'.[7] If even the most brilliant historians of our era have been taken to task for taking literary 'outbursts of emotion' as proxy for *real* 'outbursts of emotion',[8] why take the risk? Given this distrust of the literary, historians of emotion have shown little interest in adopting the methods of literary analysis, except insofar as these can help them to detect and 'discount' the literariness that 'infects' certain sources.[9]

Meanwhile, in literature departments, few medievalists currently situate their work in the context of the 'history of emotion'. One could, perhaps, see this feeble participation in a burgeoning enterprise as the yawn of a self-styled avant-garde—for in some senses literary scholars have always known that feelings, too, have histories. The manifest alterity of many of the emotional gestures and logics in pre-modern texts (swooning knights, and so on) has begged for attention—and began to receive it from the moment English departments first opened their doors. The nonchalance with which C. S. Lewis speaks of the invention of romantic love itself, and not just a new kind of love poetry, is worth noting ('Real changes in human sentiment are very rare ... but I believe that they occur, and that this is one of them'), as is J. A. W. Bennett's confident assertion that the pathetic style in early vernacular Passion lyrics represents 'one of the greatest revolutions in feeling Europe has ever witnessed'.[10] Of course, these avuncular dons were fond of the sweeping claim, and could get away with it in print in that gentler era; whether

---

presents literature and literary scholarship as secondary; they essentially show how a crux in a literary text can be illuminated by historical scholarship.

[7] As cited in Victor Erlich in *Russian Formalism: History-Doctrine* (The Hague: Mouton Publishers, 1969), 183.

[8] See, for instance, reviews of John Boswell's *Christianity, Social Tolerance, and Homosexuality: Gay People in Western Europe from the Beginning of the Christian Era to the Fourteenth Century* (Chicago: University of Chicago Press, 1980).

[9] These are the terms used by William Ian Miller in *Bloodtaking and Peacemaking: Feud, Law, and Society in Saga Iceland* (Chicago: University of Chicago Press, 1990), 47; 48. In this book, Miller offers the most spirited defence to date of using literature for the history of emotion, but he does so because 'the historian of early Iceland has no choice' (p. 45): apart from legal codes, sagas are the only sources available.

[10] C. S. Lewis, *The Allegory of Love: A Study in Medieval Tradition* (Oxford: Oxford University Press, 1936), 11; J. A. W. Bennett, *Poetry of the Passion: Studies in Twelve Centuries of English Verse* (Oxford: Clarendon Press, 1982), 32.

they would wager to eat their hats, pending further evidence, is another question. Since the 1980s, literary scholars have tended to avoid forays into the diachronic (avoiding, especially, the question of whether large-scale shifts in sensibility happen, and how) but have certainly continued to assume the historicity of emotion; the premiss that even the most intimate aspects of the self are moulded by culture—and allied with worldly structures of power—is not only commonplace, but has served as the basis for some of the very best work in recent decades, from Dinshaw's *Chaucer's Sexual Poetics* to Holsinger's *Music, Body and Desire in Medieval Culture*.

Certain self-imposed limits, however, have kept this recent work from attaining visibility and participatory vitality as a branch of the history of emotion. The chief symptom and cause of these limits is, as I see it, the very reluctance to claim this affiliation. *Other* histories have named and framed these studies and provided their guiding questions: histories of the body, sexuality, gender, subjectivity, devotion, social relations. Perhaps this tendency to treat emotion only obliquely has been driven by collective embarrassment at the very frankness and untheorized ease with which that earlier generation of Middle English scholars took up the subject; or perhaps it has been fuelled by worries that engaging openly with the 'soft' subject of emotion could only underscore the reputation of literary scholars as disciplinary softies in an academic universe that values the hard. Whatever the reasons, the reluctance to look at emotion directly, to hold it up to the light as an entity separate from as well as linked to the sexual or political or devotional, has had three significant consequences. First, it has kept the range of subjects quite narrow: the lively attention to 'desire' (under the rubrics of sexuality and subjectivity) and to 'pity/compassion' (under the rubrics of affective devotion and social relations) has failed to inspire serious investigation of other emotions in Middle English texts and contexts. Second, it has prevented us from seeking out and using the conceptual tools offered by work on emotions across the disciplines. Third, it has prevented us from imagining a future—from considering how literary scholars might participate *as literary scholars* in shaping the aims and methods of what is still an excitingly malleable field.

One quick fix to the first and second of these problems would be to follow the lead of our neighbours just around the corner in the Renaissance. Historicist work on the early modern passions has been flourishing in literature departments for the past decade, and it shows no signs of abating.[11] Taking a cue from this scholarship would not—indeed *could* not—be a matter of bringing a set of prefabricated questions to a different body of texts. Middle English scholars would still have the pleasure of inventing the questions, not only because so many features of the landscape differ (language, literacy, print, Church, state, globe, cosmos), but

---

[11] For an introduction to this body of work, see the essays collected in Gail Kern Paster, Katherine Rowe, and Mary Floyd-Wilson (eds.), *Reading the Early Modern Passions: Essays in the Cultural History of Emotion* (Philadelphia: University of Pennsylvania Press, 2004). The essay introducing this volume provides a very useful overview of the field and of the 'cultural history' approach taken by the contributing scholars.

because the central variable changes: Galenic humoral theory is not the governing model of emotional production in medieval England. What *is* the dominant model? That's a good question, one in urgent need of answering.[12] Criseyde's speculations on the ontology of emotion may actually be more representative than Galen's; as she sensibly observes, no one *trips* over love ('no wight on it sporneth').[13] Starting with a Criseydian, non-materialist model would raise a different set of questions for us medievalists, and tracing these out in Middle English literature would, in itself, enable us to contribute in productive and surprising ways to the discussion which the early modernists have so energetically begun.

Whatever possibilities of emulation, reconsideration, and extension this body of Renaissance scholarship offers, however, it provides little guidance for that third, more ambitious, task: that of questioning the way literature currently figures in this discipline-in-the-making. In general, literary scholars working in this vein openly espouse the 'cultural history' model of history–literature relations. This is not the place to assess the premises, politics, or heuristic value of this model, or its merits in relation to the old historicism or the New. Simply put, however, the cultural history model tends to collapse the literariness of literature (literary texts are typically mined for *content*) while confirming Auden's pronouncement: 'poetry makes nothing happen'. In other words, while this model grants that literary texts may absorb and replicate theories or discourses of emotion (including discourses of dissent or resistance), the literary is not typically acknowledged as a primary site or mechanism for the *making* of emotion, in any direct or historically consequential sense.

This is the problematic disciplinary juncture at which Middle English scholars can offer a high-impact intervention and can help to shape the field into one that is more capacious, fruitful, and respectful of literature's fleshy literariness. The way forward, as I see it, is through performance. Performance is the means through which the feelings embedded in literary texts became, potentially, *performative*, thus entering and altering history. Historians of emotion have long used a *vocabulary* of performance; the term 'emotion scripts' has come to stand for the loosely affiliated cultural prescripts that aid in establishing and maintaining what they have helpfully termed 'emotional regimes' or 'emotional communities'.[14] And medieval historians have recognized the affective performativity of ritual formulae, particularly in the context of feuding and reconciliation. But, on the whole, the term 'script' has been used as a metaphor for general social forces, or as a synonym for discourse.

---

[12] To date, there have been no surveys of the vernacular models of emotional production in late medieval England. Latinate theory—in the form especially of Aquinas on emotion, or Bernard on affective devotion, or medical treatises—continues to stand in for what I see as a far more multi-faceted reality. Close attention to embodied theory (to theory as it emerges from particular affective texts and practices) is, in my view, the most promising way forward.

[13] *Troilus and Criseyde*, II. 797, in *The Riverside Chaucer*, ed. Larry D. Benson, 3rd edn. (Boston: Houghton Mifflin Co., 1987), 500.

[14] The first term comes from Reddy, *The Navigation of Feeling*; the second, from Rosenwein, 'Worrying'.

What I suggest is a more imaginative, large-scale experiment with the literal; with conceiving of a wide array of Middle English texts as literal scripts that vigorously enlist *literariness* as a means of generating feelings and putting them into play in history.

To consider Middle English texts as scripts for the performance of feeling is, from one point of view, the most reasonable of propositions. Many Middle English genres (affective meditations, the drama, carols, conduct books, love lyrics, books of consolation) openly seek to 'write on the hearts' of their users. This resonates not only with certain medieval understandings of affect as something willed and performed, but with contemporary research on emotion: recent empirical studies in psychology, anthropology, and linguistics suggest that naming emotions, and acting them out, are primary ways in which they are brought into being, in culturally specific iterations that may have only the most minimal hard-wired bases. Beyond these theoretical considerations rests the practical reality that most Middle English texts were—far more often than not—*performed*. What appears to us on page or parchment is shard-like, fragmentary, even though it may 'present' as complete: the speaking voice, the listening ear, and audiences—whether human or divine—were integral to the medieval experience, even if only in *imagined* form (see Coleman, Symes, and Brantley in this volume). It is but a short step from registering this robust performance dimension of Middle English literature to seeing its potentially performative functions.[15] Analysing our texts as scripts, then, can not only expose more fully the *synchronic* historicity of emotion, but take up where Lewis and Bennett left off: it can potentially expose the mechanisms of the *diachronic* as well.

Affective scripts in the history of feeling

Having come this far with the 'history of emotion', I now wish to make a slight adjustment, and advocate 'the history of feeling' as the more useful rubric for Middle English specialists. The term 'emotion' is unlikely to be supplanted; despite the anachronistic model of affective production it implies—an expressive or 'hydraulic' model, in which pre-existing passions move outward from the inside—it

---

[15] J. L. Austin himself, of course, asserted that language could operate performatively only under 'ordinary circumstances', and *not* in the realm of the literary, claiming that a performative utterance would be 'in a peculiar way hollow or void if said by an actor on a stage, or if introduced in a poem, or spoken in soliloquy' (*How to Do Things with Words* [Cambridge, MA: Harvard University Press, 1962], 22). Austin, however, was not a medievalist. He thus had no reason to refine his theory in light of a linguistic and cultural context in which *game* and *earnest* were so intimately intertwined. My understanding of performativity is informed by the medieval context, as well as by Judith Butler's more extended definition of the performative, which includes a wide range of speech acts, gestures, and events; see especially her 'Performative Acts and Gender Constitution: An Essay in Phenomenology and Feminist Theory', in Sue-Ellen Case (ed.), *Performing Feminisms: Feminist Critical Theory and Theatre* (Baltimore: Johns Hopkins University Press, 1990), 270–82.

has irrevocably entered the interdisciplinary lingua franca. But 'feeling' is more apt in our subfield, not only because it is an authentic Middle English term, or because it serves as a reminder of the integration of the somatic, affective, and cognitive in a pre-Cartesian universe ('to feel' can mean 'to know'; see *MED*, 'felen', v. 1), but because it embeds a grammatical doubleness. Its gerundive form gestures towards process, as well as thing, or both at once. Adopting the rich verbal-nounness of 'feeling', then, can encourage us to search not only for the *what* of emotions (what were they feeling, back then?) and the *why* (what personal, social, or political functions did feeling serve?) but the *how*, especially as it is visible through literary texts: *how* did they feel?

The method I suggest for exploring such questions is a straightforward one. First, reconstruct the historical conditions of the performance of a text, through empirical research and informed speculation; next, examine how a text seeks to produce emotion, through careful attention to its affective stylistics; then see how it all adds up, kinetically. This general strategy of 'actualizing absence' by bringing external and internal features together has been used to very positive effect in various branches of historical performance studies.[16] Several more specific adjustments might be of use to Middle English scholars in their adaptation of this model.

Where the externals are concerned, a key strategy in my view is to combine the usual forms of textual research with considerations of what is likely to have been seen, heard, touched, even *tasted* at the moment of a text's performance. Speculation, I suggest, can and indeed must be harnessed as an intellectual tool in such an endeavour. Yes, there is a real risk of being wrong. But without engaging regularly in speculative acts, we are continuing to prop up the manifest fiction that what we cannot decisively document did not exist or was not operative, in any essential way, in the production of affect. In disregarding what is left to the imagination, in other words, we risk throwing the proverbial baby out with the bathwater. Indeed *real* babies have been thrown out with the bathwater in our text-centred assessment of medieval lyrics. Certain lullabies and laments of the Virgin, for instance, are highly likely to have been performed with real babes in arms, and this surely must be factored into any assessment of the historical questions such lullabies and laments prompt, such as whether babies were used as living devotional objects by their mothers, or the larger question of whether maternal love for infants is a post-medieval invention.

As for the close reading of a text's affective stylistics, what I wish to emphasize is the word 'affective'. As instituted by Stanley Fish and used by reader-response critics, this phrase has come to stand for the process through which literary texts

---

[16] I take this term from the introductory essay by Mark Franko and Annette Richards, 'Actualizing Absence: The Pastness of Performance', in their edited collection *Acting on the Past: Historical Performance across the Disciplines* (Hanover, NH: Wesleyan University Press, 2000).

make *meaning*.[17] Let's make an honest term of it: how do texts make *feeling*? The raw stuff of our texts—words, words, words—requires close attention in this quest. If, as the ethnolinguists suggest, the words *are* the feelings, philological work is essential—particularly in a multilingual culture, where multilingual manuscripts, macaronic poetry, and acts of translation were common. What were the consequences, for instance, of having *Middle English* feelings, as distinct from Anglo-Norman, Welsh, French, or Latin ones? In addition to the specific features of the language, literary techniques of many kinds—emplotment, rhythm, repetition, imagery, narrative pace, and so on—manifestly invite attention for the way they can generate feeling. But here I offer two less obvious aspects of affective stylistics for consideration: 'affective dissonance' and 'disaffection'. The first is a species of irony, and therefore highly productive in relation to Chaucer. Noticing the ways in which a text elicits opposing emotions can expose the way it functions *cognitively*, producing a desire to resolve affective conflict through new ways of thinking; such dissonance, then, can operate as a progressive force in history. 'Disaffection' has perhaps a more narrow applicability, but important nonetheless; it can illuminate, for instance, texts related to Lollardy and the demise of Catholic hegemony in England. Such texts usually seek to minimize affective response. But instead of dismissing these writings as irrelevant to the history of feeling, we might ask why the *aversion* to feeling; why the attempt to minimize the workings of the heart? This might, in turn, lead us to question the notion that to understand Lollard iconoclasm, for instance, we must go to theology. Could it have been that the ubiquitous image of Christ on the cross, an image so many Middle English lyrics cast as that of Christ the lover—leaning down to embrace and kiss the meditator-as-beloved, and demanding passionate compassion in return—had become a threat to sexual identity for certain categories of readers in late medieval England? If so, we have an interesting possibility on our hands: the possibility that feelings, including the aversion to feeling certain feelings, can be instrumental in effecting large-scale historical change.[18]

I would like to show how such strategies can be put into practice through readings of two very different Middle English texts, *The Wooing of Our Lord* and *Sir Gawain and the Green Knight*. I have chosen these texts not only because they illustrate the synchronic and diachronic historicity of emotion, respectively, but because they exemplify two distinct operations of the performative in Middle English texts: its enactment by a performer on the one hand and by an audience on the other.

---

[17] Stanley Fish sets out his definition in 'Literature in the Reader: Affective Stylistics', reprinted in Jane Tompkins (ed.), *Reader Response Criticism: From Formalism to Post-Structuralism* (Baltimore: Johns Hopkins University Press, 1980), 70–100.

[18] This line of argument has been drawn out more fully in my paper 'Lollard Disaffection and the History of Emotion', delivered at the International Medieval Congress, Kalamazoo, MI, May 2005.

Because the performative efficacy of *listening* is not a familiar concept, my reading of *Gawain* will be the more extended of the two.

Wooing Christ

That the thirteenth-century *Wooing of Our Lord* is, in the most literal sense, a script for the performance of feeling is clear. In its concluding colophon, the author asks the anchoress to say these words often, for 'wordes ofte quemen [allure] the heorte to thenken on ure lauerd' (ll. 647–9); repeat performances will 'opne thin heorte to his luve & to reowthe of his pine' (ll. 656–8).[19] This text, then, aspires to performativity, to effecting real change in the anchoress's heart. On its own, of course, this is unsurprising: affective devotions of all kinds are supposed to do such work. But if we investigate the particular historical conditions in which the *Wooing* was performed, and scrutinize its affective stylistics more carefully, we can see that it exceeds its ostensible devotional function. Embedded in this relic from the history of feeling is a peculiar, and fascinating, phenomenon, one linked to the specific social situation of women who, like the anchoress for whom the text was written, were betrothed to Christ as *sponsae Christi*. By scripting a potent affective exercise—one which leads the anchoress through an experience of intense, eroticized compassion for her lover, who suffered to win her love—the *Wooing* appears to have served a *legally* performative function: in short, it aided in the enactment of a legally valid marriage to Christ.

As I have explained in detail elsewhere, it did so through facilitating the anchoress's performance of *maritalis affectio*, 'marital affection', the concept that Gratian and other theorists of marriage-making described as the affective core that ought to underwrite the all-important legal criterion of consent.[20] I cannot, for reasons of space, explain here the complexities of how the *Wooing* is embedded in a network of legal thinking (indeed, this very impossibility reinforces an important point: that there *are* rich complexities underlying what seem to be unremarkable and easily understood configurations of affect in Middle English texts). But to put it simply, the playful, witty first half of the *Wooing*, in which the anchoress speaks of Christ as if he is, or can become, her *husband* (and not merely her lover, in the Bernardine, mystical sense), invites a closer look at precisely how an anchoress living in the Welsh Marches in the early thirteenth century would have been situated, socially and legally, in relation to Christ. The answer appears

---

[19] This and subsequent citations are from W. Meredith Thompson, *The Wohunge of Ure Lauerd*, EETS 241 (London: Oxford University Press, 1958).

[20] See 'Compassion and the Making of a *Sponsa Christi*', in my forthcoming book on affective meditation and the history of feeling.

to be that she lived out her days in a liminal realm: legally betrothed to Christ as *sponsa Christi*, yet unable to confirm or ratify this marriage through the route available to most couples—consummation. The moment of death, then, when Christ will either accept or reject her as what many texts for female religious pointedly call his *true* bride, becomes the moment towards which the daily practices of the anchoress are oriented. Indeed, palaeographical evidence suggests that the performance of the *Wooing* was considered central to those daily practices. In the sole manuscript in which the *Wooing* survives, British Library, Cotton MS Titus D. xviii, it alone is marked for easy finding, with a rubricated title that its companion pieces lack.

Turning to the text's affective stylistics, we find that this script is rich in deictic rhetoric ('here', 'there'), sensuous alliteration, and above all, rhythm. Indeed the *Wooing* is so profoundly, ecstatically rhythmic that it and its few kin have been given the generic designation, unique in all of English literature, 'prose rhapsodies'. The anchoress would have performed this rhythmic language *aloud*, doubling its somatic effects as she not only said the words (experiencing them bodily as they rise from the vocal passages as if from the heart, feeling the words on the lips and tongue) but heard herself saying them (they double back into her body, through the ear). In the Passion section, the language builds to an affective and somatic climax, and this is staged not only through the greater intensity of the rhythm but through the collapse of grammatical structure. Sentences become fragmentary, exclamations abound; even the phrase at the very centre of the drama lacks a logic-lending verb: 'A that luuelike bodi that henges swa rewli [pitifully] swa blodi & swa kalde' (ll. 532–4). These literary techniques add up to a powerful affective experience, as this text scripts an event of great intimacy, immediacy, and intensity. Enclosed in her cell—an intimate space which the anchoress was asked to imagine as both bower and tomb—the anchoress overlays these spatial poetics with those of another site, the crucifix, at the climactic conclusion of her script: 'A swete iesu mi liues luue ... Hwat mai thole [suffer] for the for al that tu tholedes for me? ... Mi bodi henge with thi bodi neiled o rode sperred querfaste [transfixed] with inne fowr wahes [walls] ... ' (ll. 577–93). This compassionate identification with Christ, this total union of affect and will, is, for the *sponsa Christi*, the equivalent of consummation. But unlike consummation, this event is not simply experienced once. As a demonstration of marital affection, here configured as intense compassion for the suffering lover, it must be repeated often. Thus, this text appears to have been instrumental in a lifelong process of marriage-making: each time the *sponsa* enters into the affective role scripted for her here, she enacts a 'wooing' of her would-be husband, demonstrating to him the depth of her marital affection. She thus moves one step closer to becoming Christ's true bride, a title that can only be confirmed after death. Only then can she be 'crowned', as she puts it, by her bridegroom, her marriage made secure.

Feeling green

Chivalry is dead. How did it die? With this stark historical fact and its complex causes I wish to frame *Sir Gawain and the Green Knight* as a performance script in which diachronic history might be glimpsed in the making.

This romance is now generally thought to have been written for the extended court of Richard II, and to comment on the crisis of chivalry during Richard's reign.[21] Precisely how it does so continues to be a subject of debate, but the dominant view has been that the romance questions traditional chivalric values—particularly the keeping of *troth*, upon which the entire edifice of chivalry rests—and reaffirms them in the end. Analysing how emotion is performed both in and through the romance, however, suggests that it is proposing something more: it presents 'loving one's life' as an affective state embedding serious ethical claims, claims upon which a new vision of aristocratic culture might be founded.

'Loving one's life', of course, is the basis on which the Green Knight tempers his criticism of Gawain for keeping the life-saving green girdle, thus breaking his *troth*: 'ye lufed your lyf—the lasse I yow blame' (l. 2368).[22] This is puzzling logic, in the late fourteenth century, and previous readings of the poem have had to import ideas from outside the text (many of them subsequently condemned as liberal humanist anachronisms) in order to fill what appears to be a selfish motive with significance and keep it in interpretative play even as Gawain himself rejects it as 'cowarddyse' and 'couetyse' (l. 2374). When we treat this text as a script for performance, we gain another perspective. In short, the poem can then be seen as a kind of experimental theatre, staging an affective and cognitive event that is potentially transformative. Through its vivid evocation of the joys of courtly culture at Hautdesert, it seeks to give its audience a vibrantly felt *experience* of 'loving one's life', an experience that the episodes before and after pointedly—and quite innovatively—frame as a serious value, one worthy of serious consideration as aristocratic culture seeks to realign itself in a changing world. In this sense, the *Gawain*-poet is, like Chaucer in the 'Franklin's Tale' and *Troilus and Criseyde*, exploring the grounds for a more supple configuring and contextualization of *troth*; and, like Chaucer, he sees the investigation of emotion as fundamental to this quest.

---

[21] The work by John M. Bowers on the relation between the works of the *Pearl* manuscript and the Ricardian court is especially thorough: see *The Politics of Pearl: Court Poetry in the Age of Richard II* (Cambridge: D. S. Brewer, 2001).

[22] This and all subsequent citations are from Malcolm Andrew and Ronald Waldron (eds.), *The Poems of the Pearl Manuscript*, 4th edn. (Exeter: Exeter University Press, 2002). Modern English glosses come from Marie Borroff, *Sir Gawain and the Green Knight, Patience, and Pearl* (New York: Norton, 2001).

The affective underpinnings of chivalry are themselves staged in the first fitt as a carefully sequenced emotion script. What must be banished above all, in chivalric culture, is primal fear—the fear of killing and of being killed. So, when the Green Knight issues his doubly terrifying challenge (mortal blow for mortal blow) and the instinctive reaction of one and all is a stunned and petrified silence—a silence whose duration heightens suspense, suggesting that what happens next is not inevitable—Arthur sets the chivalric machine in motion by leaping into the politically correct emotion script. In a remarkable display of affective prowess, he performs four feelings in quick succession:

> Wyth this he [the Green Knight] laghes so loude that the lorde [Arthur] greued;
> The blod schot for scham into his schyre face
>   And lere; [pride]
> He wex as wroth as wynde;
> So did alle that there were.
> The kyng, as kene [bold] bi kynde [nature]
> Then stod that stif mon nere ... (ll. 317–22)

That Arthur could execute such fancy feeling in the blink of an eye is itself comic, but all the more so when we recognize that this seven-line *abbreviatio* contains, in a sly parenthesis, its own highly dramatic shadow play as *the entire court* copies Arthur's sequence—even its somatics. The striking image of the collective face of the court instantly flushing red in shame and anger in imitation of their king exposes the top-down model of affective production as one of Camelot's primary fictions. Here in Camelot, emotions are produced by fiat: 'I know no gome [man] that is gast of thy grete wordes', Arthur proclaims, clearly intending his declaration to have performative efficacy (l. 325). This crucial pivot in the plot, then, establishes three things at once: that chivalric action rests on an affective foundation; that this foundation is not instinctive, like fear, but a complex, cultural script; and that this script is, from one point of view, comic—thus available for critique.

It is also, of course, deadly, and thus potentially productive of grief. This dark coda to the chivalric script has become, in late fourteenth-century England, harder to contain and control.[23] And so, when Gawain's chivalric gesture locks him into a death sentence, the text cannot fail to generate a form of affective dissonance in its audience—a state of profound discomfort on which the poet relies to pave the way for the thought that there must be a better way. The latent pathos and manifest injustice of the situation are admitted into the text even as they are aggressively covered up by a king who will 'let no semblaunt be sene' (l. 468) of the serious dismay that he, his queen, courtiers, and Gawain are at risk of feeling. Identification is one obvious and powerful strategy the poet exploits to get

---

[23] For another sphere in which similar ideas are being worked out in late medieval England, see my essay 'The Virgin and the Voice of Protest', in *Speaking Images: Essays in Honor of V. A. Kolve* (Asheville, NC: Pegasus Press, 2001), 505–23.

his audience to feel the wrongness of this suppression of grief: the poet returns repeatedly to Gawain's fellow knights and courtiers, whose efforts to hide inner sorrow with outward cheer grow increasingly unbearable, until the pressure of this disjunction issues in open critique of Arthur and his stubborn adherence to chivalric *troth* and 'angardez pryde' (empty pride) (l. 681). In addition to fostering identification with the courtiers who weep for their friend, whose life they cannot see as the 'trifel' (l. 547) which chivalry considers it to be, the poet conscripts his audience into an experience of affective dissonance through a well-placed joke. This comes just after the Green Knight rides away, after reiterating that Gawain must, in a year's time, bow to a beheading. It is a tense moment, and Arthur seizes control of it through the serious weapon of humour: 'He glent [glanced] vpon Sir Gawen and gaynly [gaily] he sayde, "Now sir, heng vp thyn ax, that hatz innogh hewen"' (ll. 474–5). You had to be there, but this is in fact a zinger of a pun. To 'hang up one's axe' meant to stop whatever one has been doing (call it a day, throw in the towel); and there stands Gawain, holding an enormous bloody axe, the wielding of which has just sealed his gruesome fate. We can assume that this joke was planted to produce explosive, involuntary laughter in the audience, thus getting the audience not only to see but to *feel*—to experience affectively and somatically—the forced gaiety that Arthur manufactures in his court. By giving the audience this felt experience of forced gaiety, the poet strengthens the basis for critique that he places in the mouths of the distraught courtiers as Gawain rides away. Affective dissonance, then, exposes the crack in the 'unalloyed gold' (l. 633) of the chivalric ideal, even as it paves the way for a new experience: feeling green.

'Feeling green' is the alternative emotion script that the poem goes on to perform, not only in the text but in and through its audience.[24] Greenness, in one sense, stands for the inevitability of growth and change, and, as the second fitt opens, the poet's evocation of the changing seasons and the newness of every year serves as an image for how tradition must make way for innovation, how a 'yere yernes ful yerne and yeldez neuer lyke; | The forme to the fynishment foldez ful selden' (a year passes apace, and proves ever new: | First things and final conform but seldom) (ll. 498–9). But overlaid upon this sense of 'green' as growth is 'green' as an affective state—a state of longing, of desiring—for although the text itself never uses the word 'green' as a verb, this colour's verbal sense seems to underwrite the whole of the mirthful experience at Hautdesert. 'To green' in Middle English is 'to desire, long' (*MED*, 'grenen', v. 2); and the particular form of desire the poet seeks to induce in his audience is one of *loving their own lives*. The reflexivity

---

[24] The argument summarized here derives from my essay 'Feeling Green: Affect and Audience in *Sir Gawain in the Green Knight*', in progress. In exploring 'green' as a feeling in medieval England, I have taken inspiration from Bruce R. Smith's rich and provocative essay on early modern greenness, 'Hearing Green', in Paster et al. (eds.), *Reading the Early Modern Passions*, 147–68.

of this formulation, the most pointed and enigmatic phrase in the entire text, is crucial. It not only describes what is, in the fourteenth century, a newly articulated emotion—new in its emphasis on one's own, particular life, rather than the more generalized concept of 'love of life'; it also describes the reflexive *process* that the poet exploits as a means of getting his listeners to see their own lives as valuable, as worth preserving.

The operations of such reflexivity become clear upon consideration of the specific conditions in which *Gawain* is likely to have been performed. What is striking about such conditions is how similar they are to the world conjured in the text. In the scenes at Hautdesert, the poet has attempted to mirror not only the familiar landscapes and particular manners of the Cheshire contingent of the court of Richard II, but even such elements of the material culture of that court as its silks and pearls, embroidered tapestries, rich carpets from the East, even the novelty of silver spoons (fastidious Richard's pet idea) on the eye-delighting table. Temporally, too, *Gawain* mirrors its own probable performance at a Yuletide feast, when time was given over to *mirth* in its many forms of hunting, dalliance, dancing, music-making, feasting, drinking, and the reading of romances. Through such mirroring, then, the poet creates a performance that overlays his fiction on a base of the real. He can thus enlist the audience as extras, the material features of the hall as backdrop, and the entire, fulsome, sensual surroundings of an elegant Yuletide feast—candles, silks, gems, music, laughter, banter, kisses, dancing, whispers, delicacies, wine—as aural, visual, tactile, fragrant, even edible props. Like the medieval drama, then, which typically conscripts audience as participants and site as scene, this script doubles the efficacy of its own story even as it blurs the boundaries between performance and life.

The aim of such mirroring and blurring is to elicit a powerful attraction, in the audience, to the lives they are living at that very moment. Gawain's journey through the wilderness in the second fitt serves a crucial framing function in this regard, for the profoundly bleak image of man *en route* to death, dwarfed and threatened by a radically inhospitable universe, paves the way for a sensory, emotional, and cognitive apprehension of the castle (and the courtly culture it represents) as a wonder, a marvel. Gawain's re-entry into a familiar world thus facilitates, in the audience, an affective and somatic double-take: as Gawain experiences, as if for the first time, the pleasures of dressing in fine clothes, feeling the warmth of the fire, eating and drinking well, engaging in banter and laughter, the audience is invited to do so too, and to identify these pleasures as primary goods.

Fitt three is, of course, a *tour de force* of kinetic art: for sheer vividness and sustained narrative vigour, it is in unequalled in the the whole of Middle English literature. Most obviously, this fitt generates narrative intensity through the unprecedented challenge of the triple plot, in which hunting, seduction, and the exchange of winnings heighten suspense on three levels at once—as if suspense itself is one of the things of time that this text wants its listeners to love. Then there are the sound effects. Knowing that his is, above all, an aural art, the poet exploits sound as the sense through which he can enter directly into the bodies of his audience members, pushing somatic buttons that produce emotion: witness the pounding, pulse-heightening rhythm, the clamorous tumult of horses and dogs, the sharp blasts and exclamations ('Hyghe!' … 'Hay! Hay!', l. 1445), and percussive alliteration on plosives (p, b) in the hunting scenes, and the way these contrast with the exquisite delicacy of the seduction scenes. Consider, in this regard, the softness of the 'littel dyn at hys dor' (l. 1183) and the lady's light footsteps, the sensuousness of the alliteration on sibilant and liquid letters (s, l, r), the pleasurable sounds of sweet talk and light laughter.

This third fitt persistently employs reflexivity as a means of attracting its listeners to the wonders of the courtly culture they already inhabit. The hunting scenes, for instance, activate memory as a means of doubling their felt appeal. For the hunters in the crowd (presumably most of the men, including Richard himself, if he was there, for he was an avid huntsman) the hunting passages would replay the vivid thrill of the chase, the kill, and the evisceration of deer. These passages would in turn be memorable, feeding into the actual experience of setting forth to hunt on a crisp morning, the fair fields sparkling with frost, as the red sun rises (ll. 1694–5). The seduction scenes, too, seek to enfold life into literature through that powerful technique so frequently deployed in the medieval love lyric: through leaving the lovely lady nameless, and free from the narrowing specificity that a fleshing out of her physical particularities would effect. Capturing the essence of flirtation in its own bare hints at hidden beauties, this script offers only the most fleeting glimpse of the lady's face ('chynne and cheke ful swete | Both quit [white] and red in blande [complexion] | Ful lufly con ho lete [playfully converse] | Wyth lyppez smal laghande', ll. 1204–7), and leaves her height, eye and hair colour, and so on to the imagination. Significantly, the text underscores the interplay such imagery allows (she's *your* beloved; yes, the one sitting across the table, glancing at you even now; *feel her attractiveness*) with rapid alternations between past and present tense, thus breaking down the barriers between distant and immediate pleasures even at the level of its temporal technique.

This passage suggests not only an intensification of present joys, but a fundamental stance towards life, one stated boldly by the host (who is presented, significantly, as a *mature* version of lordship—bearded, not boyish like Arthur): 'Make we mery quyl we may and mynne vpon joye, | For the lur may mon lach whenso mon lykez' (Be we merry while we may, and mindful of joy, | For heaviness of heart can be had for the asking)(ll. 1681–2). Performed on the brink of a new year—a liminal moment when real change can be contemplated—the affective experience this text generates is set up to do serious cognitive work. The green garter comes to stand not only for the desire to preserve one's life, but for the newly felt knowledge underwriting this desire. The text's *listeners*, as well as Gawain, are thus armed with that garter as the castle is left behind. Greenness, then, can feed into those otherwise puzzling words of the Green Knight ('ye lufed your lyf—the lasse I yow blame') and permit *disidentification* with Gawain when he rejects what the audience has been led to experience as a core value. Instead, listeners can identify with Arthur and the courtiers at the romance's end, thus imagining, in their own lives, a similar conversion experience, in which the greenness of loving one's life tempers the gold of rigid chivalric *troth*.

FURTHER READING

For a sampling of recent work on emotion across the disciplines, see the books listed in McLemee's 'Getting Emotional' (n. 1 above). The shortest route to establishing a bibliography for the history of emotion as it relates to medieval studies is to mine the rich endnotes in Rosenwein's 'Worrying' (n. 5). The essays collected and introduced by Rosenwein in *Anger's Past: The Social Uses of an Emotion in the Middle Ages* (Ithaca, NY: Cornell University Press, 1998) exemplify the range of questions and methods motivating work in this field. For full-length studies of emotion as it relates to political, legal, social, and intellectual history, see the recent and ongoing work of C. Stephen Jaeger, Paul Hyams, Rachel Fulton, Fredric L. Cheyette, and Daniel Lord Smail.

Gail Kern Paster has initiated much of the work on the early modern passions. Along with Katherine Rowe and Mary Floyd-Wilson, she provides a sweeping yet concise overview of how emotions research in the literature/cultural history nexus has been informed by—and in turn might contribute to—work in cognitive psychology, anthropology, sociology and linguistics; see the introduction to *Reading the Early Modern Passions* (n. 11). Most of the scholars contributing to this volume have also published books meriting close attention from medievalists.

Cultural studies offers richly provocative questions and methods that I have not had room to address in this essay. The prolific work of William Ian Miller, who started out as a medieval historian, is especially interesting for the movement it traces from history to cultural studies; see his books on revenge, courage, humiliation, and disgust. Eve Kosofsky Sedgwick's *Touching Feeling: Affect, Pedagogy, Performativity* (Durham, NC: Duke University Press, 2003) offers much food for thought, as do the essays collected in Lauren Berlant (ed.), *Compassion: The Culture and Politics of an Emotion* (New York: Routledge, 2004).

Reception theory and performance studies are foundational to the method I propose; bibliographies are readily available, but I recommend supplementing the former with Elaine Scarry's *Dreaming by the Book* (New York: Farrar, Straus and Giroux, 1999), which has important implications for the ways literary texts generate feelings as well as thoughts. Historical performance studies is continuing to evolve as a distinct subspeciality; in addition to *Acting on the Past* (n. 16), see the innovative work of Joseph Roach. The issues raised by the historically informed performance ('HIP') movement in music are worth considering in relation to the performance of Middle English texts, as is recent work on the history of the senses; for the latter, see David Howes (ed.), *Empire of the Senses: The Sensual Culture Reader* (Oxford: Berg, 2005).

Gesture has recently claimed more attention from medievalists, in part for its role in the performativity of emotion; see J. A. Burrow, *Gestures and Looks in Medieval Narrative* (Cambridge: Cambridge University Press, 2002) and papers that may issue from the International Congress of Medieval Studies, Leeds 2006, whose central thematic strand is 'Emotion and Gesture' (**www.leeds.ac.uk/ims/imc2006.html**).

CHAPTER 17

CONFLICT

MARION TURNER

The most dynamic period of English literary production and growth in the medieval era was also a period of extraordinary turmoil. The maelstrom—both political and textual—centred on the London-Westminster area, a site riven by 'a "discursive turbulence" as intense as the Guildhall wrangles and streetfighting chronicled by Ruth Bird'.[1] Steven Justice comments that 'texts do *happen*... they do not just *mean* or *exist*'.[2] Why, and how, did quite so many texts, of so many different kinds, *happen* in the last quarter of the fourteenth century? The upheavals of these years are well known: Richard's reign saw the Great Revolt, the development of Lollardy, dramatic mayoral disputes crystallized in the Brembre–Northampton antagonisms, the Wonderful, Merciless, and Revenge Parliaments, the taking of the city into the king's hand and, finally, usurpation. These decades also saw the emergence of writers such as Chaucer, Gower, and Langland, as well as numerous other literary practitioners such as Clanvowe and Usk. Many cultural and political events at this time bear witness to the political nature of textual production: books were burned both by the rebels of 1381 and by the mayor of London (Nicholas Exton), the first English petition was entered into the Rolls of Parliament, a trend for vernacular bill-posting developed, scribes formed themselves into guilds, and vernacular Bible translation became a controversial issue.[3] Were literary practice and socio-political conflict mutually dependent? Were poems and rebellions enabled by the same cultural changes?

---

[1] Sheila Lindenbaum, 'London Texts and Literate Practice', in D. Wallace (ed.), *The Cambridge History of Medieval English Literature* (Cambridge: Cambridge University Press, 1999), 284–309. See also Ruth Bird, *The Turbulent London of Richard II* (London: Longman's, Green, and Co., 1949).

[2] Steven Justice, *Writing and Rebellion: England in 1381* (Berkeley and Los Angeles: University of California Press, 1994), 255.

[3] On the rebels' book-burning see ibid. 40–8; on Exton's burning of the Jubilee Book see Bird, *Turbulent London*, 94 n. 4; for the petition see R. W. Chambers and Marjorie Daunt (eds.), *A Book of London English 1384–1425* (Oxford: Clarendon Press, 1931), 34–7; on bill-posting see Justice, *Writing and Rebellion*, 29; on the scribal guilds see Graham Pollard, 'The Company of Stationers before 1557', *The Library*, 4th ser. 18/1 (1937), 1–38, 6; on Bible translation see Anne Hudson, *The Premature Reformation: Wycliffite Texts and Lollard History* (Oxford: Clarendon Press, 1988), 238–47.

Texts are always inconsistent and self-contradictory. Language is an inherently conflicted phenomenon, an entity constituted by 'objective antinomies' where 'intentional meaning' and 'articulated system' exist in constant tension. Moreover, in Fredric Jameson's terms, all texts emerge out of antagonistic relationships with other voices; they exist in dialogical positions vis-à-vis other texts, many of which have been suppressed, marginalized, or appropriated, and are therefore not fully present to us. Jameson argues that conflict is constitutive in language and in texts, that writings exist in constant tension with themselves, with other generic possibilities, and with the voices that oppose them. But his emphasis in *The Political Unconscious* is, of course, on the pressures of history: plot must fall into history, genre shape-shifts and adapts itself to its historical conditions. In analysing a text we can perceive the structural norm, the deviation from that norm, and, finally, history itself as the 'absent cause' of these narrative shifts.[4] History limits and enables the possibilities of the text. During the reign of Richard II, possibilities were simultaneously expanded beyond anything previously seen in English letters and brutally limited, most obviously by hostility to certain kinds of writing, and by a heightened awareness of the importance of controlling writing.[5] In the late fourteenth century political documents, protest writing, literary texts, and the inevitably conflicted institutions of government were drawn together particularly tightly.

The kind of people who were writing and reading in the late fourteenth century suggests a great deal about how texts happened at this time. Michael Clanchy describes the subject of his seminal *From Memory to Written Record* as 'the beginnings of this growth of practical literacy, of depending for daily business on written record instead of the living memory'. The legal profession, seigneurial administration, and commerce grew in the twelfth century, and exploded in the thirteenth, from which time, 'increasing reliance and importance was placed upon the written word'.[6] By the second half of the thirteenth century, these structural changes in society were creating a new class of reader. Accustomed to reading documents in the course of their work, these people also wanted to read literary texts. This was made easier by changes in the material production of books. Cursive script, which had long been used for writs and rolls but not for books, was now pressed into service for many more kinds of texts. The lawyer or administrator accustomed to reading documents in this script could easily read books written in the same style. Moreover, books written in cursive script did not use 'drastic abbreviation', and so were more reader-friendly, and they could be produced more quickly and

---

[4] Fredric Jameson, *The Political Unconscious: Narrative as a Socially Symbolic Act* (London: Methuen & Co. Ltd., 1983), 109, 108, 84–7, 130, 145–6.

[5] Lindenbaum discusses the 'local climate of hostility to clerkly writing' in London ('London Texts', 291).

[6] Michael Clanchy, *From Memory to Written Record: England 1066–1307* (Oxford: Blackwell, 1993), 334; M. B. Parkes, 'The Literacy of the Laity', in David Daiches and Anthony Thorlby (eds.), *Literature and Western Civilization: The Mediaeval World* (London: Aldus Books, 1973), 555–77, 572.

therefore more cheaply. Increasing demand for books encouraged the development of a more organized book trade, and by the end of the fourteenth century much cheaper books were available. In London, scribes organized themselves into two guilds, the legal Scriveners and the Text-Writers. These scribes were producing books in a very different atmosphere from those working in monastic scriptoria, and they were also writing for a readership at least partly made up of men like themselves, men working and engaging with texts within 'new pressures of secular business as contrasted with the studied calm of the monastic tradition'.[7]

The kind of person who became a literary practitioner at this time was also a product of this new world of bureaucrats and lawyers, customs officers and Chancery scribes. The fourteenth century saw the demise of the minstrel and the rise of the amateur man of letters, squeezing his literary endeavours into the spare time allowed him by his day job. Paradoxically, with the demise of the professional literary practitioner we also see, I think, the diminishing of the (always deceptive) idea of literature as pleasure, as pure entertainment. Now that literature was no longer paid work, strangely, it was perceived and described as labour. Langland, for instance, who criticizes minstrels as time-wasters, goes on to describe his own writing as 'werk' (*Piers Plowman*, B. XII. 27).[8] In the *House of Fame*, Chaucer evokes an image of himself trudging home to Aldgate from the customs house to sit wearily amongst his books, trying to dredge up a poem despite his lack of inspiration (ll. 644–60). These men were not writing because they had endless leisure time, or because they had hopes of lavish rewards, but perhaps because writing was part of who they were. Writers and their texts were enmeshed in politics, administration, government, law, and debate; poetry was written while the poet was also occupied with his other jobs and tasks. There is little sense of the aesthetic as a separate realm; writing literature and working in the city or the court were part of a continuum.[9] The atmosphere of increasing literacy, bureaucracy, and vernacularity enabled people to produce bills and petitions in English and also allowed people such as Chaucer, Clanvowe, Gower, Langland, and Usk to write literary texts and find audiences for them. Writers were 'crossing discursive boundaries—particularly the barriers between the official languages and English and between legal and literary forms'.[10]

---

[7] See Parkes, 'Literacy', 563–5, 572, Clanchy, *From Memory*, 330, Pollard, 'Company of Stationers', 6.

[8] See Justice, *Writing and Rebellion*, 117. See also Richard Firth Green, *Poets and Princepleasers: Literature and the English Court in the Late Middle Ages* (Toronto: University of Toronto Press, 1980), esp. 111, 203–6 and Parkes, 'Literacy', 572.

[9] Focusing on the court, Green writes that 'Chaucer's literary abilities did not set him apart from his fellows at court; on the contrary, they gave him an entry into an aristocratic society fully conversant with the conventions binding the poet's imaginary world and confident in its role of literary arbiter', *Poets and Princepleasers*, 111.

[10] Lindenbaum, 'London Texts', 286. On the importance of law in medieval literature see also Richard Firth Green, 'Medieval Literature and Law', in Wallace (ed.), *Cambridge History*, 407–31, and John A. Alford, 'Literature and Law in Medieval England', *PMLA* 92 (1977), 941–51.

Poets, as well as clerks and civil servants, were objects of suspicion and hostility, and the textualizing of 'political aspirations' at this time inevitably associated all textual production with political manoeuvring.[11] In these decades, different classes of people were claiming literary culture and manipulating it. These people were not just respectable chamber knights and royal officials but also humbler Chancery scribes; indeed, their number included not only politically disgraced scriveners but even outright rebels. The activists of 1381, as Justice has argued, aimed not to destroy textual culture but to 'recreate it; they recognized the written document as something powerful but also malleable, something that, once written, could be *re*-written'.[12]

Increased access to textuality encouraged people to muster texts as political ammunition. The emergence of the petition, for instance, was bound up with the institutional changes of the thirteenth century, in particular the massive increase in the number of bureaucrats and royal officials and their liability to charges of misbehaviour. Petitions were also seen as providing access to law and to literate culture for the relatively disempowered; petitions did not require a writ, and therefore were cheaper and less formulaic than other legal recourses.[13] By the 1380s, petitions were being copied out by the same hand that copied out the *Canterbury Tales* (as Linne Mooney's research about Adam Pinkhurst has shown).[14] Elsewhere, I have examined linguistic and thematic connections between the Mercers' Petition and the *House of Fame*[15] (and much more work of this kind, reconstructing the dense textual environment inhabited by men such as Usk and Pinkhurst, remains to be done). We can trace precise linguistic parallels between these different kinds of texts, but the texts are also more fundamentally connected. They are all enabled by the institutional changes that shaped society at this time, and that affected metropolitan society—the place of government, law, commerce, and, in particular, guild life. Richard II's reign was a time of increased vernacular possibility, linked to the rapid growth of a public sector that could protest and could engage with protest.

A belief in the efficacy of deploying vernacular writing as a public statement of protest and self-belief was already apparent earlier in the fourteenth century. More powerful figures in society had occasionally posted up political documents in public places in the thirteenth and early fourteenth centuries (I am thinking of Magna

[11] Wendy Scase, '"Strange and Wonderful Bills": Bill Casting and Political Discourse in Late Medieval England', *New Medieval Literatures*, 2 (1998), 225–47, at 244.

[12] Justice, *Writing and Rebellion*, 48. He also discusses the rebels' use of *Piers Plowman* (pp. 104, 111).

[13] See A. Harding, 'Plaints and Bills in the History of English Law, Mainly in the Period 1250–1350', in Dafydd Jenkins (ed.), *Legal History Studies 1972* (Cardiff: University of Wales Press, 1975), 65–86, esp. 66, 71, and Justice, *Writing and Rebellion*, 60.

[14] Linne Mooney, 'Chaucer's Scribe', *Speculum: A Journal of Medieval Studies*, 81 (2006), 97–138.

[15] Marion Turner, *Chaucerian Conflict: Languages of Antagonism in Late Fourteenth-Century London* (Oxford: Oxford University Press, 2007), ch. 1.

Carta and Queen Isabella's accusation of the Despensers). In 1337, some Scots affixed a poem to St Peter's in Stangate, York. It reads:

> longe berde herteles
> peyntede hood wytles
> gay cote graceles
> maketh englond thriftles.[16]

Like many other later documents, also pinned up on the doors of ecclesiastical and governmental institutions—in the London area, St Paul's and Westminster Hall were favourite spots—this text brings together literary pretensions and overt political statement. By focusing criticism on the effete frivolity of the English, it constructs the speaker, or writer, as a down-to-earth person of integrity, a truthful, plain-speaking, honest man. Just as Edward II, and later Richard II, were often criticized for their interest in clothes, manners, and other 'surface' cultural attributes, so here the English are lambasted for their hairstyles and excessive outer garments, and each of the opening three lines links an interest in appearance with a failure in reality: the 'peyntede hood' makes the Englishman 'wytles'. The use of the vernacular and the placing of the text in a public place are strategies that contribute to the idea that the speaker represents the man on the street although, of course, the very use of poetic form undoes the illusion that this is 'direct' speaking.

By the last quarter of the fourteenth century, this mode of political expression was employed by a greater variety of social groups. Wyclif emerged as a political force, Chaucer, Langland, and Gower were producing a mass of literature in English, and the vernacular broadside or publicly posted bill was growing in popularity as a means of protest. Justice writes that:

> The vernacular broadside embodied a claim as well as a message: merely by existing, it asserted, tendentiously or not, that those who read only English—or even could only have English read to them—had a stake in the intellectual and political life of church and realm.[17]

This is particularly relevant if we think about the intended audience of such texts. But we should also remember that such texts seem to have been more the products of the educated, bureaucratic class than of those who really could only understand English: bills were embedded in the cultural world of Chaucer and his associates, and yet they are little discussed. We might examine, for instance, the case of Peter Pateshull. An erstwhile friar and papal chaplain, Pateshull preached against the friars, and posted a bill on the doors of St Paul's accusing them of various crimes

---

[16] Rossell Hope Robbins (ed.), *Historical Poems of the XIVth and XVth Centuries* (New York: Columbia University Press, 1959), p. xxxviii; Carleton Brown and Rossell Hope Robbins, *The Index of Middle English Verse* (New York, 1943), no. 1934, 305.

[17] Justice, *Writing and Rebellion*, 30. On bills, see also R. M. Wilson, *The Lost Literature of Medieval England* (London: Methuen and Co., 1952).

including sodomy and treason. How would we classify Pateshull's text? In subject matter, it clearly had close similarities not only to Lollard tracts, but also to poems against the friars produced in the 1380s, and to anti-fraternal satire of the kind that appears in Chaucer's General Prologue or in *Piers Plowman*. Walsingham tells us that Pateshull's 'chartam' was supported by various knights who wrote down copies of it, and he here produces his famous list of 'Lollard knights': Neville, Clifford, Clanvowe, Stury, Latimer, and Montagu.[18] If the story is true, Clanvowe may have read—may even have taken down his own copy of—this bill, and he also produced a religious tract of his own, as well as a debate poem, and was an early reader and associate of Chaucer. Different kinds of texts are connected in their concerns, and are also often linked in more material ways: the same workshops were producing texts of overt political protest and luxury 'literary' manuscripts.

Understanding of the kind of people who produced texts in late fourteenth-century London has recently been radically developed by the work of Linne Mooney and Caroline Barron, whose research has greatly enhanced knowledge about Adam Pinkhurst and Thomas Usk. The extrinsic conditions of cultural production affected texts in myriad ways that we can only hope to partially reconstruct, but more can now be known about the hectic, turbulent, textual world in which Chaucer's texts were copied. Both Usk and Pinkhurst read Chaucer's writings, worked as scribes, were hired by important, politically prominent London guilds, and seem to have written creatively. These interconnections reveal elements of the highly politicized and difficult environment in which late fourteenth-century texts were born.

Mooney's research has established that Adam Pinkhurst was the scribe of the Hengwyrt and Ellesmere *Canterbury Tales* manuscripts, and that he also penned the politically contentious Mercers' Petition. She posits that he was the 'Adam scriveyn' wearily addressed by Chaucer in his poem about the problems of scribal negligence, and that he was working for Chaucer from the mid-1380s and enjoyed a close relationship with him.[19] This scribe, who seems to have read and copied Chaucer's texts during Chaucer's lifetime, was deeply implicated in the factional politics of London. The Mercers' Petition is an extremely suggestive piece of writing (and may even have been intended for a wider audience than the other guilds' petitions—Mooney compares it to publicly posted texts such as the Lollard 'Twelve Conclusions').[20] The parliamentary petitions submitted by the guilds at this time all exploit the convention that the petition offered a vehicle for the disempowered to express their grievances;

[18] Thomas Walsingham, *Chronicon Angliae*, ed. E. M. Thompson (London: Rolls Series, 1874), 377. The surviving 'Lollard knights' may have posted the Twelve Conclusions; see Steven Justice, 'Lollardy', in Wallace (ed.), *Cambridge History*, 662–89, 673. See also Hudson, *Premature Reformation*, 112. Poems against the friars are published in Robbins (ed.), *Historical Poems*, 157–62, 163–4, 164–5, 166.

[19] Linne Mooney lists the texts written by Pinkhurst at (**www.medievalscribes.com/scribes. html**). See also Mooney, 'Chaucer's Scribe', 98, 105.

[20] Mooney, 'Chaucer's Scribe', 107.

these texts consistently emphasize how hard-done-by the guilds are, constructing them as pitiful victims, and obscuring their real identities as rich and powerful forces in London society. But the Mercers' Petition plays with the petition genre much more ambitiously and the result is a very different text from all the other petitions submitted at the same time. Responsibility for this difference appears to lie with the scribe.[21]

Writing before Pinkhurst had been identified, Sheila Lindenbaum had already compared the scribe's strategies with Gower's, Langland's, and Chaucer's, suggesting that his 'cultivation of a professional and scribal obscurity gives him something in common with the great London "authors" of the Northampton–Brembre era'.[22] If we accept that the idiosyncrasies of the text are Pinkhurst's responsibility, he seems to have been truly innovative and 'authorial'. His petition is, of course, the only one written in English, and it includes an emotive anecdote (about a 'company of gode women' who 'travailled on barfote' to the king) not included in the other petitions. He also employs word play in this text, punning on Brembre's name:

> sithen this wronges bifore saide han ben used as accidental or comune braunches outward, it sheweth wel the rote of hem is a ragged subiect or stok inward that is the forsaid Brere or brembre, the whiche comune wronge uses, & many other, if it lyke to yow, mowe be shewed.[23]

He develops the idea of Brembre as a twisted part of nature, suggesting that everything that grows out from this briar will likewise be poisonous and damaging. This use of detail and imagery suggests that the writer conceived of himself as a creative person, and his manipulation of a set form is interestingly similar to Usk's exploitation of the 'appeal' convention.[24] Pinkhurst again employs this strategy when swearing his oath to the Scriveners' Company, which he did some time between 1392 and 1404. All the oaths are somewhat different, while covering similar points, and Adam's is noteworthy for its elaboration—its great length and detail, as well as its ostentatious script.[25] Pinkhurst, like Usk, took advantage of the flexibility of forms to make his own writing stand out (and this desire to put

---

[21] Scribes could not claim that they were merely following orders, copying texts out slavishly: the fact that scriveners were sent to the pillory for forgery during this time demonstrates that they bore responsibility for what they wrote. See H. T. Riley, *Memorials of London and London Life* (London: Longman's, Green, & Co., 1868), 333–5, 527–9. The blurred boundary between scriveners and lawyers also exemplifies the fact that scriveners were expected to think about the texts that they wrote. See Pollard, 'Company of Stationers', 6. The political engagement of scribes—and their responsibility for what they wrote—is also demonstrated by evidence of Lollard leanings amongst members of the book trade. Hudson comments on the activities of a 'scriveyn' and a 'parchemyner' in the Oldcastle revolt, and adds that they were following in the footsteps of 'anonymous scribes of pamphlets such as those of Aston, Pateshull, or the writers of the *Twelve Conclusions*', *Premature Reformation*, 206.

[22] Lindenbaum, 'London Texts', 291.

[23] Chambers and Daunt (eds.), *Book of London English*, 36.

[24] See the discussion of Usk's *Appeal*, in Paul Strohm, *Hochon's Arrow: The Social Imagination of Fourteenth Century Texts* (Princeton: Princeton University Press, 1992).

[25] Francis W. Steer (ed.), *The Scriveners' Company Common Paper 1357–1628* (London: London Record Company, 1968), p. xx. Adam Pinkhurst is also discussed by C. Paul Christianson in *A Directory*

his own stamp on texts may shed light on the frustration expressed by Chaucer about 'Adam's' waywardness). The fact that the Mercers' Petition is so idiosyncratic and so 'literary' suggests that he employed his creative energies on it and that he was fully embedded in the politics of the piece. His long-term connection with the guild—he wrote their accounts for two years in the 1390s and possibly well into the 1400s—adds weight to the idea that he saw his interests as bound up with theirs.

Pinkhurst emerges as a figure comparable to Usk in several ways. We have long known that Usk was an early reader of Chaucer, whom he explicitly eulogizes, and whose texts he uses extensively. He was also a professional scribe. But, while we have been fully aware of Usk's ultimately disastrous embroilment in London factional politics, his explicit connection with a guild has only recently come to light through Barron's work. His name, previously wrongly transcribed, appears in the records of the Goldsmiths' Company—a guild which, like the Mercers' Guild, was rich and influential, and many of whose members were sympathetic to Northampton and unsympathetic to Brembre in the early 1380s. The records tell us that in 1381 or 1382 Thomas Usk was admitted as a clerk to the Company, swore his oath, and was promised one mark and livery each year. A year or so later, Thomas Usk was paid 20 shillings, seemingly for his service to Adam Bamme when the latter was sheriff. Several other goldsmiths also received payment at this time, presumably for their expenses and duties when riding with the sheriff to escort the mayor. Another record seems to refer to payments for the funeral of the wife of 'Thomas Skreveyner'.[26] At the same time as Usk was employed to write bills for Northampton, he was also a regular employee of the Goldsmiths' Guild, just as Pinkhurst was to be a regular employee of the Mercers (and, like Pinkhurst, Usk was also reading, perhaps copying out, Chaucer's texts). Goldsmiths such as Bamme and Nicholas Twyford were strongly associated with anti-Brembre feeling at this time (and Usk mentions Bamme's conspiracies with Northampton several times in his *Appeal*).[27] Usk's public engagement with political and discursive turbulence is also illustrated by his role writing bills for Northampton. These bills seem to have been circulated amongst Northampton's supporters, and presumably functioned to publish Northampton's views and plans; perhaps some were proclaimed, or even

of London Stationers and Book Artisans 1300–1500 (New York: Bibliographical Society of America, 1990), 23, 149. See also Mooney, 'Chaucer's Scribe', 100.

[26] Caroline M. Barron, 'Review of Lisa Jefferson (ed.), *Wardens' Accounts and Court Minute Books of the Goldsmiths' Mistery of London 1334–1446*. Woodbridge: Boydell Press, 2003', *Urban History*, 32 (2005), 173–5. See also Lisa Jefferson (ed.), *Wardens Accounts and Court Minute-Books of the Goldsmiths' Mistery of London* (Woodbridge: Boydell Press, 2003), 198, 208, 443, 212. The 20-shilling payment is listed in the accounts for 1383–4, but seems to refer to the previous year, 1382–3, when Bamme was sheriff.

[27] *The Appeal of Thomas Usk against John Northampton*, appendix 2 in *The Testament of Love*, ed. R. Allen Shoaf (Kalamazoo, MI: Medieval Institute Publications, 1998), 423–9. See also Bird, *Turbulent London*, 29, 67–9; T. F. Reddaway and Lorna E. M. Walker, *The Early History of the Goldsmiths' Company 1327–1509* (London: Edward Arnold, 1975), 42.

posted around the city.[28] Usk, like Pinkhurst, constructed, and bore responsibility for, highly political texts.

Expanded knowledge about Pinkhurst and Usk reveals that some of the earliest readers and copiers, of Chaucer's texts were themselves creative writers who also worked for some of the most politically active and volatile guilds existing in London at the time. These guilds, so profoundly bound up in civic conflict, were also closely connected to the literary culture of late fourteenth-century London. The example of the Puy, active in the opening years of the fourteenth century and made up largely of mercers, demonstrates guilds' engagement with literary composition, and the Goldsmiths' heavy expenditure on minstrels bears witness to guild concern with cultural production more generally. Indeed, these two guilds' continued preoccupation with self-fashioning through text and performance is exemplified in the fifteenth century by Lydgate's mummings, one written for the Mercers, one for the Goldsmiths.[29] In the 1380s, goldsmiths and mercers joined the drapers in the struggle against the grocers and fishmongers ranged alongside Brembre. These tempestuous guilds, many of whose members were at the heart of the battles raging in London, were sponsoring and employing active literary practitioners, men whose writings are of interest in their own right, and who also had connections with many of the most fêted writers of the day. The guilds were thus intimately linked to networks of cultural production that must have been influenced by the conflict dominating London civic politics at this time. The examples of Pinkhurst and Usk reveal that 'literary' texts were physically very close to the petitions, bills, records, and appeals that emerged out of London's textual maelstrom in the late fourteenth century. Indeed, the world of London textual production was geographically small, even claustrophobic, as those involved in the book trade clustered around the area of Paternoster Row and Old Chaunge, near St Paul's.[30] Petitions and bills were embedded in the same environment as 'literary' texts; they were in the same stationers' shops, literally on the same desks, as texts by Gower, Langland, and Chaucer.

A text penned and publicly broadcast in 1377 exemplifies the blurred discursive boundaries in late fourteenth-century London, as it seems to have been both a bill and a 'literary' text. This text was an attack on John of Gaunt, accusing him of

---

[28] Barron and Wright write that: 'If Northampton used "billes" to organise his party in the city, his example was soon followed by his rival, the grocer Nicholas Brembre, who during his mayoralty issued three English proclamations in 1383–4', suggesting that Northampton's use of bills was a new strategy in London civic politics. See Caroline Barron and Laura Wright, 'The London Middle English Guild Certificates of 1388–9', *Nottingham Medieval Studies*, 39 (1995), 108–45, at 114 n. 32.

[29] The mummings are discussed by Maura Nolan, *John Lydgate and the Making of Public Culture* (Cambridge: Cambridge University Press, 2005), 71–119. For the Puy, see Ralph Hanna, *London Literature 1300–1380* (Cambridge: Cambridge University Press, 2005), 36; for the Goldsmiths' expenditure on minstrels see Reddaway and Walker, *Early History of the Goldsmiths*, 78.

[30] C. Paul Christianson, 'A Community of Book Artisans in Chaucer's London', *Viator*, 20 (1998), 207–18.

being the son of a butcher of Ghent, and it was posted on the doors of St Paul's and of Westminster Hall, as well as in other places around the city. It was a highly political and inflammatory text, emphasizing the duke of Lancaster's preference for the Flemings and his oppression of the people of London, but it was a 'literary' text as well. Walsingham claims that the attack was composed in 'rhythmos', which might remind us of the Scots' public poetic attack on English beards forty years earlier. The *Anonimalle Chronicler* does not mention poetic form in his description of the document, but the amount of detail in his version of the story constructs it as a lively narrative.[31] He tells how the king and queen were in Ghent when the queen gave birth to a baby, but the baby was accidentally killed by a wet-nurse, who smothered him to death, and a replacement was hastily sought. Luckily, a butcher of Ghent had a son who resembled the dead baby, and was just two or three days old, so he was put in place of the deceased child. The true nature of the baby has now come out in his adulthood, as he loves Flemings two hundred times as much as the English, because of his Flemish origins. This sensational narrative is manifestly influenced by romance: the story of the changeling child, brought up as a prince, but who cannot suppress his natural instincts for his own people is the inverse of the 'fair unknown' narrative. In romances, the noble child, brought up away from court, but whose true knightly nature cannot be hidden, is a stock figure. The emphasis on the fact that the true self, determined by blood and parentage, cannot ultimately be suppressed underpins stories of knights such as Sir Percival or Gingalain. The duke of Lancaster, according to the bill, cannot help his love for Flemings, but he should not be in a position to indulge it. In romance, for society to be healed, the characters must fill their proper places: rusticated knights must rejoin the chivalric world; exiled princes must claim their thrones and throw out the usurpers. The Londoners are declaring, through their reversal of Gaunt's arms, and their publication of this insulting story, that Gaunt, as English duke and the most influential man in English politics, is playing the wrong part and he should return to the Ghent butcher's shop. Of course, one could appreciate the mockery of Gaunt without being familiar with romance, but an understanding of the conventions of such texts illuminates how this narrative works. The interpenetration of politics and literary forms produced a highly inflammatory text, and Gaunt was ultimately only satisfied by very public and symbolic penitence.[32]

Those implicated in publicly and poetically satirizing Gaunt got off very lightly, however, compared to fifteenth-century producers of similar texts. In this century, the production of bills increased dramatically, and such texts were firmly associated with dangerous popular sedition. In 1450, a royal proclamation banned the posting

---

[31] V. H. Galbraith (ed.), *The Anonimalle Chronicle 1333–1381* (Manchester: Manchester University Press, 1927), 104–5. Walsingham, *Chronicon*, 129.

[32] See Christopher Baswell, 'Aeneas in 1381', *New Medieval Literatures*, 5, ed. Rita Copeland, David Lawton and Wendy Scase (2002), 7–58.

of bills in public places, and the penalties for writing bills were as severe as possible: in 1456, for instance, John Hilton was executed for this crime. Documents of public protest were still frequently couched in verse: we might think, for instance, of the rhymed attacks on William Paston posted in 1424 all around Nedeham, of the ballad set on the gates of Canterbury in 1460, of the poems protesting against enclosure posted in Coventry in 1494 and 1496. One rhymed bill posted in the fifteenth century attests to how memorable such texts can be in the popular imagination—today, it is more familiar to many schoolchildren than any couplet written by Chaucer. This text, penned in 1484 and affixed to the doors of St Paul's, mocks Richard III and his counsellors:

> The Cat, the Rat, and Lovel our dog
> Rule all England under a hog.[33]

The pithy lines encapsulate dissatisfaction with the king's faction, managing to disparage the four targets of the poem through the seemingly obvious strategy of comparing them to ignoble beasts, while also revealing the wit and skill of the author by punning on the names and symbols of the targets (William Catesby, Richard Ratcliffe, Lord Lovel, whose crest was a silver wolf-dog, and Richard himself, whose badge was a wild boar). William Colyngbourne was executed for writing these lines. Such harsh penalties for writing seditious verse contrast with milder fourteenth-century responses to lampoons and bills. Similarly, in the late fourteenth century, adherents of the fledgling Lollard movement were able to express their views relatively freely and publicly; only in the fifteenth century, with Arundel as archbishop and the Lancastrians enthroned, were heretics executed. Attitudes also hardened in other ways against perceived sedition: as protesters increasingly produced and posted political texts and the authorities moved with increasing severity against them.

Texts made in the late medieval period were born out of compromise and conflict, and materially constructed in politically volatile circumstances, often by men who were themselves heavily implicated in the web of textual protests flying about London and Westminster. Seeing late medieval texts within the conditions of their material production can help us to understand much more about the political threads woven into their seams. For, although we have come a long way from believing in the idea of the sovereign Author, we still need to remind ourselves of the extent to which such texts were—or could be—mosaics, the products of several (internally inconsistent) minds. Roland Barthes describes the text as a 'tissue of quotations' a place where many different writings, none of them original, 'blend and clash'.[34] His ideas hold a particular resonance for a cultural context in which

---

[33] See Wilson, *Lost Literature*, 192–5; Robbins (ed.), *Historical Poems*, pp. xxxviii, 63–4, 207–8.
[34] Roland Barthes, *The Death of the Author*, in *Image, Music, Text*, trans. Stephen Heath (Glasgow: Fontana, 1977), 142–8, 146.

we might be talking not about the death of the author, but about a more grisly occurrence, the death of the authors. The tissue of quotations may be even more conflicted—and perhaps even more dynamic—when several individuals have had direct influence over its formation.

No text, as Don McKenzie suggests in his landmark *Bibliography and the Sociology of Texts*, is the product of a single author, but this multiplicity of origins is crystallized in medieval culture. Jennifer Summit writes that:

> The idea that authors were the sole originators of their texts is a relatively recent one, supplanting earlier models that invested those origins in divine or historically remote sources, likewise the modern idea of the author as a single, creative individual holds limited relevance for medieval textual culture, in which many texts were collaborative, anonymous, or adopted as common property.[35]

The idea of the *compilatio*, for instance, so central to monuments of medieval literature such as the *Decameron*, the *Canterbury Tales*, or the *Confessio Amantis*, draws on this idea of texts as common property. We might particularly relate the concept of the text as 'collaborative' to the roles of the patron and the scribe, as well as the 'maker' him/herself. Texts such as the *Testament of Love* or the Prologue to the *Legend of Good Women* suggest the limiting and determining role that a patron can have on a text. Usk's desire for patronage colours every aspect of his text, while Chaucer dramatizes in his poem the problems of having to please patrons, and the difficulty of insisting on fixed, approved meanings in any text. Patronage can go even further than determining subject matter; both Summit and Lee Patterson posit that patronage can become 'collaboration', with Patterson suggesting that parts of the *Book of the Duchess* may have been written by John of Gaunt.[36]

Scribes too play a crucial part in 'authoring' a text. This is most obvious when a text is dictated—indeed, A. C. Spearing has recently suggested that we should rename the so-called *Book of Margery Kempe* as '*The Book of Robert Spryngolde Aboute Margery Kempe*'.[37] Kings, Richard Firth Green argues, were eager 'that those who wrote their personal letters should be recognized literary stylists'.[38] Green's implication here is that the boundary between creative author and passive scribe is non-existent, and the number of scribes who were also 'authors' adds more

---

[35] Jennifer Summit, 'Women and Authorship', in Carolyn Dinshaw and David Wallace (eds.), *The Cambridge Companion to Medieval Women's Writing* (Cambridge: Cambridge University Press, 2003), 91–108, at 91. See also D. F. McKenzie, *Bibliography and the Sociology of Texts*, 2nd edn. (Cambridge: Cambridge University Press, 1999).

[36] Lee Patterson, 'Court Politics and the Invention of Literature: The Case of Sir John Clanvowe', in David Aers (ed.), *Culture and History 1350–1600: Essays on English Communities, Identities and Writing* (Hemel Hempstead: Harvester Wheatsheaf, 1992), 7–41, at 14; Summit, 'Women and Authorship', 103. For the *compilatio* see Alastair Minnis, *Medieval Theory of Authorship*, 2nd edn. (London: Scolar Press, 1988).

[37] A. C. Spearing, 'Margery Kempe', in A. S. G. Edwards (ed.), *A Companion to Middle English Prose* (Cambridge: D. S. Brewer, 2004), 83–97, at 93.

[38] Green, *Poets and Princepleasers*, 69.

weight to this idea (Usk and Hoccleve are the most obvious examples).[39] Scribal influence is not, of course, limited to contexts involving oral dictation. We are now used to the idea that Chaucer's early scribes were thinking about, interpreting, and editing his work. The earliest known reader of *Troilus and Criseyde* was a scribe, whose early, detailed knowledge of the text may well be attributable to his having known the poem as a work-in-progress.[40] Texts are not end products, but evolving processes, influenced by early readings and comments, rewritten by their makers, altered by editors, compilers, scribes, and illuminators. Not only were there various figures with claims to be part of the hydra-headed author who must die for the reader to be born—the twist being that the author/reader boundary cannot quite be made out—but the material putting-together of a book itself was particularly fragmented in pre-print London, involving input from multiple sources. Rather than being produced in one scriptorium, books seem to have been produced by diverse individuals, working separately.[41] The production of a book could be fraught with conflict between its differently minded producers, from patron to scribe to maker to illuminator, and this conflict was merely a prologue to the antagonism enacted between the discourses, quotations, and ideas battling for pre-eminence within each reading of the text. Chaucer's image in the *House of Fame* of tidings fighting each other and finally making an unholy alliance in order to make their way in the world encapsulates the conflicted circumstances of medieval textual production (ll. 2088–109).

The English poetry that emerged around London and Westminster at this time, drawing on French troubadour traditions, took the instability of the 'I' and the problematic multiplicity of textual authority as givens. The construction and use of the unstable 'I' figure both acknowledges the inevitability of fragmentation and seeks to protect the maker from its effects.[42] The deployment of the performative 'I' recognizes that no self, no structure is stable. It also allows the maker to hide his unstable self behind a self of his creation, to shield himself from the attacks of

[39] Another interesting example is James le Palmere; see Anne Middleton, 'Thomas Usk's "Perdurable Letters": *The Testament of Love* from Script to Print', *Studies in Bibliography*, 51 (1998), 63–116, at 99.

[40] See Ramona Bressie, 'The Date of Thomas Usk's *Testament of Love*', *Modern Philology*, 26 (1928), 17–29, at 29. On Chaucer's early scribes, see A. I. Doyle and M. B. Parkes, 'The Production of Copies of the *Canterbury Tales* and the *Confessio Amantis* in the Early Fifteenth Century', in M. B. Parkes and Andrew G. Watson (eds.), *Medieval Scribes, Manuscripts, and Libraries: Essays Presented to N. R. Ker* (London: Scolar Press, 1978), 163–210; B. A. Windeatt, 'The Scribes as Chaucer's Early Critics', *Studies in the Age of Chaucer*, 1 (1979), 119–41; Mooney, 'Chaucer's Scribe', 122.

[41] See Doyle and Parkes, 'Production of Copies', esp. 167; Christianson, *Directory of London Stationers*, esp. 29.

[42] Ardis Butterfield, 'Chaucer's French Inheritance', in Piero Boitani and Jill Mann (eds.), *The Cambridge Companion to Chaucer*, 2nd edn. (Cambridge: Cambridge University Press, 2003), 20–35, esp. 28–9. Butterfield discusses Chaucer's use of the first-person persona, and its origins in troubadour poetry, commenting that in such texts 'the figure of the speaker or singer is hard to characterize as a stable voice' as his identity is 'always at issue'. Ibid. 29.

outrageous fortune. This strategy also betrays a knowing anxiety about the use of language, a self-consciousness about expressing oneself. The men who surrounded Richard II—and Clanvowe, Chaucer, Gower, and Usk were all at some point reasonably close to the king—were renowned for using language in specific ways, for being slippery and persuasive with their voices.[43]

During Richard's reign, discourse was everywhere foregrounded as a cause of contention. Concerns about the inadequacies of language, and about wider political practices, were centred on the dynamics of a certain kind of writing and speaking. Poems such as *Mum and the Sothsegger*, Patterson argues, articulate the problem of exclusion from participation in courtly languages, and this poem's alliterative form highlights the opposition between 'monarch and nobleman, metropolis and hinterland'.[44] Ways of talking and writing came to be seen as emblematic of the factional politics that were tearing apart Richard's rule, as criticisms of courtiers frequently focused on their slippery words. In 1388, a bill posted at the heart of both London and Westminster, on the door of St Paul's and on a pillar at the Chapter House at Westminster, attacked Archbishop Neville, claiming that 'the fayrer he speketh the falser he is' and adding that if anyone is to apprise Richard of his perfidy, it must be a southerner, not a northerner. Those who have the ear of the king are associated with a way of using language that is both deceitful (fair and false) and persuasive (only a southerner can hope to persuade Richard), and that is set against other ways of talking and writing (northern traditions).[45] This dynamic (between plain speaking and courtly speaking) is also at work in debate poems—some of which, such as Clanvowe's *Boke of Cupide*, were produced at the very heart of the court itself. Archbishop Neville himself was closely connected with the 'Lollard knights' and thus with Chaucer's circle: his brother was William Neville, whose loving friendship with Clanvowe is well known. William Neville, alongside Clanvowe and others, was one of the witnesses of Chaucer's release for rape in 1380.[46]

[43] We might remember Thomas Walsingham's well-known characterization of Richard's knights as knights of Venus rather than Bellona, 'armed with words, rather than weapons' ('plus lingua quam lancea praemuniti'). *Historia Anglicana*, Rolls Series 28, 2 vols. (London: Longman's, 1863–4), ii. 156. Patterson contends, 'the court knows itself to be in fact heterogeneous and self-conflicted, a complexity its writing inevitably if uneasily acknowledges'. 'Court Politics', 29.

[44] Patterson, 'Court Politics', 19.

[45] William Illingworth, 'Copy of a Libel against Archbishop Neville, temp. Richard II', *Archaeologia*, 16 (1812), 80–8, at 80, 82. Scase reads the text somewhat differently, suggesting that the bill implies that a southerner must speak against Neville because no northerner would dare to do so. ' "Strange and Wonderful Bills" ', 244. (Later in his reign, of course, Richard was strongly associated with the north-west.)

[46] K. B. Macfarlane, *Lancastrian Kings and Lollard Knights* (Oxford: Clarendon Press, 1972), 162, 183. For Clanvowe's works see Sir John Clanvowe, *The Works of Sir John Clanvowe*, ed. V. J. Scattergood (Cambridge: D. S. Brewer, 1975). Patterson discusses whether or not the voice of opposition is neutralized and assimilated in Clanvowe's poem; see 'Court Politics', 23–5. For a discussion of the way that official culture can assimilate dissenting voices, see also Peter Stallybrass and

The bill against Neville interests me more generally for its crossing of generic boundaries, and for what this suggests about perceived relationships between different kinds of texts, and between texts and politics. The archbishop is addressed in the text as a tyrant; he is termed 'Alisaunder Nero'. The story of Nero was popular in medieval literature—it is told at some length by Gower and Chaucer, and is also mentioned by Usk (*Confessio Amantis*, VI. 1151–234, 'Monk's Tale', ll. 575–662, *Testament of Love*, II. 281, 557–9, 623–5). Nero was the epitome of an evil tyrant and as his crimes included matricide and incest his biography was particularly lurid and sensational. Alexander was Archbishop Neville's own Christian name, but the name also evokes the story of the Macedonian king. Alexander was a well-known romance hero, whose story was very frequently told, and, like Nero, he is associated with extreme imperial power. The 'Monk's Tale' includes both men's histories (ll. 743–82), and Gower tells the tale of Alexander's birth in a story about Nectanabus, his teacher and natural father, shortly after telling the story of Nero (VI. 1789–2366).[47] Terming the archbishop 'Alisaundre Nero' puns on 'Alisaundre Neville' but also encourages readers to associate the archbishop with both of these historical emperors—especially as the topic of the bill is Neville's assumption of kingly, even tyrannical, powers, which both Alexander and Nero wielded. Chaucer emphasized the relevance of examples such as Alexander and Nero to modern rulers by his inclusion of four modern examples in the 'Monk's Tale' (ll. 487–574) directly before telling the story of Nero. Archbishop Neville, like John of Gaunt in 1377, is presented in a bill as a character in a popular romance or tragedy, comprehensible through literary contexts. Not only can texts such as the *Canterbury Tales* be read as refracting the conflict from which they were produced, but bills of protest encouraged their audiences to read contemporary politics through the paradigms of literature. Boundaries between genres were porous; the conflict of the contemporary world was manifested both in political fiction and in literary reality.

FURTHER READING

Sheila Lindenbaum's 'London Texts and Literate Practice' (n. 1 above) provides a peerless introduction to the politics of textuality in the metropolis across the late medieval period. Also unmissable is Paul Strohm's *Hochon's Arrow: The Social Imagination of Fourteenth Century Texts* (n. 24), which is similarly concerned with locating 'literary' texts within their conflicted social contexts. My own *Chaucerian Conflict: Languages of Antagonism in Late Fourteenth-Century London* (n. 15) focuses on discourses of conflict in diverse texts written in 1380s and 1390s London, ranging from *Troilus and Criseyde* to the guild returns to Usk's *Appeal*.

Allon White, *The Politics and Poetics of Transgression* (London: Methuen, 1986). But, as the *House of Fame* shows us, texts and utterances can have lives of their own.

[47] Usk also mentions Alexander shortly before mentioning Nero, *Testament of Love*, ll. 179–82.

Nothing touches Ruth Bird's *Turbulent London of Richard II* (n. 1) as an evocation of the turmoil within late fourteenth-century London. Another wonderful London history written back in the 1940s is Sylvia Thrupp's *The Merchant Class of Medieval London* (Chicago: University of Chicago Press, 1948). All of Caroline Barron's books and articles are also required reading for anyone interested in medieval London history (most recently, she has published *London in the Later Middle Ages* (Oxford: Oxford University Press, 2004)).

Steven Justice's *Writing and Rebellion* (n. 2) is a landmark book in all kinds of ways; particularly relevant here are his discussions of protest literature and vernacular broadsides. A book about bills and complaints by Wendy Scase is forthcoming with Oxford University Press; in the meantime, she has published an article on ' "Strange and Wonderful Bills": Bill Casting and Political Discourse in Late Medieval England' (n. 11). The best piece on the John of Gaunt libel is Chris Baswell's 'Aeneas in 1381' (n. 32).

My article here builds upon the researches of Linne Mooney, published as 'Chaucer's Scribe' (n. 14). Mooney's database on scribes is in progress. Caroline Barron's discoveries about Usk can be found in her 'Review of Lisa Jefferson (ed.), *Wardens' Accounts and Court Minute Books of the Goldsmiths' Mistery of London 1334–1446*' (n. 26). On late fourteenth-century scribes and textual production, see especially A. I. Doyle and M. B. Parkes, 'The Production of Copies of the *Canterbury Tales* and the *Confessio Amantis* in the Early Fifteenth Century' (n. 40). Invaluable material on the social changes in the thirteenth century that produced new classes of readers and writers can be found in Michael Clanchy, *From Memory to Written Record* (n. 6) and M. B. Parkes, 'The Literacy of the Laity' (n. 6).

Readers interested in the kind of texts discussed in this essay could usefully explore chronicles such as the *Anonimalle Chronicle* and the *Westminster Chronicle* (ed. L. C. Hector and Barbara Harvey (Oxford: Clarendon Press, 1982)), the texts printed in *A Book of London English* (n. 3), the documents printed by H. T. Riley in *Memorials of London and London Life* (London: Longman's, Green and Co., 1868), or the poems included in Robbins's *Historical Poems of the XIVth and XVth Centuries* (n. 16). The most stimulating theoretical work on the relationship between conflict and texts is, in my view, Fredric Jameson's seminal *The Political Unconscious* (n. 4).

PART III

TEXTUAL KINDS AND CATEGORIES

CHAPTER 18

GENRE WITHOUT SYSTEM

ALFRED HIATT

The first stanza of the *balade* 'To Rosemounde', tentatively ascribed to Chaucer, describes the beauty and good cheer of the poet's lady. The second commences with the poet filling a barrel with his weeping, but ends with him finding consolation in the sound of her voice. The third describes the poet as more steeped and bound around by love than a 'pyk walwed in galauntyne' (a pike steeped in galantine sauce):

> Nas never pyk walwed in galauntyne
> As I in love am walwed [steeped] and ywounde [bound]
> For which ful ofte I of myself devyne [imagine]
> That I am trewe Tristam the secounde.
> My love may not refreyde nor affounde [grow cool or fail],
> I brenne ay [burn always] in an amorous plesaunce. (ll. 17–22)

The pike in galantine sauce creates a moment of confusion in this poem. The fish caught on the line, even the pike in jelly in a barrel, is part of an established poetic repertoire; the lover as dead fish in bread sauce is something different. The bound fish embedded in the text represents stasis, immersion in opposition and apposition to the barrel of tears previously wept by the speaker. The fish is inside the text but also seems to enter from some other place, speaking from and for the market, the pantry, the economy. A clammy, slippery presence, it renders the poem inconsistent, 'indecorous', 'primitive', grotesque, uncontrolled.[1] And in part for this reason it has been seen as the sign of Chaucer's un-authorship of the poem. What seems particularly confusing is that the pike 'walwed in galauntyne' destabilizes the complaint, stands outside of generic system, but does so from within the text.

An earlier version of this essay benefited from the comments of Margaret Clunies Ross.

[1] See the review of scholarship in George B. Pace and Alfred David (eds.), *A Variorum Edition of the Works of Geoffrey Chaucer*, v: *The Minor Poems* (Norman: University of Oklahoma Press, 1982), 161–70; also the suggestive analysis of V. J. Scattergood, 'The Short Poems', in A. J. Minnis et al., *Oxford Guides to Chaucer: The Shorter Poems* (Oxford: Clarendon Press, 1995), 455–512, at 479–82.

It also, nevertheless, speaks to 'trewe Tristam the secounde', the romance hero preserved and embedded in the succeeding lines of this unstable poem, another fish out of water, between laughter and tears, trans-genred (and de-genred?), perversely generated by the first (true) Tristam. This second Tristam is patently untrue, both an incompatible extension of the idea of the pike, and an incompatible extension of Sir Tristram, a cold fish burning with 'plesaunce'. Chaucerian irony, parody, disdain for the traditional alliterative English romance? Or a systematic destabilization of two genres—romance and *balade/compleynte*? (Systematic, that is, in its resistance to system.) The fish in the text disrupts genre but it does not suffice to construct a mixed or hybrid genre. Nor does it precisely represent an anti-genre, since what it opposes is not genre but classification. Instead, it might be described as a moment of *ungenre*, of disorientation within a text, when the unexpected, unclassifiable, and generically inexplicable takes place. The ungenre is, or seems to be, an insertion. It is the spanner in the works, the stone in the shoe, the grit in the eye: an impediment to categorization, order, function. It represents a 'breach of contract' between author and audience that brings system, and systematic understanding, to a halt. What if the act of naming a genre were similarly an act that served to disorient rather than locate?

Is there a fish in this text?

Increasingly, and across several different medieval literatures (including French, German, Dutch, and Old Norse), medievalists have pointed out the problematic nature of attempting taxonomies of medieval genres, particularly when such classificatory schemes are insensitive to the contexts—performative, political, gendered—in which literature was produced and received. They have instead emphasized the fluidity of genres: not only did authors move between and mix genres, they also very often had flexible or imprecise understandings of what and how particular genres were constituted. Further, scholars have for some time now insisted upon the importance of audience as a shaping force on the construction of genres, advancing the notion of genre as a 'contract' between author and audience. Seminal to this reconceptualization of genre was the dictum of Hans Robert Jauss that 'for each work a preconstituted horizon of expectations must be ready at hand ... to orient the reader's understanding and to enable a qualifying reception'.[2] Crucially, Jauss rejected a quasi-scientific conception of genre as a naturalistic phenomenon subject to evolution and decay, opting instead for 'a process of the continual founding and altering of horizons'. In other words, where earlier critics had seen genre in terms of cycles of birth and death, of creation, disintegration and reconstruction, Jauss saw a complex process of reciprocal relations between

---

[2] Hans Robert Jauss, 'Theory of Genres and Medieval Literature', in *Toward an Aesthetic of Reception*, trans. Timothy Bahti (Brighton: Harvester Press, 1982), 76–109, at 79.

authors and audiences, and between genres themselves, susceptible of analysis on both diachronic and synchronic axes. Nevertheless Jauss did not renounce system. Far from it: '[w]here there is no initially posited and described generic norm, the establishing of a generic structure must be gained from the perception [*Anschauung*] of individual texts, in a continually renewed pre-conceiving [*Vorgriff*] of an expectable whole or regulative system for the series of texts.'[3] I suggest that the tortured nature of this formulation is not simply a function of German academic prose—it is also the function of an attempt to describe a system where there is none.

To cease to speak of medieval literaure in terms of genre would require a considerable intellectual reorientation and/or powerful acts of self-censorship. That in itself does not prove the concept's validity. But there is undeniable evidence that genres did exist in the Middle Ages—even if, at times, in name only. One might also wish to posit the converse, that genres could exist in and across various medieval literatures *without* being named. In either case, the absence of clear statements of generic systems in the later Middle Ages must be acknowledged. To think of genres existing without a system is not to deny their existence, nor the utility of genre as a tool of critical analysis. This acknowledgement does, however, require the interrogation of generic categories. Some generic statements do exist, but they do not appear to have been meant, and certainly were not taken, as prescriptive, comprehensive codifications of generic rules: they are either partial, contingent, or retrospective in nature to the point of antiquarianism.

The well-known distinctions made by Dante and his followers between comedy, tragedy, satire, and lyric poetry appear to have been an attempt to establish a set of distinctions between genres, on the basis of content more than form, in order to construct classical poetic order in dialectical relation to their own poetics. In the late fourteenth-century treatise *L'Art de dictier* (*The Art of Composing Poetry*), Eustache Deschamps enumerated the forms and structures of 'natural music' (i.e. lyric poetry, as opposed to 'artificial', instrumental or vocal, music), and 'the method of composing balades, chansons and rondeaux in several diverse manners'.[4] The descriptions of *balade, sirventes, virelai, rondeau,* and *lai* that Deschamps provided set out precise instructions for each genre, but they also acknowledged the existence of multiple forms of these genres, their changing nature, the differences between previous and present customs (such as the composition of envoys in types of *balade* that had not customarily had them), as well as the social status of particular genres (*sirventes*, for example, were not previously composed by noblemen).

No comparable statement of generic organization exists for Middle English literature. That lack of codification indicates neither an inability to think metacritically

---

[3] Ibid. 93–4.

[4] Eustache Deschamps, *L'Art de dictier*, ed. and trans. Deborah M. Sinnreich-Levi (East Lansing, MI: Colleagues Press, 1994), 67.

on the part of medieval authors and their publics, nor a state of 'disintegration', nor any kind of 'immaturity' of literary production, but rather an active resistance to classificatory schemas. Whose interests would generic classification have served? Certainly not those of authors who revelled in the flexibility, open-endedness, and vagueness of generic expectations. And, for all their importance in contributing to the emergence, popularity, and revival of particular genres, certainly not those of audiences, rarely the source of classification. The classification of genres is an intellectual, not commercial, exercise that is almost always driven by particular assumptions and expectations of the social function of literature, and that seeks to shape as well as represent literary form. The absence of generic schema might best be explained by an equally normative resistance to classification. Evidently Old English generic terms—such as 'giedd' (a song, speech, or proverb), 'talu' (a tale or talk), 'spel' (a story, narrative, or sermon), 'sang' and 'leod' (both usually denoting a song, or poem)—were either neglected or left unrefined in Middle English; equally, the association of Middle English generic literary terms with other artistic fields (particularly song and dance) is very strong. These two observations suggest, first, that written texts did not generate their own generic nomenclature, but adapted pre-existing terms from oral and physical performance arts. They may also indicate the tendency of literary texts to desystematize existing performance structures. Writing, that is, invokes the terminology of performance but only in order to appropriate and reshape—perhaps unshape—its meaning.

In *European Literature and the Latin Middle Ages*, E. R. Curtius described the efforts of Dante to distinguish genres and concluded that the 'ancient system of poetic genres had, in the millenium before Dante, disintegrated until it was unrecognizable and incomprehensible'.[5] Most medievalists continue to oppose, as Curtius did, a stable system of classical genres to the labile, fluid, flexible practice of medieval authors, whether or not the latter constitute a 'system'. Recent work of classicists unsettles this binarism. G. B. Conte, in particular, has made an eloquent defence of the validity of the concept of genre as a means of analysis (his target is a naive, author-focused mode of interpretation prone to the exaggeration of biographical context—e.g. Horace writes about lascivious old women because of his own encounters with them). But he also makes a strong case for the fluidity of the classical 'system' of genres. Echoing Jauss, Conte describes genres as 'matrixes of works, to be conceived not as recipes but as strategies; they act in texts not ante rem or post rem but in re'.[6] Authors, with Ovid the epitome, experiment in and around genres. They take the sign of one genre, and use it to introduce another: in the *Metamorphoses* the word 'arma', redolent with epic diction, is applied to Cupid;

---

[5] Ernst Robert Curtius, *European Literature and the Latin Middle Ages*, trans. Willard R. Trask (London: Routledge and Kegan Paul, 1953), 358.

[6] G. B. Conte, *Genres and Readers: Lucretius, Love Elegy, Pliny's Encyclopedia*, trans. Glenn W. Most (Baltimore: Johns Hopkins University Press, 1994), 112.

elsewhere the virga—attribute of Mercury, an element of epic—is also used by shepherds, including shepherds of the bucolic genre. If genre, for classical authors, is strategic, if it operates within expectations, signs, and resonances but not codes and rules—if, moreover, genres are open to appropriation and refiguration (isn't that what Virgil did so spectacularly?)—then can we continue to oppose a static, fixed, and agreed-upon classical genre system to the medieval? Might we not see instead the fluidity of classical genres channelled in various directions?

In Middle English writing generic terms certainly exist. But what did they mean, and was there a system regulating them, however fluid and opportunistic their deployment? I propose to address these questions by discussing the use of three generic markers, each representative of a different strand of influence in literature written in Middle English: *romaunce, balade,* and *tragedye.* My not entirely arbitrary choice of these particular terms is designed to provide an indicative, certainly not comprehensive, sense of the ways in which generic nomenclature could signify in Middle English, and also the shifts that could occur in signification. One aspect of the names of writing is their tendency to appear in combination with other generic markers, rather than in isolation. The implications of that tendency toward combination, or mixing, will be considered at the conclusion of this essay.

Romaunce

No one will be surprised to hear that the semantic range of Middle English *romaunce* was very broad. Indeed, at times *romaunce* could function as a meta-literary term denoting all narrative production. Nevertheless, if the essential feature of the genre seems simply to have been the presence of a narrative of some kind, *romaunce* is more particularly characterized by a widespread association with verse narrative, as well as by specific associations with certain kinds of content. The obvious, synonymous, association with chivalry ('romaunses ... Of knightes') has perhaps masked a more fundamental affiliation with historical narrative. The *Cursor mundi*'s opening comparison of devotional literature with 'rimes ... And romans red on maneres sere [in diverse forms] | Of Alisaunder ... Iuly Cesar ... brut ... kyng arthour ... How charles kyng and rauland [Charlemagne and Roland] faght ... tristrem and hys leif ysote [dear Isolde] | ... O Ioneck and of ysambrase [Yonec/John and Isumbras], | O ydoine and of amadasse [Idoyne and Amadas]',[7] certainly draws attention to the capacious, epic-subsuming, qualities of *romaunce*, but it also follows a logic that is temporal, spatial, and generic. The progression of romances is chronological, but also tracks the translation of empire from Greece to Rome to Britain and France, as well as moving from history to chivalry. The nomenclature used in the passage

---

[7] Richard Morris et al. (eds.), *Cursor mundi, or the Cours of the Werlde,* 7 vols., EETS, os 57, 59, 62, 66, 68, 99, 101 (London: Oxford University Press, 1874–93; repr. 1961–6), ll. 21–6.

is also revealing of the multilingual variety of narrative embraced by romance. The subject matter of 'rimes' and 'romans' includes 'ferlys' and 'aunters' (wonders and adventures) of Arthur and his knights, but romance extends to:

> Storis als o ferekin [different] thinges
> O princes, prelates and o kinges;
> Sanges sere [different] of selcuth [wonderful] rime,
> Inglis, frankys, and latine,
> to rede and here Ilkon [each one] is prest [ready],
> the thynges that tham likes best.

In similar mode, the opening catalogue in the *'Laud' Troy Book*, echoing and expanding Chaucer's 'romances of prys [value], | Of Horn child and of Ypotys, | Of Beves and sir Gy, | Of sir Lybeux and Pleyndamour' ('Sir Thopas', ll. 897–901), looks back over several centuries of romance terrain and finds a diverse assortment of historical, pseudo-historical, and mythical figures:

> Many speken of men that romaunces rede
> That were sumtyme doughti in dede,
> The while that god hem lyff lente,
> That now ben dede and hennes wente:
> Off Bevis, Gy, and of Gauwayn,
> Off kyng Richard, & of Owayn,
> Off Tristram, and of Percyuale,
> Off Rouland Ris, and Aglauale,
> Off Archeroun, and of Octouian,
> Off Charles, & of Cassibaldan,
> Off Hauelok, Horne, & of Wade;—
> In Romaunces that of them ben made.[8]

The heterogeneous nature of this list seems representative of the scope of romance: it betrays no obvious rationale in its construction, moving between British and continental romance heroes, incorporating legendary with historical figures, more interested in alliteration than chronology. One thing that accrues to *romaunce*, then, is names. But what does its *own* name mean?

Swinging without angst between the poles of truth and 'leysyng', the term *romaunce*, characteristically of its narratives, crosses temporal and spatial barriers, unites past and present; it is fundamentally generative. It can be used of historical narratives, above all those concerned with origins; yet it also embraces anti-foundational histories of internecine destruction, such as the 'romaunce of Thebes'. Aligned with its associations with the foundational, the historical, and the redemptive is the application of 'romance' to devotional literature. The *Myrour of Lewed Men*, a reworking of Robert Grosseteste's *Chateau d'Amour* by a monk of

---

[8]   J. Ernst Wülfing (ed.), *The Laud Troy Book*, 2 vols., EETS, os 121–2 (London: Kegan Paul, Trench, Trübner, 1902–3), ll. 11–22.

Sawley, proclaims itself to be 'a romance of englische of the begynnyng of the world and of al that a lewed [uneducated] man has nede for to knawe for hele [healing] of soule'.[9] As this usage suggests, whatever it might have signified, the romance genre could be associated with instruction, with audience both elevated and humble. Several instances of usage of the term *romaunce* indicate a strong association with the act of reading, whether aloud or silent. Indeed romance can signify the book itself, to the extent that *romaunce* and *bok* may be used interchangeably. In *Havelok*, a description of joyous celebration includes harping and piping, the singing of 'gestes' (songs) beaten out by 'gleumen on the tabour' (minstrels on the drum), but also 'Romanz-reding on the book' (ll. 2325–9). The narrator in the *Book of the Duchess* seems to use *romaunce* to mean a book that contains multiple poetic narratives ('fables ... put in rime', ll. 52–4), whose subject matter was the lives of queens and kings, '[a]nd many other thinges smale' (l. 59). Similarly, Pandarus' enigmatic act of pretending 'for to looke upon an old romaunce' (*Troilus and Criseyde*, III. 980) blurs the distinction between genre and material object, between age of narrative and age of codex. In other contexts, particularly chivalric romance ('as romawns vs tellis', '[i]n romaunce as we rede', 'the romance it wittnes', 'as tellyth the romaynes'),[10] *romaunce* could be translated simply as 'source'. One might suggest, then, that *romaunce* comes close to occupying the same semantic field as the word 'text' when used by modern literary critics.

The foreignness of romance never goes away, its interest in border and cultural crossings, in translations and transformations, in textual, sexual, and artefactual commerce. The term itself contains a vague gesture towards ancient and contemporary Rome; that gesture is augmented and complicated by its particular association in English writing with France and the French language. In Mannyng's *Chronicle*, for example, the term 'romance' signifies a verse narrative ('the romans sais that is of Richardyn'), but also the French tongue itself ('Frankis spech is cald romance').[11] Romance does not signify as native. Indeed, in this context it is intimately connected with acts of translation, acting as a mediating linguistic and generic term between reworkings of antique and pseudo-antique history: Latyn-Romance-Inglis and, hovering behind Latin, Geoffrey of Monmouth's 'Breton speche' (ll. 163–200). Romance may be the genre *par excellence* for the 'matter' of Britain, along with much else, but no claim is ever made for it as a peculiarly British or English genre.

---

[9] 'The Myrour of Lewed Men', in Carl Horstmann (ed.), *The Minor Poems of the Vernon MS: Part 1*, EETS, os 98 (London: Kegan Paul, Trench, Trübner, 1892), 407–42, at 407.

[10] Respectively, *The Alliterative Morte Darthur*, l. 3200; *Athelston*, l. 383; *The Wars of Alexander*, ll. 488, 3026, also 3478 ('said the romance'), 1201 ('we rede the romaunce it callis'); Thomas Malory, *The Works of Sir Thomas Malory*, ed. Eugène Vinaver, rev. P. J. C. Field, 3rd edn., 3 vols. (Oxford: Clarendon Press, 1990), 216, ll. 9–11.

[11] Robert Mannyng of Brunne, *The Chronicle*, ed. Idelle Sullens, Medieval and Renaissance Texts and Studies 153 (Binghamton: State University of New York, 1996), II. 4688; I. 15921.

The example of a legal document may help to give some further sense of the unstable and non-systematic meaning of *romaunce* in late medieval England. The will of Lady Matilda Bowes from 1421, copied in the register of the bishop of Durham, records the gift of four books to two goddaughters and two other women: 'j romance boke [that] is called *The gospelles* ... unam romance boke ... the boke with the knotts ... j librum that is called *Trystram*'.[12] The mode of designation is interesting: the books are identified in the first case ('j romance boke [that] is called *The gospelles*') by title and language, if we assume that 'romance' means French; in the second ('unam romance boke') by language alone, unless 'romance' here refers to content, in which case we have a designation by genre; in the third ('the boke with the knotts') by a physical feature—'knotts', tentatively glossed in the *Middle English Dictionary* as 'clasps'; and in the fourth ('j librum that is called *Trystram*') by title alone. 'Boke' and 'librum' appear to be used interchangeably, characteristic of the document as a whole, which shifts between Latin, French, and English. The designation of the Gospels as a 'romance boke' seems to me to be problematic: if it indicates that they, along with the other untitled book, are in French, then why give the title in English? Is this why *Trystram* is not designated a 'romance boke'? Could *romaunce* here have the capacity for the quasi-blasphemous inclusion of biblical narratives? One is reminded of Borges's reference to the categories of animals in 'a certain Chinese encyclopedia called the *Heavenly Emporium of Benevolent Knowledge*', which consists of: 'a) those that belong to the emperor; b) embalmed ones; c) those that are trained; d) suckling pigs; e) mermaids; f) fabulous ones; g) stray dogs; h) those that are included in this classification; i) those that tremble as if they were mad; j) innumerable ones; k) those drawn with a very fine camel's-hair brush; l) etcetera; m) those that have just broken the flower vase; n) those that at a distance resemble flies'.[13] But one is only reminded of this list because, habituated to classificatory systems that appear to operate on principles of uniformity and coherency, Matilda Bowes's division of her books, with its apparent duplications, contradictions, and omissions, does not seem to us to obey a system.

Balade

Among the many generic terms used in Middle English writing *balade* would appear to have possessed, at least at first, a set of quite specific, technical applications. As I have suggested, Deschamps attempted to set down a clear definition of the form of *balades* in *L'Art de dictier*; he gives no clear indication as to the

[12] *The Register of Thomas Langley, Bishop of Durham 1406–1437*, ed. R. L. Storey, 6 vols., Surtees Society 164, 166, 169–70, 177, 182 (Durham: Andrews, 1957), ii. 195–7, at 196.

[13] Jorge Luis Borges, 'John Wilkins' Analytical Language', in *The Total Library: Non-Fiction 1922–1986*, ed. and trans. Eliot Weinberger (Harmondsworth: Penguin, 1999), 229–32, at 231.

subject matter of *balades*, but his own works range reasonably broadly in content and purpose from the amorous to the moral/aphoristic and historical/political. Deschamps's definitions of different types of *balade* rest on distinctions between number of lines, number of strophes, types of rhyme (leonine, sonant), and rhyme patterns, syllable count, and the presence or absence of a refrain. In making these definitions Deschamps, himself an innovator of the form despite or because of his deep consciousness of the achievements of his master Guillaume de Machaut, acknowledged that contemporary practice, such as the inclusion of envoys in *balades*, differed from what had occurred in the past. The genre, in other words, had changed and by implication would continue to change: one obvious development was the conception of *balades* as texts to be read silently, appreciated on the page, as well as performed. That emergence of a non-musical—or in Deschamps's terms 'natural musical'—*balade* in late fourteenth-century French literature seems to have had a liberating effect on its usage in England. To be sure, references to *balade* in English writing from the late fourteenth century repeatedly associate it with *rondelai* and *virelai*, as part of a trilogy of musical lexis. Gower's Amans admits to have 'ofte assaied | Rondeal, balade, and virelai | For hire on whom myn herte lai | To make ... ',[14] while in the Prologue to the *Legend of Good Women* Alceste specifies that Chaucer's 'hymns' composed for the God of Love consist of 'balades, roundels, virelayes' (F. Prol. 422–3; G. Prol. 410–11); 'compleyntis, baladis, roundelis, virelaies' form part of Lydgate's list in the *Fall of Princes* of 'fressh dites [compositions]' made by Chaucer. The specific instances of these references are not always clear; Amans's subsequent description of his compositions as 'caroles' sung in halls and chambers does clarify their musical setting, but at the same time seems to blur their signification by associating them with publicly performed popular song. Nevertheless, while it could have more specific applications, already in Chaucer's work, and increasingly during the fifteenth century, *balade* referred to part or whole of a poem written in rhyme royal, with or without a refrain. Chaucer used rhyme royal stanzas for 'Fortune', 'Truth', 'Complaint unto Pity', 'Complaint to his Purse', 'Gentilesse', 'Complaint to his Lady', 'Lak of Stedfastnesse', and 'Against Women Unconstant', all of which appear under the heading 'Balade' in certain manuscripts, as do poems with eight- or nine-line stanzas such as 'Womanly Noblesse', 'Complaint of Venus', 'Lenvoy a Bukton'. A *balade*, consisting of three stanzas in rhyme royal with a refrain, is inserted into the Prologue of the *Legend of Good Women* (F. 249–69; G. 203–23), while Lydgate's 'Stans puer ad mensam' (thirteen stanzas in rhyme royal, plus an eight-line envoy) is described in one manuscript as his 'godely tretis of the norture [nourishment] atte the table compiled in balade'.[15] By the middle of the fifteenth century Vegetius' *De re militari*

---

[14] *Confessio Amantis*, in *The English Works of John Gower*, ed. G. C. Macaulay, 2 vols., EETS, ES 81–2 (London: Oxford University Press, 1900–1), vol. i, I. 2726–9.
[15] Oxford, Bodleian Library, MS Bodley 686, fos. 186–7.

had been translated 'into Balade', which is how John Hardyng describes the form of his *Chronicle*.[16]

As these references indicate, *balade* may have signified certain poetic forms, but seems to have imposed no boundaries on content. History (Hardyng), military treatise (Vegetius), *The Chaunse of the Dyse*, were all described as written in, or translated into, *balade*. If, as Gower's use of the term suggests, the primary matter of *balades* in English was initially amorous (the *balade amoureuse* was an established subgenre), in certain contexts amorous could transmute into 'lewde', sung in taverns along with 'rondelettes and verelaies':

> Also vse not to pleye at dyes and tables [dice and gambling]
> Ne no maner of games vppon the holy dayes;
> Vse no tauernes wher be gestis and fable [songs/entertainments],
> Synggyng of lewde baladis, rondelettes, and verelaies[17]

The range of subject matter that could appear within *balades* attests to an impressive capacity of the form, but also to a rapid modification and extension of its meaning following its entry into the language. Deschamps could not possibly have accepted that Hardyng's *Chronicle* was composed 'in *balade*'. But this new range of subject matter and fluidity of form also indicate the wide variety of contexts and registers in which *balades* were now operating. If the performance space of a certain kind of *balade* was the tavern, for another it was the court; if one audience was popular, another was royal, and another was the gentry, members of which composed as well as collected, read, and transmitted *balades*. Manuscript evidence—such as the compilation of 'balettbokes'—might suggest a recognized genre under which texts were gathered, but equally will, I suggest, reveal heterogeneous assortments of texts alongside one another. One might see this term then as an import, like *romaunce* and *tragedye*, but an import that is easily domesticated, and that loses or at least loosens its specific technical meaning, indicative of the de-systemizing tendencies of what can only unsatisfactorily be termed literary culture, since the very term *balade* denotes a complex interaction of written and oral, of performance and composition.

Tragedye

The most obvious clue to the strangeness of *tragedye* as a generic term in Middle English is its orthography. Tragidie, trajedi, targedie, trejardi, treajde, tragetrie,

---

[16] *Knyghthode and Bataile*, ed. R. Dyboski and Z. M. Arend, EETS, os 201 (London: Oxford University Press, 1935), l. 53; *The Chronicle of Iohn Hardyng*, ed. Henry Ellis (London, 1812), 16.

[17] *Peter Idley's Instructions to his Son*, ed. Charlotte d'Evelyn (Boston: Modern Language Association, 1935), II(A). 1028–31; cf. Robert Mannyng of Brunne, *Handlyng Synne*, ed. Idelle Sullens, Medieval and Renaissance Texts (Binghamton: State University of New York, 1983), ll. 1041–4; 997–1001.

traladie, tegerte, trede ... : the word is foreign, as the efforts of scribes to transcribe it attest. And it is deployed in Middle English writing as an alien genre. Formulaic definitions associate it more with content than form. For Chaucer's Monk, tragedy is a narrative, 'a certeyn storie', with a clear trajectory, namely the fall of a man from 'greet prosperitee' and 'heigh degree' into misery and wretchedness, whereas its form, initially identified as hexametric verse, turns out to be non-specific, including prose and 'different kinds of metre': 'they ben versified communely | Of six feet ... | In prose eek been endited many oon, | And eek in meetre in many a sondry wise'; by the end of his tale, the genre has acquired a rather more pointedly political meaning: 'that Fortune alwey wole assaille | With unwar strook the regnes [kingdoms/monarchs] that been proude' ('Monk's Tale', VII. 1973–81; 2763–4). As has been noted, this does not accord precisely with the definition propagated by Dante and Boccaccio, according to which the genre (a 'goat-song', from tragos-goat and oda-song) should consist of narratives in poetic form, admirable and pleasing to begin with but at the end stinking and fear-inspiring.[18] Lydgate's definition of the genre in the *Troy Book* echoes and arguably broadens Chaucer's deployment of the term. While 'Tragidie' is described again as representing the transformation from prosperity to adversity, it 'also doth the conquest trete | Of riche kynges and of lordys grete'.[19] Yet Lydgate—like Chaucer—quite deliberately blurred the definition of tragedy by aligning it with another genre recognized by medieval authors and audiences, and one that was a favourite of Chaucer, the *compleynte*.[20] In Lydgate's *Fall of Princes*, extracts from which were sometimes entitled 'Tragedy of Prynces', reference to the figure of Chaucer unleashes a deluge of generic terms:

> My maister Chaucer, with his fresh **comedies**,
> Is ded, allas, cheeff poete off Breteyne,
> That whilom made ful pitous **tragedies**;
> The fall of pryncis he dede also **compleyne**,
> As he that was of makyng souereyne,
> Whom al this land sholde off riht preferre,
> Sithe off oure language he was the lodesterre [lodestar].
> Senek in Rome, thoruh his hih prudence,
> Wrot **tragedies** of gret moralite;
> And Tullius, cheeff welle off eloquence,

---

[18] Henry Ansgar Kelly, 'Interpretation of Genres and by Genres', in Piero Boitani and Anna Torti (eds.), *Interpretation: Medieval and Modern* (Cambridge: Brewer, 1993), 107–22, at 119; Kelly, *Chaucerian Tragedy* (Cambridge: Brewer, 1997), 12–91.

[19] *Lydgate's Troy Book*, ed. Henry Bergen, 4 vols., EETS, ES 97, 103, 106, 125 (London: Kegan Paul, 1906–25), vol. i, II. 852.

[20] See Nigel Mortimer, *John Lydgate's Fall of Princes: Narrative Tragedy in its Literary and Political Contexts* (Oxford: Clarendon Press, 2005), 215: 'One of the most certain conclusions to be drawn from Lydgate's work is that his understanding of tragedy overlaps to a large degree with the category of the *planctus*.' On the 'Tragedy of Prynces', see Eleanor Prescott Hammond, 'Ashmole 59 and Other Shirley Manuscripts', *Anglia*, 30 (1907), 322–48, at 323.

> Maad in his tyme many fressh **dite**;
> Franceis Petrak, off Florence the cite,
> Made a **book**, as I can reherce,
> Off too Fortunys, welful and peruerse.[21]

The adjective 'pitous' echoes Lydgate's description in the *Troy Book* of tragedies 'al to-tore and rent [ripped apart and torn], | In compleynynge pitously in rage | In the theatre, with a ded visage [colourless face]' (III. 5440–2). The idea of tragedy seems here to veer towards lyric, towards the emotional display of narrator and audience, and perhaps, given the courtly connotations of 'pitous', towards chivalric romance. The 'also' not only serves to elide the genre of tragedy with that of complaint, it establishes a triangular relationship between Chaucer, Lydgate, and their mutual source, Boccaccio. But Lydgate's next, deliberately classicizing, move seems contrary to Chaucer's representation of the term. The rather slick genealogy from Seneca and Cicero (and Rome) to Petrarch (and Florence) is one of standard humanist construction, but it leaves unclear whether Chaucer is a branch of the same line, or whether he represents a disjunction, a fresh start. Lydgate's own position, then, seems to lie at the intersection of these two distinct lineages connected by the writing of 'tragedies': Seneca–Cicero [Rome]–Petrarch–Boccaccio [Florence]; and Boccaccio [Florence]–Chaucer [Breteyne].

Certainly the capacity of generic terms to become extraordinarily broad applies to tragedy as much as to most other Middle English nomenclature. The fourteenth-century treatises by John Arderne on the treatment of anal fistulae, haemorrhoids, and clysters, for example, contain an introductory section on 'the manere of the leche'. Arderne advises doctors to have a stock of 'gode talez and of honest that may make the pacientes to laugh, as wele of the biblee as of other tragediez; & any othir thingis of which it is noght to charge whilez that [doesn't matter as long as] they make or induce a light hert to the pacient or the sike man'.[22] The casual connection of 'tragediez' with the Bible is striking, as is the notion that they might induce levity in a patient about to undergo rectal surgery. In other contexts tragedy marks death, and the response to death, but crucially also imprisonment within life. Within one of his *ballades*, Charles d'Orléans turns the term into a trope to describe both the state of a lover after the death of his 'nobille princesse' and the event itself: 'For leuyr [rather] had y hastily forto dy | Than langwysshe in this karfulle [sorrowful] tragedy.'[23] 'Tragedy' here serves to extend the moment of the beloved's death into a heaviness from which the only exit is a second, reciprocal death.

---

[21] John Lydgate, *Fall of Princes*, ed. H. Bergen, EETS, es 123, 4 vols. (London: Oxford University Press, 1924–7), ll. 246–59.

[22] John Arderne, *Treatises of Fistula in Ano, Haemorrhoids, and Clysters*, ed. D'arcy Power, EETS, os 139 (London: Kegan Paul, Trench, Trübner, 1910), 8, ll. 10–14. Kelly, *Chaucerian Tragedy*, 42, suggests that (in the original Latin text) Arderne 'clearly takes tragedia to mean nothing more than "book"'.

[23] *The English Poems of Charles of Orleans*, ed. Robert Steele and Mabel Day, EETS, os 215, 220 (London: Oxford University Press, 1941, 1946; repr. 1970), 68 (ll. 2000–1).

Undeniably, as well as a general sense of heavy and sorry narratives, the genre retains its classical associations. Capgrave revealed the unfamiliarity of the term when he subsumed genre into author, describing Sophocles and Euripides as themselves tragedies: 'In this tyme lyued these too poetes, Sophodes and Euripides, that were cleped [called] tragedies. Trajedi is as mech to sey as he that writith eld stories with ditees heuy and sorowful.'[24] As Lucas has argued, there is little reason to think that Capgrave conceived of these 'tragedies' as dramatists;[25] instead, he emphasizes tragedy's poetic form, and its serious content. Seneca, more than Sophocles, seems to have acted as the figure of the tragedian for fifteenth-century English writers. As well as in the *Fall of Princes*, Lydgate cited him in his *Siege and Destruccioun of Thebes*, inviting readers who wanted to hear more about Edippus to

> ... reden in a Tragedye
> Of Moral Senyk fully his [i.e. Edippus'] endynge,
> His dool [grief], his meschief [affliction] and his compleynyng,
> How with sorow and unweldy [infirm] age
> This Edippus fille into dotage,
> lost his wit and his worldly delit ... [26]

Once again linked with complaint (although, as V. J. Scattergood has noted, 'compleynyng' may signal more a 'type of expression' than a form or a genre[27]), the term tragedy is used here as a marker of distance and difference rather than identity. Lydgate distinguishes Seneca's work from his own, which is described in various places as a 'tale' and a 'story' (narrative, history), with frequent references to source material that informs it (the *Roman de Edipus*, Boccaccio's *De genealogia deorum*). What precisely these classical associations of tragedy meant—whether they operated on the level of formula or invoked a deeper knowledge of classical literature, whether they sought to align literature in English with classical texts or to mark their distance—remain open questions.

As some of the uses of the term discussed so far make evident, tragedy's obvious opposition to comedy pertained also for medieval authors. However, comedy was apparently a term rather less used, and it seems to have enjoyed a different trajectory from tragedy. Its origins, located by Higden, following Bede, in Sicily ('ibique primum inventa fuit comoedia' (and there comedy was first invented/composed), cf. Trevisa's 'commedy a song of gestes'),[28] comedy was certainly defined by Lydgate,

---

[24] *John Capgrave's Abbreuiacion of Cronicles*, ed. Peter J. Lucas, EETS, os 285 (Oxford: Oxford University Press, 1983), 40.

[25] Ibid. 259; elsewhere in the *Abbreuiacion* Capgrave uses 'trajedies' to refer to poems (specifically those of Terence), rather than authors: Kelly, *Chaucerian Tragedy*, 43.

[26] John Lydgate, *Lydgate's Siege of Thebes*, ed. Axel Erdmann and Eilert Ekwall, 2 vols., EETS, es 125 (London: Oxford University Press, 1911–30), vol. i, ll. 994–9.

[27] Scattergood, 'The Short Poems', 465.

[28] *Polychronicon Ranulphi Higden monachi Cestrensis Together with the English Translations of John Trevisa and of an Unknown Writer of the Fifteenth Century*, ed. Churchill Babington, 9 vols., Rolls Series 41 (London: Longman, 1865–86), i. 314–15.

for example, as the antithesis of tragedy—'A comedie hath in his gynnyng | At prime face [initially], a maner compleynyng, | And afterward endeth in gladnes' (*Troy Book*, II. 847–9)—and the two terms were apparently opposed in Chaucer's 'go, litel myn tragedye, | Ther God thi makere yet, er that he dye, | So sende myght to make in som comedye!' (*Troilus and Criseyde*, V. 1786–88). But Lydgate's description of Chaucer in the *Fall of Princes* as a maker of both 'fresh comedies' and 'pitous tragedyes' may indicate either a binary opposition or simply two different, perhaps even complementary genres. Surely—as Trevisa's use of the term 'gestes' suggests—the term *comodye* struggled to insert itself into the semantic space filled by *romaunce*. Whereas the rather more clearly defined content of tragedy, allied to its better-known classical ancestry, seems to have allowed it points of entry, if not assimilation into literature written in English, comedy as a generic marker failed to take off, and retained its exteriority.

Without system

To be without a system–what does that mean? To see literature within a system, regulated, generated by the system, one need only look at the production of official documents. The high and later European Middle Ages possessed a clear sense of the different genres of document (papal, royal, local; governmental, personal), and of the rules of each, such as physical form (e.g. letters patent, letters close), and formulae. Certainly audience expectations, as well as those of the producers of documents, were crucial: to signify, the form of the document needed to be recognized. Documentary genre expresses power and position within hierarchy, both of text and of producer/receiver; it is thus unavoidably social, and has historically specific effects. This is not to say that documentary genres did not change, that they cannot be analysed from diachronic as well as synchronic perspectives. But this ordered system of documentation contrasts starkly with the non-system of the production of literary texts. The work of clerk-poets such as Thomas Hoccleve may appear to straddle the dichotomy between bureaucratic and literary production. But perhaps, having identified the 'bureaucratic muse' at work within Hoccleve's writings, we need also to see his literary work as an escape from official documentation, or rather, as a heightened response to its restrictions.

For Derrida, genre and the law of genre could be seen as gendered and generative. To name a text in terms of genre, to insert a genre-clause (for example, subtitling a novel 'a novel') is to create a fold, a moment/blink of the eye (*Augenblick*).[29] Such a clause is neither within nor without the text, neither part nor whole. Can the genre-clause be connected with the idea, suggested at the beginning of this

[29] Jacques Derrida, 'The Law of Genre', *Critical Inquiry*, 7 (1980), 55–81.

essay, of the ungenre? It would be going too far to argue that the genre-clause in Middle English writing (naming a text a *balade, fable, geste, romaunce, tale, tragedye*, etc.) was exactly the opposite of its apparent intention, acting precisely as the ungenre, the destabilizing moment of the inexplicable, the fish in the text. But rather than equating nomenclature with ungenre, it might be possible to see the names of writing and ungeneric moments within texts as related, and strategic, boundary-disturbances. Instead of confirming parameters—including parameters such as the audience's 'horizons of expectations'—nomenclature and ungenre, both enfolded, self-contained moments simultaneously inside and outside literature, unsettle expectations but also create new ones. Genre is not originally an English word, and its connotations—as Derrida remarked—are much wider in French and much more obviously connected to gender. And, as he and others have noted, the German *Gattung* carries another semantic range (marriage, classification, coupling) absent from the English 'genre', which seems somehow isolated, cut off from its linguistic environment. In English, in other words, genre is both less imposing, less institutional than *Gattung* and at the same time less obviously fecund than both its German and French equivalents. Remembering these differences may help us to understand the rather pallid signification of genre as a critical concept within English studies; it may also encourage us to reconceptualize genre as a mode of mixing. Mixing genres—*tragedye-compleynte; tragedye-comodye; balade-rondelai-virelai; romaunce-comodye-compleynte; romaunce* itself, the mother of all genres, a sign of mixing and mixture—may turn out to be the fundamental trait of Middle English literature.

Borges was the enemy of systems, including generic ones, not because he disliked or attempted to dismantle them, but precisely because he loved them so much, understood and eulogized their heroism, their hermeticism, and their tyranny. In exalting them, in envisioning rationality in its ultimate and extreme manifestation, he revealed the threads of irrationality that run through system. The converse is that threads of rationality run through non-system. To talk of a non-system of genre in Middle English writing does not mean that there were no established literary practices, modes of composition, or associations attached to particular terms; it does not mean that there were no genres, nor that there was no means of ordering and categorizing literary production. 'Non-system' proposes, however, that what existed was more organic, decentred, and unpredictable, than the idea of a system demands. An analogy may be found in spatial organization. The lack of a system of genres means that the names of genres, generic markers, do not locate and do not signify place within a system. No map of genres can be drawn, because maps show movement only by means of external symbols (think of the arrows on maps of migrations, troop movements, or the weather), and what characterizes genre in the Middle Ages is rapid movement across subject matter, mode, and even technique: the voracious expanse of romance; the nomadic quality of tragedy; the fluidity of *balade*. Rather than signifying place, what the names of writing seem to do is mark passages, the trajectories and directions of which were continually subject to alteration on the part of authors, translators, and even scribes.

FURTHER READING

The heroic scholarly projects of Middle English studies in the twentieth century have left us with an invaluable basis for the investigation of the names of writing. The obvious point of entry is Hans Kurath et al. (eds.), *Middle English Dictionary* (Ann Arbor: University of Michigan Press, 1954–2001): even if many of its definitions remain open to challenge, the *MED* serves as a comprehensive if not exhaustive finding list, and can direct attention well off the beaten track. A. E. Hartung, (gen. ed.) *A Manual of the Writings in Middle English, 1050–1500*, 11 vols. (New Haven: Connecticut Academy of the Arts and Sciences, 1967–2005) in part organizes the field by genre in ways that are immensely helpful yet not always responsive to the instability of generic markers in Middle English. For this essay I have relied almost entirely on published sources: further investigation would need to examine unpublished texts and manuscript contexts much more closely. One suggestive starting point in this area, of particular relevance to the presentation of lyric in late medieval scribal practice, is Ardis Butterfield, '*Mise-en-Page* in the *Troilus* Manuscripts: Chaucer and French Manuscript Culture', *Huntington Library Quarterly*, 58 (1996), 49–80.

For classical generic categories the obvious starting points are the *Poetics* of Aristotle and Horace. Medieval discussions of literary theory include Matthew of Vendôme's *Ars versificatoria* (*The Art of the Versemaker*), trans. Roger P. Parr (Milwaukee: Marquette University Press, 1981); statements of literary theory by Dante, Boccaccio, and many others are conveniently collected and translated in A. J. Minnis and A. B. Scott (eds.), *Medieval Literary Theory and Criticism c.1100–c. 1375: The Commentary Tradition* (Oxford: Clarendon Press, 1988); Deschamps's *L'Art de dictier*, ed and trans. Deborah M. Sinnreich-Levi (East Lansing, MI: Colleagues Press, 1994) is, as I have tried to suggest, a particularly intriguing document. Although Middle English lacks a comprehensive statement on generic nomenclature, some purchase on this issue may be gained from A. L. Mayhew (ed.), *The Promptorium parvulorum: The First English–Latin Dictionary*, EETS, ES 102 (London: Kegan Paul, 1908).

On Middle English romance there is of course a vast literature. For the question of generic names I found helpful Paul Strohm's 'The Origin and Meaning of Middle English Romaunce', *Genre*, 10 (1977), 1–28; and his 'Middle English Narrative Genres', *Genre*, 13 (1980), 379–88, as well as Judith Weiss, Jennifer Fellows, and Morgan Dickson (eds.), *Medieval Insular Romance: Translation and Innovation* (Cambridge: Brewer, 2000), particularly the introduction and the articles by Elizabeth Archibald on the Breton lay (pp. 55–70), and W. A. Davenport on 'composite romance' (pp. 111–31). For a brisk discussion of the musical context of literary forms such as the *lai*, see Christopher Page, *Voices and Instruments of the Middle Ages: Instrumental Practice and Songs in France 1100–1300* (London: Dent, 1987), 92–107. Helen Cooper's *The English Romance in Time: Transforming Motifs from Geoffrey of Monmouth to the Death of Shakespeare* (Oxford: Oxford University Press, 2004) suggests that 'family resemblance' might be the best way of understanding and establishing connections between different romance texts (pp. 8–9), an idea previously broached in Ad Putter's 'Historical Introduction' to Ad Putter and Jane Gilbert (eds.), *The Spirit of Medieval English Popular Romance* (Harlow: Longman, 2000), 1–15; Putter's discussion also contains a useful summary of manuscript evidence for the 'packaging' and reception of genre.

A remarkable burst of scholarly energy was directed towards the question of genre from the early 1970s to the early 1980s. Hans Robert Jauss's 'Theory of Genres and Medieval Literature' (n. 2 above) has some claim to being the single most influential statement in this field over the past three decades. Paul Zumthor's *Essai de poétique médiévale* (Paris: Éditions du Seuil, 1972) is an attempt to refine a typology of medieval literary texts on structuralist principles, while Tzvetan Todorov, 'The Origin of Genres', *New Literary History*, 8 (1976), 159–70, provides a speculative account of the 'transformations that certain speech acts undergo in order to produce certain literary genres' (p. 165). Fredric Jameson, *The Political Unconscious: Narrative as a Socially Symbolic Act* (Ithaca, NY: Cornell University Press, 1981), ch. 2: 'Magical Narratives: On the Dialectical Use of Genre Criticism', 103–50, contains important critiques of Propp, Lévi-Strauss, Frye, and Derrida, and advances the notion that '[g]enres are essentially literary *institutions*, or social contracts between a writer and a specific public, whose function it is to specify the proper use of a particular cultural artifact' (p. 106). For Benedetto Croce's earlier, provocative ideas about genre see *The Aesthetic as the Science of Expression and of the Linguistic in General*, trans. Colin Lyas (Cambridge: Cambridge University Press, 1992).

From the mid-1990s the beginnings of a quieter, but perhaps equally radical, re-examination of genre can be discerned. Of general relevance is the 'Theoretical Postlude' to Thomas O. Beebee's *The Ideology of Genre: A Comparative Study of Generic Instability* (University Park: Pennsylvania State University Press, 1994), 249–83. Simon Gaunt's *Gender and Genre in Medieval French Literature* (Cambridge: Cambridge University Press, 1995) affirms the significance, if instability, of genre, and emphasizes its inextricability from representation of gender. More recently, Tison Pugh's *Queering Medieval Genres* (New York: Palgrave Macmillan, 2004) has viewed generic play, particularly in Middle English texts, through the lens of queer theory. The collection Bert Roest and Herman Vanstiphout (eds.), *Aspects of Genre and Type in Pre-Modern Literary Cultures* (Groningen: Styx Publications, 1999) contains a valuable article by Anda Schippers on fable and the question of genre in Middle Dutch writing. An admirably judicious discussion of the emergence of romance genres in medieval (principally German and French) literature can be found in D. H. Green, *The Beginnings of Medieval Romance: Fact and Fiction, 1150–1220* (Cambridge: Cambridge University Press, 2002) — see p. 27 for a discussion of the wide range of medieval terms used to describe what modern scholars regard as romance. See also Fritz Peter Knapp, *Historie und Fiktion in der mittelalterlichen Gattungspoetik: Sieben Studien und ein Nachwort* (Heidelberg: Universitätsverlag C. Winter, 1997; 1st pub. 1980), and Walter Haug, *Vernacular Literary Theory in the Middle Ages: The German Tradition, 800–1300, in its European Context*, trans. Joanna M. Catling (Cambridge: Cambridge University Press, 1997). William D. Paden, 'Principles of Generic Classification in the Medieval European Lyric: The Case of Galician-Portuguese', *Speculum*, 81 (2006), 76–96, uses keyword analysis to reassess traditional generic categories, while William D. Paden (ed.), *Medieval Lyric: Genres in Historical Context* (Urbana: University of Illinois Press, 2000) provides an introduction to the study of lyric genres across a range of European languages and literatures, demonstrating in its breadth and commitment to historicization the pitfalls of making generalizations about the role of genre in medieval literature. New directions in the study of the interrelation between documents and literature in late medieval English culture have been opened out by Ethan Knapp, *The Bureaucratic Muse: Thomas Hoccleve and the Literature of Late Medieval England* (University Park: Pennsylvania State University Press, 2001); Emily Steiner, *Documentary Culture and the Making of Medieval English Literature* (Cambridge: Cambridge University Press, 2003); and by the work of Wendy Scase (see for example 'Writing and the "Poetics of Spectacle": Political Epiphanies in *The Arrivall of Edward IV* and Some Contemporary Lancastrian and Yorkist Texts', in Jeremy Dimmick, James Simpson, and Nicolette Zeeman (eds.), *Images, Idolatry and Iconoclasm* (Oxford: Oxford University Press, 2002), 172–84).

CHAPTER 19

LITURGY

BRUCE HOLSINGER

Liturgy lives an amorphously ubiquitous existence in the Middle Ages and in medieval studies. Both everywhere and nowhere in the cultural history of premodern England, liturgy goes all but unmentioned in the recent *Cambridge History of Medieval English Literature* even as Eamon Duffy's *Stripping of the Altars* treats it as the social glue that 'gave meaning and purpose to [the] lives' of the medieval English populace.[1] One of the master organizing categories of medieval culture, liturgy resides in books and ceremony, in cathedral naves and household chapels, and in the symbolic lexicon of early English literature; and yet the particular character of its inherence in so many medieval cultural forms can be difficult to specify. Those who seek to account for liturgy's impact on the pre-modern literary field thus risk lapsing into a rhetoric of obsessive fascination worthy of a D. W. Robertson or an Henri de Lubac, both of whom faced a similarly boundless domain in their studies of medieval biblical exegesis. Through the simultaneously fixed and cyclical conventions of mass and divine office, medieval liturgy was at once an inspiration for endless musical and literary composition and a precise formal mechanism for fitting innumerable existing fragments of text and song together to shape stories eternally worth retelling. Liturgy was as well the great medieval frame narrative, unrivalled by any vernacular in its capacity to subsume, illuminate, substitute, and juxtapose narratives both human and divine. The mass may well be a locus of divine mystery, but it also supports a degree of aesthetic invention that is fully human in its knack for contradiction, subversion, and error. The divine office, too, proved an enduring provocation to musical and poetic innovation, practically all of it anonymous and including a great corpus of insular rhymed offices that have remained largely unstudied.

Despite the looming presence of liturgy behind so many aspects of literary making, though, and several fine studies over the years of liturgy's thematic influence on specific literary artefacts, some of the fundamental questions that

---

[1] Eamon Duffy, *The Stripping of the Altars* (New Haven: Yale University Press, 1992), 9.

might be posed about the relationship between liturgy and vernacular literary production have remained unasked. These questions are simultaneously historical and bibliographical, and they embrace a remarkable array of political, institutional, aesthetic, and formal concerns—all with great implications for the understanding of medieval literary culture. Where does liturgy reside in relation to literature? How do these two categories inhabit one another, and in what sense can they (or should they) be distinguished at certain historical moments and within particular textual communities? What modes of convergence and mutuality affiliate the liturgical and the literary? How are such affiliations negotiated within specific religious and political localities, and how do they determine the forms and aesthetics of specifically literary writing? More radically, perhaps, in what sense might literature be seen as in part an *effect* of liturgy, a curious by-product of the immense cultural industry invested in the Work of God by the institutions that performed it?

In medieval England, liturgy formed a boundless provocation to and repository of literary production and invention. Anglo-Saxon, Latin, Anglo-Norman, and English hagiographies are in large part organized according to its calendar. Ælfric's Catholic Homilies, the longest prose work in Old English, builds an influential pastoral rhetoric on its temporal foundation. William Langland professes himself schooled in it: the 'lomes that y labore with', the dreamer avows in C5, 'Is *paternoster* and my primer, *placebo* and *dirige*, | And my sauter som tyme and my seuene psalmes'.[2] It is surely what the Benedictine monk John Lydgate, the most prolific Middle English author, spent most of his time enacting—or, rather, was supposed to have spent most of his time enacting—when not making poetry. Productions of the mystery cycles were tied intimately to liturgical occasions, the plays themselves often interweaving Latin liturgical incipits and refrains into their scripts, and the liturgies of Advent and Palm Sunday feature constantly in the staging of royal entries and other displays of public power.[3] Liturgy, too, allowed William Caxton and Wynkyn de Worde, the earliest English printers, to fund significant portions of their vernacular print enterprises through the production and sale of Sarum service books from their shops within the walls of Westminster Abbey, London's own most prestigious liturgical community. So pervasive was the formal, authorial, and economic impact of liturgy on medieval English writing that one runs the danger of recruiting practically all of this writing for the history of liturgical production.

One thing liturgy cannot do, though, is abet the current tendency to overcome strong boundaries of periodization between the medieval and early modern eras. If anything, the study of liturgy will only reinforce these boundaries, for better or worse, and it may in fact help to explain them. For one of the most distinctly

---

[2] William Langland, *Piers Plowman*, C-text, v. 45–7; ed. Derek Pearsall (Berkeley and Los Angeles: University of California Press, 1978), 99.

[3] On liturgy and royal entries, see Gordon Kipling, *Enter the King: Theatre, Liturgy, and Ritual in the Medieval Civic Triumph* (Oxford: Clarendon Press, 1998).

medieval things about medieval literature, I believe, is its intimate affiliation with the institutional, aesthetic, and formal complexities of liturgical culture. These complexities would not survive the Reformation, when a 'centralized jursidiction', in James Simpson's felicitous phrase, violently displaced the 'jurisdictional hetero-geneity' characterizing late medieval writing.[4] Conversely, we will not come close to understanding the liturgical character of Middle English literature if we continue isolating this writing from the corpus of Anglo-Saxon literature that preceded it, as has been the practice in virtually all of the most influential historicist work in our field over the last twenty years. Although a full-scale engagement with Old English materials would exceed the brief of this collection, liturgy forms one of the strongest threads of cultural continuity linking the pre- and post-Conquest eras, and in what follows I will freely draw examples and provocations from both.

Detheologizing liturgy

Whatever else it will entail, the pursuit of a liturgical history of early English writing demands what I want to call a detheologizing vision of liturgy and its objects: a critical self-consciousness toward the auto-ontological function of liturgy in medieval culture. By this I mean an awareness of the metaphysical process by which liturgy arrogates to itself the power to explain, reveal, and enact the properties, essences, and relations of all things, of all beings. Medieval typology enlists the participant in liturgical ritual in re-enacting, in bodying forth on earth, the course of sacred history in all its dazzling totality. The liturgical represents perhaps the most successful ontological category for Western medieval Christianity, capable of revealing by explaining and embodying the relation of past and present, of object and spirit, of human and divine. If the domain of sacrament encompasses the many ritual ways in which 'we are present to each other', in Sarah Beckwith's terms, the domain of liturgy embraces all of these and more, for only through liturgy can sacrament enter material culture.[5]

I am using the term 'detheologizing' here in something of the way it was employed by Teodolinda Barolini in *The Undivine Comedy*.[6] For Barolini, to detheologize Dante is neither to abnegate his religiosity nor to deny the centrality of belief and its expression to the *Comedy*, but rather to recognize and resist the theologizing habits of readers themselves as well as the hermeneutical determinism built into the form and rhetoric of the poem. A detheologizing approach to the massive cultural

[4] James Simpson, *Reform and Cultural Revolution*, Oxford English Literary History 2 (Oxford: Oxford University Press, 2004), 1.

[5] Sarah Beckwith, *Signifying God: Social Relation and Symbolic Act in the York Corpus Christi Plays* (Chicago: University of Chicago Press, 2001), p. xv.

[6] Teodolinda Barolini, *The Undivine Comedy: Detheologizing Dante* (Princeton: Princeton University Press, 1992).

apparatus of liturgy, of course, will require more than a 'new formalism' of the sort advocated by Barolini, though, as I will suggest, formalism is indeed part of the complex of problems at issue here: the formalisms of liturgical studies vis-á-vis the books, texts, objects, and traditions that make up the grand unifying field it claims to know and study.

The history of liturgical commentary (including modern liturgical study) can be seen as an enduring debate between theologizing and detheologizing approaches to its subject. O. B. Hardison's classic work on liturgy as drama, for example, identified a deep-seated tension within medieval liturgical communities themselves between a theologizing sacramentality and a detheologizing theatricality. In his infamous analogy of the liturgical celebrant as an actor taking on the role of Christ, Honorius Augustodunensis was hardly denying the theology of the liturgy; yet he was promoting a demystified explication of its spectacle, encouraging practitioners of liturgical ritual to recognize its function not simply as performed salvation, but as analogy, as metaphor, as mimetic deployment of the rhetorics of gesture, motion, and personification. As Hardison recognized, Honorius had fierce opponents in his own day invested in maintaining the non-theatricality of liturgy (a theologizing insistence echoed in the tendencies of present-day critics such as Lawrence Clopper to dismiss the very notion of liturgy as theatre).[7]

In calling for a detheologizing analysis of liturgy, then, I seek to recover those moments when medieval culture stands outside its own overwhelming and overdetermined claims to be the ritual embodiment and continuity of the presence of God on earth: claims iterated within the liturgy proper and supported by the external institutional practices that surround it. On these terms, liturgy can be understood not simply as the ritual fusion of religious belief and religious practice, but also and simultaneously as the *space between professed belief and material practice*: a space, perhaps, where theology, whether vernacular or otherwise, becomes radically localized, particularized, decentralized, and miniaturized. Such a situated comprehension of pre-modern liturgical cultures may allow us to loosen liturgy's firm hold on broad swaths of medieval knowledge by opening up the predetermined typologies and classificatory schemes which, in literary studies, at least, have long denied the liturgical its rightful place among the defining modes of medieval cultural production. (To put this another way, our field typically tends to take an all-or-nothing approach to liturgy: its cultural claims are so vast and their implications so far-reaching that we either swallow them wholesale or ignore them altogether. Yet liturgy functions as a constant incentive to more localized creative gestures, and we need not subscribe to the universalizing imperatives of liturgical

---

[7] See O. B. Hardison, *Christian Rite and Christian Drama in the Middle Ages: Essays on the Origin and Early History of Modern Drama* (Baltimore: Johns Hopkins University Press, 1965), 37–79; Lawrence Clopper, *Drama, Play, and Game: English Festive Culture in the Medieval and Early Modern Period* (Chicago: University of Chicago Press, 2001), esp. 50–2.

theology—nor assume that our medieval subjects ascribed to them—in order to account for the particular character of these gestures.)

On a certain level, it makes sense that our own discipline's predominant models of historical understanding so strongly resist the importance of liturgical materiality to the literary artefacts they situate. Our historicist age prefers the history of kings, royalist politics, civic rule, gender relations, diplomatic exchange, rural revolt, heresy, Church–state struggle—in short, we prefer 'the time of the Agent', in Emmanuel Lévinas's terms, in contrast to 'liturgical time', with its implied willingness 'to act for remote things'.[8] Liturgy can only rarely be regarded as a historically specific or specifiable thing; liturgical labour in turn is patient, enduring work, never asking to be recognized as the historical present of textuality, publication, circulation, and reception, though in important ways it clearly was. N. R. Ker's exhaustive *Medieval Libraries of Great Britain* lists hundreds of insular religious houses—Benedictine abbeys, Bridgettine convents, Franciscan friaries, Carthusian hermitages, and so on—along with the books scattered throughout the modern world's libraries that can be securely affiliated with each house. Liturgical books—graduals, psalters, missals, lectionaries, tonaries, breviaries, sacramentaries, antiphonals, hymnaries, and many other subgenres that have remained virtually untapped by literary history—constitute as much as a third, in many cases half, or more of the surviving attributable books from the vast majority of medieval English libraries. Five books, for example, are attributable to the Benedictine priory of nuns in Amesbury (Wilts.): a selection from Lydgate's works, an Exhortation to nuns in English, and three liturgical books: a breviary, a psalter, and a Book of Hours. From the Cluniac priory of St John the Evangelist in Pontefract (Yorks.), three books are known to survive: writings of Augustine, a missal, and a breviary. The same pattern holds true for well-known institutions such as Syon Abbey, the great Bridgettine house in Middlesex known as a centre for vernacular literary production in the fifteenth century. Yet fully half of the surviving books from Syon are liturgical books: diurnals, processionals, psalters, breviaries, hymnaries, ordinals, and numerous liturgical miscellanies.[9] These institutions performed the liturgy daily, of course, so we would expect them to own numerous liturgical books. But Ker only grudgingly included liturgical books in his extensive lists; service books are less likely to have belonged to or ended up in ecclesiastical libraries per se because they were used in worship, and technically they belonged to the chapel or choir more often than to the library itself in many institutions.

[8] See Emmanuel Lévinas, 'On the Trail of the Other', trans. Daniel J. Hoy, *Philosophy Today*, 10 (1966), 34–44.

[9] See the relevant entries in N. R. Ker, *Medieval Libraries of Great Britain: A List of Surviving Books*, 2nd edn. (London: Royal Historical Society, 1964). Compare the surviving pre-modern lists from Syon edited and traced in the monumental work of Vincent Gillespie, *Syon Abbey*, Corpus of British Medieval Library Catalogues (London: British Library in association with the British Academy, 2001).

English print culture, too, was in many ways organized around liturgical production. The Pollard and Redgrave *Short Title Catalogue* (*STC*), a standard reference work for medievalists and early modernists listing all known books printed in the British Isles during the first century and a half of printing, begins its section on printed liturgies with this warning to the prospective researcher:

> Most bibliographers are hesitant to deal with liturgies from the period before, during and after the Reformation. For the Latin-Rite liturgies the variety of texts is the main source of confusion; for Anglican liturgies it is primarily the multiplicity of editions. For both the problem is compounded by the sad state of the majority of copies, some surviving only as fragments rescued from bindings and others having undergone contemporary, near-contemporary, or modern mutilation and/or sophistication: 'made-up' copies in every possible sense … What [the *STC*] can do is to help indicate the large heaps into which the various texts can be sorted.[10]

The *STC* rarely resorts to this kind of rhetoric ('large heaps' and so on), which here imagines liturgy as the bibliographer's worst nightmare. The section on liturgies in the *STC* is forty pages long with thousands of entries for separate editions of liturgical books in Latin and English. More editions of liturgical books are listed than those of Ovid, Virgil, Horace, Chaucer, Gower, Lydgate, Shakespeare, Sidney, Marlowe, Jonson, Spenser, and Milton combined. The only rival to liturgical books in terms of sheer number of editions is the Bible, and even here it is possible to claim at least a third, perhaps half of the *STC*'s 'Bible' list as liturgical books, since many of them are liturgically arranged into calendrical epistle collections, Gospel lectionaries, psalters, and other service-oriented forms.

A solid plurality of manuscript and printed books in pre-modern England may well have been liturgical books. More broadly, this detour into enumerative bibliography suggests that liturgy provides an economic, material, and even creative foundation of literary production through the first decades of the English Reformation. Far from exercising a conservative or regressive grip upon vernacular invention, liturgical cultures functioned as powerful engines of vernacular making. In a certain sense, English literature from the seventh century to the fifteenth might be conceived in part as an *effect* of liturgy, demanding that we account for the sheer industrial might of liturgical culture—and the amount of concealed human labour indispensable to its production—not as a theologizing, ideological constraint upon vernacular literary history, but as its very ground. Liturgy and literature create modes of writing, performance, textual production, preservation, and memorialization that need to be understood in direct institutional and causal relation to each other; liturgy forces linguistic and formal innovation in the vernacular even as its central texts and mysteries reach their audience mostly (but not always) in Latin.

---

[10] A. W. Pollard and G. R. Redgrave, *A Short-Title Catalogue of Books Printed in England, Scotland, & Ireland and of English Books Printed Abroad, 1475–1640*, vol. ii (London: Bibliographical Society, 1976), 68.

The phenomenology of the 'service book'

The modern theologized category of the 'service book' has exerted a strong organizing pressure on the descriptive bibliography of medieval manuscripts. While many manuscripts clearly fit into the conventional liturgical genres, numerous liturgically affiliated books not only fail to gel with these categories, but challenge the basic schema that liturgists have long employed to classify the liturgical culture of the book. This is particularly true for the early periods. Cambridge, Corpus Christi College, MS 41 transmits a well-known Anglo-Saxon translation of Bede's *Ecclesiastical History of the English People* that was given by Bishop Leofric to Exeter sometime in the eleventh century. The margins of this vernacular Bede are filled with Latin liturgical texts and formulae: masses for Sexagesima, Quinquagesima, Good Friday, and the Common of the Saints, among numerous others; antiphons and homilies for various occasions; offices for Advent, Easter Eve, and the Invention of the Cross; and many more. So prodigious are this book's liturgical offerings that it has been included in more than one bibliography of Anglo-Saxon service books—but as a copy, not as an actual service book. As Richard Pfaff writes in his handlist, 'Though the liturgical material copied out does not amount to anything like a complete service book, it is so extensive that something can be inferred about the liturgical text(s) from which it was copied ... We are left wistful for the massbook from which the scribe copied.'[11] Yet not counting Corpus 41, fewer than a dozen 'massbooks' survive from Anglo-Saxon England, only five or six of them considered at all complete. Given the deep investment in liturgical making that characterized Bede's own life and oeuvre, not to mention the fascination with local liturgical conventions on display throughout the *Ecclesiastical History*, Corpus 41 may have been understood, and even perhaps employed, as a 'liturgical text' in its own right.

A very different case in point is provided by *Ancrene Wisse*. Living out their enclosed lives in anchorholds adjacent to churches, the users of *Ancrene Wisse* participated with some directness in the liturgical rhythms of their communities, listening to the mass and office performed by monks, canons, or secular clergy and receiving particular instructions in various parts of the book regarding their own devotional duties relative to the larger liturgical life of their chosen communities. Liturgy infuses *Ancrene Wisse* most thoroughly in part I, the detailed instructions regarding the daily performance of hours and other devotions that have provided fruitful evidence regarding the text's sources, dating, and authorship. Yet what is perhaps most remarkable about part I is its frank acknowledgement of its

---

[11] Richard Pfaff, *The Liturgical Books of Anglo-Saxon England*, published as *Old English Newsletter Subsidia*, 21 (1995), 25. For a study of the manuscript see Raymond J. S. Grant, *Cambridge, Corpus Christi College 41: The Loricas and the Missal* (Amsterdam: Rodopi, 1979).

own liturgical identity, its explicit adequation of *Ancrene Wisse* with and even *as* liturgy. This becomes especially clear in the rubrications of the Corpus manuscript, generally considered the most authoritative and probably closest to the author's final version of the text. On these grounds alone, the manuscript's characterization of the *Wisse*'s first part must be taken very seriously: 'Her biginneth the earste boc of Vres 7 Vreisuns the god beoth to seggen' (Here begins the first book of hours and prayers which are good to say).[12] Written as the descriptive opening to part I, this sentence could be understood in several different ways: *Here begins the first book containing Hours and prayers which are good to say*; or, perhaps, *Here begins the first book, which concerns Hours and prayers which are good to say*; or even, perhaps, *Here begins the first Book of Hours, and of prayers that are good to say*. The idiosyncratic choice of phrasing here stands out in relation to the authorial designations of the other seven parts, some of them rubricated as actual headers, others as preparatory descriptives appearing in the final sentences of preceding parts. Part II, for example, begins, 'Her Biginneth þe other dale [part] of the heorte warde thurhe þe fif wittes'; at the beginning of seventh part we read, 'Nu me thuncheth we beoth icumen in to the seouethe dale that is al of luue'; and part VII leads into part VIII by promising to arrive 'scheortliche i the eahtuthe dale'. Only part I, that is, identifies itself as a 'book' rather than a 'dale' or 'part'. Yet the author goes out of his way in the introduction to stress how the eight parts should be considered in relation to one another: 'I divide this book into eight distinctions, which you call parts [*dalen*]. And each, without confusion, speaks all by itself of separate things, and yet each follows properly after the one before, and the latter is always tied to the former.'[13]

How, then, are we to understand the self-conscious gesture that initiates part I? This sentence, rubricated in red ink in the Corpus manuscript (distinguishing it from the seven other part headings in the remainder of the text, which are written in black), contains what I believe to be the first recorded appearance of the phrase 'Book of Hours' in the English vernacular. In this respect, the heading makes a kind of claim to the veritable invention of an English genre: Here begins the *first* Book of Hours. That *Ancrene Wisse*'s efforts in this respect were abortive can be appreciated if we read this phrase alongside a paragraph from a definitive survey of Books of Hours, published in a recent handbook on the medieval liturgy: 'Until around 1400, Books of Hours were entirely in Latin. Around this time, some French appeared in Horae made in France, but it was not a significant amount (calendars, some rubrics, and a few accessory prayers might be in the vernacular). The same can be said about the extent of English in Books of Hours

---

[12] J. R. R. Tolkien (ed.), *The English Text of the 'Ancrene Riwle'*, EETS, os 249 (London: Oxford University Press, 1976), 12.

[13] From the translation by Nicholas Watson and Anne Savage in *Anchoritic Spirituality: Ancrene Wisse and Associated Works* (New York: Paulist Press, 1991), 51.

made in England or made for use there … Books of Hours are books of Latin.'[14] The *Wisse* author, however, seems to be exploiting the generic fluidity of such books in this period, and doing so in order to make an argument about the cultural translation of liturgical devotion between clerical and lay ways of life—a process of devotional *translatio* also embodied in the Book of Hours itself. Bella Millett may then not be entirely correct to say that *Ancrene Wisse* part I 'is not itself a Book of Hours', particularly in a period when the Book of Hours had yet to emerge as a recognizable liturgical or paraliturgical genre (as Millett points out, the earliest extant insular Book of Hours was written in about 1240).[15] The *Wisse*'s relationship to the Book of Hours is more one of invention and formation than of reflection or consultation: the author is in a sense proposing part I *as* a 'boc of Vres', an interpolated liturgical book in the vernacular compiled as the opening part of another, larger 'boke' that is *Ancrene Wisse*. To put it another way, no comprehensible distinction may finally be drawn between *Ancrene Wisse* and liturgy.

Liturgy and lyricism

As these examples begin to suggest, previous theologizing habits of liturgical understanding have important bearing on the critical dispositions of the genres and forms of discrete literary objects, which so often seem to get categorized precisely in order to avoid too close an affiliation with liturgy. The Middle English religious lyric has been another victim of this tendency, often subsumed under the rubric of 'private devotion', a category that has served as an alibi for a hard scrutiny of this genre's liturgical complexities (and here readers may want to refer to Carol Symes's insightful comments on lyric and the manuscript matrix on pp. 7–22 of this volume). As Douglas Gray writes of the many surviving Middle English lyrics based directly on interpolated Latin liturgical texts, 'We do not really know what purpose these were intended to serve; probably they were to be used in preaching, possibly as private poems for devotion (the hymns of the liturgy itself were of course in Latin).'[16] But what exactly is 'the liturgy itself', particularly in the context of religious lyrics whose function is entirely a matter of speculation? The first *Deo gracias* poem from the Vernon manuscript seems a particularly likely candidate for some kind of liturgical designation, with its

---

[14] Roger Wieck, 'The Book of Hours', in Thomas J. Heffernan and E. Ann Matter (eds.), *The Liturgy of the Medieval Church* (Kalamazoo, MI: TEAMS, 2001), 475–6.

[15] Bella Millett, '*Ancrene Wisse* and the Book of Hours', in Denis Renevey and Christiana Whitehead (eds.), *Writing Religious Women: Female Spiritual and Textual Practices in Late Medieval England* (Lampeter: University of Wales Press, 2000), 26.

[16] Douglas Gray, *Themes and Images in the Medieval English Religious Lyric* (London: Routledge, 1972), 12.

explicit reference to its devotional role in 'the seruise' and the lyric fusion of the priest's and the poem's liturgical Latin in the refrain: 'I seigh a Clerk a book forth bringe, | that prikked was in mony a plas; | Faste he soughte what he scholde synge, | And al was *Deo gracias*'.[17] Also appearing in the Vernon manuscript is a lyric that Carleton Brown titled 'The Bird with Four Feathers', which employs a refrain on *Parce michi domine* (Job 7: 16) based on the incipit of the first lesson of matins in the Office for the Dead. To this catalogue of liturgical lyricism we might add the *Pety Job*, a fascinating mid-fifteenth-century work found in several manuscripts alongside 'The Bird with Four Feathers', with which it shares the liturgical refrain from Job. The readership of this penitential monologue, associated with Barking Abbey and Dartford Priory, was almost certainly in orders rather than lay, and, though the suggestion has been made (without evidence) that the poem was intended for public reading at extraliturgical occasions such as meals, I see no good reason to deny a specifically liturgical function for a poem that, after all, builds its devotional idiom and metrical framework around the Latin 'leccioun' it incorporates: 'I may nat from Thy respeccioun | By no way, Lorde, hyde now me; | Therfore seye I thys leccioun | Of *Parce michi, Domine!*'[18]

Some surviving vernacular lyrics, in fact, appear in narrative and codicological contexts that make their liturgical affiliations unambiguously clear. In his widely read *vita* of Thomas Becket, William of Canterbury relates a miracle story about the origin of a particular English antiphon. In this account, a Norfolk priest named Reginald sees in a vision a choir of monks singing the office. Upon the completion of the litany, the cantor requests that an antiphon be performed in honour of Becket; since Becket had not yet been canonized, however, it would not have been proper to honour him with an official Latin composition. The choir opts for an alternative language while maintaining the liturgical form of the antiphon: ' "Saltem," ait, "Anglice decantetur" ' ('At least', [the cantor] said, 'let it be sung in English'). William then transcribes the new English antiphon in its entirety:

> Haly thomas of heoueriche
> alle apostles eueliche,
> the Martyrs the vnderstonde
> godfullyche in heore honde.
> Selcuth dud vre dryhtin [wondrously did our lord],
> That he water wende [changed] to win;
> Thu ert help in engelaunde
> Vre stephne vnderstonde.

---

[17] Carleton Brown (ed.), *Deo Gracias I*, in *Religious Lyrics of the XIVth Century* (Oxford: Clarendon Press, 1924), 131.

[18] *Pety Job* stanza 32, ll. 381–4, in Susanna Greer Fein (ed.), *Moral Love Songs and Laments* (Kalamazoo, MI: TEAMS/Western Michigan University, 1998), p. 322.

> Thu ert froure [comfort] a-mong mon-kunne,
> Help vs nv of vre sunne. Euouae.[19]

The poem is explicitly labelled an *antiphona* in all of the sources, and in the Becket *vita* William immediately paraphrases the English antiphon in Latin. More remarkably, though, the Latin word *Euouae* appears at the end of the vernacular lyric in its best copy (Jesus 29) and following the Latin paraphrase in the Winchester manuscript of William's *vita*. In medieval liturgical practice, *Euouae* functions as a musical 'nonsense word' composed of the vowels of the final two words of the Doxology (... *seculorum. Amen.*), and it appears in office manuscripts at the conclusion of antiphons in order to make clear the reciting tone and *differentia* or melodic cadence of the succeeding psalm or canticle. The inclusion of an *Euouae*, in other words, represents a technical liturgicalism that strongly implies musical performance, and despite the visionary origins of the antiphon itself, the evidence suggests that this vernacular antiphon in honour of Becket was understood and even performed as an official liturgical remembrance of the martyr. In this respect, the story of Reginald evokes Bede's more famous account of Cædmon, the *rusticus* whose spontaneous performance of English lyric grants him entry into the liturgical community of Whitby.[20] Whatever the actual ritual function of these forms of vernacular lyricism, both stories powerfully locate the institutional origins of the English religious lyric in the liturgical ceremonial of insular monasticism.

Liturgical making

One way to begin approaching such liturgico-literary conundra is through the detheologizing stances taken by medieval liturgical practitioners themselves toward the ecclesiastical subcultures to which they belonged. Throughout the history of liturgical making in pre-modern England, in multiple languages and in a variety of institutional circumstances, some of the most prolific musical and literary makers exploited the resources of liturgical culture as occasions for flights of poetic innovation and even daring. In these cases, liturgy more often functions as provocation to new cultural production than a conservative hindrance to aesthetic and stylistic creativity, in no small part because of liturgy's own constant tendency toward expansion, dilation, and interpolation of new musical and textual materials into the fabric of ritual performance.

---

[19] From William of Canterbury, *Vita et passio S. Thomae*, discussed by Carleton Brown, *English Lyrics of the Thirteenth Century* (Oxford: Clarendon Press, 1932), on pp. 196–8 (the version cited here appears on p. 42).

[20] On the Cædmon story and liturgy, see my essay 'The Parable of Caedmon's *Hymn*', *Journal of English and German Philology*, 106 (2007).

The liturgical culture of Anglo-Saxon Winchester affords a particularly rich perspective on the formal interplay between literary and liturgical invention, beginning with the so-called Winchester Tropers, two books containing proper and common additions to chants of the mass and divine office. As its rhetorical designation implies, troping, a compositional practice that involved the addition and insertion of newly composed monophonic or polyphonic music within the existing corpus of plainchant, embodies a particularly strong predilection among liturgical communities for the artful expansion and dilation of even the most centrally authoritative ritual materials. In the Winchester Tropers, such expansion is carried out through a jarring process of parenthesis that often borders on hysterologia, a disruption of the syntax and *ordinatio* of established liturgical chants through the interpolation of newly composed materials. Thus, the simple, familiar, and quite ancient introit to the Christmas mass of the day becomes an occasion for a figurative display that doubles the word count of the original chant (in italics here): 'Quod prisco vates cecinerunt tempore sancti, cernitis impletum, psallentes dicite cuncti *puer natus est nobis* Daviticae stirpis genuit quem Virgo Maria *et filius datus est nobis* perdita restaurans et restaurata gubernans *cujus imperium super humerum ejus et vocabitur nomen ejus, magni consilii Angelus.*' (That of which, in ancient times, the holy prophets sang, you see fulfilled: proclaim it, all of you, with a psalm. *Unto us a Boy is born,* from the stock of David, whom the Virgin Mary bore, *and unto us a Son is given, redeeming those things that were lost, and governing those that have been redeemed,* whose government shall be upon his shoulder, and his name shall be called Angel of the Great Council.)[21]

The same liturgical subculture that gave us the Winchester Tropers produced the *Old English Benedictine Office*, a fascinating but under-studied text that intersperses newly composed vernacular verse among the Latin texts of the divine office.[22] The minor doxology at prime shares with the chants of the Winchester Tropers an interest in the performative glossing of the original liturgical chant—not with Latin, however, but with densely lyrical poetry in alliterative long lines:

> *Gloria patri*
> Sy The wuldor and lof wide geopenod
> Geond ealla Theode, Thanc and wylla
> Mægen and mildse and ealles modes lufu …

[21] Introit trope *Puer natus est*, ed. Alejandro Planchart, *The Repertory of Tropes at Winchester* (Princeton: Princeton University Press, 1977), ii. 301–2; trans. David Hiley, *Christmas in Royal Anglo-Saxon Winchester: 10th-century Chant from the Winchester Tropers* (Farnham: Herald AV Publications, 1992), 4. On the Winchester Tropers more generally, see Susan Rankin, 'Winchester Polyphony: The Early Theory and Practice of Organum', in Rankin and David Hiley (eds.), *Music in the Medieval English Liturgy* (Oxford: Oxford University Press, 1993), 58–99.

[22] Peter A. M. Clemoes, 'The Old English Benedictine Office, Corpus Christi College, Cambridge, MS 190, and the Relations between Ælfric and Wulfstan: A Reconsideration', *Anglia*, 78 (1960), 265–83; John Houghton, 'The *Old English Benedictine Office* and its Audience', *American Benedictine Review*, 45/4 (1994), 431–45.

Patri et filio et spiritui sancto
Thu eart frofra fæder and feorhhyrde,
Lifes latteow, leohtes wealdend ...
Sicut erat in principio

[*Glory to the Father*
To You be glory and praise, gratitude and devotion
Everywhere offered among all peoples,
Virtue and mercy and all the mind's lovingness ...
To the Father and to the Son and to the Holy Ghost.
You are the Father of all Solace and the Shepherd of the Soul,
Life's Leader, Light's Ruler ...
As it was in the beginning ...][23]

Even more than the Winchester tropes, this vernacular *dilatio* of a common office chant seems intended to bejewel the base liturgical text with the new, arguing for a fusion of the devotional diction of the Latin and the theological grammar of the vernacular. The deliberate repetition of *patri* in the second Latin line highlights the string of datives in the doxology—*Patri et filio et spiritui sancto*—that are then paralleled in the characteristically Anglo-Saxon appositive parataxis in the succeeding lines ('frofra fæder and feorhhyrde, | Lifes latteow, leohtes wealdend'). The vernacular functions here not simply to gloss or comment on the Latin, let alone to supplant its liturgical role, but rather to bring out its grammatical logic through juxtaposition with an alternative lyric idiom that is no less liturgical in its doxological style. Despite its categorization as a literary or poetic text, I would argue that the *Old English Benedictine Office* might be reconceived as a kind of vernacular troper, for there is no other genre from *c.*1000 Anglo-Saxon England that comes close to explaining either its form or its intricately complex treatment of the Latin text of the liturgy.

The actual practice of troping, or 'farsing' as it was sometimes termed, was but one of many forms of liturgical expansion in English use from the ninth century to the close of the Middle Ages, forms that also include the new composition of *prosulae*, sequences, and rhymed offices, polyphonic and rhythmic embellishments of the liturgy through *clausulae*, *contrafacta*, and motets, and many others.[24] Tropes, farses, *prosulae*, *contrafacta*, *clausulae*: the point worth emphasizing here is that many of the creative impulses that inspire vernacular literary innovation in the Middle Ages have strong roots in liturgical practice, which frequently drew on rhetorical and grammatical conventions of discursive embellishment in its approach

---

[23] *The Service of Prime from the Old English Benedictine Office*, ed. and trans. Bill Griffiths (Pinner: Anglo-Saxon Books, 1991), 6–9; the standard edition is James Ure (ed.), *The Benedictine Office: An Old English Text* (Edinburgh: Edinburgh University Press, 1957).

[24] On sequences and the theology of liturgical change, see Margot Fassler, *Gothic Song: Victorine Sequences and Augustinian Reform in Twelfth-Century Paris* (Cambridge: Cambridge University Press, 1993).

to and engagement with an inherited body of authoritative ritual matter.[25] In this sense, the literary history of pre-modern England might be envisioned as in part the product of a creative *habitus* or disposition that would remain fundamentally liturgical long after the demise of any specific liturgical genre or compositional technique.

Even liturgy's detractors could be articulately aware of its tendency toward aesthetic innovation, and the liturgically orthodox do not provide sole testimony to liturgy's voraciously expansive tendencies. Unlike the central figures involved in the Benedictine Reform around the year 1000, whose liturgical vernacularity was intended to supplement and enlarge rather than displace existing liturgical ceremony, Lollard writers of the Ricardian and Lancastrian eras sought to undermine the symbolic capital of liturgy by Englishing its most arcane and specialized vocabulary. In a series of treatises directed against elaborate liturgical performance, the Lollards sought to portray the culture of orthodox music-making as a wasteful spectacle of superfluous books, voices, and musics—a spectacle that resulted in the very destitution of the poor: 'For thei don not here sacrifices bi mekeness of herte and mornynge and compunccion for here synnes and the peplis, but with knackynge [improper singing] of newe song, as orgen or deschant and motetis of holouris [organum or discant or sluttish motets], and with worldly pride of costy vestymentis and othere ornementis bought with pore mennus goodis, and suffren hem perische for meschef and laten pore men have nakid sidis and ded wallis have grete plente of wast gold.'[26] This and similar passages from Wycliffite writings mark the first recorded English usages of organum, discant, and motet, liturgical forms that demanded a high level of musical skill from their often professional performers. Here the anonymous writer weds an inventive polemic against musical profligacy to a moving economic critique of liturgical waste, the gold that adorns 'dead walls' while poor men go unclothed with 'nakid sidis'. Yet, even as the Lollards object strenuously to the proliferation of musical innovation and excess in the liturgy, they themselves are forcing innovation in a vernacular unaccustomed to the specialized liturgical vocabulary they employ. After all, Lollard sermon collections and most copies of the Wycliffite Bible remain liturgically organized, their formal and imaginative structures as collections of texts regulated by ancient temporal frameworks enduring within even the most dissident Middle English textual communities. For all the passion invested in its promotion of a vernacular Bible, Lollardy rarely, if ever, pleads for an English liturgy.

---

[25] Léon Gautier, *Histoire de la poésie liturgique au Moyen Âge* (Paris: V. Palaré, 1886), marks the beginning of modern scholarly interest in liturgical poetics and the rhetoric of troping.

[26] *Of Prelates*, ch. 23; ed. Frederic D. Matthews, in *The English Works of Wyclif Hitherto Unprinted*, EETS, os 74 (London: Trübner, 1880), 91.

Liturgy and the limits of *latinitas*

What, finally, of liturgical Latin per se, the performed texts making up the Proper and the Common, the *sanctorale* and the *temporale*, that perpetually renewed cycle of song, prayer, festival, and spectacle that constitutes the proper object of liturgical study? The *Old English Benedictine Office* and William's antiphon share a close cousin in the poetry of John Skelton, the early sixteenth-century priest whose works feature a remarkable catalogue of liturgical vernacularity. Skelton's 'Phillip Sparrow' opens with a familiar incipit from the funeral liturgy put in antiphonal dialogue with a series of vernacular interrogatives and responses: '*Pla ce bo* | Who is there, who? | *Di le xi* | Dame Margery | *Fa, re, my, my* | Wherefore and why, why?'[27] Fragmenting these ubiquitous snatches of liturgical Latin into their constitutent syllables, the poem further announces their constructed artificiality by inserting a sequence of pitch syllables taken from the *ut-re-mi* solmization idiom of chant pedagogy: 'Fa re me', the first in a series of such sequences strung together across the poem's awkward stanzas and rhymed with both the English lament and the Latin liturgical snippets.

In this parodic death liturgy (as in the more extended satire of liturgical Latin in *Colyn Cloute*), Skelton deploys this species of Latinity as an externalized poetic resource rather than a predetermined theologizing solution. Skelton's adept manipulations of the liturgy recast in this sense myriad earlier attempts to absorb liturgical rhetoric and language into the idioms of literary English. 'Phillip Sparrow' makes explicit the adept macaronic (or mixed-language) toying with liturgical Latin that had become something of a literary impulse over the preceding century, from the moralizing evocations in *Piers Plowman* and *Mum and the Sothsegger* of the pedagogical discourse of 'solfe' to the rustic liturgical literacies imagined in the drama of Wakefield, Chester, and York. In the Chester 'Shepherds' play, the shepherds engage in a remarkable macaronic exchange following the performance of the major doxology, fragmenting the *Gloria in excelsis Deo* into English words and syllables that they then use to spice their own alliterative dialogue and folk song: 'Nay, on a *glor* and on *glay* and a *gly* | gurt Gabriel when he so so gloried. | When he sang, I might not be sorry. | Through my breast-bone bleating he bored.'[28] Although the late dates of some of these texts make such moments readable as Protestant anticlericalism, the irreverent and often bawdy appropriations of liturgy

[27] John Skelton, 'Phyllyp Sparowe', l. 106, in *The Complete English Poems*, ed. John Scattergood (Harmondsworth: Penguin, 1983), 71–2.

[28] From the modern-spelling edition by David Mills, *The Chester Mystery Cycle* (East Lansing, MI: Colleagues Press, 1992), 139–41.

in the mystery plays suggest less a predictable subversion of the clergy than an enduring effort to translate liturgical language into the domain of local knowledge and practice by enlisting its Latin syllables, phonemes, and syntax into the rhythms of English secular music and verse. Liturgical Latinity is in many cases a mode of practical Latinity, to adapt M. T. Clanchy's terms, often divorced from its specific performative function in religious ritual yet imbued with the institutional prestige derived from the official formulae of liturgical practice.[29]

The Book of Common Prayer and the fate of liturgical invention

These modes of formal, rhetorical, and institutional reciprocity between liturgical institution and literary vernacularity will be almost entirely obliterated by the writing and dissemination of the Book of Common Prayer. The introduction of a thoroughly vernacular liturgy in England was of course a radical step theologically that also had obvious implications for literary production over the next century. The Book of Common Prayer has always been regarded as a rare gem in the history of English, so much so that even Eamon Duffy, in casting it as a symbol of the Reformation's devastation of traditional religion, can describe in awe 'Cranmer's sombrely magnificent prose, read week by week, [which] entered and possessed [the people's] minds, and became the fabric of their prayer, the utterance of their most solemn and their most vulnerable moments' (*Stripping of the Altars*, 593). And early modernists are just beginning to appreciate the extent to which Cranmer's liturgical vernacular permeated the literature of Renaissance England, its religious idiom rivalling the Bible as a reserve of poetic symbols and literary themes.[30]

When viewed through a medieval lens, though, the triumph of the Book of Common Prayer signals not simply a new liturgical source for vernacular invention, but also, and I think much more significantly, a fundamentally new kind of social relationship between liturgical cultures and vernacular literature. One of the clearest adumbrations of Cranmer's utter rejection of the productive medieval symbiosis of literary writing and liturgical culture occurs in a slightly earlier work, the *Homily on Good Works*, one of the half-dozen or so in the 1547 homily series that can confidently be ascribed to the archbishop. The fundamental distinction underlying this homily is that between good works—those grounded in Scripture and faith, in the avoidance of idleness, in the living condemnation of idolatry—versus 'such workes as men have studied out of their owne braine, of

---

[29] M. T. Clanchy, *From Memory to Written Record: England 1066–1307* (Oxford: Blackwell, 1993), esp. 109–12.
[30] See Ramie Targoff, *Common Prayer* (Chicago: University of Chicago Press, 2001), and Judith Maltby, *Prayer Book and People in Early Modern England* (Cambridge: Cambridge University Press, 1998).

a blind zeale and devotion, without the word of God'. Although this is a familiar distinction as Cranmer articulates it, what is so striking about the homily is its argument concerning various forms of Christian 'work': good works promoted by the reformer are distinguished fundamentally from 'bad work', and specifically the medieval work of God, the *opus Dei*, the liturgical labour at the foundation of medieval religious life, yet which to Cranmer appears as 'innumerable superstitions that hath bene in strange apparel, in silence, in Dormitory, in Cloyster, in Chapter, in choise of meates, and drinkes, and in such like things'.[31]

In strictly historical terms, of course, Cranmer's polemic against liturgical institutions and their productions invokes the standard rhetoric of the Dissolution that resulted in the 'stripping of the altars' and 'bare ruined choirs' providing historians from David Knowles to Duffy with fittingly stark images of a revolutionary institutional ravishment. Yet the physical devastation of English monasteries and parish churches at the hands of Cromwell was the more spectacular counterpart of a literary removal project that reached to the heart of medieval modes of textual production. Consider, for example, Cranmer's words in the preface to the 1549 edition:

> But these many yeares passed this Godly and decent ordre of the auncient fathers, hath bee so altered, broken, and neglected, by planting in uncertein stories, Legendes, Respondes, Verses, vaine repeticions, Commemaracions, and Synodalles, that commonly when any boke of the Bible was began: before three or foure Chapiters were read out, all the rest were unread ...
>
> For this cause be cut of Anthemes, Respondes, Invitatories, and suche like thynges, as did breake the continuall course of the readyng of the scripture ...
>
> Furthermore by this ordre, the curates shal nede none other bookes for their publique service, but this boke and the Bible: by the meanes wherof, the people shall not be at so great charge for bookes, as in tyme past they have been.
>
> And where heretofore, there hath been great diversitie in saying and synging in churches within this realme: some folowyng Salsbury use, some Herford use, same the use of Bangor, some of Yorke, and some of Lincolne: Now from hencefurth, all the whole realme shall have but one use.

Cranmer's objection to the medieval liturgy derives not simply from its ceremonial diversity, but also, in my view, from its literariness: its superfluous libraries of books (graduals, antiphonals, breviaries, processionals, and so on); its myriad poetic genres and practices (stories, legends, verses, collects, antiphons, repetitions); and, more specifically, its rhetoric: its propensity to be broken up, to be 'planted' with the new—a propensity, of course, that goes all the way back to the Winchester Tropers and beyond. In Cranmer's prefaces we can track an implicit but almost obsessive policing of what I would call the literary *elocutiones* or styles of medieval

---

[31] The homily is cited here from the discussion in Diarmaid MacCulloch, *Thomas Cranmer* (New Haven: Yale University Press, 1996), 372 ff.

liturgy. *Amplificatio, abbreviatio, interpretatio, divisio, dilatio, occupatio*: all of these discrete rhetorical arts of division, contraction, expansion, delay, arrangement, and so on inspire Cranmer's polemic against the diverse liturgical cultures that had been practising them for a millennium. The Book of Common Prayer is itself nothing if not a rhetorical document, of course, but its rhetoric at least aims for a kind of stability that the medieval liturgy only rarely possessed. In the case of Cranmer, Reformation scholars and early modernists have been missing the forest for the trees—as indeed have many medievalists in their curious willingness to grant the Reformation a kind of historical monopoly on liturgical vernacularity. Thus James Simpson, in his powerful Oxford English Literary History volume, wrongly imputes to Cranmer the very origins of English prayer: 'In 1548 a commission presided over by him produced the first English prayer book, the Book of Common Prayer, which was formally instituted in 1549.'[32] As such characterizations of the Book of Common Prayer reveal, one of the most truly 'revolutionary' (Simpson's term) effects of Cranmer's liturgical industry was to erase the memory among even *modern* scholars of centuries of production of the 'English prayer book' and its many incarnations, whether in the Old English *Advent Lyrics*, the devotional lyric of the Vernon manuscript, the prayerful *dalen* of *Ancrene Wisse*, or the prayers in surviving English primers that provided thriving vernacular *contrafacta* of the Latin rites of Sarum from which Cranmer would poach, translate, abbreviate, and delete.[33]

In short, we have accepted the Reformation's thoroughgoing *translatio* of the liturgy as such a remarkable step forward for English literature and language that we have largely failed to see its constraining effects upon the poetic and rhetorical making within the liturgical cultures that gave rise to so much of early English literature. The diachronic lens of Anglo-Saxon and Middle English writing reveals the uniformity and finality of the Book of Common Prayer and its ilk, a monolith to which we might counterpose medieval liturgy not for its traditional and static character, but for its ability to sustain over centuries its own massive level of literary renewal, innovation, and growth. These were the same characteristics that allowed liturgical cultures to inspire and shape the bulk of the vernacular literature of medieval England, from the metrical hybridity of Cædmon's *Hymn* to the neologistic antiphony of *The Owl and the Nightingale*, from the liturgical rhythms and poetics of *Piers Plowman* to medieval English drama with its liturgical temporalities and its constant recreational use of liturgical Latin, from the liturgical regimen of the *Ancrene Wisse* to the lyric poems of the Benedictine monk John Lydgate.

[32] Simpson, *Reform and Cultural Revolution*, 570–1.

[33] On the liturgical affiliations of the Advent Lyrics (aka *Christ I*) from the Junius manuscript, see Susan Rankin, 'The Liturgical Background of the Old English Advent Lyrics: A Reappraisal', in *Learning and Literature in Anglo-Saxon England: Studies Presented to Peter Clemoes on the Occasion of his Sixty-Fifth Birthday* (Cambridge: Cambridge University Press, 1985), 317–40.

If this claim for the liturgical foundations of pre-modern English literature risks totalization, it does so with an awareness that many of our field's recent models of historical criticism have been grounded in the text of Chaucer, one of medieval England's least liturgical poets. This might seem a counterintuitive observation, of course, given the Prioress's appropriation of the Mass of the Holy Innocents to heighten the pathos of the clergeon's martyrdom, the Miller's parodic eroticizing of the divine office, and the many other appropriations of liturgical idioms in Chaucer's writings.[34] Yet if the Canterbury pilgrimage marks its progress with the rhythms of the liturgical year, the *Tales* themselves embody a profound disregard for the material cultures of liturgy. The Wife of Bath will always beat the other parish wives to the offering, but only to flirt and possibly seduce. Chaucer's continental urbanity masks a remarkable aesthetic bypassing of what was perhaps the most vital force sustaining vernacular writing in his epoch: the slow, patient accumulation of liturgical labour on behalf of remote things that grounds the literary culture of pre-Reformation England.

FURTHER READING

One aspect of medieval liturgy that often deters literary scholars from pursuing it in depth is its overwhelming organizational and textual complexity, which can make the transmission histories of works like *Piers Plowman* or the *Canterbury Tales* seem like a walk in the park. Liturgy does not form part of the standard training for graduate students in medieval literary studies in the way that it does for, say, musicologists, and it can take several months of hard work with handbooks, finding guides, charts, rubrics, editions, and so on before one begins to understand how the liturgy 'works' and to feel capable of getting around in the sources. The most helpful modern studies of and guides to medieval liturgy available in English include Cyrille Vogel's *Medieval Liturgy: An Introduction to the Sources*, rev. and trans. William G. Storey and Niels Krogh Rasmussen (Washington: Pastoral Press, 1986); Eric Palazzo, *A History of Liturgical Books from the Beginning to the Thirteenth Century*, trans. Madeleine Beaumont (Collegeville, MN: Liturgical Press, 1998); Margot Fassler and Rebecca Balzer (eds.), *The Divine Office in the Latin Middle Ages* (Oxford: Oxford University Press, 2000); John Harper, *The Forms and Orders of Western Liturgy from the Tenth to the Eighteenth Century: A Historical Introduction and Guide for Students and Musicians* (Oxford: Clarendon Press, 1991); Thomas J. Heffernan and E. Ann Matter (eds.), *The Liturgy of the Medieval Church* (Kalamazoo: Medieval Institute Publications, Western Michigan University, 2001); and Andrew Hughes, *Medieval Manuscripts for Mass and Office: A Guide to their Organization and Terminology* (Toronto: University of Toronto Press, 1982). For a helpful critique of the category of 'private devotion', see Susan Boynton, 'Prayer and Liturgical Performance in Eleventh- and Twelfth-Century Monastic Psalters', in Roy Hammerling (ed.), *A History of*

---

[34] Compare the argument made in Beverly Boyd's older study *Chaucer and the Liturgy* (Philadelphia: Dorrance, 1967).

Prayer, i: *From the Early Church to the Reformation* (Leiden: Brill, 2006). A wonderful tool for teaching the mechanics of the divine office is a film produced by Margot Fassler and the Yale Institute of Sacred Music, *Work and Pray: Living the Psalms with the Nuns of Regina Laudis*.

Much of the most innovative scholarship on medieval liturgy focuses on the liturgical cultures of particular institutions while laying out provocative methodologies at the intersections of musicology, literary criticism, performance studies, religious studies, codicology, and cultural and institutional history. See Anne Walters Robertson, *The Service-Books of the Royal Abbey of Saint-Denis: Images of Ritual and Music in the Middle Ages* (Oxford: Clarendon Press, 1991); Susan Boynton, *Shaping a Monastic Identity: Liturgy and History at the Imperial Abbey of Farfa, 1000–1125* (Ithaca, NY: Cornell University Press, 2006); and Margot Fassler, *Making History: The Virgin of Chartres and the Liturgical Framework of Time* (New Haven: Yale University Press, 2007). On liturgical commentary and liturgical drama, see the recent article by Donnalee Dox, 'The Eyes of the Body and the Veil of Faith', *Theatre Journal*, 56/1 (2004), 29–45.

The study of English liturgy is a particularly active subfield these days, with long-term projects in the works by Margot Fassler and Richard Pfaff on the history and historiography of insular liturgical culture; Eamon Duffy's *The Stripping of the Altars* (n. 1 above), which addresses with immense learning the liturgical lives of the late medieval English laity; and Katherine Zieman's much-anticipated *Reading and Singing: Literacy, Liturgy, and Literature in Late Medieval England* (forthcoming from University of Pennsylvania Press), which promises a fundamental reassessment of the role of liturgical and devotional practice in relation to literacy, modes of literary representation, and 'voice'. Recent work on Anglo-Saxon liturgy that touches in particular on issues of vernacularity includes M. Bradford Bedingfield, *The Dramatic Liturgy of Anglo-Saxon England* (Woodbridge: Boydell, 2002); several of the essays collected in Bedingfield and Helen Gittos (eds.), *The Liturgy of the Late Anglo-Saxon Church* (London: Boydell and Brewer, 2005); Gittos, 'Is there Any Evidence for the Liturgy of Parish Churches in Late Anglo-Saxon England? The Red Book of Darley and the Status of Old English', in Francesca Tinti (ed.), *Pastoral Care in Late Anglo-Saxon England* (Woodbridge: Boydell Press, 2005); Christopher A. Jones, 'The Book of the Liturgy in Anglo-Saxon England', *Speculum* 73 (1998): 659–702; and my own essay, 'The Parable of Caedmon's *Hymn*: Liturgical Invention and Literary Tradition', *Journal of English and Germanic Philology*, 106 (2007). Provocative recent work on the Book of Common Prayer includes Ramie Targoff, *Common Prayer: The Language of Public Devotion in Early Modern England* (Chicago: University of Chicago Press, 2001) and Judith Maltby, *Prayer Book and People in Early Modern England* (Cambridge: Cambridge University Press, 1998).

CHAPTER 20

VISION, IMAGE, TEXT

JESSICA BRANTLEY

Late medieval English reading depends on seeing. This may seem an extraordinary claim to make for an era in which iconoclastic controversies regularly set the enticements of the image against the purity of the text, and in which, following Gregory the Great, pictures were often considered merely 'books for the illiterate'.[1] It may also seem odd in material terms, since English manuscripts are less often and less lavishly illustrated than continental ones; to understand Chaucer's visual imagination one must frequently turn to illustrated copies of his sources: Boccaccio or Jean de Meun.[2] But even when text and image are ostensibly antagonistic, the two modes of representation depend closely upon each other for their sense of themselves: literary texts are defined by their sophisticated uses of 'imagery', and semioticians 'read' images as closely as they read words. As W. J. T. Mitchell has

For insightful early readings of this essay, I would like to thank Thomas Fulton, Amy Hungerford, Pericles Lewis, Nicholas Perkins, and Elliott Visconsi.

[1] Gregory wrote: 'What Scripture is to the educated, images are to the ignorant, who see through them what they must accept; they read in them what they cannot read in books' (trans. Caecilia Davis-Weyer, *Early Medieval Art, 300–1150: Sources and Documents* (Toronto: University of Toronto Press, 1986), 48). This dictum is not to be understood simplistically, however: see Herbert L. Kessler, 'Pictorial Narrative and Church Mission in Sixth-Century Gaul', in Herbert L. Kessler and Marianna Shreve Simpson (eds.), *Pictorial Narrative in Antiquity and the Middle Ages*, Studies in the History of Art 16 (Washington: National Gallery of Art, 1985) 75–91; Lawrence G. Duggan, 'Was Art Really the "Book of the Illiterate"?', *Word & Image*, 5 (1989), 227–51; and Celia M. Chazelle, 'Pictures, Books, and the Illiterate: Pope Gregory I's Letters to Serenus of Marseilles', *Word & Image*, 6 (1990), 138–53. For Lollard attitudes towards Gregory's dictum and towards images generally, see W. R. Jones, 'Lollards and Images: The Defense of Religious Art in Later Medieval England', *Journal of the History of Ideas*, 34 (1973), 27–50; Margaret Aston, *Lollards and Reformers: Images and Literacy in Late Medieval Religion* (London: Hambledon Press, 1984); and Ann Eljenholm Nichols, 'Books-for-Laymen: The Demise of a Commonplace', *Church History*, 56 (1987), 457–73.

[2] For this observation, see John Fleming, 'Chaucer and the Visual Arts of his Time', in Donald M. Rose (ed.), *New Perspectives in Chaucer Criticism* (Norman, OK: Pilgrim Books, 1981), 121–36, at 127; also V. A. Kolve, 'Chaucer and the Visual Arts', in Derek Brewer (ed.), *Writers and their Background: Geoffrey Chaucer* (London: Bell & Sons, 1974), 290–320; and Kolve, *Chaucer and the Imagery of Narrative* (Stanford, CA: Stanford University Press, 1984).

argued for more modern periods, every seemingly discrete artwork should really be considered an 'imagetext', since the arts never achieve the separation towards which they sometimes aspire, and textuality is inescapably mixed up with visuality.[3] In the Middle Ages, examples of such imagetexts include the narrative images that proliferate in wall painting and manuscript illumination—sequences of pictures that tell stories—or the many emblematic images that summon up familiar histories, and depend for their interpretation upon the viewers' knowledge of associated texts. They also include the many medieval literary works that organize themselves around visionary experience—literary works that are the subject of this essay.

Narratives of vision constitute one of the most persistent and popular genres of the Middle Ages, in part because of their malleability: courtly fantasies, spiritual revelations, prophetic allegories, and philosophical meditations all commonly take the form of dreams. From a late antique dialogue such as Boethius' *Consolation of Philosophy* to John Skelton's political satire *The Bouge of Court*, published in 1499, the wide appeal of the visionary genre spans the medieval centuries. Texts as different in their subjects and aims as the Old English *Dream of the Rood* and the thirteenth-century French *Roman de la Rose* cast themselves fundamentally in the shared form of a dream. The great fourteenth-century alliterative poems *Piers Plowman* and *Pearl* can be counted among this diverse company, along with some of Chaucer's earliest work—the *Book of the Duchess*, the *House of Fame*, and the *Parliament of Fowls*, as well as the Prologue to the *Legend of Good Women*. English poets building upon the Ricardian legacy in the fifteenth century composed a number of dream-visions that follow in this courtly tradition, and at the same time both Julian of Norwich and Margery Kempe wrote prose accounts of their waking revelations that draw on literary traditions of spiritual seeing. The range of visionary texts is so vast that disparate examples are rarely drawn together in modern discussions. But whether early or late, whether spiritual or courtly, whether alliterative or 'Chaucerian' verse—or, indeed, prose—these texts that record acts of looking constitute a distinct medieval literary genre and a distinctly medieval way of knowing.[4]

---

[3] 'Beyond Comparison: Picture, Text, and Method', in *Picture-Theory: Essays on Verbal and Visual Representation* (Chicago: University of Chicago Press, 1994), 83–107; esp. 94–107. See also *Iconology: Image, Text, Iconology* (Chicago: University of Chicago Press, 1986); and 'Spatial Form in Literature: Toward a General Theory', in W. J. T. Mitchell (ed.), *The Language of Images* (Chicago: University of Chicago Press, 1980), 271–99.

[4] For varying views on whether dream-vision can properly be called a medieval genre, see A. C. Spearing, *Medieval Dream-Poetry* (Cambridge: Cambridge University Press, 1976), 1–6; and Steven F. Kruger, *Dreaming in the Middle Ages* (Cambridge: Cambridge University Press, 1992), 1–7. Barbara Newman has recently argued for a necessary association between 'real' visions and 'literary' ones; see *God and the Goddesses: Vision, Poetry, and Belief in the Middle Ages* (Philadelphia: University of Pennsylvania Press, 2003) 24–35; and 'What Did It Mean to Say "I Saw"? The Clash between Theory and Practice in Medieval Visionary Culture', *Speculum*, 80 (2005), 1–43.

For these wide-ranging works address some basic questions of representation and meaning in a common way. Visionary imagetexts insist upon an intimate relation between seeing and reading, linking words with pictures in closely interdependent systems of signification.[5] Although visionary writing in English is no more likely than other medieval genres to appear in illustrated manuscripts, these texts rely crucially upon the verbal representation of visual experience to suggest the possibility of a special kind of wisdom. Both reading and seeing are venerable metaphors for perception; one 'reads' situations and develops 'insight'.[6] So if the iconographic is basic to the experience of reading and writing medieval visions, their conflation of representational modes raises questions of right understanding more directly than other genres generally do. In relating text to image so closely, the literary vision explicitly places problems of interpretation in the foreground of the narrative. The dream-vision asks whether the seeing eye is trustworthy, or the speaking voice, and dramatizes a fundamental uncertainty about where any knowledge comes from, and whether any source is reliable. What is real and what fiction? What is true and what false? Who should decide? And on what basis? These metafictional questions are raised by the interpretative dilemma most elemental to the visionary genre: how do dream-narrators read what they see? The answer is rarely clear, and the openness of the visionary hermeneutic explicitly represented in the text stages readerly engagement with the problems it presents, forcing every reader to confront those problems directly, and individually. The critical puzzles that arise from the interpretation of visionary images throw into relief the problems that arise from the interpretation of the words in which they are conveyed. How securely, and by what process, do things shown lead to things known?

Reading pictures, seeing words

The genre of visionary writing can be defined most broadly as a personal narration of a remarkable sight. Whether the narrator falls asleep formally by literary convention, or experiences a waking revelation presented as true, visionary texts are structured by a sequence of images: it is a constitutive convention that the dreamer's verbal report emerges from the ravishment of his visual senses, from an overpowering experience of seeing that demands description. In the opening of *Piers Plowman*,

[5] For an influential analysis of these connections in twelfth- and thirteenth-century manuscript illumination from an art historical point of view, see Michael Camille, 'Seeing and Reading: Some Visual Implications of Medieval Literacy & Illiteracy', *Art History*, 8 (1985), 26–49.

[6] Like its modern equivalent, the Middle English verb 'reden' (to read) can have a number of metaphorical meanings, including 'read with understanding', 'learn by reading', 'teach', 'interpret', and 'perceive'. Similarly, 'sen' (to see) can mean 'discover', 'perceive', and 'consider'. *Middle English Dictionary*, s.v. 'reden', v. 1, and 'sen', v. 1.

for example, a compelling bodily sight leads Will to a series of equally iconic dream-images:

> And as I lay and lenede and loked on the watres,
> I slombred into a slepyng, it sweyed so murye.
> Thanne gan (me) to meten a merveillous swevene [dream]—
> That I was in a wildernesse, wiste I nevere where.
> As I biheeld into the eest an heigh to the sonne,
> I seigh a tour on a toft trieliche ymaked,
> A deep dale bynethe, a dongeon thereinne,
> With depe diches and derke and dredfulle of sighte.[7]

The vision that so overwhelms the dream-narrator typically includes an other-worldly geography populated by allegorical figures—whether it is Langland's 'fair feeld ful of folk', a courtly garden inhabited by lovers (as in the *Roman de la Rose*) or purgatorial fires burning with sinners (as in Guillaume de Deguileville's *Pilgrimage of the Soul*). The allegorical elements of both landscape and population are marked legibly by their visible form, for allegory itself (literally *other-speaking*) can be understood as a mode of writing that engages representational modes other than itself, and that depends more often than not upon visual signs.[8] Whether the allegorical figures envisioned are formal personifications, such as Dame Nature from Alain de Lille's *Complaint of Nature*, or simply 'wondirful examples', such as the lord and the servant that God reveals to Julian of Norwich 'gostly in bodily liknes', merely seeing them is a vital way of apprehending their significance.

Moreover, the narrator's visionary landscape is often filled with actual artefacts: *ecphrasis*—the literary trope of describing an art object—is a crucial element of many dream-visions. In ecphrastic set-pieces, the dreamer-narrator dwells in extensive visual detail on material objects such as gates, temples, buildings, or tapestries. In Chaucer's *House of Fame*, for example, the dreamer recounts his sight of a temple of Venus,

> In which ther were moo ymages
> Of gold, stondynge in sondry stages,
> And moo ryche tabernacles,
> And with perre moo pynacles,

---

[7] William Langland, *The Vision of Piers Plowman: A Critical Edition of the B-Text Based on Trinity College Cambridge MS B.15.17*, ed. A. V. C. Schmidt (London: Everyman, 1995), Prol. 9–16. Subsequent quotation of Langland will be from this edition.

[8] For the dependence of allegory as a mode upon visual experience, see, e.g., Rosamind Tuve, *Allegorical Imagery: Some Mediaeval Books and their Posterity* (Princeton: Princeton University Press, 1966). It is one of the paradoxes of Spenser's *Faerie Queene* that a poem with such iconoclastic politics should take the form of an allegory, relying on a sumptuous visionary narrative surface and rich correspondences with the emblem tradition.

> And moo curiouse portreytures,
> And queynte maner of figures
> Of olde werk, than I saugh ever.[9]

Interestingly enough, however, some of the 'curiouse portreytures' and 'olde werk' described in words turn out to represent texts—specifically here Virgil's *Aeneid*. As the dreamer reports:

> But as I romed up and doun,
> I fond that on a wal ther was
> Thus writen, on a table of bras:
> 'I wol now synge, yif I kan,
> The armes and also the man ... '
>
> (ll. 140–4)

Following these engraved words, a series of pictures the dreamer unambiguously says he 'saw' represent Aeneas' adventures from the fall of Troy to the founding of Rome. In homage to the influential ecphrases in the *Aeneid* itself, the pictorial narrative of Virgil's epic occupies all of book I of Chaucer's poem.[10] In the *Book of the Duchess*, Chaucer's dreamer sees 'wyndowes wel yglased' not only with the story of Troy, but also with the 'text and glose' of that great high-medieval dream-poem, the *Roman de la Rose* (ll. 323, 333). Chaucer's suggestion that his dreamers see inscriptions, as well as narrative pictures, concretizes the close links between seeing and reading in these poems. Whether images generate texts in descriptive ecphrasis, or texts generate images in this sort of intertextual visualization, oscillations between word and picture provide the mechanism through which these imagetexts work.

As these examples show, even though the defining feature of visionary writing is the reported experience of visual images, very often those images themselves depend upon the productive power of the words that lie behind them. Even beyond the direct textuality of ecphrastic conventions, a dreamer's 'vision' is usually composed of both sights and sounds, for the figures and guides he encounters typically speak to him, making the vision also a colloquy, and the narration of seeing also inevitably a reporting of speech. From Lady Philosophy's ministrations to Boethius, to the speaking cross in the *Dream of the Rood*, what the dreamer 'sees' is very often spoken language. The first-person account of both 'what I saw' and 'what I heard' implies significant connections in visionary writing between that seeing and that hearing. What is more, many dream-visions emerge from a concrete text, in the form of the material book the dreamer brings to bed as he struggles to fall asleep. In Chaucer's *Book of the Duchess*, for example, the dreamer reads the 'romaunce'

---

[9] *The Riverside Chaucer*, ed. Larry D. Benson (Boston: Houghton-Mifflin, 1987), ll. 121–7. Subsequent quotation of Chaucer is taken from this edition.

[10] The most direct allusion is to the murals Aeneas sees in Dido's Temple of Juno (book I). For a study of the importance of ecphrasis throughout Virgil's poem, see Michael C. J. Putnam, *Virgil's Epic Designs: Ekphrasis in the* Aeneid (New Haven: Yale University Press, 1998).

of Ceyx and Alciyone 'to rede and drive the night away' (ll. 48, 49). In a neat bit of visionary intertextuality, the dreamer of the *Parliament of Fowls* reads one of the touchstone texts of medieval dream-theory—Macrobius' commentary on the dream of Scipio—and the dreamer of the *Kingis Quair* reads Boethius' popular *Consolation of Philosophy* for the same purpose. Each text in one way or another produces the vision that follows, for the book that enables the narrator to fall asleep is a necessary precondition for his dream.

Most clearly, of course, the images of the dream-vision ultimately produce a text in the form of the visionary narration itself, the poem that we read—an etiology of visionary texts that is frequently given in their concluding words. Once the landscapes and artefacts of his vision are described in imagistic terms, the dreamer awakes and the whole experience becomes a book. The dreamer of the *Book of the Duchess* connects this process of textual transmission, however, directly to the Ovidian story that inspired his dream. The poem ends:

> Therwyth I awook myselve,
> And fond me lyinge in my bed;
> And the book that I hadde red,
> Of Alcione and Seys the kyng,
> And of the goddes of slepyng,
> I fond hyt in myn hond ful even.
> Thoghte I, 'Thys is so queynt a sweven
> That I wol, be processe of tyme,
> Fonde [attempt] to put this sweven in ryme
> As I kan best, and that anoon.'
> This was my sweven; now hit ys doon.   (ll. 1324–34)

Thus the book that caused the dream—the 'romaunce' of 'Alcione and Seys the king'—also obliquely prompts the poem that comes from it; as this dreamer awakes to find the book in his hand, he is inspired to put his own 'sweven' into rhyme. The convoluted connections in a passage such as this raise interesting interpretative questions: how do texts produce images, and images texts? How does bedside reading relate to a subsequent dream? And how does the older text, or the dream itself, relate to the new poem in which it is set down? Chaucer's poem relates intertextually to Ovid's, but not through any direct connection; instead, the indeterminate mechanism of the vision asserts a relationship without specifying exactly what it might be. Medieval dream-poems are texts about visions, but are also just as clearly visions about texts.

Varieties of visionary writing that do not follow these conventions of courtly dreams depend just as obviously upon the self-conscious mixing of textual and visual forms of representation. In *Piers Plowman*, as we have seen, Langland's Will wanders in an allegorical landscape structured not as an aristocrat's garden, but instead as a devotional polity through which he hopes he can come to understand what it means to 'Do-Wel'. Stemming from sources as fundamental to the Christian imagination as the biblical book of Revelation, and the apocryphal apocalypses of Saints Peter and Paul, the early visions that influenced the late medieval vogue for the genre tended to have spiritual dimensions. The related genre of voyages to the underworld has an epic inheritance, of course, but it also engages early Christian hagiographic texts, such as the *Voyage of St Brendan* or *The Voyage of St Patrick*, and might be understood to culminate in the *Divine Comedy*. Christian visions drew also upon the ancient philosophical traditions that informed (for example) Boethius' *Consolation*, or Macrobius' commentary on the dream of Scipio. Among later English texts, *Pearl* borrows from these visions and voyages of spiritual and philosophical revelation, as the dreamer attempts to cross over to the heavenly Jerusalem to join his saintly guide—even though the poem breaks off with the failure of that attempt. Women's visions take a particularly prominent place in this tradition of spiritual seeing; both Julian of Norwich and Margery Kempe produced visionary writings in English that constitute not so much courtly allegory as mystical autobiography. Religious visions are different from wholly literary ones in some ways: they are more likely to be in prose, to employ third-person reporting, to make claims for their authenticity that go beyond the truths of fiction. Nevertheless, both use the combination of image with text in similar ways to explore questions of representation and interpretation, investigating specifically how visionary experience can lead to sure knowledge.

Julian of Norwich, for example, describes her revelations of 1373 as a kind of hybrid imagetext, asserting:

> Alle this blessyd techyng of oure lorde god was shewde by thre partys, that is to sey by bodely syght, and by worde formyd in myne vnderstondyng, and by gostely syghte. For the bodely syghte, I haue seyde as I sawe, as truly as I can. And for the words, I haue seyde them ryght as oure lorde shewde them me. And for the gostely syghte, I haue seyde sum dele, but I may nevyr fulle telle it; and therfore of this gostely syght I am steryd to sey more, as god wylle geue me grace.[11]

In this passage from the long version of her text, Julian describes three ways of knowing God's will: by physical sight, by intuiting language, and by 'gostely' sight. Each one of these 'partys' combines image with text in one way or another. Julian expresses a hope and an expectation that bodily visions can be 'seyde' truthfully—that is, that they can be related verbally. And, in a reversal of this text/image relation, the 'worde formyd in her vnderstondyng' is in fact 'shewde' to her by the Lord. Spiritual sight is the closest to inexpressible, but precisely because of the very difficulty of translating divine image into human words, the visionary is 'steryd' to keep trying. The fundamental incommensurability of vision and language is precisely what drives the creation of Julian's imagetext.

---

[11] Julian of Norwich, *A Book of Showings*, ed. Edmund Colledge and James Walsh, 2 vols. (Toronto: Pontifical Institute of Mediaeval Studies, 1978), II. 666. Subsequent quotation of Julian of Norwich is taken from this edition.

Not only do devotional visions explore a close relation between words and images, but, again like courtly dreams, they stage the complex interaction between waking and visionary worlds. In Julian's *Showings*, as in the opening of *Piers Plowman*, material visions lead to ephemeral ones—'bodely syght' guides the visionary towards 'gostely syghte'. The way in which Julian's spiritual revelations derive from physical visions is clear in her account of the first one, which comes in the midst of a great, seemingly terminal, illness:

> My curate was sent for to be at my ending, and before he cam I had set vp my eyen and might not speake. He set the crosse before my face, and sayd: I haue brought the image of thy saviour; looke ther vpon and comfort thee ther with. My thought I was well, for my eyen was sett vpright into heauen, where I trusted to come by the mercie of god; but neuertheles I ascentyd to sett my eyen in the face of the crucyfixe, if I might, and so I dide, for my thought I might longar dure to looke even forth then right vp. After this my sight began to feyle. It waxid as darke about me in the chamber as if it had ben nyght, saue in the image of the crosse, wher in held a comon light; and I wiste not how. All that was beseid the crosse was oglye and ferfull to me as it had ben much occupied with fiendes.
>
> After this the over part of my bodie began to die so farforth that [to the extent that] vnneth [scarcely] I had anie feeling. My most payne was shortnes of breth and faielyng of life. Then went I verily to haue passed. And in this sodenly all my paine was taken from me, and I was as hole, and namely in the over parte of my bodie, as ever I was befor. I merveiled of this sodeyn change, for my thought that it was a previe [private] working of god, and not of kynd [nature]; and yet by feeling of this ease I trusted never the more to haue liued.   (II. 290–2)

Julian's curate offers her a crucifix, which she initially dismisses: she has been looking 'vpright into heauen', and suspects that she has bypassed bodily sights for eternal ones. Accepting that looking at the crucifix might be a simpler spiritual exercise, however, she lowers her eyes—punning, perhaps, on the similarity between 'ascentyd' ('assented') and 'ascendyd' (ascended)—whereupon her spiritual vision begins with a kind of devotional ecphrasis.[12] Everything except the cross fades away, or becomes 'oglye', like the 'fiendes' that assail Christ in medieval iconography, but the artefact itself glows with a 'comon light'.[13] At this, Julian is suddenly relieved of her pain through a supernatural agency. She knows that the miracle—'a previe working of god, and not of kynd'—nonetheless comes from the sight of a human artefact, the crucifix.

Julian's initial refusal of the crucifix is unsurprising, for late medieval contemplatives such as the author of the *Cloud of Unknowing* aspired to an absolutely imageless devotion, in which only novices must rely on physical sights, and more advanced spiritual athletes can achieve a higher understanding through immaterial ones. This kind of division mirrors the traditional iconoclastic preference for the

---

[12] I am grateful to Nicholas Perkins for pointing out the pun.
[13] For the comparison to crucifixion iconography see *A Book of Showings*, ed. College and Walsh, I. 209 n. 37.

disembodied word over the corporeal image. Yet, as Julian's story finally shows, the two cannot be so easily separated; earthly images often aid a would-be visionary to achieve a glimpse of the divine, and most spiritual visions are not so categorical in their denial of material spectacles.[14] The Old English *Dream of the Rood*, for example, (which is explicitly a dream dreamt 'to midre niht', or 'in the middle of the night'), centres on a speaking artefact, the glorious cross ('sigebeam', literally 'victory beam') that betokens Christian redemption. The inscription of the rood's words on the Ruthwell Cross asserts concretely the link between mystical vision and tangible object that the poem implies. [15] Equally material are not only Julian's crucifix, but her great 'homely' devotional images of the water dripping from the eaves of a roof, or the numerous scales on a fish, or the insignificance of a hazelnut. As Nicholas Watson has argued, the *Cloud*-author himself is dependent on such visions, in his treatise's 'self-deconstructing attempt to undo the carnality of the language in which it is written, devoting an entire chapter to the meaning of the word "up", and sketching satiric pictures of "fleshly" contemplatives'.[16] Texts such as the *Cloud* that ostensibly advocate imageless devotion nevertheless rely on imagining images to express an ineffable experience of the divine—even the act of pushing out worldly visions inscribes them powerfully upon a reader's mind. Despite the spiritual hierarchies that such intellectualizing texts proclaim, late medieval affective piety depended upon the senses to lead the devout closer to God, and the sense of sight was primary among them.

A painted image, in fact, can show more clearly than any text the ways in which visionary devotion joins the material and the immaterial, touchable images with ethereal words (see Fig. 6). This late thirteenth-century manuscript illumination prefacing the French *Trois estaz de bones ames* enshrines many layers of visualization through prayer, and serves as a diagram to show how spiritual vision might be achieved.[17] In the first quadrant, a nun prays before her Dominican adviser, an earthly authority who supervises her spiritual progress. That progress begins with speech,

[14] Jeffrey F. Hamburger, 'Seeing and Believing: The Suspicion of Sight and the Authentication of Vision in Late Medieval Art', in Alessandro Nova and Klaus Krüger (eds.), *Imagination und Wirklichkeit: Zum verhältnis von mentalen und realen Bilder in der Kunst der frühen Neuzeit* (Mainz: Philipp von Zabern, 2000), 47–70; Michael Camille, *The Gothic Idol* (Cambridge: Cambridge University Press, 1989).

[15] For ways in which the prosopopoeic monument engages visionary experience, see Éamonn Ó Carragáin, *Ritual and the Rood: Liturgical Images and the Old English Poems of the Dream of the Rood Tradition* (London: British Library, 2005).

[16] See Watson's discussion of 'mysticism' as it relates to 'vernacular theology' in David Wallace (ed.), *The Cambridge History of Medieval English Literature* (Cambridge: Cambridge University Press, 1999), 552.

[17] The manuscript is London, British Library, MS Yates-Thompson 11 (Add. 39843), fo. 29[r]. For discussion of this image in particular, see Jeffrey F. Hamburger, 'The Visual and the Visionary: The Image in Late Medieval Monastic Devotions', in his *The Visual and the Visionary: Art and Female Spirituality in Late Medieval Germany* (New York: Zone Books, 1998), 111–48, at 131–4; and Michael Camille, ' "Him whom you have ardently desired you may see": Cistercian Exegesis and the Prefatory

Figure 6 Four stages of spiritual vision. (London, British Library MS Yates-Thompson 11 [Additional 39843], fo. 29ʳ; by permission of the British Library)

as a supervising angel hints; his text-scroll reads 'Si uis delere tua crimina dic miserere' ('If you want to erase your sins, say "have mercy"'). Then, the angel directs the supplicant towards a material image situated on an altar, represented in the pages of this manuscript as an image of an image, a physical object depicting the Coronation of the Virgin. A process that begins with verbal prayer continues with silent gazing at a devotional artefact. In the next stage, the nun prostrates herself in front of a speaking vision of a less material sort: Christ leaning down from a penumbra of heavenly clouds to fill a chalice set upon the altar. The angel holds the cross, making clear how this eucharistic vision is to be understood, and Christ speaks to the nun through another text-scroll, as if to emphasize the intimacy of the occasion. He, too, calls for *looking* to form a part of her devotions: 'Pro vita populi respice quanta tuli' (See how much I bore for the life of the people'). These visions take place in the sacred liturgical space of the church, but they are not limited to that earthly space; after the initial scene, no priest is necessary to oversee this nun's eucharistic devotion, and what she sees in the church transcends its earthly space. In the final image of this series, the Trinity manifests itself in an immaterial vision of stupendous power, one that hovers over the jewel-encrusted altar without resting on it, breaking the architectural boundaries that delimited even the previous vision. Heavenly clouds with sun and moon even venture into the woman's human space, showing the power of meditation upon physical objects to provide her with access to divine territory. Word has become flesh—or image—in this final ecstatic experience, as the text-scroll proclaims 'Pater uerbum spiritus sanctus hii tres unum sunt' ('Father, word, holy spirit: these three are one'). The series of four images shows plainly the utility of material images in a teleology that nonetheless concludes with supernatural ones. It also shows the increasingly close interaction of word and image—for earthly speech and the contemplation of physical objects prompt verbal as well as visual communication with the divine—as a crucial indicator of success in approaching God.

Seeing and writing, seeing and reading

Visionary writing depends on seeing—for very often visions prompt texts, whether literary accounts of dreams or testimonials to words exchanged with God. But in this body of texts seeing is also connected to reading, for one consequence of this intertwining of representational modes is that the status of interpretation itself becomes uncertain. The dreamer of the *Parliament of Fowls*, for example, retreats from his vision into a dogged textuality—but it is not his own composition to which he turns. At the completion of the birds' roundel, he wakes from his dream and begins vigorously to *read* the written word:

Pictures in a French Apocalypse', in Meredith P. Lillich (ed.), *Studies in Cistercian Art and Architecture* vol. iii (Kalamazoo, MI: Cistercian Publications, 1987), 137–60.

> And with the shoutyng, whan the song was do
> That foules maden at here flyght awey,
> I wok, and othere bokes tok me to,
> To reede upon, and yit I rede alwey.
> I hope, ywis, to rede so som day
> That I shal mete som thyng for to fare
> The bet, and thus to rede I nyl nat spare.   (ll. 693–9)

The deliberate and immediate movement here from vision to text is striking: this dreamer instantly begins to 'rede alwey' when he wakes, hoping that texts will give him the answers he (evidently) has not found in his vision of the birds' convocation. The 'othere bokes' he finds to occupy him stand in for the text of the dream he might otherwise be deciphering—and as the narrator moves on to other kinds of discernment, the task of interpreting Chaucer's poem is left to the reader of the *Parliament*.

The task of interpreting both texts and images is assigned more explicitly to the reader of John Skelton's *Bouge of Court*. Skelton, who was Tudor poet laureate and tutor to the young Henry VIII, wrote a sixteenth-century dream-vision that moves courtly imagery securely into a political realm, but still presents itself as a visionary enigma to be interpreted. The *Bouge of Court* opens with a conventional dream-scene: because the speaker has been having trouble writing—he feels he does not have the authority of the ancient poets—he falls into a troubled sleep, whereupon he sees a ship approaching. The first figures on the scene, Drede and Danger, might seem to come from amorous allegory, but soon enough the text takes another turn, and concentrates on the intrigues that surround a courtier's life. Perhaps because of its interpretative opacity and its authorial deniability, the dream-vision furnished a vehicle for trenchant political commentary and satire in the late Middle Ages. Visions of the alliterative tradition, such as *Piers Plowman* and its progeny, can be thought as much political as spiritual in their goals. The close of Skelton's poem reflects this tradition of political dreaming by offering a characteristic challenge to the reader—make of 'this lytyll boke' whatever you will:

> I wolde therwith no man were myscontente;
> Besechynge you that shall it see or rede,
> In every poynte to be indyfferente,
> Syth all in substaunce of slumbrynge doth procede.
> I wyll not saye it is mater in dede,
> But yet oftyme suche dremes be founde trewe.
> Now constrewe ye what is the resydewe.[18]

Skelton employs a version of the familiar modesty topos to leave his book and its interpretation in the hands of his readers. He begs pardon for any offending

---

[18] Julia Boffey (ed.), *Fifteenth-Century English Dream Visions: An Anthology* (Oxford: Oxford University Press, 2003), ll. 533–99.

sections, 'syth all in substaunce of slumbrynge doth procede'—dreaming is not reality, and the dreamer of a dream cannot be held accountable for what he saw while asleep. Skelton's dreamer overtly discounts the claim that his dream is significant or meaningful; yet, he says, 'oftyme suche dremes be founde trewe'. Finally, he demands that his reader assume the task of interpreting the significance of the dream correctly: 'Now constrewe ye what is the resydewe.' Importantly, he conceives of this challenge precisely in terms of modes of representation. Skelton's dream-book is something a reader might either 'see or rede'—thus the form of the vision-narrative transforms the reading of the poem into a vision in its own right. Like Chaucer's famous waffling between oral and literate modes of reception in the Prologue to the 'Miller's Tale'—'whoso list it nat yheere | Turne over the leef and chese another tale' (I. 3176–7)—this poem ends with an oscillation between reading and seeing that the genre of the dream-poem exploits, but never fully resolves. The oscillation opens the way to interpretative questions that the poem also never fully resolves, leaving the reader, instead, challenged to 'constrewe' the meaning of the text and its visionary images.

The question of how to understand an image—always explicit in this kind of writing—is also the question of how to understand a word; fundamentally, how is the business of interpretation done? Both the speaker's authority and the reader's judgement are at stake in this question, and, by approaching the question of interpretation directly, some medieval texts provide an impression of how contemporary readers made these judgements. One of the most influential examples of this kind of general medieval dream-theory is Macrobius' commentary on Cicero's *Dream of Scipio*. Macrobius understands 'the substaunce of slumbrynge' (in Skelton's phrase) to vary according to five varieties of dream. Two of these have no serious meaning, since they arise from naturalistic causes, such as indigestion: the *insomnium* (nightmare) and the *phantasma* or *visum* (apparition). Three are more significant: the *somnium* (enigmatic dream), the *visio* (prophetic dream), and the *oraculum* (in which a figure of great authority imparts wisdom directly). The *somnium* (incidentally the most neutral Latin word for dream) is the most intriguing of these categories, for it stands precisely between the meaningless and the meaningful and makes the greatest demands on the interpretative capacities of the dreamer.[19] Macrobius claims the *somnium* 'conceals with strange shapes and veils with ambiguity the true meaning of the information being offered, and requires an interpretation for its understanding'—that is, in literary terms, it is an allegory.[20]

The most influential courtly dream-allegory of the later Middle Ages was overtly concerned with questions of how to construe an authoritative hermeneutics. The *Roman de la Rose*, begun by Guillaume de Lorris as a love-vision set in the garden

---

[19] On the 'doubleness and middleness' of dreams, see Kruger, *Dreaming in the Middle Ages*, 17–34.
[20] Quoted in Spearing, *Medieval Dream-Poetry*, 10. Spearing also makes a connection between Macrobius' *somnium* and the allegorical mode, though not by tracing the visual elements of both.

of Narcissus, became in the hands of its continuator Jean de Meun both more bawdy and more philosophical. The opening image of the *Rose*, in which the lover sees his own reflection in the fountain of Narcissus and falls in love with the rosebud, allies the poem's insistent questions concerning right interpretation with the experience of sight, and the right interpretation of an allegorical landscape with the right interpretation of the self. Through Guillaume's vision of the lovers' dalliance, Jean de Meun raises a series of encyclopedic topics and questions—most famously, about the relationship of words to things—that make the status of artistic representation and the hermeneutic abilities required to understand it central to the poem. The *Rose* was enormously popular in both France and England—parts of it were translated into 'Chaucerian' verse that sometimes has been ascribed to Chaucer—and it left a lasting impression on visionary writing for centuries. Not only Chaucer's more obvious dream-poems—the *Book of the Duchess*, the *House of Fame*, and the *Parliament of Fowls*—but also the confessional self-scrutinizing of the Pardoner and the Wife of Bath develop from this visionary inheritance.

The worlds of political machinations and lovers' intrigues are famously unstable and hard to read. A courtier's career can hang on his ability to judge which way Fortune's wheel is turning, and a lady's smallest look can spell despair for an unsuccessful suitor. But the question of right interpretation is equally urgent—if not more so—in visions that can be considered spiritual. Religious visions constitute a special category of dream, since they address ultimate questions utterly fundamental to human life and seem to offer certain answers. They also make a special kind of claim to absolute authority—most often prophetic or oracular, in Macrobius' terms, they speak with the power of the divine. When visionary experience has divine sanction, no human understanding could be more assured. But visions that seem to emanate from God could also have other, more infernal sources—hellish visions are false ones, sent to trick or delude or entrap the seeming visionary and those who listen to him. A human who is graced with visible access to the divine is an incontestable authority; one who pretends to that authority in error is supremely culpable. As 1 Corinthians suggests—'We see now by a glasse in a darke sort: but then face to face' (Douay-Rheims 13: 12)—clear sight is the equivalent of spiritual understanding, but Paul insists that this clarity is reserved for eschatological time. The question of how to understand what we can only see on earth 'in a darke sort' is as critical for spiritual or philosophical visions as it is for courtly texts.

One problem with distinguishing right vision from misunderstanding has to do with the relation between these spiritual sights and the earthly world. As we have seen, the images that can prompt and respond to visionary writing are sometimes fantasies, sometimes concrete artefacts. But how are we to interpret the role of the physical in estimating the validity of the vision? Julian's meditation upon the crucifix turns miraculous when she sees the object bleeding:

And in this sodenly I saw the reed bloud rynnyng downe from vnder the garlande, hote and freyshely, plentuously and liuely, right as it was in the tyme that the garland of thornes was pressed on his blessed head. Right so, both god and man, the same that sufferd for me, I conceived truely and mightily that it was him selfe that shewed it me without anie meane.

(II. 294)

The material sight becomes immaterial when it is animated, and Julian knows by this that her vision comes from God 'without anie meane'—or without any intermediary. She claims here a direct access to the divine that authorizes her showings, in spite of her modesty elsewhere in calling herself 'a symple creature vnlettyrde' (II. 285).

This modesty is telling, since the late medieval subjects so often graced with visions—whether in texts like Julian's or in images like the *Trois estaz de bones ames*—are women. The manuscript illumination represents the complex place of the feminine in this image-driven piety—how both woman's authority (borrowed from her confessor) and her experience help to create a personal relationship to the visible divine. Women's experiences played an increasingly important role in visionary writing in the centuries after this picture was made. Questions of authority surface repeatedly in visionary writing in connection with issues of proper interpretation. On the one hand, the grace of heavenly visions allowed women who otherwise would not be authorized to speak a privileged place from which to do so. Sometimes feminine weakness was even invoked as a sign of certain (and greater) access to the divine: if a weak and uneducated woman knew such things, who else could have revealed them but God? No extraneous learning on her part could provide an impediment to the pure essence of divine love. As Jennifer Summit has put it, 'women's perceived weakness, humility, and unlearnedness was thought to make them into privileged conduits of God's word'.[21] But although medieval women who had spiritual visions effectively claimed a kind of authority to speak outside of the ecclesiastical structures of this world, their visions could easily be turned against them, branding them lunatics or heretics. Margery Kempe, for example, records in her *Book* many instances of institutional suspicion and persecution of her unauthorized revelations. Of course, late medieval visionary women neither simply wallowed in a pious negation of the self, nor simply usurped the authority of priests, but used the complex negotiations between lowliness and authority offered by visionary experience to find a place from which to speak. Julian's reputation as a famous anchoress and sought-after divine, combined with her powerful humility, or Kempe's obstreperousness, combined with her need for official (and even scribal) sanction for the writing of her *Book*, show that women's

---

[21] Jennifer Summit, 'Women and Authorship', in Carolyn Dinshaw and David Wallace (eds.), *The Cambridge Companion to Medieval Women's Writing* (Cambridge: Cambridge University Press, 2003), 91–108; esp. 95–9.

visionary voices were not negated by the conventions of modesty that allowed them to write in the first place.

If medieval women were often the subjects experiencing and writing visions, female figures were often also their objects. As Barbara Newman has recently argued, allegorical 'goddesses' such as Suso's Eternal Wisdom, or Langland's Holy Church, or even the mysterious *Pearl*-maiden, played a large role in the medieval imagination, not in conflict with Christian monotheism, but reconciled fruitfully with it.[22] But here again, the question of how to interpret what is seen becomes central, for the narrator's experience of the dream sometimes conflicts with the seemingly authoritative voices heard in the course of it. Dame Nature, Lady Philosophy, and Lady Reason are allegorical figures to be both seen and heard, but should a dreamer trust every vision he sees, or every voice he hears? In the works of Christine de Pisan, subject and object come together: Christine is a female author constructing a female visionary persona, who most frequently sees visions of allegorical women. In the debate over misogyny in the *Roman de la Rose*, Christine used her own authorial voice to argue powerfully for women's virtue. Her concern with the dream of the *Rose* occasioned her own great visionary text, the *Book of the City of Ladies*, which set a pantheon of virtuous women against the kind of scurrilous vision promoted by the earlier poem. As she falls asleep, troubled not by misfortune in love (cf. Chaucer's dreamers), but by unbridled misogyny, three allegorical figures—Reason, Rectitude, and Justice—come to her and charge her with the construction of a 'city of ladies', a community of women who will uphold women's virtue in the face of masculine criticism. These ladies channel Christine's own perspective through their allegorical mouths, and provide an added layer of feminine authority, answering vision with vision.

Christine's visionary writing is often explicitly autobiographical, still more so in the Boethian complaints to Fortune of *Christine's Vision* than in the *Book of the City of Ladies*. Just as Julian of Norwich and Margery Kempe took up a visionary mode in order to find their own authorial voices, Christine fashioned hers through visionary experience, as well. The visionary mode plays with autobiography even in the masculine visions of Chaucer, where the dense Geoffrey is an adumbration of the poet, or Langland, where an authorial signature announces that 'Longe Wille' has 'lyved in londe' (XV. 152).[23] Other visionary poems with female dreamer/narrators have prompted biographical questions about their anonymous authors. Even though the *Assembly of Ladies* is anonymous—not certainly written

---

[22] Newman, *God and the Goddesses*.

[23] For discussions of Chaucer's narrative personae, see e.g. David Lawton, *Chaucer's Narrators* (Cambridge: D. S. Brewer, 1985). For Langland, see Anne Middleton, 'William Langland's "Kynde Name": Authorial Signature and Social Identity in Late Fourteenth Century England', in Lee Patterson (ed.), *Literary Practice and Social Change in Britain, 1380–1530* (Berkeley and Los Angeles: University of California Press, 1990), 15–82.

by a woman—the fact that it is written in a female narrative voice shows an interest in a feminine perspective, and in representing a woman as a speaking 'I', that seems to be linked to historical women's writings.[24] If we imagine the narrative recorded in Margery Kempe's *Book* to constitute a female visionary autobiography written in the third person, these texts are the inverse: first-person accounts of a female visionary experience that might owe more to literary convention than to personal narrative.

As all of these connections show, distinctions between secular and sacred are always fluid; in both words and images the same vocabulary is often used to describe courtly passions and the soul's ecstatic longing for union with Christ. But we can imagine formal, generic connections, as well as imagistic ones: the category of visionary writing posits a relationship between devotional poems requiring intense visualization and courtly 'meditations'. Secular poetry sometimes adapts the same meditative mode to present material quite different from the religious ones. The history of the *blazon*, or *effictio*—the literary trope of describing a beloved figure from head to toe—might be considered from this perspective, for example. Does this secular 'meditation' on the image of the beloved's beauty derive from religious devotional practice, or does it prompt it? Is it possible to determine specific links, or directions of influence? It may be that in some poems the techniques of meditation and visualization developed to accelerate progression up spiritual ladders were appropriated in a secular mode. Or perhaps the conventions surrounding the vision of a courtly beloved were adapted to bridal mysticism. In either case, the common interest in the way visionary experience shapes literary texts and readers' responses to them argues that these works should be considered together.

Parodic visions

One of the most subtle medieval treatments of the problems inherent in the interpretation of visionary writing comes in parody: the dilemma faced by the rooster Chauntecleer and the hen Pertelote in the wake of his prophetic dream in Chaucer's 'Nun's Priest's Tale'. In a dream, Chauntecleer sees a frightening beast 'bitwixe yelwe and reed' (VII. 2902) that threatens his safety, and, indeed, in the course of the day a fox makes an attempt to eat him. Before the outcome is known, however, the hen and the rooster debate the question of interpretation at great length: should they heed the warning of a nightmare, or not? From Pertelote's dismissive quotation of Cato—'ne do no fors of dremes' (VII. 2941)—to Chauntecleer's opinion that 'many a dreem ful soore is for to drede' (VII. 3109), the tale acknowledges the many

---

[24] The anonymous *Isle of Ladies* and the *Flower and the Leaf* are not explicitly dream-poems, but they might be considered, alongside the *Assembly of Ladies*, visionary writing in a feminine voice. See Derek Pearsall (ed.), *The Floure and the Leafe; The Assembly of Ladies; The Isle of Ladies* (Kalamazoo: Western Michigan University for TEAMS, 1990; repr. 1992).

conflicting voices in medieval dream-theory. Pertelote takes the medical, scientific, rationalist position that dreams are meaningless; they can be explained by physical ailments, treatable with herbs, that have nothing to do with the larger workings of the universe. Chauntecleer, on the other hand, marshals both authorities and exempla to assert that 'experience' shows that, in fact, dreams do have predictive power:

> By God, men may in olde bookes rede
> Of many a man moore of auctorite
> Than evere Caton was, so moot I thee [thrive],
> That al the revers seyn of this sentence,
> And han wel founden by experience
> That dremes been significaciouns
> As wel of joye as of tribulaciouns
> That folk enduren in this lif present.
> Ther nedeth make of this noon argument;
> The verray preeve sheweth it in dede.   (VII. 2974–83)

The two lovers allude to Macrobius and the biblical authority of Daniel and Joseph, as well as to the experiential evidence of herbal treatments, in their efforts to understand the significance of the mysterious vision. And in this question of Chauntecleer's dream lie other grand questions of medieval literature: how can human free will coexist with God's foreknowledge? And should you listen to your wife? Chaucer's tale exploits the genre of visionary writing, placing the vision in the farmyard, in order to present a complex representation of dreaming that poses the problem of right reading in the most grandiose and yet most humble terms.

Even though its lofty debates are voiced by a couple of chickens, the 'Nun's Priest's Tale' explores many of the elements that constitute visionary writing in more straightforward examples of the genre—courtly, philosophical, and even spiritual. The fashion for aristocratic love-visions in the form of dreams finds reflection in the courtly manners aped by farm animals—the blazon that describes the rooster upon his first appearance:

> His coomb was redder than the fyn coral,
> And batailled as it were a castel wal   (VII. 2859–60)

And his wooing of his favourite hen:

> Madame Pertelote, so have I blis,
> Of o thyng God hath sent me large grace;
> For whan I se the beautee of youre face,
> Ye been so scarlet reed aboute youre yen [eyes],
> It maketh al my drede for to dyen.   (VII. 3158–62)

The question of women's authority, too—familiar both from courtly parliaments in which women decide the fate of men, and from religious visions in which women must claim divine authorization before speaking—is opened by Pertelote's disagreement with her husband, and his ironic mistranslation of *Mulier est hominis confusio* as ' "Womman is mannes joye and al his blis" '(VII. 3164–6). The narrator's subsequent coyness on the subject, in which he suggests both that 'Wommennes conseils been ful ofte colde' (VII. 3256) and also that he 'kan noon harm of no womman divyne' (VII. 3266), does not close the question, but makes it, if ambiguous, central to the humour of the tale. The heady theological and philosophical questions addressed by so many dream-visions in the tradition of the *Consolation* appear in the guise of discussions of free will and God's foreknowledge sparked by the threat of a fox among the chickens. And even though the narrator insists that his tale 'is of a cok' (VII. 3252), and he need not address such profound questions, nonetheless the tale flirts with wondering whether 'what that God forwoot moot nedes be' (VII. 3234).

Finally, the explicit injunction at the end of the text to the reader to figure out the meaning of it all, as the authorial voice backs enigmatically away, echoes the constitutive interpretative ambiguity of visionary writing:

> But ye that holden this tale a folye,
> As of a fox, or of a cok and hen,
> Taketh the moralite, goode men.
> For Seint Paul seith that al that writen is,
> To oure doctrine it is ywrite, ywis;
> Taketh the fruyt, and lat the chaf be stille.   (VII. 3438–43)

The combination here of absolute authority—there *is* a moral, we are assured—and uncertainty about how to construe what that authority is saying marks Chaucer's work in general, but also the genre of dream-vision that he parodies here. When readers ask themselves what they are to conclude from this sequence of events, and who has the authority to interpret the dream, they find themselves in a hall of mirrors. The dreamer Chauntecleer would seem to have the experiential authority to interpret his own dream, he can certainly marshal numerous authorities in his cause, and of course the fox intends to do him harm. But in the end the rooster is not eaten by the fox, the dream is not finally prophetic, and Pertelote's opinion that this meaningless vision does not forebode death is in some strange sense borne out.

The consequences of the rooster's dream-vision are finally unclear, and with them the distinction between interpretative 'fruyt' and 'chaf' so important to so much medieval literature. But this very hermeneutic uncertainty—as Chaucer seems so well to understand—is the impetus behind the voluminous production of visionary texts in the period. Visions produce texts only uneasily, and texts describe visions incompletely and with difficulty. But the incommensurability of text and image is why we find them again and again together, as medieval and modern artists try to reconcile the contradiction, or perhaps use it to understand more about the representational capacities of both word and picture. The delicate balance of these two representational modes, and the impossibility of final interpretation that their combination produces, suggests that the complications of the imagetext are endlessly productive. To recall Julian's hopeful words, 'And for the gostely syghte, I haue seyde sum dele, but I may nevyr fulle telle it; and therfore of this gostely syght I am steryd to sey more, as God wylle geue me grace.'

FURTHER READING

Several helpful studies have described the form and historical development of medieval dream-poetry in late medieval England: A. C. Spearing, *Medieval Dream-Poetry* (Cambridge: Cambridge University Press, 1976); J. Stephen Russell, *English Dream-Vision: Anatomy of a Form* (Columbus, OH: Columbus University Press, 1988); Kathryn L. Lynch, *The High Medieval Dream Vision: Poetry, Philosophy, and Literary Form* (Stanford, CA: Stanford University Press, 1988); Robert R. Edwards, *The Dream of Chaucer: Representation and Reflection in the Early Narratives* (Durham, NC: Duke University Press, 1989); and Steven F. Kruger, *Dreaming in the Middle Ages* (Cambridge: Cambridge University Press, 1992). More recently, the collection of essays edited by Peter Brown, *Reading Dreams: The Interpretation of Dreams from Chaucer to Shakespeare* (Oxford: Oxford University Press, 1999), investigates similar territory.

For connections between visual and literary experience, see several influential articles by Michael Camille, 'The Book of Signs', *Word & Image*, 1 (1985), 26–49; 'Seeing and Reading:' (n. 5) 'Visual Signs of the Sacred Page', *Word & Image*, 5 (1989), 111–30. See also Mary Carruthers, *The Book of Memory: A Study of Memory in Medieval Culture* (Cambridge: Cambridge University Press, 1990); Mary Carruthers, *The Craft of Thought: Meditation, Rhetoric, and the Making of Images* (Cambridge: Cambridge University Press, 1998); Denise Despres, *Ghostly Sights: Visual Meditation in Late-Medieval Literature* (Norman, OK: Pilgrim Books, 1989); V. A. Kolve, *Chaucer and the Imagery of Narrative: The First Five Canterbury Tales* (Stanford, CA: Stanford University Press, 1984); and Barbara Newman, *God and the Goddesses* (n. 4). For art historical perspectives on questions of vision, particularly relating to spiritual sight, see Jeffrey F. Hamburger, *The Visual and Visionary: Art and Female Spirituality in Late-Medieval Germany* (New York: Zone Books, 1998); and Michael Camille, *The Gothic Idol: Ideology and Image-Making in Medieval Art* (Cambridge: Cambridge University Press, 1989).

A number of anthologies offer useful collections of medieval visionary texts apart from the visions of Chaucer, the *Pearl*-poet, and Langland. For the early history of other-worldly visions, see Eileen Gardiner (ed.), *Visions of Heaven and Hell before Dante* (New York: Italica Press, 1989). Julia Boffey, *Fifteenth-Century Dream Visions: An Anthology* (Oxford: Oxford University Press, 2003) includes post-Chaucerian courtly love-visions, including Lydgate's *Temple of Glas*, James I of Scotland's *Kingis Quair*, and the anonymous *Assembly of Ladies*. For a selection of women's spiritual visions in translation, see Elizabeth Alvilda Petroff (ed.), *Medieval Women's Visionary Literature* (Oxford: Oxford University Press, 1986).

CHAPTER 21

SAINTLY EXEMPLARITY

KAREN A. WINSTEAD

In the *Life of St Katherine* composed *c*.1445 by the Augustinian friar John Capgrave, Katherine of Alexandria begins her debate against the pagan philosophers with a sarcastic challenge: let them explain which of their gods is the 'worthyest' (IV. 1514).[1] The pagan gods, she notes, are hardly models of behaviour:

> ... your Saturn, pardé,
> Whyl that he lyved was a fals traytoure—
> Homycyde cruell, debatere and robboure.
> His wyffe was a woman nye of that same vyce:
> Veniable, dispytous, chydere every tyde,
> Of hir condycyon unstable and ful nyce.   (IV. 1517–22)

Likewise, she continues, there is Vulcan the cuckold, Mercury the sorcerer, Apollo the drunkard, and Pluto the rapist, not to mention other perpetrators of 'grete vylonyes' (IV. 1538). Her embarrassed opponents concede that their gods are not moral exemplars but argue that they are, rather, symbols of 'natures whech that be eterne' (IV. 1584). As such, they are the purveyors of 'good provydens', despite their 'schamful dede' (IV. 1564–5).

Rapists and homicides are scarcer (though not entirely absent) within the medieval Christian alternative to the Roman pantheon, the community of saints; yet even the better-behaved saints are not wholly unproblematic models of conduct. Katherine is a case in point. As Capgrave presents her, she is an unruly daughter and negligent queen. And what inspiration should readers draw from her denunciation of idols and declaration that she would 'withdrawe' her 'servise' from the Emperor Maxentius until he mends his ways? These are admirable acts for a saint in a book, but, in the daily world of Capgrave's readers, the only people decrying 'ydols' and withholding service (tithes) owed to figures they deemed unworthy were the reviled Lollards. Capgrave's Katherine, moreover, is no anomaly. The saints whose lives

---

[1] John Capgrave, *The Life of Saint Katherine*, ed. Karen A. Winstead (Kalamazoo, MI: Medieval Institute Publications, 1999).

are most frequently told in Middle English, and thus most available to a broad public, include few staid matrons, devout knights, or pious clerics; instead, we find rebels, failed monarchs, disobedient children, virginal spouses, social radicals, and cross-dressers. If these saints are examples for the reader, it is difficult to believe that they are always meant as *good* examples.

Until the late twentieth century, the standard view was, indeed, that saints in medieval legends were not to be seen as exemplars of proper *behaviour* but as exemplars of the Christian spirit: pious, devout, penitent, or patient as called for, steadfast in the faith. The martyr who rebelled against her parents, spouse, religion, and ruler inhabited a remote, *pagan* past; how could her actions possibly be relevant to a *Christian* present? One of the achievements of late twentieth-century criticism was to recognize that saints' lives are 'about' not just piety and spirituality but also politics, economics, social control, gender, and sexuality, and that what their authors have to say on these topics is intended to be relevant to, and sometimes critical of, contemporary life. Their saints' careers are available to suggest, or to criticize, contemporary courses of action. But not available to the authors only; another powerful strain in late twentieth-century criticism was to demonstrate that a multivalent figure such as the virgin martyr is susceptible to appropriation by the reader, who is free to read her as something quite other than the author intended—and, in so doing, perhaps, to recover meanings the author has suppressed.

Thus, at the beginning of the twenty-first century, the issue of saintly exemplarity has been deepened and complicated. What remains to be done? As hinted above, I think we should take a hard look at the often-unconscious assumption that saints, where meant as exemplars, are always meant as exemplars of the good and not the bad. From there I will move to a consideration of the fifteenth century; this period of remarkable innovation in hagiography will reward far more attention than the twentieth century gave to it. Also up for re-examination is the critical practice of considering the saint's exemplarity as if it were directed mostly if not solely at members of his or her own sex. Finally, I will urge more creative attention to the meaning of the saints to ordinary medieval people.

Examples ... of what?

Some saints' lives present themselves as exemplary in the straightforward sense.[2] The earliest Middle English saints' lives—the early thirteenth-century lives of Margaret, Juliana, and Katherine within the so-called Katherine Group—are prime examples. These lives, part of a larger body of devotional literature directed at

---

[2] I am not at all suggesting that this apparently straightforward model cannot be—or has not been—complicated. See, for example, Sarah Salih, 'Queering *Sponsalia Christi*: Virginity, Gender, and Desire in the Early Middle English Anchoritic Texts', *New Medieval Literatures*, 5 (2002), 155–75.

religious women and at anchoresses in particular, echo the themes found in that literature.[3] (Anchoresses were recluses who never left their small cells, or anchorholds, which usually shared a wall with a church. They were encouraged to think of their anchorholds as prisons.) The virginity treatise *Hali Meidhad*, for example, urges its female readers to forsake earthly lovers and to give themselves to their heavenly bridegroom, Christ, and Katherine, Margaret, and Juliana do exactly that. The Katherine Group authors emphasize Christ's role as 'lefmon [lover]' and the saint's role as his 'iweddede wif'.[4] The author of *Hali Meidhad* explicitly invokes the virgin martyrs as exemplars: 'Thench o [Think of] Seinte Katerine, o Seinte Margarete, Seinte Enneis, Seinte Iuliene, Seinte Lucie, ant Seinte Cecille, ... hu ha ... forsoken kinges sunes ant eorles, with alle worldliche weolen [wealth] ant eorthliche wunnen [pleasures].'[5] Though a thirteenth-century anchoress would not be called upon to endure grisly tortures for Christ's love, the Katherine Group legends create common ground between the saints and late medieval readers by inscribing long prayers that would have been appropriate for religious women, especially anchoresses. Their thirteenth-century hagiographers may have chosen to translate the lives of Margaret, Katherine, and Juliana precisely because their legends pay special attention to the saints' activities in prison—praying, being comforted by angels, and combating demons. The anchoress's contact with the outside world was mediated through windows in her cell: through those portals, she received food and other essentials, participated in church services, and conversed with her spiritual advisers and with members of the community. Margaret sounds very much like a contemporary anchoress, both provisioned with the 'bread and spring water that kept her alive' ('bred ant burnes drunch, thet ha bi liuede') and admiringly observed by her supporters through a window ('thurh an eilthurl') in her prison cell.[6]

The Katherine Group legends, with their ostensibly straightforward models, stand in sharp contrast to the martyr legends composed a generation later as part of the *South English Legendary*, the most widely circulated collection of saints' lives in late medieval England. Although the legends comprising the *SEL* are abridged from Latin texts that were similar in tone and structure to the Katherine Group legends, their Middle English redactors consistently removed facets of the martyrs' character and experience that might make them exemplary in any conventional sense (that is, as examples of proper speech and behaviour).[7] They say little of the martyrs' virtues

---

[3] On this literature and its context, see Elizabeth Robertson, *Early English Devotional Prose and the Female Audience* (Knoxville: University of Tennessee Press, 1990).

[4] Bella Millett and Jocelyn Wogan-Browne (eds.), *Medieval English Prose for Women from the Katherine Group and 'Ancrene Wisse'* (Oxford: Clarendon, 1990), 46, 50.

[5] Ibid. 41.

[6] Ibid. 58–9. On the anchorhold as a prison, see Ann K. Warren, *Anchorites and their Patrons in Medieval England* (Berkeley and Los Angeles: University of California Press, 1985), 8–9, 92–5.

[7] It is surely no accident that these distancing techniques are not systematically employed in the lives of the non-martyred saints, whose actions are less susceptible to radical interpretations. Anne B.

beyond that they are 'holy' or 'good', and their narratives focus almost exclusively on the saints' defiance of civil and religious authority figures, which is relayed in scathing insults, and on the grisly punishments those figures devise in retribution. These authors seem far from encouraging any sort of *positive* identification between the reader and saint; indeed, the *SEL*'s martyrs contemptuously reject sympathy offered by onlookers, and some of their contempt seems to be directed at the reader, or at least at the reader's presumed sentimentality. Far from inviting it, the writers of the *SEL* seem to warn readers against imitation of the martyrs, who have—and need—courage and other-worldliness beyond that of ordinary folk.[8] This lesson was apparently not lost on Margery Kempe, who, in the fifteenth century, longed to imitate the lives of the martyrs but not their painful deaths. We should allow that she wasn't misreading, but rather reading clearly what we have misread.

Fifteenth-century departures

The nature of saintly exemplarity was profoundly affected by the turn to more 'literary' saints' lives during the fifteenth century. Though Chaucer is usually said to have inaugurated this trend with his Cecilia legend, whose polished rhetoric set it apart from popular Middle English legends of the past, John Lydgate—Benedictine monk, avid Chaucerian, and Lancastrian poet laureate—did more than anyone else to transform the saint's life into a literary genre. His legends, composed during the first four decades of the fifteenth century, are not merely rhetorically ornate but also evince an interest in history and character that was rare in earlier Middle English saints' lives. Unfolding in multiple books, with elaborate prologues, epilogues, and addresses to the reader, as well as carefully drawn characters and complex plots, his 'epic' lives of Edmund and Alban present themselves as hagiographical equivalents to Chaucer's *Troilus and Criseyde*.

The protagonists of fifteenth-century saints' lives often model qualities only loosely tied to holiness. Thus, Lydgate's George is the ideal knight, debonair and skilled at arms; his Margaret is 'benygne', 'gracyous', and 'softe of hir speche'; and his Petronilla is a paragon of courtesy who uses tact rather than insults to deflect an unwelcome suitor.[9] The concern with deportment found in the legends of Lydgate

Thompson discusses some of the saints whose lives are more accessible to ordinary readers in *Everyday Saints and the Art of Narrative in the 'South English Legendary'* (Aldershot: Ashgate, 2003).

[8] I consider the possibility that some martyr legends, particularly those in the *South English Legendary*, were designed to frighten readers into social conformity in 'Fear in Late-Medieval Martyr Legends', in Johan Leemans (ed.), *More than a Memory: The Discourse of Martyrdom and the Construction of Religious Identity in the History of Christianity* (Leuven: Peeters, 2005), 201–21.

[9] For the quotes from Lydgate's *Margaret*, see Sherry L. Reames (ed.), *Middle English Legends of Women Saints* (Kalamazoo, MI: Medieval Institute Publications, 2003), 150, ll. 95, 97, 105. I discuss the trend in fifteenth-century hagiography to more exemplary virgin martyrs, with particular attention to Lydgate and Osbern Bokenham, in *Virgin Martyrs: Legends of Sainthood in Late Medieval England* (Ithaca, NY: Cornell University Press, 1997), 112–46.

and many of his followers, including Osbern Bokenham and Capgrave, is consistent with a broader concern with conduct among gentle and bourgeois readers. (See Stephanie Trigg's essay in this volume.)

Many fifteenth-century narratives convey the reassuring message that genteel fifteenth-century readers might, just by being themselves, already have much in common with the elect; others, even within the oeuvre of a conservative figure such as Lydgate, portray more ambiguous and unsettling models. Just, generous, and prudent, Lydgate's Edmund is the ideal monarch—until he decides that it is better to be captured and killed by the marauding Danes than to defend his kingdom against them.[10] Prior hagiographers confined themselves to praising Edmund's Christ-like suffering, but Lydgate reports its unpleasant collateral: the maidens raped, the old men killed, the churches burned, the priests murdered, the sacraments 'hangyng in Jupartye' (III. 457). Lest readers miss his point, Lydgate follows his account of Edmund's martyrdom with God's summons to his cousin Fremund, recalling him from eremitic life to vanquish the Danes and restore order to the realm. Fremund objects that 'to been armyd' is 'contrarye' to his vocation, but he is told in no uncertain terms that the welfare of the realm trumps his 'professioun forto lyue solitarye | Teschewe werre and shedyng eek off blood' (III. 470–476). Capgrave is as hard on Katherine of Alexandria as Lydgate is on Edmund, vividly describing the chaos that ensues when she neglects her duties as ruler to pursue a life of study and contemplation. When Maxentius takes over her capital, burning churches and forcing Christians to sacrifice to the pagan gods, Katherine innocently wonders, 'Why sufferth my spouse now swech cursyd men | To breke His chirchis, His servauntis for to kyll?' (IV. 512–13), but Capgrave invites us to wonder whether the responsibility for all that misery is Christ's or Katherine's.

Fifteenth-century hagiographers eschew simple moral lessons to explore the doubts and vulnerabilities of their characters. The prose life of St Barbara included in several manuscripts of the 1438 *Gilte Legende* devotes extraordinary attention to Barbara's pre-conversion anxieties. She intuits that the paganism she has been raised in is wrong-headed, but filial piety initially controls her: she 'durste nat ... displese'

---

[10] I consider Lydgate's ambivalence towards Edmund's actions in 'Lydgate's Lives of Saints Edmund and Alban: Martyrdom and *Prudent Pollicie*', *Mediaevalia*, 17 (1994), 221–41. For discussions of Lydgate's Edmund specifically as a model for the reigning king, Henry VI, see Katherine J. Lewis, 'Edmund of East Anglia, Henry VI and Ideals of Kingly Masculinity', in P. H. Cullum and Katherine J. Lewis (eds.), *Holiness and Masculinity in the Middle Ages* (Cardiff: University of Wales Press, 2004), 158–73; and Fiona Somerset, '"Hard is with seyntis for to make affray": Lydgate the "Poet-Propagandist" as Hagiographer', in Larry Scanlon and James Simpson (eds.), *John Lydgate: Poetry, Culture, and Lancastrian England* (Notre Dame, IN: University of Notre Dame Press, 2006), 258–78. I compare Lydgate's *Edmund* and Capgrave's *Katherine* as commentaries on Henry VI's rule in *John Capgrave's Fifteenth Century* (Philadelphia: University of Pennsylvania Press, 2007), emphasizing the hagiographers' ambivalence towards their protagonists. On Lydgate's martyrs, see also Ruth Nisse, '"Was it not Routhe to Se?": Lydgate and the Styles of Martyrdom', in Scanlon and Simpson (eds.), *John Lydgate*, 279–98. Lydgate's life of Edmund was edited by Carl Horstmann in *Altenglische Legenden: Neue Folge* (1881; repr. Hildesheim: Georg Olms, 1969), 376–440.

her father and so accompanies him to the temple 'with body but not with herte'.[11] But her hypocrisy troubles her: 'What schal I do? And if I knele not before theym [the idols], what schalle I answere to theym that aske of me why I knele not? Yif I knele with my body and not with my herte, what schal it advayle me or what schalle it hurte me?' She asks for an intellectual basis to persist in her faith, but the pagan priests can't or won't provide it. Yet in the *Gilte Legende*, the transition into Christianity can be as difficult as the transition out of paganism. When its Alban first hears the tenets of the Christian religion, he objects, 'What is this that thou spekyst, thow mad man? ... There is no reson in thy talkyng!'[12] Contrast his scepticism here to his blind faith in the *South English Legendary*, where his mere observation of a priest at his prayers evokes a renunciation of his paganism.

Apparent in the fifteenth century, then, is not just a trend to realistic literary characters who need motivation for their actions and decisions, but also to saints who demand a reasoned basis for their faith: the importance of faith grounded in knowledge and understanding becomes a recurring theme, conveyed in part through the kinds of saints hagiographers were choosing (intellectuals and founders of religious orders, for example), in part through their selection of source texts, and in part through the ways they tweak or embellish those sources. Extended conversion narratives, non-existent in Middle English hagiography of the late thirteenth and fourteenth centuries, start to appear in saints' lives around 1420. They peak during the second quarter of the century, in Lydgate's life of Alban and Amphibalus, John Capgrave's lives of Katherine and Augustine, and the anonymous prose lives of Barbara, Alban, and Katherine included in the 1438 *Gilte Legende*. But they continue to be written into the sixteenth century, as Alexander Barclay's 1515 life of St George illustrates. Accounts of saints' conversions repeatedly portray conversion as a *process*, often involving doubt, hesitation, and anguish. They also show that fear and force, censorship and repression, are ineffective means of securing religious conformity.

Uncoincidentally, these intellectually engaged saints' lives appear at a time when the open discussion of religion had been severely curtailed in response to concerns about the Lollard heresy. If Arundel's 1409 Constitutions, as Rita Copeland has argued, introduced 'a systematized pedagogy of infantilization, an "education" structured around conserving ignorance', could hagiography—not an obviously pedagogical genre—have functioned as a vehicle of orthodox resistance to the church hierarchy's policies of censorship and repression?[13] Could it have formed part of the ' "underground" fifteenth-century theological tradition', that Nicholas Watson has speculated might have arisen in response to the Constitutions and have

---

[11] Richard Hamer and Vida Russell (eds.), *Supplementary Lives in Some Manuscripts of the 'Gilte Legende'* EETS, os 315 (Oxford: Oxford University Press, 2000), 391–2.

[12] British Library, Add. MS 35298, fo. 58ʳ.

[13] Rita Copeland, *Pedagogy, Intellectuals, and Dissent in the Later Middle Ages: Lollardy and Ideas of Learning* (Cambridge: Cambridge University Press, 2001), 123.

been 'carried on mainly through the processes of translation and compilation'?[14] Saints' lives would have provided an ideal medium for orthodox dissent: the very act of writing a saint's life was an assertion of orthodoxy, for the saints were part of a traditional Catholicism that most Lollards despised, and their lives were, or were said to be, derived from authoritative sources whose authority the Lollards denied.

My work with Capgrave convinces me that he, at least, was using the saints to model an alternative orthodoxy, whose roots pre-date Archbishop Arundel's strictures.[15] Capgrave's Norbert preaches without being properly licensed. His Gilbert criticizes oaths. His Cecilia reads Scripture. His Katherine, as noted earlier, rails against devotional images and expounds abstruse subjects ranging from the Trinity to the theory of Adoption. At one point, she launches into an apparently gratuitous discussion of spiritual baptism—the teaching that those who 'stedfastly troste' (V. 276) may be baptized through their faith and God's mercy alone—which, though orthodox, might nonetheless have been labelled Lollard in 1445 England. Capgrave, staunchly anti-Lollard himself, appears to be criticizing the heretication of views that were once either accepted or at least freely debated among the orthodox. How many other hagiographers, I wonder, were engaged in similar projects? The saints in many fifteenth-century legends are suspiciously long-winded in their denunciations of pagan statuary—an odd topic to belabour unless their hagiographers intended a contemporary allusion.[16] Could one really, in the first half of the fifteenth century, have read about a saint's alarm at the 'erroure and supersticion' of venerating 'dyvers ymages' without being reminded of Lollard critiques of devotional imagery?[17] The contemporaneousness of Alban's denunciation of the gods might explain the *nota bene* mark placed beside it in one manuscript of the 1438 *Gilte Legende* (British Library, Add. 35298, fo. 59[r]).

We only began in the twentieth century to look at hagiography as a possible vehicle of religious dissent. The writings of John Lydgate, Osbern Bokenham, Simon Wynter, and George Barclay; the Digby plays of Mary Magdalene and Paul; and the narratives of countless anonymous writers still contain untapped information about the complexion of orthodoxy in pre-Reformation England. When Jacobus de

---

[14] Nicholas Watson, 'Censorship and Cultural Change in Late-Medieval England: Vernacular Theology, the Oxford Translation Debate, and Arundel's Constitutions of 1409', *Speculum*, 70 (1995), 836.

[15] *John Capgrave's Fifteenth Century*. On Capgrave's complex orthodoxy, see also Sarah James, ' "Doctryne and Studie": Female Learning and Religious Debate in Capgrave's Life of St Katharine', *Leeds Studies in English*, NS 36 (2005), 275–302; and James Simpson, *Reform and Cultural Revolution, 1350–1547* (Oxford: Oxford University Press, 2002), 420–9.

[16] See Kathleen Kamerick, *Popular Piety and Art in the Late Middle Ages: Image Worship and Idolatry in England, 1350–1500* (New York: Palgrave, 2002), 64–7; Sarah Stanbury, 'The Vivacity of Images: St Katherine, Knighton's Lollards, and the Breaking of Idols', in Jeremy Dimmick, James Simpson, and Nicolette Zeeman (eds.), *Images, Idolatry, and Iconoclasm in Late Medieval England* (Oxford: Oxford University Press, 2002), 131–50; James, ' "Doctryne and Studie" '; and Simpson, *Reform and Cultural Revolution*, 424–6.

[17] 'St Barbara', *Supplementary Lives*, 386.

Voragine's *Legenda aurea* was translated into English Golden Legends, various of Jacobus' brief saints' lives were replaced with more elaborate and morally complex renditions, and other such lives were added. What do the protagonists of these lives have to say about the sacraments, clerical poverty, preaching, pilgrimage, devotional imagery, and other hot-button topics? And what do their *antagonists* have to say on these subjects? (In Capgrave's *Life of Saint Katherine*, the pagan philosophers defend their religious statuary with arguments remarkably similar to those that orthodox apologists were advancing against the Lollards!) Are the saints' lives being used to teach Christine doctrine, or perhaps to model an appropriate Christian pedagogy (which may or may not be consistent with Arundel's 'pedagogy of infantilization')? How do Christian intellectuals, such as Jerome or Augustine, deal with the heretics of *their* day? And does the portrayal of those intellectuals vary among the different versions of their lives, particularly in their approach to error? Does Bokenham's Augustine express the same attitudes as Capgrave's Augustine?[18]

Such questions may be addressed by looking not only at different legends of the same saint, but also at different copies of the 'same' legend. Consider, for example, the prose *Life of Saint Katherine* composed *c*.1420, an early example of the more historically and psychologically complex saints' lives that were written in fifteenth-century England.[19] Its first half is an extended account of Katherine's life before her confrontation with Maxentius, including information about her ancestry, upbringing, experiences as queen of Alexandria, and conversion and mystical marriage to Christ. Its second half, which recounts her passion, includes an unusually detailed account of her debate with the pagan philosophers, including her arguments and their replies on a variety of religious topics. About a dozen copies of the prose life are extant, many as part of the 1438 *Gilte Legende*, but a number of these replace the extended debate with a shorter summary of it based on the *Legenda aurea*. This replacement appears to suggest discomfort with extended vernacular theologizing. What else might close attention to editorial practices reveal about the producers and consumers of hagiography?

The 'French connection'

Many of the innovations in fifteenth-century Middle English hagiography were anticipated in the saints' lives composed in Anglo-Norman French during the

[18] By Bokenham's Augustine, I mean the life of Augustine found in the Abbotsford *Legenda aurea*, which appears to be by Bokenham. At least, Simon Horobin has made a compelling case for Bokenham's authorship. See Horobin, 'A Manuscript Found in the Library of Abbotsford House and the Lost Legendary of Osbern Bokenham', *English Manuscript Studies 1100–1700*, forthcoming. For Capgrave's life, see *Life of Saint Augustine*, ed. Cyril Lawrence Smetana (Toronto: Pontifical Institute of Mediaeval Studies, 2001).

[19] This life is discussed at length in Katherine J. Lewis, *The Cult of St Katherine of Alexandria in Late Medieval England* (Woodbridge: Boydell Press, 2000). For the earliest version, see *The Life and Martyrdom of St. Katherine of Alexandria*, ed. Henry Hucks Gibbs (London: Nichols, 1884).

twelfth, thirteenth, and early fourteenth centuries. Anglo-Norman hagiography includes saints and martyrs whose comportment is more in keeping with normative behaviour for contemporary men and women. It also pays greater attention to history and character, and offers a wider variety of exemplars, especially for women. The early fourteenth-century Franciscan Nicholas Bozon, for example, was the first English hagiographer to compose a vernacular life of a continental holy woman, Elizabeth of Hungary. He also produced lives of Martha and Mary Magdalene along with lives of six virgin martyrs.

Despite the richness of Anglo-Norman hagiography, only the life of Katherine composed by the twelfth-century nun Clemence of Barking has received much attention. Jocelyn Wogan-Browne has taken the first major steps toward recifying this situation; her *Saints' Lives and Women's Literary Culture* shows how French-language lives composed between 1150 and 1300 differ from contemporaneous English lives.[20] However, the strong affinities between thirteenth- and fourteenth-century Anglo-Norman lives, on the one hand, and fifteenth-century Middle English lives, on the other hand, remain to be explored. For example, one might compare the hagiography of Nicholas Bozon to that of Osbern Bokenham. Both wrote mostly about female saints, especially virgin martyrs, both wrote lives of Mary Magdalene and Elizabeth of Hungary, and both revise a common source—the *Legenda aurea* of Jacobus de Voragine—to emphasize imitable virtues rather than inimitable feats. Just as one can ask why the projects of contemporary Anglo-Norman and Middle-English hagiographers differ, one can ask what had changed, by the fifteenth century, to inspire Bokenham in a project so similar to Bozon's.

Gendered exemplarity?

Middle English hagiography furnishes a large and varied body of literature about women, many of whom transgressed gender norms. Though no Middle English saints' lives are known to have been written by women, many were written for women, read by women, and commissioned by women. Since the 1990s, scholars have analysed the role of saints' lives in the construction of gender. They have scrutinized the unstated assumptions about women, examined the models intentionally or unintentionally offered to women, and looked at evidence of how actual women read and 'misread', used and 'misused', those models. Indeed, Middle English hagiography developed into a serious field of enquiry thanks largely to the efforts of feminist scholars. Yet, surprisingly, most lives of female saints have scarcely been looked at, for scholarship to date has focused on a very small set of works: mostly on the virgin martyr legends of the Katherine Group, Chaucer's

---

[20] Jocelyn Wogan-Browne, *Saints' Lives and Women's Literary Culture, c.1150–1300: Virginity and its Authorizations* (Oxford: Oxford University Press, 2001).

Cecilia legend, and Bokenham's lives of holy women, although lives of St Katherine (especially Capgrave's) and the *Digby Mary Magdalene* have lately begun to receive more attention.

Marked by its attention to female holiness and its promotion of new, more inclusive, paradigms of holiness for women, fifteenth-century hagiography is especially rich. Fifteenth-century hagiographers told the stories of classic favourites, such as the virgin martyrs, in new ways, sometimes aligning holy radicals more nearly with contemporary norms of femininity. They also were more likely to write about holy wives and mothers. All six extant versions of the life of St Anne date from the fifteenth century. The first Middle English life of St Monica was composed during the first half of the fifteenth century and appears within the Abbotsford *Legenda aurea*, while Capgrave's life of Augustine diverts so much attention to Augustine's mother that it might also be considered a life of Monica. The first Middle English life of St Helen was composed during the fifteenth century, as were the first Middle English lives of Marie d'Oignies, Elizabeth of Hungary, and Birgitta of Sweden. The lives of Marie and Birgitta point to another important trend in fifteenth-century hagiography: the production of the first Middle English lives of 'modern' holy women. Others include Catherine of Siena, Christina Mirabilis, and Elizabeth of Spalbeek.

Particularly intriguing are the prose lives of three thirteenth-century holy women of Liège—Elizabeth of Spalbeek, Christina Mirabilis, and Marie d'Oignies—found in Bodleian Library, MS Douce 114, which also includes a translation of Stephen of Siena's letter supporting the canonization of Catherine of Siena and an English translation of Henry Suso's *Horologium sapientiae*. The 'apolege of the compilour' preceding the three lives declares that 'this Englysche that folowth heere' is intended for 'the worschep of God and edificacyone of deuoute soulles that are not leeryd [learned] in Latyn tunge'.[21] Perhaps to forestall accusations of inappropriate vernacular theologizing, the compiler claims to have omitted 'legeauns and auctorites of holy writt that wolde be ful dymme to vndirstonde if they were turnyd into Englissh withoute more declarynge of glose'.

The heroines of the Douce 114 lives engaged in devotional practices that, so far as we know, had no counterparts in late medieval England. Elizabeth daily delivers a performance of Christ's Passion that on Fridays culminates in her reception of the stigmata. Her Middle English life, translated from the eyewitness account of Philip of Clairvaux, vividly details the cruelties she inflicts on her own body as she plays out the roles of both Christ and his tormentors. Christina, following a near-death experience, becomes 'the Astonishing', cartwheeling through the streets, dangling from gibbets, leaping into hot ovens, and drinking from her own breasts.

---

[21] Jennifer N. Brown, 'A Critical Edition of and Commentary on MS Douce 114: The Middle English *Vitae* of Elizabeth of Spalbeek, Christina *Mirabilis*, and Marie d'Oignies' (Ph.D. dissertation, City University of New York, 2003), 230.

Marie d'Oignies parts company with her husband to pursue a life of asceticism and charity in the company of like-minded women who would become known as the first beguines. Though less spectacular than Elizabeth or Christina, the beguines were likewise radical. They left behind the bonds of family without accepting those usually associated with religious vocations: they remained unbound by the rules of any order, uncloistered, unconfined to any anchorhold. Few other medieval women, lay or religious, knew such autonomy.

The scant discussion to date that is ostensibly about the lives of Douce 114 has in truth focused on the meanings of their Latin sources and the motivations of those Latin authors. Nobody has yet drawn more meaning from the English texts in late medieval England than to observe that they participate in a broader interest in continental spirituality. But why were these particular lives translated? And why were they translated when they were? It is certainly consistent with the conservative reputation of English spirituality that, as the beguine movement swept the Continent during the late thirteenth and fourteenth centuries, the lives of its participants were *not* being made available in English. But isn't it odd that they *were* translated when the English Church had become more conservative than ever, and even though the beguine movement had faded on the Continent, in part because it had become associated with heresy?

The theme these three lives most obviously share is the heroine's self-inflicted 'martyrdom'. Yet this may not have been the theme that stood out for the medieval translator and motivated his selection. Neither Elizabeth, Christina, nor Marie seems exemplary in the straightforward sense. Indeed, Jacques de Vitry, the author of Marie's Latin life, explicitly discourages readers from imitating her excesses, and his disclaimer is faithfully translated into Middle English: 'priuilege of a fewe makith not a commun lawe' (p 299). But the three lives also share a less obvious theme: reverence for the sacraments, particularly penance. Elizabeth's 'reuelacyouns and spiritual lyfe … figurith … the sacramente of the auter, and of confessyon' (p 257); Christina's example shames those who 'dreed to do penauns for oure selfe and for oure synnes' (p 293); Marie's penitential practices are detailed at length. These religious radicals of thirteenth-century Belgium were perhaps being recast as models of orthodoxy, counters to the more dangerous brand of radicalism found among the Lollards of fifteenth-century England.

The penitential message of the Douce 114 lives would, of course, have applied broadly, not just to women. Gender-oriented critics have tended to consider saints principally in relation to members of their own sex. During the late twentieth century, that mostly meant looking at what female saints meant to or for female readers: what ideals of femininity did the lives of female saints promote, or make available? Were they empowering models for women, or were they vehicles for controlling female desire and sexuality? How were their lives tailored to the perceived needs and interests of female readers, or how might female readers have appropriated male-authored *vitae* to their own ends? More recently, analogous questions have been posed of male saints:[22] What ideals of masculinity are conveyed by, or latent in, saints such as George or Edward the Confessor? While there is no denying that much can be and has been learned from such gender-specific enquiry, other, more complex avenues of identification await exploration.

We need to step beyond the presumption that the life of a female saint is either intended for women or that gender is its primary subject. —and likewise for male saints. Chaucer's 'Second Nun's Tale', a life of St Cecilia, is a well-known case in point. As indicated by the Prologue's reference to the author as 'I, unworthy sone of Eve', and also by its time of composition,[23] Chaucer did not write the life of Cecilia merely to have a gender-appropriate tale to put into the mouth of the Second Nun, nor is there any evidence he intended it especially for female readers. To appreciate fully the cultural significance of saints' lives, we must ask why and how a fourth-century virgin martyr appealed to a fourteenth-century layman like Chaucer.[24] Or like William Paris, who wrote a life of Christine while imprisoned for treason on the Isle of Man in 1397–9.[25] Paris's life of Christine is a superb example of the fast-paced martyr legends popular in his day, in which witty, resilient saints make fools of the bumbling authorities who try to intimidate or to harm them. Far from feeling divided by gender from Christine, Paris probably felt united with her by common experience as a prisoner. Yet why did he identify more readily with an adolescent girl than with one of the many soldier-martyrs who also defy hapless captors—St Sebastian, for example, or St George? And, just as men could be drawn to female saints, women could be drawn to male saints. Based on her study of wills from the first half of the sixteenth century, Christine Peters concluded that, 'logical' as it might seem 'for women to favour female saints over male saints ... this does not seem to have been the case'.[26] If many women were more attracted to holy men than to holy women, why? Did they consider

---

[22] Samantha J. E. Riches and Sarah Salih promote the study of 'masculine holiness' as 'a necessary adjunct to the study of female holiness' in their essay collection *Gender and Holiness: Men, Women and Saints in Late Medieval Europe* (London: Routledge, 2002), 3. See also the essays comprising Cullum and Lewis (eds.), *Holiness and Masculinity in the Middle Ages*.

[23] *The Riverside Chaucer,* ed. Larry D. Benson, 3rd edn. (Boston: Houghton Mifflin, 1987), 'Second Nun's Tale,' l. 62. Chaucer's allusion to his 'lyf ... of Seynt Cecile' in both prologues to his *Legend of Good Women* (l. 426 in F, 416 in G) indicates that he composed the life before most scholars believe he had begun work on his *Canterbury Tales.*

[24] I cannot even try to do justice to the mass of criticism that has been written about Chaucer's Cecilia legend, the single most-studied Middle English saint's life; however, I will mention Lynn Staley Johnson, 'Chaucer's Tale of the Second Nun and the Strategies of Dissent', *Studies in Philology*, 89 (1992), 314–33. Staley's view that hagiography can function as a screen to address contemporary politico-religious issues applies to many other Middle English saints' lives and is an early example of what has become a particularly fruitful approach to the Middle English saint's life.

[25] See Mary-Ann Stouck, 'Saints and Rebels: Hagiography and Opposition to the King in Late Fourteenth-Century England', *Medievalia et humanistica* NS, 9 (1997), 75–94.

[26] Christine Peters, *Patterns of Piety: Women, Gender and Religion in Late Medieval and Reformation England* (Cambridge: Cambridge University Press, 2003), 47.

them more efficacious intercessors? Were their stories more exciting? Were they more appealing as exemplars? If so, as exemplars of what? At the limit of such questioning, we can ask whether the Katherine Group lives really tell us what their (presumably male) authors considered fit reading for their (presumably female) readers, or whether they tell us what those (presumably male) authors wanted to write about.

Indeed, a major issue that early twenty-first-century criticism has only begun to address is whether and when a binary framework of gender is appropriate for reading saints' lives. Salih's essay, noted above, proposes that medieval virginity is better understood not as abstinence from sexuality but as an alternative sexuality. Karma Lochrie has persuasively challenged the assumption that medieval culture was heteronormative, and critics such as Robert Mills are proposing that saints' lives were particularly suitable—both in their ostensible distance from contemporary life and in their explicit engagement with violent and sexual themes—for exploring alternative desires and sexualities.[27]

Audience

All questions of audience and authorial intent are difficult to answer. Many of the difficulties are exemplified in the case of the unnamed woman who, c.1450, asked Capgrave to write her a life of St Augustine because she was born on his feast day. Capgrave responded not with a simple life of Augustine but with one that incorporates an extended account of his mother Monica, not found in his Latin source. The inclusion of this Monica material seems meant to produce a life that would be exemplary, in the straightforward sense, for a fifteenth-century gentlewoman. Monica copes with unruly servants, a cantankerous mother-in-law, and an irascible spouse. She doggedly instructs Augustine in discipline and morality even as her husband's laxity undercuts her at every turn. One can wonder whether Capgrave is engaging in a certain amount of gender stereotyping by assuming that a reader who had asked for the life of a 'grete doctoure of the cherch' will prefer to read about that doctor's mother.[28] Or is it gender bias on our part to suppose that Capgrave's inclusion of the Monica material reflects concern for his female reader rather than his own interest in a woman who was, after all, specially venerated by his own Augustinian order? Of course, these possibilities are not mutually exclusive, and we can best understand how a particular saint's life attained its form—its emphases, its exclusion or inclusion of certain elements, its style—by considering the broadest range of possibilities.

[27] Karma Lochrie, *Heterosyncrasies: Female Sexuality When Normal Wasn't* (Minneapolis: University of Minnesota Press, 2005); Robert Mills, *Suspended Animation: Pain, Pleasure & Punishment in Medieval Culture* (London: Reaktion Books, 2005).
[28] *Life of Saint Augustine*, 15.

Given the paucity of evidence, how might knowledge about the reception of saints' lives by ordinary readers be gained? The lives of Christina of Markyate and Margery Kempe are often mined for indications of how women responded to the saints, especially to the virgin martyrs, but such would-be saints are hardly ordinary. Prologues and/or epilogues, including those to Wynter's life of Jerome, Capgrave's life of Katherine, and various of Bokenham's lives, provide information about patrons and readers, but that sort of information is scarce, sketchy, and filtered through the hagiographer. Municipal and guild records have been scoured for mention of performances of saints' plays, but one can only learn so much from such passing references, especially when the plays themselves are lost. Against this dearth of data, manuscripts are a source well worth exploring.

An interesting example is British Library, Arundel MS 168.[29] This fifteenth-century manuscript comprises an ABC poem in honour of the Virgin Mary, a translation of Benedict Burgh's *Distichs of Cato*, Lydgate's *Life of Our Lady*, and three virgin martyr legends: an anonymous life of Dorothy dating from the early fifteenth century, Paris's life of Christine, and Capgrave's life of Katherine. Some of these contents suggest the manuscript may have been used to educate gentle or bourgeois children. Such a use would explain the apparent incongruity of setting Lydgate's life of Mary and the virgin martyr lives alongside a conduct book for schoolboys. Yet that incongruity exists only if we assume that gender and sexual status were the attributes of saints most important to the manuscript's intended readers. Arundel 168 suggests otherwise. What its saints' lives have in common—and what makes them eminently suitable as educational literature for children—is an emphasis on family life. Dorothy is the rare virgin martyr who belongs to a devout Christian family and can piously wish to grow up to be like her father, 'goddis lovere'.[30] Her life models acceptable behaviour both for children and for adults: Dorotheus flees Rome with his family to avoid persecution, and Dorothy doesn't set out to antagonize or defy; she merely persists in her faith, politely but firmly, despite unjust persecution by a lecherous official. In contrast, Paris's Christine is a 'classic' virgin martyr who ridicules and repudiates both father and mother. Her defiance might well invite identification by a rebellious child, but her suffering, so vividly described, sends the useful message that rebellion has its cost. Capgrave's life of St Katherine devotes much attention to Katherine's relationship with her parents and makes the value of filial piety explicit: Katherine defies her mother by refusing to marry, and later, when Maxentius overthrows her, a servant reminds her that marriage would have forestalled that disaster. My own sense is that Capgrave himself was interested in family issues, but that William Paris would have

---

[29]   On this and similar manuscripts, see A. S. G. Edwards, 'Fifteenth-Century Collections of Female Saints' Lives', *Yearbook of English Studies*, 33 (2003), 131–41. Like other commentators on Arundel 168, Edwards concludes, 'its subject matter *obviously* suggests a female audience' (p. 136, my emphasis).

[30]   Carl Horstmann (ed.), *Sammlung Altenglischer Legenden* (1878; repr. Hildesheim: Georg Olms, 1969), 191, l. 11.

been surprised to see his Christine used to instruct children in filial piety. The context provided by manuscripts such as Arundel 168 may be most valuable when it points to uses and readings at odds with those envisioned by the original hagiographers.

If individual lives are capable of accommodating diverging interpretations, legendaries are even more so, and this flexibility surely goes a long way toward accounting for the ongoing popularity of the *South English Legendary*, which circulated widely for more than a century. Later *SEL* manuscripts omit some lives and/or add lives not originally part of the collection, and they often contain very different versions of some saints' lives from the earliest copies. For example, the life of Katherine of Alexandria in Bodleian Library, MS Bodley 779, a fifteenth-century manuscript, includes an account of the saint's mystical marriage with Christ. Even in the fifteenth century, when the legendary as a whole was less frequently copied, individual items were excerpted, rewritten, and incorporated into other collections, such as the 1438 *Gilte Legende*. Though the textual tradition of the *SEL* has been carefully charted, the themes introduced by variant legends and the interests exhibited in the overall 'tailoring' of specific manuscripts remain largely unexamined.[31] These variations might reveal much about the reception of the legends and the contest over the saints' meanings in late medieval England.

Illustrations are unfortunately rare in Middle English hagiographical manuscripts—though this absence in itself tells us something about intended function and audience. Only one manuscript of the *SEL* contains illustrations, Bodleian Library, MS Tanner 17, which dates from the fifteenth century. The decorous, serenely prayerful saints depicted contrast strongly with the vituperative rebels celebrated in the accompanying text and suggest an attempt to project paradigms of holiness more suited to the tastes of conservative readers. To my knowledge, the only manuscripts to include actual scenes from a saint's life are manuscripts of Lydgate's *Life of Saint Edmund*. That produced for presentation to King Henry VI c.1433–4 includes 118 scenes, which seem to reinforce Lydgate's emphasis on good governance. Thirty years following its composition, Lydgate's *Edmund* underwent 'a somewhat surprising revival of interest'.[32] Two of the manuscripts produced during the 1460s include cycles of fifty-odd images. Might the selection of images for these later manuscripts help explain what about Edmund's life appealed to consumers in the wholly different political climate that followed the deposition of Henry VI and the ascension of Edward IV? One can also look beyond the boundary of the hagiographical manuscript for visual evidence of the saints' meanings and interpretation—to Books of Hours, sculpture, wall paintings, and stained glass.

[31] Manfred Görlach, *The Textual Tradition of the 'South English Legendary'* (Leeds: University of Leeds, School of English, 1974).

[32] Kathleen L. Scott, 'Lydgate's Lives of Saints Edmund and Fremund: A Newly-Located Manuscript in Arundel Castle', *Viator*, 13 (1982), 335–66 (quote on 335). For a facsimile of the presentation copy of *Edmund*, see A. S. G. Edwards, *The Life of St Edmund King and Martyr: John Lydgate's Illustrated Verse Life Presented to Henry VI* (London: British Library, 2004).

This reflection on directions for a new century of research on hagiography is of course idiosyncratic and indicates only a few of the ways to fruitfully complicate the notion of saintly exemplarity and revise assumptions about the saints and their roles in late medieval culture. These seem to me the most salient questions that the past half-century or so of criticism has left both unanswered and ready to answer. I hope, though, that readers and scholars will be asking yet other questions and revising yet other assumptions long before the end of this century; the best compliment the next generation of scholarship could pay to the topics proposed here would be to exhaust them and pass beyond.

FURTHER READING

A seminal essay, which challenged late twentieth-century scholars to think in new ways about the saints' roles in medieval culture, is Kathleen Ashley and Pamela Sheingorn, 'Introduction', *Interpreting Cultural Symbols: Saint Anne in Late Medieval Society* (Athens: University of Georgia Press, 1990), 1–68. The following monographs represent a variety of late twentieth and early twenty-first-century approaches to Middle English saints' lives, mostly concerned with gender or cultural studies: Gail Ashton, *The Generation of Identity in Late Medieval Hagiography: Speaking the Saint* (London: Routledge, 2000); Theresa Coletti, *Mary Magdalene and the Drama of Saints: Theater, Gender, and Religion in Late Medieval England* (Philadelphia: University of Pennsylvania Press, 2004); Sheila Delany, *Impolitic Bodies: Poetry, Saints, and Society in Fifteenth-Century England; The Work of Osbern Bokenham* (New York: Oxford University Press, 1998); Lewis, *The Cult of St Katherine of Alexandria* (n. 19 above); Catherine Sanok, *Her Life Historical: Exemplarity, England, and Female Saints' Lives* (Philadelphia: University of Pennsylvania Press, forthcoming); Robertson, *Early English Devotional Prose* (n. 3); Sarah Salih, *Versions of Virginity in Late Medieval England* (Woodbridge: D. S. Brewer, 2001); Thompson, *Everyday Saints* (n. 7); Winstead, *Virgin Martyrs* (n. 9) and *John Capgrave's Fifteenth Century*; (n. 10) and Wogan-Browne, *Saints' Lives and Women's Literary Culture* (n. 20). The earliest monograph treating Middle English hagiography to exhibit the concern with culture and gender that continues to prevail today is Thomas J. Heffernan, *Sacred Biography: Saints and their Biographers in the Middle Ages* (New York: Oxford University Press, 1988).

For over a century, the Early English Text Society has been producing and keeping in print many of the major hagiographical source texts. Horstmann's *Sammlung Altenglischer Legenden* (n. 30) and *Altenglische Legenden: Neue Folge* (n. 10) also include many major lives and are available in reprint editions. The publication of previously unedited material and of more reliable editions of previously published saints' lives is transforming the field. Some notable new and forthcoming editions of which I'm aware include Hamer's edition of the *Gilte Legende* and Horobin's edition of the Abbotsford *Legenda aurea* for EETS; E. Gordon Whatley, *Saints' Lives in Middle English Collections* (Kalamazoo, MI: Medieval Institute Publications, 2004); and Reames, *Middle English Legends of Women Saints* (n. 9).

An indispensable reference, even if somewhat out of date, is Charlotte D'Evelyn and Frances A. Foster, 'Saints' Legends', in J. Burke Severs (ed.), *A Manual of the Writings in Middle English, 1050–1500* (Hamden, CT: Archon Books, 1970), vol. ii. 410–29, 553–635. Another essential reference is John Scahill's annotated bibliography, *Middle English Saints' Legends* (Woodbridge: D. S. Brewer, 2005).

CHAPTER 22

SPECULATIVE GENEALOGIES

MATTHEW GIANCARLO

On a chylde is al my thoght. . .
(Octavian, l. 1102)

In the tail-rhyme romance *Octavian*, this dreamy evocation is spoken by the beautiful Saracen princess Marsabelle.[1] The knight Florent has killed a pagan giant, Araganour, who 'lovyd that maydyn par amour' (l. 806) and who, as a warrior of the invading Sultan, was threatening Paris. Marsabelle is the Sultan's daughter, but, being freed from the unwanted attentions of the giant and briefly abducted—and unceremoniously kissed—by the victorious Christian, she finds later that she cannot get 'Chylde Florent' off her mind. He invades her thoughts and desires. In the end the two are united and Marsabelle is converted, but at this point in the story Florent remains the distant object of ambivalent affection as Florent himself is still a child of ambiguous parentage. Born to the emperor and empress of Rome, separated from his family by lies, betrayals, and fantastic events, raised as a foundling by a Parisian burgess, Florent adopts the identity of 'Florent of Paresche ... thoghe he ther were noghte borne' (ll. 1126–8). In true romance style, the road to Florent's reunion with his family (which includes his brother Octavian of the eponymous but misleading title) is thus also the road to the re-securing of his Christian nation and the return of his true identity, finding who he is and where he belongs. Nor is he the

---

[1] Citations from the romances and chronicles come from the following easily accessible editions: *Sege of Melayne, Emaré, Octavian, Sir Isumbras,* and *Sir Gowther* are from Maldwyn Mills (ed.), *Six Middle English Romances* (London: J. M. Dent & Sons, 1992); *Havelok, Athelston, Gamelyn, Sir Orfeo,* and *King Horn* are from Donald B. Sands (ed.), *Middle English Verse Romances* (Exeter: University of Exeter Press, 1993); Stephen Shepherd (ed.), *Turpines Story* (Oxford: Oxford University Press, 2004); Robert Mannyng of Brunne, *The Chronicle,* ed. Idelle Sullens (Binghamton, NY: Binghamton University, 1996); Layamon, *Brut,* ed. G. L. Brook and R. F. Leslie, 2 vols. (London: Oxford University Press, 1963, 1978); Ralph Hanna and David Lawton (eds.), *The Siege of Jerusalem* (Oxford: Oxford University Press, 2004). Shepherd has also edited *Middle English Romances* (New York: W. W. Norton, 1995); and the *Stanzaic Guy of Warwick* (*Guy* 2) is also recently available, ed. Alison Wiggins (Kalamazoo, MI: Medieval Institute Publications, 2004).

only 'child' of the narrative, as we ourselves are meant to identify emotionally both with Florent's broad social context and with his familial and intimate milieu. As the romance moves towards its resolution, all our thoughts too are on these children: they are the objects of our own pleasurable longings for a happy narrative and for a familiar story of family reunion, 'evil' defeated, and love triumphant.

I want to begin with this infinitely repeated—and infinitely repeatable—plot trajectory to structure this review of Middle English romance reading and scholarship. Romance is the most capacious and protean of medieval genres—Bakhtin's novelistic genre *avant la lettre*—even as it is the most recognizable in its motifs, themes, structures, and memes. Very little indeed can escape from the purview of romance, then or now. Much recent criticism has refrained from defining 'the' romance genre by way of any simple criteria or a priori elements, settling instead on the sensible recognition that a wide network of motifs, broadly defined, can instead give us a better understanding of its 'family resemblances'.[2] Ironically this flexible notion of genetic-generic relatedness is also meta-generic, as 'romance' is the genre among genres where *family resemblances*, undefinable but foundational kinship ties, are a singular organizing principle and thematic obsession of narrative and its inhabitants.

This emphasis on family and lineage will be the main aspect of my overview here. But, in the spirit of romantic deferral, I would also like to frame these speculations with an example of storytelling that is both distant and, at the same time, recognizably a near cousin to the romances we find and enjoy in Middle English. Lila Abu-Lughod's book *Veiled Sentiments*, published some years ago, is a remarkable study of the Awlad 'Ali, Bedouins of the Western Deserts of Egypt. An isolated, Islamic, strongly patriarchal, and fiercely proud culture, one pressured by modernity and by its own persistent internal tensions, the Awlad 'Ali place high value on oral poetry and storytelling. Their poems, *ghinnawas* or 'little songs', are the focus of Abu-Lughod's analysis. They provide a key for understanding many aspects of the Awlad 'Ali culture: kinship ties and marital relations, the importance of honour and modesty, as well as the socio-sexual roles and self-understandings of Awlad 'Ali women and men. This poetry is short and plaintive (Abu-Lughod describes it as a cross between Japanese haiku and American blues), short songs of loss and desire; lovers in the romantic stories of the Awlad 'Ali speak exclusively in *ghinnawas*. However it is not a *ghinnawa* but a little parable, told by an old Bedouin woman to explain the difference between sons and daughters, that captures some of the resemblances I want to trace here:

> There once was a woman with nine daughters. When she became pregnant again she prayed for a boy and made an oath to give up one of her daughters as an offering if she

2 The term is used in the Wittgensteinian sense: see Helen Cooper, *The English Romance in Time: Transforming Motifs from Geoffrey of Monmouth to the Death of Shakespeare* (Oxford: Oxford University Press, 2004), 7–10; Ad Putter, 'A Historical Introduction', in Ad Putter and Jane Gilbert (eds.), *The Spirit of Medieval English Popular Romance* (London: Longman, 2000), 2.

were granted a son. She did give birth to a boy. When they moved camp, riding off on their camels, she left behind one daughter.

Soon a man came by on a horse and found the girl tied up. He asked her story, untied her, took her with him, and cared for her.

Meanwhile, the boy grew up and took a wife. His wife demanded that he make his mother a servant. He did this, and the old mother was forced to do all the household work for her daughter-in-law.

One day they decided to move camp. They loaded up the camels and traveled and traveled. The old mother had to walk, driving the sheep. She got tired and was eventually left behind. Lost, she wandered and wandered until she came upon a camp. The people in the camp called to her and invited her in. They asked her story. She told them she had not always been a servant and recounted her tale. When the people heard this story they went running to tell one of the women. It turned out that she was the old woman's daughter who had been abandoned as a child. She came, questioned the old woman, and, once convinced that it really was her mother, embraced and kissed her, took her to her tent, washed her clothes for her, fed her, and cared well for her.

By and by, the son came looking for his mother. He rode up to the camp and asked people, 'Haven't you seen an old servant wandering around?' The woman who (unknown to him) was his sister invited him into her tent. She demanded that a ram be brought and slaughtered in his honor. She then asked him, 'Where is the *rihm* [womb] of the ram?' The brother looked at her in surprise answering, 'A ram has no *rihm*, didn't you know?'

She then revealed her identity and told him her story. She refused to let him take his mother back and scolded him for having so mistreated her. [3]

To understand the story, one must first understand the overwhelming cultural preference among the Awlad 'Ali (as among other Arabs) for sons over daughters; that daughters-in-law are supposed to serve mothers-in-law, not vice versa; and the profound transgression of treating an elder kinsman (or kinswoman) as a mere servant. As Abu-Lughod explains, 'the moral of the story turns on the double meaning of the triliteral root *rahama*, from which the word *rihm* (womb), as well as a word meaning pity, compassion, or mercy is derived. Thus the story links wombs (femaleness) with compassion and caring.'[4] The conclusion 'a ram has no *rihm*'—a male has no womb/compassion—thus carries the force of a critical pun and a parabolic little critique of the assumed superiority of men over women and sons over daughters. While women among the Awlad 'Ali also strongly prefer sons (for various reasons, as Abu-Lughod makes clear), this little narrative gives evidence for a resistant, if somewhat clandestine, perspective on family relationships among the Awlad 'Ali.

This story is also, clearly, a little romance. It has separations, chance encounters, family betrayals and reunions, and a clever play on language—a revelatory turn that hinges on the recognition of a punning kinship between terms. A daughter,

---

[3] Lila Abu-Lughod, *Veiled Sentiments: Honor and Poetry in a Bedouin Society* (Berkeley and Los Angeles: University of California Press, 1986), 128–9.

[4] Ibid. 129.

rather than a son, is abandoned; a mother, not a father, is unjustly dispossessed; felicitous resolution follows the re-establishment of right family relations (parent and child) as well as right social relations. The parable combines elements familiar from biblical analogues (like the story of Joseph and his brothers) as well as medieval narratives of the 'Constance' type; the unnamed daughter is not too distant from a Cordelia. Despite its differences—indeed, partly because of them—this Bedouin story stands as a small example of the extents of 'romance' narrative. Given that medieval European romances began to flourish at about the time of the Crusades in the eleventh and twelfth centuries, some historical connection might possibly exist between these modes of circum-Mediterranean narrative art. But as Abu-Lughod makes clear, the deeper motivation for stories like these, and for the *ghinnawas*, is a system of cultural reproduction deeply embedded among the Awlad 'Ali and also deeply relevant to medieval Europe: strong agnatic or patrilineal descent and (in Europe as in North Africa) male primogeniture, the systems of social authority through males' inheritances. What romance responds to, and what Abu-Lughod's old woman's tale partly reacts against, is the social system of *genealogy* itself, of the conception of family relation, power, and descent that is at the core of the temporal arrangement of narrative consciousness. As such, romances are almost always, in some manner, thoughts on a child.

Chronicle and genealogy

Although the distance from this kind of romantic family story to the genre of historical chronicle may seem far, in fact they are demonstrably close kin. In medieval literature, the genres of romance and chronicle are connected by their thematic and structural focus on the genealogical foundations of social organization. Both are about, and *are,* genealogy, family and individual histories. Like storied twins, 'romance' and 'chronicle' have the same point of birth and their wanderings intersect; they grow up together, and somewhat apart. In a way, the unstated object of much medieval historiography was to bring these two narrative impulses home in reconciled reunion. As Francis Ingledew, Gabrielle Spiegel, Howard Bloch, and others have demonstrated, the development of Western European systems of genealogy was coterminous with the development of secular and vernacular historiography, especially in the adoption of an 'Aeneidized' history for the ascendant Normans of the twelfth century.[5] Neo-Virgilian history, tracing

---

[5] See Francis Ingledew, 'The Book of Troy and the Genealogical Construction of History: The Case of Geoffrey of Monmouth's *Historia regum Brittaniae*', *Speculum*, 69 (1994), 665–704; Gabrielle Spiegel, 'Genealogy: Form and Function in Medieval Historiography', in *The Past as Text: The Theory and Practice of Medieval Historiography* (Baltimore: Johns Hopkins University Press, 1997), 99–110; and R. Howard Bloch, *Etymologies and Genealogies: A Literary Anthropology of the French Middle Ages* (Chicago: University of Chicago Press, 1983).

speculative national genealogies back to the diaspora of Troy, rendered genealogy itself the mode not only of political legitimization but of socially significant narrative. The appropriation of land, its ties to an agnatic scheme of familial descent and inheritance, and the stories told to justify it all, all took on the form of a family story of separation, travel, conflict, and conquest, a providential (but secular) movement forward that was really a movement *back* to a patrimony or 'true' home. Especially in the *Historia* of Geoffrey of Monmouth, that source and cathexis not only for Arthurian romance but for a whole range of historical narratives, 'British history is thus systematically genealogized for the first time at the same moment that it is first systematically imperialized'[6]—and, one could add, first systematically *romanticized*, as it would later be adopted and adapted by the earliest chronicles and romances. But the broader point is that, as Spiegel has summarized, 'it is genealogy as symbolic form ... that had the greatest impact on the patterning of historical narrative and the formation of its expressive meaning. Through the imposition of genealogical metaphors on historical narrative, genealogy becomes for historiography not only a thematic "myth" but a narrative *mythos*, a symbolic form that governs the very shape and significance of the past.'[7]

As *mythos*, 'ritual', 'mode', 'socio-symbolic message', 'story form', or whatever else, romance has this fundamental kinship with the shape of historical narration that also opened it up to the possibilities of individual narrative as well, the story-form for singular persons as the focus of sentiment. The romance landscape in England and elsewhere is populated by figures mythic, heroic, and historic: Tristran, Horn, Orestes, Guy, Alexander, Havelok, Arthur, Bevis, Orfeo, Charlemagne, Aeneas, Constantine, Robert, Godfrey, Turpin, Gawain, and others, as well as Emaré, Constance, Blancheflour, Griselda, Florence, Paulina, Canacee. An interweaving of national and personal destinies creates a narrative field or nexus wherein the shape of an individual life, usually an exemplary one in some way, can find a similarly exemplary style. In this way saints' lives also overlapped with romances. But it was, almost exclusively, members of the secular aristocracy—preferably kings—who were imagined through the tropes of romance. A good example is Robert Mannyng's very self-aware vernacular romanticization of his king Edward I,

> The hardy Kyng Belyn the cite of Rome wan,
> & sithen Constantyn & Maximian;
> Arthure wan alle ffraunce, slouh the emperour of Rome;
> thise of suerd ne lance doubted dynt no dome ...
> Among all thise hardie may Edward, our kyng,
> be sette fulle solempnelie & made of grete praisyng;
> sen the dede of Arthure, in Inlond was ther non
> that so wele stode in stoure ageyn his foos ilkon [each one].
> This was Edward, Kyng Henry sonne, the last,

---

[6] Ingledew, 'The Book of Troy and the Genealogical Construction of History', 678.

[7] Spiegel, 'Genealogy', 105.

tithing haf we hard, the dede him doun has kast.
Now may men sing & say, in romance & ryme,
Edward is now away, right has lorn [lost]his tyme.

(Chronicle, II. 8309–12, 8317–24)

Here in Mannyng's 'romance and rhyme' Edward, child of Henry, receives his
chronicling, placed in the Galfredian pantheon of great British conquerors along
with others such as Havelok (whose missing story Mannyng explicitly interpolates
into the temporal sequence). This chronicle is neither uniformly laudatory or
uncritical, nor entirely credulous. Layamon's sceptical but not dismissive comments
about Arthur in his own Brut—whose accomplishments, he says, the Welsh Britons
are wont to overinflate 'because they love him greatly' ('ah Bruttes hine luueden
swithe' (l. 11471))—can also stand as a cue to the veridical sensibilities of romance
historiography. The boundaries between romance and chronicle are fluid, but this
fluidity is not just a symptom of 'generic vacillation', or even that 'at the deepest
levels, most writers of romaunces seem indifferent to the historicity or fictionality
of their narratives'.[8] In some of the most imaginative Arthurian romances, as Ad
Putter has shown, care was taken by authors to make the temporal sequencing
of events fit into recognized and plausible gaps in the chronicled 'true' narrative
history.[9] And even the wildly imaginative excesses of a story like The Siege of
Jerusalem can give way to a dry and fairly accurate chronicle of the Roman
year of four emperors (ll. 925–52). Rather, we can see the historical/historicist
ambiguity of romance-chronicle form as the hybridized result of precisely this
originary condition of narrative in genealogical order, an order which 'makes the
real desirable, makes the real into an object of desire, and does so, by its formal
imposition, upon events that are represented as real, of the formal coherency
that stories possess'.[10] If medieval romances appeal to historical veracity, medieval
histories—like later ones—also appeal to romantic promise and attraction: the
promise of a good story, well fulfilled, that makes a certain sense or order of things
and that provides an acceptable genealogy of events in a recognizable and repeatable
arc or form.

Romances and chronicles are thus both obsessively concerned with the stories
of kings and knights, the rise and fall of reigns and rules, the 'subjects of history'
at various levels of authoritative social organization and genealogical order. They
also display a continual fascination with the sheer improbability of events and the

[8] Lee Patterson, 'The Romance of History and the Alliterative Morte Arthure', in Negotiating
the Past: The Historical Understanding of Medieval Literature (Madison: University of Wisconsin
Press, 1987), 204; Paul Strohm, 'The Origin and Meaning of Middle English Romaunce', Genre, 10
(1977), 19.

[9] Ad Putter, 'Finding Time for Romance: Medieval Arthurian Literary History', Medium Aevum,
63 (1994), 1–16.

[10] Hayden White, 'Narrativity in the Representation of Reality', in The Content of the Form: Narrative
Discourse and Historical Representation (Baltimore: Johns Hopkins University Press, 1987), 21.

strange potentialities of temporal unfolding itself that may or may not be 'magic'.[11] It is axiomatic that romance is the genre of magical wonders and wish-fulfilment, but these wishes—like the chance encounter of a child with a lost parent, the return of a person long gone, the recognition of a thing forgotten—are often not other-worldly so much as they are, unsettlingly, *more* of this world than we normally experience. In Jameson's evocative formulation, 'romance is precisely that form in which the *worldness of the world* reveals or manifests itself, in which, in other words, *world* in the technical sense of the transcendental horizon of our experience becomes visible in an inner-worldly sense'.[12] Similarly, Gradon characterizes the magic in and of romance as a form of immanence: 'The supernatural of romances is essentially a way of making the familiar unfamiliar and remote. Where the ice of reality is so thin we are always aware of the dark waters beneath, and the familiar world becomes strange.'[13] 'Worldness' is revealed in the defamiliarized liminality of familiar experience occurring at the borders of wonder, a space romances love to evoke and chronicles frequently strive to record. Here truth is strange *as* fiction, or fiction is merely a species of barely estranged truth; and here medieval chronicles and romances often tend to tread on the same thin ice between historicity and sheer absurdity.

Childish romances

Often the objective correlative of Gradon's strange immanence is the child, the strangeness in it or around it, 'child-ness' real and symbolical. The childish youth of Arthur's court in *Gawain and the Green Knight* calls forth the threatening marvels of the green knight; in *Havelok* the young foundling prince Havelok exudes a phosphorescent glow in his sleep, an aura that clearly signals him as both uncanny and elect. In *Emaré*, Emaré's son Segramour is so beautiful that he naturally captures the eye of his unknowing father, the King of Wales, and Emaré herself has also been a single child around whom marvellous events have unfolded. In the beginning of *King Horn*, the beautiful fairness of child Horn is what keeps him and his captured companions from being slain by the invading Sultan. In *Octavian*, after the Empress has been falsely accused of adultery and exiled, the fate of her two children is like a scene out of *Raising Arizona*. Baby Florent is stolen by an ape, which is then defeated by a knight, who is then set upon by brigands, who then sell the baby to the Parisian merchant Clement for twenty pounds (Clement bargains them down

---

[11] See Michelle Sweeney, *Magic in Medieval Romance from Chrétien de Troyes to Geoffrey Chaucer* (Dublin: Four Courts Press, 2000).

[12] Fredric Jameson, 'Magical Narratives: On the Dialectical Use of Genre Criticism', in *The Political Unconscious: Narrative as a Socially Symbolic Act* (Ithaca, NY: Cornell University Press, 1981), 112.

[13] Pamela Gradon, 'The Romance Mode', in *Form and Style in Early English Literature* (London: Metheun, 1971), 236.

from forty). Baby Octavian has it comparatively easy since he is only abducted by a lioness, and both the lioness and the baby are then taken away by a griffin to an island where the child (who has been suckled by the lioness) is eventually reunited with his mother.

Such child-centric flights of fancy are common stuff in romances. But even in romances where children are not the discrete focus of wonders and adventures, the conditions of genealogical lineage and descent still provide narrative and symbolical focus. A strangely resonant example could be drawn from the martial *Turpines Story*. Christian soldiers under Charlemagne, gathered to fight the Saracens in Spain, camp the night before the battle and fix their spears into the ground: 'But what wonder whas there? Treuly, on the morne alle the speris that where pyhtte so, they where ryndyd, buddede, and grene' (p.12). This marvel happens twice: when planted into the earth, the spears of soldiers fated to die in battle sprout new growth overnight, symbolizing the soldiers' imminent rebirth of martyrdom. The implicit genealogical image of the *virga de radice Iesse* (Isa. 11:1) here indicates they will be new children of God. In *Athelston* the political plot is driven by multiple marriages and by the pregnancy of the wife of Egelond, the earl of Stane—as well by as Athelston's wife's own pregnancy, which Athelston ruins when he kicks her and kills his unborn son and heir. In *The Sege of Melayne*, the military campaign of the Christians against the Sultan Arabas is motivated by the Saracen invasion of Lombardy, but also by the Sultan's threat that he will kill Duke Alantyne's 'wyffe and his childire three | Byfore his eghne that he myghte see' (ll. 58–9). The threat to Alantyne's family partly motivates the Christian resistance. More subtly, the romance appeals to kinship by making Alantyne the 'cosyn nere of kyn' of Charlemagne (l. 149), and by making the conflict between 'Ganyenn'/Ganelon and Roland one of genealogy and inheritance: Ganyenn has married Roland's mother and covets Roland's landed patrimony, so he treasonously tries to have him slain (ll. 169–80). In these examples as in many others—not to mention the familial upheavals of the Griselda and Constance traditions—the principle of historical emplotment as genealogy, the succession of generations and the histories of families, provides the background for the unfolding of the world in all its familiar strangeness, conflicts, and resolutions.

In this manner just about every medieval romance, and most chronicles, could be characterized as 'family romances', and not just in the way Freud defined the term as a childish fantasy of discovering a better and nobler parentage (reflecting the child's lost adoration for his or her real mother and father).[14] Rather, the wish to discover or recover a truer, nobler self, and a legitimizing lineage, is a form of ideological narrative reiterable at almost every level: the individual, the family, the tribe, the class, the region, the estate, the nation. Proceeding from Adorno's

[14] See Sigmund Freud, 'Family Romances', in *Collected Papers*, vol. v, ed. James Strachey (New York: Basic Books, 1959), 74–8.

dictum that identity is the primal form of ideology, we can see various romances as chronicles (and vice versa) of various identity-fantasies, ideologically selective emplotments of the way things were, or should have been, or ought to be. *The Sege of Melayne* focuses largely on the warrior-bishop Turpin, whose power lies not only in his ecclesial office and bullying of the secular barons, but also in his ability to muster, literally, an army of clerics: 'a hundrethe thowsande were redy bownn | Of prestis that werede schaven crownn | And fresche men forto fighte' (ll. 632–4). This massive priest army threatens the secular European forces just as Turpin draws his weapon against the recalcitrant Charlemagne, eventually forcing him, and them, to fight the heathens as they are supposed to. The warrior priests are even given the vanguard in the fight (ll. 923–5). In reading *Melayne* we are in the midst of an estates-mixing, quasi-clerical fantasy of priestly martial power. At the end it is 'Oure Bretons' (ll. 1517, 1526, 1532) under the Duke of Brittany, Sir Lyonelle, who turn the battle for the Christians. This British connection recuperates the chronicle-story as a glorious British-English story as well. Similarly the author of *Turpines Story* attempts to make Roland's father Milo into an Englishman, and so to appropriate Roland's glory, genealogically, to the English nation.[15]

Other examples are both distant but similar in their fantastic exploration and rewriting of the boundaries of the social world. *Havelok* has an attractive combination of class-mixing monarchialism, as the prince and destined king, the supposed son of an upright fisherman, works as a porter and lackey. Everyone loves him for his noble bearing, which wins him the hand of a similarly displaced and mistreated princess, Goldeboru. Like others, this romance seems to want to teach us that real ethical nobility—which stands *with* noble genealogical lineage, not in place of it—can flourish precisely in these intersections of working-class and productive bourgeois values with 'good birth'. A similar cross-class fantasy operates in *Octavian*. Florent is adopted by 'Clement the Velayn' (l. 573) and comes to conflict with him over Florent's innate noble tendencies (he wastes good money on things like falcons and beautiful horses). A slapstick moment occurs when Clement and his wife literally fall over themselves trying to help Florent with Clement's old rusty armour and sword; the son is deeply embarrassed when his foster-father acts like a money-grubbing merchant at a noble feast. Still, even after Florent has learned his true lineage, he goes back to Clement for help in his fight against the heathens and he still calls him 'father' (and Clement calls Florent 'son') in the latter parts of the story (ll. 1489–1560).

A more aggressive social examination of the stresses of family and genealogy underlies the romance of *Gamelyn*. *Gamelyn* is usually classed as a romance of the 'greenwood' since the hero retreats to the forest when disinherited by his elder brother. But the larger trajectory of the story shows that Gamelyn

---

[15] This is noted by Stephen Shepherd (ed.), *Turpines Story* (Oxford: Oxford University Press, 2004), p. xxxix.

reacts violently against all of the social institutions enforcing the primogenital inheritance driving the conflict—and denied by the dying father, who tries to partition his lands equitably for all three of his sons. Gamelyn fights against family (his eldest sibling), the Church (he arranges a sound beating for the clerical 'brothers' assembled at his elder brother's feast), and even the state, as he opposes the king's sheriff and officers who come to subdue him. This is a fantasy for younger brothers. The young men who gather in the forest with Gamelyn are a striking image of all those (male) children cut out of the deal by the rules of the inheritance game. The eventual reconciliation hinges on the reorganization of all the principal elements as well as on Gamelyn's display of true filial and political fidelity. The eldest brother dies, making the more reasonable middle sibling the elder, and Gamelyn rescues him from unjust execution at the hands of the shire court. The two are easily reconciled and Gamelyn also reconciles with the king. But this is not before Gamelyn himself has been made 'maister outlawe' of the forest brigands and crowned their king (l. 694), an oppositional ascendancy he can leave only when the system recognizes his just claims to a place in the family inheritance.

Indeed so many adapatations of this basic medieval kinship/inheritance plot have been made, from Shakespeare to the Brontës, that one easily forgets how socially resonant it must have been for a contemporary audience. A story like *Sir Gowther* offers another version of the romance of an outsider child who cannot fit into the heritable order of things. Gowther is the child of a demon who lay with his unwitting mother. Baby Gowther is a little devil-spawn (Merlin's 'halfe brodur' (l. 95)) who suckles his nursemaids to death, terrorizes his family and community, attacks churches, and generally raises hell all throughout his childhood. But when he learns his true parentage from his mother—that he is not, in fact, the son of the Austrian duke (l. 31)—he grieves pitifully and goes on pilgrimage to Rome. This is a child who wants to repudiate his infernal biological paternity in favour of an adopted 'holy fadur' (l. 281). After fighting heathens and doing a long and self-abasing penance, Gowther is shriven by the Pope who declares, 'Now art thou Goddus chyld; | The thar not dowt tho warlocke wyld' (ll. 667–8). This spiritual conversion is emotionally satisfying, and it also works to satisfy the original motivation for Gowther's birth: to provide the duke with an heir 'that schall owre londus weld' (l. 81). Where before Gowther was a threat to the social system, in the end he becomes a pillar of it: defending Christianity and Europe, endowing lands and churches, protecting his (foster) father's patrimony. This can come about only through a quasi-paradoxical *denial* of a 'true' paternity in favour of a truer adopted one, an inheritance that turns out to be both spiritual and material. Like the (justly) more famous conversion of Guy of Warwick from the secular to the religious world, Gowther's history suggests another kind of social co-option in the context of an agnatic system that wants to recuperate its own demons. But in all cases, another *true* child of narrative is the system of familial descent that gives rise to the conflicts, and shape to the stories, in the first place. This other, abstract object of desire is what is fostered and recuperated—given a restored identity—by the energies of imaginative 'history' put into a romantic form.

Visceral conventions

As these examples suggest, Middle English romances in fact do quite a bit of symbolical work in the representation and exploration of their contemporary social systems.[16] Some of this representation is fairly direct. The English version of *Havelok* contains references to parliament that may reflect actual parliamentary assemblies of 1301 and 1307 (*Athelston* also has interesting references to judicial parliaments); *Gamelyn* portrays shire court legal proceedings in the case brought against the outlaw hero; *Sir Orfeo* raises questions of kingly succession and regency rule, with a surprisingly (romantically?) smooth transition of power at the story's end; *Athelston* depicts not only the process of trial by ordeal but also, in the strained relations of the principals, an exploration of conflicts among the governmental elite. Looking at the English romances overall, there could scarcely be a group less illustrative of Auerbach's assertion that 'in the courtly romance the functional, the historically real aspects of class are passed over'.[17] Far from passing over class and historical differences, English romances frequently show a barely concealed desire to foreground them, play with them, to take trouble over them in various ways. And in the great 'matters' of national romance traditions—Britain/England, France, Rome/antiquity, and, in John Barbour's *Bruce*, the often-overlooked national history of Scotland—medieval cultures produced chronicle-narratives of direct political resonance that appeal to the visceral bases of family, inheritance, and patrimony.

This appeal to a recuperable and felt immediacy, the emotional and sometimes violent attractions of a good story, also characterizes the intersections of romance and chronicle. Fantastic and bloody violence is another hallmark of medieval romances, from the endless and repetitive trepannings of Malory's Arthuriad to the gory excesses of *Siege of Jerusalem*, to the casual head-chopping and Saracen-splitting antics of heroes like Guy and Beves.[18] Geraldine Heng has recently argued that the entire genre of post-Galfredian romance has at its origin the foundationally excessive and fantastic violence of the first crusades, with episodes of cannibalism

---

[16] In this regard, see esp. Susan Crane, *Insular Romance: Politics, Faith, and Culture in Anglo-Norman and Middle English Culture* (Berkeley and Los Angeles: University of California Press, 1986); and *Gender and Romance in Chaucer's Canterbury Tales* (Princeton: Princeton University Press, 1994).

[17] Erich Auerbach, 'The Knight Sets Forth', in *Mimesis: The Representation of Reality in Western Literature*, trans. Willard R. Trask (Princeton: Princeton University Press, 1953), 136.

[18] For discussion see the essays collected in Albrecht Classen (ed.), *Violence in Medieval Courtly Literature: A Casebook* (New York: Routledge, 2004).

and wartime atrocity obliquely reflected in texts like *Richard Coer de Lyon*.[19] Lurid latecomers like the *Alliterative Morte Arthure* only continue this well-established tradition. In this regard, the romances are not too different from the often-noted violent excessiveness of Layamon's *Brut*. The attractions of the visceral also help explain the presence and delight in romantic wonders. Additionally, the chronicle-romantic imperative for a recuperable and significant story appears to lie at the heart of the genres' other kinds of violence, emotional and sentimental. Romance is—or tries to be—the genre that cuts close to the bone in episodes of pathos and feeling: familial separations, deep-felt attachments between men and women, men and men, even people and animals, and, of course, parents and children. Domestic relations especially are the focus of stress and sentiment, as most romances will find a way to turn all sorts of conflicts into family affairs. A somewhat absurd set of examples can be drawn from one of the most popular metrical romances, *Sir Isumbras*. The knight Isumbras, a worldly and successful nobleman with a perfect family (a beautiful wife and three sons), is punished for his pride, 'that of God yafe he ryghte nowghte' (l. 38). He loses all his property and possessions; his children are stolen away by wild animals (a lion, a leopard, and a unicorn, naturally); his wife is abducted, and later married, by a heathen king. For years Isumbras becomes a lowly bog-digger and smith's assistant, forging the armour for Christian warriors opposing the heathen. When he gets his chance to fight the enemy, he wins the battle for the Christians and then goes on a seven-year pilgrimmage to Jerusalem. After he receives a divine message that his penance has been lifted, Isumbras visits the heathen queen, his long-separated wife. There is a token-recognition scene and a touching reunion, and then Isumbras is—without any explanation—'crowned kynge … of many ryche londes thare' (ll. 716–17). He declares a new war on the Saracens. Isumbras's forces desert him, but before he goes into battle, his wife dons armour 'as she were a knyghte' (l. 746) and the two stride off to face the enemy together. When they reach the battlefield, who should come to their aid but their three boy children, now grown, riding the wild animals that had abducted them. Like a superhero family the Isumbras-clan defeats the entire Saracen army by themselves, killing 'thrytty thowsand and thre' (l. 762). All's well that ends well as they return home and Isumbras endows each son with lands and a kingdom.

This is a ridiculous but fun example of the kind of story that might have been read with pleasure around a family table or gathering, because it gives fantastically romantic shape to the chronicle of one gentry family's loss, recovery, and victory. Isumbras's crowning as a Christian king in a heathen land is at once inevitable and inexplicable. The romance motifs make the story silly and wondrous, but also more emotionally engaging. The darker counterparts to this playful exaggeration are the internecine struggles of the Arthurian tradition and, as Helen Cooper has suggested,

[19] Geraldine Heng, *Empire of Magic: Medieval Romance and the Politics of Cultural Fantasy* (New York: Columbia University Press, 2003).

the trend towards family tragedy and father-killing in the fifteenth-century prose romances, which might reflect the increasingly violent kin struggles of the Wars of the Roses.[20] And many romances also react to the undeniably visceral anxieties surrounding the institution of the household itself: the fear of the loss—and perhaps equally stressful, the unexpected gain—of wealth and social status, the desire for advancement along with the worries of fitting into a real home. Narratives such as *Sir Launfal* and *Sir Amadace*, which are almost exclusively focused on domestic economic loss and gain, give fantastic imagining and refraction to this other, quotidian emotional turmoil.[21] Even in those later grim prose chronicle-romances where a ram truly has no *rihm*, the form of romance itself implicitly holds out the attraction of a homely, recuperable story that can make critical sense out of violent and harmful history.

What I want to suggest in part, then, is that when medieval English writers appealed to romance stories or conventions—when in Passus XIX/XX of *Piers Plowman*, for example, Langland dresses up Jesus Christ as a knight to have him joust for the salvation of mankind—such typified gestures would have made stories *more* immediate, not less, for their audiences. Again, this immediacy goes back to the genealogical assumptions of the genre. Much good work is yet to be done on what we might call, after Bourdieu, the 'practical logics' of kinship and family that inform these texts. As numerous and popular stories, romances form a unique literary field that can be interpreted in ways simply unavailable to the more limited 'high' literature of a Gower and Chaucer, and different again from the clerical-social criticism of *Piers Plowman*. They also resonate in more direct ways with the historical chronicles that were their fellow travellers in subjects and audiences. Many of these chronicles for the medieval period (the differing versions of Geoffrey's *Historia*, Layamon, Gaimar, Wace, Langtoft, Mannyng, Robert of Gloucester, Castleford's *Chronicle*, Trevisa and Higden, Walsingham, Knighton, the prose *Brut*, the political poems and prophecies collected by Thomas Wright, and others) are still neglected or only recently re-edited and re-encountered. The task is not so much trying to fit specific romances to specific historical episodes, real or not, nor to specific chronicles. Rather the challenge is to see them *as* a field, as a mutually informing body of historical, speculative, and creative authorship both reflecting and establishing the cultural assumptions of genealogical propriety, and property. The breadth of romance's ideological reach is simply undeniable. As Chaucer himself must have been aware (despite his snide remark), it was not just women who believed in the historical veracity of the romances of Lancelot du Lake,

---

[20] Helen Cooper, 'Counter-Romance: Civil Strife and Father-Killing in the Prose Romances', in Cooper and S. Mapstone (eds.), *The Long Fifteenth Century: Essays for Douglas Gray*, (Oxford: Clarendon, 1997), 141–62.

[21] See generally D. Vance Smith, *Arts of Possession: The Middle English Household Imaginary* (Minneapolis: University of Minnesota Press, 2003), for a provocative study of how 'in Middle English, the romance is as often an economic designation as it is a formalist generic designation' (p. 77).

but his own king, Edward III, who (like his grandfather Edward I) was one of the most vigorous promoters of the Arthurian *mythos* in the Middle Ages. In a socially real sense, *everyone* lived in a romance-world, because that is how the world was discursively constituted; any chronicle would have told you so.

The homes of romance and chronicle

As ongoing editorial and critical study has also made clear, the textual nexus of that historical-romantic world was the medieval household, and with it, the family. The great collections and miscellanies of medieval English romances owe their textual form and patterned randomness to the institutional needs of the household.[22] The Auchinleck manuscript, Ashmole 61, the Thornton manuscript, the Ireland–Blackburn manuscript, and other compilations containing romances are clearly the products and possessions of (or were intended for) bourgeois and gentry households. The particular codex form in which many of these are found, the slender 'holster book', is now recognized to be not the format of a travelling minstrel's collection but rather—in a fitting hypostasization of so many romances' domestic focus—a format adopted from the convenient and cost-effective books of household accounting ledgers. Along with the romances these collections contain a wide range of texts for domestic topics and concerns: saints' lives, conduct literature, lyrics, exempla and proverbs, catechistic and meditative texts, comic tales and burlesques, and histories and chronicles. The Auchinleck manuscript, for example, contains an anonymous short English metrical chronicle as well as a copy of the Battle Abbey roll. The romances are sometimes mixed up quite intimately with these other genres. When read in context, then, the oft-repeated self-declarations in the romances that they come from 'cronekill' and 'historie' would have seemed much less dissonant than they do today, since all of them—romance, history, life, and legend—came out of the same books, literally. Families appear to have consciously cultivated the texts both of the contemporary domestic life of the household *and* of its genealogical-historical fantasies in the same book space.

The challenge still facing current scholarship is to account for the nuances of those imaginings in a way that will do justice to the simultaneous challenge of editing and interpreting the romances themselves. The Auchinleck *Guy of Warwick*, for example, which survives in either three parts (*Guy* 1, *Guy* 2, and *Reinbroun*) or two, or as a single whole, poses a unique problem for editorial practice that simultaneously requires an interpretative positioning on the ideal shape of the romance itself. An increasingly attractive solution is the current trend towards reproducing such texts

---

[22] See Putter, 'A Historical Introduction'; Murray Evans, *Rereading Middle English Romance: Manuscript Layout, Decoration, and the Rhetoric of Composite Structure* (Montreal: McGill-Queen's University Press, 1995); and Smith, *Arts of Possession*.

in something approximating their 'original' context. The miscellany Ashmole 61 is currently being edited as a whole with all forty-one of its disparate texts retained together. Reading the romance *Lybeaus Desconus* not just with *Sir Orfeo* and *Sir Isumbras* (items 20, 39, and 5) but also with texts like *The Life of St Eustace*, *The Short Charter of Christ*, and Lydgate's *Stans puer ad mensam* (items 1, 29, and 7) promises to alter our own understanding of how all of them were situated and received by a medieval domestic audience. Much as the work of the last thirty years has improved our knowledge of the courtly-bureaucratic contexts of a poet like Chaucer, and as recent scholarship on the 'professional readers'—and rebellious misreaders—of Langland has refined our understanding of *Piers Plowman*, so too the broader domestic contexts of the chronicles and romances stand to be investigated for their selective and formative influence on the texts as we have received them. This is not to promote a programme of 'un-editing', as it is sometimes called. If one thing is clear, it is that the romances are always already edited; they were the products of a domestic book market.[23] But where romances have usually been gathered and anthologized into monogeneric collections, the judicious de-anthologization and re-miscellanization of the romances will, perhaps, return these literary-historical children to their more rightful home, however messy and foreign it may in fact be.

This, of course, is itself a romantic desire. As genres of the visceral and as symbolic structures of both events and narrative, romances and chronicles stand in a unique position to demonstrate to modern audiences that such modes 'tell us in what direction to think about the events and charge our thought ... with different emotional valences'.[24] The greatest impact that medieval romance has had over the succeeding centuries is in the development of what has recently been called the 'bardic nationalism' of Anglo-European literary history. Recent work on nationalism and communal identity in the romances, as well as the long-standing ambivalences about the 'nation' that romances and chronicles display, can be correlated thematically to the impact that romances themselves have had as textual vehicles of national identity-fantasies.[25] Nationalism *is* a form of chronicle-romance and romantic chronicling, the aggressive and creative recuperation of the past through desired stories and historically 'true' narratives, and an activity that is at once radical *and* conservative; a return to a new home. Recent historiographical work by David Matthews has demonstrated how central medieval romances were in the editorial and philological projects of recuperating the 'reliques' of a national

---

[23] For discussion of this point see Putter, 'A Historical Introduction', and Evans, *Rereading Middle English Romance*.

[24] Hayden White, 'The Historical Text as Literary Artifact', in *Tropics of Discourse: Essays in Cultural Criticism* (Baltimore: Johns Hopkins University Press, 1978), 91.

[25] I adopt the phrase from Katie Trumpener, *Bardic Nationalism: The Romantic Novel and the British Empire* (Princeton: Princeton University Press, 1997); see esp. the introduction and ch. 1, 'Harps Hung upon the Willow'. For medievalist examples of such enquiries, see Heng, *Empire of Magic*; Daniel Donoghue, 'Layamon's Ambivalence', *Speculum*, 65 (1990), 537–63; and several essays collected in Carol Meale (ed.), *Readings in Medieval English Romance* (Cambridge: D. S. Brewer, 1994).

past.[26] Equally importantly, the competitive frameworks of historically conceived bardic-minstrel traditions (Celtic-bardic versus English-minstrel) provided the foundation for the conceptualization of an English literary tradition, one defined both with and against the internally colonized peoples of the British isles. A medieval enquiry could do more than simply (but critically) reconnect the art of 'Child Florent' and *Horn Childe* to the national wanderings of Byron's *Childe Harold*, or to Walter Scott, or even to Samuel Johnson. But this in itself would not be such a bad start. As Christopher Cannon has recently noted, 'the whole of romance form is never more than an approximation of the idea it exists to capture'.[27] Substituting the subject 'nation' for romance form, we could make the exact same observation with the same terms. That is, through a re-encounter with 'romance' and 'chronicle' we can also begin to recognize how the medievalism of later eras was so immanently present—a childlike family resemblance—in the specifically romantic and historiographical desires of the medieval period itself. The epiphenomenal effects of romance, in other words, include both the individual *and* communal longings so durably figured forth in the homely products of this genre, which are still waiting to be recognized and recuperated as our kin, for better or worse, in the increasingly contested critical assessments of our literary and national cultures.

FURTHER READING

For basic background, probably the best single-volume overview of medieval English romances remains W. R. J. Barron's *English Medieval Romance* (London: Longman, 1987). Also extremely valuable are the entries on romance in the new *Cambridge History of Medieval English Literature* (Cambridge: Cambridge University Press, 1999), ch. 6 by Rosalind Field, 'Romance in England, 1066–1400', ch. 26 by Helen Cooper, 'Romance after 1400', and ch. 10, 'Writing History in England', by Andrew Galloway, on the overlap of chronicle and romance. Helen Cooper's magisterial recent study, *The English Romance in Time: Transforming Motifs from Geoffrey of Monmouth to the Death of Shakespeare*, (n. 2 above) should become a standard resource for most of the subjects I have mentioned. These have excellent bibliographies. The standard reference works remain vol. i 'Romances' of J. B. Severs (ed.), *A Manual of the Writings in Middle English, 1050–1500* (New Haven: Connecticut Academy of Arts and Sciences, 1967–) and Gisele Guddat-Figge, *Catalogue of Manuscripts Containing Middle English Romances* (Munich: W. Fink, 1976).

---

[26] David Matthews, *The Making of Middle English, 1765–1910* (Minneapolis: University of Minnesota Press, 1999), esp. ch. 3, 'The Last Minstrel: Walter Scott and the Decade of Romance'; see also John M. Ganim, 'The Myth of Medieval Romance', in R. Howard Bloch and Stephen G. Nichols (eds.), *Medievalism and the Modernist Temper* (Baltimore: Johns Hopkins University Press, 1996), 148–66.

[27] Christopher Cannon, 'The Spirit of Romance: *King Horn, Havelok the Dane*, and *Floris and Blancheflour*', in *The Grounds of English Literature* (Oxford: Oxford University Press, 2004), 189.

As mentioned, we can look forward to an edition of the Ashmole 61 manuscript, currently being edited for TEAMS by George Shuffelton. The entire Auchinleck manuscript is available in an accessible website provided by the National Library of Scotland. But the English romances continue to need increased attention to their re-editing and renewed publication. Many, if not most, are available only in relatively rare editions dating to the end of the ninteenth and early twentieth centuries.

In addition to the volumes already referenced, romance is the subject of several recent essay collections: see Carol Meale (ed.), *Readings in Medieval English Romance* (Cambridge: D. S. Brewer, 1994); Derek Brewer (ed.), *Studies in Medieval English Romances* (Cambridge: Brewer, 1988); and Nicola McDonald (ed.), *Pulp Fictions of Medieval England: Essays in Popular Romance* (New York: Manchester University Press, 2004). A capacious literary history is provided by Corinne Saunders (ed.), *A Companion to Romance: From Classical to Contemporary* (Malden, MA: Blackwell, 2004). A handy chronological list of all the Anglo-Norman and Middle English romances is provided at the end of Lee C. Ramsey's accessible study *Chivalric Romances: Popular Literature in Medieval England* (Bloomington: Indiana University Press, 1983).

My thoughts on the genealogies of romance were stimulated by Lila Abu-Lughod's *Veiled Sentiments* (n. 3); also valuable is her follow-up study, *Writing Women's Worlds: Bedouin Stories* (Berkeley and Los Angeles: University of California Press, 1993), and her essay 'Shifting Politics in Bedouin Love Poetry', in Catherine Lutz and Lila Abu-Lughod (eds.), *Language and the Politics of Emotion* (Cambridge: Cambridge University Press, 1990). Also influential for me, from a sociological/anthropological perspective, are the chapters on kinship and matrimony in Pierre Bourdieu's *The Logic of Practice*, trans. Richard Nice (Stanford, CA: Stanford University Press, 1990).

CHAPTER 23

INCARNATIONAL (AUTO)BIOGRAPHY

NANCY BRADLEY WARREN

Lives and afterlives

When Augustine Baker took over the spiritual direction of the English Benedictine nuns in exile in Cambrai in 1624, he encouraged their serious engagement with modes of spirituality and texts drawn from the English Middle Ages. To better train the nuns in contemplative prayer, in a form of spiritual life that Gertrude More (descendant of Thomas More and founder of the Benedictine nunnery at Cambrai), echoing Julian of Norwich's emphasis on divine love, calls 'the way of love', Baker directed them to read the 'classics' of English spirituality from the fourteenth and fifteenth centuries.[1] Julian's *Showings* accordingly formed a mainstay of the nuns' collections; indeed, we largely owe our knowledge of the Long Text to the English Benedictine community in Cambrai and its daughter house in Paris.[2] As I shall discuss in more detail below, the example of Margaret Gascoigne, who included excerpts of the *Showings* in a contemplative anthology that she wrote, demonstrates how avidly the nuns read, copied, and meditated upon Julian's writings, engagements that played fundamental roles in shaping the nuns' distinctive form of Benedictine spirituality.

Margaret Gascoigne's copy of Julian's text and the accompanying record of her contemplative experiences were copied by Brigit More, sister of Cambrai's founder

---

[1] The phrase 'the way of love' as a description for the Benedictine nuns' distinctive form of spiritual life occurs in Gertrude More's epistle 'To the Reader' that precedes *The Spiritual Exercises of the Most Vertuous and Religious D. Gertrude More* ... (1658; Wing/M2632), biiii, hereafter cited parenthetically by page number.

[2] On the manuscript and early print versions, see Edmund College and James Walsh, *A Book of Showings to the Anchoress Julian of Norwich*, part 1 (Toronto: Pontifical Institute of Mediaeval Studies, 1978), 1–18; hereafter I cite the Long Text of the *Showings* parenthetically from part 2 of this edition.

Gertrude More, and also by Barbara Constable for the daughter house in Paris at a time when the Cambrai nuns were under threat of having all their manuscripts confiscated. The threat was the result of a conflict with Benedictine authorities about the distinctive mode of spiritual life the nuns practised under Augustine Baker's direction. This threat to the nuns' corporate identity, which was an identity grounded on union with Christ and union with the English religious past, was perceived by the nuns as a suffering of the corporate body and suffering of the textual corpus, sufferings through which the processes of union and embodiment were, perhaps paradoxically, furthered.

Gertrude More's exposition of the contemplative life as taught by Father Baker, published in 1658 under the title *The Spiritual Exercises of the Most Vertuous and Religious D. Gertrude More*, highlights breakdowns of the boundaries separating individual bodies, communal bodies, Christ's body, and a textual corpus. Much as Julian re-embodies Christ's suffering in her own body and in her text, this volume sets up a chain of explicitly English reincarnations of Christ's suffering in which those who successively re-embody Christ's Passion also re-experience the sufferings of their English forebears.

Placed after the title page and before the dedicatory epistle to Brigit More in this volume is an engraving of Gertrude More; on the page facing the engraving is a poem. The poem begins with an apostrophe to Gertrude's ancestor Thomas More and transitions into praise for Gertrude:

> Renowned More whose bloody Fate
> England neer yet could expiate,
> Such was thy constant *Faith*, so much
> Thy *Hope*, thy *Charity* was such,
> As made thee twice a Martyr proue;
> Of *Faith* in Death, in Life of *Loue*
> View heer thy Grandchilds broken *Hart* ...   (ll. 1–7)

By invoking More's martyrdom, the poem aligns his suffering, like that of all the martyrs, with the crucified Christ's suffering. The poet then instructs More to view his grandchild's suffering (as we perhaps are to view and experience it via the image on the facing page?); her 'broken Hart' seems to be a response to, even a re-enactment of, More's 'bloody Fate' at England's hands. Her suffering, and that of the community (in their exile from England and at the hands of those who would rob them of their manuscripts and Baker's spiritual direction), *are* More's suffering and, like Julian's, also Christ's. The past is written in and known through their bodies as well as in and through their books.

As bodies suffer, so too can books: the dedicatory epistle to the *Spiritual Exercises* even discusses a kind of textual experience of the Passion, suggesting that the body of Gertrude's text suffers in common with her body, the monastic body, More's body, and Christ's body. The author, who signs the epistle 'F.G.' and whom I take to be Francis Gascoigne, writes—making reference to another work of Gertrude's published in 1657—'If it chance to fal into the hands of any such as may reiect, or cry it down: (as some did the Ideots Deuotions of the same Spirit lately set forth) it will (as that did) but receive the greater luster thereby, and be more highly prised' (p. 4).

Individual, corporate, and textual reincarnations of suffering make the past live in the present; suffering, however, is not the end of the story in the *Spiritual Exercises*, much as it is not for Julian. In the poem placed opposite Gertrude More's engraved portrait, her 'broken Hart' is the fulcrum on which the poem makes an important turn. In the first part of the poem, the pain of her 'broken Hart' is the pain of shared martyrdom. However, the poem continues:

> View heer thy Grandchilds broken *Hart*
> Wounded with a Seraphick Dart.
> Who while she liu'd mortals among
> Thus to her *Spouse Diuine* she sung.   (ll. 7–10)

The nature and meaning of her 'broken Hart' shift—the heart is broken because it is pierced, like that of St Teresa in ecstasy, with a seraphic dart. Martyrdom gives way to mysticism and prayer (her hymn to Christ fills out the remaining fourteen lines of the poem). Corporeal suffering and union with the 'Spouse Divine' are for Gertrude, as for Julian, inseparable. Experiencing Christ's bodily suffering is the beginning: the beginning of a revelation of divine love, the beginning of knowledge of self and other, the beginning of a text, and, so the English Catholics in exile hope, the beginning of a reincarnation in England of 'the old religion'.

The reincarnations I have traced in this discussion of texts by and about Gertrude More highlight something essential about the *Showings* specifically and medieval life writings generically. Middle English life writing is fundamentally incarnational, both in its poetics and in its epistemologies. This incarnational quality sows within Middle English life writings the seeds of textual and corporeal afterlives that have profound personal, theological, and political implications.

Beginning my exploration of life writing in Middle English with processes of identity formation within communities of Benedictine nuns is also appropriate because, given the incarnational poetics and epistemologies of Middle English life writing, these texts are closely related to a genre strongly associated with monastic life, the *forma vitae*. A *forma vitae* is a text that seeks to order a life, that seeks to become a lived life, to take bodily form. Medieval life writings are texts in which the experiences of an 'I' that exists in history (experiences admittedly themselves shaped and mediated to various extents by and through texts) take on a textual body, become a textual corpus.

The relationship of life writings and the *forma vitae* does not, however, end with this observation that the two genres are flip sides of a coin. I see it as a constitutive aspect of Middle English life writings that these texts fundamentally seek to insinuate themselves into and to shape other lives, to become—as we have just seen with the case of texts by and about Gertrude More—shared experiences in their own day and afterwards. As a textual corpus they bear witness to embodied human experience in history and simultaneously seek reincarnation in the lives of their readers through human history. Strikingly, Julian of Norwich ends the Long Text of her *Showings* by calling it a book 'begonne by goddys | gyfte and his grace, but ... nott yett performyd'.[3]

The 'I' of Middle English life writings is individual, but simultaneously is—or strives to be—not simply individual, but more than individual. It is an 'I' constituted around a reach outward and forward, defined not just in opposition to others, but with reference to others. In making this claim, I do not mean to join the camp that doubts the existence of 'the individual' or 'the subject' in the Middle Ages; surely most medievalists no longer find this a necessary argument to have. I am also making a rather different point about self and others than that encapsulated by David Lawton. Although the 'I' of which I speak exists as a 'social production' in Lawton's use of the phrase, it is also social in a different sense—constituted by plurality, by union with rather than distinction from a 'you' and a 'he' or 'she'.[4]

Pondering the question of precisely which Middle English texts exhibit the qualities outlined above—incarnational poetics, a commitment to incarnational epistemology, a performative imperative, an 'I' paradoxically individual and plural at once—I found myself thinking, not surprisingly, of the aforementioned *Book of Margery Kempe* as well as of accounts of visions and revelations by such figures as Richard Rolle, St Catherine of Siena, and St Birgitta of Sweden (the latter two were both translated into Middle English). Far more surprisingly, I found myself insistently drawn to *Piers Plowman*. Although works such as the *Showings* and *The Book of Margery Kempe* are often read as some species of life writing, one currently shows one's sophistication as a reader of *Piers Plowman* by denying its autobiographical relevance. Nearly 150 years ago Walter Skeat called *Piers* 'a true autobiography in the highest sense of the word', but the idea of reading *Piers* through the lens of autobiography has become more, rather than less, problematic in the intervening years.[5] I became convinced, however, that the *Showings* and *Piers* share a great deal and may productively be read together in order to identify constitutive elements of Middle English life writing.

---

[3] My exploration of the performative imperative of the *Showings* is influenced by Frederick Bauerschmidt's work in *Julian of Norwich and the Mystical Body Politic of Christ* (Notre Dame, IN: University of Notre Dame Press, 1999), especially his conclusion entitled 'Performing the Book'. Hereafter I cite this book parenthetically as *Mystical Body Politic*.

[4] David Lawton argues for interpreting *Piers Plowman* through poststructuralist understandings of subjectivity in which 'The sense of being "I" arises from dialogue with another, "you", or in distinction from a third person. .... [O]ur sense of identity is predetermined by another or others' ('The Subject of *Piers Plowman*', *Yearbook of Langland Studies*, 1 (1987), 1–30, quote from 5).

[5] Walter W. Skeat, *Langland's Vision of Piers Plowman: The Vernon Text; or Text A*, EETS, o.s. 28 (London: Oxford University Press, 1867), p. xxxviii.

Both the *Showings* and *Piers* are life writing projects in the basic sense that each occupied the author for a lifetime; the multiple, and complexly related, iterations and revisions of each text appear to comprise the life's work undertaken by the author.[6] Additionally, the *Showings* and *Piers* wrestle with a great deal of overlapping subject matter concerning how one negotiates life in the world and life in God—problems of human sin, divine love, and the mysteries of salvation. And in *Piers Plowman*, whatever else the controversial 'tearing of the pardon' scene in the B-text may mean, it surely suggests that words must be translated off the page and embodied in action in order to attain meaning that reaches the standards of the Truth who sent the pardon.[7] As is the case with the *Showings*, *Piers*'s performative thrust ensured it an afterlife in early modern religious culture. Finally, precisely the same relation of author and text holds for Julian and the *Showings* as does for William Langland and *Piers Plowman*. That is, in both cases, beyond what the texts (perhaps) tell us, little is known from other sources about the authors' lives.

I do not mean to suggest that Will the dreamer in *Piers* 'is' William Langland; of course this text cannot be read as an uncomplicated record of authorial lived experiences, and surely few critics would now attempt do so. But, no more should the *Showings*, or *The Book of Margery Kempe*, be seen in this way, even though they might seem to invite such interpretations. To put it another way, *Piers* and the *Showings* may be construed as autobiographical life writings, but not as *the* autobiography of historical people named William Langland and Julian of Norwich. To signal this distinction, rather than speaking of 'autobiography', I adopt the term '(auto)biography', borrowed from Douglass Catterall, both to signal the blurry boundary between biography and autobiography and to signal that my understanding that 'life writing' in Middle English does not entirely align with the genre as it is understood in much contemporary criticism on the subject, a great deal of which explicitly excludes medieval material to focus exclusively on works written from the seventeenth century onward.[8]

---

[6] I am quite deliberately sidestepping the authorship controversy surrounding *Piers Plowman*. I do believe that the same person had at least something to do with the versions of the poem labelled the A-, B-, and C-texts. Paradoxically, however, although I am reading the poem through the lens of autobiography, it does not particularly matter to my interpretation of the poem whether that person was William Langland, or what the historical details of William Langland's life may have been. My thanks to Larry Clopper for helpful conversations about *Piers Plowman*, especially in conjunction with Julian of Norwich.

[7] C. David Benson makes the same point about the significance of the tearing of the pardon, albeit to rather different ends, also quoting the end of the *Showings*, in *Public Piers Plowman: Modern Scholarship and Late Medieval English Culture* (University Park: Pennsylvania State University Press, 2004), 57.

[8] Catterall explains his use of the (auto)biography by saying, 'The term (auto)biography is used to indicate that from the perspective of the present we are looking at biographical information; it was also autobiographical with respect to its contemporary generation' (Douglass Catterall, 'Drawing Lives and Memories from the Everyday Words of the Early Modern Era', *Sixteenth Century Journal*, 36/3 (2005), 652 n. 8).

Julian of Norwich and (re)incarnations

In an essay on the Chinese Manchu prince Yihuan's poetry about the destruction of the Summer Palace by British and French troops in 1860, Vera Schwarcz elegantly declares, 'Precisely because the past is a fragile, slippery dream, it can hardly be contained by something as exacting as words.'[9] As my discussion of Gertrude More and her fellow nuns has already begun to suggest, in examining Julian of Norwich's *Showings* and the text's afterlives, my concern is precisely with the ways in which words can, and cannot, contain the fragile dream of the remembered past. Furthermore, I am interested in what beyond words is necessary in the constitution of memory, of relationships between past and present, and additionally in the bodies of writers and readers who translate fleshly experience into words and words into flesh once more. Or, to put it another way, my focus is on the shifting and intersecting lines demarcating embodied writers and readers, the divine Logos, and a textual corpus; lines that animate, shape, and disturb so much life writing in Middle English.

Christopher Abbot has argued that 'in Julian's case, the personal and the theological are best taken together'.[10] I take this assessment, with which I tend to agree not only with reference to Julian's *Showings*, but with reference to Middle English (auto)biography generally, as a starting point. But, following Frederick Bauerschmidt, I would add the category of 'the political' to the theological as something to be considered with the personal, and in discussing the personal I would also place particular emphasis on 'the bodily'. To vary the classic feminist claim, this revised 'personal' is both political and theological.

A multi-faceted, though ultimately unified, quest for knowledge of God, self, and human others lies at the heart of the Long Text of Julian's *Showings*. As Julian writes, 'It longyth to us to haue three manner of knowyng. The furst is that we know oure lorde god. The seconde is that we know oure selfe, what we ar by him in kinde and grace. The thyrde is that we know mekely that oure selfe is a gaynst our synne and agaynst oure febylnes' (p. 665). The opening of Julian's *Showings* highlights not only that these types of knowledge are coextensive but also that for Julian spiritual knowledge must be bodily knowledge. The *Showings* originates, as is well known, with a series of revelations that Julian experiences in 1373. When she is 30 $\frac{1}{2}$ years of age, Julian, who has long desired not only to have an in-depth awareness of Christ's Passion comparable to that of the eyewitness Mary Magdalene but also to have bodily illness, suffers from a near-fatal episode of disease. In her

---

[9] Vera Schwarcz, 'Circling the Void: Memory in the Life and Poetry of the Manchu Prince Yihuan (1840–1891)', *History and Memory*, 16/2 (2004), 32–66, quote from 60.

[10] Christopher Abbot, *Julian of Norwich: Autobiography and Theology* (Woodbridge: Brewer, 1999), 3; hereafter cited parenthetically as *Autobiography and Theology*.

suffering, she concentrates her attention on a crucifix, and at what she perceives to be the point of death, she says, 'sodenly all my paine was taken from me, and I was as hole ... as ever I was befor' (p. 292). She is initially unhappy not to have been 'deliured of this world', but is subsequently moved anew to desire that 'my bodie might be fulfilled with mynd and feeling of his blissed passion ... for I would that his paynes were my paynes' (p. 292). With this desire to unite with the suffering body of Christ, to have his pains as her own, Julian has a revelation of 'the reed bloud runnyng downe from vnder the garlande, hote and freyshely, plentuously and liuely, right as it was in the tyme that the garland of thornes was pressed on his blessed head' (p. 294).

This quick synopsis of the opening of the *Showings* illustrates that seeing and knowing are 'intensely somatic', and that perception and knowledge cannot be restricted 'within the domain of consciousness' (Bauerschmidt, *Mystical Body Politic*, 50). Christ the Word made flesh is most fully known to Julian through her own suffering female flesh, and that embodied knowledge becomes the textual corpus of her *Showings,* a text that records the very bodily processes of coming to know 'oure lords menyng' (p. 732). In Julian's spirituality, bodies are not, to appropriate the philosopher Stanley Cavell's formulation, veils or things that 'come between [one's] mind and the other'.[11] Bodies are the site of and means to knowledge of self and others, both divine and human. Indeed, Julian's ways of knowing God, knowing herself, and knowing her fellow members of Christ's body are characterized by what I term incarnational epistemology.

Christ's bodily experiences as Julian comes to know them are, furthermore, expressible in and knowable through a textual corpus, which can in its own turn be incorporated and embodied by a reader. Julian's pains and Christ's can—indeed, even *must*—be conveyed in language for others to know for themselves. As Julian says, 'Alle that I sawe of my selfe I meene in the person of alle myne evynn cristene' (p. 219). Through her text, others may have her bodily sights, her bodily knowledge, and so share in incarnational epistemology.

Because Julian's life writing about herself and her experiences is so 'other-oriented' (and because it shares this characteristic with much life writing in Middle English), I want to consider at greater length some of the others who read Julian's text. The nuns of Cambrai and Paris incorporated Julian's writings into their own lives and their own textual corpus; Julian's engagement with 'interlocking problems of identity, faith, religious authority, and writing' (Abbot, *Autobiography and Theology*, 3) becomes part of the nuns' negotiation of these same issues. The ways in which Christ's embodied experience, Julian's embodied experience, and the experiences of the corporate body of her 'evynn cristene' (p. 219) who read her text are mutually knowable, are central to the role of Julian's *Showings* in the

---

[11] Stanley Cavell, *The Claim of Reason: Wittgenstein, Skepticism, Morality, and Tragedy*, new edn. (Oxford: Oxford University Press, 1979), 369; hereafter cited parenthetically.

development of these nuns' spirituality, their monastic identity, and their distinctive version of English Catholic identity.

Bauerschmidt claims that in reading Julian's *Showings* he is 'trying to read the text that Julian herself read, the text of Christ's crucified body that she describes' (*Mystical Body Politic*, p. x). I would argue that in reading and writing Julian's *Showings*, the Benedictine nuns of Cambrai and Paris did precisely this, reading Christ's suffering body in Julian's bodies both corporeal and textual. In turn they came to embody Christ's and Julian's experiences corporeally, corporately, and textually. To borrow Julian's language, the English nuns in exile simultaneously engage in 'oneing' with Julian, with Christ, with their 'evynn cristene' within the monastic community, and, as we shall see, with the departed 'evynn cristene' of a Catholic England. The nuns' engagement with Julian's text accordingly bears witness to the long reach both of a medieval *forma vitae* and of medieval textual forms.

Margaret Gascoigne's copy of an excerpt from Julian's *Showings* is illustrative. Before her death in 1637, Margaret wrote an account of her own devotions in which she includes fragments of Julian's text intermingled with her own meditations. Margaret begins by quoting and identifying Julian. She writes, 'Thou has saide, O Lorde, to a deere child of thine, 'Lette me alone, my deare worthy childe, intende (or attende) to me, I am inough to thee; rejoice in thy Saviour and Salvation' (this was spoken to Julian the Ankress of Norwich as appeareth by the book of her reuelations).'[12] Margaret continues by aligning herself with Julian; her relationship with Christ is in effect a reincarnation of Julian's. Margaret says, 'This o Lorde I reade and thinke on with great joie, and cannot but take it as spoken allso to me' (p. 444). That Margaret perceives her own experience to be contiguous with Julian's, even to *be* Julian's, emerges even more clearly when the focus turns to the body and its pains. Margaret repeats Christ's words to Julian, 'Intende to me', and then links these words with Julian's experience of bodily sickness. Then, after invoking Julian's experience of suffering and divine love, Margaret immediately repeats another excerpt of Christ's words to Julian, 'I am inough to thee', in the context of her own suffering. She says, 'those thy most delicious words, "I am inough to thee," is so great a joie to my hart, that all the afflictions, that are, or (as I hope) euer shall fall upon me … do and shall cause me to receave from them so much comforte, solace, and encouradgment, as that I hope by thy grace, they shall be most dearlie welcome unto me' (p. 444).

Margaret Gasgoigne's devotional writings reveal a complex process of subject formation taking place as she engages with Julian's text. Julian's experiences and

---

[12]   From St Mary's Abbey, Colwich, MS Baker 18, included in 'Appendix: Records and Responses, 1394–1674', in *The Writings of Julian of Norwich: A Vision Showed to a Devout Woman and A Revelation of Love*, ed. Nicholas Watson and Jacqueline Jenkins, (University Park: Pennsylvania State University Press, 2006), 443–4, hereafter cited parenthetically by page number from this edition.

her text are implicated in Margaret's constitution as a contemplative, but the inverse is also in a sense true—Margaret, as one of Julian's 'evynn cristene' is implicated in, and has always been implicated in, Julian's constitutive spiritual experiences and their textual expressions. As Abbot observes, 'One crucial effect of Julian's rigorously pursued emphasis on the incarnation, and on all this implies for humanity as a whole and for the individual, is to create certain intellectual and imaginative conditions in which a *theological* interpretation of contingent personal experience might credibly be made. It creates, that is, the conditions for *shareable religious autobiography*' (*Autobiography and Theology*, 140; his emphasis). One might say that Julian and Margaret do just this—share a religious autobiography. Indeed, they do so to such an extent that, according to Augustine Baker, in dying Margaret 'relived' the experience that Julian had on what she believed would be her deathbed, the contemplation of the crucifix that preceded, not her death, but her revelations. As she was dying, Margaret

> caused one, that was most conversant and familiar with her, to place (written at and underneath the Crucifix, that remained there before her, and which she regarded with her eyes during her sickness and till her death) these holy words that had sometime ben spoken by God to the Holie Virgin Julian the ankresse of Norwich ...: 'Intend (or attend) to me, I am enough for thee: rejoice in me thy Savior, and in thy salvation.' Those words (I say) remained before her eyes beneath the Crucifixe till her death.[13]

Another way of viewing the multidimensional bonds among Christ, Julian, and Margaret is a solution to the dilemma Cavell posits in working through what he calls 'Wittgenstein's attempts to realize the fantasy of a private language' (*Claim of Reason*, 348). Cavell considers the case of one who writes an 'S' in his diary to mark the occurrence of a particular sensation; the question at stake is whether another person could have that sensation and use the same token to express it. Cavell arrives at the idea that one cannot deny either the sensation or the method of expression to another. I would suggest that the *Showings* itself provides us with virtually the opposite of private experience and private language, and in this, the *Showings* exhibits what I see to be an elemental quality of Middle English (auto)biography. Julian experiences Christ's pain—not simply pain *like* his, but the identical pain he suffered. After the pain caused by her illness has been miraculously removed, Julian says, 'And in alle thys tyme of Cristes presens, I felte no peyne, *but for Cristes paynys*' (p. 364; emphasis added). The *Showings* is itself the token of Christ's/Julian's pains. Margaret Gascoigne's text reveals that through reading the textual tokens of Julian's/Christ's sensations, and through writing them in her contemplative anthology, she *uses* Julian's textual token and simultaneously *experiences* Julian's/Christ's sensation.

Reading Julian's token, experiencing Julian's/Christ's sensation, and recounting her own experience by reinscribing Julian's token (which is never really just Julian's)

---

[13] Downside Abbey, MS Baker 42, pp. 232–4; quoted ibid. 438–9.

in her own text become for Margaret a virtually seamless whole. The shared token and the shared sensation work to constitute communal identity that transcends the space between self and other and the time between past and present, as well as, Margaret Gascoigne perhaps hoped, the time between her present and that of future readers of her text.

That Julian and Margaret understand their individual experiences as having not only meaning but also spiritual benefits for others also suggests something central to much Middle English (auto)biography: it is, yet simultaneously is not, or at least is not only, personal. To turn again to Cavell, his assertion that, however far one has got with the interior life (which is by no means separate from the bodily life), one will find that 'what is common was there before you were' seems particularly apt (*Claim of Reason*, 361).

Piers Plowman as (auto)biography

Like the *Showings*, *Piers Plowman* is a text in which an 'I' seeks knowledge of self, God, and human others. In the opening of Passus XI, at the beginning of the climactic second half of the text, Scripture raises the subject of self-knowledge and the detriments to the lack thereof: 'Thanne Scripture scorned me and a skile tolde, | And lakked me in Latyn and light by me sette, | And seide, "*Multi multa sciunt et seipsos nesciunt*"' (XI. 1–3).[14] Here *Piers* encompasses the epistemological trajectory of an 'I', a trajectory in which the body is always implicated, and it translates embodied knowledge into a textual corpus that strives to breach the boundary between the body of the text and the body of the reader, to become 'reincarnated' in readers. Unlike C. David Benson, I propose no necessary conflict between the 'personal' and the 'public' in reading *Piers Plowman* because, as in the *Showings*, the personal *is* 'public'—or, to use the term that Benson rejects but I prefer, 'common', and 'common' (again as in the *Showings*) in specifically political and theological ways.[15]

Critics now by and large reject the idea that *Piers Plowman* is structured as a *visio* (consisting of the first seven passus) and a *vita* (consisting of Passus VIII to XX). The poem, however, undoubtedly consists, as does the *Showings*, of a series of visions, an account of the efforts of the textual 'I' to make sense of those visions, and various *vitae*, including numerous accounts of the life and death of Christ. Both the *Showings* and *Piers* involve dynamics of recursiveness and repetition that are intimately linked to their epistemological methodologies and theological content.

---

[14] Quotations from *Piers Plowman* are cited by passus and line number from William Langland, *The Vision of Piers Plowman: A Complete Edition of the B-Text*, ed. A. V. C. Schmidt (London, Everyman, 1991).

[15] Benson notes, 'I decided not to use *common*, because of its pejorative modern connotations, though it seems to be the word most frequently used in Middle English for what I mean by *public*' (p. xv n. 4).

In the process of coming to terms with what has been revealed, both Julian and the dreamer have to negotiate complex Trinitarian theological systems in which terms proliferate and meanings shift and accrete (for instance, Jesus the Son who is also our Brother and our Mother in the *Showings*; Dowel, Dobet, and Dobest in *Piers*). Because of the nature both of revelation and the 'I' of the text, neither the *Showings* nor *Piers* unfolds in a simple chronological fashion (something also true of *The Book of Margery Kempe*). As Carolyn Dinshaw has said of Margery Kempe, the 'I' in the *Showings* and in *Piers* exists at times simultaneously, and at times sequentially, in earthly time and in holy time.[16] Accordingly, even in its forward trajectory, *Piers Plowman*, like the *Showings*, proceeds according to a logic of spiralling, coming back again and again to ideas and figures (sometimes ideas *as* figures) that are simultaneously the same and different each time.

Furthermore, in *Piers*, as is the case in the *Showings*, types of revelation are quite complex and shifting—we have dreams within dreams, different types of dreams, just as we have 'bodily' and 'ghostly' sight in the *Showings*. Indeed, given the complicated modes of perception that inhere in both texts, one wonders how different the ontological status as textual 'artefact' of *Piers*'s dream-visions and the *Showing*'s accounts of visionary experience really is. I am reminded of the beginning of Chaucer's *House of Fame*:

> Why that is an avision
> And why this a revelacion,
> Why this a drem, why that a sweven,
> And night to every man lyche even;
> Why this a fantome, why these oracles ...[17]

To explore the ways in which the combination of revelatory experience and incarnational epistemology in *Piers Plowman* resembles the dynamics of the *Showings*, I want to turn briefly to an immensely complex sequence in *Piers*. In Passus XVI, upon hearing the name of Piers Plowman, the Dreamer falls into one of the text's 'inner dreams', in the C-text significantly called a 'louedreem'.[18] In this dream within a dream, Piers explicates the Tree of Charity, a tree that, as Anima

---

[16] Carolyn Dinshaw, 'Margery Kempe', in Carolyn Dinshaw and David Wallace (eds.), *The Cambridge Companion to Medieval Women's Writing* (Cambridge: Cambridge University Press, 2003), 222–39; the reference is to p. 236.

[17] Geoffrey Chaucer, *The House of Fame*, in *The Riverside Chaucer*, ed. Larry D. Benson, 3rd edn. (Boston: Houghton Mifflin, 1987), ll. 7–11; hereafter I cite *The House of Fame* as well as *The Canterbury Tales* parenthetically from *The Riverside Chaucer*. Lawton makes a similar point when he considers the 'radical' claim that *Piers Plowman* might offer 'unmediated access to God' (p. 24). He closes 'The Subject of *Piers Plowman*' by arguing that 'If the term "mysticism" ... can usefully be employed of Margery Kempe's meditations on Love's *Mirror* or Rolle's affective piety of the Passion, then I think ... that it can be fruitfully applied to the subject's vision of the Crucifixion and Harrowing of Hell in *Piers Plowman*' (p. 28).

[18] See XVI. 20 in the C-text; on the significance of this label for the vision, see Schmitt, introduction, *The Vision of Piers Plowman*, p. xxiii.

has already explained, grows within the human body (XVI. 13–14). Much of the explication is taken up with a 'biography' of Christ from the Annunciation to the Crucifixion (XVI. 86–166). The dreamer, however, cannot yet fully process what Piers, so strongly associated with the incarnate Christ ('Piers the Plowman, *Petrus id est Cristus*' (XV. 212)), tells him. At the end of the passus, he awakes from the inner dream 'And after Piers the Plowman pried and stared' (XVI. 168).

To achieve the knowledge of self, God, and human others that so occupies him in the second half of the poem, the dreamer must, in effect, convert the biography of Christ into an autobiography. He must, as must Julian, have experiential, embodied knowledge, the kind of knowledge that is gained through processes of incarnational epistemology that *Piers* calls 'kynde knowing'. Indeed, the resonant Middle English word 'kind' is absolutely central to the epistemological and theological systems of the *Showings* and *Piers Plowman*. 'Kind' links the individual 'I' with the God who took human form as well as with human others. 'Kynde knowing' is what occurs in Passus XVIII, when the dreamer falls asleep in Lent and, just as does Julian, just as does Margery Kempe, 'lives' the events of Christ's Passion. The boundaries between the dreamer, Christ, Piers—and ultimately, as I shall argue, the reader—blur. As many critics have remarked, Christ and Piers are in many ways inseparable; in the Crucifixion, Jesus jousts 'in Piers armes | In his helm and in his haubergeon—*humana natura*' (XVIII. 22–3), and the dreamer later cannot distinguish between Jesus and Piers (XIX. 10–11). Additionally, Robert Crowley, in the first printed edition of the poem (1550; *STC* 2nd edn., 19906), assigned it the title *The Vision of Pierce Plowman*, a title printed on a page that bears no mention of the 'Robert Langland' whom, in his prefatory material, Crowley designates as the author. His title page thus emphasizes another blurry boundary, the one between the author and Piers—a boundary whose blurriness would soon be exploited.

As is also the case in the *Showings*, 'kynde knowyng' is not only individual, personal, and embodied knowledge, but also knowledge that constitutes the individual as 'one' with her or his 'evynn cristene' (to blend crucial terms from the *Showings* and *Piers*). In each case, the knowledge has to be translated into a textual corpus that can then be 'reincarnated' once again. The opening line of Passus XIX foregrounds the process of textualization: 'Thus I awaked and wroot what I hadde ydremed' (XIX. 1). This, of course, is not the end of the poem. The passage that is the end, however, joins the reader with the text's 'I' and carries an imperative of performance, a demand that this text, like the *Showings*, be embodied and put into action:

> 'By Crist!' quod Conscience tho, 'I wole bicome a pilgrym,
> And walken as wide as the world lasteth,
> To seken Piers the Plowman …
> And siththe he gradde after Grace, til I gan awake.   (XX. 381–3, 387)

As the 'I' that is Conscience (a representation both of ethical faculties and consciousness) departs on pilgrimage, continuing his own passus-by-passus progress after Piers, the 'I' of the dreamer, now implicitly linked with Conscience, regains consciousness and must, like the reader now the text has ended, do—what? We don't know, of course, but *Piers Plowman* is on such a basic level preoccupied with *doing* (given its extended focus on Dowel, Dobet, and Dobest) that its call to action is impossible not to perceive.

That call to action was heard, quickly and famously, by the rebels of 1381, who 'reincarnated' *Piers Plowman* in ways that were, in their day, even more politically and religiously transgressive than the reincarnations of the *Showings* performed by the exiled nuns of Cambrai and Paris. For the rebels, *Piers* represented just the sort of 'repeatable autobiography' that the *Showings* represented to Margaret Gascoigne. Appropriately in light of the text's 'spiral logic', the 1381 repetition is at once the same and different—and possibly different enough from what Langland had in mind that it prompted the transformation of the B-text into the C-text. The rebels do not precisely do what the text says; rather, they 'perform' the text, embodying it in human action as well as creating for it a new textual corpus. Key parts of what the rebels reincarnate have to do with epistemology and language. As Steven Justice puts it, the rebels take from *Piers Plowman* 'the mode of thought enabled by its grammatical form'. He continues, '*Piers Plowman* gave the rising a language and a style, an imaginative model of rural articulacy that conferred on empirical language a conceptual utility and public force.'[19]

As we have seen with the nuns of Cambrai and Paris as well as with the rebels of 1381, Middle English (auto)biography in its textual history mimics the processes of recursiveness, repetition, and (re)incarnation that characterize the forms of the *Showings* and *Piers* textually. Appropriately, *Piers Plowman* too has early modern reincarnations of its own. Sarah Kelen wittily observes, 'the Plowman's age does not slow him down at all in the sixteenth century; in fact, he seems to get around better than ever, and to raise just as much of a ruckus as he had in his youth'.[20] Robert Crowley attributed the authorship of his 1550 printed edition of the poem to Piers himself. Crowley, a Protestant clergyman who also printed polemical texts, clearly had religious and political aims that, he probably hoped, might be served by making available the words of the text to be made flesh and performed in his own day.

Interestingly, Crowley was later one of the group of men appointed by Archbishop Whitgift officially to license books to be printed.[21] Whitgift's censorship crackdown, which, in 1588, led to Crowley's appointment, was largely sparked by the controversy

---

[19] Steven Justice, *Writing and Rebellion: England in 1381* (Berkeley and Los Angeles: University of California Press, 1994), 134, 137.

[20] Sarah A. Kelen, 'Plowing the Past: "Piers Protestant" and the Authority of Medieval Literary History', *Yearbook of Langland Studies*, 13 (1999), 101–36 (quote from 136). Kelen's brilliant essay provides much more detailed analysis than I am able to offer here of the early modern printings of *Piers Plowman* and the figure of Piers in the Marprelate controversy.

[21] Basil Morgan, 'Crowley, Robert (1517 × 19–1588)', in H. C. G. Matthew and Brian Harrison (eds.), *Oxford Dictionary of National Biography* (Oxford: Oxford University Press, 2004), www.oxforddnb.com/view/article/6831 (accessed 7, Feb. 2006).

instigated by the Martin Marprelate pamphlets. In another dramatic instance of repetition that embodies sameness and difference at once, this controversy included its own reincarnation of *Piers Plowman*. In 1588–9, while the pseudonymous Marprelate tracts excoriating the Church of England as an outpost of popery were in full flow, along with anti-Marprelate responses, an earlier sixteenth-century polemical piece called *I Playne Piers* (not itself one of the Marprelate texts, but in harmony with them) was put out in a second edition. This second edition links the figure of Martin Marprelate to Piers Plowman, declaring on the title page that Piers is 'Gransier of Martin marprelitte' (*STC* 19903a.5).

This is my body: (auto)biography as transubstantiation

Having extended the term (auto)biography from likely texts (the *Showings*) to a more resistant text (*Piers Plowman*), I wish now to attempt a further and more challenging extension to the works of the Chaucerian corpus in which a character bearing Chaucer's name speaks as a textual 'I'. In book II of *The House of Fame*, incarnational poetics and incarnational epistemology closely intertwine as 'Geffrey' is taken in a dream on a journey to enlighten him on the dynamic workings of language in human relations of selves and others. After swooping up the surprised Geffrey, the Eagle educates him on the mechanisms by which 'every speche, or noyse, or soun,/ ... Mot nede come to Fames Hous' (ll. 783–6). Significantly, the Eagle's didactic speech begins by invoking, and subsequently almost obsessively repeating variations of, the same Middle English term that is so important in the *Showings* and *Piers Plowman*— 'kind':

> Geffrey, thou wost ryght wel this,
> That every *kyndely* thyng that is
> Hath a *kyndely* stede ther he
> May best in hyt conserved be ...[22]   (ll. 729–32; emphasis added)

The speech is designed to prepare Geffrey for his own moment of what we might call 'kynde knowyng' in the House of Fame—the knowledge he will acquire, not through the books he so relentlessly reads without fully being able to make use of the information they contain (ll. 665–60), but through 'experience', and particularly experience involving the body (shades of the Wife of Bath—words embodied through experience and put into action trump text on the page!). The Eagle declares to Geffrey:

> 'By God', quod he, 'and as I leve,
> Thou shalt have yet, or hit be eve,
> Of every word of thys sentence
> A preve by *experience*,

[22] For other repetitions and variations in the course of the speech, see ll. 734, 749, 824, 829, 831, 834, 836, 841, 842, 852.

> *And with thyne eres heren wel,*
> Top and tayl and everydel,
> That every word that spoken ys
> Cometh into Fames Hous, ywys ...'   (ll. 875–82; emphasis added)[23]

What Geffrey comes to know by experience in the House of Fame is virtually a dramatization of incarnational poetics in which boundaries between words and bodies break down. Geffrey wonders if the noise in the House of Fame is produced by living bodies (l. 1063), and the Eagle denies that this is the case (l. 1066). The Eagle, however, goes on to warn him of a phenomenon which will cause him to 'wonder' (l. 1070). He says that when any speech comes into Fame's palace

> Hyt wexeth lyk that same wight
> Which that the word in erthe spak ...
> And hath so verray hys lyknesse
> That spak the word, that thou wilt gesse
> That it the same body be
> Man or woman, he or she.   (ll. 1076–81)

In a twist on the transformation of substance but persistence of accident in the transubstantiated host, in the House of Fame words take on the outward attributes of bodies without ceasing to be words. These words do become embodied again, however, when Geffrey experiences them, only to turn them into words once again as a textual corpus, a process that the Invocation to book III (an invocation that follows only seven lines after the Eagle's speech) foregrounds with its emphasis on the technical aspects of verse-making (ll. 1091–109).

The *House of Fame* ends abruptly with the appearance of a 'man of gret auctorite' into a confused scene that might be read as a nightmarish version of incarnational epistemology and incarnational poetics. As he comes into view, members of a 'congregacioun | Of folk' (ll. 2034–5) frantically seek to consume the latest tidings and transmit the words from their mouths 'in others ere' (l. 2044). Words, virus-like, move from body to body, in the ear, out the mouth, into another ear, to increase in the process. The frenzy is so great that bodies themselves are damaged—heels are trampled and stamping ensues (ll. 2150–4).

Incarnational poetics and incarnational epistemology appear again in a far more positive guise at the end of another unfinished Chaucerian text, the *Canterbury Tales*. The Parson's extended disquisition of sin and penance in the final tale is, by definition, a text with a performative imperative. His are words that demand embodiment and action so that the penitent may enjoy the 'fruyt of penaunce', which is 'the endlees blisse of hevene' (l. 1076). In heaven, as the Parson says in his closing speech, the body will be transformed; one will experience both absolute 'oneing' with 'evenn cristene' and absolute 'kynde knowing' of the divine: 'ther as

---

[23] See also ll. 782–8, where the Eagle reiterates that Geffrey will learn by experience.

the body of man, that whilom was foul and dark, is moore cleer than the sonne; ther as the body, that whilom was syk, freele, and fieble, and mortal, is inmortal … | ther as ne is neither hunger, thurst, ne coold, but every soule replenyssed with the sights of the parfit knowynge of God' (ll. 1078–9). The Parson seeks to mobilize incarnational poetics to effect incarnational epistemology in this world and the next.

Some readers of the *Canterbury Tales*, unwilling to read the 'Retraction' as the author Chaucer's sincere expression of penitent renunciation of 'worldly vanitees', have read it as Chaucer the pilgrim's response to the Parson's call to action. I prefer not to make the 'I' of the Retraction an either/or proposition—that is, I do not wish to dismiss the 'I' of the author in favour of the 'I' of Chaucer the pilgrim, or vice versa. Instead, I read the 'Retraction' as (auto)biography; its 'I' is individual but also multivocal, it reaches outward, backward, and forward at once. The 'Retraction' is a statement that directly demands an embodied response by its reader ('preye for me that Crist have mercy on me'). It is also an ending that calls for interpretative action. The reader must, for instance, determine precisely which of 'the tales of Caunterbury' are those 'that sownen into synne'. And that decision depends on 'kynde knowing' of and performance of the text, for how else but by the reader's own embodied response to the tale within human history is such a determination to be made? In short, the 'Retraction', like the end of the Long Text of the *Showings*, tells us that the book is begun, but it is not yet performed—and what the book *is* depends on its embodiment.

What *Piers Plowman*, the *Showings*, and Chaucer's texts share as exemplars of Middle English (auto)biography might be called 'transubstantiativity' (somewhat ironically, I admit, since *Piers Plowman* figures so prominently in early modern Protestantism and since Chaucer was so readily claimed as a proto-Protestant poet). In the mass, the Word made Flesh is made over and over again through the priest's words, to be ingested and hence embodied by the members of the body of Christ that is the Church. Likewise, Middle English (auto)biographies endlessly transform fleshly experience into words (experience that may include becoming one with the incarnate Christ), words that are consumed and made into flesh and then words over and over again.

FURTHER READING

With the exception of the nuns of Cambrai and Paris, on whom relatively little work has been done, all of the key figures I discuss in this essay are the subject of vast amounts of excellent, and relevant, scholarly work. Furthermore, the topic of life writing itself boasts a substantial critical tradition. For foundational works of life writing, some of which established the field in such a way as largely to exclude women's life writings, see James Osborn, *The Beginnings of Autobiography in England* (Berkeley and Los Angeles: University of California Press, 1960) and the influential essay collection edited by James Olney, *Autobiography: Essays Theoretical and Critical* (Princeton: Princeton University Press, 1980). For feminist revisions and correctives, see the essays in Estelle Jelinek (ed.), *Women's Autobiography: Essays in Criticism* (Bloomington: Indiana University Press, 1980); Sidonie Smith and Julia Watson (eds.), *Women, Autobiography, Theory: A Reader* (Madison: University of Wisconsin Press, 1998); and Shari Benstock (ed.), *The Private Self: Theory and Practice of Women's Autobiographical Writings* (Chapel Hill: University of North Carolina Press, 1988). Additionally, see Leigh Gilmore's book *Autobiographics: A Feminist Theory of Women's Self-Representation* (Ithaca, NY: Cornell University Press, 1994). Gilmore discusses Julian in this book, and her concept of 'autobiographics' helped shape my readings of the *Showings*.

On Julian of Norwich and autobiography, see Christopher Abbot, *Julian of Norwich: Autobiography and Theology* (n. 10 above). On the performative imperative of the *Showings*, see Frederick Christian Bauerschmidt, *Julian of Norwich and the Mystical Body Politic of Christ* (n. 3). My understanding of the *Showings* owes much to both of these scholars. On Julian and modes of perception, see Nicholas Watson, 'The Trinitarian Hermeneutic in Julian of Norwich's *Revelation of Love*', in Sandra J. McEntire (ed.), *Julian of Norwich: A Book of Essays*, Garland Medieval Casebook 21 (New York: Garland, 1998), 61–90; the other essays in this collection provide a good survey of critical approaches to Julian's writings. Nancy Coiner's work on Julian of Norwich has important implications for considering the epistemological quests for knowledge of self, others, and God in the *Showings*; see 'The "Homely" and the Heimliche: The Hidden, Doubled Self in Julian of Norwich's *Showings*', *Exemplaria*, 5/2 (1993), 305–23.

For an overview of the *Showings*' reception with the Benedictine communities at Cambrai and Paris, as well as excerpts from the nuns' manuscripts, see Nicholas Watson and Jacqueline Jenkins, *The Writings of Julian of Norwich* (n. 12). On the influences of Julian on Gertrude More's devotional practices and writings, see Dorothy Latz, 'The Myastical Poetry of Dame Gertrude More', *Mystics Quarterly*, 16/2 (1990), 66–75.

On *Piers Plowman* and issues related to autobiography, see the collection of essays edited by Steven Justice and Kathryn Kerby-Fulton, *Written Work: Langland, Labor, and Authorship* (Philadelphia: University of Pennsylvania Press, 1997) as well as David Lawton, 'The Subject of *Piers Plowman*' (n. 4), and C. David Benson, *Public Piers Plowman* (n. 7). Many others have remarked upon the centrality of Passus XVIII in the process of achieving 'kynde knowyng'. A. V. C. Schmidt claims that the passus has 'a single concentrated purpose—to give the audience experiential knowledge, *kynde knowyng*, of the nature of charity, God's love in action' (*The Vision of Piers Plowman* (n. 14), p. xxix); similarly Mary Clemente Davlin states, 'The experience the poem recreates is that of a believer struggling to find a *kynde knowyng* of God, at the same time God is seeking him', 'Chaucer and Langland as Religious Writers', in Kathleen M. Hewett-Smith (ed.), *William Langland's Piers Plowman: A Book of Essays* (New York: Routledge, 2001, 119–41; quote from 123).

CHAPTER 24

DRAMA AS TEXTUAL PRACTICE

SHEILA LINDENBAUM

The most enduring principle of medieval drama study has been the conviction that plays become fully accessible only in the moment of performance. So naturalized is this axiom in our work that only recently has it been questioned, and it still seems counterintuitive to examine it at all. As with the Théophiliens of the 1930s, and their desire for an 'incarnational identification' with medieval experience, we have laid particular value on the 'vital blood of dramatic representation', the active embodiment and visual imagining that has escaped the written text.[1] This approach has been as important for literary scholars as for theatre historians, and in fact has been the main ground of rapprochement between the two. For the great biblical cycles, particularly, modern reconstructions by theatre historians are said to provide 'essential' access to the plays' incarnational aesthetic. The verbal text is 'subordinate to the incarnate spectacle'; it is 'the imaging of scripture in human flesh that is the generating force of the medieval religious drama'.[2]

Yet the privileging of performance over the text is not the inevitable corollary of drama study. Until recently, Shakespearians privileged the verbal script, measuring modern performances against 'the text' in hope of a faithful realization. Modernists too have treated the verbal script as the 'authentic ground or source of theatrical

---

[1] The 'vital blood of dramatic representation' ('le sang vif de la représentation') is the central theme of Henri Rey-Flaud's *Pour une dramaturgie du Moyen Âge* (Paris: Presses Universitaires de France, 1980), 23. He writes: 'Le théâtre du Moyen Âge n'existe qu'à la représentation. C'est un leurre de le chercher ailleurs'. The intellectual debt of Rey-Flaud and other French medievalists to the Théophiliens, the medieval performing group originating at the Sorbonne, is discussed in Helen Solterer's 'The Waking of Medieval Theatricality: Paris 1935–1995', *New Literary History*, 27 (1996), 357–90, at 384. For North American academics, an important source of interest in medieval dramatic performance was the Modern Language Association seminar on the subject organized by Arnold Williams in the 1960s, from which stemmed the Poculi Ludique Society for medieval performance at the University of Toronto.

[2] These are Gail McMurray Gibson's eloquent statements in 'Writing before the Eye: The N-Town *Woman Taken in Adultery* and the Medieval Ministry Play', *Comparative Drama*, 27 (1993–4), 401–2.

meaning', with performance following as a side effect.[3] It is medievalists who have located the source of meaning in the act of performance, on the assumption that performativity pervades the whole of medieval culture and its representational forms. For a drama 'before the playwright', performance enables identification with the past in lieu of a compelling authorial presence. Enactment accesses behavioural regimes and other intangibles of medieval culture which a text cannot convey.

What we have demanded of the text, therefore, is that it be an instrument for reviving a medieval performance, along with the support provided by dramatic records and iconographic research. An imagined reconstruction of a medieval performance by these means has seemed the ideal starting point of critical enquiry. Yet manuscript studies have shown that many texts as we have them are not ideal for this purpose. Some have survived in literary compilations; others are antiquarian copies that correlate imperfectly with the theatrical records from their supposed locales. Some may never have been used in connection with any medieval performance, or the surviving copies may have been made for readers rather than performers.[4] The texts are certainly performable, but less and less have they seemed transparent witnesses to medieval theatrical enactments.

Attention has consequently shifted slightly but perceptibly to the text itself as the main focus of critical enquiry. Dramatic texts have become more important 'registers of meaning' and 'sources of knowledge' about the cultural context. Performativity has increasingly been relocated to textual operations, so that we now have studies of 'Performative Exegesis', 'Performative Reading', and 'Performance of the Literary'.[5] There is a growing sense that a play belongs first and foremost

[3] For the Shakespearians, see Janette Dillon, 'Is There a Performance in this Text?', *Shakespeare Quarterly*, 45 (1994), 74–86. Dillon remarks on the Shakespearians' recent shift to the 'primacy of performance'. For the modernists' tendency to treat performance as a 'side effect' of dramatic writing, see W. B. Worthen, 'Drama, Performativity, and Performance', *PMLA* 113 (1998), 1093–107, at 1094.

[4] For a discussion of whether the N-Town cycle, now regarded as a compilation, was intended for literary or dramatic purposes, see Lawrence M. Clopper, *Drama, Play, and Game: English Festive Culture in the Medieval and Early Modern Period* (Chicago: University of Chicago Press, 2001), 190–1. David Mills has suggested that the sixteenth-century copies of the Chester plays, the only ones to survive, may have been written because the plays were 'suitable for private devotional study': 'The Chester Cycle', in Richard Beadle (ed.), *The Cambridge Companion to Medieval English Theatre* (Cambridge: Cambridge University Press, 1994), 115. Peter Meredith discusses whether the Bodley *Burial and Resurrection* was originally a play or a meditation in 'The Bodley *Burial and Resurrection*: Late English Liturgical Drama?', *Between Folk and Liturgy* (Amsterdam: Rodopi, 1997), 133–55.

[5] Theresa Coletti, *Mary Magdalene and the Drama of Saints: Theater, Gender, and Religion in Late Medieval England* (Philadelphia: University of Pennsylvania Press, 2004), 15. Susan Boynton, 'Performative Exegesis in the Fleury *Interfectio puerorum*', *Viator*, 29 (1998), 39–64; Robert A. Clark and Pamela Sheingorn, 'Performative Reading: The Illustrated Manuscripts of Arnoul Gréban's *Mystère de la Passion*', *European Medieval Drama*, 6 (2002), 129–54; Maura B. Nolan, 'The Performance of the Literary: Lydgate's Mummings', in Larry Scanlon and James Simpson (eds.), *John Lydgate: Poetry, Culture, and Lancastrian England* (Notre Dame, IN: University of Notre Dame Press, 2006), 169 ff.

to its material manuscript and manuscript context, as opposed to an ephemeral performance in the past which is difficult to recreate.[6]

While in sympathy with all these approaches, I would like to propose a somewhat different line of enquiry, one that also shifts attention to the text, both verbal and material, but not to its performative qualities. My suggestion is to focus on the literate practices set into motion in the text's articulation and transmission. The practices I have in mind are the skills and procedures that trained professionals regularly employed in their ordinary lines of work—in the record office, choral establishment, and schoolroom—and then applied more incidentally to drama. From this perspective, drama becomes a consequence of other, more primary cultural activities rather than a special ludic occasion; it resonates primarily through its connection with everyday life. The work of practitioners on this level, moreover, can take us closer to the mainsprings of drama's aesthetic and cultural effects than the activities of its sponsors—the urban governments, guilds, and noble patrons who often assume an authorial function in medieval drama studies.[7] This approach certainly does not foreclose attention to the theatrical moment, since the professional groups examined here were also actors on occasion. It does, however, show that much of the cultural work of drama was accomplished in other phases of engagement, prior to, or even separate from, the undertaking of an actual performance.

Spectacle in the archives

The process of copying a great London spectacle into the city's official books would seem to produce something of a dead letter, a text more than normally drained of the lifeblood of dramatic representation. The job of the city's common clerk was, after all, to mediate the eventfulness of public affairs through the standardized forms and continuities of the written record. Yet in the compiling of records the clerk was also doing a great deal of creative work—identifying the documents most important to the 'common good', establishing precedents in regard to the city's liberties and property, and helping the city to communicate with its political allies and other towns. Located in the heart of the Guildhall, he was in the business of

---

[6] A seminal article that works brilliantly with the manuscripts of medieval plays while remaining acutely sensitive to their theatricality is Carol Symes's 'The Appearance of Early Vernacular Plays: Forms, Functions, and the Future of Medieval Theater', *Speculum*, 77 (2002), 778–831. For a trenchant critique of modern reconstructions of medieval drama and their desire to 'salvage' the past, see Claire Sponsler, 'Medieval Plays and Medievalist Players', in *Ritual Imports: Performing Medieval Drama in America* (Ithaca, NY: Cornell University Press, 2004), ch. 6.

[7] For a turn toward the study of practice in historical studies, with implications for drama study as well, see the introduction by Gabrielle Spiegel to *Practicing History: New Directions in Historical Writing after the Linguistic Turn* (New York: Routledge, 2005). Paul Strohm expertly sums up what attention to practice can accomplish, from a theoretical perspective, in *Theory and the Premodern Text* (Minneapolis: University of Minnesota Press, 2000), 47–8.

articulating civic policy, and his recording of spectacle was part of that productive activity.

The account of Henry VI's entry into London in the city's Letter Book K illustrates all these aspects of documentary practice. This account exists in the form of a report by John Carpenter, the city's common clerk, and it seems at first a rather perfunctory piece of Latin record-keeping. Carpenter tells us that the boy king progressed from London Bridge to Cheapside, and that gifts of Nature, Fortune, and Grace were symbolically bestowed on him at seven pageants along the route. He briefly describes the allegorical figures who come forth to bestow the gifts, and he records the Messianic verses inscribed on each pageant. In all of this, the account is strangely lacking in affect, especially in comparison with Lydgate's poetic version of the same material in English. Carpenter mentions the huge mechanical giant with a sword ('gigas mirae magnitudinis … extendens gladium'), but does not go on to imply, as Lydgate does, the phallic figure's associations with the king's warlike father. Carpenter's account conveys no sense of awe when the king encounters a simulacrum of his royalty, whereas, in Lydgate's version, an enthroned child of 'beaute precellyng' radiates pure presence.[8]

Carpenter achieves other important objectives, however, in the process of entering the report. The first is to establish a precedent; he begins with the words 'Memorandum (est)'—'let it be remembered', signifying that the item is being recorded for consultation in the future. The report would indeed provide a model for the royal entry of Edward VI, but, more importantly, like other precedents, it would set the limits of the city's responsibility in financial affairs. In matters of ceremony, such responsibility was frequently in dispute: how many new pageants should be provided as opposed to recycled old ones, in what degree of splendour, and at whose expense; and precedent was important in such deliberations. On a future occasion of note, the city proposed to offer Anne Boleyn only three pageants because they had not been given the customary notice. In 1432, the issue was whether the city could afford to mount a royal entry when it was also customarily obliged to present the king with a huge gift of money when he returned from abroad. If the city was to proceed with its property developments in Leadenhall, it would not have enough money for both.[9] Carpenter's report was thus part of

---

[8] Corporation of London Record Office, Letter Book K, fos. 103ᵛ–104ᵛ. Carpenter's report is edited by H. T. Riley in *Munimenta Gildhallae Londoniensis, Liber Albus, Liber Custumarum, et Liber Horn*, Rolls Series 12 (London: Longman Green, 1862), iii. 457–64. Lydgate's poem is edited by Henry Noble MacCracken in *The Minor Poems of John Lydgate*, part II, EETS, os 192 (London: Oxford University Press, 1934), 630–48. For the pageant verses, and a detailed visualization of the pageants as they would have been performed, see Gordon Kipling, 'The Civic Triumph as Royal Epiphany', in *Enter the King* (Oxford: Clarendon, 1998), 142–69. The Letter Books were alphabetized to facilitate access to the city archive.

[9] Gordon Kipling, 'A Horse Designed by Committee: The Bureaucratics of the London Civic Triumph in the 1520s', *Research Opportunities in Renaissance Drama*, 31 (1992), 79–89. Letter Book K, fo. 94ᵛ.

the continuous process by which the city balanced loans and gifts to the crown, including customary gifts of homage, against its own financial needs, never losing sight of the commercial advantages the king could offer in exchange.

From this standpoint, the decision to mount a royal entry was an important expression of the city's corporate will. In this respect as well, Carpenter's report differs from Lydgate's version. As Maura Nolan has eloquently shown, Lydgate uses the occasion of the royal entry to construct a public audience, an alliance of London and aristocratic elites, who are addressed in their native tongue as participants in a classical Roman triumph, and imagined by these means to be the representative body of the realm.[10] Carpenter too is interested in forms of address and issues of representation, but mainly from the viewpoint of who speaks rather than the public addressed. For the elite clerks of monarchs and municipalities, giving authority a voice was what their practice of *dictamen*, the art of diplomatic letter-writing, was all about, particularly in Carpenter's time, when ideas of representation aired at the councils of Constance and Basle were finding their way into high-level correspondence. To appreciate this aspect of Carpenter's report, we have only to look at the many items in Letter Book K which ventriloquize the voices of corporate bodies in fascinating ways. In the item preceding the royal entry, for example, the besieged governors of Paris beg for help in the plaintive tones of a legal petitioner: 'Jeo suis Parys qui ne faiz que languir | Loing de secours, en douleur et martire … Loups ravissans me viennent assailir' (I am Paris, who can do nothing but languish | Destitute of aid, in misery, a martyr … beset by hungry wolves).[11]

The voice Carpenter employs for London's mayor and aldermen originates in diplomatic correspondence. When these authorities speak as the 'city of London' in their letters, they speak as sovereigns, as if to exemplify the belief that the true city is 'what is most sovereign in it' and 'what the ruler of a city does, the whole city is said to do'.[12] When they speak as officers of the city, they likewise style themselves as hereditary powers: they are 'the full honourable Lord the Maire' and 'all the worthy Soverayns Al(d)remen'. So when Carpenter tells us that the city ('nobilis illa Civitas Londoniarum') has ordained the 1432 royal entry, or that the city speaks 'through' the mayor in offering the king their 'litelle yefte' of 1,000 pounds, these statements have the force of a diplomatic utterance. The city is defining the terms on which it will relate to another authority or respond to its requests. It is addressing the king as a feudal power would do, deferring to its superior not slavishly but in the manner of a hereditary vassal.

At the end of his report, Carpenter informs us that it was originally written as a letter to an unnamed friend, signed with his title, 'secretarius', and 'Faber', a

[10] *John Lydgate and the Making of Public Culture* (Cambridge: Cambridge University Press, 2005), 238, 240.

[11] Corporation of London Record Office, Letter Book K, fo. 103[r].

[12] Antony Black, *Monarchy and Community: Political Ideas in the Later Conciliar Controversy, 1430–1450* (Cambridge: Cambridge University Press, 1970), 55, 65.

playful reference to his name in Latin. As these signatory practices suggest, it was important to authenticate city policy with a display of Latin learning. Carpenter was a prosperous Londoner and influential in city affairs—he had been an MP and executor of Richard Whittington's will—but it was more crucial to his position that he be a learned man. No mere clerk, he was at the other end of the professional scale from the parish clerks of London, the much humbler men who had once performed London's cycle of biblical plays, and who by this time were presenting indoor entertainments for the city companies.[13] His education probably included a mix of dictaminal training and classical literature under a prestigious teacher; in his will, he left his junior clerks not only his books of documentary forms but copies of Alain de Lille, Petrarch, Cicero, and other literary writers. He also appears to have been in touch with London intellectuals: adopting a playful pseudonym like 'Faber' was common in the circle of John Seward, a classical scholar who kept a school in the parish of St Peter Cornhill where Carpenter lived. Interestingly, Seward wrote poems on the Lady Liberal Arts and the royal antelope device, two of the pageant themes in the 1432 royal entry.[14] Such associations suggest that, in London, the aesthetic of civic spectacle may owe something to the work of the common clerk's office, where dictaminal practice and classical learning joined forces to serve the oligarchic elite.

Given his privileged position in London, we may wonder to what extent Carpenter's work was duplicated in other towns. Provincial clerks may have recorded royal entries in similar circumstances, but they may not have equalled Carpenter's dictaminal skills or learned associations. The chief clerks of York, who kept the register of that city's dramatic cycle, seem to have employed a set of practices more appropriate to tracking the responsibilities of the city's constituent guilds.[15] They are much more concerned with accuracy and completeness than Carpenter, who tells us that he has not set down the whole of his report because of the pressure of other business. The common denominator may not be what the clerks specifically accomplished but rather that spectacle was validated in each case by the practices of trained clerks. What clerks in large and small municipalities had in common was that they were employed for their professional skills and diligence, qualities which immunized them from the charges of personal gain often levelled at civic authorities. Whatever their skills or the specific practices they employed, whether they were setting precedent or accomplishing another objective, their particular contribution was to give the appearance of disinterestedness to their

[13] Anne Begor Lancashire discusses the parish clerks' plays in *London Civic Theatre: City Drama and Pageantry from Roman Times to 1558* (Cambridge: Cambridge University Press, 2002), 61.

[14] James G. Clark, *A Monastic Renaissance at St Albans: Thomas Walsingham and his Circle c.1350–1440* (Oxford: Clarendon, 2004), 213 (dictaminal and grammar masters) and 218–26 (John Seward). Carpenter's will is Guildhall Library, MS 9171/4, fos. 84^v–86^v.

[15] For the York register, see Peter Meredith, 'Scribes, Texts, and Performance', in Paula Neuss (ed.), *Aspects of Early English Drama* (Cambridge: D. S. Brewer, 1983), 15–16 and 'John Clerke's Hand in the York Register', *Leeds Studies in English*, ns 12 (1981), 245–71.

employers' highly interested policies. Others may have determined the content of the great civic spectacles, but the clerks provided the magic by which they seemed to spring from the collective will.

Liturgical practice and Resurrection drama

Late medieval English drama took shape in a period of intense liturgical development. From the early fourteenth century, the exponential growth of intercessory observances for the dead turned even modest parish churches into monasteries in miniature. Growth was accompanied by increasing complexity, as new feasts and votive observances collided with one another in the liturgical calendar. The feast of Corpus Christi alone is said to have 'unhinged the course of the Temporale', the seasonal progression of services within the church. A more complex observance required specialized skills: ritualists to solve the problems of the calendar, colleges of priests to sing for the souls of the nobility, priests for altars funded by chantries and parish guilds, and lay clerks to supplement the music, along with troupes of singing boys.[16] As these developments suggest, the English liturgy was not just a familiar body of texts that dramatists could raid for themes and formal principles, but a set of dynamic textual practices that could be activated in the various phases of play production.

The most influential of these practices can be identified in the objections of Wycliffite preachers. First and foremost was the tendency to elaborate the scriptural content of the liturgy, whether by sequences and other non-scriptural matter, votive offices of the saints, or Marian observance. The preachers particularly despised the musical forms of these elaborations: the various forms of polyphony ('deschaunt, countre note and organe') and highly ornamented singing of chant. They also resented the number of books required to produce the services: the new Sarum Ordinal, which gave instructions for incorporating innovations, and the 'portos, antifeners, grales, & alle othere bookis' connected with highly developed musical rites. They mocked the punctilious attention to detail, 'all the studie & traveile' that the elaborated round of observance demanded. Above all, they deplored the aestheticizing of liturgical rites at the expense of scriptural understanding: 'oure fleschly peple hath more lykynge in here bodily eris in sich knachynge & tateringe than in erynge of goddes lawe'.[17]

To see how these practices were activated in drama, we can turn to the late medieval Resurrection plays, a group whose subject matter is familiar from the

---

[16]   The 'multa inconueniencia' caused by new feasts are discussed in Christopher Wordsworth (ed.), *Ordinale Sarvm sive Directorivm sacerdotvm* (London: Henry Bradshaw Society, 1901), i. xviii, xxi, and *passim*.

[17]   *The English Works of Wyclif Hitherto Unprinted*, ed. F. D. Matthew, EETS, os 74 (London: Trübner, 1880), 191, 193, 192.

liturgical ceremonies of Easter week. Resurrection plays survive in a variety of forms, including liturgical plays from Dublin, Barking, and York, the bilingual 'Shrewsbury' fragments with liturgical music, the Burial and Resurrection plays in the York cycle, and the intriguing Bodley *Burial and Resurrection*, which has been called a vernacular liturgical drama.[18] Modern scholars usually call the Latin versions performed in church 'ceremonies' to distinguish them from actual 'drama', but in focusing on the Latin version from Barking, I will simply call it a 'play'. The Barking play is of interest because it emerges so clearly from the practice of a specific liturgical community, having been composed for Benedictine nuns in the latter half of the fourteenth century around the same time as the Wycliffite attacks on liturgical excess.

Barking was an ancient convent in Essex, on the outskirts of London. Its aristocratic abbesses held extensive property as barons of the realm as well as having spiritual charge of numerous parishes on their lands. At the time of Abbess Katherine Sutton (1356–76), when the convent's play was composed, the Barking area had begun to see religious dissent and hostility to monastic landlords. By the time the play was copied into its surviving manuscript, the new ordinal compiled under Abbess Sybil Felton in 1404, unrest in Essex had greatly increased. In 1378, insurgents had destroyed buildings at Hatfield Priory; in 1381 they had burnt the estate archives of Waltham Abbey. By 1395, the abbess's relations with the local parish of St Margaret had deteriorated to the point that the bishop of London had to halt 'strife and debate between her and her parishioners'.[19] This history of local strife may have affected the way the play was entered into the ordinal, with a 'nota' on the local parishioners' slackness in devotion ('populorum concursus … uidebatur deuocione temporibus illis frigessere').[20] Whatever the precise form their delinquency took, the 'nota' emphasizes the need to 'excite the devotion of the faithful', to which the convent responded with a play for Easter day.

Barking certainly possessed the expertise to support such an effort. A highly literate community throughout its long history, it had nine priests, along with other

---

[18] Alexandra F. Johnston surveys the forms of the Easter play, ranging from 'purely liturgy' to 'purely narrative', in 'The Emerging Pattern of the Easter Play in England', *Medieval English Theatre*, 20 (1998), 3–23. See also Susan Rankin's important article, 'Shrewsbury School, Manuscript VI: A Medieval Part Book', *Proceedings of the Royal Musical Association*, 102 (1975), 129–44 and Meredith, 'The Bodley *Burial and Resurrection*'.

[19] Lawrence R. Poos, *A Rural Society after the Black Death: Essex, 1350–1525* (Cambridge: Cambridge University Press, 1991), 235, 249, 239. Winifrid M. Sturman, 'Barking Abbey: A Study in its External and Internal Administration from the Conquest to the Dissolution' (Dissertation, University of London, 1961), 135–7. Parishioners attended services at the abbey on certain important feasts.

[20] J. B. L. Tolhurst (ed.), *The Ordinale and Customary of the Benedictine Nuns of Barking Abbey: University College, Oxford, MS. 169*, 2 vols. (London: Henry Bradshaw Society, 1927–8), 106–10 (text), 107 ('nota'). A useful English translation appears in Peter Meredith and John E. Tailby (eds.), *The Staging of Religious Drama in Europe in the Later Middle Ages* (Kalamazoo, MI: Medieval Institute Publications, 1983), 83–7. Photographs of the manuscript are included in Pamela Sheingorn, *The Easter Sepulchre in England* (Kalamazoo, MI: Medieval Institute Publications, 1987), plates 10–17.

clerks and boys, together with a cantrix and choir nuns who specialized in musical performance of liturgical rites. The 1404 ordinal, written in Latin for the cantrix, required her to execute a complex round of observances with the aid of numerous service books. The cantrix directed the choir nuns in two different liturgical uses, the Benedictine for the daily office and St Paul's for the mass, as well as special rites of the house: hymns for the first abbess, St Ethelburga, a special liturgy for novices at St Lawrence's altar, and a misrule ceremony on Holy Innocents day. The nun chosen to be cantrix had sufficient knowledge of liturgical texts to work creatively with them. Much was left 'ad uolantatem cantricis'—whether or not to sing the Christmas hymn *Te Lucis* 'cum nota' (with polyphony), or which Kyrie melody to have on the feast of St Andrew. She was also responsible for a formidable amount of detail, such as knowing what to do if Christmas Eve fell on a Sunday or the different routes the priests should take in processions around the vast abbey church.[21]

Practices well rehearsed in previous liturgical activity could thus be set in motion for the new Resurrection play. There was no need to start from scratch, since such plays typically synthesized new material with old. As Susan Rankin has shown, this is what happened at the convent of Origny, where the early fourteenth-century play was based on a much older version. But the process inevitably produced a great deal of verbal and musical elaboration. Because the Barking manuscript lacks notation, musicologists have been unable to trace which of its details are new, but we know that at Wilton, another Benedictine convent, one-third of the material was newly composed.[22]

At Barking, the idea for developing the material seems to have come from the liturgy of Easter Saturday, where the Harrowing of Hell signifies the redemptive power of the Resurrection that is symbolized in the Host. This is the initial action of the play: the entire convent of about thirty nuns is locked in the chapel of Mary Magdalene, like the souls about to be released from hell. Then the fact of the Resurrection is celebrated in three further actions in various parts of the church: the removal of the Host from the Easter Sepulchre (the *Elevatio*), the visit of the three Maries to the tomb (the *Visitatio*), and Mary Magdalene's recognition of Jesus in the person of a gardener (*Hortulanus*), all concluding with the liturgical sequence *Victimae paschali*: 'We know Christ to have been risen truly from the dead'. The emphasis throughout is on witnessing the truth of the Resurrection beyond any question; the only role specified for the parishioners is to gaze at the Host in confirmation of this fact.

Every aspect of this play, for some forty participants, reflects intense attention to ritual detail. The normal time for an Easter ceremony is changed from before matins

---

[21] *Ordinale*, 22 (*Te Lucis*), 166 (Kyrie), 27 (routes).

[22] Susan Rankin, *The Music of the Medieval Liturgical Drama in France and England* (New York: Garland, 1989), 141–4 (Wilton).

to afterwards, a fine tuning that would encourage more parishioners to attend. The priest who represents Christ at the gates of hell does not simply approach the chapel; he must do so wearing an alb and cope, accompanied by two deacons, one with a cross and banner, the other with a censor, together with other priests and clerks and two boys with candles. Moreover, every moment is highly aestheticized, not only by the sung text, whose directives for sighing or employing a joyful voice seem to invite musical embellishment, but also by lights, incense, splendid surplices, and rich properties, like the crystal pyx containing the Host.

Because it includes all this detail, the text gives us a clear idea of how the performances at Barking Abbey may have been visually realized. Yet the liturgical practices that produced the text reveal the play's dramatic mode. Thinking in terms of those practices, we may not need to puzzle over the degree of impersonation intended when the priest assumes Christ's 'Persona', or whether the Maries' surplices are ritual garments or naturalistic costumes—the performance-based questions asked by Karl Young. In terms of practice, the Barking play proceeds from habits of textual and musical elaboration that belong exclusively to the nuns and priests who perform the action and experience the revelations it contains. The laity in the nave are witnesses to the ritual experience rather than participants themselves; this is the substance of their devotion, however much their knowledge of the Resurrection is heightened by aesthetic means. The Barking play thus differs from the Bodley *Resurrection*, which proceeds from a liturgical practice directed primarily to the laity—that is, meditations on the mass, which provide an intensely affective account of the Passion to read during the priest's symbolic sacrifice. A late Carthusian text, the Bodley play invites the audience to participate in extended passages of self-reproach and weeping, the loss of Christ prompting his mourners to feel the full burden of their sins. The York Resurrection plays follow from yet another practice: that of identifying with the biblical characters particular to liturgical observances and extrapolating from their stories. Much as the liturgical hour of the Resurrection in Love's *Mirror* encourages the worshipper to imagine the Magdalene and Christ actually touching, the York plays invite a personal experience of Christ's human presence.[23] Of course, nothing would have prevented the laity at Barking from bringing affective practices with them to the play, especially in its later years. One thinks, in this respect, of the resident gentlewomen who may have read Abbess Felton's copy of Love's *Mirror*. But such private devotions would not have nullified the play's affirmation of clerical privilege for the officiating priests or its implied justification of the nuns' vocational labours in the choir.

[23] 'Meditatyons for goostly exercyse. In the tyme of the masse', in J. W. Legg (ed.), *Tracts on the Mass* (London: Henry Bradshaw Society, 1904), 19–29. For the 'presencing of Christ' at York, Sarah Beckwith, *Signifying God: Social Relation and Symbolic Act in the York Corpus Christi Plays* (Chicago: University of Chicago Press, 2001), 72–89.

Terence and translation

The Terence revival in England is usually dated from the early sixteenth century, the first known performance taking place at King's Hall in Cambridge in 1510–1. Shortly therafter Terence's *Phormio* was performed at court under the auspices of Cardinal Wolsey, part of a double bill celebrating Pope Clement's rescue from captivity. In the years that followed, Terence was frequently performed in a rich schedule of classical drama at the universities and grammar schools. In the 1540s, a 'Terence man' at Westminster School, Alexander Nowell, mounted productions of *Adelphi* and *Eunuchus* with prologues that appropriated Terence for the Protestant cause. Terence was in the repertory of the children's troupes who played at the Elizabethan court, and, as dramatic histories would have it, the rest is Shakespeare, whose comedies continue the tradition of Terentian intrigue.[24]

This is the Terence revival according to the familiar contours of theatre history, an account that is based on known performances and so fixes him firmly in the annals of early modern drama. If we think of the textual and pedagogic traditions of Terence, however, an earlier phase of the revival comes into view, one not as tied to documented performances, but significant for drama nevertheless. From 1483, the grammar pupils of Magdalen College school, where Wolsey himself taught, were learning Terence by 'new' methods under their master John Anwykyll. The great reform of the Cambridge arts faculty which put Terence at the head of the curriculum also dates from the 1480s, and the first Cambridge lecturer in Terence was appointed in 1488–9. At about the same time, William Horman, headmaster of Eton, gave his students the phrase 'we haue played a comedy of latten' to translate in Terentian style. New print editions of the plays with illustrations of stage 'houses' and declaiming actors had also begun to appear, as if to announce that Terence's identity as a playwright had not been lost in the course of the Middle Ages.[25]

This earlier phase of interest in Terence deserves to be more fully explored, in part to make significant connections with vernacular drama. As plays about delinquent youth, Terence's comedies have a great deal in common with the early

---

[24] Alan H. Nelson (ed.), *Records of Early English Drama: Cambridge* (Toronto: University of Toronto Press, 1989), i. 84. See also John R. Elliott and Alan H. Nelson (eds.), *Records of Early English Drama: Oxford* (Toronto: University of Toronto Press, 2004). For Wolsey's entertainments in 1522–9, W. R. Streitberger, *Court Revels: 1485–1559* (Toronto: University of Toronto Press, 1994), 129–36. Alexander Nowell, *A True Reporte of the Disputation … Had in the Tower of London*: STC 18744, F.iiii.a. Bruce R. Smith, *Ancient Scripts and Modern Experience on the English Stage, 1500–1700* (Princeton: Princeton University Press, 1988), ch. 4 convincingly tracks a romanticized Terence into the Shakespearian period.

[25] Damian Riehl Leader, 'Professorships and Academic Reform at Cambridge: 1488–1520', *Sixteenth Century Journal*, 14 (1983), 220. William Horman, *Vulgaria*: STC 13811. *Shakespeare Quarterly*, 13 (1962), 462, 486, 498 (illustrations).

Wit moralities as well as the Reason and Sensuality plays exemplified by Medwall's *Nature*. Destined to provide household drama for elite audiences, Terence occupied the same cultural niche as these English plays, which likewise circulated in print: indeed, it is likely that the brisk market for Terence editions opened up the world of print to vernacular drama on similar themes.[26]

In the late fifteenth century, however, Terence belonged first and foremost to the schoolroom, and the work being done there on the Terentian text also deserves greater attention. Beyond simply saying that the plays were valued for their style, morality, and ways of modelling behaviour, we also need to understand how specific classroom practices were activated in their use. The most important of these practices was the textual commentary that was incorporated into the Latin print editions—the work of Donatus and his successors, a combination of genre criticism and close reading with attention to metre, plot, and style. But most characteristic of the period was the practice of translation whereby schoolmasters produced an English Terence for their students, first in the phrase books called Vulgaria and then in actual plays. These efforts may not always be linked to performances, but, because they were reinforced daily in the schoolroom and promulgated in print, they had extensive publicity and significant cultural effects.

The initial project in translating Terence was to compile Vulgaria from bits and pieces of dialogue in his plays. These Vulgaria have the look of dual-language phrase books: they pair up Latin phrases with their English equivalents in order to provide exercises in translation from one to the other or 'double translation' back and forth. They are more or less performative and charming, or moralistic and crude, depending on the compiler's disposition. They refer to everyday activities, the master—pupil relationship, and points of common wisdom, the latter either as a boy would utter them or as he might be spoken to: 'To se as tesipho seyth in terence I am afraid to prece [praise] ye to yor face lest ye thinke I do it more to flatter the than to say as I thinke.'[27]

The earliest Terentian Vulgaria, all from the milieu of Magdalen College school, promote conversational skills. John Anwykyll heads his collection with a statement to that effect:

> Let the pupil, who desires to speak English as well as Latin, eagerly commit this book to memory, because it teaches our everyday speech extensively, by which he becomes accustomed to enlarge his discourse. So too these comedies of Terence, with which they are made familiar, will give them much enlargement of their faculties.

Anwykyll then culls and adapts useful phrases from Terence's six plays, beginning with a greeting to the character Crito from the *Andria*:

[26] Greg Walker, 'Early Drama and the Printed Text', in *The Politics of Performance in Early Renaissance Drama* (Cambridge: Cambridge University Press), 6–50.

[27] BL, Royal MS 12.B.xx, fo. 39[v].

gOdd spede you. saue you or rest mery.
Saluete. Salue. Saluus sis chrito[28]

The ultimate goal of these exercises is to qualify the student for gainful employment. In the anonymous *Vulgaria* BL, Arundel MS 249, a boy determines to earn his master's favour by industrious study, for 'my master hath promysed to do for me if it lye euer in hys power'. The boy will have to earn his reward, for 'euery man must be servede after his meryttes', but he can expect satisfaction along the way ('Lo what a wyt I haue') when he learns the relevant skills.

In a later group of Vulgaria, the focus shifts from the schoolboy to the master, and from linguistic competence to teaching methods. By the time these later texts are published, the genre has become a point of contention in the Grammarians' War of 1519–21. The masters use Vulgaria to stake out their opposing positions, whether to teach Latin by imitation or by the rules of grammar, and they carry on the struggle in public through the medium of print. The larger issue in these debates is whose Vulgaria will be approved by the state. England was moving toward the era of official grammars and catechisms: a contract with the printer Richard Pynson seems to imply royal approval for William Horman's Vulgaria, which had a run of 800 copies, presumably for use in schools.[29] To improve their chances in this competition, the masters court literary distinction: Robert Whittington, who favoured the rules of grammar over imitation, styles himself the 'chief poet of England'. In title pages and dedicatory verse, masters are identified as authors of their compilations. Terence is no longer so important as a source of material; William Horman's is the name that is writ large on the decorative title page of his Vulgaria.

The relationship of the Vulgaria to drama is problematic: the translated bits of Terence can sound like dramatic dialogue without ever achieving dramatic form. Yet traces of both kinds of Vulgaria can be detected in plays. A striking example is *Terens in Englysh*, a translation of the *Andria*, published around 1520 but possibly composed at an earlier date. On one level of its discourse, *Terens in Englysh* purports to be about linguistic competence. It is much like a school exercise written to please a master. The English translation has the Latin alongside it: the English in black letter, the Latin in a smaller roman font. At the end of the play, a judgement is sought as to how well the English translates the Latin: 'The translatours know well it may be Amendyd | By theym that be wyse & wold take the payne | It for (to) rede & to corect again.' In keeping with this purpose, the book has a simple format, without the elaborate commentary or dedicatory verses that are a master's province: 'if it had a long expocysyon | Then were it a comment & no translacion.'

---

[28] Alexander H. Brodie, 'Anwykyll's *Vulgaria*: A Pre-Erasmian Textbook', *Neuphilologische Mitteilungen*, 75 (1974), 425 (Brodie's translation); John Anwykyll (attrib.), *Vulgaria quedam abs Terencio in Anglicam linguam traducta*: STC 23904.

[29] F. J. Furnivall, *Pynson's Contracts with Horman for his Vulgaria* (London: Philological Society, 1868).

On another level, however, *Terens in Englysh* is not about the translators' competence but their supposed contributions to a national literature. Here the translators are not students but masters, attempting to achieve the kind of distinction at stake in the Grammarians' War. The playtext is not translated into conversational prose, as we might expect, but into the high literary style of English rhyme royal. A prologue spoken by a Poet invokes the legacy of Gower, Chaucer and Lydgate, the 'poetys ornate that vsyd to indyte | Of dyuers maters in theyr moder tong'. The goal is not linguistic competence, with a career in view, but to authorize the work according to a national standard and to employ a literary aesthetic—in this case, writing 'compendious & elegantly'—that is officially approved.[30]

Observing the schoolmasters at work on these Terence translations, we find them in an ambiguous position, caught between exercising their skills in a manner that quietly signals merit and promoting their skills to a wider public in a more deliberate way. In this, they resemble their counterparts in documentary and liturgical practice, who tend to remain invisible contributors to dramatic activity until some social imperative—a shaky government in need of validation, a parish lacking in devotion—brings them into public view. In their public postures, however, these figures can seem pretentious or out of place: affecting to belong to literary circles, reforming local dissidents, or assuming a laureate's role, they abandon their primary vocations with varying degrees of success. In their engagements with dramatic texts, they make their most significant contributions when using their everyday skills to articulate policy, enact ritual, or teach the young.

FURTHER READING

Lawrence Clopper's *Drama, Play, and Game* (Chicago: University of Chicago Press, 2001) is an invaluable overview of the entire field, speaking to the regionality and variety of early drama as it is now perceived, and bridging the gap between theatre historians and literary scholars. Richard K. Emmerson's 'Dramatic History: On the Diachronic and Synchronic in the Study of Early English Drama', *Journal of Medieval and Early Modern Studies*, 35 (2005), 39–66, puts one immediately in touch with the major trends in recent work, including those stemming from the Records of Early English Drama series. The introduction to Theresa Coletti's *Mary Magdalene and the Drama of Saints* (Philadelphia: University of Pennsylvania Press, 2004) explores current critical issues in considerable depth.

Drama and documentary practice: For the common clerk of London, Caroline M. Barron, *London in the Later Middle Ages: Government and People 1200–1500* (Oxford: Oxford University Press, 2004), 185–8. For an account of a London royal entry that employs recording practices different from the ones discussed here, Sidney Anglo, 'The Coronation of Edward VI and Society of Antiquaries Manuscript 123', *Antiquaries Journal*, 78 (1998),

---

[30] *Terens in Englysh*: STC 23894.

452–7. For theory, Pierre Bourdieu, 'From the King's House to the Reason of State: A Model of the Genesis of the Bureaucratic Field', *Constellations*, 11 (2004), 16–36.

Drama and liturgical practice: C. Clifford Flanigan's groundbreaking work on the subject, published from the late 1970s to mid-1990s, is frequently cited in liturgical studies today. A partial list of his articles can be found in the online Early Drama Arts and Music bibliography under 'Part IV: Early Drama, Liturgical Drama'. To see how the text of a liturgical play expands when the music is supplied, see Máire Egan-Buffet and Alan J. Fletcher, 'The Dublin *Visitatio sepulchri* Play', *Proceedings of the Royal Irish Academy*, Section C, 90 (1990), 159–241. Carol Symes includes a jongleur's version in 'A Few Odd Visits: Unusual Settings of the *Visitatio sepulchri*', in John Haines and Randall Rosenfeld, *Music and Medieval Manuscripts* (Aldershot: Ashgate, 2004), 300–22. A politically motivated surge of liturgical activity is studied by Jeremy Catto in 'Religious Change under Henry V', in G. L. Harriss (ed.), *Henry V: The Practice of Kingship* (Oxford: Oxford University Press, 1985), 97–115.

Terence and academic drama: Ludmilla Evdokimova analyses the translator's work and the commentary in *Therence en françois*, a much more elaborate sister publication of *Terens in Englysh*. See 'Commentaires des comédies de Térence dans l'édition de Vérard et leurs sources', *Le moyen français*, 54 (2004), 95–152. In 'The Performance and Preservation of Medieval Latin Comedy' (*European Medieval Drama*, 7 [2003], 29–50), Carol Symes challenges the paradigm that 'requires Latin to remain static and conventional ... while the vernacular takes off in new directions'. Paul White's *Theatre and Reformation* (New York: Cambridge University Press, 1993) offers a context in which to consider Protestant appropriations of Terence.

CHAPTER 25

VERNACULAR THEOLOGY

VINCENT GILLESPIE

The rise of 'lewed clergie'

Seamus Heaney has written that his experience of the Scriptures and the Catholic liturgy in English was marked by 'a nostalgia for the original undifferentiated linguistic home'. The vernacular versions expressed 'a form of diaspora, a diminished life lived in exile from a fullness available in the old country of the Latin'.[1] Most discussions of vernacular theology position it in a linguistically and intellectually subordinate relationship to the discipline's meta-language of Latin and its main practitioners, the clerical cadre. Ian Doyle, who first used the phrase in relation to Middle English texts in 1953, comments that 'writing in English which may be called, broadly, theological was not, like that in Latin, made by clerics for clerics but immediately or ultimately for other sections of the community ... This is an important part of ecclesiastical and an equally essential part of general social history.' He reinforces this narrative of social and linguistic subsidiarity by remarking that 'there was little or no original thought in the vernacular'.[2]

Doyle's model of vernacular theology was at least broadly based, embracing catechetic as well as contemplative texts, but 'vernacular theology' has recently been equated with a more particular role as the site of audacious attempts to explore complex ideas and articulate advanced spiritual experiences. Bernard McGinn, in his panoptic accounts of contemplative writing in Europe, suggests that vernacular theology takes its place alongside the cognate fields of scholastic and monastic theology, and that its methodology is most akin to the affective and ruminative

---

[1] 'The Drag of the Golden Chain. The 1999 St Jerome Lecture', *The Times Literary Supplement* (12 Nov. 1999), 14–16, both quotations at 14. Also published as 'Fretwork: On Translating *Beowulf*', *Saltana*, 1 (2001–4), accessed online at www.saltana.org/1/1eng.html.

[2] A. I. Doyle, 'A Survey of the Origins and Circulation of Theological Writings in English in the 14th, 15th and Early 16th Centuries with Special Consideration of the Part of the Clergy therein', 2 vols. (unpublished Ph.D. dissertation, Cambridge, 1953), i. 5–7.

modalities of the latter. For McGinn, 'late medieval vernacular theology not only created distinctive theological models, it also produced new, and sometimes challenging, insights into the mysteries of the faith'. It also allowed a new female vocalization and a fresh examination of gender roles and paradigms of power within theological discourse. This imagery of new beginnings is central to his model: 'the explosion of religious writing in the vernacular was not just a case of simple translation, but was a complex and still inadequately studied creation of new theological possibilities.'[3]

McGinn's account nevertheless overlooks the fact that very few acts of translation into medieval vernaculars are what could be called 'simple'. They invariably involve complex editorial acts of selection, reordering, lexical choice, and responsiveness to the needs and abilities of a real or imagined audience. Issues of manuscript context, genre, register, and style are often as important as issues of content or theology.[4] Vernacular theology is ultimately more about the pragmatic and devotional literacies of different target audiences than about the status or cultural worth of the different languages in which it is performed.[5]

The history of vernacular theology in England is a history of intralingual ambition, aspiration, and achievement. Sophisticated and challenging religious texts moved from Latin into French and English, from French into Latin and English, and from English into Latin and French. Ambitious vernacular texts, like Hilton's *Scale of Perfection* or the *Cloud of Unknowing*, were translated into Latin. Ambitious Latin texts, like Rolle's *Incendium amoris*, were translated into English for lay readers. High-grade Latin exegetical and academic materials are quarried and redeployed in new vernacular contexts. Originally monastic works like the *Speculum ecclesiae* of Edmund of Abingdon enjoyed sprightly textual careers and widespread insular circulation in Latin, French, and English versions. Latin sermons reappear in vernacular clothing. And, of course, innovative and original vernacular theology of

---

[3] 'Introduction', in Bernard McGinn (ed.), *Meister Eckhart and the Beguine Mystics* (New York: Continuum, 1994), 1–14, these comments at 7, 10. See also, more generally, Bernard McGinn, *The Flowering of Mysticism: Men and Women in the New Mysticism (1200–1350)* (New York: Crossroad Herder, 1998), *passim*.

[4] Ian Doyle's publications represent an extraordinary foundation for scholars in this field. See the list in Richard Beadle and Alan J. Piper (eds.), *New Science Out of Old Books: Studies in Manuscripts and Early Printed Books in Honour of A. I. Doyle* (Aldershot: Scolar Press, 1995), though his output has hardly slackened in the intervening period. For some illustrations of the importance of manuscript study in vernacular theology, see my 'Vernacular Books of Religion', in Jeremy Griffiths and Derek Pearsall (eds.), *Book Production and Publishing in Britain 1375–1475*, Cambridge Studies in Publishing and Printing History (Cambridge: Cambridge University Press, 1989), 317–44; Ralph Hanna, *Pursuing History: Middle English Manuscripts and their Texts*, Figurae: Reading Medieval Culture (Stanford, CA: Stanford University Press, 1996).

[5] For the concepts of devotional and pragmatic literacy, see Margaret Aston, 'Devotional Literacy', in her *Lollards and Reformers: Images and Literacy in Late Medieval Religion* (London: Hambledon Press, 1984), 101–33; M. B. Parkes, 'The Literacy of the Laity', in David Daiches and A. K. Thorlby (eds.), *The Medieval World, Literature and Western Civilisation* (London: Aldus Press, 1973), 555–77.

a complex and challenging kind appeared in England in particular abundance in the fourteenth century. Such texts were challenging both in their intellectual ambition and in their potential threat to the authority and power of the clerical institution with their espousal of 'lewed clergie' (lay learning).[6] But all this innovative writing is rafted on the assumptions, ideologies, and even idiolects of Latin theological writing, with which it is in constant and creative dialogue. And if the bulk of surviving vernacular translation and compilation is of texts aimed at catechetic or devotional audiences, that emphasis partly reflects the breadth of the available market for such texts, and the number of environments in which they might be used.

This less 'original' vernacular theology constitutes the horizon of expectation within which the more eye-catching compositions emerge: vernacular theology is not simply about intellectual innovation. The rapid advances in Latin pastoral theology and penitential psychology in the thirteenth century university schools have yet to be fully explored in their vernacular instantiation.[7] In England, catechetically ambitious and capacious vernacular verse *summae* like *Speculum vitae* and *Prick of Conscience* deserve much more sustained intellectual and literary analysis. The strength and resourcefulness of vernacular theology emerges precisely from its ability to recombine a wide spectrum of cognate theological discourses robustly and flexibly available in the mother tongue.

The advanced and highly sophisticated vernacular theology of Julian of Norwich, for example, derives much of its pliability and playful responsiveness to key issues such as universal salvation and the problem of sin and evil from her virtuoso command of the full range of contemporary didactic and devotional vernacular writing. Attending deeply to the texture of the writing, the reader becomes aware of Julian's skilful use of different linguistic codes and registers, narrative voices, and rhetorical levels of style. Shifts between such registers and codes often signal themselves with verbal punctuation ('as if'; 'as thus'; 'as if he had said'). But just as often her ventriloquial employment of, for example, the adjectivally supercharged language of affective meditations on the Passion is signalled only by a sudden and unheralded change in the specific gravity of the prose. (Students with expertise in stylistics would, for example, find much to comment on in chapter XII of Julian's Long Text.) She is the master of multiple discourses, capable of alluding to and pastiching various contemporary styles of religious and philosophical writing, without ever allowing any of them to become dominant or specifying. Her text is a vast echo chamber of allusion and imitation, but her source can rarely be unequivocally identified, as several generations of editors have found to

---

[6] For this concept, see Fiona Somerset, *Clerical Discourse and Lay Audience in Late Medieval England*, Cambridge Studies in Medieval Literature 37 (Cambridge: Cambridge University Press, 1998), esp. 22–61, 154–7.

[7] For a recent attempt to explore this field, see Masha Raskolnikov, 'Confessional Literature, Vernacular Psychology, and the History of the Self in Middle English', *Literature Compass*, 2 (2005), accessed online via **www.blackwell-compass.com/subject/literature/**.

their frustration. This is one of the key ways in which her text subverts normal critical (and perhaps theological) reading. Originality is not the issue: truth to her showing is. Again and again, she demonstrates the ability to deploy religious and philosophical discourses in tightly controlled tactical ways without ever putting her faith or reliance on any of them to describe or account for the essence of her showings. Instead she uses the local velocity of those discourses and registers to project her own text into new and surprising directions. These provisional discourses, codes, and registers are only 'means' to be discarded on the journey to the promised end revealed by Christ who seeks to lead Julian and her reader to perfect understanding.[8]

Julian's skill at textual construction is not only manifested at the micro-textual level; at the macro-textual level of chapters or indeed whole revelations, she displays equal skill at 'borrowing' textual velocity and narrative texture from familiar genres of religious writing. Julian is a hospitable but highly controlled writer, allowing these discourses to discharge their narrative potential in carefully constructed tactical deployments, without ever letting any one of those guest discourses or genres swamp the deliberate and deliberative procedures of her own metanarrative. She displays unusual sensitivity to her own textual construction by being alert to the way that her conscious mind slides into the registers and narrative conventions of dominant contemporary genres. In chapter VI of the Long Text, for example, she introduces a long excursus on prayer. Arguing that good prayer is a naked cleaving to the goodness of God in its most abstract form, she ruminates on the ways that mechanical prayer can occlude this abstract goodness with its emphasis on 'means'. She then transcribes her own immediate thoughts on the subject, which 'cam to my mind in the same time', and the texture of the writing immediately shifts to reflect the devotional clichés of her time (and perhaps of her own earlier life):

> For thus as I shall say cam to my mind in the same time. We pray to God for his holy flesh and for his precious bloud, his holy passion, his dereworthy death and worshipful woundes: and all the blessed kindnes and the endlesse life that we have of all this, it is of his goodnes. And we pray him for his sweete mothers love that him bare: and all the helpe that we have of her, it is of his goodnes. And we pray for his holy crosse that he died on: and all the helpe and all the vertu … , it is of his goodnes.
>
> (ed. Watson and Jenkins, 143)

The usual suspects of contemporary vernacular prayers and meditations are lined up for inspection in this sentence, each noun clinging pathetically onto its clichéd adjective. Against this array of tawdry and jaded religious language, Julian simply

---

[8] Julian quotations are taken from *The Writings of Julian of Norwich: A Vision Showed to a Devout Woman and A Revelation of Love*, ed. Nicholas Watson and Jacqueline Jenkins (University Park: Pennsylvania State University Press, 2006). For longer consideration of Julian's style, see my '(S)he do the police in different voices: Pastiche, Ventriloquism and Parody in Julian of Norwich', in Liz Herbert McAvoy (ed.), *A Companion to Julian of Norwich* (Cambridge: D. S. Brewer, forthcoming).

reiterates her understanding of the true nature of prayer with the bare clause 'it is of his goodnes'. She strips away the verbal decoration to reveal a core theological truth of how creation works. But this revelation acquires its force from her acutely sensitive and tactical flexibility in the deployment of the popular vernacular religious discourses of her time. In effect she is creating an intertext between a range of current vernacular theologies.

Issues of tactical flexibility, and its scope and domain, arise in Nicholas Watson's influential discussions of the English instantiation of vernacular theology in the fourteenth and early fifteenth centuries.[9] Watson's laudable aim was to challenge the segregation of contemplative writings ('The Middle English Mystics') away from the broad spectrum of other religious writings in the vernacular, to which they often refer and from which they often draw, in acts of verbal parody, pastiche, or contestation. In a recent essay reflecting on the impact of his work, he observes that 'writing about religion in the vernacular is a political act (in a more specific sense that that in which writing in general is political); and that, because this is so, all vernacular writing about religion is connected, part of a single field or arena of discourse'.[10] Secondly, he sought to demonstrate the vigour, occasional theological innovation, and general level of intellectual aspiration in vernacular religious texts. He saw this as 'an attempt to distance scholarship from its habitual adherence to a clerical, Latinate perspective in its dealings with these texts'. Thirdly, he wished to 'focus attention on the cultural-linguistic environment in which religious writing happens'.[11]

Watson pivots his arguments around what he sees as a defining moment in English religious history: the promulgation in 1409 of Archbishop Thomas Arundel's repressive decrees aimed at controlling unlicensed preaching, setting a limit to catechetical instruction, policing speculation on matters of faith and doctrine, and outlawing vernacular translation or commentary on scriptural texts without express licence from the episcopate. Watson argues that this intervention radically changed the nature and texture of English spirituality, bringing to a shuddering halt

---

[9] Watson's most influential publications on the subject of vernacular theology have been 'Censorship and Cultural Change in Late-Medieval England: Vernacular Theology, the Oxford Translation Debate, and Arundel's Constitutions of 1409', *Speculum*, 70 (1995), 822–64; 'Visions of Inclusion: Universal Salvation and Vernacular Theology in Pre-Reformation England', *Journal of Medieval and Early Modern Studies*, 27 (1997), 145–87; 'The Middle English Mystics', in David Wallace (ed.), *The Cambridge History of Medieval English Literature* (Cambridge: Cambridge University Press, 1999), 539–65; 'The Gawain Poet as a Vernacular Theologian', in Derek Brewer and Jonathan Gibson (eds.), *A Companion to the Gawain Poet* (Cambridge: D. S. Brewer, 1997), 293–314; 'Conceptions of the Word: The Mother Tongue and the Incarnation of God', *New Medieval Literatures*, 1 (1997), 85–124.

[10] Nicholas Watson, 'Cultural Changes', *English Language Notes*, 44 (2006), 127–37, at 130. See also his 'The Politics of Middle English Writing', in Jocelyn Wogan-Browne, Nicholas Watson, Andrew Taylor, and Ruth Evans (eds.), *The Idea of the Vernacular: An Anthology of Middle English Literary Theory 1280–1520* (Exeter: University of Exeter Press, 1999), 331–52.

[11] Watson, 'Censorship and Cultural Change', 823–4 n. 4. This seminal article remains the most richly nuanced and powerfully contextualized discussion of vernacular theology in Middle English, and asks many questions that still require answering.

the growing momentum he observes in intellectually challenging and exploratory thinking in the vernacular during the fourteenth century in texts intended for both clerical and lay audiences. He suggests that 'from a few years after 1410 until the sixteenth century there is a sharp decline both in the quantity of large theological works written in the vernacular and in their scope and originality' ('Censorship and Cultural Change', 832). The tightness of Watson's focus on the fourteenth and early fifteenth centuries has led his version of vernacular theology to become the most richly implemented model in the Middle English academy. But the boldness of his arguments has, perhaps inevitably, led to some overstatement and tabloidization in writings of other scholars building on his observations, which are often more tentatively and cautiously expressed than might appear from their headline impact on the field. Watson not only focused on a limited chronological period, but also on a restricted range of treatises written for reading rather than for oral or public performance, excluding from his argument most preaching texts and all drama texts, which afford particularly clear evidence of lively and challenging theological work being performed in the vernacular and in very public environments.

But recent essays responding to Watson's work have shown the benefits to be gained by enlarging his context of consideration.[12] They have demonstrated that the broad cultural and socio-political outline of a 'vernacular theology' can also be found in Anglo-Saxon literature, thirteenth-century religious writing (where the public concern and private anxiety about vernacularity so central to Watson's model seems to have been largely absent, and where richly dynamic theological multilingualism is most acutely focused), and in fifteenth-century religious drama. So it might now be better to work with the assumption that each subperiod in medieval England produced multiple, interlocking, and overlapping vernacular theologies, each with complex intertextual and interlingual obligations and affiliations.

The next stage in mapping vernacular theology must involve further expansion of this model in order to understand why issues of vernacular translation and composition continued to resonate in such powerful ways.[13] Sometimes, as with texts like *The Chastising of God's Children*, this will require careful attempts to reconnect vernacular texts with their Latin hinterland. Sometimes, as with Julian of Norwich, it will be necessary to explore mundane sites of textual didacticism. While Watson's work has usefully encouraged broader debate about the intellectual

---

[12] See the short articles by Elizabeth Robertson, Daniel Donoghue, Linda Georgianna, Kate Crassons, C. David Benson, Katherine C. Little, Lynn Staley, and James Simpson in *English Language Notes*, 44 (2006), 77–126.

[13] Important recent synoptic discussions of translation issues in medieval England can be found in Roger Ellis, 'Figures of English Translation, 1382–1407', in Roger Ellis and Liz Oakley-Brown (eds.), *Translation and Nation: Towards a Cultural Politics of Englishness* (Clevedon: Multilingual Matters Ltd., 2003), 7–47; Andrew Cole, 'Chaucer's English Lesson', *Speculum*, 77 (2002), 1128–67. On recent sociolinguistic approaches to vernacularity, see Tim William Machan, *English in the Middle Ages* (Oxford: Oxford University Press, 2003).

and spiritual capacities of the laity, a phenomenon also found in much recent work on non-academic Lollardy, this emphasis has perhaps led to a privileging of the lay perspective over the clerical, and a downplaying of the continuing agency of the orthodox clergy in the production and dissemination of vernacular texts. But the socio-political tension between continued clerical agency and growing lay self-determination remains a key issue in exploring the contested rise of vernacular theology. As Barbara Newman has recently commented, 'Discussions of vernacularity call attention to the problem of who could write theology and who could read it ... What credentials did the theologian require? Could the mere love of God suffice, or were Latin literacy and priestly ordination de rigueur?'[14]

Precisely this question is posed by *Piers Plowman*, which enacts the moment in the literary history of medieval England when hermeneutic skills in the production and navigation of interior spiritual landscapes began to pass over from the enclosed and clerically directed world of anchoritic and monastic readers to the much less securely regulated and less stable world of lay spiritual ambition.[15] At the end of Passus XI of most A-text manuscripts of *Piers Plowman*, Will resoundingly affirms the power of simple faith and the sanctity of the working poor, contrasting their devotion and dedication with the inflated learning and *scientia* of the educated and 'clerkes':

> *Ecce ipsi ydiote rapiunt celum vbi nos sapientes in infernum mergemur.*
> [The uneducated seize heaven, and we with all our learning are sunk
>   into hell]
> And is to mene in oure mouth, more ne lesse,
> Arn none rathere yravisshid [seduced] fro the righte beleve
> Thanne arn thise kete [illustrious] clerkis that conne many bokis,
> Ne none sonnere [more quickly] ysavid, ne saddere [more steadfast/
>   righteous] of consience,
> Thanne pore peple, as ploughmen, and pastours of bestis,
> Souteris [supplicants] & seweris [petitioners]; suche lewide iottis
> Percen with a *paternoster* the paleis of hevene,
> Withoute penaunce at here partyng, into the heighe blisse.   (A. XI. 305–13)

In the B-text, Will's advocacy of a lay spirituality constituted by patient poverty, simple faith, and reliance on knowledge of the Latin *Pater Noster* is immediately questioned by Scripture:

> Thanne Scripture scorned me and a skile tolde,
> And lakked me in Latyn and light by me sette.   (B. XI. 1–2)

[14] Barbara Newman, *God and the Goddesses: Vision, Poetry, and Belief in the Middle Ages* (Philadelphia: University of Pennsylvania Press, 2003), 297.
[15] References are to the following editions of *Piers Plowman*: A-text: *Piers Plowman: The A Version*, ed. George Kane (London: Athlone Press, 1960); B-text: *The Vision of Piers Plowman: A Complete Edition of the B-Text*, ed. A. V. C. Schmidt (London: J. M. Dent, 1978).

This scornfully stages the debate between Will and the academic discipline of Scripture as a conflict founded on linguistic competency and access to the magic circle of Latinate theological understanding. Scripture challenges not his spiritual optimism, but his linguistic deficiency ('lakked me in Latyn'), just as Holy Church had previously rebuked him for his failure to apply himself to the master language in childhood:

> 'To litel Latyn thow lernedest, leode, in thi youthe.' [You learned
>   insufficient Latin in your childhood, young man]   (B. I. 141)

His A-text eulogy attempts to praise a catechetic staging of pious lay obedience and simple faith that is neither applicable to himself (as a questing, intelligent cleric in minor orders), nor representative of developing pastoral reality in contemporary England. This is Will the cleric expressing the party line on lay spirituality. But Will is later also chided by Ymaginatif that 'thow medlest thee with makynges [poetry or literature] - and myghtest go seye thi Sauter [Book of Psalms]' (B. XII. 16). The charge against Will here is not primarily against 'makynges' as such. Rather it is that his vernacular theology is not needed. Ymaginatif asserts that 'ther are bokes ynowe | To telle men what Dowel is, Dobet and Dobest bothe | And prechours to preve [demonstrate] what it is' (B. XII. 17–19gg). In other words, Ymaginatif argues that there is already in place a didactic system that provides teaching materials and magisterial exposition as part of a stable and holistic programme of religious education administered by the Church. Will's objection to this didactic matrix of book and preacher is that it has not worked for him: he has failed to find the answer in books, nor can any man tell him what Dowel, Dobest, and Dobet in fact are. This is Will the layman complaining about the deficiencies of clerical teaching models.

Ymaginatif's words to Will serve as a cardinal moment in the poem. They provide a hinge between the earlier search for knowledge (*scientia*) along initially catechetic, then didactic, and finally academic pathways and Will's subsequent (and progressive) search for understanding or 'kynde knowynge' (*sapientia*) along pathways that mimic the more affective, devotional, and intuitive features of the meditative and psychologically catalytic 'monastic' spirituality reflected in the religious prose that appeared in the vernacular in such rich abundance in the years after 1380, and continued to enrich it throughout the fifteenth century. It is a long way from catechesis to contemplation, but the field of vernacular theology necessarily embraces them both. Will's point of departure ('How may I save my soul?') is a search for a deeper personal understanding of the catechetic basics of the Church's teaching tradition, and his most profound spiritual experiences take place because of his progressively deeper engagement with the liturgical and sacramental life of the institutional Church. Even his rude awakening at the end of the poem enacts an apocalyptic trajectory of abandonment and fear caused by the collapse of that institutional life. In his powerful critique of contemporary religious life, Langland anticipates both the Wycliffite rejection of the Church and clergy as beyond reform, and the dynamic sense of the need for institutional and personal renewal that powered the post-Wycliffite generation of orthodox reformers. As a cleric in minor orders, poised liminally between clergy and laity, Will's journey towards truth is at once a profound and challenging exercise in what Barbara Newman has recently called 'imaginative theology' and a progressive and sequential dramatization of the difficulties and rewards of vernacular theology.

Arundel and after

Langland's staging of the issues surrounding vernacular theology emerged before Wyclif and Lollardy further complicated an already labile theological environment. In 1382, vernacular theology moved firmly onto the public intellectual agenda of the English Church with the Blackfriars council, an attempt to address the problems arising from the breakout of academic (and therefore Latinate) Wycliffism into wider clerical circulation and into vernacular Lollardy. Blackfriars responded to the Wycliffite version of vernacular theology with an order against 'unauthorised explication of scriptures in either Latin or the vernacular'. Twenty years later, many of these issues were still in active play within the academic community at Oxford, and the parameters of the debate are discernible in a series of academic determinations and responses staged or compiled in the years around 1401.[16]

Masters and doctors at medieval universities routinely used academic disputations and other scholastic acts as the proving ground for exercises in logical and theological analysis. Usually such speculative debate was controlled by the self-sealing discipline of the university community. But as university graduates increasingly moved into parish work (a development which was itself a result of the new pastoral emphases of the post-Lateran Church which had done much to fuel the market for vernacular theology), so too the debates, issues, and contentions of the university went with them. Mostly such debates remained safely restrained in

---

[16] For Blackfriars, see Ellis, 'Figures of English Translation', 7. The Oxford 'debate'on Bible translation has received much attention, but key Latin texts remain unedited. In particular the fullest form of Ullerston's *determinacio* exists in a still unedited manuscript, Vienna, Österreichische Nationalbibliothek, Codex Vindobonensis Palatinus 4133, fos. 195–297ᵛ. I am grateful to Professor Anne Hudson for permission to consult her transcription of this text. The arguments of Butler and Palmer, and a vernacular version of Ullerston's tract, have been edited by Margaret Deanesly, *The Lollard Bible and Other Medieval Biblical Versions* (Cambridge: Cambridge University Press, 1920); and by Curt Bühler, 'A Lollard Tract: On Translating the Bible into English', *Medium Aevum*, 7 (1938), 167–83. The first modern discussion was Anne Hudson, 'The Debate on Bible Translation, Oxford 1401', *English Historical Review*, 90 (1975), 1–18, repr. *Lollards and their Books* (London: Hambledon Press, 1985), 67–84. Important recent discussions include Watson, 'Censorship and Cultural Change', 840–6; Ellis, 'Figures of English Translation', 20–31; Fiona Somerset, 'Professionalizing Translation at the Turn of the Fifteenth Century: Ullerston's *Determinacio*, Arundel's *Constitutiones*', in Fiona Somerset and Nicholas Watson (eds.), *The Vulgar Tongue: Medieval and Postmedieval Vernacularity* (University Park: Pennsylvania State University Press, 2004), 145–57.

scholastic Latin and within the covers of clerical miscellanies and handbooks. But as the laity began increasingly to exercise their pragmatic literacy, the subjects of some of those disputations spilled over into the vernacular.

In the third quarter of the fourteenth century, John Trevisa, himself a former Oxford academic who had been at the university in the fierce heat of Wyclif's most torrid teachings, constructs for his aristocratic patron a dialogue between an intelligent and literate lord and his clerical servant as an urbane discussion between two thoughtful and reflective men. But the genre of dialogic debate in which he carefully positions his protagonists is clearly a local parody of those academic discussions to which he would have been party during his university career.[17] Wyclif himself had used the debate form in his polemical Latin *Dialogus* and *Trialogus* (though in the latter he was indebted to the form and dramatis personae of the *Ecloga* of pseudo-Theodolus, a popular text in Latin grammar school reading collections throughout the Middle Ages). In English, under the pressure of such academic and classical models, the dialogue form was to become the genre in which many of the most vibrant discussions of vernacular theology would be aired.[18] Vernacular theology inherently potentiates dialogue. About the same time as Trevisa's work, *The Lyf of Soule* presents a catechetic and devotional programme through the medium of a dialogic discussion. The early fifteenth-century *Dives and Pauper* reveals many of the perils of debate and the tactics of dialogue form. Its author, clearly a man of some sympathy with the Wycliffite position on the use of the vernacular in theological debate, explores many contentious aspects of contemporary English church teaching, including a checklist of the main areas of Lollard complaint. But he does so in a forum that allows patristic and biblical examples to spill freely into his discussions. Like Trevisa, he presents his dialogue as taking place between a quizzical and naturally sharp-witted layman and a cleric, and similarly here (as in the sermons preserved in Longleat 4, plausibly linked to the same author) the cleric finds himself in some difficulty (indeed positive intellectual discomfort and distaste) at the orthodox teachings of his hierarchy and at the restraints placed upon him in discussing such theological matters in the suspicious atmosphere of what appears to be the first decade of the fifteenth century.[19]

[17]   For a recent overview of Trevisa's life and writings, see A. S. G. Edwards, 'John Trevisa', in A. S. G. Edwards (ed.), *A Companion to Middle English Prose* (Cambridge: D. S. Brewer, 2004), 116–26. This volume discusses many texts and authors engaged in vernacular theology.

[18]   On the classical (non-scholastic) hinterland of the dialogue and debate genre, see my 'The Study of Classical and Secular Authors from the Twelfth Century to c.1450', in Alastair J. Minnis and Ian Johnson (eds.), *The Cambridge History of Literary Criticism*, ii: *The Medieval Period* (Cambridge: Cambridge University Press, 2005), 145–235; Marjorie Curry Woods and Rita Copeland, 'Classroom and Confession', in Wallace (ed.), *The Cambridge History of Medieval English Literature*, 376–406.

[19]   On the link between *Dives and Pauper* and the Longleat sermons, see particularly Anne Hudson and Helen L. Spencer, 'Old Author, New Work: The Sermons of MS Longleat 4', *Medium Aevum*, 53 (1984), 220–38.

The Oxford debate on translation was on one level just another series of Latin scholastic acts to explore the topography of an issue in pastoral theology. But on other levels it staged a much larger struggle: a struggle to establish the orthodoxy and reliability of the post-Wyclif university as a centre of advanced study of theology as well as a struggle between two very different ideas of how to respond to the growing threat of heterodox ideas at large among the laity and parochial clergy of the English Church.[20] On one side, the Franciscan William Butler and the Dominican Thomas Palmer argued against any extension of the use of the vernacular for theological discourse, and in particular against the sanctioning of the translation of the Bible into English. On the other side, Richard Ullerston led the line for those who felt that there were pastoral and spiritual advantages to be gained for the national Church from a cautious and moderate extension of the use of the English vernacular, which, with the gradual eclipse of Anglo-Norman, was now widely establishing itself as the nation's linguistic common denominator. In the event, the measures in Thomas Arundel's 1409 decrees against the use of the vernacular in religious speculation and against translation of religious texts into English, which were drawn up by him at a meeting of his senior clergy in Oxford in 1407, marked the apparent triumph of the more suspicious, even potentially repressive, attitude to vernacular theology. But in 1401 there still seems to have been everything to play for.

In mounting their arguments, both sides chose to look back over the history of the English Church and, while their conclusions may have been rather different, their analyses of the historical role and didactic importance of native vernaculars in the formation of what was already coming to be called *ecclesia anglicana* share a lot of common ground. Both sides accept that preaching in the vernacular establishes a methodological precedent for theological translation. Both recognize that in such instructional contexts material recorded in Latin might usefully and appropriately be delivered in the vernacular, collapsing the intellectual boundary between them. Both accept the existence of many precedents for the translation of the Bible into native vernaculars across the world (indeed that argument had first been made in England as early as Bede and had been repeated in English by Ælfric in his Preface to Genesis). Both sides recognize that the vernacular had long been used in catechetic instruction. But the two sides draw different conclusions from their consideration of the evidence. Butler and Palmer argue that English is linguistically, lexically, and syntactically inadequate to render the complexity and sophistication of the Word of God as revealed through Scripture. Palmer in fact argues that the laity should only have access to those things strictly 'necessary for salvation'. Ullerston too recognizes that Latin offers a kind of pan-European linguistic gold

[20] In addition to the helpful overview in Anne Hudson, *The Premature Reformation: Wycliffite Texts and Lollard History* (Oxford: Clarendon Press, 1988), I have found invaluable two superb essays by Jeremy Catto, 'Wyclif and Wycliffism at Oxford 1356–1430', and 'Theology after Wycliffism', both in Jeremy Catto and T. A. R. Evans (eds.), *The History of the University of Oxford*, ii: *Late Medieval Oxford* (Oxford: Clarendon Press, 1992), 175–261, 263–80.

standard, and reports some opponents as arguing that Latin, Greek, and Hebrew should be regarded as the principal languages of theology, with other languages relegated to a lesser second-order status. Moreover he reports that they fear that in the face of widespread translation into English, knowledge of Latin and other learned languages would decay, as knowledge of French had done in the recent past (a decline also noted by Trevisa). The opponents of translation also fear that the availability of texts in the vernacular will marginalize the role of the clergy as intermediate transmitters (and local policers and enforcers through confession) of matters of faith and doctrine. The anxiety here is that foolish and naive reading of sophisticated and challenging scriptural and theological texts will generate error and heterodox belief, and that the institutional Church will lose its pastoral role as the centre of communal life and the source of communal belief, and its sacramental role as dispenser of grace and as vehicle for personal and collective salvation. Old women, Ullerston reports his opponents as arguing, will become teachers; laity will teach rather than learn; women will talk philosophy and dare to instruct men, and rustics will set themselves up as teachers.

At a time of political upheaval, social unrest, and religious turmoil, the opponents of translation feared that its further extension might destabilize society and encourage the unravelling of its social fabric (and of their own privileged role in it). Unmediated access to Scripture and other religious texts threatened what was seen as the proper instructional hierarchy, with knowledge trickling down through the strata of society until it reached a laity grateful (or in the Lollard view impatient) to slake its thirst. The orthodox campaign against Lollardy often uses these same arguments in its attacks on the heretics. John Lydgate, Thomas Hoccleve, and John Audelay echo them in their anti-Lollard poems, and the diatribes against Margery Kempe reported in her *Book* often draw on the same vocabulary of censure and dismay. So the opposition has a socio-political as well as a linguistic dimension, and that socio-political dimension soon became embodied in the person of Thomas Arundel and inscribed in his Oxford decrees. History is written by the victors, and Arundel was already preparing the script.

But Ullerston's arguments in favour of translation, many of which were picked up and included in a still unpublished collection of vernacular texts discussing the subject from a position sympathetic to Lollard views, should not be disregarded even if they apparently failed to persuade those in power in the early years of the century. Ullerston's defence creates a moderate and thoughtful model of an English Church at ease with its national linguistic identity, where a well-informed laity would gratefully receive vernacular instruction from a clerical cadre newly freed by the wide availability of suitably authoritative translations to exercise innovative and imaginative pastoral and missionary work. Ullerston counters most of the more apocalyptic views of his intellectual opponents by arguing that heresy has never been confined to or even largely the result of vernacular theology (as his generation of academic theologians at Oxford knew only too well). Ullerston recognizes that translation is understood not only to involve the movement of sense and meaning from one language to another, but also to embrace a process of intralingual commentary and exposition 'by expounding, revealing, explaining, or unlocking the meaning latent in words'. In what might, therefore, be considered as a coded defence of 'doing theology' in the vernacular, he implicitly suggests that the process of moving theological and scriptural truths from one language to another, and expounding those truths in the vernacular, could involve a parallel process of theological explication and exploration that might be analogous to the agendas and procedures of academic theology, which takes the hidden truths of Scripture and subjects them to technical scrutiny through the specialized languages of the university schools. Ullerston is groping towards a justification of vernacular theology that anticipates in embryo the arguments used later by Reginald Pecock. Moreover, like Pecock, he argues that a properly educated laity could take more responsibility for their own spiritual well-being, entering into a cooperative covenant with the clergy and working within clearly defined theological parameters. He accepts that the laity need access to those things that are 'necessary for salvation', but in his mind those necessities include an understanding of the Bible 'grosso modo' (in a basic manner). Invoking a model of linguistic development and evolution, he argues that languages change over time, and that older texts therefore stand in need of constant refreshment to make them intelligible (he cites the difficulty he has had in reading copies of works in his possession written 'in vetustissimo anglico' (in the most ancient English) by Bede or some other ancient author).

Ullerston recognizes that English may yet be a language of limited flexibility and responsiveness, but its relative barbarousness can be mitigated by a clerically led campaign of linguistic borrowing. (This may be the opening move in the turn to aureation so characteristic of English religious writings in the next two decades.) With vigorous policing by the episcopate and other church leaders, a newly democratized laity might share in the spreading of the Word. Women would instruct other women rather than try to preach (again prefiguring the terms of Margery Kempe's self-defence); rustics would not teach, except for those matters of faith and practice in which the episcopal decrees had long since required them to instruct members of their families and households. Ullerston envisages society configured as an utopian pyramid, where bishops will instruct the clergy; clergy (many of whom will themselves benefit from having books of religion available to them in the vernacular because of their limited and imperfect Latinity) will instruct the laity; masters will instruct servants; husbands will instruct women and children; and women will instruct each other, 'talking about the things of God'.

After Ullerston's determination, the voice of moderate reform largely falls silent. But many of his arguments and manoeuvres are repeated in texts that carefully walk the line between outright Lollardy and engaged and reform-minded orthodoxy. The first of the vernacular treatises in favour of translation collected together in Cambridge, University Library, MS Ii. 6. 26, for example, mounts several arguments with which Ullerston would have had little problem.[21] The programme of this text, although reflecting the kind of exchange between layman and clergy staged in *Dives and Pauper*, with which it has some material in common, envisages no radical extension in the ownership of religious books beyond that emerging class of gentle and mercantile readers who were already exercising their literacy in such materials long before the end of the fourteenth century, and who continued so to do after the imposition of Arundel's limits on vernacular theology. It argues, rather, that it is 'spedful [profitable] to hem that kunne rede, and nameliche [in particular] to gentellis [those of gentry status], to have Goddis lawe writen in bookis, that thei mowon red it and so the better kunne [know or understand]' (p. 278). This moderate and quietly clerical treatise regularly cites chapter and verse of canon law and episcopal decrees to demonstrate how problems of clerical illiteracy have hindered the efficient delivery of the Church's teaching. It argues that many priests 'kunnen not construe ne expoune [do not know how to analyse/understand or explain]' (p. 258) the basic catechetical syllabus in Latin, despite being obliged to instruct their parishioners in it. Therefore, it argues, grammar schools have been established precisely for the purpose of teaching children who 'ben disposid to be [intend to become] men of holy chirche schulden lerne what Englische answerith to [relates to] what latyn' (p. 262). The author very carefully lays the ground of his argument here: Latin remains the master language of the Church; the clergy remain the primary vehicle for religious exposition and instruction, serving as two-way valves between the deposit of faith as interpreted by the universal Church and its local delivery in national vernaculars. He distinguished between the illiterate laity (who need only to know the basics of the faith) and those who can read, who may know more than clerics and should have their understanding nurtured. He concedes that the most obscure and difficult issues ought to remain the preserve of academics: 'highe materes schulden be descuscid and disputid amongis clerkis and men of skoole [academics]' (p. 277). But, in a decisive widening of the vernacular agenda, he argues that parish priests must not only instruct the laity, but also be ready and eager to answer their questions when issues arise in what they have heard or read (pp. 265–6).[22] Clergy should, as canon law requires, consider the needs and abilities of their audiences when they speak or preach. This requires them to 'turne latyn into Englische not Englische into latyn currup [corrupt/hybrid] as men don theise days to blende [mislead] the peple and to magnifien hemselfe' (p. 269), he argues, perhaps already reacting to attempts to enrich the vernacular by lexical

---

[21] The only edition to date is Simon Hunt, 'An Edition of Tracts in Favour of Scriptural Translation and of Some Texts Connected with Lollard Vernacular Biblical Scholarship' (unpublished D.Phil. thesis, Oxford, 1994). Reference in the text is by page to this edition.

[22] A short tract, *Deus expediat me*, interpolated into Mirk's *Festial* suggests that such questions were becoming more frequent and troublesome around the turn of the century, and that priests were often ill equipped to answer such queries. Karl Young, 'Instructions for Parish Priests', *Speculum*, 11 (1936), 224–31.

borrowing and aureation, or maybe just warning against stilted word-for-word translation. Unlike his opponents, who feared vernacular translation would unleash social unrest, the author of the treatise, like Ullerston, fears that denying the laity access to such materials would make the laity false, unstable, ready to rebel against their 'sovereyns [rulers]' and more apt to murder and manslaughter. Another treatise in the Cambridge collection uses material from St Augustine (beloved of both orthodox and heterodox reformers) to exhort priests to use the Bible to work against heresy and for the reform and renewal of the Church. Another says that the life of Christ reported in the Gospels is of far more value to laymen than any saints' lives they might come across. Yet another reuses materials from the prologue to Robert Greatham's *Mirur*, an Anglo-Norman sermon collection that proved a key text in the incipient vernacular theology of fourteenth-century gentry readers in London.[23] Between them these treatises address and invoke most of the major genres of non-contemplative and non-heretical vernacular religious writing in circulation in England in the early fifteenth century: catechetics, sermons, saints' lives, lives of Christ, Gospel harmonies and commentaries. Although the debate was ostensibly about the translation of the Bible, and centrally important though that was, also at stake was the viability of any religious text that used scriptural materials directly (through citation and translation) or indirectly (by paraphrase or retelling). This was, in fact, a battle for control over the direction of vernacular theology.

No doubt like Thomas Arundel, Richard Ullerston's views on translation were coloured by his wider perspective on the state of the universal Church, riven by schism and in dire need of reform in root and branch, and by the perceived threats to the stability of the English state and the viability of the English Church. But, unlike the somewhat older Arundel, Ullerston was among many in his generation at Oxford who seem to have felt that much of what Wyclif had criticized in the institutional Church did indeed need to be addressed, even if they did not subscribe to his doctrinal aberrations.[24] Ullerston was not without powerful and influential friends, even if some of them achieved their greatest influence after the death of Thomas Arundel in 1414. In 1408 Ullerston wrote sixteen petitions, designed to be presented by the English delegates to the Council of Pisa, and to be brought to the attention of Henry IV. These called for widespread reform of the Church militant on issues such as simony, the appropriation of benefices, exemptions,

---

[23] An edition of the Middle English translation is under way: *The Middle English Mirror: Sermons from Advent to Sexagesima*, ed. Thomas G. Duncan and Margaret Connolly, Middle English Texts 34 (Heidelberg: Universitätsverlag C. Winter, 2003). See the brilliant discussion of this text in Ralph Hanna, *London Literature, 1300–1380*, Cambridge Studies in Medieval Literature 57 (Cambridge: Cambridge University Press, 2005), 177–202, and *passim*.

[24] On this cultural environment, see the recent essays in Helen Barr and Ann M. Hutchison (eds.), *Text and Controversy from Wyclif to Bale: Essays in Honour of Anne Hudson*, Medieval Church Studies 4 (Turnhout: Brepols, 2005), and in Fiona Somerset, Jill C. Havens, and Derrick G. Pittard (eds.), *Lollards and their Influence in Late Medieval England* (Woodbridge: Boydell Press, 2003).

plurality of benefices, the abuse of privileges, clerical apostasy, and the holding of secular office. Most of these had been on Wyclif's own reform agenda. Ullerston also wrote a defence of tithes, and a handbook on chivalry for the king's son, the future Henry V, known by Lollards, according to Hoccleve, as the Prince of Priests. Henry was an energetic advocate of many of the reforms undertaken at the Council of Constance, where Ullerston's reforming influence could still be discerned in the positions advocated by the English delegates (and enshrined in the English version of the final concordat issued by the Pope), and in a document of *articuli* drawn up by the University of Oxford in 1414, after the death of Thomas Arundel. The Oxford *articuli* in fact contained a section 'de anglicatione librorum' (on the Englishing of books) which complained that inept and incompetent translation into the vernacular was misleading the simple and unlearned, and asked the king to legislate to order the confiscation of books in English until proper scholarly translations were available. This probably reflects the aspiration in chapter 6 of Arundel's decrees for a university-based system of examination and distribution of such texts through exemplars held by university stationers.[25] But it shows that the issue of translation and the status of the vernacular was never far away from the intellectual agenda in the decade after Arundel's decrees. The Oxford *articuli* argue only for a deferral of translation, not a prohibition of it, and in calling for proper scholarly translations to be made under orthodox clerical supervision in effect concede the cautious case for the transmission of theological materials in the vernacular outlined by Ullerston in 1401.

Arundel's decrees cast a long shadow across the following decades and encourage a sense that the role of the vernacular in innovatory religious writing was diminished, and its advocates cowed and anxious. Yet, though Ullerston's reform writings are only one strand in a skein of reform texts emerging from Oxford in the early fifteenth century, they give a voice to a movement for engagement with the vernacular and institutional reform that was never entirely silenced, and grew in confidence in the following decades. During the long episcopate (1414–43) of Arundel's successor as archbishop of Canterbury, Henry Chichele, the English Church came to adopt positions that arguably reflect those of Ullerston more closely than those of his opponents in the translation debate. Chichele, an Oxford doctor of civil law, was part of that generation of career clerics and bishops, like Ullerston, Robert Hallum, and Richard Flemyng, who had trained in Oxford alongside intellectual supporters

---

[25] On Ullerston's writings, see Richard Sharpe, *A Handlist of the Latin Writers of Great Britain and Ireland before 1540* (Turnhout: Brepols, 1997), 516–17; on his career, see Margaret Harvey, Richard Ullerston', *Oxford Dictionary of National Biography*, accessed online at **www.oxforddnb.com**. Ullerston's *Petitiones pro ecclesiae militantis reformatione* are edited by Hermann Von der Hardt, *Magnum oecumenicum Constantiense Concilium*, 4 vols. (Frankfurt: Christian Genschius, 1699), i, cols. 1126–71. The *Articuli concernantes reformationem universalis ecclesiae editi per universitatem Oxoniensis* are edited by David Wilkins, *Concilia Magnae Britanniae et Hiberniae*, 4 vols. (London: R. Gosling, 1737), iii. 360–5. Arundel's 1409 decrees are edited by Wilkins, *Concilia*, iii. 314–19.

of and advocates for Wycliffite views on the institutional Church. That generation shared more common ground with the *Wyclivisiti* than Arundel's, and their analysis of the state of the institutional Church would have frequently overlapped, even if they disagreed about the necessary remedies. Chichele promised to blow away the 'pulvis negligentiae' (the dust of neglect) from the English Church (which is, after all, hardly a ringing endorsement of the achievements of his predecessor).[26] Chichele and his men gave English orthodoxy a newly European, but also a newly austere, tenor in the wake of the Council of Constance. In their liturgical and institutional reforms they set a new course for the English Church. The orthodox reformers also placed a new emphasis on preaching as the primary medium of scriptural instruction and exposition in the wake of Arundel's cautions about the dangers of written vernacular translations of Scripture. The style of English sermons changed, and their importance was enhanced both in parochial practice and in English pastoral theory. Richard Flemyng introduced a new form of preaching to Oxford that moved away from scholastic distinction towards a clearer and more easily digested form of exposition. The stress on the primacy of the scriptural text and on the avoidance of rhetorical and scholastic tricks reflects Wyclif's own homiletic concerns and priorities. The orthodox reformers would have agreed wholeheartedly with the Lollard William Thorpe that 'we demen that we doon not the office of presthood if we leeuen oure preching'.[27]

The Latin sermons delivered by Englishmen at Constance establish a vocabulary of orthodox reform that spills over into vernacular poetry. The Church as a ship needing careful steering, the need for rebuilding Syon, the imperative to guard and maintain the walls of the vineyard are all themes that recur in these sermons, just as they do in the English vernacular poetry of the time. John Lydgate's *A Defence of Holy Church* is a deliberate checklist of the lexis of the episcopal reform project. Thomas Hoccleve, John Audelay, and the poet of Oxford, Bodleian Library, MS Digby 102 reveal assumptions about vernacular theology that often engage respectfully and seriously with the institutional critique initiated by Wyclif, while seeking to reinforce the centrality of the priesthood.[28] Lydgate offers scathing

[26] The *pulvis negligentiae* comment is made in a 1416 statute against Lollards issued at a Convocation of the Province of Canterbury: see Wilkins, *Concilia*, iii. 352–78, and the translation in Foxe's *Acts and Monuments*, ed. J. Pratt, 4th edn. (London: Religions Tract Society, 1877), iii. 534–5. Jeremy Catto, 'Religious Change under Henry V', in Gerald L. Harriss (ed.), *Henry V: The Practice of Kingship* (Oxford: Oxford University Press, 1985; repr. Stroud: Sutton, 1993), 97–115.

[27] *The Testimony of William Thorpe 1407*, ed. Anne Hudson in *Two Wycliffite Texts*, EETS, os 301 (London: Oxford University Press, 1993), 47; cit. Hudson, *Premature Reformation*, 354. On post-Arundel preaching, see Helen Leith Spencer, *English Preaching in the Late Middle Ages* (Oxford: Clarendon Press, 1993); Catto, 'Wyclif and Wycliffism', 255, see similar comments at 240 and 259; *Loci e Libro veritatum: Passages from Gascoigne's Theological Dictionary*, ed. J. E. Thorold Rogers (Oxford: Clarendon Press, 1881), 34–5.

[28] Only a few of the sermons preached by Englishmen at Constance have been edited, e.g.: Chris L. Nighman, ' "Accipiant Qui vocati" ': Richard Fleming's Reform Sermon at the Council of Constance',

criticism of clerical covetousness in the *Troy Book* (see, for example, IV. 5846–67), and Digby 102's criticism of careless curates is linked to passionate denunciation of usury, simony, 'and holy chirche rebel to goddis sawe' (XIV. 93). Sometimes its poems verge on a Lollard ecclesiology ('the folk is cherche' (VIII. 27)):

> There as gadryng of goode men ys,
> Is holychyrche of flesch and bones.   (XXIII. 103)

Several Digby poems (e.g. XXI, XXIII), describe priests as 'lanterns of light', perhaps reflecting Lollard diction (a popular Lollard compilation had this title), as does John Audelay in his echoically titled *The Council of Consciens* ('thai are the lanternys of lyf the leud men to lyght' (II. 12)). The largely unstudied prose moralizations in Hoccleve's *Series* explicitly read their antecedent fables in terms of broad issues of contemporary ecclesiastical reform, religious observance, and clerical idealism.

The membrane between the registers and lexis of clerical Latin and those of the English vernacular seems to have become increasingly permeable in the early fifteenth century. Aureation created a lexical and stylistic bridge between the Latin language of formal theology and the vulgar tongue of vernacularity. Far from eschewing vernacular theology, these writers of Chichele's generation created for it a whole new high-style register, seeking to reclaim the vernacular for orthodoxy, and to make it fit for precise and nuanced theological thought, just as Ullerston had said they should.[29] The real story about vernacular theology is that in the end John Wyclif had more impact on the language and attitudes of the English Church in the fifteenth century than his arch-enemy Thomas Arundel.

For the early fourteenth-century *Northern Homily Cycle*, the agenda of vernacular theology was apparently straightforward: 'To wirke sum god thing on Inglisse' (Wogan-Browne et al. (eds.), *The Idea of the Vernacular*, 128). By 1400, vernacular theology, responding to and perhaps providing a voice for successive waves of

---

Journal of Ecclesiastical History, 51 (2000), 1–36; Thomas E. Morrissey, ' "Surge, Illuminare": A Lost Address by Richard Fleming at the Council of Constance', *Annuarium historiae conciliorum*, 22 (1990–1), 86–130. For Lydgate's *Defence*, see *The Minor Poems of John Lydgate*, part 1, ed. Henry Noble McCracken, EETS, es 107 (London: Oxford University Press, 1911; repr. 1962). For the *Troy Book*, see *John Lydgate: Troy Book*, ed. Henry Bergen EETS, es 97 (London: Oxford University Press, 1906), 103 (1908), 106 (1910), 126 (1935). For the *Series*, see Thomas Hoccleve, *'My Compleinte' and Other Poems*, ed. Roger Ellis, Exeter Medieval Texts and Studies (Exeter: University of Exeter Press, 2001). For Digby 102, see J. Kail (ed.), *Twenty-Six Political and Other Poems*, EETS, os 124 (London: Oxford University Press, 1904), reference by poem number and page. Dr Helen Barr is at work on a new edition of these poems, and I am very grateful to her for discussing them with me, and for reading early drafts of some of these ideas. For Audelay, see *The Poems of John Audelay*, ed. Ella Keats Whiting, EETS, os 184 (London: Oxford University Press, 1931), reference by poem number and page. *The Lanterne of Light*, ed. Lillian M. Swinburn, EETS, os 151 (London: Oxford University Press, 1917).

[29] Contemporary writers sometimes complained that preachers used 'English latin': see Spencer, *English Preaching*, 118. A 'clerycall manere' may reflect that fact that the lexis and syntax of many priests were profoundly macaronic, and that code-shifting was a way of life for many clerics preaching in the vernacular from notes and texts recorded in Latin.

social and religious turmoil, had developed into a complex and contested field, characterized by significant nuance of opinion within its orthodox and heterodox supporters and opponents. The next phase of work on vernacular theology needs to respond to that complexity and nuance in its local analyses. The growing vernacularity of the broad spectrum of English religious writing needs to be historicized more acutely, perhaps particularly in pre–1400 writing, and in its full range from didactic and catechetic to contemplative and visionary texts. The interaction between oral and written discourse (perhaps especially in preaching and the written circulation of sermon texts) requires sustained attention to the status, identity, and authority of the speaking subject in such texts. Orthodox and clerical engagement with vernacularity deserves more sympathetic treatment, especially in the context of the sociolinguistic mediation of vernacular theology in the fifteenth century (and not just in regard to the atypical views of Reginald Pecock). The diversity of genres, implied audiences, and linguistic registers consciously invoked by acts of vernacular theology (and often imported from other discourses) should be attentively tracked. The growing generic importance of dialogic encounters (real or staged) within and across social, gender, and spiritual categories will reward closer investigation. Dialogue provides a fictive locus for the performance of vernacular theological debate, and for the voicing of potentially contentious views. The linkage between such dialogic textual encounters and the public realm of religious drama merits further sustained analysis. Vernacular theology became a contested category, but the power and potential of the vernacular as a vehicle through which all could have access to theological understanding through speech or writing meant that it had always been worth arguing for:

> Ofter haly kirkis state [following the church's decree]
> This ilke [same] boke ys translate
> Until [into] Ingeles tonge to rede
> For the love of Englis lede [people],
> Englis lede of Engelande
> The commune for til understande [so that the commons
>   will understand].   (*Cursor mundi*, c.1300, in Wogan-Browne et al. (eds),
>   *The Idea of the Vernacular*, 270)

FURTHER READING

The 'religious turn' in medieval studies over the last fifteen years has been dramatic, though the publication of editions has not kept pace. Vernacular theology is a fast-expanding area, and I have restricted reference to works published since the turn of the century. The cluster of short papers in *English Language Notes*, 44 (2006) is a good place to take the temperature of the subject. In synoptic terms, David Wallace's *The Cambridge History of Medieval English Literature* (1999) contains many articles that severally and collectively sum up the state of the subject at the turn of the millennium and offer hints and nudges for new directions. James

Simpson's *Reform and Cultural Revolution, 1350–1547*, Oxford English Literary History 2 (Oxford: Oxford University Press, 2002) makes a powerful implicit case for the centrality of vernacular theology as an underpinning bass-note throughout late medieval and early modern culture. Roger Ellis's volume for *The Oxford History of Literary Translation in English* (forthcoming) will give sustained attention to issues of vernacularity from Anglo-Saxon to the end of the Middle Ages. For pre–1300 writing, Christopher Cannon, *The Grounds of English Literature* (Oxford: Oxford University Press, 2004) offers challenging readings of thirteenth-century religious texts and contexts. Jocelyn Wogan-Browne, *Saints' Lives and Women's Literary Cultures: Virginity and its Authorizations* (Oxford: Oxford University Press, 2001) opens up the multilingual world of post-Conquest England in exciting ways, and her ongoing project The French of England Translation Series (FRETS) (published by the Medieval and Renaissance Text Society, Arizona State University, Tempe) will make available translations into English of important but understudied Anglo-Norman texts. Ralph Hanna, *London Literature* (n. 23 above), ruminates profoundly on the codicological issues behind vernacular theology, as does his 'Yorkshire Writers', *Proceedings of the British Academy*, 121 (2003), 91–109.

Barr and Hutchison's *Text and Controversy from Wyclif to Bale* (n. 24) contains many essays that begin to explore the 'grey area' that lies between the certainly orthodox and the unequivocally heterodox, as does Somerset, Havens, and Pittard's *Lollards and their Influence* (n. 24). Kantik Ghosh has opened up Wycliffite exegesis in *The Wycliffite Heresy: Authority and the Interpretation of texts* (Cambridge: Cambridge University Press, 2002). Mishtooni Bose's 'Reginald Pecock's Vernacular Voice' in Somerset et al. (eds.), *Lollards and their Influence* (pp. 217–36) contributes valuably to mapping the academic and intellectual contours of English theology in the first half of the fifteenth century, as does Andrew Taylor ('Translation, Censorship, Authorship and the Lost Work of Reginald Pecock', in *Middle Ages and the Renaissance. The Politics of Translation in the* Renate Blumenfeld-Kosinski, Luise von Flotow, and Daniel Russell (eds), (Tempe: Arizona Center for Medieval and Renaissance Studies, 2001), 143–60).

The categories and procedures of medieval theology (including those of McGinn and Watson) are reviewed by Barbara Newman in *God and the Goddesses* (n. 14). She proposes a new category of 'imaginative theology' which 'focuses on how theology might be performed'. A theology where 'the devices of literature … are its working tools' had already been hinted at by Jim Rhodes, *Poetry Does Theology: Chaucer, Grosseteste and the Pearl-Poet* (Notre Dame, IN: University of Notre Dame Press, 2001), and by M. B. Pranger, *The Artificiality of Christianity: Essays on the Poetics of Monasticism*, Figurae: Reading Medieval Culture (Stanford, CA: Stanford University Press, 2003).

CHAPTER 26

HERESY AND HUMANISM

ANDREW COLE

Ecclesiastical dampness causes prematurely gray hair.

John Cheever

Until very recently, settled knowledge about religious culture in the late Middle Ages has gone something like this: To consider yourself a part of mainstream religion in the fifteenth century is to be acutely aware of your difference from heretics. If you are a religious writer in this period you must hew closely to orthodox teachings lest you be mistaken for a heretic in your lyrical or prosaic musings about Church hierarchies, the Scripture, or the sacraments. Some specialists in Middle English literature—though by no means all—have begun to quarrel with this model. My purpose is to extend this quarrel and explore other paradigms that may broaden our notions about religious writing in fifteenth-century England. The paradigm that interests me does not include heretics so much as their persecutors—bishops. One reason for this focus is that the underdogs in the conflicts between orthodoxy and heterodoxy—namely, the Wycliffite heretics—have received much expert attention recently, with, thankfully, no sign of this attention faltering. Another reason is that bishops are in large part responsible for innovations that are elided in a focus on Wycliffism, in which bishops appear as, frankly, the bad guys. My aim here is not to take or even switch sides (I partly work in the subfield of Wycliffite studies) but only to focus on the critically neglected innovations within what I call 'ecclesiastical humanism', which is a cultural efflorescence of literary, educational,

My gratitude goes to the British Library and the Bodleian Library for use of their resources, including the New College manuscripts temporarily in possession of the latter; thanks also go to the Department of English and American Literature at Harvard for a Morton Bloomfield Fellowship, which allowed me to write this essay and present it to the Medieval Doctoral Conference at Harvard. Both the Dean of the Franklin College of Arts and Sciences and the Research Foundation at the University of Georgia supplied two semesters of paid leave during which time this project was imagined and executed. The input of Maura Nolan, James Simpson, and Nicholas Watson is everywhere in this essay, to its credit.

and artistic endeavours in the fifteenth century that eschewed a world view of 'the Church vs. heresy'.

In this essay, I read a manuscript illustration and a play written by a chancellor of Oxford University as ways of opening a window onto this new cultural scene. I show how 'ecclesiastical humanism' emerged during the fifteenth century and describe some of its features—particularly, the rhetoric of petitions to patrons and the related 'advice to bishops' genre, a phrase I have coined from the mint of the more familiar 'advice to princes' tradition. My conclusion is that between the 1430s and the 1480s the prevailing cultural obsession with the Wycliffite heresy had largely disappeared and was replaced, in part, by new ambitions to imagine ecclesiastical institutions as centres of patronage and humanist literary culture.

Whither Wycliffism? The mid-fifteenth century

I begin, however, with Wycliffism, because its emergence in the fourteenth century and surprising submergence in the fifteenth will be crucial to this account. Wycliffism is a reformist movement that began in the late 1370s at Oxford University—particularly around the teachings of the theologian John Wyclif (d. 1384). Wyclif and his followers sought great changes in the Church's sacramental theology and ecclesiastical structures. They insisted, for instance, that the eucharist—by far the most important of devotional forms of expression in late medieval religion—was a source of deception for believers. Specifically, they claimed that the Church rationalized its own power by obscuring the meaning of the sacrament itself, failing to recognize the symbolism of the eucharistic wafer as Jesus had intended it in the Gospels as a *sign* of his imminent sacrifice, and not as a *trompe l'oeil* whereby Christ's real, crucified body appears in the bread but remains invisible to the senses. They also argued strenuously that a Church that held property was a Church mesmerized by worldly things, and that the only way to direct its attention back to spiritual concerns would be a systemic disendowment of the prelacy. Small wonder, then, that in 1382 the Church deemed these and other teachings to be heresy at a provincial synod, which now goes by the name of the Blackfriars Council (held at the Blackfriars house in London). After this condemnation, and from the mid-1380s on, many persons disparaged Wycliffites publicly by calling them 'lollards', a Latin and Middle English word that loosely meant 'heretic'. Wycliffism—which should be our word of choice to describe this heresy so as to free ourselves from transparently transmitting medieval prejudices—is, then, in most respects an academic heresy that became exceedingly popular. In the mid-1380s the dissident ideas of Wyclif and his students at Oxford connected, by processes not fully visible today, with a portion of the laity, and from then on spread with increasing diversity and reach among the peasantry and gentry alike, relying for expression on religious books written in English rather than Latin.[1] Because of the spread of Wycliffism among the laity and its continuing appeal within vernacular cultures, the Church—specifically, successive archbishops of Canterbury—sought measures to eradicate it, virtually inaugurating the fifteenth century with some very sobering business.

In 1401, the Wycliffite priest William Sawtre became the first person to be executed in England for the crime of heresy. Then in 1409 Archbishop Thomas Arundel published his Constitutions, a set of provincial mandates designed to monitor the discussion of theology in the schools and its preaching in the parishes—all in the effort to make sure that Wycliffites were not gaining students or audiences.[2] Just a year later, an obscure smith, John Badby, was burned in a barrel at the stake during a royal spectacle in London, becoming the first layman in England ever to be executed as a heretic—killed for the explicit purposes of setting an example to would-be Badbys.[3] In 1413, Sir John Oldcastle (the distant original of Shakespeare's Falstaff) became the first aristocrat to be tried and condemned for heresy and treason. He was executed in 1417. Then, in the next year and quite far afield from England in what is now south-western Germany, the Council of Constance convened. Meeting between 1414 and 1418, this remote ecumenical council had implications for England, because the English Church was beholden to its decrees and keenly interested in the effort to end the great papal schism. England's own problems with heresy were among the topics discussed at Constance, to the conclusion that Wyclif and the contemporary Czech reformer John Hus were to be condemned as heretics; Hus was burnt at the stake, and Wyclif's bones were ordered to be exhumed and burned, which happened, belatedly, in 1428. In that same year, Archbishop Chichele (Arundel's successor) called together the bishops in the see of Canterbury in an attempt to regularize the procedures related to the inquisition of heretics. This convocation seems to have motivated a series of trials in Norwich between 1428 and 1431, which were the first major inquisition into the beliefs of numerous lay persons suspected of heresy.

Recent scholarship has been intensively focused on the problems related to late medieval orthodoxy and heresy, and literary critics have found the literature of the age to be responsive to these circumstances. Authors have been thought to align themselves with one side of this binary or the other. Indeed, obvious

---

[1] In my *England after Heresy* (forthcoming), I offer my position on the words 'lollardy' and 'lollard' as social typologies, describe the legal processes and politics of the Blackfriars Council, and explore how Wycliffism bears on the work of Chaucer, Langland, Hoccleve, Lydgate, Kempe, and a host of minor authors.

[2] See Nicholas Watson, 'Censorship and Cultural Change in Late-Medieval England: Vernacular Theology, the Oxford Translation Debate, and Arundel's Constitutions of 1409', *Speculum*, 70 (1995), 822–64.

[3] See Peter McNiven, *Heresy and Politics in the Reign of Henry IV: The Burning of John Badby* (Woodbridge: Boydell, 1987).

alignments may be observed. Wycliffites would refuse to kowtow to any attempts at theological censorship; one Wycliffite, for instance, would publish (i.e. 'circulate' in manuscript form) the *Lanterne of Light*, which, among other things, directly impugns Arundel's Constitutions as yet another contrivance of the devil.[4] And orthodox polemicists would continue to rally to the causes of orthodoxy, such as William Woodford or Thomas Netter, who would endeavour to show that Wycliffism was not only a heresy but an intellectual fraud, a gross misreading of scriptural and exegetical texts.

Nevertheless, other persons sought the best of both worlds—compilations of texts that did the seemingly unthinkable for Arundel, mixing orthodox and Wycliffite items together. These readers accepted that the 'Wycliffite' or 'orthodox' difference between such works is usually a matter of emphasis on the received traditions: the seven sacraments, the seven deadly sins, the seven virtues, the seven works of mercy, the Ten Commandments, the Pater Noster (or 'Lord's Prayer'), the Creed, and so forth. For instance, a Wycliffite would perhaps not wish Mary to be mentioned in the Creed and have her name removed without any carping about why. Conversely, an orthodox person might wish to underscore the fact that the sacrament of the altar does indeed contain Christ's own flesh and blood, but forgo blaming 'lollards' for holding a contrary view. Yet both persons believed in the Creed and the sacrament of the altar, broadly formulated, and both could attend services in the same church, participating in the same rituals but silently interpreting them within their own frame of reference. Even with such a seemingly unresolvable binary afoot, then, people worked around it by working between it.[5]

So that is what happened. But what sort of literary history is this? What are its methodologies and limits? Typically, when scholars set about interpreting these texts in their historical context, they first try to assess their ideological content so then decisions can be made about what sort of cultural work these texts may be doing, what sort of audiences they may be addressing. Scholars usually place these texts on a spectrum of religious views that runs from things outright Wycliffite—so positively against established religion that the critique is the substitute religion itself—to things so stringently orthodox that anti-Wycliffism seems to be the only concern. Wycliffites on one end, orthodox persons on the other. A generally disinterested or 'neutral' party or even an author who happens to make a wry comment about a cadging friar, say, is then placed somewhere in the centre of things, perhaps close to the persons reading mixed compilations.

---

[4] Lilian M. Swinburn (ed.), *The Lanterne of Liȝt*, EETS, os 151 (London: Kegan Paul, Trench, Trübner, 1917), 17–18.

[5] See Jill C. Havens, 'Shading the Grey Area: Determining Heresy in Middle English Texts', in Helen Barr and Ann M. Hutchison (eds.), *Text and Controversy from Wyclif to Bale: Essays in Honour of Anne Hudson* (Turnhout: Brepols, 2005), 337–52.

Is this, however, the best way to organize literary history? In many cases, yes—especially when attention is given to texts that have escaped rigorous analysis, such as the corpus of English Wycliffite prose texts that still reside in crumbling, acid-paper nineteenth-century editions. But I must question the relevance of this approach for the fifteenth century as a whole, especially the great middle portion from the 1430s to the beginning of the Tudor period in 1485, and I do so on account of a curious historical fact: in the mid-fifteenth century, as Hudson puts it, 'the authorities for some reason lost interest in pursuing heretics'.[6] Did Wycliffites go away or underground, only to reappear later by way of new prosecutions in the late fifteenth and early sixteenth century—the Coventry, Lichfield, and Kent heresy trials? Perhaps. Did bishops perceive the problems and politics of heresy in the mid-fifteenth century differently from their predecessors in the earlier part of the century? These questions are best left answered for a more elaborate version of this argument but the latter question especially gets at my ultimate concern for this chapter about the cultural and theological preoccupations of bishops and those in their circle.

For now, however, suffice it to make a point about how Hudson's claim pertains to literary history. We may note that Hudson did not explore how her observation relates to the literature of the period. Her literary historical chapter, entitled 'The Context of Vernacular Wycliffism', is largely focused on materials from around the 1380s to the 1430s, with the addendum of one later author from the 1440s and 1450s, Bishop Reginald Pecock, whom I discuss below. No subsequent scholarship, such as the recent *Cambridge History of Medieval English Literature* or James Simpson's literary history entitled *Reform and Cultural Revolution*,[7] has accounted for this peculiar historical moment in literary historical terms. In sum, when I ask the question, 'whither Wycliffism?' I mean to draw attention to the fact that something is interfering with the familiar narratives about religious writing in the fifteenth century and that something is disturbing our settled sense of a fifteenth century caught up in a larger teleology moving from late medieval Catholicism to early modern Protestantism, a movement generated precisely by Wycliffite problems all along. That something is, I suggest, 'ecclesiastical humanism', which might offer a partial explanation as to why 'the authorities lost interest in pursuing heretics'—or at least why, in part, they appear that way in literary materials. Indeed, this

---

[6] Anne Hudson, *The Premature Reformation: Wycliffite Texts and Lollard History* (Oxford: Clarendon Press, 1988), 446; after this claim, Hudson discusses the few heresy trials that did transpire. The point here is not that the prosecutions against heresy disappeared. No such totalizing claim can be sustained, but the point is that the pursuit of heretics in the mid-fifteenth century is considerably less active than in the earlier part of the century.

[7] Simpson charts the course of literary history in terms of the waxing and waning of various kinds of reformist writing from the 1350s to the Reformation, at which point the multivalency of reform is trampled by the march of the magisterial revolution: see *Reform and Cultural Revolution: The Oxford English Literary History, ii: 1350–1547* (Oxford: Oxford University Press, 2002).

precocious humanism may account for why a set of neglected texts authored by persons patronized by bishops seem to be very different from the sorts of texts that worked within the orthodox-heterodox binary in the earlier part of the century.

Ecclesiastical humanism

My phrase of choice here, 'ecclesiastical humanism', is not perfect.[8] But it seeks to account for some of the institutional settings within which humanist activity flourished after new classical texts from the Continent began to circulate in England in the first quarter of the fifteenth century, a development amply documented by Roberto Weiss. I wish, however, to go one step beyond Weiss who, having described a multitude of such humanist manuscripts, concluded that there was no humanism in England at the time.[9] *What were all those texts for*, then? My effort here is not to describe but to interpret—to explore how such a humanist background begins to figure into 'ecclesiastical humanism' in the fifteenth century. Specifically, I will offer a sketch of how new texts by and translations of Plato, Cicero, Aristotle, and others motivated correspondingly new forms of self-fashioning among the following group of persons: deans, deacons, archdeacons, bishops, wardens of colleges, and chancellors—all of whom move among a variety of sacred and secular spaces in late medieval England, some holding the highest offices in the kingdom. Such persons obviously already bore a relation to one another, by virtue of holding (in most cases) offices in the Church. Yet some within these ecclesiastical relations were additionally connected to one another by relations of patronage—typically, between a bishop and an ecclesiastical subordinate—and these sometimes produced literary exchanges. In the literary forms that emerge within such contexts of patronage, the institutional settings of the *ecclesia* itself appear and are themselves imagined in classical terms: an influential bishop will be hailed as the modern-day equivalent of a Greek or Roman leader or author. Yet in describing ecclesiastical persons in light of a new Latinity, authors were not only finding novel ways to praise great persons; they were, rather, supplying new models of identity that are not 'theological', 'religious', or preoccupied with heresy, but rather resonant with the secular virtues and germane to the obligations of running the institutions of the *ecclesia* successfully. While 'ecclesiastical humanism' should be understood as diverse in nature—involving art and architecture, as much as literature—the focus here will be specifically on the literary matters related to patronage.

---

[8] Richard Southern, in his *Medieval Humanism and Other Studies* (Oxford: Basil Blackwell, 1970), explored medieval humanism among religious writers, but he confined his enquiries to continental authors in the period 1100–1350.

[9] R. Weiss, *Humanism in England during the Fifteenth Century*, 3rd edn. (Oxford: Basil Blackwell, 1967).

A picture of episcopal patronage: New College MS 288

I now turn to a picture of patronage at Oxford University, as shown in Oxford University, New College MS 288, fo. 4[r] (see Fig. 7). This illustration is a perfect example of a relation of patronage and, more importantly, a relation of patronage within a relation of patronage. In the top centre of the picture is Bishop William Wykeham, founder of New College, chancellor of England, and Keeper of the Privy Seal under Edward III. He was one of the most powerful and influential churchmen of late medieval England.[10] Surrounding Wykeham are eleven ecclesiasts, identified by their first names written on their robes, ranging from the archbishop of Dublin to bishops, archdeacons, and the dean of St Paul's. Note that Wykeham himself is holding in his right hand a building, as well as a small structure in his lap in his left hand. These are, respectively, New College at Oxford and Winchester College, Wykeham's famous foundations of the late fourteenth century that are typically seen as revolutionary educational establishments. Winchester was a 'feeder school' for New College itself, with the idea that a grammar school can prepare one for graduate work. And when a student graduated from New College, he would typically benefit from what A. B. Cobban calls 'the central utilitarian aim of Wykeham's foundation'—that is, 'a career in the service of the church or state'.[11] The first generation of scholars bears this out, for New College produced a class of public intellectuals and high office holders who were Keepers of the Privy Seal, chancellors of Oxford University, tutors to the young King Henry VI, and so forth. Not a bad placement record for a graduate institution!

But more interesting still is the relation of patronage within the relation of patronage. Observe the figure touching Wykeham's New College. He is two places from Wykeham's right hand, and he is Bishop Thomas Bekynton, who served as Henry VI's tutor and was a patron of New College. Bekynton's gesture may be read as one of support and influence, which, judging by the visual semiotic, flows not only up but down.[12] That is, notice Bekynton's robe, which flows into the hands of a man just beneath him. That is Thomas Chaundler, a graduate of New College who enjoyed the patronage of Bekynton, and who was once chancellor of Oxford and warden of New College. Were Chaundler actually grasping Bekynton's hem,

---

[10] Jean Froissart indicated that Edward III did nothing without first consulting Wykeham; see *Chroniques*, ed. George T. Diller, vol. iii (Geneva: Droz, 1992), 465.

[11] A. B. Cobban, 'Colleges and Halls 1380–1500', in Jeremy Catto and Ralph Evans (eds.), *The History of the University of Oxford: Late Medieval Oxford*, vol. ii, (Oxford: Clarendon Press, 1992), 586.

[12] If this gesture symbolizes Bekynton's bequest to New College—Bekynton died in 1465—then the image perhaps can be dated after that year. On the bequest, see Robert W. Dunning's entry, 'Beckington, Thomas', in H. C. G. Matthew and Brian Harrison (eds.), *Oxford Dictionary of National Biography*, 60 vols. (Oxford: Oxford University Press, 2004), iv. 740.

Figure 7
Bishop William Wykeham
(seated) and his circle,
among whom are several
noted humanists. Grisaille
illustration. (Oxford, New
College MS 288, fol. 4ʳ. By
permission of the Master
and Fellows of New
College)

I would be tempted to cite Luke 8: 46, where 'virtutem' (virtue or power) is said to flow out from Jesus when his hem is touched. Yet there is actually something of a flow of patronage and power represented here in the way Wykeham, Bekynton, and Chaundler are all visually, physically connected, each touching the other, directly or secondarily, as it were. And the reason has to do with what I believe are some of the more interesting moments of literary patronage in fifteenth-century England. Granted, much ado can be made over portraits; the presentation portraits of Chaucer, Hoccleve, and Lydgate in Corpus Christi College, MS 61, British Library Arundel MS 38, and Huntington Library, MS HM 268, respectively, always seem to stand out for special notice, perhaps on account of the implied intimacy or exclusivity between one patron and one author. But here we have something different. Chaundler, so far as we know, is both the compiler of New College 288 and *perhaps* the artist of this illustration, which of course betrays a semiotic that in essence puts him in the symbolic centre as the maker of books and the recipient of patronage—thereby also elevating his cultural importance while acknowledging those who stand above him, literally and figuratively. Furthermore, the contents of the manuscript itself actually duplicate this situation in which Chaundler's importance is acknowledged. The manuscript contains seven *collocutiones* in praise of Wykeham written by a student of Chaundler and two *allocutiones* by Chaundler himself in tribute to Wykeham.[13] The student's contribution is especially interesting, because Chaundler is clear to say that he instructed this individual ('quem ego in teneris annis philosophiam docui' (whom I instructed in philosophy in his earlier years) (ii. 320)).[14] Such words bolster Chaundler as an educator and patron himself, making literary opportunities available to his students, and then presenting these student efforts along with his own work to a patron, Bekynton. Of course, Chaundler makes sure that Bekynton emerges from all of this looking good. In his dedicatory prologue to all of these works, Chaundler offers Bekynton counsel on forbearance during adversity and in the process refers to the sayings or circumstances of Cicero, Epicurus, Aristippus of Cyrene, Democritus, Plutarch, and other classical authorities that, save for a few exceptions, were uncommon several decades before. Essentially, Chaundler makes Bekynton out to be a patron worthy of counsel in the new classical forms.

The Mirror for Bishops tradition, or, how do you talk to a bishop?

Let us unpack that claim, first by acknowledging that these particular discourses in which one even addresses a bishop are themselves unusual and generally unavailable to literary criticism so far. Were critics to acknowledge the discursive stakes in the very act of 'speaking to a bishop', they would probably think of examples that bring us back to Wycliffite problems and to the more prominent instances of ecclesiastical patronage or claims to patronage, both of which are typically instrumental in their aim to combat heresy. For example, we might think of Archbishop Arundel's commissioning of Friar William Woodford to refute the positions of Wyclif, or of the same archbishop's commendation of Nicholas Love's *Mirror of the Blessed Life of Jesus Christ*.[15] Further, judging by present interests in the field, critics might respond to the question of 'How do you talk to a bishop?' with the answer, 'You talk to a bishop by talking back as a "lollard"!' The familiar examples

---

[13] See *Duke Humfrey and English Humanism in the Fifteenth Century: Catalogue of an Exhibition Held in the Bodleian Library* (Oxford: Bodleian Library, 1970), 21.

[14] See *Official Correspondence of Thomas Bekynton*, ed. George Williams (London: HMSO, 1872), ii. 15–20; 323, 325.

[15] *Nicholas Love: The Mirror of the Blessed Life of Jesus Christ: A Full Critical Edition*, ed. Michael G. Sargent (Exeter: University of Exeter Press, 2005). John Gower includes a 'dedicatory epistle' to Archbishop Thomas Arundel in a manuscript of *Vox clamantis* (Oxford University, All Souls MS 98), and although I do not have the space here to deal with this epistle at length, I can proleptically say that this item lacks the main rhetorical features that characterize dedications in the tradition of 'ecclesiastical humanism'.

then come to mind: the records related to the heresy trials in Norwich, Coventry, or Kent, the *Testimony of William Thorpe*, or the *Book of Margery Kempe*.[16]

But this problem of 'talking to a bishop' has other elements, and we can frame the issue by drawing from some generalities from the Mirror for Princes tradition—a tradition comprised of texts that compile stories or exempla aimed to counsel and instruct a prince or king in the virtues. Insofar as clerkly authors offered their secular rulers texts befitting their stations—namely, exempla—so, too, must authors think about the literary appropriateness of the works they present to episcopal superiors. In the same way that offering advice to rulers often straddles the fine line between wisdom and flattery—indeed, the overlap between these terms confers upon this tradition its most interesting features—authors writing within what I would call the Mirror for Bishops tradition must walk an analogous fine line. There is a difference between presuming to instruct an ecclesiastical superior on points of theology and offering such a person a literary handling of theological traditions and sources that seems, in essence, relevant to the dedicatee's station.

What is initially interesting about New College MS 288 is that the binary of orthodoxy vs. heresy is not operative. For instance, the authors of the *collocutiones* do not praise any of the prelates as hunters of heresy[17]; for the record, Chaundler refers to Bekynton's brooking 'horribles dissensiones ac schismata [horrible dissentions and schisms]' (ii. 316), but the reference is tellingly vague and is absorbed into general reflections about brooking hard times. Instead, these authors are more concerned to construct in their literary portraits an episcopal person as a virtuous man of learning and letters. For instance, the laudation of Wykeham within the dedication to Bekynton states that if the Greeks and Romans have their 'scribae, poetae, comici' (scribes, poets, and comedians (dramatists)), we have our 'Willelum de Wykam' (ii. 319)—a literary figure of a different sort by virtue of being the subject of literature himself. What is at issue here is not the praise of great persons so much as the elements of that praise.

References to the secular virtues and the new classical figures are a feature of 'ecclesiastical humanism' and are motivated by a need to draw, if you will allow, the institutionality of the *ecclesia* into the literary imagination and to do so in a way that is not strictly 'theological' or, better, ecclesiological.[18] Indeed, ecclesiology does not

---

[16] See the 'Testimony of William Thorpe,' in Anne Hudson (ed.) *Two Wycliffite Texts*, EETS, os 301 (Oxford: Oxford University Press, 1993); *The Book of Margery Kempe*, ed. Lynn Staley (Kalamazoo, MI: Medieval Institute, 1996).

[17] *Bekynton Correspondence*, ii. 325–6; Doris Enright-Clark Shoukri (ed.), *Liber apologeticus de omni statu humanae naturae* (London: Modern Humanities Research Association, 1974), 3–4, 8, 9. Chaundler's *Liber apologeticus* will be cited from Shoukri's edition by page, parenthetically, in the main text.

[18] Chaundler's 'Libellus de laudibus duarum civitatum' (in New College MS 288) is, in its details about the institutional establishments at Wells and Bath, a remarkable example of 'ecclesiastical humanism'; see George Williams (ed.), *Proceedings of the Somersetshire Archaeological and Natural History Society*, 19 (1873), 99–121.

suffice as an explanation here, neither the study of the Church hierarchy from pope to acolyte as if it were a pseudo-Dionysian Great Chain of Being, nor ecclesiologies that are overtly theological in their reflections on the Church as 'body of believers' or the 'Corpus Christi'—that is, the various models by which theologians conceive of the Church as a collective of persons oriented around a shared concern with salvation or a community drawn together in the partaking of the sacrament of the altar. Rather, the *ecclesia* that is imagined here is one in which classical references are useful not as theological sources but as models of identity and virtue for patrons and authors alike.

Thomas Chaundler and *Liber apologeticus*

The bracketing of certain kinds of theological discourse in favour of the secular virtues is evident in another gift-text, Thomas Chaundler's *Liber apologeticus de omni statu humanae naturae* in Cambridge, Trinity College, MS R.14.5, fos. 10^r–35^v. Chaundler wrote the *Liber apologeticus* as a play, complete with a long opening dialogue from God on the fall of Lucifer; then follows a series of exchanges between God and the first man (named 'homo', not Adam). There are also speeches by Reason (*Racio*), Sensuality (*Sensualitas*), and the four cardinal virtues (justice, prudence, fortitude, and temperance). The sheer existence of this work—a Latin drama written by a university chancellor—is remarkably interesting. My main concern here, however, will be to address those details related to some of the main features of 'ecclesiastical humanism' and the 'advice to bishops' genre—unfortunately forgoing the *explication de texte* this work merits.

Sometime between 1457 and 1461, Chaundler completed this text and gave it to Bekynton. In the dedication to Bekynton, Chaundler announces that the purpose of his *Liber apologeticus* is to offer a defence of humanity or, as he boldly puts it in his title, *de omni statu humanae naturae* (of human nature in every condition). Yet Chaundler knows that this topic must be made appealing to Bekynton. He writes in the dedication:

> This your devotion which you poured out most abundantly, not only to a great many but also to myself, most blessed Father, inspired my weakness so that I might reflect on piety more closely. So it happens that I seemed to travel in mind to the bowels of divine piety. I beheld indeed the orb of the heavens and earth, God the omnipotent creator of both, and I saw how the piety of God had been stamped on his creatures. ... And that is why it is like the labour to comprehend what is incomprehensible to fashion a little book about that divine and ineffable piety, which I decided to prepare for you, O holy pastor of souls.
> (p. 51)

Chaundler's language of modesty is thinly veiled, for what it takes to make this deceptively 'little book' is tantamount to the no mean task of comprehending 'what is incomprehensible'—i.e., this gift was impossible to pull off and thus deserves due consideration. 'I worked hard on this', Chaundler is saying. He further demands

Bekynton's attention in the following words: 'Receive now, Father, the first fruits of my labours [and] … do use the authority of a holy Chancellor, [and] … strengthen in substance this little work of mine' (p. 53). To unpack this compressed syntax: 'when you enact your great office, you strengthen this work'—which is another way of saying that this work is pointless unless it is applied.

Chaundler furthers the interest of his text by appealing to Bekynton's own interests in classically inspired humanism.[19] He goes so far as to compare his *Liber apologeticus* to Plato's *Apologia*:

> The book is called *Apologeticus* because it is intended to excuse and refute, from apologia, which is a defence or refutation. Whence also the book which Plato published on the death of Socrates is called *Apologia Socratis* from its excusing or refuting defence of Socrates.   (p. 53)

Not only is Chaundler's apology on behalf of 'homo [man]' equivalent to Plato's defence of Socrates, making the protagonist of the drama an idealized Socratic figure worthy of defence, but Chaundler himself comes out of this as a modern Plato—a Plato of the mid-fifteenth century. Here there is no 'medieval Plato'—no reference to the few commonly read works by Plato that were cited in various disquisitions on the nature and immortality of the soul. This is the new Plato—the Plato newly exported to England.[20] Pertinent to the question of Bekynton's familiarity with this talk of Plato is the partial evidence of two formularies, associated with Bekynton, that contain copies of Duke Humphrey's letters to Decembrio concerning the acquisition of Plato's *Republic*.

In the play itself, Chaundler continues to make this work suitable for an episcopal superior. How so? First, and again, Chaundler names the protagonist of the play 'homo', and not Adam, and in so doing generalizes the identity of the protagonist so that it resonates more as a category of person than as a specific biblical character. This is not a minor adjustment. For while Chaundler does place 'homo' within biblical history—from Creation, to the Fall, to the redeeming Crucifixion—his version of this history suggests that 'homo' is not only a man from the scriptural past but a figure of the everlasting present, a figure for whom the problems of self-rule and good counsel are a defining feature of personhood. Indeed, I would go further to suggest that Chaundler renders 'homo' as the mirror image of Bekynton—literally, a symmetrically opposite persona: rather than ruling, patronizing, and making opportunities available to others, which is the Bekynton of the dedication, *homo*'s purpose in the play is self-rule and the lessons of self-rule, first and foremost. When in the play God creates 'homo', he issues to him the royal accoutrements of orb and sceptre in what appears to be a mock coronation ceremony (pp. 63–9). Are these external items of rule sufficient for self-rule? That is the question posed by

---

[19] On Bekynton's interests, see Weiss, *Humanism in England*, 71–83.
[20] A copy of the *Apologia Socratis* survives in Balliol College MS 315 and was once owned by the bishop of Ely, William Grey; see Weiss, *Humanism in England*, 86.

the play during the temptation of 'homo', who hears the counsel not of Eve but of two competing figures—*Sensualitas* and *Racio*, both of whom are called *dominae* (women). Predictably for us, he accepts the counsel of the wrong adviser—the wrong Eve, if you will—and thus begins the narrative where bad counsel must be undone by good counsel, bringing us to the climax of the drama, where 'homo' seeks counsel from the cardinal virtues about his errors. By accepting their wisdom, and by the virtues recognizing that 'homo' is indeed worth saving (see pp. 149–51; 157–9), the protagonist is redeemed and achieves self-dominion, as a person governed chiefly by these virtues. Although this might still sound like ordinary theology, it is not. For the moral or theological virtues are excluded, as well as (with few exceptions) the efficacy of the sacraments (see pp. 115, 133–5); Christ's crucifixion goes by in a flash, and what is emphasized instead is *homo*'s reacquisition of the royal symbols of the political and ethical self—orb and staff—thanks to God becoming Christ in an utter instant (pp. 131, 164–5) without a pause for the Ascension. The lesson here for a bishop is as clear as the lessons in the exempla of the Mirror for Princes tradition: rule your kingdom, rule your temporalities, by first ruling yourself.

Bishop Reginald Pecock

I wish now to turn to a very different case, Bishop Reginald Pecock. Pecock assumed his episcopal seat at Chichester after his predecessor, Bishop Adam de Moleyns, was murdered in the earliest disturbances of the Wars of the Roses. Incidentally, Moleyns was Keeper of the Privy Seal after none other than Bishop Bekynton. And Andrew Holes, the Keeper of the Privy Seal after Moleyns, is depicted in the illustration of New College MS 288 (second figure from the bottom left—the figure looking outward). Because Pecock was also briefly in the employ of Bekynton, we can question how his work might be construed within the literary-historical terms posed here.[21]

Like Moleyns, who authored *The Libelle of Englyshe Polycye*, Pecock was himself an author-bishop.[22] In the 1440s and 1450 s, he wrote a number of vernacular works that offered spiritual, ethical, and moral instruction, such as his Seven Matters and Four Tables—an interconnected set of precepts on all aspects of Christian teaching that appear in the *Reule of Crysten Religioun* and the *Donet*.[23] In an effort to rationalize this novel systematic theology, Pecock assumed a specific audience with pressing needs: a laity that is either grossly ignorant of basic Christian theology or,

---

[21] Wendy Scase, *Reginald Pecock* (Aldershot: Ashgate, 1996), 101.

[22] See *The Libelle of Englyshe Polycye* (Oxford: Clarendon Press, 1926).

[23] See *Reule of Cristen Religioun*, ed. W. C. Greet, EETS, os 171 (Oxford: Oxford University Press, 1927); *The Donet of Reginald Peacock*, ed. E.V. Hitchcock, EETS, os 156 (London: Oxford University Press, 1921).

what is worse, taught by the wrong persons—heretics. Many lay persons, argued Pecock, were easily seduced into heresy, and so his intention was to instruct the laity away from Wycliffism and into a more moderate form of orthodoxy. He even wrote in English to assure that those persons who might have been reading vernacular Wycliffite writings would also read his series of texts. Yet for all of this, and surely for so much more, Pecock was accused of heresy—with the result that he was removed from office, standing as the first bishop in England to be unseated as a heretic.

So here we are with the problem of heresy in the mid-fifteenth century, but a closer look at Pecock's situation will suggest its consistency with my working thesis about this period. First, Pecock was never branded a Wycliffite. Even Thomas Gascoigne, who offers one of the major accounts of Pecock's problems and who hems and haws at every turn ('heu! heu!', 'vae! vae! vae!', and 'O Deus!'), could never apply the word 'lollard' to Pecock, nor count him among the 'Wyclivistae' of the earlier generation.[24] That accusation might not have made sense in Gascoigne's own historical present. This is odd because, namely, Pecock's singular obsession seems to be the Wycliffite heresy—an obsession that is so great that he in fact appears, as Anne Hudson puts it, 'in the last resort, anachronistic: his reliance upon logic, and his exaggeratingly pedantic style, might have been an appropriate weapon [against Wycliffism] up to about 1420', but not 1440.[25] I concur. The fact that Pecock had to resurrect Wycliffite adversaries from twenty and thirty years ago shows that in some fundamental way, although a product of his age in other respects, he is not representative of the mid-fifteenth century: the orthodox vs. Wycliffite binary had gone away, and he had put it back on the table. Even the fine scholarship that does assess Pecock in the (vanishing) Wycliffite context finds the author-bishop to be fundamentally displaced from his own present: 'he stepped outside [the catechetical] tradition'; 'Pecock's dismissal of affective theology and hermeneutics set him clearly apart from his times.'[26] Granted, Pecock cannot simply

---

[24] Thomas Gascoigne, *Loci e Libro veritatum*, ed. James E. Thorold Rogers (Oxford: Clarendon Press, 1881), 141. Royal and archiepiscopal letters did associate Pecock with Wyclif in orders that the reading of their works cease, but such an association reveals an effort to fashion the former as a heresiarch—a heretical man with followers, much like Wyclif; see the two replies to these injunctions in Henry Anstey (ed.), *Epistolae academicae Oxon. (Registrum F)*, 2 vols. (Oxford: Oxford Historical Society, 1898), ii. 338–39; 412–13; in forthcoming work, I discuss this interesting collection of epistles.

[25] Hudson, *Premature Reformation*, 442.

[26] Margaret Aston, 'Bishops and Heresy', in *Faith and Fire: Popular and Unpopular Religion, 1350–1600* (London: Hambledon Press, 1993), 73–93 at 87; Kantik Ghosh, 'Bishop Reginald Pecock and the Idea of "Lollardy"', in Barr and Hutchison (eds.), *Text and Controversy from Wyclif to Bale*, 251–65 at 258. Mishtooni Bose writes, in a somewhat similar vein, that Pecock 'was abandoning the clerical inscrutability [of] the academic and polemical idioms … favoured by his predecessors, Woodford, Dymmok, and Netter' ('Reginald Pecock's Vernacular Voice', in Fiona Somerset, Jill C. Havens, and Derrick G. Pitard (eds.), *Lollards and their Influence in Late Medieval England*, (Woodbridge: Boydell Press, 2003), 217–36 at 203). I especially admire Bose's article but on this point tend to agree with Hudson about Pecock's 'pedantic style': I find much in his work to be inscrutable, and many passages require several rereadings.

be dismissed as an anachronism, and his entire project can hardly be confined to its anti-Wycliffite elements. A fuller understanding requires that more work on Pecock and humanism ('ecclesiastical' or otherwise) be done.[27]

Second, secular persons were responsible for securing Pecock's downfall, and among those persons was, in the first instance, a Lancastrian by the name of John, Viscount Beaumont, who in seeking to bring charges of heresy against Pecock 'recalled', as Wendy Scase argues, 'the moves taken against heretics by ... Henry V, after which he had had victory over his enemies'.[28] In other words, Pecock looked back to the time of Henry V and the age of Wycliffite heretics, and so did Beaumont, but rather than a bishop coordinating his anti-heresy initiatives with the secular arm, or rather than a bishop seeking to bring charges of heresy against a lay person (the standard protocol), we see here that secular and ecclesiastical authorities are at cross-purposes, to the detriment of a bishop. While Pecock was the first bishop in England to be removed from his seat as a heretic, then, the larger point of interest is that that event signals a new politics of heresy at work, a split between the secular and the episcopal versions of heresy.

The fifteenth century: bishops and literary history

'Ecclesiastical humanism', as I have tentatively presented it here, identifies an inward turn within a portion of the English episcopate itself; literary responses seem to correspond to this turn by drawing attention to the *ecclesia* as a context for patronage. Such texts were probably circulated among a coterie of other ecclesiasts, a circumstance that tended to elevate their cultural importance while at the same time narrowing their ostensible audiences to an elite group.[29] As for the specific question of heresy, the rise of 'ecclesiastical humanism' signals that the cultural conversation about heresy was different in the mid-fifteenth century and that anti-heresy initiatives no longer figured as a primary form of episcopal self-fashioning, as they seem to have done in the earlier part of the century for Archbishops William Courtenay and Thomas Arundel, or Bishops John Buckingham and John Trefnant. Indeed, in the early fifteenth century, archbishops

---

[27] We need more on this topic besides the albeit helpful suggestion that Pecock writes a kind of 'floating library ... without walls', accessible to the laity and, as such, a parallel effort to Bishop John Carpenter's own in opening libraries specifically for the laity, a totally recent development. See Margaret Aston, 'Bishops and Heresy', in *Faith and Fire*, 73–93, at 87; Scase mentions Pecock's connections with John Colop: 'the two men shared an interest in the provision of religious books for lay readers' (*Reginald Pecock*, 90).

[28] See Scase, *Reginald Pecock*, 104; see 103–5.

[29] Maura Nolan (*John Lydgate and the Making of Public Culture* (Cambridge: Cambridge University, 2005)), traces a phenomenon analogous to the self-referentiality of 'ecclesiastical humanism', looking at how secular elite groups view themselves as representative of the social whole during the minority of Henry VI.

and the most prominent bishops fashioned their public personae as heresy hunters at a time when secular authorities did the same—namely the Lancastrians, keenly devoted to promoting their royal selves in the terms of orthodoxy and anti-heresy. Yet what we see instead are bishops and their subordinates staking a claim on the world of letters, typically the province of clerks addressing kings, but now also the preserve of ecclesiasts addressing their superiors and each other with literary forms that seem in some ways analogous to those presented to secular rulers.

My concern in this essay, then, has been threefold. First, to ask whether Hudson's observation about the relative disappearance of Wycliffism can be connected at all with 'ecclesiastical humanism'—with this form of episcopal self-fashioning in which the pursuit of heretics and the routing out of 'lollards' are no longer the defining features of a bishop's public image, nor the desirable ways in which authors chose to extol and advise bishops. Second, to insist that literary history in the fifteenth century can seem very different if we look more closely at authors who appear to be on the 'bad side' of the binary of 'orthodoxy' vs. 'heresy'. I have sought to broaden paradigms about religious writing in the fifteenth century by conceiving of 'religious writing' as a larger category, not only as 'writing about religion' or 'religious topics', but as including writings by ecclesiastical persons that rework theological genres within humanist terms and which appropriate secular genres (such as the Mirror for Princes tradition) from time to time. Third, and finally, a scholarly focus on heresy, Wycliffism, and orthodoxy—even when complicated by looking at those interesting mixed compilations—offers only a partial view of literary production in the fifteenth century. The result is overemphasis on religious writing with a pastoral and theological interest, and (with the exception of Pecock, whom scholars of Wycliffism study) an automatic exclusion of the episcopal contexts of writing.

I have only discussed one small element of a very complex social picture. I have not addressed problems in contemporary secular politics (such as the War of the Roses) that may also partly explain this phenomenon among certain bishops. I have purposely omitted a discussion of the transitions from medieval to Renaissance, despite the fact that the word 'humanism' in any sentence always raises questions about nascent modernities within the medieval period and problems of longer historical trajectories or diachronic history. I have excluded such a discussion in favour of a more rigorous attention to the synchronic instance itself—to the multitude of particulars (persons, texts) that fall within the ambit of 'ecclesiastical humanism' in the fifteenth century. Future work in this area can account not only for Chaundler's other efforts but also for the work, activities, and social circles of Bishops William Grey, Richard Flemyng, John Carpenter, Edmund Lacy, Adam Moleyns, William Waynflete (to name a few). Meanwhile, we cannot forget the generation before Chaundler's who were alive at the time, a generation that was of extreme political importance and that persecuted heretics—again, before 1430 especially: Archbishop Chichele (c.1364–1443) who was a graduate of New College, and Bishop Henry Beaufort (1374–1447), who brought the continental humanist Poggio Bracciolini to England in 1418 for a four-year visit. By way of contrast, Chaundler was born a year later and wrote his *Liber apologeticus* several years after both men were deceased. Chichele, of course, is depicted in the illustration of New College MS 288, but note that he is depicted only as 'Chichele the educator', holding a miniature of his own foundation, All Souls College at Oxford. If Chichele fashioned his public identity one way—as a heresy hunter—then it seems unsurprising to find that the artist of the illustration fashioned him in yet another way.

In the final analysis, the relevance of generational distinctions and perceptions cannot be ignored when accounting for historical changes, even those as seemingly sweeping as the submergence of Wycliffism in the mid-fifteenth century. Indeed, when figuring out how the cultural activities of bishops and those in their circle bear on our view of the fifteenth century, we need a method of historical enquiry that fully understands what a difference a generation makes.

FURTHER READING

Starting up a research project in the area of humanism requires consultation of and continual return to Roberto Weiss's *Humanism in England* (n. 9 above). Although rife with prejudices about the English fifteenth century, it is nonetheless an indispensable compendium of information about persons and manuscripts (though on occasion the manuscript designations are incorrect). A useful corrective to Weiss and a broad workable definition of humanism can be found in James Simpson, 'Humanism', in William Chester Jordan (ed.), *Dictionary of the Middle Ages: Supplement 1* (New York: Charles Scribner's Sons, 2004), 279–82. Specialized work on humanism in the fifteenth century is: David Carlson, *English Humanist Books: Writers and Patrons, Manuscript and Print, 1475–1525* (Toronto: University of Toronto Press, 1993); Chris Lee Nigham, 'Reform and Humanism in the Sermons of Richard Fleming at the Council of Constance' (dissertation, University of Toronto, 1997); David Rundle, 'Humanism before the Tudors: On Nobility and the Reception of *Studia humanitatis* in Fifteenth-Century England', in Jonathan Woolfson (ed.), *Reassessing Tudor Humanism*, ed. (New York: Palgrave, 2002), 22–42; Susanne Saygin, *Humphrey, Duke of Gloucester (1390–1447) and the Italian Humanists* (Leiden: Brill, 2002); David Wallace, 'Dante in Somerset: Ghosts, Historiography, Periodization', *New Medieval Literatures*, 3 (1999) 9–38; Daniel Wakelin, 'Vernacular Humanism in England c.1440–1485' (dissertation, Cambridge University, 2002; forthcoming, Oxford University Press).

PART IV

WRITING AND THE WORLD

CHAPTER 27

AUTHORIAL WORK

KELLIE ROBERTSON

Foucault has observed that 'texts, books, and discourses really began to have authors (other than mythical, "sacralized", and "sacralizing" figures) to the extent that authors became subject to punishment; that is, to the extent that discourse could be transgressive'.[1] In the late fourteenth century, not only 'discourse' but the very act of writing itself could be seen as transgressive, a perception that gave rise to a new kind of authorial self-representation in England. The first national labour laws passed in 1349 did not specifically mention 'writer' as a category of worker to be surveyed. Even so, in the wake of these laws, authors began to take seriously the need to justify their writing as work, to discriminate between the moral utility of aesthetic labour and mere idle 'lolling' that lacked any recognizable social value. At the same time, literate practices became more central to ensuring a steady pool of workers within any given locale: letters patent were mandated for workers travelling from one town to the next, affidavits were issued against renegade labourers, and written descriptions of work proliferated in legal statutes, guild ordinances, and sermon literature. The technology of writing became the scaffolding on which work (and workers) were displayed. And yet writing outside of officially sanctioned spaces also came to look suspiciously like non-work, an unregulated activity potentially damaging to society insofar as it was not adding any concrete 'good' to the common good. Writing thus came to occupy an ambiguous position by the late fourteenth century: it was the means by which social norms regarding labour were communicated and enforced, while, at the same time, it could potentially be the object of such enforcement.

To understand how late medieval texts came to have authors is to understand medieval literary production in the context of contemporary discourses about everyday work. Post-plague labour laws indelibly marked post-plague authors who

---

[1] Michel Foucault, 'What is an Author?', trans. Josue V. Harari, in Josue V. Harari (ed.), *Textual Strategies: Perspectives in Post-Structuralist Criticism* (Ithaca, NY: Cornell University Press, 1979), 148.

were, for the first time, asked to think about their own writing in terms of its productive value rather than, primarily, its relation to a past literary tradition. They were forced to situate their work not just between the venerable poles of *imitatio* and *inventio* but also between the social polarities of idleness and industry. The embodiment of authorial labour was no longer merely confined to an academic prologue addressing a text's relationship to previous *auctores*. With increasing frequency, post-plague writers meditated on the value of literary work in the marketplace of work more generally. The task of situating late medieval writers in these contemporary conversations has already begun—notably in studies of Langland such as those by David Aers and Anne Middleton—but this conversation should include the voices of other late medieval writers as well.[2] The first part of this chapter surveys the strategies available to late medieval writers who self-consciously positioned their writings in a literary landscape marked by newly emphatic understandings of the material value of labour. The second half focuses on the particular case of Chaucer's Prologue to the *Canterbury Tales*, using it as a lens through which to view the critical stakes in thinking about a medieval poet's work in terms of wider discourses about medieval labour.

In thinking about the relation of work to the biopolitical body of the writer, this chapter also acts as a complement—a kind of 'prehistory'—to criticism on the ideology of written work in later periods such as that undertaken by Nancy Armstrong and Leonard Tennenhouse in the seventeenth century and Clifford Siskin in the eighteenth and nineteenth centuries. As such, it is intended to encourage further exploration of the social spaces in which narrativized labour occurs, investigation into what we might call the 'topologies of work' created by medieval writers.[3]

Between labour and leisure: the work of writing

According to the late fourteenth-century writer John Gower, his poetry was made 'between work and leisure'—as he claims, 'inter labores et ocia'. He makes this claim in a colophon discussing how and why he writes poetry (the author's 'account of his books') found in some of the earliest manuscripts of the *Vox clamantis*

---

[2] David Aers, 'Justice and Wage-Labor after the Black Death: Some Perplexities for William Langland', in *Faith, Ethics and Church: Writing in England, 1360–1409* (Cambridge: D. S. Brewer, 2000), 56–75; and Anne Middleton, 'Acts of Vagrancy: The C Version "Autobiography" and the Statute of 1388', in Steven Justice and Kathryn Kerby-Fulton (eds.), *Written Work: Langland, Labor, and Authorship* (Philadelphia: University of Pennsylvania Press, 1997), 208–317.

[3] Nancy Armstrong and Leonard Tennenhouse, *The Imaginary Puritan: Literature, Intellectual Labor, and the Origins of Personal Life* (Berkeley and Los Angeles: University of California Press, 1992); and Clifford Siskind, *The Work of Writing: Literature and Social Change in Britain, 1700–1830* (Baltimore: Johns Hopkins University Press, 1998).

(*c.*1382) and the *Confessio Amantis* (*c.*1390). Gower must have spent a significant amount of time in this 'in-between' space, since he produced more than 74,000 lines of verse in French, English, and Latin.[4] His claim interests me as a literary historian because it focuses our attention on a peculiarly medieval space—a hybrid of work and leisure that was reducible to neither. Gower creates a literary 'third space' that can be seen as analogous to other medieval spaces of 'non-work', such as feast days and pilgrimage. Just as medieval people who stood watching Corpus Christi plays experienced their spectatorship as not exactly work-like, but neither as repose, so too the poet (according to Gower) wrote in the twilight between vocation and avocation. Yet more can be said about this literary third space than that it is merely 'liminal' with regard to usual social practices (in Victor Turner's phrase) or that it serves as an instance of 'carnivalesque inversion' (in Mikhail Bakhtin's). Gower's desire to situate his own written work outside of the binary of work and leisure suggests that he was attempting to escape the constraints of contemporary discourses about the social usefulness of writing as labour. Indeed, Gower's assertion that writing takes place in a space of non-labour looks unusual (even anomalous) when placed in the context of an increasing literary self-consciousness about writing as work in late medieval England.

A model of writing as something 'other' than explicitly work or leisure did exist, but this model was usually only applied to explicitly scriptural acts of writing. This model is described in a late fourteenth-century English poem, 'The Song of Creation' (*Canticum de Creatione*), an apocryphal retelling of the postlapsarian wanderings of Adam and Eve found in Trinity College, Oxford, MS 57. Instead of focusing on the Cain and Abel story, this poem focuses on Adam and Eve's bodily penance, their post-Edenic labours, and the birth of their third son, Seth. After Adam's death, his son Seth is granted visions of paradise and then instructed to write his parents' history on stone tablets. These tablets are later discovered by Solomon, to whom God sent an angel to explain the meaning and the provenance of the foreign writing. Solomon names the tablets in honour of their unusual method of production:

> And tho[se tablets] 'archilaykas'
> Salamon dede hem calle,
> That is to sayn: 'withoute trauaylle',

---

[4] Gower makes this assertion at the end of the *Confessio Amantis* in the colophon to book VIII. It appears in the first paragraph of 'the author's account of his books', which is followed by descriptions of his French, Latin, and English works. See *The English Works of John Gower*, ed. G. C. Macaulay, EETS, ES 81–2 (London: Kegan Paul, 1900–1), ii. 479. This colophon is attested in at least twenty-seven manuscripts according to Siân Echard, 'Last Words: Latin at the End of the Confessio Amantis', in Richard Firth Green and Linne R. Mooney (eds.), *Interstices: Studies in Middle English and Anglo-Latin Texts in Honour of A. G. Rigg* (Toronto: University of Toronto Press, 2004), 99–121. On Gower's productivity, see John Fisher, *John Gower* (New York: New York University Press, 1964), 94.

> And withouten wit saunfayle
> Seth wrot hem alle,
> For an angel held his hond rigt.   (ll. 944–9).[5]

The otherwise unattested Middle English word 'archilaykas' translates the phrase 'sine laboris doctrina' in the earlier *Vita Adae et Evae*. Seth's tablets thus represent a model of divinely inspired inscription, writing without work, since the angelic hand guided Seth's pen as he wrote literally 'without knowledge'. The ending of the poem makes clear that this 'writing without work' occurs only in an originary Hebrew, which then must be translated into Latin and then into 'Englisch speche' by the poet in the year 1375 (ll. 1183–91). Seth's writing here does not participate in the punitive cast of work, written or otherwise, after the Fall. Yet Seth's Hebrew writing is a counterpoint to the writing of the English poem we are actually reading here: it is an unfallen foil for the vernacular *Creation*-poet's travail, since the vernacular poet must translate the work, presumably *with* travail. Even as it asserts the unfallenness of Seth's divine composition practices, the poem dramatizes the fallenness of vernacular poetic work undertaken not in the 'angelic' but in the 'English' key. The *Creation*-poet ultimately shows us that the idea of writing without work is a deeply nostalgic one, an act made possible only through divine intervention and presumably unavailable to contemporary vernacular poets.

Late medieval English poets often dealt with the fallenness of the poetic enterprise by positioning their work as an antidote for idleness, taking up pen against the sea of sloth to which writers (then as now) were assumed to be prone. Chaucer dramatizes this predicament in the *Canterbury Tales*, when the Second Nun claims that her verse translation of St Cecilia's life fends off idleness by replacing it with its opposite, 'leveful bisynesse' or lawful industry (VIII. 5). Chaucer here ventriloquizes the monastic view of authorial or scribal labour, locating writing in opposition to 'roten slogardye'. Writing can prove a moral tonic not only to writer but to reader as well. The pro-Lancastrian poet John Lydgate claimed that, while the chivalric content of his *Troy Book* would surely edify its intended patron, the future Henry V, the very act of reading would encourage the young prince 'to eschewe | The cursyd vice of slouthe and ydelnesse' (Prol. 82–3).[6] Reading engages the prince in 'vertuous besynesse', just as physical exercise drives away lethargy. Although claims for the prophylactic value of writing against the malaise of *accidia* (or spiritual sloth) in both writers and their readers would seem to be a conventional platitude gleaned from penitential manuals, they have an important topical valence as well. Arguments for the social utility of writing implicitly validated intellectual labour as 'work', positioning writing not just as private penance but as public service.

---

[5] Brian Murdoch and J. A. Tasioulas (eds.), *The Apocryphal Lives of Adam and Eve* (Exeter: University of Exeter Press, 2002). For an overview of the 'Adambook' tradition, see Michael Stone, *A History of the Literature of Adam and Eve* (Atlanta: Scholars' Press, 1992), and Marinus de Jonge and Johannes Tromp, *The Life of Adam and Eve and Related Literature* (Sheffield: Academic Press, 1997).

[6] *Lydgate's Troy Book*, ed. Henry Bergen, EETS, ES 97 (London: Kegan Paul, 1906), 3.

Although post-plague labour laws were designed to regulate primarily artisanal and manual labour (the work of carters and ploughmen), they began to
be applied to what we might call 'intellectual labour'—the work of preachers and pilgrims—as well. Poets were not (to our knowledge) regularly hauled
before local peace commissions, though the work of travelling pilgrims, preachers, and university students—fellow labourers in the immaterial vineyards—was
regularly surveyed under these increasingly stringent laws. Pilgrims and university students (just like itinerant manual labourers) were forced to carry letters
patent that approved their movements from one town to the next. Parish
priests whose main duties were associated with 'cure of souls'—preaching and
the administration of the sacraments—could be prosecuted for shoddy spiritual work. The compulsion writers felt to prove that they were not merely
'idle' (and therefore liable for compulsory impressment in the corn harvest) or,
even worse, 'lollers' (vagrant writers with heterodox leanings) started to influence their self-representation from the second half of the fourteenth century
onwards.[7]

Poets like Langland and Hoccleve dramatized this new continuum of work on
which manual and intellectual labours occupied adjoining positions. The well-
known addition to the C-version of Langland's *Piers Plowman* (*c*.1385) finds the
narrator Will forced to justify his apparent lack of productive occupation before
the allegorical figure of Reason. Just as the labour laws demanded otherwise
unoccupied labourers to join the corn harvest, Reason—having met Will in 'an hot
heruest'—questions him about his apparent idleness:

> 'Can thow seruen', [Reason] sayde, 'or syngen in a churche,
> Or koke for my cokeres [bundle hay for my haymakers] or to the cart piche,
> Mowen or mywen [stack] or make bond to sheues,
> Repe or been a rypereue and aryse erly,
> Or haue an horn and be hayward and lygge theroute nyhtes
> And kepe my corn in my croft from pykares [pilferers] and theues?   (C. V. 12–17)

Will claims that he is physically unfit for such manual labour (his arms are too
long); instead, he labours with prayer-book and psalter rather than with scythe

---

[7] The foundational work on the labour laws is Bertha Putnam, *The Enforcement of the Statutes of
Labourers during the First Decade after the Black Plague* (New York: Columbia University Press, 1908).
More recent work includes L. R. Poos, 'The Social Context of Statute of Labourers Enforcement',
Law and History Review, 1 (1983), 27–52; Chris Given-Wilson, 'Labour in the Context of English
Government', in James Bothwell, P. J. P. Goldberg and W. M. Ormrod (eds.), *The Problem of Labour
in Fourteenth-Century England* (York: York Medieval Press, 2000); W. M. Ormrod, 'The English
Government and the Black Death of 1348–49', in W. M. Ormrod (ed.), *England in the Fourteenth
Century* (Woodbridge: Boydell & Brewer, 1986), 178–9; and A. Musson, 'Reconstructing English
Labor Laws: A Medieval Perspective', in Kellie Robertson and Michael Uebel (eds.), *The Middle Ages
at Work* (New York: Palgrave Macmillan, 2004), 113–32. On the regulation of ecclesiastical labour,
see Bertha Putnam, 'Maximum Wage-Laws for Priests after the Black Death, 1348–1381', *American
Historical Review*, 21 (1915–16), 12–32.

or reaper.[8] Reason here plays the role usually enacted by the local justice of the peace interrogating a renegade worker, enquiring into Will's capacity as well as his willingness to work. Both Reason's questions and Will's answers make it clear that spiritual work (serving or singing in church) and manual labour (hay mowing and corn harvesting), although discrete occupations, are both embodied labours that need to be regulated.

This concatenation of seemingly different species of labour also appears in a well-known passage in Hoccleve's *Regement of Princes* (c.1412). Interrogated by an unnamed Old Man as to the source of his mental and physical lethargy, Hoccleve meditates on his professional anxieties, relating manual labour to intellectual labour in terms similar to those employed in *Piers Plowman*:

> With plow can I nat medlen ne with harwe,
> Ne woot nat what lond good is for what corn,
> And for to lade [load] a cart or fille a barwe,
> To which I never usid was toforn [before];
> My bak unbuxom hath swich thyng forsworn,
> At instaunce of wrytynge, his werreyour [enemy],
> That stowpynge hath him spilt with his labour.
> Many men, fadir, weenen [think] that wrytynge
> No travaille is; they holde it but a game;
> Aart hath no fo but swich folk unkonnynge.
> But whoso list desporte him in that same,
> Let him continue and he shal fynde it grame [bitter];
> It is wel gretter labour than it seemeth;
> The blynde man of colours al wrong deemeth.   (ll. 981–94)[9]

Hoccleve asserts his unfitness for agricultural labour as he points out that writing takes a similar toll on the body: hunching over the scribe's desk has given him back problems. He then complains against those who refuse to acknowledge the physical strenuousness of written work. Whereas Langland's Will argues for the superiority of the *via contemplativa* over the *via activa*—intellectual labour over manual labour—Hoccleve claims that scribal labour *is* manual labour. What the two passages share, however, is an imperative need to figure out how writing,

[8] This passage has been much discussed in relation to the labour laws; see the articles of David Aers and Anne Middleton cited above, n. 2. See also Lawrence M. Clopper, 'Need Men and Women Labor? Langland's Wanderer and the Labor Ordinances', in Barbara Hanawalt (ed.), *Chaucer's England* (Minneapolis: University of Minnesota Press, 1992), 110–29; and Derek Pearsall, '*Piers Plowman* and the Problem of Labour', in Bothwell et al. (eds.), *The Problem of Labour*, 123–32.

[9] Ethan Knapp compellingly discusses this passage in the context of scribal labour more generally; see *The Bureaucratic Muse: Thomas Hoccleve and the Literature of Late Medieval England* (University Park: Pennsylvania State University Press, 2001), 89–93. On this passage, see also Steven Justice, 'Inquisition, Speech, and Writing: A Case from Norwich', in Rita Copeland (ed.), *Criticism and Dissent in the Middle Ages* (Cambridge: Cambridge University Press, 1996), 289–322; and Antony Hasler, 'Hoccleve's Unregimented Body', *Paragraph*, 13 (1990), 164–83.

and other 'immaterial' labours, relate to more 'material' ones. A long ecclesiastical history viewed the plough as a symbol for the productive intellectual duties of the preacher: the masses, preaching, and ministry that disseminated God's word. So too the scribe's pen was the intellectual equivalent of the plough as it prepared the Christian mind for the planting of theological ideas.[10] But the second half of the fourteenth century saw a revision of this relation between intellectual and agricultural labour. When Langland and Hoccleve dramatize their own immaterial labour, it is marked by a new and urgent competition between pen and plough, even as statutory initiatives sought to make both kinds of labour amenable to similar types of regulation in the wake of the plague. The legal and social need to justify one's labour (whether as carter, priest, or pilgrim) made these labours continuous whereas previously this relation had only been analogous. This new conception of work produced what we might think of as a Möbius strip of material and immaterial labours, an alternative to the trifunctional conception of society based on discrete 'orders' or 'estates' of work.

Hoccleve's indignation that the act of writing may be perceived as *game* rather than *travaille* returns us to Gower's claim that writing poetry is neither. Although there is an obvious difference between the paid scribal labour to which Hoccleve refers and the gentry gentleman's *belle lettriste* endeavours, Gower's view that writing occurs in an interstice between 'work' and 'leisure' also responds to post-1349 conversations about the productive value of various kinds of work. Gower could no longer merely affirm a Virgilian notion of the pastoral poet, a writer living in *ignobilis oti*, the 'ignoble ease' first set out in the *Georgics*. The social and legal pressures that had made all work subject to intense scrutiny by the end of the fourteenth century also had their effect on Gower, particularly as his own symbolic labour often explicitly echoed and affirmed the norms spelled out in the labour laws. Gower's poetic project in the 1370s and 1380s, as expressed in the *Miroir de l'omme* and the *Vox clamantis*, was to chastise those who worked badly, those who shirked their divinely ordained labours, those who failed the 'common profit'. These early poems read much more like *sermones ad status*, or satiric reviews of the social responsibilities of the varied estates, than his later *Confessio Amantis*. By asserting that poetic work is not 'labour', Gower seems to acknowledge the tacit ambiguity that plagued writing at this time: that it was both an instrument of enforcing social norms about labour and (potentially) an activity of concern itself under the labour laws. This ambiguity—and perhaps a preference for being the surveyor of others' labours rather than the surveilled—may have led him to place writing 'outside' of this binary.

---

[10] On the symbolic nature of the plough, see Paul Freedman, *Images of the Medieval Peasant* (Stanford, CA: Stanford University Press, 1999), 33–7; and Stephen A. Barney, 'The Plowshare of the Tongue: The Progress of a Symbol from the Bible to *Piers Plowman*', *Mediaeval Studies*, 35 (1973), 261–93.

Gower's choice to create a third space for his writing—a space outside of debates about labour—finds an analogy in the visual self-representation of the poet that appears in an early manuscript of the *Vox Clamantis*, BL Cotton Tiberius A.iv (Fig. 8).[11] The *Vox Clamantis* reimagines the events of the 1381 rebellion with the rebels turned into animals and the world turned upside down. Interestingly, this bestial transformation is itself subject to the social division of labour: carters are transformed into asses, ploughmen into oxen, and so forth. The poetic voice crying in the wilderness denounces the irrational and rebellious peasants who have left their work to bloody their betters and attempts to corral them back inside estates confines, however monstrously reimagined. In this manuscript illustration, a figure (presumably Gower) takes aim at the world with his arrows, just as the satirist takes aim at earthly sins through his purgative writings. Like the extraterrestrial space of the satirist, so too the poet's written work is not of this world and hence cannot fall under either of the sublunary rubrics of labour or leisure. Writing cannot be an embodied (and hence regulatable) practice for Gower because only bad labourers have bodies (to which they can be mercilessly reduced for transgressions against the social order). Such a stance can be read as the antithesis of the positions staked out by Langland and Hoccleve, writers who felt compelled to justify their own intellectual labours in terms of their physical bodies rather than in spite of them. If, as the manuscript illustration suggests, the space of writing for Gower is a disembodied and hence unregulatable one, it is also a potentially precarious one; so too, we might conclude, the counterfactual position of the late medieval poet whose own work exists outside of contemporary debates about productive labour.

Representing work: Chaucer's third space

If many medieval poets were interested in labour, Geoffrey Chaucer was arguably the medieval poet most attuned to the problems attendant on representing labour in writing, the difficulties of transferring phenomenal experience to the page. So where does Chaucer stand in the literary landscape that I have been outlining, a terrain whose features included statutory prohibitions against idleness, ecclesiastical exhortations to contribute to the common profit, as well as the more 'literary' depictions found in the works of other poets? Chaucer was obviously fascinated by working bodies and makes spectacular use of them in the Prologue to the *Canterbury Tales*. Despite the fact that all of the pilgrims are described in terms of the work that they do, previous critical approaches to the question of work in relation to

---

[11] This manuscript is dated to 1408, the year of Gower's death. The same illustration appears in Glasgow University Library, MS Hunter 59 (T.2.17) and in San Marino, Huntington Library, MS HM 150.

Figure 8 Archer shooting at the world. 1408 Illustration of Gower's *Vox Clamantis*. (London, BL Cotton Tiberius A. iv., fo. 9ᵛ, by permission of the British Library)

Chaucer's composition practices are surprisingly few.[12] Chaucer's everyday work experience was significant to an earlier generation of scholars who believed that it brought him into contact with the living, breathing models for his Canterbury pilgrims. John Manly's 1926 *Some New Light on Chaucer* is the best-known—and now most commonly derided—exponent of this view.[13] Critical consensus moved away from seeing the General Prologue as an elaborate *roman à clef* based on Chaucer's professional contacts; Chaucer was not, after all, David Lodge.

Since 1973, our view of the representations of work in the *Canterbury Tales* has largely been guided by Jill Mann's influential study *Chaucer and Medieval Estates Satire: The Literature of Social Classes and the General Prologue of the Canterbury Tales*. In part a reaction against Manly's view, Mann's book sought to demonstrate that the portraits were conventional rather than individualized by showing Chaucer's dependence on a sermon literature that categorized by profession and then critiqued each class's failure to fulfil its professional duties. While Mann's book is surely one of the most significant and insightful contributions to Chaucer studies in the last several decades, it framed discussion of work in the *Canterbury Tales* in purely binary terms: Chaucer's portraits could be seen as either conventionalized or individualized. With the most recent consideration of Chaucer's representation of work, David Carlson's 2004 book *Chaucer's Jobs*, the pendulum seems to have swung back to the sphere of the individual. Carlson analyses Chaucer's writings through the lens of his administrative and diplomatic appointments, concluding that 'serving and keeping the dominant order is what Chaucer did' in his administrative as well as his poetic life. This analysis allows little nuance in differentiating between the life and the art. Because Chaucer served the interests of both monarch and mercantile class, the poet's writing 'did the same kind of work in the cultural sphere as he had contributed by his other employments to the concrete, less mediated work of social management'. Chaucer was, to use Carlson's provocative formulation, a 'counterrevolutionary factotum'.[14] Whereas Mann's approach assumes the literary to be sealed off from the everyday and thus has no way of accounting for historical or phenomenological aspects of lived labour, Carlson's argument, on the other hand, has no way of accounting for

---

[12] Good discussions of Chaucer's representation of specific types of work within the tales include Peggy Knapp, 'Robyn the Miller's Thrifty Work', in *Chaucer and the Social Contest* (London: Routledge, 1990), 32–44; and Lee Patterson, 'The *Miller's Tale* and the Politics of Laughter', in *Chaucer and the Subject of History* (Madison: University of Wisconsin Press, 1991), 244–79.

[13] *Some New Light on Chaucer* (Gloucester: Henry Holt & Co., 1926).

[14] See Jill Mann, *Chaucer and Medieval Estates Satire: The Literature of Social Classes and the General Prologue of the* Canterbury Tales (Cambridge: Cambridge University Press, 1973); and David R. Carlson, *Chaucer's Jobs* (New York: Palgrave Macmillan, 2004), 39, 33. My own discussion of the Prologue to Chaucer's *Legend of Good Women* in relation to his time spent as justice of the peace is perhaps guilty of this same conflation of life and art, though I take a rather more optimistic view of Chaucer's life and his art than Carlson; see *The Laborer's Two Bodies: Labor and the 'Work' of the Text in Medieval Britain, 1350–1500* (London: Palgrave Macmillan, 2006).

specific aesthetic choices found in Chaucer's poetry nor does it have a sufficiently theorized way of placing the life in relation to the literature.

A way of synthesizing these two approaches—which might respectively be called the 'literary' and the 'biographical'—would be to situate their insights in the context of the wider, social conversation about labour (manual and intellectual) that would have been available to late fourteenth-century subjects themselves. More specifically, such a synthesis would involve seeing where Chaucer 'stands' in relation to his own labour as well as that of his pilgrims; it would also need to map the contours of the narrative space in which he chooses to stage these complicated representational issues about labour and leisure. For Chaucer, a viable 'third space' from which to speak could not spring *ex nihilo* from the poetic imagination (like the medial space imagined by Gower). Instead, he chose the third space of pilgrimage, a framing device that takes advantage of a socially recognized space of non-labour. The interspace of pilgrimage allows Chaucer a topos from which to speak about work outside of the overtly moralizing genre of estates literature—as found in the sermon tradition and as adapted by the moral Gower. Similarly, it provides an alternative to the everyday legal language that demanded exhaustive documentation of authenticity in work, a demand that Chaucer was familiar with from his own administrative appointments.

Discussions of Chaucer and pilgrimage are legion and I will not review them here; instead, I will emphasize the singularity of Chaucer's choice to stage the most concentrated medieval meditation on the relation between work and individual identity in the most culturally conspicuous arena of non-work. Pilgrimage is, as the anthropologist Victor Turner has pointed out, a liminal phenomenon insofar as it is an experience of the social margin, a momentary boundary crossing before the pilgrim passes back into social stability.[15] My point, however, is that its liminality and enchantment materialized in opposition, specifically, to work. Lollard-inspired debate over pilgrimage would have made Chaucer's choice a controversial one, and not necessarily only on account of the well-known Wycliffite antipathy to relics and images. Lollards also vehemently objected to feast days and pilgrimage because both interfered with the performance of necessary, everyday work in the community. A contemporary critic of religious mores, the writer of British Library, Add. MS 24202, claims that pilgrims 'veynly spenden hore [their] good and leeue [leave] the trewe labour that thei shulden do at home in help of hemsilf and hore negheboris'.[16] The relationship of pilgrimage and work had become a legal and not just a moral problem with the advent of the 1388 labour statutes that cautioned

---

[15] Victor Turner, 'Introduction: Pilgrimage as a Liminoid Phenomenon', in Victor Turner and Edith Turner, *Image and Pilgrimage in Christian Culture* (Oxford: Basil Blackwell, 1978), 1–39.

[16] Reproduced in Anne Hudson (ed.), *Selections from English Wycliffite Writings* (Toronto: Medieval Academy of America, 1997), 86/137–8. According to Anne Hudson, Lollard attacks on feast days claim that 'no days were to be restricted with regard to work, food, or drink'; see *The Premature Reformation* (Oxford: Clarendon Press, 1988), 114. Lollard opinion on this question was not uniform,

local officials to be vigilant in pursuit of labourers travelling to other villages in search of higher wages. In order to guard against this type of identity fraud, all travelling workers were to carry letters patent stating the reason for and dates of their travel. Unlicensed pilgrims, like able-bodied vagrants, were to be put in stocks until surety could be found at the discretion of the local justices of the peace.[17] Chaucer, as a justice of the peace in Kent in the late 1380s, would presumably have been called upon to write such letters. While we need not necessarily see the pilgrim portraits in the General Prologue as the literary equivalent of the letters patent issued to travelling pilgrims, Chaucer certainly shows an abiding interest in the tension between spiritual and material works.

Critics often note that, despite the availability of an extensive guide literature listing routes and expenses incurred on trips to the Holy Land as well as European pilgrimage sites—a kind of *Fodor's* for the travel savvy medieval pilgrim—this literature provides no real analogue to what Chaucer undertakes in the *Tales*.[18] Rather than previous pilgrimage narratives, the *Tales* may be more usefully compared to other medieval frame tales. Tellingly, Chaucer eschews the most common frame narrative that situates the tellers in a leisurely idyll: for example, the pastoral dream-vision settings of poems like Gower's *Confessio Amantis* or Chaucer's own earlier *Legend of Good Women*. He similarly eschews Boccaccio's rotating cast of manor houses where leisured ease contrasts with the horror of plague-ridden Florence. On the other hand, he also avoids spaces of everyday work such as Christine de Pisan's *cité des dames*, an urban edifice continually under construction—a fifteenth-century, women-only work camp. If contemporary frame tales tend to place their narratives in either a space of leisure or a space of work, Chaucer chooses the middle road of pilgrimage, a space of neither work nor leisure.

Although this line of thought is necessarily speculative, I hope it serves to defamiliarize Chaucer's altogether too familiar pilgrimage frame and to foreground

---

but many disapproved of fasting and the prohibition of labour on Sundays and feast days because it was extra-biblical.

[17] A. Luders et al. (eds.), *Statutes of the Realm, 1101–1713*, 11 vols. (London: Record Commission, 1810–28), ii. 56–9.

[18] Despite the opening lines of the *Canterbury Tales*, Chaucer seems unfamiliar with or (perhaps more accurately) uninterested in actual accounts of pilgrimage. After reviewing extant pilgrimage guides, Donald Howard comments that the *Canterbury Tales* 'has no counterpart in travel literature'; *Writers and Pilgrims* (Berkeley and Los Angeles: University of California Press, 1980), 83. This lack of substantive interest understandably led previous scholars (like D. W. Robertson) to pursue the more allegorical and metaphorical aspects of pilgrimage at the expense of its material history in fourteenth-century England. More recent critics interested in the meaning of pilgrimage in relation to the frame tale have included Dee Dyas, *Pilgrimage in Medieval English Literature, 700–1500* (Cambridge: D. S. Brewer, 2001); Frederick B. Jonassen, 'The Inn, the Cathedral, and the Pilgrimage of *The Canterbury Tales*', in Susanna Greer Fein, David Raybin, and Peter C. Braeger (eds.), *Rebels and Rivals: The Contestive Spirit in* The Canterbury Tales (Kalamazoo, MI: Medieval Institute Publication, 1991), 1–35; and David Lawton, 'Chaucer's Two Ways: The Pilgrimage Frame of the *Canterbury Tales*', *Studies in the Age of Chaucer*, 9 (1987), 3–40.

the peculiarity of interrogating medieval labour practices in a socially controversial setting of non-work. Even as the pilgrimage frame conveniently assembles a heterogeneous group of tellers, it ultimately may have intrigued the poet less for its literary possibilities and rather more for its ethical ones. Pilgrimage as an interstitial narrative space functioned in relation to work much the same way that the classical, pagan past functioned elsewhere in Chaucer's poetry. In *Troilus and Criseyde* and the 'Knight's Tale', for example, the pagan past allows Chaucer to explore questions of free will and agency in ways not sanctioned by contemporary religious discourse. So too, the pilgrimage frame allows Chaucer an ethical space in which to consider questions of truth in labour that contemporary legal and social discourses had largely foreclosed in the wake of the 1348 plague and the labour shortages that followed.

For the analysis of Chaucer's own relation to these contemporary discourses, the biographical provides a useful context for understanding the indexical (but indirect) influence they exert on his rhetorical practices and aesthetic choices. Chaucer's administrative appointments would have frequently seen him engaged in the regulation and oversight of labourers throughout the 1380s and 1390s. His stint as a justice of the peace in Kent in the late 1380s would have found him primarily occupied with enforcing the controversial labour statutes in a county that had a long (and sometimes violent) history of resistance to the statutes. This peace commission on which Chaucer served would have been responsible for investigating not only workers who took higher wages but also the employers who paid them, as well as issuing letters patent to travelling workers, pilgrims, and university students. Chaucer's subsequent (and final) administrative appointment as clerk of the king's works in the early 1390s would have found him engaged in worker oversight of a more direct nature: the rebuilding of the chapel at Windsor Palace and Tower Wharf as well as more mundane maintenance of storm drains and ditches. His responsibilities would have included engaging labourers, setting them to work, and disciplining those who failed to do their work properly. Like most middle management, however, Chaucer was unlikely to have been out strong-arming labourers in the marketplace; instead, records show that he was issuing writs for building, construction, and repair around the city of London.[19]

Chaucer does not just soak up the bureaucratic ideology of labour regulation like a sponge, however, but rather acquires the habits of the bureaucratic rhetoric that divide up labour to make it legible for surveillance. He also appreciates the shortcomings of such attempts to textualize identity (as I will argue later). Biographical knowledge is here invoked not in the name of an author-subject who exhibits full agency in his writings but rather as a kind of rhetorical 'habitus' (to

---

[19] For Chaucer's service as clerk of the king's works, see Martin M. Crow and Clair C. Olson (eds.), *Chaucer Life-Records* (Oxford: Oxford University Press, 1966), 402–76. For the clerkship more generally, see R. Allen Brown, H. M. Colvin, and A. J. Taylor, *The History of the King's Works: The Middle Ages*, 2 vols. (London: HMSO, 1963).

borrow Bourdieu's terminology). As such, this knowledge can be used heuristically to situate written work among the 'schemes of perception' that structure everyday experience. This model does not imply that a writer consciously or unconsciously 'applies' the ideology of his working life to his writing.[20] The General Prologue of the *Canterbury Tales* documents the division of labour in society; so too Chaucer's job demanded that he make legible the divisions of labour necessary to the smooth economic functioning of the city and the commonwealth. The writer that we know as 'Geoffrey Chaucer' is constituted by, as Ruth Evans reminds us, not only the poetry that he left us but the life records that give us insight into how he made his living.[21] I would add that this 'Chaucer' is also made up of the statutes that he enforced, the writs that he wrote and received, and the habits of thought that such work encouraged. These statutes and documents describe fourteenth-century labour in all its copiousness: here we find the carpenters, masons, tilers, coverers of fern and straw (and their knaves), the cordwainers, shoemakers, goldsmiths, saddlers, horsesmiths, sporriers, tanners, tailors, and other servants.[22]

Work in the General Prologue to the *Canterbury Tales*

When we look at the catalogue of portraits in the General Prologue we should see not only the tendency of estates satire and sermon literature to divide up society but also the technology of enumeration with which Chaucer would have been familiar from his secular work life. Indeed, the estates satire tradition leaves unexplained a major aspect of Chaucer's pilgrim portraits. According to Jill Mann,

> [W]e must note one paradoxical aspect of the Prologue's estates content. The neutral and detailed enumeration of the daily duties of each occupation increases our awareness of the estate, rather than the individual—but this sort of *enumeratio* is rarely found in estates literature itself. Where the satirists use concrete detail, it is not neutral, but illustrative of failings; where they are not criticising failings, they offer generalised moral advice rather than instruction in a trade.   (*Chaucer and Medieval Estates Satire*, 15)

This model of 'neutral' enumeration that was lacking in estates analogues can be found frequently in contemporary legal and mercantile records, precisely the kind that Chaucer was asked to keep usually 'in his own hand' throughout his

---

[20] Pierre Bourdieu, *The Logic of Practice*, trans. Richard Nice (Stanford, CA: Stanford University Press, 1990), 53.

[21] Ruth Evans, 'Chaucer's Life', in Steve Ellis (ed.), *Chaucer: An Oxford Guide* (Oxford: Oxford University Press, 2005), 9–25. For an alternative view of the relation of history and literature in biographical criticism, see Paul Strohm, *Social Chaucer* (Cambridge, MA: Harvard University Press, 1989); see also Strohm's more recent, psychoanalytically inflected understanding of the relation between authorial agency and text in 'What Can We Know about Chaucer that He Didn't Know about Himself?', in *Theory and the Premodern Text* (Minneapolis: University of Minnesota Press, 2000), 165–81.

[22] For such a list, see, for example, Luders et al. (eds.), *Statutes of the Realm*, i. 311–12.

administrative career. Thinking about biographical detail here as 'habitus' helps to explain formal choices like descriptive enumeration in the General Prologue without having to fall back on a model of biographical effects that would crudely equate the narrator of the *Tales* with Chaucer the clerk of the king's works.

Moreover, the pilgrim-narrator is able to talk about labour in ways that Chaucer the medieval bureaucrat certainly could not (at least not around the water cooler). Chaucer's poetry differs from both estates literature and the bureaucratic description of labour in that it makes transparent the difficulty of making identity legible in a text. The General Prologue shows that the fantasy of a regulated society is ultimately based on the fantasy of knowable, narrated labour. Chaucer's major administrative jobs all involved the narration of labour—its supply and regulation, its procurement and punishment—and the General Prologue shows how difficult it is to textualize personhood in this way. The labour laws demanded that everyone (and not just the enforcers) have access to the interiority of labourers, be able and willing to map inner intention onto outer persona. To take just one example: the first labour ordinance of 1349 demanded that no one should give alms to able-bodied beggars; if they did, the giver (not the receiver) was to be imprisoned. These laws assumed an impossible knowledge on the part of the giver, simultaneously demanding that society at large (and not just local law enforcement officials) regulate the labour of others.

A similar fantasy of omniscient labour knowledge haunts the descriptions of work found in Chaucer's General Prologue to the *Canterbury Tales*. The portrait of the Merchant can provide one example:

> A Marchant was ther with a forked berd,
> In mottelee [parti-colored cloth], and hye on horse he sat;
> Upon his heed a Flaundryssh [Flemish] bever hat,
> His bootes clasped faire and fetisly [elegantly].
> His resons [remarks] he spak ful solempnely,
> Sownynge [tending toward] alwey th'encrees of his wynnyng.
> He wolde the see were kept fro any thyng
> Bitwixe Middelburgh and Orewelle.
> Wel koude he in eschaunge sheeldes selle.
> This worthy man ful wel his wit bisette [used]:
> Ther wiste [knew] no wight that he was in dette,
> So estatly [dignified] was he of his governaunce
> With his bargaynes and with his chevyssaunce [borrowing].
> For sothe he was a worthy man with alle,
> But, sooth to seyn, I noot how men hym calle.   (General Prologue, ll. 270–84)

Lines 280–1 are a perfect example of Chaucer's much-vaunted technique of ambiguous description that leaves unanswered the question of whether or not the Merchant is, in fact, in debt. However these lines are interpreted, they imply an omniscient narrator, one capable of seeing that this pilgrim may be in debt despite an exterior persona that seems to militate against it (the beaver hat, the nice boots). This omniscient perspective cannot be that of the pilgrim-narrator—the 'I' that lies at Southwark with the band of pilgrims. The knowledge must reside somewhere else. It is in the omniscient voice that 'knows' whether this merchant is a 'true' merchant or a false one, has engaged in sound labour practices or not. The paradox of pronouncing on the secrets of the Merchant's work life but disavowing knowledge of his name highlights the problem of aligning work with identity. The pilgrim-narrator may have simply failed to enquire after the name, but this paradox could signal a larger hermeneutic crisis, an inability to connect a person's inner intentions to work truly with his outer, public persona.

Like almost all of the Canterbury portraits, the Merchant's description is ruled by the bureaucratic regimen of parataxis, the 'and then and then and then' of bureaucratic time. Although parataxis was much more common in Middle English than in Modern English, we have to recognize its obsessive repetition as a stylistic choice on Chaucer's part, since Chaucer was also a recognized master of hypotaxis ('Whan that April ... '). The portraits rely heavily on the bureaucratic idiom of parataxis because, as a formal choice, it implies causality even where none exists. In the Merchant's description, it is unclear whether the line 'This worthy man ful wel his wit bisette' ('this noble man used his brains well') applies to what comes before or what comes after it (does he use his wits to exchange money and goods or does he use his wits to hide his debts?). The appositive parataxis implies that it could be the latter just as easily as the former. If labour statutes and bureaucratic lists produced artificial divisions that attempted to make phenomenal acts of labour legible to those interested in its surveillance, so too does the General Prologue, complete with all its ambiguities. Chaucer turns the reader-listener into the bureaucratic surveyor—he puts us in charge of finding out the 'truth' of his pilgrims' labours. In so doing, he interpellates his audience into the same subject position that he occupied in his administrative jobs just as efficiently as the labour laws attempted to interpellate every potential almsgiver by enlisting them in the process of surveying a given person's capacity and willingness to work. The General Prologue is not so much a 'disciplinary machine' (as Carlson and others would have it) as a meditation on the complexities of trying both to live and *work* inside a newly created and ever-evolving disciplinary machine, a machine that produced unnuanced definitions of 'good' and 'bad' labour that had become sedimented in the legal and moral discourses of the late fourteenth century.

If Chaucer asks his audience to occupy the position of labour inquisitor, how are we to understand his allotment of the role of bad labourer to himself in almost all of his major works? In the early *House of Fame*, the poet 'Geffrey' is chastised by his eagle-guide for being too dull to write well; in the Prologue to the *Legend of Good Women*, the narrator 'Geffrey' is on trial for his bad translations; in the *Canterbury Tales*, the pilgrim-narrator tells the 'Tale of Sir Thopas', a story of such parodically bad metrics and such an inane storyline that it gives the Host Harry Bailey an earache. Finally, the Retraction to the *Canterbury Tales* is Chaucer's most famous (and most ambivalent) *apologia* for the failings of his written work. The staging of failed narrative labour becomes a kind of 'authorial signature' for Chaucer, a self-dramatization similar to those found in Langland and Hoccleve but more obsessively pursued. The realization that labour—whether manual or intellectual—can and may and perhaps always will go astray despite best intentions is ubiquitous in Chaucer's representation of his own work. This narrative pose was not just a perverse modesty topos or case of extreme literary self-abjection. It was, as I have been arguing, a reaction to social and legal pressures that demanded transparency in one's intention to work truly. Chaucer meets this demand by staging the failure of his own narrative labour, while, at the same time, undermining this judgement on account of the audience's awareness of the virtuoso literary performance of the poetry taken as a whole. The ontological ambiguity of 'written work' is thus restaged and transformed into a literary argument about the quality of the writer's labours.

Chaucer's self-mocking feints at his own failings as a writer uncover a more serious representational crisis: the difficulty of representing or narrativizing work as an outer expression of inner identity. Unlike his contemporary Gower, Chaucer had an insight (perhaps attributable to his work life) that the textualization of identity was a fraught process at the best of times. Chaucer adopts bureaucratic rhetoric in part to show us that identity is an effect, an effect produced both by the structural position of the individual and by available linguistic positions. If there is no such thing as a 'core' identity that exerts completely conscious control over the choice to labour truly or labour badly, then there is no guarantee that such an identity can be represented as a conspicuously readable text. What estates satire and the labour statutes share—and what I think Chaucer rejects—is the expectation that writing can reproduce the authentic, reclaimable value of social labour in words, whether the words are spoken by a preacher, a bureaucrat, or a poet.

I have been arguing that contemporary legal and moral discussions of work contributed to the ways in which medieval poets framed their own written work. These debates offer us hermeneutic help not only on a macrocosmic, ideological level but also on the local level by helping us understand the formal, aesthetic choices employed by these poets. This type of analysis is intended to supplement previous literary and biographical discussions of medieval labour, while steering a course between 'merely conventional' on the one hand, and the pitfalls of identity politics, on the other. Tellingly, both Chaucer and his contemporary John Gower sought a space outside of the increasingly polarized binary of work and leisure in the late fourteenth century, a space in which they could consider the anomalous activity of writing as work. For Gower, this space of non-work allowed him to declare poetry to be exempt from contemporary debates over work. For Chaucer in the *Canterbury Tales*, pilgrimage—the paradigmatic social space of non-work—allowed him the freedom to explore the paradoxical position of writing, both in its poetic role of identity creation and in its coercive bureaucratic role of identity certification. To occupy the middle is to be aware of the usual binaries without necessarily affirming them, an awareness Chaucer displayed as a writer, and one that we must cultivate as belated readers of medieval work and culture.

FURTHER READING

My thinking on medieval literary practices in relation to everyday work has been most obviously influenced by the work of Pierre Bourdieu, *The Logic of Practice* (n. 20 above), and *The Field of Cultural Production* (New York: Columbia University Press, 1993). For the division between so-called 'material' and 'immaterial' labours, see Michael Hardt and Antonio Negri, *Empire* (Cambridge, MA: Harvard University Press, 2000) and Maurizio Lazzarato, 'Immaterial Labor', in Michael Hardt and Paolo Virno (eds.), *Radical Thought in Italy: A Potential Politics* (Minneapolis: University of Minnesota Press, 1996), 133–47. For rethinking social space in terms of use-value, see Henri Lefebvre, *The Production of Space*, trans. Donald Nicholson-Smith (Oxford: Blackwell, 1991) and Maurice Blanchot, *The Space of Literature*, trans. Ann Smock (Lincoln: University of Nebraska Press, 1982). For a provocative meditation on the problem of intellectuals representing workers, see Jacques Rancière, *The Nights of Labor: The Worker's Dream in Nineteenth-Century France*, trans. John Drury (Philadelphia: Temple University Press, 1989).

Explorations of medieval work in specific literary texts are to be found in the essays gathered in Steven Justice and Kathryn Kerby-Fulton (eds.), *Written Work: Langland, Labor and Authorship* (Philadelphia: University of Pennsylvania Press, 1997), see especially Anne Middleton's essay 'Acts of Vagrancy'; David Aers, 'Justice and Wage-Labor after the Black Death: Some Perplexities for William Langland', in *Faith, Ethics and Church: Writing in England, 1360–1409* (Cambridge: D. S. Brewer, 2000), 56–75; Lisa H. Cooper, 'Urban Utterances: Merchants, Artisans, and the Alphabet in Caxton's *Dialogues in French and English*', *New Medieval Literatures*, 7 (2005), 127–61; and Kellie Robertson, *The Laborer's Two Bodies: Labor and the 'Work' of the Text in Medieval Britain, 1350–1500* (n. 14). For examinations of the social value of labour more generally, see James Bothwell, P. J. P. Goldberg, and W. M. Ormrod (eds.), *The Problem of Labour in Fourteenth-Century England* (York: York Medieval Press, 2000); Kellie Robertson and Michael Uebel (eds.), *The Middle Ages at Work* (New York: Palgrave Macmillan, 2004); and Allen J. Frantzen and Douglas Moffat (eds.), *The Work of Work: Servitude, Slavery, and Labor in Medieval England* (Glasgow: Cruithne Press, 1994).

CHAPTER 28

LEARNING TO LIVE

STEPHANIE TRIGG

First, the question of aesthetics and reader fatigue. At the conclusion of his study of medieval courtesy books, Jonathan Nicholls sounds exhausted:

> An examination of a typical courtesy book...does not leave the reader with an immediate sense of its cultural worth or importance. The precepts seem crude and basic, the style, at best a hackneyed pastiche of the prevailing literary fashion, is at worst the heavy and unpalatable dough of pedagogy.[1]

Nicholls's candour is refreshing. It allows us to acknowledge that medieval books of nurture, courtesy, conduct, and advice are often intractable; instead of delighting us, or bringing us to the point of the sublime, as we conventionally expect of literary texts, they make us feel uncomfortable, and are almost impossible to read from beginning to end. Anyone spending much time with these texts starts to feel grateful to the glossing conventions of nineteenth-century editors, whose marginal notes on many such works help us navigate our way through them. We should probably acknowledge, too, that our attention is most often engaged when the manners or precepts being expressed are curiously unfamiliar, when these works seem to promise a neat codification of the daily alterity of the Middle Ages. And yet the content of many of these books—especially those concerned with table manners and social decorum—is not that alien to modern principles of social governance. We similarly train our children not to put food they have touched back in the common dish, not to speak with their mouths full, and not to wipe their noses on the tablecloth. The play of similarity and difference between ourselves and the medieval past is thrown into sharper relief when we compare the content and the use of these texts in the medieval period and our own. Aspiring courtiers might read one such text and be glad to hold a precious collection of time-honoured advice in their hands as the key to social success; aspiring students and scholars feel

---

[1] Jonathan Nicholls, *The Matter of Courtesy: Medieval Courtesy Books and the Gawain-Poet* (Woodbridge: D. S. Brewer, 1985), 140.

obliged to read as many as they can, while also trying to read behind and around these texts, for glimpses into the lived reality of the medieval period implied by its various principles and rules for living. Medieval conduct literature forces the question: what do *we* do with such texts?

Writing in 1985, Nicholls resolves the question of perspective by adopting the familiar approach of putting these texts where scholars used to agree that historical background belonged: *behind* works of literature. His study is divided into two parts: first, a rich scholarly description of medieval secular and religious texts of courtesy and nurture, in Latin, French, and English; and second, a study of the four poems of the *Gawain*-manuscript and their relation to that tradition. He also includes a number of texts and translations of rare works. For Nicholls, conduct texts are to be read in the service of better understanding medieval literature. He knows these texts intimately, and is able to recognize features of the courtesy tradition in the four poems. His division into background and foreground does have the effect, though, of reducing our interest in works of conduct and nurture as textual artefacts, and of helping to maintain a hierarchical distinction between the literary and the non-literary that was not such a strong feature of the medieval textual landscape.

A more recent collaborative foray into this material articulates a very different approach, as we might expect in a different critical era. Kathleen Ashley and Robert L. A. Clarke introduce their edited collection of essays, *Medieval Conduct*, with a discussion of the relationship between 'documents or texts and lived practice or performance'.[2] Instead of using conduct and courtesy texts to illuminate 'literature', their emphasis is divided equally between 'texts, theories, and practices'. Ashley and Clarke also consider the reception history of the texts, the way they have been subordinated to literary works as if 'contaminated' by their association with material and social history; their damaging association with popular culture (especially in the case of books addressed to women); the sometimes artificial distinction between texts addressed to men and women; and the recent recuperation of these texts as valuable cultural artefacts, no longer to be rigorously set apart from literary texts. Emphasizing the circulation of discourse between late medieval texts, many of the essays in Ashley's and Clarke's collection effectively reverse Nicholls's priorities, encouraging the reading of both 'literary' and other kinds of texts such as Lollard trial records and confraternity documents for their capacity to serve as forms of conduct literature, as they tease out the 'behavioral ideologies' at work in different sorts of texts.

Recent theories of ritual practice and social behaviour also help us examine the representation of nurture and conduct in the medieval period and the reality of medieval behaviour, thought, and feeling about the proper conduct of the self,

---

[2] Kathleen Ashley and Robert L. A. Clarke (eds.), *Medieval Conduct* (Minneapolis: Minnesota University Press, 2001), p. ix.

whether that self is conceived primarily in spiritual, social, or ethical terms. Key texts here are Pierre Bourdieu, *Distinction* and *Outline of a Theory of Practice*, Michel de Certeau, *The Practice of Everyday Life*, Norbert Elias, *The Civilizing Process*, and Michel Foucault, *The History of Sexuality*.[3] None of these writers is specially concerned with medieval English life, but we can fruitfully draw on their various methods of interpreting the social world: the customs, practices, and rituals of daily life.

My focus is, however, principally textual. Unlike the sociologists, I am interested in the textual effects of these works, across a range of forms: narrative, didactic, exemplary, prescriptive, and satiric. These texts are always layered, and so, too, should be our critical paradigms. With these possibilities in mind, I will explore several different approaches to this material. This chapter offers no taxonomy of conduct literature, no fine discriminations between its genres, no historical account of its development; my focus throughout is on the questions raised by these texts, and I will move freely amongst different genres and types.

Medieval conduct books: writers and readers

> Qwo so wylle of curtasy lere,
> In this boke he may hit here!
> Yf thow be gentylmon, yomon, or knaue,
> The nedis nurture for to haue.[4]

The production of conduct books increases rapidly in the fourteenth and fifteenth centuries, suggesting the increasing instability of class boundaries and a concern at various levels either to maintain or acquire the manners and customs of 'courtesy'. According to conservative early medieval ideology, such manners were the natural preserve of the aristocracy alone. By contrast, these opening lines from the *Boke of Curtasye*, dated around 1460, confidently address men of several classes, suggesting that all are in need of training, whether to acquit themselves honourably at court, to further a career of service in a noble household, or even to 'pass', as we might say, as a member of a higher class. The *Boke* proceeds with a detailed set of instructions as to how to be a gracious guest when you visit a lord's household, and how to eat

---

[3] Pierre Bourdieu, *Distinction: A Social Critique of the Judgement of Taste*, trans. Richard Nice (Cambridge: Cambridge University Press, 1984); *Outline of a Theory of Practice*, trans. Richard Nice (Cambridge: Cambridge University Press, 1977); Michel de Certeau, *The Practice of Everyday Life*, trans. Steven Rendall (Berkeley and Los Angeles: University of California Press, 1984); Norbert Elias, *The Civilizing Process: Sociogenetic and Psychogenetic Investigations* (1930), trans. Edmund Jephcott, rev. edn. ed. Eric Dunning, Johan Goudsblom, and Stephen Mennell (Oxford: Blackwell, 2000); Michel Foucault, *The History of Sexuality*, trans. Robert Hurley (New York: Pantheon, 1978).

[4] *The Boke of Curtasye*, BL, Sloane MS 1986, ed. F. J. Furnivall, in *Early English Meals and Manners*, EETS, os 32 (London: Kegan Paul, Trench, Trübner & Co., 1868), 177, ll. 1–4.

your meal, with due attention to bodily decorum and social manners. The second part is addressed to young children, with a greater emphasis on moral instruction; and the third part is a series of job descriptions for the officers in a noble household, starting with the four who carry rods of office—porter, marshal, steward, and usher (the porter's rod is longest; the usher's the smallest; and the steward's is rather a staff 'to reule the men of court ymong'), and finishing with the chandler, who snuffs out the candles at the end of the day. Like most such texts, this *Boke* ranges freely between the normative and the prescriptive, the present and the future tense. Characteristically, the style of address is anonymous, impartial, classless: it can be used alike by teacher and student, parent and child.

The mobility and fluidity of address here are thrown into sharper contrast by comparison with earlier works of instruction for men and women in religious orders, which are conceived within a far more stable and specialized structure of authority. They often begin as if responding to a request for a disciplinary regime, like the English translation of Ailred of Rievaulx's *De institutione inclusarum*: 'Suster, thou hast ofte axed of me a forme of lyuynge accordyng to thyn estat, inasmuche as thou art enclosed.'[5] The author of *Ancrene Wisse* echoes Ailred: ' … And ye my leue sustren habbeth mony day icraued on me after rule.'[6] Life in an anchorhold often seems the most extreme example of disciplinary subjection, a concentration of institutional and internalized surveillance. The modern spirit has difficulty imagining itself in that situation, and wanting yet *more* discipline, but the request for a rule might reflect a need for structure, as much as further subjection. In any case, the convention of seeking advice, of 'craving a rule', is one of long standing.

This trope is developed most fully as a narrative starting point in John Russell's *Boke of Nurture*, which opens in the mode of pastoral or *chanson d'aventure*. The narrator is wandering through a forest, and meets a young man who is 'semely' but 'sklendur' and 'leene'. He is unable to find a good master because he 'cowd no good', and was 'wantoun & nyce, recheles & lewde | as Iangelynge as a Iay'.[7] The narrator offers to teach him, and soon launches into a long disquisition that will help him find employment. The petitionary frame is not found in all works, of course, though it appears in a vestigial form in a number of shorter works. Many poems begin this way: 'Who-so wilneth to be wiis, & worschip desirith'; 'Who-so wylle of nurture lere'; and 'Who se euer wylle thryue or the'.[8] Or the presumption of a petitionary wish appears in the title, as in 'A generall Rule to teche euery man that is willinge for to lerne to serue a lorde or mayster in euery thyng to his plesure'.[9]

[5] Ailred of Rievaulx, *De institutione inclusarum: Two English Versions*, ed. John Ayto and Alexandra Barratt, EETS, os 287 (Oxford: Oxford University Press, 1984), Bodley MS 423, p. 1.

[6] Arne Zettersten and Bernhard Diensberg (eds.), *The English Text of the Ancrene Riwle: The 'Vernon' Text*, introd. H. L. Spencer, EETS, os 310 (Oxford: Oxford University Press, 2000), 3.

[7] Furnivall (ed.), *Early English Meals and Manners*, 3, l. 36.   [8] Ibid. 260, 262, 266.

[9] R. W. Chambers (ed.), *A Fifteenth-Century Courtesy Book* and Walter W. Seton (ed.), *Two Fifteenth-Century Franciscan Rules*, EETS, os 148 (London: Kegan Paul, Trench, Trübner & Co., 1914).

The desire for instruction finds its most dramatic expression in *Sir Gawain and the Green Knight*, where Bertilak's court hovers around the knight hoping to receive training in good manners and good discourse from him. In this case, nurture is better learned *without* asking ('vnspurd'). Clearly, nurture and conduct are learnable, desirable techniques: there is little room here for the idea of any kind of innate knowledge of behaviour particular either to the aristocracy or indeed any class. Indeed, this is an important contrast between Arthur's and Bertilak's court, with the provincials aspiring to the artless grace of Camelot. If these are disciplinary regimes they are represented in these texts, at least, as voluntary ones.

Many texts simply assume the desirability of their advice. The fifteenth-century prose 'General Rule', quoted above, begins with the first action of the day: 'The marshall in the mornyng ought to come into the hall and se that it be clene of all maner thyng that may be fond unhoneste ther In ... ' (p. 11). Many of the shorter texts similarly present their instructions quite baldly. As Elias remarks, many of these books probably encapsulate an oral tradition of material that is seen as unauthored, though no less authoritative on that account.

At the other extreme are texts that carefully address the concerns of a more readerly audience. The Knight de La Tour Landry is the most expansive and bookish of all such writers. He expresses his desire to teach his daughters, by asking a team of clerics and priests to assemble examples of good and bad women. Literary and popular anecdote provide his chief examples across a range of cultural fields from the exotic to the familiar. Narrative pleasure plays an important role in framing and softening the exemplary mode, a luxury reserved for texts directed at gentlemen and gentlewomen, though this is a contested and mutable category, especially in the fifteenth century.

Caxton's prefaces provide an intriguing insight into this issue, as they often seem concerned to frame particular texts for particular audiences. These prefaces give readers and consumers the sense that they may choose the text that best fits their situation. Perhaps this indirectly implies they may be able to choose which class to belong to, or at least, identify with. Moreover, if the performance of a social role can be learned and improved through the purchase of a book, this is a major concession that the ideology of the estates, as a codification of divisions that were supposed to be 'natural', is dissolving. Caxton's world is strikingly different from the world of *Piers Plowman*, for example, on the topic of knighthood. Where Langland appeals to the traditional ideal of the knight's primary role as defending the Christian community, his static allegory never suggests that those not born to knighthood might wish or be able to aspire to its ideals (B. VI. 21–54).

Caxton's introduction to the *Ordre of Chyvalry* is ostensibly addressed to the upper classes:

Whiche book is not requysyte to every comyn man to have, but to noble gentylmen that by their vertue entende to come and entre into the noble ordre of chyvalry, the whiche in these late dayes hath not ben used accordying to this booke heretofore wreton.[10]

But the key clause is the one addressed to those who 'entende to come and entre into the noble ordre of chyvalry', a reminder that entry into the status of 'knight' in the Middle Ages was not contingent simply on birth or hereditary title; it presumed a certain income and involved payment of a fee. Having acknowledged this mobility, though, Caxton offers a traditional lament on the decline of knighthood which moves quickly into a practical solution, the reading of romance:

> O ye knyghtes of Englond, where is the custome and usage of noble chyvalry that was used in tho dayes? What do ye now but go to the baynes [the baths] and playe atte dyse? And some not wel advysed use not honest and good rule ageyn alle order of knyghthode. Leve this. Leve it and rede the noble volumes of Saynt Graal, of Lancelot, of Galaad, of Trystram, of Perse Forest, of Percyval, of Gawayn and many mo. Ther shalle ye see manhode, curtosye and gentylnesse.

One of his imperatives is downright impatient. 'Rede Froissart', he orders. Caxton's knights are dissolute, unruly, and lazy, but his passionate vision for their improvement through reading and studying is entirely secular and courtly. It may also be commercial: as the publisher of Malory's tales, Caxton is actively creating a market for such works.

Caxton's preface to Higden's *Polychronicon*, on the other hand, appeals to a different audience, distinguishing less between common and knightly men, than between old and young.

> Historyes ought not only to be juged moost proffytable to yonge men whiche by the lecture, redyng and understandyng make them semblable and equale to men of greter age and to old men, to whome longe lyf hath mynystred experymentes of dyverse thynges, but also th'ystoryes able and make ryght pryvate men digne and worthy to have the governaunce of empyres and noble royammes.   (p. 129)

This last clause also hints that the reading of history has the capacity to elevate 'pryvate men' to the status of rulers and governors. Again, Caxton appeals to a sense of class and social mobility for middle-class men, while also invoking the 'advice to rulers' genre, the *Secretum secretorum* tradition. By contrast, his *Eneydos* is emphatically not for 'rude men'; and there is very little sense in any of Caxton's prefaces or in any of the conduct books that women might also rise through modifying their behaviour. Where women readers are mentioned it is in far more static terms. The romance of *Blanchardin and Eglantine*, for example, is 'honeste and joyefull to all vertuouse yong noble gentylmen and wymmen for to rede therin, as for their passe-tyme' (p. 57).

---

[10] *Caxton's Own Prose*, ed. N. F. Blake (London: Andre Deutsch, 1973), 126. All further citations from Caxton refer to page numbers in this edition.

Social advancement is not possible for the lower classes: they need more direct forms of instruction to bring them up to the level of the human. Here is Caxton's prologue to the *Book of Good Manners*, translated from French:

> Whan I consydered the condycions and maners of the comyn people whiche without enformacion and lerning ben rude and not manerd, lyke unto beestis brute (acordyng to an olde proverbe he that is not manerd is no man, for maners make man), thenne is it requesite and necessary that every man use good and vertuous maners.   (p. 60)

This preface closes with a benediction on those who shall 'rede or here it'; like many such texts, it is perhaps directed for training others. Caxton is not alone in his equivocations between the idea of texts that train, or bring to perfection; and texts that can improve or advance one's situation. Such evidence must indeed be employed with caution. Sponsler and Krueger 'show that the actual consumers of these texts are not necessarily the inscribed or intended readers',[11] while Mark Amos makes the argument that 'courtesy literature represented a site of struggle between the nobility and non-noble urban elites, as these two proximate classes attempted to control definitions of "gentle" behaviour': 'Each of the constituencies involved in the struggle over class honour in the late Middle Ages sought the distinction offered by such rarefied and artful behaviour, and each sought to naturalize those behaviours into an innate and unquestioned code of superiority.'[12] Writing of the sixteenth century, Frank Whigham makes a similar point: if Castiglione's *Book of the Courtier* was designed to expose those social upstarts who aspired to the status of courtier, it also codified the desired behavioural norms both for the 'members of an endangered aristocracy' *and* for anyone else who could read.[13]

Three illustrative topics

1. Carving: 'dysfygyre that pecocke   transsene that ele'

Despite its very practical orientation, equivocation of address and purpose is a regular feature of conduct literature. These works characteristically presuppose a subject-in-process, but in process of becoming ... what? Grown up? Socially mobile? Further advanced in one's career? Many of the nurture books are concerned with the rules governing the preparation, serving, and consumption of food at the courtly table: the feast is an important occasion for conspicuous consumption and display,

---

[11] See the essays by Claire Sponsler and Roberta L. Krueger in Ashley and Clark (eds.), *Medieval Conduct*, and also Tracy Adams, '"Noble, wyse and grete lordes, gentilmen and marchauntes": Caxton's Prologues as Conduct Books for Merchants', *Parergon*, 22/2 (2005), 53–76.

[12] Mark Addison Amos, '"For Manners Make Man": Bourdieu, de Certeau, and the Common Appropriation of Noble Manners in *The Book of Courtesy*', in Ashley and Clarke (eds.), *Medieval Conduct*, 30.

[13] Frank Whigham, *Ambition and Privilege: The Social Tropes of Elizabethan Courtesy Theory* (Berkeley and Los Angeles: University of California Press, 1984), 18–19.

and the exercise of social command of the self and of others. The self-in-training addressed here is often the young man, inhabiting the ambiguous territory between the roles of servant, courtier, and the squire being prepared for a knightly career.

The most famous such figure is Chaucer's Squire, exemplifying the nobility of youth as he carves and serves meat to his father. The squire also carves before his lord in Chaucer's 'Summoner's Tale' and 'Merchant's Tale', where Damian carves for January. In the earlier *King Horn*, Aylmar has his steward Athelbrus take charge of young Horn's education, that he might learn the noble arts of hunting, playing the harp, carving, and serving. In the public rituals of the courtly household, the carving and serving of meat is a rich social act, often worthy of special comment in both chronicle and romance. The squire proves he is learning the kind of discipline that will make him a knight; the king does honour to his guests; the senior courtier claims an intimacy with the king's household.[14]

The complex terminology of service reflects some of the ambiguities here. Kate Mertes shows how many of the titles of household occupations as they appear in account books, such as '*generosus* or armigerous, *valettus, garcio*, and pagettus/puer', encrypt an elaborate series of changing relationships between service and gentility, and between youth and experience.[15] Squires and junior knights might serve in a lord's household: child servants, too, might be well-born children serving in another aristocratic household to receive a 'military, social, and academic education'. But the term *pagetti* or *pueri* might also be used to describe children from much humbler families who were employed in the household with the hopes of reaching a permanent position there, rather than receiving training for an aristocratic career. As Mertes writes, 'one must caution that all these ranks, while constant in themselves, did not fix or define individuals. … The household could be a signal way of social and material advancement; the ranks within it were, as we have seen, a matter of relative and rather loosely defined status, but imposed no ultimate restrictions on the servant who was named with them.'[16]

Unlike nearly every other aspect of serving meals, carving required special skills, and so it is one of the richest and most ambiguous social acts. The trope of the 'kitchen knight' in romance indicates how porous are some of these boundaries. Sir Kay's job, as the steward, is to serve the king, from a position of honour, but when knights like Gareth or Lancelot are put to work in the filth of the kitchen, this is one of the most humiliating fates for a knight. However, such knights never remain there. Gareth eventually fights his way to courtly pre-eminence, so that the three most powerful knights he defeats petition to be given posts respectively as his carver, chamberlain, and butler. Sarah Gordon comments of three such romances:

---

[14] Ernest P. Kuhl and Henry J. Webb, 'Chaucer's Squire', *English Literary History*, 6 (1939), 282–4.
[15] Kate Mertes, *The English Noble Household 1250–1600: Good Governance and Politic Rule* (Oxford: Basil Blackwell, 1988), 26.
[16] Ibid. 31.

'The contrast of noble/servant is given a complex, ironic treatment related to the dichotomies of appearance/reality and nature/nurture, omnipresent themes in medieval literature … the discourse of knights in the kitchen begins to reveal the possibility, threat and promise of upward and downward social mobility.'[17] If romances can rehearse these possibilities, the conduct books provide the manuals for such upward mobility. Treatises about carving and serving complement the display of feasting celebrated in the menus of poems like *Wynnere and Wastoure* and the *Alliterative Morte Arthure*.

The young man in Russell's *Boke* has some sense of the complexities to be learned:

> 'Good syr, y yow praye the connynge of kervynge ye wille me teche,
> and the fayre handlynge of a knyfe, y yow beseche,
> alle wey where y shalle alle maner fowles breke, unlace, or seche,
> and with Fysche or flesche, how shalle y demene me with eche.'[18]

Russell's *Boke* expounds in some detail how to hold one's three knives, how to prepare the bread trenchers on which the meat is served, and the particular methods of serving the appropriate food for the appropriate occasion. Like many such books that expound a *techné* in this way, Russell's text loves the signifier. Carving demands a specific and precise vocabulary and procedures: it is a very textual art. The first point is to know which meats are 'fumose', and Russell offers this alliterative (and remarkably unmemorable) mnemonic:

> **F** is the furst that is, **F**att, **F**arsed & **F**ried;
> **R**, **r**aw **r**esty, and **r**echy, ar comberous vndefied;
> **S** salt **s**owre and **s**owse all such thow set a-side.   (ll. 357–9)

The *Boke of Kervynge*, printed by Wynkyn de Worde in 1508, has hardly begun before it launches into a surreal list of imperatives, a string of matching verbs and meats:

Breke that dere	tyere that egge
lesche that brawne	chyne that samon
rere that goose	strynge that lampraye
lyft that swanne	splatte that pyke
sauce that capon	sauce that playce
spoyle that henne	sauce that tenche
frusshe that chekyn	splaye that breme
vnbrace that malarde	syde that haddocke
vnlace that cony	tuske that barbell
dysmembre that heron	culpon that troute
dysplaye that crane	fynne that cheuen
dsyfygyre that pecocke	transsene that ele[19]

---

[17] Sarah Gordon, 'Kitchen Knights in Medieval French and English Narrative: Rainouart, Lancelot, Gareth', *Literature Interpretation Theory*, 16 (2005), 189–212, at 209.

[18] Furnivall (ed.), *Early English Meals and Manners*, 21, ll. 313–16.   [19] Ibid. 151, ll. 1–12.

Reading this list produces a similar response to the hunting scenes in poems like *Sir Gawain*. Modern readers tend to glaze over the difficult vocabulary, appreciating the narrative patterning of the poem and the symbolism of the hunt but without really wanting to absorb or own the details. In each text, every kind of animal requires its own special method of capture and killing, dismemberment in the field, preparing in the kitchen, and carving at the table. The *public* interaction between gentleman and animal, at first raw and then cooked, is crucial in both hunting and carving. The carver is on public display in the formality of the hall, and may be carrying out his task before lords who were once themselves squire-carvers in other households. No wonder the man in Russell's book wants to know 'how shalle y demene me with eche', referring to his comportment with each different kind of meat. The meat is to be presented to the lord, again in different fashion according to the animal, and on the carefully prepared bread trenchers, and always subject to what the lord wants. The instructions are detailed to the left and right hand to be used with each knife, whether the legs or wings or left or right wing of the bird are to be served first, whether the rabbit is to be laid on its back or its belly at different stages in the carving. The art of carving is the art of the proper, the love of the right way to handle and serve the right meat at the right time of the year; the *Boke of Kervynge* is closely concerned with menus for feasts at different times of the liturgical year.

The *Babees Book* explains why carving and consumption of food are important to the noble household:

> Kutte nouhte youre meete eke as it were Felde men,
> That to theyre mete haue suche an appetyte
> That they ne rekke in what wyse, where ne when,
> Nor how vngoodly they on theyre mete twyte [hack, cut] ... [20]

Readers of *The Book of Margery Kempe* know that food and its consumption are crucial theatres for the performance of spiritual virtues and their sometimes uncomfortable relation to courtly or social ones.[21] The possibilities for social decorum to go astray seem endless, at every level of gesture, discourse, and comportment of the body: the art of fine eating is the art of not seeming to need to eat.

2. The Mouth

> Grennynge and mowes at the table eschowe;
> Cry nat to lowde; kepe honestly silence;
> To enboce thy Iowis withe mete is nat diewe;

---

[20] Furnivall (ed.), *Early English Meals and Manners*, 256, ll. 175–8.
[21] See for example, Margery's trials with her fellow pilgrims at Seryce, in *The Book of Margery Kempe*, ed. Barry Windeatt (Harlow: Longman, 2000), ll. 1966–98, and 2045–80, pp. 151–2, 154–6.

> Withe ful mowthe speke nat, lest thow do offence;
> Drynk nat bretheles for hast ne necligence;
> Kepe clene thy lippes from fat of flesshe or fisshe;
> Wype clene thy spone, leve it nat in thy dissche.[22]

Of all the body parts these regimes seek to discipline, the eyes, hands, and mouth feature most extensively. The mouth constellates two sets of anxieties about consumption of food and proper speech. This is particularly the case at the monastic table, as Nicholls shows, where rules and principles of conduct sometimes seem haunted by the familiar barbs of estates satire, and their sense that monastic orders sometimes had trouble with the vows of abstinence. The dreamer's experience at Conscience's feast in Passus XIII of *Piers Plowman* similarly shows how highly charged is feasting as a focus for ethical and religious issues.

Much of the discourse of the mouth, like carving, is implicitly about distinguishing one's social class by one's behaviour. The *Babees Book* commends the babies, those of royal blood, to wipe their mouths clean with a cloth (like the young lady in *Le Roman de la Rose* (ll. 13385–456) and Chaucer's Prioress). The knife is not to be brought into the mouth, and the children are particularly instructed not to stuff their cheeks full of food. Here they are threatened by the comparison with the non-human:

> Let neuer thy cheke be Made to grete
> With morselle of brede that thou shalle ete;
> An apys mow men sayne he makes,
> That brede and flesshe in hys cheke bakes.   (p. 179, ll. 57–60)

The mouth is an organ dangerously close to being uncontrollable. Not only is eating a natural function that animals perform without constraint of manners; the mouth is also the site of so many ungovernable, involuntary acts such as yawning, choking, vomiting, excessive laughter, and so on. We might argue that these texts construct the proper behaviour of the mouth so attentively because they are haunted by their opposite, the carnivalesque body, and the carnivalesque feast as the site of excess, animalistic appetite, and the threat of social reversal.

Eating and drinking, like the service and distribution of food, are highly charged activities, as Caroline Walker Bynum shows so powerfully.[23] Even in the secular court context, physical and especially culinary conduct are frequently linked to moral conduct. The Knight de La Tour Landry specializes in making these connections; he tells of a young woman who habitually spoiled her two little dogs, even though she had been warned by a friar against this practice, 'and the pore pepille so lene and famisshed for hunger'.

---

[22] *Stans puer ad mensam*, in Furnivall (ed.), *Early English Meals and Manners*, 277, ll. 29–36.
[23] Caroline Walker, Bynum *Holy Feast and Holy Fast: The Religious Significance of Food to Medieval Women* (Berkeley and Los Angeles: University of California Press, 1987), esp. ch. 3, 73–111.

And after she happed she deied, and there fell a wonder mervailous sight, for there was seyn euer on her bedde. ij. litelle blake dogges, and in her deyeng thei were about her mouthe and liked [licked] it, and whanne she was dede, there the dogges had lyked it was al blacke as cole.[24]

The *Male Regle* of Thomas Hoccleve also gives us a characteristically dramatic vision of what happens when the body refuses and resists this discipline, when 'Excess' becomes one's dining partner, 'at borde hath leyd his knyf with me':

> The custume of my repleet abstinence,
> My greedy mowth, receite of swich outrage,
> And hondes two, as woot my negligence,
> Thus han me gyded and broght in seruage
> Of hir that werreieth euery age,
> Seeknesse, Y meene, riotoures whippe,
> Habundantly that paieth me my wage,
> So that me neithir daunce list, ne skippe.[25]

No problem with readerly fatigue, here: Hoccleve's readiness to expound on his bad habits, and the temptations of the tavern—sweet wine, thick wafers, and the 'fressh repeir' of pretty women—offers a fascinating glimpse of everyday misrule. Like the confessions of the Deadly Sins in *Piers Plowman*, this seems to reveal a more individualized subject than we find in the perfect, compliant, and unhurried eaters of the model texts. Hoccleve's misrule of mouth and belly leads not only to sickness, but also to the disordering of the social. In summer it is too hot to walk, and in winter the road is too muddy, so in any season, weighted down by 'superfluitee', Hoccleve takes the boat home, overtipping the boatmen, who in turn flatter him and call him 'maistir'. His vanity gratified, he tips them some more. 'Methoughte I was ymaad a man for euere', he says, the impersonal verb reminding us that on the contrary, he is in the process of unmaking himself. Like many writers, Hoccleve associates excess in eating and drinking with the misrule of speech.

Many texts make the same easy transition from eating to conversing, like the *Young Children's Book*, written around 1500.

> And whylle thi mete yn thi mouth is,
> Drynk thou not; for-gete not this.
> Ete thi mete by smalle mosselles;
> Fylle not thy mouth as done brothellis.
> Pyke not thi tethe with thy knyfe;
> In no company begynne thow stryfe[26]

---

[24] *The Book of the Knight of La Tour-Landry*, ed. Thomas Wright, EETS, os 22 (London: N. Trübner & Co., 1868), 29.

[25] Thomas Hoccleve, '*My Compleinte' and Other Poems*, ed. Roger Ellis (Exeter: University of Exeter Press, 2001), 67, ll. 113–20.

[26] Furnivall (ed.), *Early English Meals and Manners*, 267, ll. 35–40.

The emphasis on careful speech segues easily into the category of political poetry, which abounds in cautions about the dangers of loose speech and flattery. The relationship between the physical governance of the mouth and the monitoring of its counsel warrants fuller study.

3. Touch

'The ancre ne hire meiden ne plohien worldliche gomenes ed te thurle, ne ne ticki togederes ...'

[The recluse and her maid should not play worldly games at the window, or romp together.]

Human touch is rarely foregrounded in the literature of conduct, unless the lesson is specifically about sexuality. The Knight de La Tour Landry, for example, writes in detail about the dangers of touch as the prelude to further sexual engagement, while Mirk's *Instructions for Parish Priests* mentions touch as one of the five wits to be enquired after in the confessional. The various prescriptions about separate beds in monastic houses are predicated on similar concerns. Touch is nearly always invoked only in a sexual context, and often quite graphically. Calling on the hysteria that often surrounded the chastity of women, the Knight writes of a virtuous daughter who prays assiduously for the dead. She is rewarded when an amorous knight comes to her room but sees her as if lying surrounded by the dead. At this sight, his erotic imperative is short-lived.

Sexual touch is usually less Gothic, and more quotidian. Another daughter is not so well governed, to the point of being spoiled and indulged when she pleads a headache as a reason not to spend longer at her devotions. When she is married, her husband turns for her in the night, but finds her in the wardrobe with her ladies and two men singing and crying out. One man has his hand 'vnder one of the wommanes clothes'. The virtuous husband strikes him, but a splinter blinds his wife, whereupon the husband stops loving her and the household falls into ruin. This is a story of wild disproportion at every level, but its mention of the casual hand under the dress seems to bring the cheerful and sexually explicit marginalia of medieval devotional texts into much closer dialogue with the everyday world of the household.

These texts have much less to say about social (non-sexual) touch, though this is a promising area of speculation. Why are we so struck when Criseyde pulls Pandarus by the hood, or when he stuffs Troilus' letter down the front of her dress? When Bertilak's lady puts her hands on either side of Gawain's body, making him her prisoner? When Bertilak himself 'laches' him by a fold of his clothing, to bring Gawain to sit next to him, instead of with the ladies? What can texts of conduct and nurture tell us about the social boundaries of the medieval self, in an era well before the concept of 'personal space' became so intimately tied to our own sense of self?

The evidence is slight, but suggestive. An intriguing prohibition is offered by Mirk, who specifies that when the godparents bring the child to be baptized, they should not 'holde' the childe during the service.[27] A more expansive example is found at the very end of the *Ancrene Wisse*: 'The ancre ne hire meiden ne plohien worldliche gomenes ed te thurle, ne ne ticki togederes.'[28] The author quotes St Bernard on the capacity for 'every such pleasure of the flesh' to diminish the spiritual life. This is intriguing not only for the glimpse into the relationship between anchoress and maid and the vision of the worldly games they might play at their window, but also for the acknowledgement that comfort and pleasure are to be derived from casual physical contact. The *MED* offers only this one instance of 'ticki', and glosses it thus: 'To touch or pat a person as part of a game, dally frivolously'. Did medieval people touch, hold, and pat each other to the same extent we do? What other hints can we find of human touch in the Middle Ages?

Fashioning a self

Confessional manuals reveal the medieval self as a work in progress, subject to reform, scrutiny, and development. The growth in the literature of instruction in the fourteenth and fifteenth centuries also suggests a growing consciousness that one might lead a different kind of life from one's parents, and experience dramatic shifts in one's social sphere and social role as well as spiritual life.

In this final section, I want to consider briefly the extent to which we might use the literature of conduct to worry away at the boundaries of the Middle Ages, and the sense of self we associate with them. This remains one of the important preoccupations of medieval studies: the extent to which late medieval selves might anticipate the sixteenth-century sense, in Stephen Greenblatt's famous formulation, 'that there were both selves and a sense that they could be fashioned'.[29] Greenblatt's first example is one that resonates powerfully with this chapter, and with the late medieval preoccupation with feasting as social situation: Sir Thomas More's account of a dinner party at Cardinal Wolsey's, in which a clever priest stages a brilliant, if wordless piece of flattery of his host. Greenblatt further diagnoses More's own court performances, all the while citing contemporary evidence for the understanding of the life of the courtier as a play, a deliberately orchestrated drama of the self.

---

[27] John Myrc, *Instructions for Parish Priests*, ed. Edward Peacock, EETS, os 31 (London: Trübner & Co., 1868), 6, l. 16.

[28] Bella Millett and Jocelyn Wogan-Browne (eds.), *Medieval English Prose for Women, from the Katherine Group and Ancrene Wisse* (Oxford: Oxford University Press, 2000), 148, ll. 4–5.

[29] Stephen Greenblatt, *Renaissance Self-Fashioning: From More to Shakespeare* (Chicago: Chicago University Press, 1980).

To what extent do medieval texts begin to anticipate such consciousness? Greenblatt is the first to admit that medieval writers like Chaucer certainly evince something of the 'manipulation' of identity, while writers such as Margery Kempe and Thomas Hoccleve testify to a high degree of consciousness about social fashioning. Hoccleve's famous leaps in front of his mirror, trying to catch himself in the act of looking normal, are the most poignant example, but these would be exceptional in any age. Kempe's social and religious performances, too, are hardly indicative of any quotidian or normative understanding of the self.

Susan Crane has explored the 'formal, festive, and most often ritual contexts' in costume, heraldry, and social ritual,[30] but the literature of conduct seems a promising place to look for less formal instances of social performance. If behaviour can be learned and taught, is there any sense that the squire carving before his lord, for example, is fashioning a self? Or is he only ever rehearsing his carefully acquired skills, and wearing the mask of politeness that was recognized as a feature of court life from the early medieval period?[31] The Middle English literature of conduct does not address this issue in a frontal way. Hoccleve himself, when diagnosing his own *male regle*, assumes a conventional understanding of vice as the absence of virtue: he ignores the advice of reason and as a result becomes ill through excessive consumption. Similarly, when Damian carves before January, he can hardly stand, so beset is he with desire for May. But the Merchant narrator sees simple treachery:

> O perilous fyr, that in the bedstraw bredeth!
> O famulier foo, that his servyce bedeth!
> O servant traytour, false hoomly hewe,
> Lyk to the naddre in bosom sly untrewe,
> God shilde us all from youre aqueyntaunce!   (IV. 1783–7)

This is a simple opposition between outward demeanour and inner desire: dissimulation, not self-fashioning.

Yet we should not overlook the subtlety of conduct literature's strategies, offering advice for social survival in what could be potentially very fraught and tense situations, especially eating a meal with one's superiors. These conventions, linking manners, ethics, and morals, persist well into the Renaissance and beyond: only much later are manners and morals more profoundly separated. The spectacular court performances of the Renaissance take place against a background that maintains and enforces many of the conventions and the technologies of selfhood established in the fourteenth and fifteenth centuries.

A further investigation might focus on the kind of writerly performances the texts represent, particularly in the 'advice to rulers' genre. The careful self-positioning of

---

[30] Susan Crane, *The Performance of Self: Ritual, Clothing, and Identity during the Hundred Years War* (Philadelphia: University of Pennsylvania Press, 2002).

[31] C. Stephen Jaeger, *The Origins of Courtliness: Civilizing Trends and the Formation of Courtly Ideals 939–1210* (Philadelphia: University of Pennsylvania Press, 1985), 7.

the poet giving advice, needing to condemn the ruler's flatterers without seeming, himself, to flatter; needing to warn the ruler against those who give bad advice without seeming, himself, to give bad advice—might well be seen as at least prefiguring the self-fashioning of which Greenblatt writes. The narrative framing and the gendering of advice might also be instructive here. Although Chaucer has his male advice-givers, like Placebo and Justinus in the 'Merchant's Tale', his *Canterbury Tales* foreground several instances where Chaucer writes of wives and mothers giving advice: Prudence, the old woman in the 'Wife of Bath's Tale', the Manciple's other. Similarly, Felicity Riddy has suggested that the female narrator of *The Good Wife Teaches her Daughter* might well represent the performance of a male writer.[32] How do male and female parents, speakers, and writers differ in the giving of advice, and the raising of children? To what extent can these examples be seen as performances, or indeed, as exhibiting the performativity we now associate with all exercise of gendered behaviour? Medieval literature is full of philosophical women who give advice. How many such figures appear in early modern literature and in what contexts? Does the gradual separation of ethics from courtesy have implications for the role of women as nurturers and teachers, as the Middle Ages pass into the Renaissance?

FURTHER READING

The very broadest contexts for the study of medieval conduct literature are works of sociology and anthropology that explore the ways humans have shaped and organize society. Key works in this field have been Norbert Elias, *The Civilizing Process*, Pierre Bourdieu, *Distinction: A Social Critique of the Judgement of Taste* and *The Logic of Practice*, Michel de Certeau, *The Practice of Everyday Life*, and Michel Foucault, *The History of Sexuality* (n. 3 above). Many of the essays in Kathleen Ashley and Robert Clarke's collection *Medieval Conduct* (n. 2) develop methods of analysis drawing on these methodological perspectives, in greater detail than has been possible in this essay.

Claire Sponsler's *Drama and Resistance: Bodies, Goods, and Theatricality in Late Medieval England* (Minneapolis: University of Minnesota Press, 1997) similarly includes a chapter on 'Conduct Books and Good Governance' that explores the insights of conduct books into the inner workings of the late medieval 'habitus', a term coined and used by Bourdieu in *The Logic of Practice*. Like Susan Crane in *The Performance of Self* (n. 30), Sponsler ranges over literary and historical texts, and other documents in the social construction of the medieval self. Less theoretical in orientation, Jonathan Nicholls's *The Matter of Courtesy* (n. 1) remains an excellent starting point as a survey of the relevant literature in Middle English.

C. Stephen Jaeger's *The Origins of Courtliness: Civilizing Trends and the Formation of Courtly Ideals 939–1210* (n. 31), provides a longer, older, and European context for the

---

[32] Felicity Riddy, 'Mother Knows Best: Reading Social Change in a Courtesy Text', *Speculum*, 71 (1996), 66–86, at 73.

medieval English tradition of court culture, and a thoughtful critique of some aspects of Elias's work.

Judith Ferster, *Fictions of Advice: The Literature and Politics of Counsel in Late Medieval England* (Philadelphia: University of Pennsylvania Press, 1996), and Nicholas Perkins, *Hoccleve's* Regiment of Princes: *Counsel and Constraint* (Cambridge: D. S. Brewer, 2001) both present subtle accounts of Middle English books that offer conduct advice to rulers, and of the difficulties of offering counsel to lords.

Much current interest in this field is focused on texts directed to a female audience. Essays by Daniel T. Kline, Ruth Evans, and Sarah Salih, in Carolyn Dinshaw and David Wallace (eds.), *Medieval Women's Writing* (Cambridge: Cambridge University Press, 2003) explore some of the expectations of women's social conduct in this period. Kim M. Phillips, *Medieval Maidens: Young Women and Gender in England, 1270–1540* (Manchester: Manchester University Press, 2003) draws on a broad range of sources to consider the upbringing, education, and training of women.

CHAPTER 29

GOSSIP AND (UN)OFFICIAL WRITING

SUSAN E. PHILLIPS

The Yeoman's gossip

The Prologue to the 'Canon's Yeoman's Tale' would appear to be a cautionary narrative about the dangers that gossip poses to the master–servant relationship. It depicts in vivid detail a conversational exchange in which a loyal servant succumbs to the pleasures of idle talk, betraying his master's closely held secrets in the process. The master's stern reprimand, 'Thou sclaunderest me heere in this compaignye, | And eek discoverest that thou sholdest hyde', proves to be no match for the conversational manoeuvres of an inveterate gossip, as the Host assails the unsuspecting Yeoman.[1] In his attempt to penetrate the Yeoman's code of silence, the Host deploys everything from polite encouragement, 'Telle me that, and that I thee biseche' (l. 639), to feigned concern for the Canon's affairs, 'Where dwelle ye, if it to telle be?' (l. 656); from forced intimacy, 'yit lat me talk to the' (l. 663) to the promise of safe haven, 'telle on, what so bityde, | Of al his thretyng rekke nat a myte!' (ll. 697–8). The Canon can do nothing but listen helplessly while his servant's speech yields to this persuasion, as rehearsed professional patter gives way to shared conversational intimacy: 'therefore keepe it secree, I yow preye' (l. 643). Seeing that exposure is inevitable, the ashamed Canon quickly flees the group, leaving his servant to gossip freely about his misdeeds, an opportunity the Yeoman immediately seizes: 'Syn that my lord is goon, I wol nat spare; | Swich thyng as I knowe, I wol declare' (ll. 718–19).

This scene could be interpreted as a demonstration of gossip's capacity for and tendency toward social transgression, its usefulness as a weapon of the

---

[1] 'The Canon's Yeoman's Prologue', VIII. 695–6, in *The Riverside Chaucer*, ed. Larry D. Benson, (Boston: Houghton Mifflin, 1987).

disempowered. Indeed the pressure to arrive at such a reading is almost irresistible. At the level of the text, the Host frames the Yeoman's speech in exactly this way, attempting to broker an alliance with him by repeatedly asking him to speak not about himself but about his 'lord'. For the Host, the Canon's Yeoman's membership in the community of pilgrims is predicated on his willingness to talk about his master, as gossip forges a conversational bond between social equals at the expense of a hierarchical professional relationship. Late medieval authorities would encourage precisely this reading of gossip's 'evil werke'. Warnings about the subversiveness of idle talk fill the pages of penitential manuals and courtesy books, as young men are warned not be to 'tale-wijs', avoiding both the unmannerliness of gossip at their lord's table and the sedition of gossiping about his affairs.[2] What is more, recent critical debate about gossip would all but require this reading of idle talk as social transgression. Building on the pioneering work of Patricia Spacks, scholars have interpreted gossip as a mode of resistance, a subversive speech that '*will not be suppressed*'.[3] Feminists, queer theorists, and scholars of minority discourses have suggested the larger social and literary stakes of this subversive speech, arguing that gossip is the 'resistant oral discourse of marginalized groups', a means of critiquing majority culture and protecting community interests.[4]

Such a reading of the Yeoman's exchange with the Host, however, would miss the myriad ways in which gossip functions, not only in the 'Canon's Yeoman's Tale', but also, I would suggest, in late medieval English culture more generally. Much more is at stake in this scene than the damage that a servant's idle talk can do to his master; for the Canon's Yeoman's gossip does not simply divulge the Canon's shortcomings, but also illuminates the ways in which gossip is both implicated in and fundamental to the narrative experimentation at the heart of this tale. Moreover, although the 'Canon's Yeoman's Tale' explicitly takes gossip as its thematic, the lessons it teaches about the relationship between gossip and narrative practice are not reducible to this fact. Rather, the tale reveals the ways in which gossip might inform and indeed provide the model for late medieval narrative, suggesting that idle talk functions not just as the transgressive speech of the disempowered, but, more centrally, as the discursive tool of 'official' culture.

---

[2] Frederick J. Furnivall (ed.), *How the Wise Man taught his Son, The Babees Book*, EETS, os 32 (London: Oxford University Press, 1868), 48–52, l. 26.

[3] Patricia Meyer Spacks, *Gossip* (Chicago: University of Chicago Press, 1985), 263. I am indebted to Spacks's suggestive study, particularly her first two chapters, on gossip's reputation and its 'problematics'.

[4] Karma Lochrie, *Covert Operations: The Medieval Uses of Secrecy* (Philadelphia: University of Pennsylvania Press, 1999), 57. See also Patricia Turner, *I Heard it Through the Grapevine: Rumor in African-American Culture* (Berkeley and Los Angeles: University of California Press, 1993); Deborah Jones, 'Gossip: Notes on Women's Oral Culture', *Women's Studies International Quarterly*, 3 (1980), 193–8; and Jennifer Coates, 'Gossip Revisited: Language in All-Female Groups', in Jennifer Coates and Deborah Cameron (eds.), *Women and their Speech Communities: New Perspectives in Language and Sex* (London: Longman, 1988), 94–122.

This revelation has implications not just for the larger literary canon of Chaucer's works, but for stories which scholars typically treat as a wholly distinct narrative form—the exemplary tales of late medieval English preachers. For, as I will suggest, gossip is as central to Robert Mannyng's exemplarity as it is to Chaucer's narrative experimentation. Moving gossip from the transgressive margins to the official centre will turn out to have quite far-reaching consequences, forcing us to rethink our understanding not only of Chaucerian poetics but of late medieval pastoral practice.

Gossip's narrative alchemy

Troubled by its incongruous asides, ill-fitting moral commentary, structural incon-sistencies, and genre bending, scholars have branded the 'Canon's Yeoman's Tale' an 'imperfect' narrative, an earlier Chaucerian text that has been unsuccessfully adapted to the *Canterbury Tales*.[5] Although the tale may indeed have been written for another occasion, its problematic features need not be the result of careless revision. Rather, I would suggest this tale, which takes as its subject all manner of alchemical intrigue, adopts alchemy as its *modus operandi*, combining and transmuting its 'problematic' narrative features by means of an unexpected and therefore overlooked catalyst: gossip's idle talk. More than simply a demonstration of the dangers of a servant's wagging tongue or a comic illustration of the Host's penchant for idle talk, the gossipy exchange between the Canon's Yeoman and the Host initiates the narrative alchemy of the tale. Over the course of the Prologue, the Canon's 'tale' is supplanted by the Yeoman's gossip—a substitution and conflation that will continue to characterize this narrative. Indeed, it is this intermingling of fiction and idle talk that enables the structural, rhetorical, and generic experiments that define this tale.

What precisely constitutes the Canon's Yeoman's 'tale' has been long been the subject of contention among Chaucerians, for the Yeoman's promise of full disclosure—'I wol nat spare; | Swich thyng as that I knowe, I wol declare' (ll. 718–19)—introduces not one narrative but two. In the first, he recounts the failed alchemical endeavours of his employer and mentor; in the second, he depicts the infamous swindling of a morally bankrupt canon. The two potentially distinct narratives, however, comprise the singular 'Canon's Yeoman's Tale'. What would be autobiographical prologue for another pilgrim is for the Canon's Yeoman the first part of his tale, while the tale proper, the 'pars secunda' as it is commonly

---

[5] 'Incongruous' asides have often served as the focal point for this dissatisfaction. The critical reception of the 'Canon's Yeoman's Tale' has been amply documented by John Reidy in his notes to the *Riverside Chaucer*, 946–8. More recently, George Kaiser has surveyed scholarly frustration with the tale's conclusion. 'The Conclusion of the *Canon's Yeoman's Tale*: Readings and (Mis)readings', *Chaucer Review*, 35 (2000), 1–21.

called, begins without any formal marker to distinguish it from what has preceded. Indeed, the structural instability of 'prologue' and 'tale' is more pronounced in the Canon's Yeoman's narrative than at any other point in the *Canterbury Tales*. The Canon's Yeoman does not offer the 'My tale I wol bigyne' of the Pardoner (VI. 462) or the Wife of Bath (III. 828), but instead refers to both parts as his 'tale'.[6] Although modern editors insist on the separation of the two parts, inserting the rubric 'pars secunda', medieval readers were unwilling or unable to make that distinction: the manuscripts that preserve the tale fail to offer a consistent division between its two halves.[7] Without editorial intervention, the separation between autobiography and fiction collapses, as the audience is left to wonder whether the Yeoman's Canon and the wicked canon of the second part are one and the same—left to wonder, that is, where gossip ends and narrative begins.

The blurring of the personal and the fictional that takes place in the 'Canon's Yeoman's Tale' is more than an incidental structural conflation owing to the absence of formal divisions between the tale's component parts; it is a defining feature of the narrative's rhetoric. Caught up in the permissive atmosphere created by the Host, the Canon's Yeoman is at constant pains to assure his audience both that his 'tale' will disclose closely held secrets—'Now he is goon, I dar seyn boldely' (l. 902)—and that this narrative 'shal tellen more' (l. 1167), titillating his audience with the promise of his unexpurgated and illicit gossip.[8] What is more, when he moves from the first tale to the second, he continues to represent his narrative as gossip, insisting on the actual rather than merely fictive presence of the second tale's canon—'Ther is a chanoun of religioun | Amonges us' (ll. 972–3). Forgoing the fictional distance of 'whilom', he proceeds to tell a present-tense story of a canon who lives among us now, who beguiles today, who practises his mischief perhaps at this very moment. Here, in the Yeoman's rather unorthodox use of the present tense, gossip commandeers conventional narrative rhetoric, so that

---

[6] The Canon's Yeoman concludes both narratives with a similar formulation, ending the first with 'By that I of my tale have maad an ende' (l. 971) and the second with 'And there a poynt, for ended is my tale' (l. 1480). The Wife of Bath similarly refers to both prologue and tale as her 'tale'; exclamations like 'Now wol I telle forth my tale' (III. 193) and 'A ha! By God, I have my tale ageyn' (III. 586) both refer to her Prologue. Yet the beginning of the 'Wife of Bath's Tale' is clearly marked by both the Wife's own remarks, 'Now wol I seye my tale, if ye wol heere' (III. 828) and the Friar's frustrated recognition that the initial 'tale' was merely a 'preamble' (III. 831).

[7] Of the extant manuscripts, twenty-nine indicate no division whatsoever at l. 972 (the point at which the 'pars secunda' conventionally begins); ten mark this line with a capital; a further three use marginal notation to call attention to it; and only Ellesmere offers the Latin rubric adopted by the *Riverside Chaucer*, 'Explicit prima pars, Et sequitur pars secunda'. John M. Manly and Edith Rickert, *The Text of the Canterbury Tales* (Chicago: University of Chicago Press, 1940), III. 533–7. For a detailed discussion of the manuscripts and the consequences of their inconsistent divisions, see Albert E. Hartung, ' "Pars secunda" and the Development of the *Canon's Yeoman's Tale*', *Chaucer Review*, 12/2 (1977), 111–28.

[8] In just over 900 lines, the 'Canon's Yeoman's Prologue and Tale' uses the verb 'to tell' thirty-three times, more than any other text in the *Canterbury Tales* with the exception of the much longer offerings of the Man of Law and the Wife of Bath.

the 'tale' continues to sound like idle talk, implicating ever more narratives and characters in its proliferating conversation.

So clear is gossip's capacity for discursive appropriation that the Yeoman makes numerous disclaimers attempting to proscribe the limits of his speech. He not only informs his audience that he is no longer discussing his former employer, but also reassures the potential canons in his audience that the trickery he describes pertains only to this particular 'shrewe' (l. 995). Taken as awkward and intrusive, these remarks have been interpreted as evidence that Chaucer has not adequately adapted to the *Canterbury Tales* a narrative originally written for another context.[9] Far from incongruous, however, the Yeoman's remarks, understood as disclaimers, make perfect sense in relation both to the Prologue and to the *Canterbury Tales* more generally. That these disclaimers constitute an abrupt shift in the Yeoman's usual mode of address, turning from the audience as a collective to specific individuals within it, need not be taken as proof of the tale's disunity. Although it is true that elsewhere in the 'pars secunda' the narrator refers to his audience with the plural 'sires', his singling out of the Host is far from arbitrary:

> This chanon was my lord, ye wolden weene?
> Sire hoost, in feith, and by the hevenes queeene,
> It was another chanoun, and nat hee,
> That kan an hundred foold moore subtiltee.   (ll. 1088–91)

Given the Host's aggressive interest in the Canon's affairs, the Yeoman's specific address to the potential misconceptions of the overly curious Host is perfectly understandable, especially since the Host is the character most likely to assume ('weene') and indeed hope that the tale is a further exposé. Similarly, the reassurances offered to the 'worshipful Chanons religious' reflect the Yeoman's concern over the offensive and proliferating potential of his speech.

In fact, the Yeoman is so disconcerted by the ever-expanding implications of his narrative gossip that, immediately following his apology to the canons, he retreats into the safety of the fictional past: the canon who used to be among us now tricks a priest who *was* in London. That the shift is significant rather than accidental, that it denotes not a seam between unassimilated texts but a transition to the past tense of fiction, is evidenced by that fact that it occurs in all of the manuscripts containing the tale and remains in effect for the duration of the narrative. Indeed, several of Chaucer's early readers acknowledged the significance of the shift, identifying the Yeoman's adoption of the past tense as the beginning of the 'tale'.[10] Even as

---

[9] Hartung, following Manly and others, has argued that in combination, the two remarks indicate the ambiguous state of Chaucer's draft (O[1]). Hartung, 'Pars secunda'; John Matthews Manly, *Some New Light on Chaucer* (London: Bell, 1926), 235–52.

[10] Three manuscripts of different textual traditions make this claim: Holkham Hall, MS 667 opens l. 1012 with a large capital; Fitzwilliam Museum, MS McClean 181 offers the heading, 'The Chanons Yeman'; and most striking of all, Harley 7334 uses a marginal 'Narrat' to declare that the tale begins

the Canon's Yeoman attempts to distance himself from the blurring of gossip and fiction he has created here, explicitly rejecting the present tense of idle talk, he continues to demonstrate gossip's potential as a poetic device. Despite his pretence to fictional distance, his idle talk remains the tale's narrative mode.

Accompanying and indeed superseding gossip's rhetorical appropriations and structural conflations is its generic alchemy, as idle talk in the Canon's Yeoman's narrative enables a seemingly endless series of generic experiments. What begins as an individual confession, in which the Yeoman reveals how destitute alchemical enquiry has made him personally—'Al that I hadde I have lost therby' (l. 722)—quickly becomes a tell-all exposé of his infamous profession, 'I wol speke of oure werk' (l. 749), as the atmosphere of speaking everything draws professional secrets into the conversation. Under the guise of both, the Yeoman delivers an alchemical treatise, an amalgamation of scientific lore drawn from a variety of authorities.[11] The genre-shifting here is not superficial: the 'tale' did in fact pass for a legitimate scientific treatise; late medieval readers identified Chaucer as an alchemical authority on the basis of this *Tale*.[12] The Canon's Yeoman's narrative does not, however, read like the Parson's penitential manual, in which the text stands *as* treatise. Instead, by presenting lists of substances, equipment, and techniques as disclosed secrets, Chaucer uses gossip to translate treatise into 'tale'.

The generic alchemy of the 'Canon's Yeoman's Tale' serves not only to enliven scientific discourse, but also to lend legitimacy to this unconventional narrative. Concluding the first part of his tale with a moral, the Yeoman combines confession, exposé, and treatise to create an exemplum: 'he that semeth the wiseste, by Jhesus, | Is moost fool, whan it cometh to the preef; | And he that semeth trewest is a theef' (ll. 967–9). Couched as a disclosure about his alchemical community—'Right so, lo, fareth it amonges us' (l. 966)—the moral is both a continuation of the Yeoman's idle talk and his attempt to recuperate it as instructive. This recuperative manoeuvre is repeated in the 'pars secunda', where generic alchemy consists not

---

at 1012. Manly and Rickert, *Text*, 535. While none of these manuscripts is considered 'authoritative', they nonetheless give evidence that fifteenth-century readers recognized the past tense as a marker of the fictional.

[11] While the precise identity of Chaucer's alchemical sources remains uncertain, several scholars have shown his borrowings from particular texts. Pauline Aiken argues that he relies exclusively on Vincent of Beauvais's *Speculum naturale*, while Edgar Duncan demonstrates Chaucer's indebtedness to late medieval alchemical texts, such as the *book Senior*, Gerber's *Sum of Perfection*, and Arnaldus of Villanova's works. Pauline Aiken, 'Vincent of Beauvais and Chaucer's Knowledge of Alchemy', *Studies in Philology*, 41 (1944), 371–89; and Edgar H. Duncan, 'The Literature of Alchemy and Chaucer's Canon's Yeoman's Tale: Framework, Theme, and Characters', *Speculum*, 43 (1968), 641–6.

[12] As George Kaiser demonstrates, late medieval and early modern alchemy enthusiasts 'regarded Chaucer as a fellow student of the art (or science)'. 'Conclusion', 3. Kaiser provides a detailed and insightful discussion of the tale's early reception history. Two citations form the basis for the scholarly consensus about Chaucer's status as alchemical authority: Thomas Norton's 1477 reference to the tale in the *Ordinal of Alchemy* (1159–66) and Elias Ashmole's inclusion of the tale in his 1652 alchemical compendium, *Theatrum chemicum Britannicum*.

in the translation of treatise into exposé, but in the fusing of generic opposites, as fabliau trickery compounds with sober exemplarity.[13] Chaucer has of course tested the permeability of the boundaries between these two genres elsewhere in the *Canterbury Tales* in the hybrid offerings of the Friar and Summoner, but here the reaction runs in reverse. Rather than an exemplum operating under fabliau rules, the 'pars secunda' is a fabliau about alchemical trickery transmuted into a moral tale. The transformation into exemplum does not consist solely in the addition of a concluding moral. Not only does the tale end with the lesson that Christ is the source of true alchemy (ll. 1472–81), but throughout the narrative the Yeoman encourages his audience to condemn rather than laugh at the false canon's trickery. He does so, however, through a series of exclamatory asides, which, in the context of his previous gossip, establish conversational intimacy rather than exemplary distance. Declarations like 'the foule feend hym fecche!' (l. 1159) and 'yvele moot he cheeve [fare]!' (l. 1225) cannot help but resonate with his earlier complaints about his master, 'the foule feend hym quelle!' (l. 705). Perpetually anxious that his 'tale' not be taken as gossip, the Yeoman insists that he takes no pleasure in revealing the Canon's trickery, claiming that he only offers it as a public service:

> It weerieth me to telle of his falsnesse,
> And nathelees yet wol I it expresse,
> To th'entente that men may be war therby,
> And for noon oother cause, trewely.   (ll. 1304–7)

Although he insists that his intent is virtuous, what comes across most clearly in the Yeoman's disclaimer is not his weariness at having to expose such behaviour, but his willingness to disclose yet more details about it. That is, he protests too much, implying the very motive he pretends to eschew. For the Canon's Yeoman, the turn to exemplum, like the retreat into the past tense of fiction, is an attempt to distance himself from the proliferating dangers of idle talk. Yet it is in precisely these moments of abjuration that the Yeoman reveals the unlimited potential of gossip as a poetic technique, for his tactics of renunciation are themselves wholly dependent upon idle talk.

Recognizing gossip as the *modus operandi* of the 'Canon's Yeoman's Tale' allows us not only to recuperate the 'problematic' details of this narrative as its essential

---

[13] The tale's straddling of the two genres is reflected in the variety of sources and analogues scholars have proposed for it. While no exact source for the tale has been found, several analogues have been proposed, both fabliau and exemplum. Willa Folch-Pi connects the tricks in the 'tale' to a story by Ramón Lull. Willa Babcock Folch-Pi, 'Ramon Llull's Felix and Chaucer's Canon's Yeoman's Tale', *Notes and Queries*, 212 (1967), 10–11. Spargo suggests that a similar trick occurs in the *Novelle* of Sercambi. John W. Spargo, 'The Canon's Yeoman's Tale', in W. Bryan and G. Dempster, *Sources and Analogues of Chaucer's Canterbury Tales* (Chicago, 1941), 685–95. Reyes has recently argued that Chaucer was influenced by Exemplum 20 of Don Juan Manuel's 'El Conde Lucanor'. Jesus L. Serrano Reyes, *Didactismo y moralismo en Geoffrey Chaucer y Don Juan Manuel* (Córdoba: Universidad de Córdoba, 1996), 251–368.

features, but also to view this 'imperfect' tale as emblematic of the larger project of the *Canterbury Tales*. That is, considering this alchemical tale from the perspective of idle talk reveals how central gossip might be to Chaucerian poetics. Whereas the Host certainly demonstrates his gossiping acumen in the Prologue to this tale, he acts as gossip's agent throughout the *Tales*. Commenting on the tales of his fellow pilgrims and stirring up an atmosphere of speaking everything with his repeated injunctions to 'spare it nat' (III. 1763), he enables verbal exchanges which seem to reproduce actual gossip. His gossip in fact serves as the framework for the *Canterbury Tales*, providing not only the links between them but also the mechanism by which Chaucer transforms old stories into new tales. Moreover, treating gossip as a fundamental feature of Chaucerian poetics might allow us to recognize the Wife of Bath, not simply as a marginalized woman who uses her gossip (both with her audience and her female gossips) to subvert 'auctoritee'—although she certainly is this—but as the apotheosis of Chaucerian small talk. Through gossip, Chaucer transforms a text composed almost entirely of antifeminist stereotypes into a larger-than-life character.

Gossip and pastoral narrative

If gossip can prove to be so fruitful a tool in the hands of a vernacular poet, can it be equally productive for other types of narrative? Could gossip, for example, prove useful for pastoral purposes as well as literary ones, influencing and perhaps structuring late medieval exemplary practice? Given the perpetual complaints of late medieval preachers against idle talk, this suggestion might initially seem improbable. Clerical condemnation of gossip is universal in Middle English pastoral literature, as clerics across England attempt to gain verbal control over their chattering congregations. Preachers browbeat parishioners with seemingly endless lists of verbal transgressions and turn countless exempla to the purpose of condemning idle talk, depicting the gruesome fates awaiting those sinners who delight in idle tales. So pervasive is the problem of gossip that it merits its own devil, Tutivillus, the recording demon who is invoked by clerics with such frequency that he becomes part of the cultural imagination.[14] However, preachers do not simply rail against gossip; they traffic in it, enticing parishioners with detailed stories that come dangerously close to the congregation's unlicensed tale-telling. That is, exemplarity emulates gossip.

---

[14] In addition to his countless appearances in the exempla of Middle English penitential manuals and sermon collections, Tutivillus menaces parishioners in numerous wall paintings, stained glass windows, and misericords, creates mischief on manuscript flyleaves, and plays a starring role in late medieval morality plays. For a comprehensive account of the demon's popularity and an extensive catalogue of his literary and pastoral appearances, see Margaret Jennings, 'Tutivillus: The Literary Career of the Recording Demon', *Studies in Philology*, 74 (1977), 1–95.

The line between idle tales and orthodox exemplary practice is nowhere more blurred than in Robert Mannyng's *Handlyng Synne*. Mannyng's exemplary practice trades on the entertainment value of the exemplum, a tactic he makes explicit in the introduction to his text. He has undertaken the task of translating this work into English, he declares, because so many parishioners love to listen to 'trotouale' (idle tales).[15] Taking advantage of the fact that so many men 'wyl blethly here' tales in any venue—'Yn gamys, yn festys, & at the ale' (l. 47)—Mannyng entices his audience into pastoral instruction through the promise of compelling tales of his own. By substituting his authorized narratives for his congregation's idle tales, Mannyng attempts to replace sinful recreation with the more spiritually productive work of religious devotion, recognizing all the while, however, that he can only achieve this substitution by catering to the sinful tastes of his audience.

Although Mannyng embraces the exemplum's ability to entertain, he recognizes that his narratives have a dangerous affinity with idle talk. He brushes past the more common criticism of exemplary practice—that it supplants the Gospels with classical fables and new verse chronicles, sullying the pulpit with 'newe soteltes'[16]—but admits instead to a more particular anxiety: that, even when performed by an authorized preacher and derived from an authoritative source, exemplary narration might nonetheless be a species of gossip. When he describes the contents of his text, Mannyng asserts that his exemplary practice is above reproach, offering the following protective disclaimer:

> Talys shalt thou fynde ther ynne,
> And chauncys that haue happyd for synne;
> Merueylys, some as y fond wretyn,
> And outhyr that haue be seye & wetyn [witnessed; known];
> None be ther ynne more ne lesse
> But that y fond wrete or hadde wytnesse.
> Tharfore may hyt & gode skyl why [for good reason],
> Handlyng synne be clepyd oponly.
> For hyt touchyth no pryuyte [private matters],
> But opon synne that callyd may be.   (ll. 131–40)

---

[15] *Handlyng Synne*, ed. Idelle Sullens (Binghamton, NY: Medieval and Renaissance Texts & Studies, 1983), l. 48. As Mark Miller observes, 'trotouale' appears to be a 'favorite word' of Mannyng's. 'Displaced Souls, Idle Talk, Spectacular Scenes: *Handlyng Synne* and the Perspective of Agency', *Speculum*, 71 (1996), 606–32, at 626. Indeed, Mannyng seems to have been one of the few English writers to use the word; and while the other two texts in which the word appears offer only a unique instance, Mannyng uses the word four times in this text. *OED, MED*, s.v. 'trotëvale'.

[16] *The Order of the Priesthood, The English Works of Wycliffe*, ed. F. D. Matthew (London: Kegan Paul, Trench, Trubner & Co., 1880), 175. Even as ecclesiastical authorities championed the exemplum's persuasive powers, anxiety over the questionable use of these stories was widespread, as authorities attempted to determine which sources were acceptable for exemplary narratives. While most orthodox commentators accept patristic writers as exemplary sources, they cast suspicion on chronicles, romances, and classical texts. For a detailed discussion of this controversy, see H. Leith Spencer, *English Preaching in the Late Middle Ages* (Oxford: Clarendon Press, 1993), 78–91.

He will tell many marvellous tales, but will reveal 'no pryuyte'. Unlike the transgressive details of other people's private and backbiting gossip, his tales are in the realm of the public, they concern matters already well known, or that at least speak of sins already revealed.[17] Yet even as Mannyng establishes the legitimacy of his narratives, he advertises them as compelling. More prominent in this disclaimer than the fact that his text abjures private matters is the fact that it contains no more or less than all the tales, adventures, and marvels that have ever been recorded. While Mannyng insists that his exempla have proper authority, the nature of that authority is suspect, for he claims to rely not only on traditional *auctoritas*, what has already been written, but also on his own experience and on the experience of his acquaintances. Moreover, Mannyng's assertion of authority through stories that have 'be seye or wetyn' or that he 'hadde wytnesse' is dangerously close to gossip's own verifying rhetoric: 'I heard it from so-and-so who was there,' 'I saw it with my own eyes.'

Throughout his text, Mannyng acknowledges the potential slippage between exemplarity and gossip, as he reminds both himself and his congregation that his tale-telling sermons are always in danger of spilling over into the realm of gossip's 'ydel tales'. At the conclusion to one exemplum, appropriately about a backbiting monk, Mannyng quickly catches himself before committing the sin that he expounds:

> Thys tale y wote and vndyrstande
> Where hyt fyl yn ynglande,
> At a ful namecouth [famous] abbeye
> That y ne wyle telle ne bewreye.
> Swych peyne ys for hem dyght [prepared]
> That kun nat kepe here tung ryght.   (ll. 3617–22)

Mannyng's concluding warning, here, is a provocative variation on Scanlon's argument about the relationship between the exemplum and its moral. Here, not only is the moral 'apprehended narratively', growing organically out of, and confirming, the narrative, but also it runs the risk of being too successful a confirmation, coming dangerously close to being another instance of that narrative.[18] Proclaiming that he is withholding information in order to protect both himself and his audience from

---

[17] Mannyng's preoccupation with committing this verbal sin is evidenced by the fact that he makes a similar disclaimer even earlier in the text, as he outlines his project: 'Of pryuytees speke y nought; | The pryuytees wyl y nought name | For noun tharfore shuld me blame' (ll. 30–2). It is almost as if the very premiss of *Handlyng Synne* requires such a disavowal.

[18] Larry Scanlon, *Narrative, Authority, Power: The Medieval Exemplum and the Chaucerian Tradition* (Cambridge: Cambridge University Press, 1994), 30: 'the moral can only be apprehended narratively. Indeed, it can only be apprehended narratively because it is produced narratively.' 'The Manciple's Tale' provides a humorous echo of Mannyng's concern. To his exemplum about the dangers of not holding one's tongue, the Manciple adds a fifty-line *moralitas*, in which he ventriloquizes his mother's voice. What she provides in the form of advice from parent to child is a monotonous list of proverbs and parables about idle speech. The tale, it seems, is actually about jangling, as many of the species of

sin, he first assures them that he knows the identity of the abbey, and then refuses to reveal its name. By claiming that his tale took place in a famous abbey in England that shall remain nameless, Mannyng renders his exemplum more immediate, more transgressive, more like the tales of his chattering congregation. These moments on the verge of transgression and the tenuous disclaimers that accompany them are precisely what make Mannyng's exempla so engaging and persuasive. The problem with his sensationalizing rhetoric, however, is that it renders the exemplum an instance of that which it seeks to control. Even while this posturing gives the exemplum its power to bridle the congregation's chatter, it makes the exemplum complicit in that tale-telling.

Mannyng's identification of backbiting as the sin to which his exemplary practice is susceptible is a complicated mixture of advertising, confession, and diversion, for the sin he commits here is not backbiting. He nonetheless insists on his need to be vigilant about that particular sin. In fact, this is one of the few instances in which Mannyng calls for a general, communal shriving: 'Of thys synne y rede we vs shryue | And take oure penaunce by oure lyue' (ll. 3631–2). Whereas his moralizations usually address the congregation in the second person plural, here, he includes himself among the sinners who need to atone for this specific transgression. But Mannyng clearly stays within the letter of the law on backbiting. Not only have the Monk's transgressions been recounted in numerous exempla, but also Mannyng does not traffic in the Monk's 'privitee': he does not disclose either the abbey's identity or the Monk's name. While the Monk reveals his identity to his former colleague within the narrative—'and tolde hys name' (l. 3604)—Mannyng does not convey this private information to his audience. Nor does he attempt to slander surreptitiously this anonymous English monk. This is not, for example, the Pardoner's barely concealed slander, through which the audience knows the subject of his story despite the Pardoner's omission of proper names. Mannyng's exemplum is not malicious nor is it unprofitable, for its content is morally useful to its audience, or at least has the intent of being so. Yet, with its emphasis on the 'curiouse' and the sensational, it is a manner of deviant speech—it is the 'jangling' of idle talk. The notion of jangling I raise here is not the fear of ineffectual or unproductive speech which Mark Miller suggests haunts Mannyng throughout his text—the perhaps common concern of a priest that his words, for all his good intentions, are unprofitable.[19] Nor is this the jangling that preoccupies Langland—the idle speech

idle speech find their way into her discussion. But in its seemingly endless repetition of injunctions against too much speaking, the Manciple's *moralitas* (or at least his mother's) commits the sin against which it speaks, with jangling triumphing over its condemnation.

[19] Miller, 'Displaced Souls', 626–32. Miller's rich and suggestive essay does much to reveal both the complexity of Mannyng's exemplary practice and its connection with idle talk, but for Miller, idle talk constitutes not gossip but ineffective pastoral speech. As a consequence, he overlooks the ways in which Mannyng's pastoral practice trades on gossip's rhetoric in an attempt to maintain his audience's attention.

that inappropriately debates matters of religion.[20] It is instead a transgression both more and less obvious than these two. By hiding behind his avoidance of backbiting, Mannyng camouflages his gossip.

For all his disclaimers to the contrary, throughout this text, Mannyng plays blatantly and deliberately with the line between idle talk and productive salvific speech, repeatedly reminding his readers that his tales are no 'tryfyls' even as he draws on the attention-grabbing power of the 'trotouale' (idle tales). Not simply a favourite term or a constant preoccupation, 'trotouale' are his narrative mode—the mechanism through which he transforms narratives derived from exemplary authorities into the new and exciting tales in which his audience so delights. While he begins his text with 'a tale of autoryte' (l. 168) 'wretyn al and sum | Yn a boke of vitas patrum' (ll. 169–70), his citation of patristic authority quickly gives way to the advertising rhetoric of the 'trotouale': 'Y shal yow telle what me was told | Of a prest that sagh and fond | Thys chaunce yn the holy lond' (ll. 1252–4). Despite this titillating introduction, the narrative preceded by this claim does not come from the first-hand account of a priest who travelled to the Holy Land, but directly from his source, the *Manuel des pechiez*. That is, Mannyng cleverly alters the convention of citing 'auctoritee', using it not as a means to legitimize his narratives with actual authorities, but as a way to transform his borrowed tales into the latest news by pretending that they are eyewitness accounts. Just as Mannyng manipulates 'auctoritee' in order to make his narratives more immediate, so he alters the setting of these tales. When he adds narratives of his own to the collection, he emphasizes the novel and immediate, rather than the distant and the authoritative. Of the seven original exempla that he contributes to his text, four are set explicitly in England, with one occurring quite close to home in Lincolnshire.[21] These are tales introduced as coming not from revered 'auctoritees' but from Mannyng's own experience: 'Yn cambrygshere, yn a toune | Y herd telle of a persoune' (ll. 6173–4). Even tales he borrows from appropriate authorities

---

[20] See Joan Heiges Blythe, 'Sins of the Tongue and Rhetorical Prudence in "Piers Plowman"', in Richard G. Newhauser and John A. Alford (eds.), *Literature and Religion in the Later Middle Ages* (Binghamton, NY: Medieval and Renaissance Texts and Studies, 1995), 119–42; and Linda J. Clifton, 'Struggling with Will: Jangling, Sloth, and Thinking in *Piers Plowman* B', in Míceál F. Vaughan (eds.), *Suche Werkis to Werche: Essays on* Piers Plowman *in Honor of David C. Fowler* (East Lansing, MI: Colleagues Press, 1993), 29–52.

[21] Fritz Kemmler lists five original exempla: the tale of the witch and the cow-sucking bag (l. 499), the tale of Bishop Grosteste (l. 4743), the tale of the Norfolk bondman and the cattle that defile the churchyard (l. 8669), the tale of the derelict midwife (l. 9627), and the tale of the bishop's corpse (l. 11083). *'Exempla' in Context: A Historical and Critical Study of Robert Mannyng of Brunne's 'Handlyng Synne'* (Tübingen: Gunter Narr Verlag, 1984), appendix IV, 202–4. To these, following Idelle Sullens, I add the tale of the Suffolk man (l. 10403) and the tale of the Cambridgeshire parson (l. 6175). Sullens, *Handlyng Synne*, appendix II, 381–7. These two exempla do not appear in the *Manuel des pechiez* and are listed by Tubach (nos. 3213c and 1487, respectively) as unique occurrences. Frederic C. Tubach, *Index exemplorum: A Handbook of Medieval Religious Tales* (Helsinki: Suomalainen Tiedeakatemia, 1969).

are altered to make them more immediate both in time and place. The tale of the wicked executors gains a location as the tale of the wicked Kesteven executors, as the exemplum takes place not far away, but here in the audience's very midst: 'Y shal yow telle of a kas | That fyl now late yn kesteuene, | But the name y wyl nat neuene' (ll. 6378–80). Mannyng moves his exempla from the timeless past of gospel and patristic history into the here and now of Lincolnshire. Thus the danger of backbiting he voices here becomes quite real. Yet, read against the earlier remark from the tale of the backbiting monk, this disclaimer must be understood as something more than an avoidance of sin. Just as with that earlier disclaimer, Mannyng uses this remark to generate curiosity in his audience. He offers the temptation to privy details, but withholds those details, as a way of simultaneously denying the idleness of his narratives and exploiting it.

Mannyng's exemplary practice thus trades on—and inspires—his audience's desire for illicit specificity. While he never completely capitulates to that desire, he all but does so in his most elaborate exemplum, the 'Dancers of Colbek'. Announcing that he will tell a marvellous story that is 'as soth as the gospel' (l. 9014), he proceeds to deliver a narrative consumed with idle talk. Yet his preoccupation with idle speech, here, is not, as Miller suggests, a worry about his own potentially inefficacious teaching or his sentimentalizing rhetoric, but rather a further extension of the curious tale-telling in which that teaching often engages. A narrative obsessed with naming, this exemplum provides more specific and identifying details than any other in Mannyng's collection, a fact he makes clear as he introduces the tale. Opening with a statement of 'auctoritee' that would seem more appropriate for a conversational familiar than a congregation, he promises to admit his audience to a body of secret knowledge: 'Here names of alle thus fond ywrete [written], | And as y wote, now shul ye wete [learn]' (ll. 9027–8). In keeping with his aversion for backbiting, throughout his text, Mannyng reveals names only when they belong to holy men and church fathers who witness, but do not commit, sin. Here, however, he tells a tale of a priest named Robert, resident of the town of Colbek during the reign of King Edward, preacher at the church of St Magnus, and father of two children, Ayone and Aue, who was menaced one Christmas by carollers named Gerleu, Merswynde, and Wybessyne. The tale, as Miller has shown, is as much about Robert's failings—his unprofitable admonitions, his idle and ill-advised swearing, his inability to control both his children and his temper—as it is about the carollers' sacrilege. Thus the narrative traffics in the distressing and private details of Robert's life, instead of the transgressions of an anonymous sinner. While the tale is not backbiting, since it speaks of sins already made open by other writers, it is nonetheless reliant on the illicit specificity of gossip's idle talk. Nor need such a Robert have existed for Mannyng to trade on his secrets. Rather, it is the illusion of such disclosed 'pryuytee' that Mannyng uses to engage his audience. What he displays in the 'Dancers of Colbek' is not a concern over idle talk but an exploitation of it.

Gossip's official writing

If Mannyng's orthodox exemplarity can rely so heavily on gossip, then how many other aspects of late medieval culture might be modelled on this idle talk? Investigating gossip not as an unofficial discourse in direct conflict with official culture, but as speech that both appropriates and structures official practices, reveals the ways in which idle talk transforms the very tools that attempt to control it. Considering gossip in this way suggests the need to re-evaluate a number of authoritative discourses. The fact that preaching practice is so susceptible to and reliant upon gossip implies that other pastoral practices might be equally vulnerable. Indeed, confession is just as influenced by idle talk as is exemplarity. This is not simply because parishioners come to confession to gossip to their priests (rather than about them) nor because loose-tongued priests reveal confessional secrets, but because the rules governing confessional practice would seem to demand complete and explicitly detailed narratives that come dangerously close to idle talk. Gossip thus might be institutionally embedded, integral to both the theory and the practice of pastoral instruction, rather than merely the defiant chattering of unruly congregations.

Similarly, treating gossip as a discursive tool might require us to reconsider the relationship between idle talk and the discourse of courtesy. On pages of courtesy manuals, we see both the castigation of idle talk as immoral and unmannerly speech and the absolute reliance of courtesy discourse on gossip as the medium through which reputation is forged. We might thus be able to make sense of a declaration like the *Thewis of Gud Women*'s 'Gyf folk gud word behynd thar bak',[22] not as a clumsy formulation of a commonplace—speak well of your neighbour—but as an expression of the fundamental paradox at the heart of courtesy discourse: private gossip establishes public reputation, good or ill. The whispering in Chaucer's House of Rumor is the medium through which Fame is spread (*The House of Fame*, ll. 2110–20). Finally, recognizing the complicated ways in which gossip is deployed by 'official' culture might allow us to arrive at a more complete picture of gossip's 'unofficial' machinations. When we witness the gossips meeting in late medieval carols and ballads, we might be able to recognize in their idle talk not just their resistance to 'auctoritee', but their co-optation of it, as they remake pastoral and textual practice. Gossip was certainly as transgressive in the Middle Ages as it is in contemporary culture, but when we focus exclusively on its transgressive aspects we ignore the wider range of discursive appropriations that made idle talk both so problematic and so productive in late medieval England.

---

[22] Tauno F. Mustanoja (ed.), *The Thewis of Gud Women, The Good Wife Taught her Daughter, The Good Wyfe Wold a Pylgremage, and the Thewis of Gud Women* (Helsinki: Suomalaisen Kirjallisuuden Seuran Kirjapainon Oy, 1948), 18, l. 101.

FURTHER READING

In recent years, gossip has become something of a hot topic among scholars across a range of fields. Two competing models have dominated gossip theory in the social sciences. For explorations of gossip as an instrument of social control, see Max Gluckman, 'Gossip and Scandal', *Current Anthropology*, 4 (1963), 307–16; John Beard Haviland, *Gossip, Reputation, and Knowledge in Zinacantan* (Chicago: University of Chicago Press, 1977); and Sally Engle Merry, 'Rethinking Gossip and Scandal', in Donald Black (ed.), *Toward a General Theory of Social Control*, i: *The Fundamentals* (New York: Academic Press, 1984), 271–301. For discussions of gossip which focus on the individual speaker, interpreting this speech as 'social exchange', see Ralph R. Rosnow and Gary Alan Fine, *Rumor and Gossip: The Social Psychology of Hearsay* (New York: Elsevier, 1976); Luise White, 'Between Gluckman and Foucault: Historicizing Rumor and Gossip', *Social Dynamics*, 20/1 (1994), 75–92; Jörg R. Bergmann, *Discreet Indiscretions: The Social Organization of Gossip*, trans. John Bednarz Jr. (New York: Aldine de Gruyter, 1993) and Robin Dunbar, *Grooming, Gossip, and the Evolution of Language* (Cambridge, MA: Harvard University, 1996). For literary critical reformulations of gossip, see Patricia Spacks, *Gossip* (n. 3 above); Patricia Turner, *I Heard it Through the Grapevine: Rumor in African-American Culture* (n. 4); and Jan B. Gordon, *Gossip and Subversion in Nineteenth-Century British Fiction: Echo's Economies* (London: Macmillan, 1996).

Much less critical attention has been paid to gossip in the Middle Ages, but there is a small body of rich and suggestive work on the topic. For the relationship between medieval women and transgressive speech, see Karma Lochrie, *Covert Operations* (n. 4), esp. ch. 2, 'Tongues Wagging: Gossip, Women, and Indiscreet Secrets'; and Sandy Bardsley, *Venomous Tongues: Speech and Gender in Late Medieval England* (Philadelphia: University of Pennsylvania Press, 2006). For discussions of pastoral writing on sinful speech, see Edwin D. Craun's thorough and insightful study, *Lies, Slander and Obscenity in Medieval English Literature: Pastoral Rhetoric and the Deviant Speaker* (Cambridge: Cambridge University Press, 1997), as well as the essays in Edwin D. Craun (ed.), *The Hands of the Tongue: Essays on Deviant Speech* (Kalama 200, Medieval Institute, MI:). For 2007 gossip in Chaucer's poetry, see Stephen Manning, 'Fabular Jangling and Poetic Vision in the *Nun's Priest's Tale*', *South Atlantic Review*, 52 (1987), 3–16; William A. Quinn, 'Chaucer's Janglerye', *Viator*, 18 (1987), 309–20; and my 'Transforming Talk: The Problem with Gossip in Late Medieval England' (University Park, PA: Penn State University Press, 2007). Finally, for investigations of those suspect women known as the gossips, see Linda Woodbridge, *Women and the English Renaissance: Literature and the Nature of Womankind, 1540–1620* (Urbana: University of Illinois Press, 1984), 224–43; Gail Murray Gibson, 'Scene and Obscene: Seeing and Performing Late Medieval Childbirth', *Journal of Medieval and Early Modern Studies*, 29 (1999), 7–24; Mary Wack, 'Women, Work, and Plays in an English Medieval Town', in Susan Frye and Karen Robertson (eds.), *Maids and Mistresses, Cousins and Queens: Women's Alliances in Early Modern England* (Oxford: Oxford University Press, 1999), 33–51; Patricia Anne Anderson, 'Gossips, Ale-Wives, Midwives, and Witches' (dissertation, SUNY Buffalo, 1992); and my *Transforming Talk*, esp. ch. 4, 'The Gospel According to Gossips, or How Gossip Got its Name'.

CHAPTER 30

THE POETICS OF PRACTICALITY

LISA H. COOPER

'Quid mihi loqueris? Quid habes operis?' 'What do you say to me? What is your work?'[1] In this way, the monastic schoolmaster of Ælfric's *Colloquy*, a much-anthologized Latin vocabulary of around the year 1000, queries the boys who come to him, asking that he teach them 'to speak correctly, for we', they say, 'are unlearned, and speak badly' ('loqui latialiter recte, quia idiote sumus et corrupte loquimur') (ll. 2–3). So, from the outset of the didactic literary tradition in England, are the arts of discourse—of speaking, of writing, and ultimately, as this essay will suggest, of fiction-making—inextricably linked to labour and to the practical knowledge that makes that labour efficacious in the world. In response to his students' plea for speech ('locutio') that is both correct ('recta') and useful ('utile') (ll. 5–6), the master leads the boys to assume the roles of agricultural and craft workers—of ploughman and shepherd, of carpenter and blacksmith, to name just a few—and not only to describe but also to justify their daily tasks. 'How do you carry out your trade?' ('Quomodo exerces artem tuam?') he asks the 'hunter'; 'what do you work at for our use?' ('quid operaris nobis utilitatis?') he demands of the 'shoemaker'; and 'What do you say ... what is the use of your trade; or can we survive without you?' ('Quid dicis tu ... Cui prodest ars tua, aut si sine te possimus vitam ducere?') he presses the 'baker' (ll. 56, 167, 185–6). Within all these somewhat imperious queries, and especially within the first double-barrelled one (what do you *say* to me? what is your *work*?), lie some barely concealed assumptions about the relationship of language and action, of speech and practice, and most particularly of Latin literacy and manual labour. For the young oblates, who are being trained ultimately *not* to perform the tasks of which they talk but rather the *opus Dei*, the work of

---

[1] *Aelfric's Colloquy*, ed. G. N. Garmonsway, 2nd rev. edn. (Exeter: Exeter University Press, 1991), ll. 11–12; translation from 'Aelfric's *Colloquy*', in *Anglo-Saxon Prose*, ed. and trans. Michael Swanton (London: J. M. Dent, 1975), 107–115, at 108. The *Colloquy* is preserved in four manuscripts; one of these (British Library, Cotton MS Tiberius A.iii, that edited by Garmonsway) is provided with a continuous and interlinear Anglo-Saxon gloss; however, I quote only the Latin here, and further references will be made in the text to the line numbers of Garmonsway's edition.

prayer, to speak *is* to work and to work *is* to speak. And yet to speak, as their master here suggests, is first and foremost to speak of work *other* than the work of speaking.

The *Colloquy*—which quickly becomes a contest among the workers for pride of place (with the victory given to the monk on the one hand and, over the blacksmith's rather vociferous dismay, to the ploughman on the other (ll. 213–28))—is a fascinating text; it has long been recognized, and continues to be studied, for the way it opens up any number of windows upon the linguistic, social, technological, and of course pedagogical systems and situations of Anglo-Saxon England.[2] I turn to it here, however, as a useful springboard for some reflections about what my title refers to as the 'poetics of practicality' in the didactic literature of medieval England. My title might first, understandably, seem to imply an interest in the practicality of medieval poetics. In the opening of his *Poetria nova* (*c.*1215), for example, Geoffrey of Vinsauf famously compared the writing of a poem to the building of a house, an architectural analogy still very much alive for Geoffrey Chaucer when he made use of it almost two hundred years later in his *Troilus and Criseyde*.[3] More generally, all medieval literature is arguably to some degree 'practical', in the sense of 'didactic'; even the most outrageous of fictions produced over the course of the Middle Ages were potentially justifiable as *utile* (useful) no matter how *dulce* (sweet) they might be.

But, rather than discuss the way imaginative fictions like Chaucer's narrative poetry or non-fictional works like Vinsauf's manual were either intended to be or (mis)understood as *useful*, and also leaving aside the very complicated issue of what constitutes the 'literary' in any age, I propose to undertake a different, more thorny, perhaps even pig-headed task. I will consider whether insistently practical texts, those whose explicit goal is to assist their readers to *make* something in the world beyond the page (a book, a culinary dish, an ointment, an object), might be said to have a poetics and, if so, in what that poetics might be said to consist. I take my inspiration in part from Michel de Certeau's assertion that 'the narrativizing of practices is a textual "way of operating" having its own procedures and tactics'.[4] Although de Certeau is here referring to the way theorists of culture such as Karl

---

[2] See for example Earl R. Anderson, 'Social Idealism in Aelfric's *Colloquy*', *Anglo-Saxon England*, 3 (1974), 153–62; Joyce Hill, 'Winchester Pedagogy and the *Colloquy* of Aelfric', *Leeds Studies in English*, 29 (1998), 137–52; and John Ruffing, 'The Labor Structure of Aelfric's *Colloquy*', in Allen J. Frantzen and Douglas Moffat (eds.), *The Work of Work: Servitude, Slavery, and Labor in Medieval England* (Glasgow: Cruithine Press, 1994), 55–70.

[3] Geoffrey of Vinsauf, *Poetria nova*, trans. Margaret F. Nims (Toronto: Pontifical Institute, 1967), ll. 43–5; Geoffrey Chaucer, *Troilus and Criseyde*, I. 1065–8, in *The Riverside Chaucer*, ed. Larry D. Benson, 3rd edn. (Boston: Houghton Mifflin, 1987) (all other references to Chaucer's poetry will be to this edition and will be made in the text). On the architectural trope see Mary Carruthers, 'The Poet as Master Builder: Composition and Locational Memory in the Middle Ages', *New Literary History*, 24/4 (1993), 881–904.

[4] Michel de Certeau, *The Practice of Everyday Life*, trans. Steven Rendell (Berkeley and Los Angeles: University of California Press, 1984), 78.

Marx and Sigmund Freud write (or wrote) about what they do, I want to ask whether the 'narrativizing' of even the most mundane of medieval practices by mostly anonymous writers can also be said to have its own 'procedures and tactics', if such procedures and tactics can indeed be identified. I also want to ask how this attempt of identification might help us to read more profitably in and across the other genres that make up the (admittedly ever-shifting) canon of medieval English literature.

But before I go any further in outlining, in a deliberately exploratory fashion, what is perhaps a massively *impractical* project (for reasons that are frustrating and exciting in equal measure), I want to explain my omission of another set of texts and concepts that a reader coming to an essay on medieval practical or didactic literature might well be expecting. I will *not* be considering exempla collections, courtesy manuals, spiritual guidebooks, and other works of this sort, not only because these kinds of texts have received a great deal of recent scholarly attention (including elsewhere in this volume),[5] but also because, as fictions about—as well as scripts for—the drama of living in the world and preparing for the afterlife, such works lend themselves almost *de facto* to the kind of analysis that literary scholars are used to performing. Particularly as they were written in the later Middle Ages, instructions on how to behave in spheres both secular and sacred tend to come already complete with implied and often explicitly fleshed-out characters, a plot (even if that plot is understood simply as the tracing of the crooked line between birth and death), and a conflict (to use a medieval cliché, the constant battle against the world, the flesh, and the devil). We have at our disposal any number of ways to read stories of this sort *as stories*, just we also have many strategies for thinking about the urgent admonitions of such texts, which tend to shape behaviour largely by policing and prohibiting ('avoid this, don't do that', and so forth).

But how we might best read the largely untapped reserve of what I would call *positive* or *productive* instruction to which medieval English readers turned for help in shaping (or fixing) themselves and the world around them is almost as uncertain as the genre is vast. In addition to works like encyclopedias, calendars, dream-books, and other interpretative volumes, the 'how-to' texts of medieval English culture (a loose but nonetheless quite visible category of textual production that has to date gone largely ignored, even in critical tomes as 'broad and inclusive' as *The Cambridge History of Middle English Literature*[6]) proffer an extensive syllabus of practical knowledge: herbals, leech-books, surgical treatises, lapidaries, cookbooks, husbandry manuals, hunting tracts, and more.[7] The producers and owners of

[5] In this volume see Stephanie Trigg's chapter on 'Nurture', and its thorough bibliography, which I will not reduplicate here. See also Elizabeth Allen, *False Fables and Exemplary Truth in Later Middle English Literature* (New York: Palgrave Macmillan, 2005).

[6] David Wallace (ed.), *The Cambridge History of Middle English Literature* (Cambridge: Cambridge University Press, 1999), p. xvi.

[7] See George R. Keiser's indispensable *Works of Science and Information*, vol. x of Albert E. Hartung (ed.), *A Manual of the Writings in Middle English, 1050–1500* (New Haven: Connecticut Academy of

these works seem to have been far more optimistic than Pierre Bourdieu about the relationship of language to practical activity. While Bourdieu insists that 'the essential part of the *modus operandi* which defines practical mastery is transmitted in practice, in its practical state, without attaining the level of discourse',[8] those who penned and those who read medieval works of practice in prose and verse certainly seem to have put their faith in discourse as a reliable transmitter, if not of mastery, then at least of basic competence, in quite a staggering variety of disciplines.

Here we might pause to note that Chaucer, despite his allusion to the *Poetria nova*'s practical poetics (not to mention his own practical composition, the *Treatise on the Astrolabe*), seems to have shared Bourdieu's much later scepticism. In the 'Canon's Yeoman's Tale', he gives us an apprentice who has discovered that the *ars* of alchemy is a scam no matter how much it is either verbalized in 'termes … so clergial and so queynte' or how much it is performed with 'care and wo' in the workshop (VIII. 752, 769). In this tale, both a discourse *and* the practice it claims to teach are revealed as equally deceptive and equally disappointing. 'For all oure sleightes', the luckless worker who has learned this hard lesson complains, 'we kan nat conclude'; indeed, the only conclusion he *has* reached is that 'oure labour is in veyn' (VIII. 773, 777),[9] fruitful only in the sense that its frustrations make for a good story on the road to the Canterbury. But Chaucer's send-up of practical knowledge is not limited to the notoriously obscure craft of turning base metal to gold and the related, equally fruitless quest for the Philosopher's Stone; in fact, with the exception of the devout Parson and his silent 'brother' the Ploughman (I. 529), no pilgrim on the road to Canterbury escapes the poet's sardonic eye, particularly when it comes to the practice of his or her profession. Even more pertinently for the purposes of this discussion, in the 'Squire's Tale' Chaucer presents us with a group of readers who, while well versed in practical texts, are still unable to make much sense of the world-travelling brass horse, fortune-telling mirror, all-conquering (and all-healing) sword, and bird-decoding ring that have been presented to Genghis Khan.[10] They know of classical texts on optics and perspective, and are informed, apparently also through their reading, about the crafts of metal-smithing, medicine, and glass-making (V. 225–62). Yet their discursive knowledge of these practical arts—limited, Chaucer seems here to suggest, precisely *because* it is no more than discursive—does not bring them

Arts and Sciences, 1998). A useful edition and analysis of some of the shorter pieces in this body of material is Linne R. Mooney's 'Practical Didactic Works in Middle English' (Ph.D. thesis, University of Toronto, 1981).

[8] Pierre Bourdieu, *Outline of a Theory of Practice*, trans. Richard Nice (Cambridge: Cambridge University Press, 1977), 87.

[9] See Lee Patterson, 'Perpetual Motion: Alchemy and the Technology of the Self', *Studies in the Age of Chaucer*, 15 (1993), 25–57.

[10] For a reading that sees a similarly pessimistic view of technical knowledge in a different poem, see Andrew Galloway, 'Chaucer's *Former Age* and the Fourteenth-Century Anthropology of Craft: The Social Logic of a Premodernist Lyric', *English Literary History*, 63 (1996), 535–53.

any closer to understanding the gifts. The Squire rather cuttingly identifies this problem in a comment that, while it specifically dismisses the crowd's fear that the brass steed may be a new Trojan Horse, clearly applies to its members' subsequent bewilderment before the three remaining magical objects as well:

> Of sondry doutes thus they jangle [chatter] and trete [debate],
> As lewed [ignorant] peple demeth [judge] comunly
> Of thynges that been maad moore subtilly
> Than they kan in hir lewednesse comprehende;
> They demen gladly [habitually] to the badder end.   (V. 220–3)[11]

Some six hundred years in advance, Chaucer is here effectively anticipating Bourdieu's warning that 'artificially wrenching ... from their conditions of production and use' the 'practical taxonomies' that serve as 'instruments of cognition and communication' and subjecting them to 'strictly *internal* analysis'—as the 'lewed' folk of the 'Squire's Tale' do, particularly when they examine the mirror and ring—will always 'fai[l] to understand their [that is, the instruments'] social functions' (p. 97). But as the written traces of mostly vanished practices, and particularly the productive kind in which I am most interested, medieval works of instruction have for us, much more so than for the crowd in the 'Squire's Tale', always already been wrenched out of context. And so, despite the risk of ending up merely mired in inconclusiveness like the Canon's Yeoman, what Bourdieu calls 'internal analysis' and what I would call a close reading does not seem like such a bad place to start.[12]

The most naked encounter between the symbolic order of words and material practice occurs in the place where this essay began—namely, vocabularies, a staple of English pedagogy from the *Colloquy* to the early modern period and even beyond. Throughout the centuries of their popularity these word-books served as tools for a literate elite attempting to come to terms *with*—by defining the terms *for*—the social, intellectual, and commercial value of artisanal practice.[13] What I want to emphasize here, however, is not their variously expressed ideologies but rather their shared impulse, irrespective of the circumstances of their production, to transport

---

[11] We might note that the Squire himself is rather like the crowd he mocks, in that he appears to know what makes a 'rethor [rhetorician] excellent'—something he could have learned from a manual like Vinsauf's *Poetria nova*—yet declares himself unable to speak as one (V. 34–41). This is a self-criticism that the Franklin actually ratifies when he cuts short the Squire's meandering narrative (V. 673).

[12] A full study of English practical texts would have to include a consideration of their manuscript contexts, and the history of their production and circulation; it would also take into account, in a much more specific way than I can here, the many different types of practical literature *within* the mega-genre that constitutes the larger field, and consider their conceptual as well as thematic similarities and differences. Such questions are not truly extricable from the formal issues upon which I somewhat artificially concentrate in this essay, but they are beyond its present scope. On some of the issues raised by the clash of aesthetic form and social function in Middle English exemplary texts see Allen, *False Fables*, 22–6.

[13] As I suggest at greater length in Lisa H. Cooper, *Crafting Narratives: Artisans, Authors, and the Literary Artifact in Late Medieval England*, currently in progress.

their users from the domain of the factual to the realm of the imaginary. If Ælfric's *Colloquy*, at the beginning of this tradition, asks its users to assume personae not in fact their own, a word-book such as Alexander Nequam's *De nominibus utensilium* (*c*.1175–85) contextualizes the 'names for tools' that give the text its title in such a way that its readers are projected not only into the spaces of a country estate, shipyard, scriptorium, and goldsmith's shop, but also into at least a temporary identification with those who operate within them. In the passage on the labour of a goldsmith, for example, Nequam writes:

> Manus altera levi pulsu folles regat summa diligencia, ita ut spiritus exiens intus per fistulas prunas accendat, acque etiam crebra aspersione igni prebeat alimentum. Assit etiam incus duricie inexhauste, vel exarate, super quam ferrum positum vel aurum emoliatur, et debitam formam suscipiat. Hinc usu forcipis teneatur ad formandum, ut usu mallei produci possit et extendi.
>
> [One hand should operate the bellows with a light pressure and the greatest diligence, so that the air inside the bellows, being pressed through the tubes, may blow up the coals and that the constant spread of it may feed the fire. Let there be an anvil of extreme hardness on which iron and gold may be softened and may take the required form. They can be held for shaping with the tongs and stretched and pulled with the hammer.[14]]

Here verbal display, ostensibly intended for the Latin-learning student, becomes something more than descriptive information by an observer on behalf of a later reader: it almost becomes, by virtue of its subjunctive verbs and its overall hortative quality, actual craft instruction. At the same time, however, it is a rather curious instruction, since it is situated somewhere between the factual (*this* is how goldsmiths work) and the imaginary (this is how the reader *would* work if he *were* a goldsmith—even though, presumably, he is not).

In part because they are usually topically rather than alphabetically arranged, medieval vocabularies, no matter how schematic, tend to operate as what Werner Hüllen calls 'texts in the full semiotic sense', signifying on multiple levels and creating meaning above and beyond their primary linguistic function, that of supplying one word for another.[15] This is the case even with the simple word-lists that made up the bulk of the genre in the early phases of its development (with the striking exception of Anglo-Saxon colloquies like Ælfric's). Word-lists, however, and as Nequam's word-book exemplifies, were increasingly incorporated into narratives and dialogues. This contextualization, designed primarily for cognitive

---

[14] 'The Treatise *De utensilibus* of Alexander Neckham', in Thomas Wright (ed.), *A Volume of Vocabularies* (London: Joseph Mayer, 1857), 96–119, at 117–18. Trans. Slightly modified from U. T. Holmes, *Daily Living in the Twelfth Century* (Madison: University of Wisconsin Press, 1952), 142; see also John Cherry, *Medieval Craftsmen: Goldsmiths* (Toronto: University of Toronto Press, 1992), 24. For a slightly different version of the passage (and an edition of a different manuscript), see Tony Hunt, *Teaching and Learning Latin in Thirteenth-Century England*, 3 vols. (Cambridge: D. S. Brewer, 1991), i. 177–90, at 189.

[15] Werner Hüllen, *English Dictionaries 800–1700: The Topical Tradition* (Oxford: Clarendon Press, 1999), 22.

ease, has narratological implications; once they are embedded in descriptions of imagined situations, vocabulary words take on a life of their own that is quite distinct from the external reality they are attempting to encompass. As Gérard Genette observes, 'every narrative introduces into its story an "emplotting" which is already a "fictionalizing"'.[16] And in fact, the more contextualized they are, the more medieval collections of verbal facts acquire the characteristics not simply of narrative in general, but of various kinds of medieval fiction in particular. Nequam's observations in the *De nominibus utensilium* upon another craft, that of weaving, provide a case in point, for they open with a remarkable set of images for the operation of the loom:

> Textor terrestris eques est, qui duarum streparum adnitens apodiamento, equum admittit assidue, exili tamen contentum dieta. Scansilia autem, eius fortune conditionem representantia, mutua gaudent vicissitudine, ut dum unum evehitur, reliquum sine nota livoris deprimatur.
>
> [A weaver is an earthly knight, who leans upon two stirrups and who gives rein constantly to the horse, content with a short journey. But the stirrups, representing the condition of his fortune, enjoy mutual vicissitudes, since when the one goes up the other is depressed without any indication of rancor.[17]]

Here Nequam translates craft labour into the language not only of chivalric living, but also of chivalric literature. This is, however briefly, weaving as romance, governed by an uncharacteristically benign Fortune. Another genre makes its appearance near the end of the same book's description of the goldsmith's workshop, when technical instruction begins to become a cautionary tale about the perils of the market, one made more dramatic by way of the kind of language with which exempla and fable collections of this and later periods are rife. The goldsmith's apprentice, Nequam warns, 'must know how to distinguish solid gold from brass and copper, that he may not purchase brass for gold' ('Aurum etiam obrizum sciat discernere ab oricalco, a cupro ne pro auro elico emat auricalcum'); furthermore, he adds, 'it is difficult to escape the wiliness of the fraudulent merchant entering the forge' ('grave est institoris pellacis effugere tergiversationem fabateriam subintrantis').[18]

I may have been hasty in saying that I wanted to avoid 'admonitory' texts in this attempt to get some kind of a purchase on the language and literature of practicality. For, in the Middle Ages as now, the first step in being practical, no matter what one is saying, doing, or making, is to *be careful*. So, in fact, the warnings embedded in practical texts of all kinds may be the very places where such works, even the most non-narrative in design, stretch themselves to the fullest extent of their potential eloquence. In a collection of medical recipes from the mid-fifteenth century, for

---

[16] Gérard Genette, *Fiction and Diction*, trans. Catherine Porter (Ithaca, NY: Cornell University Press), 27.

[17] Hunt, *Teaching and Learning Latin*, 184–5; see also 'The Treatise *De utensilibus*', 106; trans. from Holmes, *Daily Living*, 146, with some slight alteration.

[18] Hunt, *Teaching and Learning Latin*, 189; see also 'The Treatise *De utensilibus*', 119. The translation of the first phrase is from Holmes, *Daily Living*, 142; the translation of the second phrase is my own.

example, a simple list of things to avoid in order to protect the eyes becomes a vocabulary of daily (but not dull) danger, a kind of compressed epic of potentially hazardous experience:

> Thou must knawe or thou come to medecynes that þies thyngis bene euel for the syght in the eyghen moch lechery for to loke moch on schynynge ymges [images] and for to rede moch on small lett(er)s to slepe at noone after thi mete (and) he that hat fawte in hys syght muste be ware that he ete nat ere mete th(a)t he ete before be defiede [digested] and drunkonnes and for to brake [vomit] before mete and to moch slepe and to moch blode lattynge w(ith) cuppynge all man(er) of metys th(at) bene salte and sharpe and stronge wyne that is trubly [turgid] and thyke lekes onyons rype olyues anete [dill] worts of cole [cabbage] and fygges garlyke wyne benes smoke fyre fume hoote blode grete travaylle laughynge chese wepynge pep(per) strokys [blows] mustarde and moch wakynge[19]

A text, writes Genette, 'is literary ... for someone who is more concerned with its form than with its content—for someone, for example, who appreciates the way it is written even while rejecting or ignoring its meaning' (*Fiction*, 17). My own appreciation of this passage from the leech-book might be accused of just this kind of ahistorical bias; what strikes me as quirky and compelling and drives me to read this book (albeit, *pace* Genette, as much for its content as its form) is probably not what primarily interested its owner. Then again, this work, like others of its kind, does seem occasionally to relish its own verbal flourishes in a way that leads me to wonder if my reading is so ahistorical after all. Note, in particular, the breathless and rather exuberant catalogue—'figs, garlic, wine, beans, smoke, fire, fume' and so forth—at the end of the passage quoted above. Likewise, another passage in the same book makes the following increasingly triumphant declarations about the virtues of blood-letting:

> it clerith thi thought it closith thi bladder it te(m)p(er)ith th(y) breyn it amendith thyn heerynge it streyngth teres it closith thy maw it defieth [digests] thi mete it clerith thy voyce it sharpith the witt it easith thi wombe [stomach] it gedirith [gathers] thy slepe it drawyth away angwysshe it norisshith goode blode wykkd blode dystroyeth and lengthith thy lyve.[20]

The appearance of such material in Middle English verse as well as in prose (many poems on blood-letting, in particular, survive) may deserve more critical consideration by students of medieval literature than it has received.[21] Although the

---

[19] Warren R. Dawson (ed.), *A Leechbook or Collection of Medical Recipes of the Fifteenth Century* (London: Macmillan, 1934), 160–3; I have spelled out abbreviated letters in brackets.

[20] Ibid. 63. Part of the texture of these two passages is determined by the placement (and the absence) of the word 'and', whose multiple functions William Gass has usefully analysed in 'And', in Allen Wier and Don Hendrie Jr. (eds.), *Voicelust: Eight Contemporary Fiction Writers on Style* (Lincoln: University of Nebraska Press, 1985), 101–25.

[21] See the editions and brief study of blood-letting poems in Tony Hunt, 'The Poetic Vein: Phlebotomy in Middle English and Anglo-Norman Verse', *English Studies* (1996), 311–22. For more

versification of much practical knowledge in the fourteenth and fifteenth centuries tends to be explained away as mnemonic device, we might want to ask whether (like their classical forebears, who were entertained as well as instructed by the didactic verse of Lucretius and Virgil) medieval readers did not themselves take aesthetic enjoyment from practical literature. That at least one reader found some degree of pleasure in practical texts is suggested by the Middle English version of a Latin agricultural handbook by the fourth-century writer Palladius.[22] Translated c.1442–3 for Humphrey, duke of Gloucester, the dedication copy of the work is equipped with a textual apparatus, including an alphabetical table of contents, that points to its having been created with a practical function in mind (this despite the fact that some of its advice, such as that for growing olives in a Mediterranean climate, would be difficult for an English landowner to follow). But the work's form—rhyme royal stanzas—suggests, as George R. Keiser observes, 'that delight was at least as important as instruction' to the work's conception (Works of Science and Information, 3596).

John Lydgate, the most prominent poet of Duke Humphrey's circle, seems to have shared as well as encouraged his patron's appreciation of the practical rendered in and as poetry. Within Lydgate's vast and largely didactic corpus, several little-studied works stand out not only because they present technical information in verse, but also because their practical content is in one way or another an integral part of their poetic form and function. The short 'Tretise for Lavandres', for example, reads on its surface as a set of versified instructions for washerwomen;[23] however, as Maura Nolan demonstrates in a forthcoming essay, the poem is actually 'embedded within a devotional discursive network' that includes biblical passages on the cleansing of sin, Marian lyrics, and vernacular allegories like Piers Plowman.[24] The singular

on blood-letting practices and texts see Linda E. Voigts and Michael R. McVaugh, A Latin Technical Phlebotomy and its Middle English Translation, Transactions of the American Philosophical Society 74, part 2 (Philadelphia: American Philosophical Society, 1984); and Pedro Gil-Sotres, 'Derivation and Revulsion: The Theory and Practice of Medieval Phlebotomy', in Luis García-Ballester et al. (eds.), Practical Medicine from Salerno to the Black Death (Cambridge: Cambridge University Press, 1994), 110–55.

[22] Palladius on Husbondrie, ed. Barton Lodge, EETS os 52 and 72 (London: N. Trübner, 1873 and 1879). For more on this translation and its role in the duke's promotion of humanism see Alessandra Petrina, Cultural Politics in Fifteenth-Century England: The Case of Humphrey, Duke of Gloucester (Leiden: Brill, 2004), 266–77. For what seems to have been a more widely used Middle English prose horticultural text in the Palladian tradition (it survives in thirteen manuscripts) see David G. Cylkowski, 'A Middle English Treatise on Horticulture: Godfridus Super Palladium', in Lister M. Matheson (ed.), Popular and Practical Science of Medieval England (East Lansing, MI: Colleagues Press, 1994), 301–29; see also Petrina, Cultural Politics, 267.

[23] The Minor Poems of John Lydgate: Part II: Secular Poems, ed. Henry Noble MacCracken, EETS, os 192 (London: Oxford University Press, 1934), 723. All other references to Lydgate's poetry are to this volume and will be made in the text.

[24] Maura Nolan, 'Lydgate's Worst Poem', in Lisa H. Cooper and Andrea Denny-Brown (eds.), Poetry and Material Culture in the Fifteenth Century: Lydgate Matters (New York: Palgrave Macmillan, forthcoming).

'Debate of the Horse, Goose, and Sheep', a kind of bickering bestiary, takes as its central theme the use-value of the animals who speak its words, right down to the sheep's explanation of the precise end to which each of his body parts may be put: his wool for cloth, his skin for gloves and parchment, his tail and (boiled) head for medicinal ointments, his intestines for harp strings (pp. 554–5, ll. 351–85). And consider the long section on the humours, uroscopy, and phlebotomy in Lydgate's *Fabula duorum mercatorum*, of which I reproduce the central stanzas:

> Effymera [ephemeratic fever] hath his original
> Whan mannys spiritys been in distemperaunce,
> Or in-to excesse yif a wiht [person] be fal
> Of mete and drynk thoruh mysgovernance:
> Of accidentis, of thouht, of perturbaunce,
> Of hoot, of cold or greef in any maneer
> This feuere cometh, as auctors tellen heer.
>
> And putrida is causyd gladly thus:
> Whan any humour synneth in quantite,
> Or whan his flowyng is to plentevous,
> That he excedith mesoure in qualite.
> Yiff by blood, anoon ye may it see;
> Yif quantite ouht erre, espyeth it thus,
> The fevere in phisyk is callyd sinochus.
>
> And, yiff the humour in qualite exceedith,
> Or heete or blood passe his temperament,
> In-to a fevere anoon a man it leedeth
> Clepith synocha by putrefaccioun shent [ruined].
> And, yif of colra he take his groundement,
> Pure or vnpure, citryn or vitellyne [deep yellow],
> Gyles you techith to iuge it by vryne.   (p. 496, ll. 288–308)

Some time ago, this passage, among others of a similar informational nature, led Derek Pearsall to 'confess to a certain bafflement' regarding the poem's story even as he admitted that 'as an exercise of style it is superb'.[25] But story and style are I think inseparable, and perhaps nowhere more so than in this passage about physical 'excesse'. Drawn almost directly, or so it would seem, from a leech-book like the one I have already quoted, or else adapted from one of many blood-letting poems in circulation, in the *Fabula* the passage actually turns practical knowledge into a poetic game. For Lydgate uses it to highlight, in ironic fashion, the way the love-sick merchant to whom its terms are applied is actually suffering *not* from a bodily surfeit but rather from the (seeming) impossibility of ever possessing the woman he desires since she is engaged to his best friend, the second merchant of the title. Furthermore, the concepts of surplus and lack that Lydgate appropriates here from the medical profession also operate as figures for the financial profit and

---

[25] Derek Pearsall, *John Lydgate* (London: Routledge and Kegan Paul, 1970), 204.

loss experienced by the two merchant-protagonists in the marketplaces where they practise their skill.

So in the vocabulary tradition does the marketplace increasingly appear both as the inspiration for further fictionalizing and also, thematically speaking, the locus of fiction—in the sense of fraud—*par excellence*. 'Deceitful drapers, led on by excessive greed', writes John of Garland in another popular word-book, the *Dictionarius* of *c.*1220, 'defraud buyers, badly measuring cloths with a short ell and false lengths' (§ 41).[26] The anxiety attendant upon possibly being deceived in the market—rather than, say, using the wrong word, since the vocabularies themselves (at least in theory) prevent that unfortunate occurrence—is in fact a central theme of one of the latest and most elaborate of medieval English word-books, Caxton's *Dialogues in French and English* (*c.*1483).[27] This bilingual phrasebook, a guide for travelling merchants, includes (along with an alphabet of artisans and many other short vignettes) a complete script whereby a buyer and seller of cloth move from friendly greeting through mutual suspicion, tense disagreement, eventual accord, payment, and courteous farewell (pp. 15–19).

Caxton's vocabulary implies by the simple fact of its *printed* existence the idea that anyone who would buy the book and equip himself with the language the text offers to teach can learn to be a merchant.[28] This suggestion—that is, that discourse can lead seamlessly to practice, and not just to the practice of proper speech, but also to other types of productive activity—is made more explicitly in the opening of another late medieval manual, John Russell's *Boke of Nurture*.[29] This work, composed around 1460 by an upper servant in the household of Humphrey of Gloucester, was meant not for a wide audience but rather for young boys raised in the households of noble men. But its opening gambit—a dialogue between an older, wiser man and a young one looking for a master—is the suggestion that such a work can in fact teach a willing learner *any* skill pertaining to *any* occupation, no matter where it falls on the social ladder: ' "Now, son, yiff y the teche, wiltow any thynge lere?" ' the older figure asks his new young acquaintance. ' "Wiltow be a seruaunde, plowghman, or a laborere, | Courtyour or a clark | Marchaund | or masoun, or an artificere | Chamburlayn, or buttillere | pantere or karvere?" ' (ll. 37–40). The

[26] 'Pannarii, nimia cupidate ducti defraudant emptores, male ulnando pannos cum ulna curta et cum police fallaci' (Hunt, *Teaching and Learning Latin*, 199); for an English translation of this work (based on a different manuscript from that edited by Hunt), see *The 'Dictionarius' of John de Garlande*, trans. Barbara Blatt Rubin (Lawrence, KS: Coronado, 1981).

[27] *STC* no. 24865. The most widely available edition is *Dialogues in French and English by William Caxton*, ed. Henry Bradley, EETS, es 79 (London: Kegan Paul, 1900); another more accurate but less accessible edition is Jean Gessler (ed.), *Le Livre des mestiers de Bruges et ses dérivés: quatres anciens manuels de conversation* (Bruges: [Fondatian Universitaire de Belgique], 1931).

[28] Lisa H. Cooper, 'Urban Utterances: Merchants, Artisans, and the Alphabet in Caxton's *Dialogues in French and English*', *New Medieval Literatures*, 7 (2005), 127–61, at 160–1.

[29] *John Russell's Boke of Nurture*, in Frederick J. Furnivall (ed.), *Early English Meals and Manners* (London: N. Trübner, 1868), 1–123.

nature of the text demands that the boy choose, as he immediately does, the last four options of learning to serve in chamber and at table. But what is striking here, particularly if we think back to the *Colloquy*'s much earlier and only temporary assignment of roles, is the idea of occupational freedom.[30]

The statement that the later fourteenth and fifteenth centuries in England were characterized by increasing social and professional mobility, at least or especially for those of bourgeois status, has become a truism. But the concept of choice is also an essential part of any poetic we might ascribe to practical works. In the later Middle Ages, most of these kinds of texts, along with many other kinds of literature, were sought out by precisely those for whom upward mobility was indeed an option.[31] This genre's seeming (if not actual) availability to and potential utility for all comers was already one of its characteristics in the early thirteenth century, as we saw above in the latent suggestion of Alexander Nequam's *De nominibus utensilium* that its reader might, by following its instructions, do some work in the goldsmith's shop. Practical texts both early and late, and however limited or broad their circulation, present a slew of options—areas of expertise, methods within those areas—and leave it up to the reader to select from among them depending on his or her need or even desire.[32] In the *Boke of Nurture*, the world of practice is presented as the young man's oyster, and only after being asked to choose from a wide professional spectrum does he opt to learn with what sauce a dish of real oysters should be served (according to this book, one of chives or gravy (l. 822)).

Recipes for sauces and descriptions of the foods to which they are applied themselves make for their own kind of drama, and not just one of the palate. Although works like the *Boke of Nurture* and other late medieval recipe collections present something of an obdurate 'centre of resistance' to close analysis,[33] I am nevertheless struck by the 'narrative' hinted at in the *Boke of Kervynge* (Wynkyn

---

[30] The same idea, albeit in its negative form, also appears in a poem uniquely preserved in Yale University, Beinecke Library, MS 163, in which a father forbids his son not only the risky profession of court counsellor, but also '[m]asons crafte and all clymbynge, | And shipmans crafte for perell of dethe' (ll. 2–3). This is more of a conduct poem than a technical treatise, to be sure, but it might also be considered severely practical in its insistence that wise men (and their sons) avoid the bodily dangers of manual labour. Notably, the manuscript in which this warning appears is otherwise a compendium of practical material, including texts on medicine, herbs, and falconry (Keiser, *Works of Science and Information*, 3596). The poem is edited in Roger Lass, 'Three Middle English Cautionary Lyrics', *Anglia*, 83 (1965), 172–5; on its use of the trope of the wise parent to proclaim its authority see Cameron Louis, 'Authority in Middle English Proverb Literature', *Florilegium*, 15 (1998), 85–123, at 93.

[31] Mooney, 'Practical Didactic Works', 125–6; Janet Coleman, *Medieval Readers and Writers 1350–1400* (New York: Columbia University Press, 1981), 43–57.

[32] On the potentially 'deterministic' ideas latent in these works see Keiser, *Works of Science and Information*, 3598. On the way recipes make possible 'an extension of the repertoires of specialist and layman alike', see Jack Goody, *The Domestication of the Savage Mind* (Cambridge: Cambridge University Press, 1977), 138.

[33] Paul Strohm, *Theory and the Premodern Text* (Minneapolis: University of Minnesota Press, 2000), p. xiv.

de Worde's prose adaptation of the verse *Boke of Nurture*, first printed in 1508) in its directions for dressing a capon: 'Take up a capon, and lyfte up the ryght legge and the ryght wynge, & so araye forth & laye hym in the plater as he sholde flee, & serve your soverayne.'[34] If on the one hand the suggested 'array', or display, of the dressed but still seemingly fleeing bird is its own kind of fiction for the table, the arrangement of the instructions in this part of the *Boke of Kervynge* attain their own kind of verbal as well as visual rhythm:

Dysmembre that heron

Take an heron and reyse his legges, and cut of his wynges as a crane and sauce hym with vynegre mustarde poudre of gynger and salte.

Unioynte that bytture [bittern]

Take a bytture & reyse his legges & his wynges as an heron and no sauce but salte onely.

Breke that egryt

Take an egryt and reyse his legges and his wynges as an heron and no sauce but salte.
(p. 162)

This section of the book in fact elaborates upon the display proffered on its first page, a list of the 'Termes of a Kerver' laid out without any further explanation (it is not really a table of contents) except, it seems, to bewilder the reader with its sheer variety and so impress upon him his need to read on (since the first half of this list appears elsewhere in this volume (see p. 467), I quote only the second half of it here):

unioynt that bytture	traunche that sturgyon
vntache that curlewe	vndertraunche that purpos
alaye that fesande	tayme that crabbe
wynge that partryche	barbe that lopster
wynge that quayle	
mynce that plouer	
thye [thigh] that pegyon	
border that pasty	
thye that wodcocke	
thye all maner of small byrdes	
tymbre [timber] that fyre [fire]	(p. 151)

This last passage is in many ways a neat précis of the narratological interest and set of problems that practical literature presents. The opening of the *Boke of*

---

[34] *STC* no. 3289; also in Furnivall (ed.), *Early English Meals and Manners*, 149–74, at 161. For a modernized translation with facing black-letter text see *The Boke of Keruynge*, ed. Peter Brears (Lewes: Southover Press, 2003). For earlier English recipes and a useful introduction to the genre see Constance B. Hieatt and Sharon Butler (eds.), *Curye on Inglysch: English Culinary Manuscripts of the Fourteenth Century*, EETS, ss 8 (Oxford: Oxford University Press, 1985); another recipe collection is Thomas Austin (ed.), *Two Fifteenth-Century Cookery Books*, EETS, os 91 (Oxford: Oxford University Press, 1888). On manuscripts of medieval recipes, see Constance B. Hieatt, 'Making Sense of Medieval Culinary Records: Much Done, But Much More to Do', in Martha Carlin and Joel T. Rosenthal (eds.), *Food and Eating in Medieval Europe* (London: Hambledon Press, 1998), 101–16.

Kervynge is a prime, if late, example of an 'intersection' of several practical genres with one another. It is at once a (mostly avian) bestiary, a vocabulary (of verbs), and a conduct book (for the kitchen if not the table). But it is something more as well. As Hayden White notes of the entries in the much earlier *Annals of St Gall*, 'It may be a mistake to call it discourse at all, but it has something discursive about it. The text summons up a "substance." '[35] White, as his placement of the word in quotation marks suggests, means 'substance' somewhat metaphorically, but medieval practical works like those I have considered in this essay literally 'summon up a substance' by definition: they ask their readers to make (or at least give them the option of making) the things to which they refer.

In fact, 'summon up' is not quite the right phrase. Though medieval practical works have an even more pronounced incantatory form than that which White senses in the *Annals*, their incantations—or, better, their more-or-less urgent imperatives—are, with perhaps the exceptions of alchemical poems and versified charms, far more mundane than magical. Furthermore, unlike the forms of *historia* upon which White focuses his attention, works of practical instruction have a rather indeterminate relationship to time, an indeterminacy that effectively redoubles their 'summoning' power by allowing them to gesture in two temporal directions at once. What I mean by this is that, on the one hand, practical literature lays claim to authority by pointing, at least implicitly, towards a past act that has met with success (this is, at any rate, the leap of faith a credulous reader must make). On the other hand, practical texts, unlike much medieval historiography, are designed less to narrate the probable past than they are to represent the quite literally possible future, *if*—and this, as I have already mentioned, is a key condition—their reader(s) should choose to follow directions. Moreover, in the (present) moment of their being read they are also outlines, or sketches, of tangible content—of the *things*, the *stuff*—that their users may choose (or not) to add to the world around them. At the same time, as literary artefacts, medieval practical works *also* and *already* have a verbal content, and any number of forms, of their own. This is something that their readers, quite as much as their writers, appear to have understood and relished. The appeal of the how-to text in later medieval England is something that literary critics have yet fully to grasp; but, practically speaking, in exploring the genre's intricate marriage of form and content, variously embodied in an amazingly copious corpus, we may find much more 'work' to do.

[35] Hayden White, *The Content of the Form: Narrative Discourse and Historical Representation* (Baltimore: Johns Hopkins University Press), 9. I thank Jacques Lezra for discussing this idea and many others in this essay with me.

FURTHER READING

The best introduction to and bibliography for the study of medieval English practical literature of all kinds is that of George R. Keiser, *Works of Science and Information*, vol. x of Albert E. Hartung (ed.), *A Manual of the Writings in Middle English, 1050–1500* (New Haven: Connecticut Academy of Arts and Sciences, 1998). See also Keiser, 'Scientific', Medical and utilitarian Prose', in A. S. G. Edwards (ed.), *a companion to Middle English Prose* (Cambridge D. S. Brewer, 2004). Linda Ehrsam Voigts, 'Scientific and Medical Books', in Jeremy Griffiths and Derek Pearsall (eds.), *Book Production and Publishing in Britain 1375–1475* (Cambridge: Cambridge University Press, 1989), 345–402, and Robert M. Schuler and John G. Fitch, 'Theory and Context of the Didactic Poem: Some Classical, Mediaeval, and Later Continuities', *Florilegium*, 5 (1983), 1–43.

There are some scattered studies of the intersection of English practical literature and fictional works, with the emphasis placed for the most part on the latter; see for example Anne Rooney, *Hunting in Middle English Literature* (Cambridge: D. S. Brewer, 1993) and Marijane Osborn, *Time and the Astrolabe in* The Canterbury Tales (Norman: University of Oklahoma Press, 2002). Though it focuses on German and Spanish material with only a brief epilogue about English texts, the editions and commentary in Richard C. Hoffman, *Fisher's Craft and Lettered Art: Tracts on Fishing from the End of the Middle Ages* (Toronto: University of Toronto Press, 1997), are also of interest.

Much work on medieval practical (sometimes called technical) literature was done in the mid-twentieth century by German scholars focusing on German texts; see for example Gerhard Eis, *Mittelalterliche Fachliteratur*, 2nd edn. (Stuttgart: J. B. Metzler, 1967) and Gundolf Keil et al. (eds.), *Fachliteratur des Mittelalters: Festschrift für Gerhard Eis* (Stuttgart: L. B. Metzler, 1968). In England and North America, the focus of didactic literature studies has been predominantly on classical Latin and early modern works. For classical material see Alexander Dalzell, *The Criticism of Didactic Poetry: Essays on Lucretius, Virgil, and Ovid* (Toronto: Toronto University Press, 1996), and Katharina Volk, *The Poetics of Latin Didactic: Lucretius, Vergil, Ovid, Manilius* (Oxford: Oxford University Press, 2002); theoretically useful for thinking about the relation of 'imperatival' form to content in this material is Roy K. Gibson, 'Didactic Poetry as "Popular" Form: A Study of Imperatival Expressions in Latin Didactic Verse and Prose', in Catherine Atherton (ed.), *Form and Content in Didactic Poetry*, Nottingham Classical Literature Studies 5 (Bari: Levante Editori, 1997), 67–98. For the later period see Elizabeth Tebeaux, *The Emergence of a Tradition: Technical Writing in the English Renaissance, 1475–1640* (Amityville, NY: Baywood, 1997); Natasha Glaisyer and Sara Pennell (eds.), *Didactic Literature in England 1500–1800: Expertise Constructed* (Aldershot: Ashgate, 2003); Yasmin Haskell and Philip Hardie (eds.), *Poets and Teachers: Latin Didactic Poetry and the Didactic Authority of the Latin Poet from the Renaissance to the Present* (Bari: Levante, 1999); Yasmin Annabel Haskell, *Loyola's Bees: Ideology and Industry in Jesuit Latin Didactic Poetry* (Oxford: British Academy, 2003); and, most recently, Henry S. Turner, *The English Renaissance Stage: Geometry, Poetics, and the Practical Spatial Arts 1580–1630* (Oxford: Oxford University Press, 2006). Two valuable studies that stand out for their inclusion of medieval material are William Eamon, *Science and the Secrets of Nature: Books of Secrets in Medieval and Early Modern Culture* (Princeton: Princeton University Press, 1994), and Pamela O. Long, *Openness, Secrecy, Authorship: Technical Arts and the Culture of Knowledge from Antiquity to the Renaissance* (Baltimore: Johns Hopkins University Press, 2001).

INDEX OF MEDIEVAL AUTHORS
AND TITLES

Note: Footnote numbers in brackets are used to indicate the whereabouts on the page of authors who are quoted, but not named, in the text. Page references in *italic* refer to illustrations.

INDEX OF NAMES

Note: Footnote numbers in brackets are used to indicate the whereabouts on the page of authors who are quoted, but not named, in the text. Page references in *italic* refer to illustrations.

SUBJECT INDEX